International Marketing

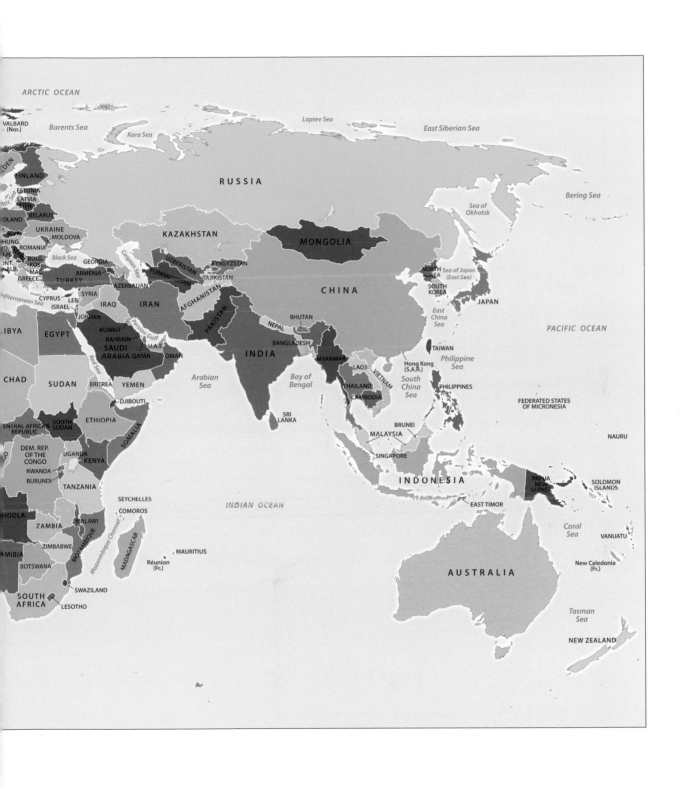

I dedicate this book to my father, Donald Baack. I have been blessed by God with many journeys, and he has been my rock for all of them. Dad, I love you deeply and am thankful for all your work teaching me to be the man I am.

—Daniel W. Baack

I dedicate this book to all future readers of this textbook—
I hope you find this book useful in your studies of international marketing.

—Barbara Czarnecka

My efforts on this book are dedicated to my wonderful aunt and uncle, Mary Lou and Forrest Kelly.

—Donald Baack

Daniel W. Baack, Barbara Czarnecka & Donald Baack

International Marketing

2nd
EDITION

⑤SAGE

Los Angeles | London | New Delhi
Singapore | Washington DC | Melbourne

Los Angeles | London | New Delhi
Singapore | Washington DC | Melbourne

SAGE Publications Ltd
1 Oliver's Yard
55 City Road
London EC1Y 1SP

SAGE Publications Inc.
2455 Teller Road
Thousand Oaks, California 91320

SAGE Publications India Pvt Ltd
B 1/I 1 Mohan Cooperative Industrial Area
Mathura Road
New Delhi 110 044

SAGE Publications Asia-Pacific Pte Ltd
3 Church Street
#10-04 Samsung Hub
Singapore 049483

Editor: Matthew Waters
Editorial assistant: Jasleen Kaur
Assistant editor, digital: Chloe Statham
Production editor: Sarah Cooke
Marketing manager: Alison Borg
Cover design: Francis Kenney
Typeset by: C&M Digitals (P) Ltd, Chennai, India
Printed in the UK by Bell & Bain Ltd, Glasgow

Library of Congress Control Number: 2018941471

British Library Cataloguing in Publication data

A catalogue record for this book is available from the British Library

ISBN 978-1-5063-8921-9
ISBN 978-1-5063-8922-6 (pbk)

At SAGE we take sustainability seriously. Most of our products are printed in the UK using responsibly sourced papers and boards. When we print overseas we ensure sustainable papers are used as measured by the PREPS grading system. We undertake an annual audit to monitor our sustainability.

BRIEF CONTENTS

DETAILED CONTENTS

LIST OF FIGURES, TABLES AND MAPS

FIGURES

TABLES

MAPS

ABOUT THE AUTHORS

Daniel W. Baack is the Academic Director of MBA Programs and Associate Professor of Marketing and International Business at the Daniels College of Business at the University of Denver. Previous positions include Ball State University and Saint Louis University, where Professor Baack received his PhD, in international business and marketing.

Professor Baack has published academic research in the *Journal of International Business Studies*, *Journal of Advertising*, *Journal of Advertising Research*, *Journal of International Management*, *European Journal of Marketing*, *Journal of Business Research*, *International Business Review*, *Journal of Product and Brand Management*, *International Journal of Commerce and Management*, *Journal of Electronic Commerce Research*, and the *International Journal of Emerging Markets*. He serves on the editorial board of the *Journal of Promotion Management*.

Professor Baack is an active member of the Academy of International Business, having attended all but one conference since 2003. When not writing or traveling internationally, he stays busy with his Taiwanese wife and their three joint ventures (or children). He also enjoys playing and watching basketball, particularly while in foreign countries.

Barbara Czarnecka is an Associate Professor of Marketing at London South Bank University. She previously held positions at the University of Bedfordshire and Middlesex University. Barbara's research and teaching interests focus on behavior change communication, the influence of culture on consumer behavior, and the interactions between international corporations, consumers, and governments. She co-authored *Marketing Communications* (Routledge).

Professor Czarnecka has published academic research in several journals including the *Journal of Advertising Research*, the *Journal of Promotion Management*, and the *Journal of Global Marketing*.

In her time away from teaching and research, She enjoys spending time with her family, cooking Asian dishes, reading historical fiction, and walking her dog Canello.

Donald Baack holds the rank of University Professor of Management at Pittsburg (Kansas) State University. He previously held positions at Southwest Missouri State University, Missouri Southern State College, and Dana College. He received his PhD, from the University of Nebraska.

Professor Baack served as a consulting editor and published in the *Journal of Managerial Issues*. He also published in the *Journal of Advertising Research*, *Journal of Euromarketing*, *Journal of Nonprofit and Public Sector Marketing*, *Journal of*

Customer Service in Marketing, Journal of Professional Services Marketing, Journal of Ministry Marketing and Management, Journal of Business Ethics, Journal of Global Awareness, Human Relations, Journal of Management Inquiry, and the *Journal of Business Strategies.*

He has authored *International Business* (Glencoe/McGraw-Hill) and *Organizational Behavior* (Bridgepoint). He co-authored *Integrated Advertising, Promotion, and Marketing Communications* (Prentice Hall), *Marketing Management* (SAGE), and *The Concise Encyclopedia of Advertising* (Haworth) with Kenneth D. Clow. He also has published three popular press books in the area of romance/self-help.

He has also been active in the Southwest Academy of Management and received SWAM's Distinguished Educator award in 2014. He has been recognized as a Distinguished Alumnus at Lincoln (Nebraska) East High School and by Dana College.

PREFACE

"Marketing is marketing, no matter where you are. There is still a marketing mix. The focus continues to be on creating value for customers and building relationships with them. It just becomes a great deal more complicated when you operate on an international scale." This observation by a noted international marketing instructor succinctly summarizes the challenges international marketers face. Globalization, technological advances, economic upheaval, political shifts, and cultural trends are transforming society at an escalating rate. In this ever-changing global environment, the field of marketing must continually adapt to remain on the cutting edge.

Communicating the complexities and nuances of marketing on an international scale in a single course can be a daunting task for instructors. Students taking this course also face a unique set of obstacles. We believe many international marketing textbooks currently available complicate these challenges by focusing too much on international business in the first portion of the book and then introducing marketing topics later on. Instead of segregating the two topics, we concluded that a better approach would be to present marketing in an international context. We wrote this book out of our desire to help resolve some of the issues confronting both students and professors.

MARKET AND COURSE

This textbook is for undergraduate courses in international marketing. It also can be used in undergraduate international business courses and in topical international marketing courses at the MBA level.

INSTRUCTOR CHALLENGES

The international marketing course is typically taught by either a marketing instructor or a business instructor. Marketing instructors, including Daniel Baack, the lead author on this book, often find the standard international marketing textbook to be fairly daunting, especially the opening chapters, which are typically packed with international business concepts. The pages are filled with charts, tables, and statistics that can overwhelm the reader. This group of instructors may be inclined to gloss over these topics and move quickly to the more standard marketing materials presented. When international business instructors teach the course, they may be more inclined to focus on international business concepts and are tempted to cover marketing material in less depth.

In essence, neither the needs of the marketing instructor nor the needs of the business instructor are met by the currently available textbooks. Our book utilizes an integrated framework designed to cover both the international business and the marketing concepts found in traditional international marketing textbooks in a new and integrated way, meeting the wants of both types of instructors.

STUDENT CHALLENGES

Students encounter several major challenges when taking an international marketing course. First, many students will have been exposed to only one of two topics areas. Some students may have already taken international business courses but have had little exposure to marketing. Other students may have backgrounds in marketing but an international marketing course might be their first and only exposure to international business. In essence, students taking this course may have little experience in marketing, international business, or both. We have endeavored to present the material in a manner that engages and reaches all three groups of students.

To assist students in learning the concepts, each chapter opens with a figure that integrates five key international business elements with the main elements in marketing. This figure provides students with a visual illustration of the connections between the marketing elements presented in the chapter with the most closely associated international business issues.

Some students may struggle when trying to integrate marketing concepts with international business concepts. The textbooks that begin with an overview of international business and then discuss marketing may worsen this problem by segregating the two topics and diluting the marketing focus. To help overcome this obstacle to learning, we outline the differences and similarities in domestic and foreign markets while maintaining a strong focus on core marketing concepts. This assists in understanding how to conceptualize the international marketing process.

The third complication some students face can be either ethnocentrism or a degree of naïveté. We try to overcome these impediments to learning with careful attention to the nature of culture and the cultural nuances of countries around the world. Our goal is to expand student awareness and understanding along with acceptance and appreciation of business practices in other parts of the world. We have created features and selected photographs designed to help students engage more deeply with the chapter materials. The International Incident boxes challenge students to make ethical or cultural decisions in international situations. The International Marketing in Daily Life boxes reveal how products they use in their everyday lives are impacted by global marketing.

OUR APPROACH

We have backgrounds in marketing, international business, brand management, consumer behavior, market research, management, and marketing communications. We hope our academic and professional experiences and areas of expertise have helped us to design a textbook that provides an important and fresh contribution to the field of international marketing. There are several primary differences and advantages between our book and the books currently available: core marketing concepts are integrated with international business principles, an emphasis on bottom-of-the-pyramid markets, and the incorporation of sustainability concepts.

INTEGRATED APPROACH

As noted, in this book we utilize an integrated framework that combines marketing concepts and international business concepts. This integrated approach was designed to ameliorate the challenges that students and instructors face. To do so, five key international business principles are defined in the opening chapter of the text:

- cultural differences
- language differences
- political and legal differences
- economic differences
- technological/operational differences

These concepts are placed into a figure along with the five key marketing elements: markets, products, prices, distribution (place), and promotion. The figure reappears in each section. Next the text moves directly into the primary marketing areas (markets and the 4 Ps) and concludes with operational, organizational, and managerial issues. International business concepts are presented in depth at points in which they have the greatest value in demonstrating international marketing concepts.

BOTTOM-OF-THE-PYRAMID

One major international target market consists of individuals who earn less than $2 per day. The bottom-of-the-pyramid segment is large and increasingly relevant to international marketing scholars and practitioners. The relatively untapped nature of the market appeals to many international companies. We argue that targeting this group of 4 billion people is viable and could lead to more efficient processing and innovations. We have incorporated issues associated with reaching this group in each chapter throughout the book.

SUSTAINABILITY

Sustainable business practices are of growing significance. Many students express strong interests in the topic. Sustainability issues are noted in the text, in various chapter-opening vignettes, and in end-of-chapter cases. We also link sustainability to bottom-of-the-pyramid marketing because these two crucial forces have generated a dramatic impact on globalization and international marketing programs. Successfully targeting the bottom-of-the-pyramid segment often necessitates the incorporation of business practices that emphasize sustainability. The synthesis of these themes provides a rich context for the exploration of international marketing concepts.

FEATURES

To help students think critically about the concepts and principles provided throughout the text, we developed a series of features designed to reinforce learning and help maintain reader interest.

OPENING VIGNETTES

The chapters begin with presentations about companies with an international marketing presence or about widely used products such as aspirin and fruit. Each vignette effectively sets the stage for the chapter material. Three questions then are posed to help students reflect on the company and prepare them to read about and discuss the issues that follow in the chapter materials.

INTERNATIONAL INCIDENTS

Each chapter contains brief boxes that describe an unusual event or challenge that arises in a specific international setting. Each hypothetical scenario is accompanied by discussion questions in a "What would you do?" type of approach. This helps foster critical thinking and prepares students for situations that will come up as they work in a global economy.

INTERNATIONAL MARKETING IN DAILY LIFE

Throughout the text, we note that many international marketing efforts deal with products that are not "sexy" or high-tech. In fact, items as mundane as toothbrushes, headache remedies, and toilets represent approachable markets for international companies. The incorporation of these products as illustrations helps explain how marketing works on a global scale when seeking to sell everyday life products, recognizing that the same concepts often apply to more glamorous and sophisticated items.

STRATEGIC, TACTICAL, AND OPERATIONAL IMPLICATIONS

This book does not provide the standard summary section at the end of each chapter. Instead, each chapter's materials will be reviewed under three headings: Strategic Implications, Tactical Implications, and Operational Implications. Strategic implications allow students to integrate materials at the conceptual level, typically at the level of decision-making directed by a company's CEO and top management teams. Tactical implications link strategic concepts to the various marketing functions, such as advertising, personal selling, and creating promotions. Operational implications explain the practical implementation of the various international marketing tools at the individual level, such as how a program might affect an individual salesperson in a retail store. This approach not only summarizes the materials but also integrates analytical thinking with actual marketing practices.

END-OF-CHAPTER RESOURCES

We created end-of-chapter resources for several reasons. We wanted to give students the opportunity to assess their understanding of the chapter, apply ideas and concepts in various settings, use mathematical and statistical methods when applicable, generate discussion, and analyze a case. Each chapter concludes with the following:

Terms. Each bolded key term defined in the text is presented in the same order each appears in the chapter to help students both review the chapter and reexamine the terms to make sure they understand them.

Review Questions. Brief questions were written for each chapter to help students quickly summarize and test their comprehension of what they have read in the chapter. These questions appear in the order that chapter concepts have been presented and are designed to highlight and test the primary points, concepts, and definitions addressed in the chapter.

Discussion Questions. These items can be used for individual analyses of marketing management concepts or to guide in-class conversations. Some of the questions require students to apply the mathematical and statistical models and formulas they have learned about in the chapters.

Analytical and Internet Exercises. Completing these exercises provides students with the opportunity to apply what they have learned in the chapter. The items are often web-based assignments that challenge students to use their analytical skills.

Cases. Each chapter concludes with a brief case designed to illustrate the major concepts in the chapter. Case questions can be used for class discussion or completed as an assignment.

BOOK DESIGN

We hope you agree that this book is visually exciting. By incorporating photographs and advertisements from around the world, we believe the text comes alive. We hope the colorful and meaningful graphs, tables, and photos will appeal to the visual learner.

ACKNOWLEDGEMENTS

There are many persons who have assisted us in the development of this book. We would first like to acknowledge Matthew Waters for his tremendous support and enthusiasm. We are very grateful to Lyndsay Aitken for assistance and editorial work. We would like to thank the following individuals who assisted in the preparation of the manuscript through their careful and thoughtful reviews:

Mark Young, Winona State University

Ruth Lesher Taylor, Texas State University

Yun Chu, Robert Morris University

Laurie Babin, University of Louisiana at Monroe

Brent Smith, Erivan Haub School of Business, St. Joseph's University

Douglas Hausknecht, University of Akron

John Gironda, Florida Atlantic University at Boca Raton

William Lesch, University of North Dakota

Eric C. Wittine, John Carroll University

Xueming Luo, University of Texas at Arlington

Nicholas Didow, University of North Carolina at Chapel Hill

Mark Burgess, Rider University

David Crain, Whittier College

Catherine E. N. Giunta, Seton Hill University

John Hadjimarcou, University of Texas at El Paso

Ron Lennon, University of South Florida at Tampa

Melissa Huffman Malabad, Mary Baldwin College

Mary Lee Stansifer, University of Colorado at Denver

Loy Watley, Nebraska Wesleyan University

Fekkri Meziou, Augsburg College

Ken Fairweather, Letourneau University

Finola Kerrigan, King's College, London

Robert A. Lupton, Central Washington University

Mark Mitchell, Coastal Carolina University

Ben Oumlil, Western Connecticut State University

Al Rosenbloom, Dominican University

Mee-Shew Cheung, Xavier University

Andrew C. Gross, Cleveland State University

Donald Hsu, Dominican College

George V. Priovolos, Hagan School of Business, Iona College

Finally, Daniel Baack would like to thank his father Donald for inviting him to work on this project, and for his incredible hard work on this edition. He carried the project, and Dan will always be grateful. He will always be grateful for the opportunity to publish a second edition of a book with his dad. Daniel would also like to thank his wife and mother, as well as his three great kids, Andy, Emilee, and Jason. His close friends Jason, Dan, Jin, Sol, Ben, and Ed, and his brother David provided a valuable stress release throughout the process. The support of individuals at the University of Denver has also been invaluable, including Pat Perella, Lisa Victoravich, Melissa Akaka, Donald Bacon, and Brad Rosenwinkel. His graduate assistant, Rondel Wright, was a huge help. Thanks Rondel.

Barbara Czarnecka would like to thank the two co-authors, Donald and Daniel, for inviting her to work on this textbook together. It has been an enjoyable experience. Barbara would also like to thank her son Alexander and husband Alejandro for giving her time and space to work on this textbook.

Donald Baack would like to thank his son Daniel for convincing him to make this journey. He is grateful to Barbara for her work on this project. He would also like to thank the administrative assistants and student workers in his department at Pittsburg State University for the help they have given. He would also like to acknowledge his other two children, Jessica and David, and his grandchildren, Rile, Danielle, Andy, Emilee, Jason, Joey, and Tommy.

ONLINE RESOURCES

FOR THE INSTRUCTOR

The password-protected **Instructor Teaching Site** available at **https://study.sagepub.com/baack2e** gives instructors access to a full complement of resources to support and enhance their course. The following assets are available on this site:

- An author-created **Test Bank** contains multiple-choice, true/false, short-answer, and essay questions for each chapter. The test bank is provided on the website in Word format as well as in an electronic format that can be exported into popular course management systems such as Blackboard or WebCT.

- The book's authors also developed **PowerPoint** slides for each chapter. They can be used for lecture and review. Slides are integrated with the book's distinctive features and incorporate key tables, figures, and photos.

- **Video Resources** vividly illustrate key information in each chapter. These links allow both instructors and students to access videos directly related to the content.

- Full-text **SAGE Journal Articles** accompany each chapter, providing extra commentary and analysis on important topics from SAGE's marketing journals.

- **Answers to End-of-Chapter and Discussion Questions** provide valuable tools for facilitating classroom discussions.

- Suggested **Class Assignments** offer instructors a wide range of group and individual activities designed to enhance student learning.

- **Learning Objectives and Chapter Outlines** from the book provide an essential teaching and reference tool.

- Sample **Course Syllabi** for quarter and semester systems include suggestions for structuring an international marketing course.

- **Country Fact Sheets** provide detailed information and unique facts about various countries highlighted in the text.

FOR THE STUDENT

The open-access **Student Study Site** available at **https://study.sagepub.com/ baack2e** is designed to maximize student comprehension of international marketing and to promote critical thinking and application. The following resources and study tools are available on the student portion of this book's website:

- **Flashcards** reiterate key chapter terms and concepts.
- **Self-quizzes** include multiple-choice and true/false questions, allowing students to test their knowledge of each chapter.
- **Learning Objectives and Chapter Outlines** from the book provide an essential study tool.
- **Video Resources** vividly illustrate key information in each chapter. These links allow both instructor and student to access videos directly related to the content.
- Full-text **SAGE Journal Articles** accompany each chapter, providing extra commentary and analysis on important topics from SAGE's marketing journals.
- **Interactive Maps** allow students to increase their knowledge of geography and engage with course content in a dynamic and meaningful way.
- **Country Fact Sheets** provide detailed information and unique facts about various countries highlighted in the text.
- Guidelines for **Developing an International Marketing Plan** are included.

PART I
ESSENTIALS OF INTERNATIONAL MARKETING

CONTENTS

1

INTRODUCTION TO INTERNATIONAL MARKETING

LEARNING OBJECTIVES

After reading and studying this chapter, you should be able to answer the following questions:

1. What are the meanings of the terms multinational corporation, born-global, home country, and host country?

2. What are the essential ingredients in the marketing mix as they relate to international markets, needs, and wants?

3. How have the drivers of globalization influenced international marketing?

4. How are the factors that create international marketing complexity linked to creating a global mindset for marketing activities?

5. Why are the concepts of sustainability and bottom-of-the-pyramid consumers linked to today's international marketplace?

IN THIS CHAPTER

LLOYD'S: A STRONG BRAND SEEKS NEW GLOBAL MARKETING OPPORTUNITIES

Over the years, many pundits have compared various aspects of life to a barracuda, that is, an entity that must keep moving forward or it will die. A case can be made that such an analogy at times applies to individual businesses and industries. In this increasingly complex and challenging global market, many firms find that they must continually adapt in order to remain competitive. Lloyd's, or Lloyd's of London, provides a quality example of a firm able to withstand such pressures and succeed through continual adaptation. A review of the firm's recent activities highlights many of the topics present in this textbook.

The service industry market continues to grow around the world. Lloyd's has primarily focused on specialty insurance and reinsurance for more than a century. Founded in the 1700s, the organization has become a major global entity. To many, the name "Lloyd's of London" has been associated with underwriting unique risk exposures, such as the legs of attractive female celebrities, the arms and legs of athletes, various contests and sweepstake prizes, and other unusual situations.

Most recently, the organization developed a Vision 2025 mandate. The features of the initiative include the items displayed in Figure 1.1.

- Lloyd's will be an international, London-based market, built on trusted relationships and focused on specialist property and casualty business requiring bespoke underwriting and broking.

- Lloyd's will be a mutual supported by a Central Fund, so it will always be more capital efficient to trade inside Lloyd's than outside.

- Lloyd's will be able to access all major international insurance markets, including emerging markets, through its global licence network.

- Lloyd's will offer access to underwriting expertise and capacity in the most efficient way to meet brokers' and clients' needs, including through a face-to-face subscription market.

- Lloyd's world class underwriting and claims management will be supported by an industry-leading infrastructure and service proposition with efficient central services and seamless processing.

- Lloyd's will be a risk selector and a market where entrepreneurialism and innovation will thrive, underpinned by robust risk and performance management.

- Lloyd's ratings will be at a level capable of attracting the specialist business it will write.

- Lloyd's will be larger than today, predicated on sustainable, profitable growth after allowing for movements in the underwriting cycle. Its performance will outstrip that of its competitor group. The increase in premium income in the largest 10 developed economies will track or slightly exceed increases in non-life premium. In the largest 10 developing economies, at times we would expect growth to exceed non-life premium as the specialist risk sector develops and insurance penetration increases.

- Lloyd's will be known around the world for its integrity. The Lloyd's brand will be globally admired and recognised. Lloyd's will be respected for its reputation as the world's specialist centre for (re)insurance.

- The Corporation will promote and protect the interests of the Lloyd's market, and provide valued support services to members and market participants.

FIGURE 1.1 Lloyd's 2025 Vision

Source: Lloyd's. Retrieved from https://www.lloyds.com/about-lloyds/strategy-and-vision

Among the features of the program are the emphasis on continuing the organization's strong brand presence, seeking to enter emerging markets, specializing activities, attracting quality employees, and maintaining a strong ethical foundation. The firm's current emphasis includes efforts devoted to improving and maintaining market access as well as adapting and transforming business processes in light of changing methods of communication and marketing.

In addition to the standard issues of developing and maintaining effective products, prices, distribution methods, and promotional programs, Lloyd's management team will need to cope with many of the drivers of internationalization noted in this textbook, including new and more sophisticated channels of communication, shifting immigration and emigration patterns, and fluctuations in governmental policies and regulations. Further, expansion into new countries as well as maintenance of programs in existing host countries requires attention to culture, language, political shifts, and other forces that

(Continued)

(Continued)

increase complexity in the environment, such as financing issues and local/departmental governance.

Due to the many political, social, and economic shifts that have transpired in global markets during this decade, the complications and obstacles that influence many companies and industries will play out in the insurance world as well. Lloyd's stands in a strong position to cope with these issues and continue to grow in the new world economy.

A Strong Brand Seeks New Global Marketing Opportunities

Source: Tommy Lee Walker/ Shutterstock.com. Retrieved from: https://www.shutterstock.com/image-photo/city-london-financial-services-companies-headquarters-1067023454?src=qU6-HAeJqluQKGzHXUAfsg-1-3

Questions for Students

1. Can you name any of Lloyd's primary competitors?
2. How have the rise of social media and Internet marketing affected a company such as Lloyd's?
3. How would you introduce the Lloyd's brand to a new country?

OVERVIEW

"The only thing constant in life is change." This roughly translated quote from François de la Rochefoucauld may require an update. More accurately, the only thing constant in life in the twenty-first century is *the increasing rate of change*. The new millennium has witnessed an abundance of dramatic new and newsworthy events. Prior to 2000, no one had used the terms "Facebook" or "Twitter." Technological advances, economic upheaval, political shifts, cultural trends, and a vast variety of smaller innovations have transformed the ways people socialize, work, and shop.

In this turbulent global environment, the field of marketing stands on the cutting edge of professions required to adapt. Products, methods of production, changes in trade agreements and treaties, financial swings, improvements in methods that can be used to reach customers as well as changes in ways customers shop require the attention of international marketers.

International marketing is the utilization and adaptation of the best marketing practices for the purposes of conducting commerce in other countries. It includes conducting commerce with customers, clients, partners, society at large, and the *overall global community*.

international marketing: using the marketing mix to meet the needs and wants of consumers in foreign markets

The first part of this book identifies the basic ideas associated with international marketing. This chapter presents marketing concepts and outlines the plan for the upcoming chapters. Chapter 2 examines economic systems and suggests potential modes of entry into new countries for companies seeking to become involved in international marketing. Chapter 3 studies global trade and integration. Chapter 4 reviews methods by which marketers choose countries to enter and the strategies involved. Chapter 5 presents basic concepts related to marketing planning programs, organizational design, and control systems.

This chapter begins with a review of some basic concepts, including the traditional definition of marketing as well as the marketing mix. Through a discussion of needs, wants, and demand, the process for creating relationships with consumers can be examined. The next section considers the grouping of these consumers and how to target them with segmentation and positioning efforts.

With the foundation in mind, this chapter introduces the basics of international marketing. Globalization and greater connectivity continually increase the numbers and types of businesses competing in many nations. Consequently the manner in which globalization influences marketing, specifically in terms of culture, language, politics, law, economics, and infrastructure receives attention. Next, this chapter outlines the organization of the entire textbook. An introduction of the topics of sustainability and bottom-of-the-pyramid marketing within the international context follows, culminating with a discussion of ethical concerns.

LEARNING OBJECTIVE #1:

What are the meanings of the terms "multinational corporation," "born-global," "home country," and "host country?"

THE WORLDWIDE MARKETPLACE

The majority of international consumers purchase numerous items over the course of the week. Some buy coffee or tea to enjoy in the morning. Many individuals prefer rice and tofu to cook for lunch while others buy fish and chips at small restaurants. People purchase clothes, electronics, insurance policies, and a growing number of items on a regular basis. An increasing number of companies from other countries now offer these products. Further, a shirt may have been sewn in Costa Rica or Vietnam. A pen may have been manufactured in Great Britain, and a purse might have been designed in China. Globalization fundamentally changed the ways marketers approach business. Consumers in many countries may be willing to try new products and brands. Companies that effectively market to them may become global business leaders.

To be successful in the international marketplace, marketers learn about new cultures as they adapt to changes in the environment. Business partners in other countries often speak different languages. Various laws and regulations govern business activities. Consumer wants and reasons for purchasing vary across and within countries. Marketing in an international context requires comprehension of these and other forces and factors.

TYPES OF GLOBAL BUSINESSES

Many types of companies are international in scope. The largest are **multinational corporations**, or MNCs. Multinational corporations conduct business activities in at least one other country that differs from the home country in which the organization is headquartered. Many multinational corporations operate in hundreds of countries. The Coca-Cola Corporation engages in commerce in more than 200 countries, with different products and brands in many of them.

Multinational corporations can be large in terms of market value, revenues, and numbers of employees. Table 1.1 compares the market value of the top fifteen global multinational corporations to the size of a country's economy, in terms of gross domestic product. The world's largest multinational corporation, Exxon Mobil, has a market value larger than the economy of Pakistan, a nation of approximately 175 million people.

Many international businesses are considerably smaller than the multinational corporations in Table 1.1. These smaller businesses are often started by entrepreneurs who have experience in international marketing or have worked in multiple countries. The organizations that operate in two or more different countries from inception are **born-global firms**. Often, the founders of these companies have existing international business relationships or knowledge of international markets that facilitate being international from inception (Oviatt and McDougall, 1994).

Global business may be as small as a family business selling items in other countries or as large as the vast expanse of various multinational firms. Many small businesses partner with multinational corporations to increase international marketing efforts (Prashantham and Birkinshaw, 2008). For each, the **home country** is the nation in which the business is located or the country that houses the company's main headquarters. A **host country** is the nation being targeted for expansion. Nestlé's home country is Switzerland. If the marketing team at Nestlé decides to enter the nation of Belarus by selling chocolate products, Belarus becomes the host country. Regardless of the organization's size or its home location, success will be determined, in part, by the effectiveness of the company's marketing operations.

COMPANY ORIENTATION

As companies diversify into a wider number of countries, the orientation of the leadership team frequently evolves. A domestic company can take on a new focus and approach to conducting commerce. Four terms used to explain these

multinational corporations: organizations conducting business activities in at least one other country that differs from the home country in which the organization is headquartered

born-global firms: businesses that operate in two or more different countries from inception

home country: the nation in which the business is located or the one that houses the company's main headquarters

host country: the nation being targeted for expansion by a company

differences in approach include ethnocentric, polycentric, regiocentric, and geocentric management.[1]

ETHNOCENTRIC COMPANIES

When an organization's leaders prefer to use its own employees, both at home and abroad, the company exhibits an ethnocentric leadership style. Management concludes that nationals from the home country are best able to drive international marketing activities, and a home country orientation results. The policies and procedures used by the company remain largely unchanged in the host country. The advantages of this type of approach include greater control over the firm and the ability to more quickly transfer core competencies to operations in the host country. The disadvantages might include greater resistance or aversion by host country employees and consumers, plus the possibility that expatriate company employees may not fully adapt to the host culture.

TABLE 1.1 Largest Multinational Corporations and Equivalent Size Countries

Company / Country	Market Value or Gross Domestic Product (in millions of U.S. dollars)
Exxon Mobil (United States)	452,505
Pakistan	448,100
PetroChina (China)	423,996
Belgium	381,400
General Electric (United States)	369,569
Sweden	333,200
Gazprom (Russia)	299,764
China Mobile (China)	298,093
Ukraine	294,300
Industrial and Commercial Bank of China (China)	277,235
Norway	276,500
Microsoft (United States)	264,131
Vietnam	258,200
AT&T (United States)	231,168
Royal Dutch Shell (United Kingdom)	220,110
Procter & Gamble (United States)	215,640
Wal-Mart Stores (United States)	210,973
Petrobas (Brazil)	208,390
Berkshire Hathaway (United States)	206,924
Israel	206,900
Nestlé (Switzerland)	197,215
HSBC (United Kingdom)	195,767
Ireland	177,000

POLYCENTRIC COMPANIES

A polycentric firm employs locals in the host country to conduct operations. The approach takes advantage of the skills and local knowledge of these individuals to more quickly adapt the company's operations in the host country, shifting the firm's orientation to that host country. Doing so may be less expensive than other approaches to international organization, because fewer expatriate employees will be trained and sent to the host site. The primary problems occur when lines of communication and coordination are not carefully constructed and maintained.

REGIOCENTRIC COMPANIES

When a company employs managers from a variety of countries within a region, such as the Pacific Rim, the organization operates in a regiocentric mode. This strategy creates a series of host countries within the region to serve as the primary orientation. The firm transmits some knowledge and experience about a region into a specific country. A manager who has successfully worked in a Japanese operation may be able to transfer what she has learned to South Korea or the Philippines. The primary management challenge will be maintaining control over a diverse set of employees.

GEOCENTRIC COMPANIES

Many global companies seek to find the best employees and systems, regardless of the country in which they are located. Geocentric companies maintain a global orientation without referencing a specific home or host country. Effective geocentric companies adapt to new international circumstances more quickly. The disadvantage may be greater costs associated with more global searches for new employees, plus challenges in the areas of coordination and control.

IMPLICATIONS

Several factors influence the type of orientation exhibited by a company. The firm's age, its number of host countries, the products and services to be marketed, differences and similarities between home and host countries, and management preferences all influence the company's orientation. A firm directed by a CEO who thinks his or her country does things best will most likely remain in an ethnocentric mode. Multinationals are logical candidates for the most geocentric orientation (Baack, 2008).

THE ESSENCE OF MARKETING

marketing:
discovering
consumer needs
and wants, creating
the products that
meet those needs,
and then pricing,
promoting, and
delivering those
products and
services

Marketing may be defined as "discovering consumer needs and wants, creating the goods and services that meet those needs, and then pricing, promoting and delivering those goods and services" (Clow and Baack, 2010, p. 6). Using this approach, *consumers and other businesses* become the key targets of the marketing process. Groups of consumers and businesses, or markets, lead companies to produce and merchandise the goods and services they desire.

The American Marketing Association (AMA) notes that marketing activities include a set of institutions, and processes for creating, communicating, delivering, and exchanging offerings that have value for customers, clients, partners, and society at large. This viewpoint expands the overall concept of marketing to include any exchange of value. The money that buyers use to make purchases has value, as do the goods and services offered by sellers.

Money is the most common vehicle used to facilitate a marketing exchange, but it does not need to be present for an exchange to be considered marketing. Individuals trade physical products, such as when an Italian teen swaps an AC Milan team jersey to another for a fashionable jacket made in Germany. Also, two people may barter for services: a man who has difficulty reading and writing could agree to help an acquaintance repaint his living room. In the exchange, the acquaintance helps the illiterate man's child fill out application forms for college. When the two trade these services, a marketing exchange takes place. Ideally an exchange satisfies both parties. In this context, the nature of international marketing takes on additional dimensions, including trading goods for services and much more complex trade practices.

THE MARKETING MIX

The **marketing mix** consists of the major activities used to develop and sell goods and services. The four Ps of the marketing mix are product, price, place (or distribution), and promotion, as shown in Figure 1.2. Effectively combining and managing these four components of marketing means that a company develops a product that consumers desire, sets a price consumers are willing to pay, distributes the product in a way that allows consumers to make purchases, and promotes the item effectively.

marketing mix: the major activities used to develop and sell goods and services, including products, prices, distribution systems, and promotional programs

---

LEARNING OBJECTIVE #2:

What are the essential ingredients in the marketing mix as they relate to international markets, needs, and wants?

Promotion incorporates the elements of the *promotional mix*, which includes every activity that transmits messages about a product. The promotional mix incorporates advertising, sales promotion, personal selling, direct marketing, and public relations programs. Trade shows and fairs have become an important part of many international marketing programs (Palumbo and Herbig, 2002). Marketers effectively integrate promotional programs to provide consistent messages about the nature of the product and the company.

Product	A good or service that satisfies consumer needs by providing value
Price	The value of what is exchanged in return for the product
Place (or distribution)	Movement of the product from the seller to the buyer
Promotion	Communication of product value from the buyer to the seller

FIGURE 1.2 The Marketing Mix

MARKETS, NEEDS, AND WANTS

market: people with wants and needs, money to spend, and the willingness to spend money on those wants and needs

A **market** consists of people with wants and needs, money to spend, plus the willingness and ability to spend money on those wants and needs.

Needs are the necessities of life that all humans require for their survival and well-being. *Physiological* needs include food, clothing, shelter, air, water, and sex for the purposes of procreation (survival of the species). Many products satisfy physiological needs. In international settings, especially nations in sub-Saharan Africa, there may be a premium on an item as simple as clean drinking water.

needs: the necessities of life that all humans require for their survival and well-being

Safety needs are met through products ranging from guns and ammunition to health insurance and life insurance policies. In Laos, the war involving the Hmong insurgency affects everyday life and safety needs become more urgent.

Love and belongingness may not be purchased; however, many products assist in meeting such needs, including flowers and cards, romantic taverns and restaurants, plus other places for social gatherings. Courtship rituals vary widely by culture. Red roses express romantic feelings in the United States and other countries. Red is often the color worn by brides in the East, whereas it is the color of mourning in South Africa (Bear, 2010).

Self-actualization refers to meeting one's potential and feeling that one has achieved something valuable by helping others or by performing meaningful work. Finding work that contributes to self-actualization in less- or least-developed countries may be nearly impossible for many.

wants: the specific expression of needs through the desire for specific objects

Wants express specific needs through the desire for individual objects. A physiological need for food may be expressed by desiring a plate of lasagne or fresh fruit. Thirsty consumers in the Middle East may desire a carbonated soda to satisfy their thirst needs. Depending on the country, Middle Eastern consumers could purchase a variety of local sodas including Mecca, Zam Zam, or Parsi Cola, or a soft drink imported from another nation.

Although consumers want many different goods or services; not all of them can be satisfied. A majority of consumers may want a luxury automobile; however, only a few consumers have the financial ability to satisfy this desire, due to the product's high price.

demand: the amount of a good or service that consumers will buy at various price levels

Demand reflects the amounts of goods or services that consumers will purchase at various price levels. A higher-priced car has a smaller demand because fewer consumers are willing and able to pay what is needed to buy one.

SEGMENTATION, TARGET MARKETS, AND POSITIONING (STP)

market segmentation: a process that involves identifying specific groups based on their needs, attitudes, and interests; the grouping of consumers based on their needs, attitudes, and interests

Any given product may have several types of customers who might wish to buy it, and they may use the same product in different ways, such as using baking soda for baking or as a tooth cleanser. Identifying the consumers who demand or want a product due to their needs, attitudes, and interests is the **market segmentation** process. Marketers group or segment consumers in ways that allow them to identify sets that express or have demand for various products. International marketers consider differences in nationalities and customs when identifying market segments (Broderick et al., 2007).

A **target market** consists of a specific, identifiable market segment that a company seeks to reach. The marketing mix can then be used to ensure that consumers within the target market both want the product and are satisfied after purchasing and using it (see Figure 1.3). A company's marketing team might identify ten market segments but choose to only target five of those segments, which is the process of *target marketing*.

The marketing mix helps establish **positioning**, which is creating a perception in a consumer's mind about the nature of a company and its products relative to those of competitors. Most companies seek to position products as being different from those of competitors. An emphasis on a unique benefit or component of a product that separates an item from competitors' products results in **differentiation**. Products may be differentiated based on price, innovations, high levels of quality, and other attributes.

target market: a specific, identifiable market segment that a company seeks to reach

positioning: creating a perception in a consumer's mind regarding the nature of a company and its products relative to those of competitors

differentiation: emphasis on a unique benefit or component of a product that separates that product from competitors

FIGURE 1.3   The Marketing Mix Applied to Target Markets

MARKETING IN AN INTERNATIONAL CONTEXT

The essence of marketing remains the same, whether in domestic or international settings. At the same time, entering a new country to sell goods or services requires many adjustments. Employees in a firm preparing to enter foreign markets first examine the new context to identify the parts of the marketing mix that may require changes along with adjustments to managerial practices, accounting methods, human resource policies, shipping and storage programs, and other activities.

International marketing begins with meeting the needs and wants of consumers in foreign markets. A home country may have a great deal of similarity with the host country in which a target market has been identified. In that circumstance, perhaps only small changes or adaptations to the marketing mix will be necessary. It is possible that consumer tastes and preferences have become increasingly homogenized as in this new global environment (Vrontis et al., 2009). At times, however, the host country target market may be markedly different in some way. This would lead to efforts to change aspects of the marketing mix to fit the new environment. Two of the most salient forces that influence the degree of adaptation necessary are:

1. the drivers of globalization, and

2. the factors that create international marketing complexity.

| Channels of Communication |
| Lower Transportation Costs |
| Immigration and Emigration Patterns |
| Governmental Actions |

FIGURE 1.4   Drivers of Globalization

These forces combine to create both opportunities and challenges for companies seeking to expand into new countries.

THE DRIVERS OF GLOBALIZATION

globalization:
the increased interconnectedness of consumers and businesses globally

Globalization is driven by a variety of forces, including those displayed in Figure 1.4. Countries around the world have become more interconnected in spite of conflicts such as terrorism, and wars. In the United Kingdom, consumers enjoy computers, games, and toys from South Korea; strawberries from Colombia; flowers from Venezuela; raspberries from Poland; and peas from Kenya (Gregory, 2006). These connections are partly derived from commerce, but also result from improved methods of communication, increased travel, and greater ties across borders.

LEARNING OBJECTIVE #3:

How have the drivers of globalization influenced international marketing?

Globalization grows out of numerous technological and structural innovations. Technology fundamentally alters communication patterns. The costs of communication combined with greater access to communication channels reduce international barriers. Social media outlets facilitate contacts between consumers. Communications between companies and consumers have also increased. As one example, British consumers calling companies often talk to customer service representatives in Estonia or Lithuania (Gregory, 2006).

Technology decreases transportation costs and enables the movements of people and products. Lower costs associated with entering new markets and moving operations to new countries create new marketing and business opportunities. Quality communication systems reduce shipping costs. *Containerization* is the process of packing goods during the manufacturing process leading to the point of distribution without the need for repacking or complex handling. Estimates suggest that shipping of a single typical ship-, train-, and truck-interchangeable container from southern China to the western United States costs $2,500 (Notteboom and Rodrigue, 2009). Reductions in air freight costs enable air transportation to play a key role in international marketing activities (Hummels, 2007).

Globalization has been enhanced by changing patterns of immigration and emigration. A dramatic increase in movement of people has affected many countries, including Estonians in Finland, Africans in China (including former President Obama's half-brother), and Guatemalans in Mexico (Martin, 2001). This movement increases the ties between countries and widens exposures to different cultures and ideas for many citizens as it presents new marketing opportunities. Someone who has moved into a new country may still desire products from her former home. If a sufficient number of individuals who have left a country share the same want, a company may be able to export that product to their new homes.

Governments play an important role in increasing connections between countries. One governmental action has been to reduce barriers to commerce. Doing so stimulates trade. Today, freer movement applies to labor and capital, which lowers the costs of moving many business processes to lower-cost or highly specialized locations. The increase in the flow of goods, people, and capital has also led, at least to some degree, to economic development in many countries, including China, India, and Brazil. *Market liberalization* refers to the removal of governmental control over economic activity. Countries which were part of the former Soviet Union, and nations in Eastern Europe, China, and Vietnam, have experienced forms of market liberalization. Liberalization removes barriers to trade and opens markets. Nations such as China have become primary destinations for foreign investments. China has become a leading global exporter as a result. Map 1.1 presents the exports of countries globally.

LEARNING OBJECTIVE #4:

How are the factors that create international marketing complexity linked to creating a global mindset for marketing activities?

Globalization provides a key marketing opportunity. A recent survey of 1,400 CEOs from forty-six countries by Price Waterhouse Cooper revealed that two-thirds of respondents thought globalization would generate positive effects on their businesses in the coming years (Nelson, 2006).

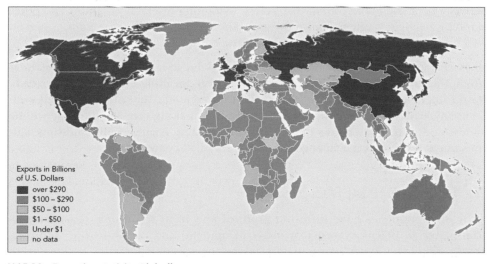

Exports in Billions
of U.S. Dollars

- over $290
- $100 – $290
- $50 – $100
- $1 – $50
- Under $1
- no data

MAP 1.1   Exporting Activity Globally

New major global exporting countries have recently emerged

THE FACTORS THAT CREATE INTERNATIONAL MARKETING COMPLEXITY

Marketers face an increasingly complex global context for many business decisions. Complexity may be found in the differences in business environments within each country. Each nation features distinct differences, as summarized in Figure 1.5.

FIGURE 1.5   Factors That Create International Marketing Complexity

CULTURE

culture: the beliefs, customs, and attitudes of a distinct group of people

The beliefs, customs, and attitudes of a distinct group of people constitute its **culture**. Culture exhibits a powerful influence on every aspect of international marketing (Yaprak, 2008). Tastes and preferences for products, interactions between coworkers, standard purchasing methods, the willingness to try a new product, and comfort levels with different types of retailing and product distribution are examples of cultural differences between countries. Finding local partners to help navigate these differences should be one of the first steps when expanding internationally. The "world teen" or "global youth" market consists of people with similar values and tastes, regardless of country of birth (Chu and Huang, 2010). Learning about segments such as these offers a promising new area to explore.

LANGUAGE

language: the system used to communicate between peoples, including verbal and nonverbal cues

The system used to communicate between peoples, including verbal and nonverbal cues, is a **language**. The movement of products across boundaries may require translation and adaptation of advertising, labels on products, and basic communication between host and home country marketers. Marketing research programs and other marketing activities often require the assistance of a *cultural assimilator*, a person well versed in the host country's language and culture.

Many classic international blunders have occurred due to language, such as Chevrolet attempting to sell the Nova automobile in Spanish-speaking countries. In Spanish, Nova roughly translates as *no va* or "no go." Consequently, the cars did not sell well. Company leaders now recognize the importance of making sure any message will be understood in the way it was intended before sending it out. Communicating with consumers represents a challenge for marketers in all contexts.

POLITICAL AND LEGAL FACTORS

political systems: the people with an organization, typically governments, who possess the power and how that power is structured

Individual countries have differing political and legal traditions. Governments administer **political systems** in order to manage and maintain the country's power structure. Types of political systems include democracies, authoritarian governments, and anarchies. In each, governments create laws that regulate commerce and establish trading treaties or arrangements with governments from other countries.

Legal systems constitute the methods for applying and implementing the laws of a country. Legal systems include common law, civil law, and theocratic law, among others. Governmental activities, through both regulations and the actions of governmental officials, constrain what marketers can do within a country's borders. These directives include packaging and labelling requirements, regulation of advertising, and may be as severe as banning certain products.

legal systems: the methods for applying and implementing the laws of a country

ECONOMIC SYSTEMS

The means by which a country allocates resources, goods, and services to citizens constitute its **economic system**. The types of economic systems present in international commerce include capitalist, communist, and mixed structures.

economic system: the means by which countries allocate resources, goods, and services to citizens

Each type of economic system will be based, in part, on the role that the government plays in the distribution of resources. Governments establish, revise, and oversee economic systems. The extent to which a ruling class exerts influence becomes the primary concern in international marketing. In communist systems, the government oversees the means of production and exerts nearly total control over business activities. The interplay between the government and the economic system in communist countries can create additional barriers for companies seeking to enter markets.

In contrast, a capitalist economy invites investment and entrepreneurship. When the system allows for the ownership of private property and protection of intellectual property, market opportunities expand at a faster rate. Companies consider the economic system of prospective host countries before attempting to enter those markets.

Economic systems affect a variety of international marketing activities. Economics play a key role in the setting of prices and in the overall international finance. Global trade, a key component of international marketing, is also affected by economic systems.

INFRASTRUCTURE

Marketers identify differences in infrastructure in host markets. **Infrastructure** contains the organizational and physical structures essential for societies to operate. Examples of the presence or lack of infrastructure include the availability of roads, the degree of Internet access, the percentage of the population owning mobile phones, the quality of educational institutions, and the availability of water, electricity, and/or natural gas.

infrastructure: the organizational and physical structures present in a country, such as roads, technology, and information systems

A poor infrastructure increases production and marketing costs. Roads in India, as one example, are notorious for being underdeveloped and crowded. Infosys Technologies Ltd, a leading Indian technology firm, spent $5 million in 2006 to pay for a fleet of buses, minivans, and taxis to transport its employees in Bangalore. Estimates suggest that, due to traffic jams, commutes can take as long as four hours per day for employees in that city (Hamm and Laksman, 2007).

Highly developed economic systems lead to major urban centers.

Source: photo courtesy of Chih-Kuo, Kuo clearspace.tw.

A well-established infrastructure presents new marketing opportunities. Most- and more-developed nations grow, in part, by strengthening a country's infrastructure. Increased investment and greater trade for the nation often result. Infrastructure influences international marketing in a number of ways. Many times throughout this text, an analysis of infrastructure will be included in the discussion of a marketing activity.

IMPLICATIONS

Responding to changes in different countries requires a global mindset. This involves learning about new places, people, and processes, and viewing business activities from a global perspective. Topography represents a key example of an issue that emerges from this broader perspective. Map 1.2 displays key topographic features across the world. Providing the foundation for a global mindset is one intention of this book, while recognizing that maintaining a global mindset should be a continuing process.

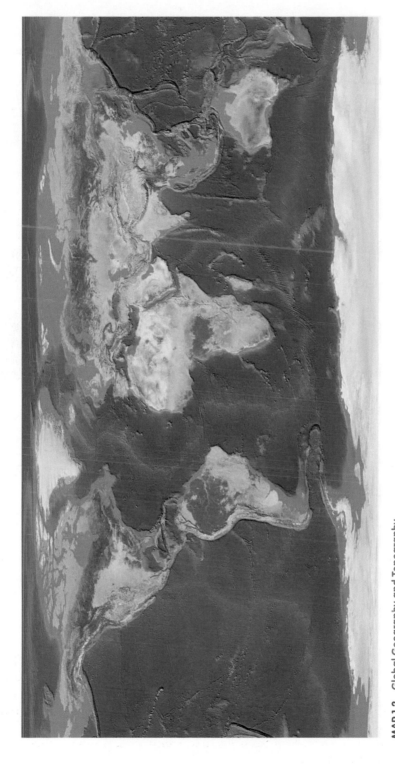

MAP 1.2   Global Geography and Topography

Topographic features can facilitate or hinder relationships between countries.

INTERNATIONAL INCIDENT

As part of an international junket, your marketing team stops to visit an important potential new client in Spain. Within a few hours of cordial discussions, the manager of the client company invites you to attend the bullfights the next day as his guest. You have little interest in attending the event and do not like the custom. What should you do? How would you respectfully decline? Or, would you accept and then bow out, claiming illness the next day? Would you consider attending? How would your response change if you were a Hindu from India or Nepal? (Hindus hold all life to be sacred and consider bulls to be religious animals that should never be harmed.)

INTERNATIONAL MARKETING IN DAILY LIFE

It may be that most people think of something "glamorous" when the term "marketing" is used. It may feel classy or sexy to consider a marketing program for the newest hand-held mobile technology, a fancy sports car, or designer clothing. At the same time, a case can be made that the majority of marketing opportunities may come from much simpler products and services—those used in everyday life.

One common theme that appears in this textbook is the marketing of products to be used daily or regularly. The approach serves a special purpose: to illustrate how the most commonplace of daily activities can lead to the identification of target markets that companies can reach with products that are adapted to individual cultures and national circumstances. Figure 1.6 lists some of the daily activities described in this textbook.

Bathing	Brushing Teeth/Dental Hygiene
Using the Restroom	Wearing Jeans
Sleeping and Beds	Methods of Transportation
Cosmetics	Candy
Dining Habits and Foods	Cooking Methods
Drinks and Milk Consumption	Coping with Headaches
Socialization	Music
Religions	Methods of Payment and Banking

FIGURE 1.6   Selected Daily Life Activities and Marketing Opportunities Presented in This Textbook

BATHING PRODUCTS AND THE DRIVERS OF GLOBALIZATION

As an example of the far-reaching impact of globalization on business practices and international marketing, consider one basic human activity: bathing and cleaning. Bathing and cleaning are routine activities worldwide, but the methods and products used vary widely. Among the methods are showers, baths, and washing using only water from a stream or river. Soap products may be solid, liquid, or gels. The same holds true for shampoo. Certain companies offer more specialized items for washing a person's face or to clean strong stains, such as oil or grease. Consequently, the simple, common everyday event of personal hygiene may present marketing opportunities for numerous companies from a variety of countries, all of them affected by international marketing complexities.

Bathing and cleaning are routine activities worldwide.

Source: Paul Piebinga/iStockphoto

The drivers of globalization and the factors that create international marketing complexity influence the types of products that may be marketed, the places where they are sold, and the methods used to reach customers in order to entice them to buy. Bathing and cleaning products are no exception.

Channels of Communication

The methods consumers use to communicate with companies are changing, as are the methods consumers use to communicate with one another. Methods of cleaning and grooming that are common in one country might be viewed as new and exciting in another. New channels of communication, such as social networks, enable consumers to gossip about products, form brand communities, as well as describe and discuss products. Customers can go online to register thoughts with companies about products. For instance, a customer might inquire about the correct method to use a new soap or cleaning agent for a shower or tub. Website FAQs (frequently asked questions) make it easier to explain product benefits and uses to a wider audience, especially when the website has been translated into more than one language.

Lower Transportation Costs

Reduced shipping costs make it possible for a greater number of companies to enter markets. Unilever sells a large number of personal grooming products around the world. Each can be adapted to the specific needs of a culture, region, or infrastructure. Salespersons from Unilever travel to remote places seeking out new markets.

Immigration and Emigration Patterns

As a group of people moves from one country to another, the individuals may seek to both maintain their previous cultural norms and adapt to others. For example, a young woman seeking to "fit in" in a Westernized culture may shave her legs for the first time. A young man attempting to adapt might bathe more or less frequently, wash his hair using a different product, and groom himself to become part of the social fabric of a new country.

Governmental Actions

Through liberalization and inner-connectivity, governments may speed up the process of exporting products that are new and innovative. A new soap form, such as a gel that turns into lather, may find a wide marketplace, especially when the container size can be made smaller than a liquid soap. Towelettes used for cleaning one's hands without the need for water may reach a wide audience of persons wishing to wash their hands before a meal in arid climates.

BATHING PRODUCTS AND THE FACTORS THAT CREATE INTERNATIONAL MARKETING COMPLEXITY

Even as the drivers of globalization open new markets, the complications remain. Washing and cleaning products require adaptation to meet the needs of consumers in various countries. This includes methods of pricing, promoting, and distributing the products.

Culture

Cultural views of cleanliness vary widely. Strong body odor may be offensive in one nation and acceptable in another, which affects the frequency and duration of personal grooming. Many religions express concepts relating cleanliness to purity. Cleansing and water are used in religious rites, such as baptisms in Christian religions. In India, water holds special meaning to some consumers, especially those from more traditional rural areas. Where water is scarce, baths are infrequent and can be seen as sacred. Many Indians observe a funeral ritual in which the individual's ashes are scattered into the Ganges River. Due to the special nature of water, Indians may find using a hot tub or taking two showers per day to be offensive (Brady, 2007).

Methods for washing hair and caring for hair are affected by views of aesthetics and beauty as well as practical matters such as hair texture and hair style. In many countries, women do not shave their legs or armpits. The use of deodorants may be widely accepted in one region and not even considered in others.

Language

The term "clean" has a variety of meanings, depending on the language and culture in which the language is spoken. Language usage would be closely watched as part of any advertising or promotional program for soaps, shampoos, and other items. In a culture with relaxed views toward nudity and sexuality, the image of a bare leg used to promote a bathing product might inspire interest and achieve the desired effect. In a culture with more strict views, such an image would be highly offensive.

Political and Legal Factors

Laws and regulations affect the ingredients that may be included in a product as well as how those ingredients are represented. A dandruff shampoo may be considered medicinal in one country if it contains certain ingredients and might be subject to strict regulation. Packaging and labeling requirements may be stringent in some nations and nearly nonexistent in others.

Any cleansing product that injures a customer would be subject to various legal systems. In some countries, a defective or injurious product might result in the execution of the person in the company who was responsible for the problem. Methods of adjudicating lawsuits as well as regulations regarding compensation for injuries would also vary depending on the government involved.

Economic Systems

A free enterprise economy encourages entrepreneurs to develop new and better cleaning agents. This would lead businesses to develop products that not only wash people but also clean the places where people bathe or shower. Mildew removers may be routinely available in one country but not in another. Glass cleaners and other cleansers may be found where showers with glass doors are available. One innovation driven by economic interests has been liquid soap dispensed from a bottle.

Economic systems that are more restrictive may limit the opportunity to develop new products. They may also limit a company's ability to export to that country. A communist or state-driven economy might utilize tariffs and other methods to keep competing companies out.

Infrastructure

The availability of water influences bathing and cleaning habits. Where water is scarce, bathing will be less frequent and the emphasis will be on conservation. In some countries, steam showers may be used. When water is readily available, people may take long, luxurious baths and showers. Water may also be available where electricity or natural gas is not. The result would be cold showers and baths.

The delivery of products to consumers may be helped or hindered by road and transportation systems. Some countries also have well-developed channels of distribution, including wholesale and retail operations. Others have only scattered and diverse shops and stores.

THE INTERNATIONAL MARKETING CONTEXT

The four drivers of globalization and the five factors that influence international marketing complexity are featured throughout this textbook. While all of the factors affect every marketing activity, these individual concepts are described in greater depth in the sections of this textbook where they exhibit prominent influence on a specific marketing function.

THE ORGANIZATION OF THIS BOOK

Figure 1.7 expresses the interactions between the five factors that influence international marketing complexity, with the topics to be described in this textbook. As shown, the marketing mix constitutes the primary set of topics presented, combined with sections about markets and international marketing management. Figure 1.8 lists the topics presented in this textbook. A brief description of each follows.

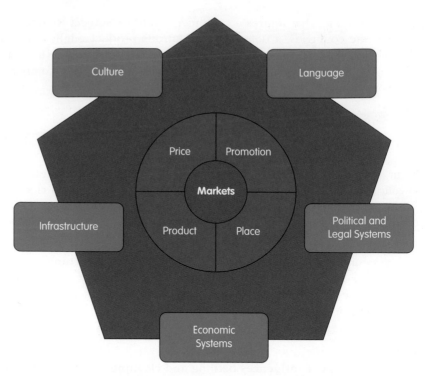

FIGURE 1.7   The International Marketing Context

PART I: ESSENTIALS OF INTERNATIONAL MARKETING

This first chapter establishes the foundation of international marketing. Marketing is an exchange of value, typically between a buyer and a seller. To provide value, marketers must understand the nature of markets in order to effectively identify the target markets a company intends to reach.

Chapter 2 introduces a more in-depth analysis of culture. The challenges of marketing across cultural differences receive attention. Techniques for adjusting to cultural variances are noted.

Chapter 3 investigates the nature of global trade. Various ideas about global trade will be presented. Then, integration, or the agreements between countries to lower limits on the movements of products, capital, and/or labor is described. Free trade has both supporters and critics.

Chapter 4 examines the factors which influence the selection of countries to enter and items that eliminate them as prospects. It also details the various modes of entry companies utilize. Modes of entry constitute the methods marketers use to place products in new host countries.

Chapter 5 reviews the critical activities associated with planning, organizational design, and control systems. Linkages between the three constitute a key ingredient in creating a successful international marketing program.

Essentials of International Marketing

Introduction to the Field

Culture and Cross-Cultural Marketing

Global Trade and Integration

Country Selection and Entry Strategies

International Marketing Planning, Organization, and Control

International Markets and Market Research

Markets and Segmentation in an International Context

International Positioning

Market Research in the International Environment

International Product Marketing

International Product and Brand Marketing

International Product Standardization and Adaptation

International Pricing and Finance

International Pricing

International Finance and Pricing Implications

International Place or Distribution

International Marketing Channel Management

International Distribution: Exporting and Retailing

International Promotion and Personal Selling

Globally Integrated Marketing Communications

International Sales Promotions and Public Relations

FIGURE 1.8 Topics Presented in This Textbook

PART II: INTERNATIONAL MARKETS AND MARKET RESEARCH

The second part of this book examines international markets and market research. Chapter 6 describes international target market segmentation and selection. The effects of culture on segmentation programs are noted. This includes an analysis of the emergence of ways to identify market segments as a business becomes more globalized. In essence, markets can be segmented at the country level and then at smaller levels, such as by consumer groups and types of businesses.

Chapter 7 continues the presentation of the international segmentation, targeting, and positioning (STP) process by examining methods used to establish positioning. Positioning differentiates products in a consistent fashion across countries. Creating brand equity, the perception that a product is different and better, will be the ultimate goal of positioning. To do so, global products must be positioned to overcome negative consumer perceptions, including attitudes toward the country of origin of an item.

To provide value to consumers, marketers must first understand what consumers want. International market research, the focus of Chapter 8, is the process marketers use to obtain this information. Market research uses the scientific method and strives for objectivity. A great deal of domestic data collection takes place at the micro or individual consumer level. Within an international marketing context, marketers often collect data at the macro or country level. Country-level analysis includes assessing political risk and determining country-level advantages.

PART III: INTERNATIONAL PRODUCT MARKETING

The third part of this text presents product-based issues. Chapter 9 addresses the fundamentals of managing the product component of the marketing mix. The product life cycle is introduced and extended internationally. Product and brand management strategies are reviewed.

Chapter 10 describes the use of product strategies and tactics to meet the needs of host country target markets. The concepts of adaptation and standardization as they apply to global marketing are explained in detail.

PART IV: INTERNATIONAL PRICING AND FINANCE

Price is the focus of the fourth part of this textbook. International pricing, the topic of Chapter 11, includes various methods for setting a price. The role of price in signaling quality is also discussed.

In Chapter 12, the role of international finance in price setting is considered. Currency is central to international price setting, and currency conversion and risk assessment are reviewed. Economic systems and global finance institutions are also integrated into the discussion of international pricing.

PART V: INTERNATIONAL PLACE OR DISTRIBUTION

The fifth part of this book studies the role of distribution in meeting the needs of international consumers. Chapter 13 reviews the marketing channel management process, including differences between various types of transportation. Infrastructure plays a central role in distribution and receives consideration in the chapter.

Chapter 14 focuses on exporting and retailing to foreign markets. The chapter examines the five primary tasks associated with physical distribution. Then retailing methods and approaches are described.

PART VI: INTERNATIONAL PROMOTION

The sixth part of the text concentrates on promotion. Marketing communications, especially advertising, are the focus of Chapter 15. Differences between communication styles across cultures influence promotional activities. The decision to either change or keep a promotion in a host market is discussed in depth.

Chapter 16 covers the topics of sales promotion and public relations. These final ingredients accompany all other messages transmitted internally to employees and externally to all other publics. Effective programs help detect negative publicity and help respond when damage to the company's image may be present.

LEARNING OBJECTIVE #5:

Why are the concepts of sustainability and bottom-of-the-pyramid consumers linked to today's international marketplace?

SUSTAINABILITY AND THE BOTTOM-OF-THE-PYRAMID

In addition to the content above, each chapter incorporates a discussion of marketing to the bottom-of-the-pyramid and the role of sustainability in international marketing. These key new forces have generated a dramatic impact on globalization and international marketing programs.

SUSTAINABILITY

Sustainability or sustainable development refers to meeting the needs of the current generation in a way that leaves future generations with the ability to also meet their needs. For example, instead of using gasoline, a new line of Brazilian cars called Flex burn ethanol made from sugar cane. Oil-based gasoline has a finite supply but sugar cane is renewable, which represents a more sustainable approach to meeting consumer needs for fuel (Downie, 2005).

sustainability: meeting the needs of the current generation in a way that leaves future generations with the ability to also meet their needs

Some businesses may view sustainability efforts as representing a cost rather than in terms of potential profit. Hopefully instead, many marketing and management professionals will begin to view sustainability not as a burden but rather as a process that can reduce costs and lead to innovations that can give a company an advantage over competitors. Many well-known firms, such as Wal-Mart, Unilever, and Staples, have changed to more sustainable business practices.

FedEx is a leader in this movement. Not long ago, the company rolled out replacements for Boeing 757 airplanes. The change was estimated to reduce the company's fuel consumption by 36% while increasing capacity by 20%. In addition, the company's IT department developed proprietary software to optimize flight schedules, and began incorporating solar panels into its energy generation. FedEx leveraged its ownership of Kinko's to become more sustainable. The company encourages consumers to print to-be-delivered documents at Kinko's location in the destination city. This reduces transportation costs for FedEx, gives individuals more time to finish their documents, and provides the greener service customers desire. FedEx's expertise in sustainable business practices has the potential to generate additional profits. The company's leadership team recently announced the launch of a stand-alone sustainability consulting business (Nidumolu et al., 2009).

In the end, being sustainable should be considered as more than promoting products as "green." Sustainability reflects a fundamental shift in business practices and can become a mindset that views sustainability as a potential source of profit. Table 1.2 presents a recently introduced framework for leveraging sustainability for business success.

TABLE 1.2   A Sustainability Framework

Stage 1. Viewing Compliance as Opportunity
Action: Comply with the most stringent rules and do so before they are enforced
Stage 2. Making Value Chains Sustainable
Action: Focus on supply chains, operations, telecommuting, and returns
Stage 3. Designing Sustainable Products and Services
Action: Leverage consumer demand for "green" products
Stage 4. Developing New Business Models
Action: Think of new ways to deliver consumer value
Stage 5. Creating Next-Practice Platforms
Action: Change the existing paradigm

BOTTOM-OF-THE-PYRAMID

bottom-of-the-pyramid: the approximately 4 billion people globally living on less than $2 per day

Approximately 4 billion people globally live on less than $2 per day. This group of consumers is referred to as the **bottom-of-the-pyramid** (Prahalad, 2006). These consumers are described throughout this book. The traditional view of marketers has been that while this group has needs and wants that are similar to other groups, these consumers lack the financial ability to transform those wants to demand. To rephrase, members of this group do not have enough money for companies to justify targeting them.

The Fortune at the Bottom-of-the-Pyramid: Eradicating Poverty through Profits, a book by C. K. Prahalad, argues against this perspective. He makes the counterpoint that at 4 billion consumers, even a small level of profit per sale can lead to a large profit across the entire segment. In addition, targeting this group can lead to more efficient processing and innovations that can then be applied to more affluent consumers (Prahalad, 2006).

ETHICAL DECISION-MAKING AND INTERNATIONAL MARKETING

Many of the chapters in this text include discussions of the ethical concerns raised by the content in that section. Proscribing certain behaviors or advocating particular viewpoints will not be the objective. Instead, the text raises issues with ethical implications in various chapters and notes the potential societal effects of marketing activities.

As business moves to a global level a marketer may be exposed to business practices that are considered unethical in the person's home country. Or, in contrast, the marketer may be tempted to use these business practices in the host country. For example, chemical companies continued to sell pesticides that were outlawed in Western countries in poorer countries that did not have that prohibition (Arvind and Habib, 1998). Is that behavior ethical or unethical?

Two separate frameworks can be applied to these questions. The first, *cultural relativism*, represents the concept that an individual's culture should inform the ethical or unethical implications of their beliefs and actions. What is accepted by one culture should be the standard when conducting business in that region. This idea has been controversial from its inception. At the extreme, the approach may tacitly approve of behavior almost universally decried as being unethical and immoral, such as child labor, oppression of women, and slavery. The focus on business education and cultural sensitivity is partially blamed by some as teaching an inappropriate level of relativism (Smeltzer and Jennings, 1998).

The *justice approach* provides a contrasting framework. Justice involves treating all people fairly and consistently when making decisions. Two types of justice are described in ethical discussions. A concentration on the fairness of outcomes, punishments, and awards is *distributive justice*. *Procedural justice*, on the other hand, is rooted in fair and reliable use of rules and protocols. The justice approach calls for equivalent pay, working conditions, rules, and ethical behaviors in all countries where the business is active. This approach would apply regardless of the legal context in which these decisions are made.

CHAPTER 1: REVIEW AND RESOURCES

Strategic Implications

Top-level managers direct the strategic courses of companies by first employing a SWOT analysis. This analysis involves assessing internal strengths and weaknesses (SW) and opportunities and threats (OT) present in the external environment. Understanding that a company enjoys an advantage based on a superior product and strong brand loyalty represents key company strengths. When that same company lacks the funds to expand further, weakness exists. Predicting changes in economic conditions or shifts in consumer preferences are examples of how to identify potential threats or opportunities.

The net result of a SWOT analysis will be the strategic choice of products and services to be offered, because opportunities and threats have been identified, some of which emerge from the analysis of a national or regional culture. Culture presents opportunities in terms of revealing wants and needs held by members of a community. Assuming these individuals have sufficient resources to acquire products that meet these wants and needs, then products can be developed, prices set, delivery systems established, and promotional programs created to reach members in the market.

To complete the strategic design, target markets are chosen with positioning approaches that match the markets. The strategic design outlines the direction the organization will take with regard to both domestic and international markets.

Decisions are made concerning the emphasis on *broad differentiation* of the product as the *low-cost provider* or as the *best-cost provider*. Broad differentiation indicates the product will be presented as being superior as well as different. The low-cost approach features an emphasis on price. A best-cost strategy combines the unique qualities of the product with its price, leading to a focus on the value offered to the customer. After specific target markets are defined, the market niche may also be reached through differentiation, low cost, or best cost. These may be adjusted to fit the requisites of the domestic or international market.

Tactical Implications

Marketing focuses on facilitating exchanges in value by understanding consumer needs and wants, which lead, over time, to relationships with consumers. This process is the same, albeit more complex, for international marketers. International marketing leads to many potential tactical changes. Every component of the marketing mix (product, price, place, and promotion) should be adjusted as companies become increasingly international. Advertising programs will be altered to fit the culture of a host country. Relationships with retail outlets will be formed.

To assist in creating successful tactics, marketers seek to understand how the external environment changes after crossing home country borders. Culture, language, political and legal systems, economic systems, and infrastructure are the primary categories for these changes. By successfully understanding and responding to these differences, marketers can establish connections with consumers.

Changes in tactics should be based on a deep understanding of consumption in each market. Local partners, along with effective marketing research, may help in this regard. Tactics not rooted in an understanding of host country consumers will eventually fail.

Marketers must be willing and able to make rapid modifications to tactics in response to changes in international locales. Predicting responses and risks in host countries is more difficult than in home countries, and it must be assumed that mistakes will be made. By being prepared to respond to these mistakes in tactics, companies will be more successful.

Operational Implications

Day-to-day operations will vary dramatically across markets. In some markets, consumer relationships are built through daily interactions. Methods of payment, body language, bargaining, and other personal contacts affect the conduct of routine business. Over time, these repeated exchanges broker trust and longer-term commitments.

At the operational level, individual advertisements and other promotions will be scrutinized to make sure they fit with the local culture. Shipping methods are studied and adjusted to meet local laws and standards. An overall strategy of broad differentiation results in the local salesperson emphasizing the product's unique features and advantages as part of the sales pitch. The key to effective daily operations will be maintaining consistency with strategic and tactical direction taken by the organization.

TERMS

international marketing	marketing mix
multinational corporations	market
born-global firms	needs
home country	wants
host country	demand
marketing	market segmentation

target market	political systems
positioning	legal systems
differentiation	economic system
globalization	infrastructure
culture	sustainability
language	bottom-of-the-pyramid

REVIEW QUESTIONS

1. Define international marketing and marketing. What is the difference between them?

2. What are the four components of the marketing mix?

3. What components are included in the promotional mix?

4. Define a market and give an example.

5. What is the difference between needs and wants?

6. How do wants lead to demand?

7. What is the market segmentation process?

8. Define target market.

9. What is the relationship between positioning and differentiation?

10. Define globalization and identify the four drivers of this process.

11. What are the five factors that create international marketing complexity?

12. Define culture.

13. Describe how language might influence marketing.

14. Compare and contrast economic systems with political and legal systems.

15. Define infrastructure.

16. Define sustainability.

17. What are the six stages for leveraging sustainability?

18. Define bottom-of-the-pyramid.

19. Define cultural relativism and the justice approach to ethical issues.

DISCUSSION QUESTIONS

1. The marketing mix is manipulated to meet target market needs and wants. How might the following companies use this process to satisfy consumers?

   • Jones Soda

   • Red Bull

- Haier

- Sony

- Hyundai

2. There are four main drivers of globalization: (1) channels of communication, (2) lower transportation costs, (3) immigration and emigration patterns, and (4) governmental actions. How have these forces influenced your own life? Consider both your social life and your interaction with businesses.

3. Identify, in simple terms, differences in the factors creating international marketing complexity for the following countries. These factors are culture, language, political and legal systems, economic systems, and infrastructure.

- India

- Brazil

- Kenya

- Slovenia

- Mongolia

4. Sustainability is increasingly viewed as a potential driver of firm success. What are the implications of this perspective with regard to the various marketing functions?

ANALYTICAL AND INTERNET EXERCISES

1. Visit the following websites. Even though they are in different languages, use the images on the websites to identify the company's target market. Can you also identify the company's position, and how it is differentiated?

    http://news.baidu.com/
    www.sony.jp/
    www.giant-bicycles.com/zh-TW/
    www.mercedes-benz.de/
    www.ethiopianairlines.com/en/default.aspx
    http://scf.natura.net/

2. Coca-Cola has an online virtual vendor at www.virtualvender.coca-cola.com/. Look at the products it sells in at least three countries from each continent. How do these products reflect differences in culture between these countries?

3. Google the terms "sustainability" and "bottom-of-the-pyramid" together. What are the results? What do the results say about how these two concepts interact?

STUDENT STUDY SITE

Visit **https://study.sagepub.com/baack2e** to access these free additional learning tools:

- Web Quizzes
- eFlashcards
- SAGE Journal Articles
- Country Fact Sheets
- Chapter Outlines
- Interactive Maps

CASE 1

Carrefour: Retailing in an International Marketplace

As the second-largest retailer in the world, the French company Carrefour dominates the global retail market. The company's first store opened on June 3, 1957. The name refers to the location of the first store near a crossroads, or a *carrefour* in French. The company expanded at a strong pace within France during the late 1950s and early 1960s. In June 1963, the company revolutionized the retail industry in Europe with the introduction of the hypermarket. A hypermarket combines a grocery store and a department store. As an early pioneer of this retailing model, Carrefour grew rapidly in France, later Europe, and eventually around the globe.

Currently the company faces many international complexities due to culture, language, economic systems, political and legal systems, and infrastructure. To overcome these obstacles, Carrefour leverages local partners when entering new markets. Carrefour was the first Western retailer to enter the Asian market when it began operations in Taiwan in 1989. The company partnered with the local Taiwanese company Uni President Enterprises Corporation. The marketing team focused on learning about the Asian business environment, especially culture, through this relationship. This knowledge led to expansion in six other Asian markets.

The same strategy of seeking local partners was used in other regions. A local partner helped open the first store in Kuwait, and today stores are located in ten Middle Eastern countries. Local partners assist in adjusting to the country's business culture, provide governmental contacts, and smooth the market entry process.

(Continued)

(Continued)

The French company Carrefour is the second-largest retailer in the world.

Source: photo courtesy of Chih-Kuo, Kuo clearspace.tw.

Carrefour experienced problems associated with the 2008 global recession and increased competition. In 2010, the company sold outlets in Japan to its Japanese partner and closed twenty-one of 627 stores in Belgium. The experiences of overcoming these difficulties will serve Carrefour well as the company encounters down cycles in the economies of the future.

Retailing behavior may vary greatly depending on the local culture. The willingness to make large or small changes in response to these differences helped Carrefour achieve success. Adapting to cultural differences in consumption in Thailand required the company to move away from hypermarkets. Instead, Carrefour introduced a mini-supermarket in Bangkok. These smaller stores still provide ready-to-eat meals, plus groceries, frozen foods, drinks, and household products. The format was created to better meet local Thai needs and leverage the company's strong position in the country.

Carrefour has made changes to account for religious differences. In the Middle East, to generate goodwill and to meet Islamic expectations of corporate giving, the company often donates to local charities. During Ramadan, the company often makes large contributions to the Red Crescent Society. Not long ago, in the United Arab Emirates, Carrefour donated food worth AED625,000 (about $170,000 U.S.) to people in need.

Carrefour deals with many host country languages, which necessitates strong translation skills and sensitivity to local or regional differences in language. At the most basic level, this means successful translation of the company's name, when necessary. In Chinese, while the sounds for the brand name remain close to the French pronunciation, the characters used to make up the name Carrefour translate to "Every Happy Family," which reinforces the company's image.

Carrefour operates in countries with vastly different economic systems. Singapore has a more open market economy than Egypt's economy. The company has been active in the relatively strong command economy of China since 1995. In these situations, the marketing program is adjusted to meet governmental restrictions. There may be limitations on the products that can be sold, the price for certain goods may be set by the government, or the company may be required to find a local partner.

Carrefour also faces political and legal difficulties. While the company's home country, France, has a traditional parliamentary democracy, the company operates in countries with less-representative or less-stable systems. Carrefour entered Pakistan in 2009 even though the marketing team faced a situation with high levels of political risk. In other markets, legal actions hinder activities. In the Indonesian market, the firm was found guilty in a recent antitrust case. The company has appealed, but if the appeal is lost, Carrefour will be forced to sell its stake in a local Indonesian retailer.

As a grocery store, Carrefour sources many of its products locally. To overcome difficulties in infrastructure, the marketing and sales departments often couple education with relationship building. In India, relationships with local suppliers of food have been established through camps for Indian farmers. The camps educate farmers on technical farming skills. This creates important bonds with the company, increases the efficiency of Indian farmers, and, most importantly, improves the sources of food.

With the skill to successfully respond to complexity in international markets, Carrefour continues to aggressively pursue opportunities in growth markets. Specifically targeting Brazil, India, and China, the company moved aggressively into these markets. Carrefour entered the Indian market using the strategy of leveraging local partners. In this case, the partner was Kishore Biyani of Pantaloon Retail. Local partners may help Carrefour counter moves by the American Wal-Mart and the British Tesco to corner the $390 billion Indian retail market.

Following the same business strategy that fostered success globally, Carrefour's managers hope to continue to be a worldwide leader in retailing. Whether the difficulty faced is cultural, linguistic, economic, political and legal, or infrastructure, the company's acquired abilities suggest a bright future.[2]

1. How is Carrefour's marketing mix kept consistent across markets?

2. What value does Carrefour provide consistently in all of the various countries in which it operates?

3. How do local partners help Carrefour overcome difficulties in new markets? What is the advantage of that approach?

4. Explain the impact of the drivers of globalization described in this chapter with regard to Carrefour.

5. How have the factors that create international marketing complexity both helped and hurt Carrefour? Has the impact been mostly positive or mostly negative?

2

CULTURE IN INTERNATIONAL MARKETING

LEARNING OBJECTIVES

After reading and studying this chapter, you should be able to answer the following questions:

1. How do culture and the various elements of culture affect consumer behaviors and marketing?

2. What are the main models of cross-cultural differences and how can they help managers when making international marketing decisions?

3. Why should a marketing team examine cultural imperatives, cultural electives, and cultural exclusives when entering a host country?

IN THIS CHAPTER

HOME DESIGN, FURNITURE, AND CULTURE

Home design and furniture style vary by culture. People surround themselves with objects that fulfill different functions and have various meanings to them. Factors that influence building design include legal regulations, building codes, availability of space, location, climate—but also culture. For example, many Scandinavians prefer functional furniture with a minimalistic design, whereas Middle Easterners tend to seek ornamental furniture that looks beautiful and impresses guests.

(Continued)

(Continued)

In traditional Japanese homes it is common to have *washitsu* room, a room that has no specific purpose and is modestly furnished with *tatami* mats (thick, woven straw mats) as flooring and may also include a low table, portable folding partitions, cushions, and futons that are folded in the closet during the day and laid out on the tatami floor in the evening.[1] In fact, a traditional Japanese house does not have a designated use for each room aside from the entrance area, kitchen, and bathroom. Any room can be a living room, dining room, study, or bedroom. This is possible because all the necessary furniture is portable and stored in closets.

In the UK, each room has a prescribed function such as living room, dining room, kitchen, or bathroom. British families like living in single family homes, but in Egypt, homes are usually multi-generational and are designed to cater to the needs of grandparents, parents, and children.

In the United States, homes are also built to be functional, but space may be less of an issue. Consequently, many Americans enjoy relatively large houses. Similarly, in Australia home owners usually choose large living spaces and gardens while Chinese homes are among the smallest in the world. In the UK, on the other hand, people must do with smaller houses and flats. Homeowners in the UK rarely build their own houses. In Poland people rarely buy ready built houses and prefer designing and building their own homes according to their own tastes and budgets. Mexicans usually surround their houses with several feet high concrete walls in order to protect their privacy and possessions; Americans opt for picket fences. These cross-national differences in approaches to home building and design make marketing furniture to consumers in different cultures challenging (Milne, 2013).

Typical Japanese Living Room.

Source: Inspired By Maps/ Shutterstock.com. Retrieved from https://www.shutterstock.com/image-photo/typical-japanese-living-room-672323509?src=pzJLdWPUQoQ3PRnFrcHx4w-1-5&drawer=open

Questions for Students

1. What function does furniture play in various cultures?
2. How would you market furniture to cultures that emphasize beauty in furniture, and how would you market furniture to cultures that value functionality and simplicity?
3. What types of market research would be best for studying furniture use and significance in a new country?

OVERVIEW

In the international context, differences in culture, language, economic systems, political and regulatory systems, technological development, and marketing infrastructures make decision-making more complex (Figure 2.1). What works well in one country might not succeed in another. International marketing managers face complex challenges of operating in multiple cultures at the same time (Kelly, 2015).

In this chapter, the various definitions of culture are discussed first, along with different models of cross-cultural differences. Next, the effects that culture has on consumer behavior are described. Finally, the chapter focuses on how culture influences the marketing mix in global marketing. The chapter concludes with an overview of the strategic, tactical, and operational marketing implications of cross-cultural similarities and differences.

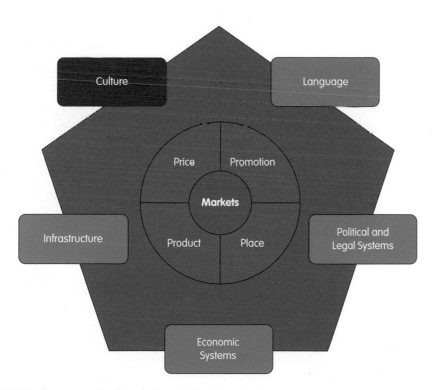

FIGURE 2.1   The International Marketing Context

> **LEARNING OBJECTIVE #1:**
>
> How do culture and the various elements of culture affect consumer behaviors and marketing?

THE MANY DEFINITIONS OF CULTURE

Culture is a concept that has many descriptions. The word culture has over 160 definitions in the English language (Jahoda, 2012). The term "culture" can be applied to a nation, a region, a city, or a single business. It influences every aspect of people's lives, including business, marketing and consumption activities. Culture includes "the ideas, values, practices, and material objects that allow a group of people, even an entire society, to carry out their collective lives in relative order and harmony" (Ritzer, 2015: 71). Culture is the human-made part of the environment and includes material culture and subjective (symbolic) culture (Triandis, 2002). There is no clear line between material and non-material culture as most material objects have symbolic meaning, and symbolic culture is manifest in material articles (Ritzer, 2015). Both aspects of culture have important implications for international marketing activities. Table 2.1 presents some descriptions of culture.

TABLE 2.1   Selected Definitions of Culture

The arts and other manifestations of human intellectual achievement regarded collectively
The way of life, especially the general customs and beliefs, of a particular group of people at a particular time[a]
"The collective programming of the mind which distinguishes the members of one group or category of people from another" (Hofstede, 2001; page 5)
"Culture provides the overall framework wherein humans learn to organize their thoughts, emotions, and behaviours in relation to their environment" (Neuliep, 2009: 38)
"Culture consists of patterns, explicit and implicit, of and for behavior acquired and transmitted by symbols, constituting the distinctive achievement of human groups, including their embodiments in artefacts; the essential core of culture consists of traditional (i.e. historically derived and selected) ideas and especially their attached values; culture systems may, on the one hand, be considered as products of action, on the other as conditioning elements of further action" (Kroeber and Klukhohn, 1952: 181)

Note: [a]Culture, accessed at http://dictionary.cambridge.org/dictionary/english/culture.

MATERIAL CULTURE

material culture: physical elements of a culture such as clothing, food, houses, tools and machines, works of art, buildings

Material culture consists of such elements as clothing, food, houses, tools and machines, works of art, buildings. Physical aspects of a culture help to define its members' behaviors and perceptions. For example, technology is a vital aspect of material culture in developed countries. Students must learn to use computers to function at university and at work, in contrast to young adults in the traditional societies of Africa who must learn to build weapons and hunt (Survival, 2017). The study of material culture focuses on how consumers relate to material objects, how they use them, and what value they place on them. For example, the style and design of clothing that consumers wear around the world differ. In India, people must protect their bodies from the harmful effects of the sun, and hence wear light clothing that covers their skin and keeps them cool. In northern Canada, people must protect their bodies from freezing temperatures and wear clothing that keeps them warm and dry in winter. In some cultures clothing is a marker of wealth and status, in others clothing fulfils very utilitarian functions. Many Americans value comfort and convenience, whereas most people in Latin American countries choose clothes to look smart and presentable in public as physical appearance is very important in those cultures. It is very common for people in Poland to iron all their clothes, even casual T-shirts and jeans to look presentable in public. This is not common in the United States.

DIETARY PREFERENCES

Food is an important aspect of material culture (Choi, 2014). Cultural dictates affect patterns of dining as well as dietary preferences. The primary meal of the day may take place in the mid- to late evening in one culture but at noon in another. Culinary preferences may be quite dramatic, especially in terms of what is deemed a delicacy. In Taiwan, one food, *chòu dòufu* or stinky tofu, has a powerful aroma that many foreigners find difficult to tolerate. Nordic countries serve fish without skinning, deboning, or even removing the eyes. It is not unusual for insects such as chocolate-covered ants to be considered delicacies in various countries (Miroff, 2013). These dietary preferences affect both business people visiting (and eating) in the locales, and businesses that create goods for consumption. In many countries, particularly in Africa, fresh food is preferred to preserved food. There, open-air markets that offer fresh food for sale serve the role that grocery stores play in other regions.

Dietary preferences may also be expressed as part of an individual's religion. McDonald's in India serves neither beef nor pork to meet the dietary restrictions of Hindus and Muslims, two of the dominant religions in the country. Instead, patrons can order a Chicken *Maharaja* Mac (Kannan, 2014).

At the least, the marketing team should make certain that any salesperson or representative visiting another country is aware of dietary differences (see Table 2.2). These preferences may also influence products to be created and the other elements of the marketing mix that will be used to vend them. For example, American consumers have grown to prefer fat-free or reduced-fat foods, such as fat-free yoghurts. The majority of European consumers choose full fat options of such products (Aubrey, 2014).

TABLE 2.2 Various Dietary Restrictions Globally

Kashrut	Jewish dietary law. Kosher foods are "fit" and the law excludes some meats, including pork. Rabbis supervise food production and verify kosher status
Halal	Muslim law, including dietary restrictions. *Haraam*, or forbidden foods, include pork and alcohol
Hindu Dietary Law	All Hindus avoid eating beef. Stricter Hindus avoid all meat, and some may avoid dairy products or eggs
Lacto-ovo Vegetarians	Do not eat meat but do eat dairy foods and eggs. Some Buddhists are lacto-ovo vegetarian on holy days
Ovo-Vegetarians	Do not eat meat or consume dairy products. Do consume eggs
Lacto-Vegetarians	Only eat dairy products and vegetables
Vegans	Do not eat anything derived from animals

SUBJECTIVE CULTURE

Subjective culture consists of ideas about what has worked in the past and thus is worth transmitting to future generations. Language and economic, educational, political, legal, philosophical, and religious systems are important elements of subjective culture. Ideas about aesthetics, and how should people live with others are also vital elements. Most important are unstated assumptions, standard operating procedures, and habits of sampling information from the environment (Triandis, 2002). People have numerous beliefs concerning what is or is not true and beautiful and good about the physical and social world in which they live. These beliefs influence the way they behave as consumers and how they respond to marketing stimuli. Values, norms, folkways and mores, roles, and behaviors that may be observed through interactions with members of a society express subjective culture (Table 2.3).

TABLE 2.3 Elements of Subjective Culture

Language	Official languages and local dialects
Values	Strongly held concepts that are present in a cultural group
Norms	Social rules that affect behaviors and actions and reflect cultural values
Folkways and Mores	Cultural customs that dictate how people act socially
Roles and Schemas	The enacted "parts" and "scripts" that members of a society play and follow in everyday interactions

ORIGINS OF CULTURE

Understanding a culture starts with awareness of the factors that created and sustain it. Traditions and customs develop slowly and then become slow to change. Two factors that influence the origins of culture are the history and the geography of a nation or region.

HISTORY

Table 2.4 identifies common characteristics that emerge as culture develops over time. Language, dialects, and slang have roots that are centuries deep. Each evolves as the context of a nation changes. Consequently, a language such as French now incorporates new technological terminology even as shifts in popular culture influence the nature of slang. These alterations depend, in part, on the nation where the language is spoken. *Francophones*, or French-speaking individuals, may be found in Africa, the Caribbean, and Canada. The dialect and slang vary depending on location. To respond to these differences, Disney introduced a television channel, *La chaîne Disney*, targeted at Francophones in Canada which is a localized version of the US Disney Channel. The programming is in French, and some of the programs spotlight authors from Quebec (Corus, 2015).

KFC is called *Poulet Frit Kentucky* in Quebec, because of the legal requirement for commercial signs to be translated into French.[2] Some global brands have challenged this interpretation of the local law (CBC News, 2012).

Customs and rituals are closely tied to religions and social institutions and practices. In East Asia, a common custom is to celebrate the new year (which is not on January 1, and instead is based on a lunar calendar) with orange juice for good luck rather than enjoying champagne or other forms of alcohol. Holidays, especially those sanctioned or honored by the government, typically reflect the primary religion of the area. The month-long celebration of Ramadan, in nations where Islam represents the prevalent religion, serves as an example. Social institutions are intertwined with religions and customs.

TABLE 2.4 Cultural Characteristics

Language, Dialects, Slang
Customs and Rituals
Religions
Social Institutions and Practices
Political Sphere
Common Attitudes and Beliefs
Aesthetics (concepts about beauty)
Views toward Education (for both genders, by wealth, income, or social status)

Not all customs and rituals are religious or were originally religious events. The *La Tomatina* festival in Spain, a massive food fight with tomatoes among members of the local community, began in 1945 with differing origin stories. One group suggests it started as a fracas among friends that included throwing tomatoes and vegetables at their opponents. Others believe that the first tomato-throwing incidents were part of an anti-Franco rally. Eventually, the government sanctioned the event, which takes place in the *Plaza del Pueblo* in the small town of Buñol in eastern Spain. Despite its secular origins, the festival is now considered to have ties to religion as a festival to honor the town's patron saint, San Luis Bertrán, and the Virgin Mary from the Catholic Christian tradition (Tapp, 2017).

GEOGRAPHY

Several factors related to the location and characteristics of a geographic region affect the development of culture. These include topography, population density, climate, and the access to other nations and cultures.

Topography, or the physical surface of a geographic area, influences lifestyles and the form a culture may take. Mountains and mountain ranges separate people, leading to differences in language, dialect, religious practices, and everyday matters such as finding, growing, and preparing food. The mountainous topography of Switzerland, and the isolation of parts of that country, have led to the emergence of four official languages within the country over time: French, Italian, German, and Romansch. The unique Romansch language in Switzerland is spoken by less than 1% of the country, and is mainly found in one of the thirteen Swiss cantons, or states (Swissinfo, 2017).

Deserts and mountainous topographies are often connected to a sparse *population density*. Bodies of water often lead to dense populations of inhabitants near them. Approximately half of the world's population lives within 200 kilometers of a body of water, generally oceans, lakes, and rivers. Population density affects patterns of daily interaction and the culture that emerges. High population density creates new target markets for companies, such as restaurants, department stores, big box stores, and specialty shops.

Climate also has a profound impact on culture. Inhabitants in extremely cold climates such as the First Nations, Inuit, and Metis in Canada lead vastly different lives compared to people in other parts of the world. Hunting and fishing are part of daily life, as is dealing with bitterly cold temperatures.

Those near the equator are likely to dress in fewer and skimpier clothes and daily activities are adjusted to cope with intense heat. Smaller differences in climate also create market segments. In countries where sunlight appears only a few hours per day at the height of winter, items such as tanning beds and snow blowers are popular. Countries in warmer climates normally feature a much stronger emphasis on outdoor recreation and may include naps or siestas during the hottest part of the day.

A common beach activity, surfing, was originally part of Polynesian culture and probably originated in either Tahiti or Hawai'i. The climate and geography of the islands—tropical and surrounded by water—facilitated the adoption of the sport.[3] Visitors to Hawai'i began to spread surfing to the continental United States during the 1930s, especially to California. The powerful waves in the Monterey Bay area, especially Santa Cruz, helped spread surfing to the continental United States (Bourne, 2013).[4]

Access to other nations and cultures affects the culture of a given region. The presence of trade routes such as the ancient Silk Road creates greater interchanges between collectives of people, and more cross-cultural influences result. Buddhism, the dominant religion in East Asia, has its roots in Indian culture. Its founder, Siddhartha Gautama Buddha, was an Indian prince, and the religion spread to East Asia along the ancient Silk Road (Hansen, 2013).

LEARNING OBJECTIVE #2:

What are the main models of cross-cultural differences and how can they help managers when making international marketing decisions?

CULTURE AND VALUES: HOFSTEDE, GLOBE, AND SCHWARTZ

values: strongly held concepts that are pervasive within a culture

A marketing technique or approach that works well in one culture may not work as well in another. Differences in values account for some of this. **Values** are strongly held concepts that are pervasive within a culture. The five main features of values that constitute the common background for social science research about values are (1) concepts or beliefs (2) about desirable end states or behaviors (3) that transcend specific situations, (4) guide the selection or evaluation of persons, behavior, and events, and (5) are ordered by relative importance.

Typical values include freedom, justice, social responsibility, loyalty to family or a spouse, and equality. Various views of the influence of values on those living in a culture and how that influence becomes manifest are available. For years, the most widely cited dimensions of culture were those proposed by Geert Hofstede, as displayed in Table 2.5.

TABLE 2.5 Hofstede's Value Dimensions of Culture

Power Distance	Distance between leaders and followers; authoritarian versus collaborative relationships
Individualism-Collectivism	Personal needs are more important than groups' needs
Masculinity–Femininity	Importance of competition, achievement versus values of harmony and quality of life
Uncertainty Avoidance	Risk-taking versus risk-avoidance societies
Short- or Long-Term Orientation	Emphasis on immediate versus distant; strategic outcomes

Hofstede's dimensions remain widely used in a number of contexts, including international marketing, although criticisms have emerged. Hofstede's data were collected in the late 1960s and, while culture is normally slow to change, the data collected and used as a guide to create the categories predate the introduction of the personal computer, the Internet, the fall of communism, and many other significant global events. A recent approach, Project GLOBE, is an international effort to respond to these criticisms and to identify and measure cultural dimensions. Project GLOBE, similarly to Hofstede's dimensions, may serve as a tool to develop awareness of cultural differences in many areas of marketing strategy, including international marketing issues. Table 2.6 identifies and defines these dimensions.

TABLE 2.6 Culture Constructs Developed in Project GLOBE

Power Distance	The degree to which members of a collective express comfort with power and differences in status
Uncertainty Avoidance	The extent to which there is an expectation that social norms, rules, and procedures will alleviate future event unpredictability
Humane Orientation	The degree to which individuals are rewarded for being fair, altruistic, generous, caring, and kind to others
Institutional Collectivism	The extent to which institutional practices encourage and reward the collective distribution of resources and collective action
In-Group Collectivism	The extent of pride, loyalty, and in-group cohesiveness individuals have for their organizations and families
Assertiveness	The preference for individual behaviors that are assertive, dominant, and demanding
Gender Egalitarianism	The degree to which a group works to limit gender inequality
Future Orientation	The extent to which future-oriented behaviors such as delaying gratification, planning, and investing in the future are encouraged
Performance Orientation	The degree to which a collective encourages and rewards group members for performance and excellence

APPLYING CULTURAL VALUES TO MARKETING ACTIVITIES

Research applying the values introduced by Hofstede's work and then further refined by GLOBE research reveals important implications for marketing practice. Marketers can first use cultural dimension scores to provide a broad conceptualization of the cultural values of countries in which a business intends to operate. These dimensions of culture may guide international market segmentation. Differences in expressions of the values provide a method for grouping consumers in terms of how these values lead to product preferences that will be accepted in a culture and further affect the methods used to identify and reach target markets. International marketers must be aware that national cultures frameworks such as Hofstede's dimensions or GLOBE dimensions must be used with caution as their ability to explain and predict consumer behavior is not straightforward. Cultural dimensions need to be used with caution as marketing practices may lead to the cultural paradoxes described in Chapter 15. For example, consumers from individualistic cultures will prefer collectivistic appeals. Researchers caution that dimensions should not be used as extremes but rather as a continuum of an expression of a preference of one value over another. No culture is purely, and entirely, individualistic or collectivistic, or masculine versus feminine.

Table 2.7 provides examples of high and low scores on Hofstede's typologies. In many cases, countries in a region overlap. Latin American nations, for example, tend to score low on individualism.

Broad implications of these scores may be drawn. Research has linked cultural values to a variety of behaviors. More than 600 articles have been published regarding Hofstede's values alone, and the findings are diverse. Overall, the research implies that Hofstede's values best predict emotional responses followed by attitudes, perceptions, and behaviors. Evidence suggests that high levels of individualism and uncertainty avoidance lead to slower rates of mobile phone adoption. Cultural values also influence relationships between market channel partners and influence which leadership style to use when managing disagreements.

A large body of research links cultural values to advertising content. Culture influences the effectiveness of banner advertising, website design, and television advertising. Differences in perceptions of what is funny in a print advertisement abound. Cultural values also influence the creation of brand meaning and positioning. Cultural values therefore should be considered before beginning any marketing process. Detailed research will reveal how values influence target market responses to marketing activities.

TABLE 2.7 Country Examples of High/Low Scores on Hofstede's Cultural Values

Cultural Dimension	Example Countries with a High Score on the Dimension	Example Countries with a Low Score on the Dimension
Power Distance	Malaysia (104), Guatemala (95)	Austria (11), Israel (13)
	Panama (95), Philippines (94)	Denmark (18), New Zealand (22)
	Mexico (81), Venezuela (81)	Ireland (28), Sweden (31)
Individualism	United States (91), Australia (90)	Guatemala (4), Ecuador (8)
	United Kingdom (89), Netherlands (80)	Panama (11), Venezuela (12)
	New Zealand (79), Italy (76)	Colombia (13), Pakistan (14)
Masculinity	Japan (95), Hungary (88)	Sweden (5), Norway (8)
	Austria (79), Venezuela (73)	Netherlands (14), Denmark (16)
	Italy (70), Switzerland (70)	Costa Rica (21), Finland (26)
Uncertainty Avoidance	Greece (112), Portugal (104)	Singapore (8), Jamaica (13)
	Guatemala (101), Uruguay (100)	Denmark (23), Sweden (29)
	Belgium (94), El Salvador (94)	Hong Kong (29), United Kingdom (35)

Cultural Dimension	Example Countries with a High Score on the Dimension	Example Countries with a Low Score on the Dimension
Long-Term Orientation	China (118), Hong Kong (96)	Sierra Leone (16), Nigeria (16)
	Taiwan (87), Japan (80)	Ghana (16), Philippines (19)
	South Korea (75), Brazil (65)	Norway (20), Zambia (25)

Note: For each of Hofstede's dimensions, a country is given a score. In the table, example countries are listed for each dimension. These examples score either high or low on Hofstede's survey for that dimension.

Source: Adapted from Clearly Cultural, "Geert Hofstede's Cultural Dimensions," updated April 21, 2009. Retrieved from www.clearlycultural.com/geert-hofstede-cultural-dimensions/.

VALUE LEVELS

Additional conceptualizations of values have emerged. The two typologies presented above, Hofstede's and Project GLOBE's, concentrate on national level values. While the nation-state arguably represents the most important grouping variable, cultural values have the most impact at the individual level. A micro approach to values can lead to additional insights.

The work by the researcher Shalom Schwartz focusing on the individual level suggests that values may be found in three types of human requirements. First, *biologically based needs* drive individuals to seek out food, shelter, sex, and other basic survival or well-being requirements. Second, *social interactional requirements* assist in interpersonal coordination and interaction, or, in more common terms, romance, love, friendships, and social relationships in locations such as the workplace or places of worship. Third, *social institutional demands for group welfare and survival* lead individuals to collectively value security, prosperity, and peace. Many times, one value may transcend all three levels. Consequently, basic biological sexual needs are transformed into values related to intimacy and love, and eventually into valuing a peaceful society in which long-term relationships can thrive.

Social motives connect the three levels of values. These motives may be categorized into ten universal and distinctive individual-level values. Table 2.8 identifies and defines each value.

The values listed in Table 2.8 may be categorized as those associated with *individualistic* or *collectivist* interests—that is, with personal versus group well-being. They also may be considered as part of reaching a goal (*instrumental*) or the eventual outcome (*terminal*).

TABLE 2.8   Individual-Level Values

1. Power	Focusing on attainment of social status, prestige, and dominance over people and resources
2. Achievement	Seeking personal success and proficiency
3. Hedonism	Seeking personal pleasure, particularly physical pleasure
4. Stimulation	Focusing on excitement, adventure, or challenges
5. Self-Direction	Valuing independence in thought and action
6. Universalism	Being concerned with understanding and protecting all people and natural resources

(Continued)

TABLE 2.8   (Continued)

7. Benevolence	Focusing on improving or maintaining the welfare of people, but only those people one is directly in contact with
8. Tradition	Seeking respect and preservation of the core components of one's culture
9. Conformity	Focusing on maintaining order and stable social interactions through observation of social norms
10. Security	Valuing safety, harmony, and stability of society or relationships

Source: Adapted from Bilsky and Schwartz (1994).

Hofstede's typology and the Project GLOBE cultural factors may be cautiously connected to individual-level values. Some of the more notable ties are mentioned in Table 2.9. Relationships between genders are influenced by a culture's masculinity/femininity dimension as well as by values associated with gender equality. Religious teachings as well as the position taken by the government may have influenced these views, reflecting social institutional demands for group welfare and survival. A prolonged war may change values related to gender, when males are away from home and engaged in conflict, because women may find they are asked to work in what had typically been male-dominated occupations.

TABLE 2.9   Links between National and Individual Values

Relationships between genders
Relationships to authority and governance
Importance of the group versus the individual
Levels of equality in the allocation of resources
How aggressively members of a culture approach the environment, including nature
Feelings about fate or destiny

TIME ORIENTATION

Time perceptions and attitudes are important factors of social order. They affect people's behaviors and general attitudes. People's relationship with time is reflected in the scheduling of tasks or the value people place on time, or how they evaluate past, present, and future. Two time-related orientations are important for consumer behavior: 1) task scheduling behavior: monochronic versus polychronic-time orientation, and 2) temporal orientations: past, present, future (Spears et al., 2000; Neuliep, 2009).

Cultures with **monochronic-time orientation** emphasise schedules and see time as a continuous line which can be divided into separate "blocks." Only one task is undertaken at any time and interruptions introduce chaos into the schedule. Most Western countries follow this time orientation.

Cultures with **polychronic-time orientation** see time as a flexible resource in which multiple tasks can be scheduled and performed at the same time. Schedules are flexible and may change if some tasks take more time than initially scheduled.

monochronic-time orientation: cultural emphasis on schedules and punctuality

polychronic-time orientation: cultural emphasis on flexibility and performing multiple tasks at the same time

These two time orientations are important for understanding buyer–seller relationships in business-to-business marketing, scheduling project completion times, deliveries, or promotional campaigns (Usunier and Lee, 2009).

Cultures which are **present-oriented**, such as Mexico, tend to see time as a cyclical process in which the future cannot be controlled or predicted, and the past will repeat itself in the future. Planning for the future is not important and people focus on the "here and now." It is not important to plan for retirement in present-oriented societies as the future cannot be controlled. In such cultures, consumers want to enjoy their purchases immediately and marketers often offer consumers the opportunity to "buy now and pay later." In cultures which are **future-oriented** such as the USA, people envisage and plan for their future, they prepare for the long-term. In such cultures, people plan for retirement, save money, or delay gratification. In **past-oriented cultures**, people appreciate the past. Such cultures value tradition, history and respect the elders. Many European and Asian countries are oriented toward the past. In such cultures, older generations help young people to buy homes or pay for education hence mortgages or loans are not as popular as in future-oriented societies.

In a study of promotional appeals in the United States (future-oriented culture), China (past-oriented culture), and Mexico (present-oriented culture), researchers found that promotional campaigns that are geared toward immediate gratification, such as credit purchases, should use different appeals across these three countries. In the United States, such campaigns should communicate the importance and benefit of such purchases on future outcomes. In countries that are past-oriented, these campaigns are more likely to be successful if they have a theme focused away from tradition. In Mexico, a campaign designed to encourage immediate gratification should emphasize the present benefits of the purchase (Spears et al., 2000).

THREE CULTURES WORLD

Recently, researchers that worked on the World Values Survey proposed a perspective of a world in which only three main cultural groups exist. These groups include: honor cultures, achievement cultures, and joy cultures which are presented in Table 2.10 (Basanez, 2016). **Cultures of honor** adhere to tradition. Members of such cultures value religion, traditional gender roles, hierarchy, and strong authority. Such cultures consider new ways of life inferior to the time-honored traditions, they value strong social and family bonds, and the interests of the group are more important than the interests of individuals.

Cultures of achievement place significant value on egalitarianism, individualism, and orientation toward economic efficiency and productivity. Religion is not valued, and secularism is the preferred social order. These cultures value gender equality and acceptance of individual differences. Marketing implications are advertising that appeals to individual values and shows gender equality, for example adverts featuring women in nontraditional roles should be more successful in such cultures than in cultures of honor.

In **cultures of joy**, individuals value the well-being of individuals and society, they are socially responsible, and work is for achieving quality of life not to demonstrate economic productivity. Cultures of joy place importance on hierarchy and obedience but not as much as cultures of honor. People in such cultures are personally religious but they reject the idea that religion should play a role in a public sphere.

present-oriented cultures: cultures which view time as a cyclical process in which the future cannot be controlled or predicted, and the past will repeat itself in the future

future-oriented cultures: cultures in which planning for the future takes priority over enjoying the present or appreciating the past

past-oriented cultures: cultures in which people value tradition, history, and appreciate the past

cultures of honor: cultures which value religion, traditional gender roles, hierarchy, and strong authority

cultures of achievement: cultures in which egalitarianism, individualism, and orientation toward economic efficiency and productivity are important

cultures of joy: individuals value the well-being of individuals and society, and work is for achieving quality of life not to demonstrate economic productivity

TABLE 2.10   A Summary of the Characteristics of the Three Cultures

	Honor	Achievement	Joy
Drivers	The state (political)	The market (economic)	The Family (social)
Priorities	Dominance	Wealth	Human relations
	Tradition	Efficiency, punctuality	Well-being
Prevalent	Ancient empires	Modern empires	Catholic and Buddhist countries
	African countries	Asian countries	Latin American countries
	Middle Eastern countries	Anglo-Saxon countries	
	Islamic countries	Western and Northern countries	

The differences in how cultures value joy, honor, and achievement may have an impact on consumption and marketing activities. Consumers from cultures of joy may respond better to advertising that features appeals to fun, joy, happiness, and relaxation executed via a soft sell strategy. Cultures of honor may respond better to advertisements of products that enhance social status. A hard sell approach and appeals to performance and effectiveness may work better in cultures of achievement. Table 2.11 presents the top 10 countries of honor, achievement, and joy.

TABLE 2.11   Top 10 Countries of Honor, Achievement, and Joy

Honor	Achievement	Joy
Zimbabwe	Sweden	Italy
Pakistan	Norway	Spain
Jordan	Denmark	Northern Ireland
Morocco	Switzerland	Croatia
Ghana	Andorra	Uruguay
Iraq	Netherlands	Israel
Algeria	Finland	Galicia
Rwanda	Iceland	Argentina
Trinidad	West Germany	Brazil
Bangladesh	France	Portugal

Source: Adapted from Basanez (2016: 120–128). By permission of Oxford University Press, USA.

GLOBAL AND LOCAL CULTURAL INFLUENCES

The forces of the modern interconnected world have an impact on the social and cultural environments of the globe. Consumers around the world are exposed to products and brands designed and produced in foreign markets. Media, music, and technology are spreading fast around the globe. Most people are aware of Netflix which is available in 190 countries. People travel for leisure or business to foreign lands. All these encounters are opportunities for cultural exchanges. Some societies and individuals are open and accepting of such global influences. Other cultures and groups resist global cultural influences. The interplay of local and global forces leads to hybridization, implying increasing homogeneity and heterogeneity of behaviors occurring simultaneously (Wang and Yeh, 2005). Some global cultural trends are more popular than others (Steenkamp and de Jong, 2010). One common theme across many societies is the increasing importance of consumption for economies and individual lives.

Hybridization is the mixing, blending, and synthesizing of different global and local elements that generate new cultural forms and connections.

CONSUMER CULTURE

In a **consumer culture**, people place importance on consumption as the primary source of meaning in life. The roots of contemporary consumer culture may be traced back to the times when department stores, world's fairs, and trade expositions became accessible to the middle and working classes. As people's ability to afford consumption improved with modernization, and as economies became dependent on consumption, consumer culture became the most dominant in Western societies (Ritzer, 2015). Consumer culture encourages the spread of market values in which individuals are seen as consumers. Marketing and branding principles are applied to most human activities such as education, health care, or running for public office (Boyte, 2016). This cultural orientation is based on spending, incurring debt, and excessive buying that was created by corporations wanting people to have "desires" instead of "needs" (Lury, 1996).

consumer culture: culture in which consumption and possessions are the primary source of meaning in life

Global consumer culture: globally recognized set of consumption behaviors, values, and brands associated with globalization and global culture

Consumer culture has spread around the world and **global consumer culture** has emerged. Global brands play a crucial role in creating consumer culture and marketing is partly responsible for the spread of global consumer culture. Some experts believe that global brands distort competition, create unrealistic consumer aspirations, contribute to serious health problems, encourage irresponsible consumer behaviors, and are not good for the environment (Benady, 2008).

Consumers react to these global cultural changes in various ways. Some consumers reject the values that are associated with global corporations and global brands. One example of such an opposition group is the Slow Food movement established in Italy with an aim to raise awareness of the impact that global brands and corporations have on local food cultures. The Slow Food movement works with other groups and individuals in order to educate consumers about the importance of regional food traditions, local communities, the impact of industrial farming on the environment, and food quality.[5]

Slow Food logo.

Source: www.slowfood.com/.

Other consumers purchase global brands willingly as they want to participate in and share the meanings of global culture. Such consumers see global brands as an assurance of good quality and reliability that local brands do not provide (Holt et al., 2004). For consumers who have positive attitudes toward global consumer culture trends,

global brands, the ones a company features when promoting the same brand name, image, and brand mark globally, such as those presented in Table 2.12 are often an important part of their social identity.

TABLE 2.12   The Top 10 Global Brands According to Interbrand, Forbes, and Financial Times Rankings

Rank	Interbrand	Forbes	FT
1	Apple	Apple	Google
2	Google	Google	Apple
3	Coca-Cola	Microsoft	Microsoft
4	Microsoft	Facebook	Amazon
5	Toyota	Coca-Cola	Facebook
6	IBM	Amazon	AT&T
7	Samsung	Disney	Visa
8	Amazon	Toyota	Tencet
9	Mercedes-Benz	McDonald's	IBM
10	General Electric	Samsung	McDonald's

CULTURAL DISTANCE AND PSYCHIC DISTANCE

Cultural distance and **psychic distance** are important aspects of international marketing managers' cultural understanding. Cultural distance is the degree to which cultural values, norms and beliefs in one country are different from those in another country. Cultural distance is usually measured by differences in economic development, level of education, language, cultural dimensions and other indicators of culture. One way of measuring cultural distance is to compare countries' scores on cultural dimensions. Table 2.13 presents cultural distance indices based on data from the European Social Survey and the European Values Survey. These indices need to be used with caution and should be combined with other measures of cross-national differences, such as for example economic development indices.

TABLE 2.13   Cultural Distance Indices for Selected European Countries

	Belgium	Bulgaria	Switzerland	Czech Republic	Cyprus	Germany
Belgium	0.00	2.51	0.61	0.16	2.26	0.05
Switzerland	0.61	4.97	0.00	1.30	2.57	0.41
Czech Republic	0.16	1.50	1.30	0.00	1.90	0.32
Cyprus	2.26	2.31	2.57	1.90	0.00	2.29
Germany	0.05	3.10	0.41	0.32	2.29	0.00
Denmark	1.48	7.51	0.50	2.58	4.93	1.14
Spain	0.41	2.33	1.43	0.27	2.13	0.39
Finland	0.47	4.15	1.09	0.84	4.11	0.39

	Belgium	Bulgaria	Switzerland	Czech Republic	Cyprus	Germany
France	0.47	3.86	1.39	0.76	4.63	0.50
Great Britain	0.03	2.34	0.79	0.10	2.20	0.07
Greece	2.64	2.31	3.05	2.21	0.42	2.81
Croatia	1.12	0.45	3.06	0.44	1.91	1.47
Hungary	1.85	1.47	3.34	1.15	1.66	2.08
Ireland	0.27	1.69	0.93	0.19	1.07	0.38
Latvia	1.42	0.67	2.93	0.76	1.06	1.73
Netherlands	0.36	4.56	0.16	1.00	3.21	0.25
Norway	0.88	5.47	0.95	1.60	4.89	0.76
Poland	0.94	0.41	2.68	0.41	1.76	1.32
Portugal	0.85	0.61	2.69	0.38	2.33	1.23

Source: Kaasa et al. (2016).

Psychic distance is the individual's subjective perception of the differences between the home country and the foreign country. The perceptions of cultural distance between home market and host market affect managerial decision-making processes in foreign market selections, as well as deciding which products and services would work in a foreign market (Shenkar, 2012).

Psychic distance influences how managers formulate international marketing strategies and how they adapt marketing programs to different circumstances. Therefore, managers should be aware of the impact of their perceptions of the foreign market on their strategic decisions. Sales and marketing professionals who have more positive perceptions of the foreign market are more likely to be successful in a particular foreign market and selection of such staff should include measuring their psychic distance toward the foreign market. An appropriate match should increase the firm's probability of success. The consequences of psychic distance may be addressed by the firm, but this is not the case with cultural distance, which is outside the firm's control (Sousa and Bradley, 2006).

LEARNING OBJECTIVE #3:

Why should a marketing team examine cultural imperatives, cultural electives, and cultural exclusives when entering a host country?

CULTURE AND BEHAVIORS

Culture and cultural value affect patterns of daily living and social interactions. These may be observed from matters as simple as greeting friends, strangers, and potential business partners, to far more complex behaviors such as those displayed in family relationships. From a marketing perspective, the most important behaviors are those that affect business relationships. The behaviors can be classified as cultural imperatives, cultural electives, and cultural exclusives.

CULTURAL IMPERATIVES

cultural imperatives: the customs and expectations that must be met and conformed to or avoided if international business relationships are to be successful

Cultural imperatives are the customs and expectations that must be met and conformed to or avoided if international business relationships are to be successful. For example, the significance of establishing friendships in business relationships often becomes a key element in successful international marketing, especially in countries that most strongly emphasize family and group relationships. Building bonds represents a cultural imperative in these countries.

Friendship, human relations, and trust are reflected by language, in the Latin American *compadre*, in China's *guanxi*, and in Japan's *ningen kankei*. Establishment of these forms of friendship takes place before business negotiations or sales presentations begin. Meetings, entertaining mutual friends, contacts, and spending time visiting develop trust. Friendship motivates local agents to make more sales and helps establish quality relationships with end users.

Also, a person's demeanor can be critical. A cultural imperative in one country may be an imperative to avoid in another. In Japan, making prolonged eye contact is considered offensive. In Arab and Latin American cultures the failure to make strong eye contact may lead to the perception of seeming evasive and untrustworthy. Also, while losing patience and raising one's voice is almost always poor etiquette, in some cultures such an outburst would end a business relationship. Correcting someone in public may have the same results. For instance, in Asian cultures, correcting someone in public causes the person to lose "face," which reflects a sense of personal integrity, an important part of an individual's social identity.

CULTURAL ELECTIVES

cultural electives: areas of behavior or customs that visitors may wish to, but are not required to, conform to or participate in

Cultural electives relate to areas of behavior or to customs that cultural aliens may wish to, but are not required to, conform to or participate in. The majority of culturally meaningful behaviors fit into this category. Greeting someone with a kiss, eating certain foods, holding hands or touching another person, engaging in gambling activities, and drinking alcoholic beverages are cultural electives that may be graciously declined or avoided.

At the same time, following a given custom might be helpful in building a positive relationship. The symbolic attempt to participate in a custom helps to establish rapport. For example, while a Japanese manager typically does not expect a Westerner to bow or to understand the bowing ritual, the attempt at a symbolic bow indicates interest and goodwill. Greeting an individual in a native language or knowing some small phrases suggests the desire to create a positive tone. In business meetings, Asian business people tend to accept an offered business card with two hands and a slight bow as a sign of respect for the new business connection. The business card is presented with the words facing the person receiving the card, allowing the other person to read it easily during the exchange. Electives such as these can play important roles in international marketing interpersonal relationships.

CULTURAL EXCLUSIVES

cultural exclusives: customs or behavior patterns reserved exclusively for the locals and from which the foreigner is barred

Customs or behavior patterns reserved exclusively for the locals and from which the foreigner is barred are **cultural exclusives**. Marketers in a foreign country need to know when they are dealing with a cultural exclusive. These often include religious ceremonies in which members of any other religion would not be welcome or when limitations are placed on activities for women. One mosque at the

Taj Mahal, the iconic mausoleum in Agra, India, has rules stating that only males are allowed to enter. For visitors to the Parliament building in London, UK citizens may visit year-round while foreign visitors may visit only on Saturdays or during the "summer opening."

SUBCULTURES AND COUNTERCULTURES

Subcultures are groups whose values and related behaviors are distinct and set members off from the general or dominant culture. Each subculture consists of a world within the larger world of the dominant culture, has a distinctive way of looking at life, but remains compatible with the dominant culture. The term *microculture* applies to smaller groups found within an overall subculture or culture.

subcultures: groups whose values and related behaviors are distinct and set members off from the general or dominant culture

Ethnic groups often form subcultures featuring their own language, distinctive foods, religious practices, and other customs. Religious subgroups also form subcultures, such as in the differences that exist in the various forms of Judaism. All nations have subcultures, and increasingly these subcultures are found in immigrant groups that may become targets of marketing activities. For example, immigrants from the Ingria region of Estonia constitute a significant subculture in Finland.

Countercultures are groups whose values set their members in opposition to the dominant culture. Countercultures challenge the culture's core values. Some are associated with controversial behaviors or attitudes, such as those present in groups that glorify Satanism or Nazism. Others simply choose differing lifestyles. Vegans, for example, exhibit dining patterns that most meat-eaters would consider to be benign even though they are part of a counterculture. The Amish avoid advanced technology as an expression of religious values.

countercultures: groups whose values set their members in opposition to the dominant culture

CULTURAL CHANGE

Cultures, and cultural influences, evolve over time. What was true about a particular culture in the last decade, or even the last year, may not be true today. As an example, the use of social media such as Facebook has dramatically influenced a variety of cultures through connections between persons from other cultures and countries. The effects of music, world views, and other aspects of daily life should not be underestimated. Cultures change slowly and gradually. Researchers have discovered drastic cultural changes and the persistence of distinctive cultural traditions at the same time. Economic development is associated with shifts away from absolute norms and values toward rationality, trust, and values of tolerance and participation (Inglehart and Welzel, 2007). The distinctive traditions of societies leave imprints on the values and attitudes of individuals; however even very traditional cultures change and these changes may become important opportunities for businesses and marketers. For example, Saudi Arabia has recently introduced a change to allow women to drive. This drastic change for Saudi Arabia may become an important marketing opportunity for car sellers.

Subcultures and countercultures are associated with the desire for cultural change. Groups that wish to protect animals or the environment, including, People for the Ethical Treatment of Animals (PETA) and Greenpeace, seek to affect laws as well as cultures. Other groups may simply push for greater freedom of expression, such as the followers of goth fashion and music in various countries.

Saudi women have now been allowed to drive.

Source: clicksahead/ Shutterstock.com. Retrieved from https://www.shutterstock.com/image-photo/ arab-women-driving-car-387728554?src=YqqjiHH3WdtQmKt9gDPkIA-1-6

There are instances in which subcultures and countercultures represent potential target markets. As part of the assessment of the dominant culture within a geographic area, the marketing team examines the presence of these groups to see if opportunities exist. Companies that successfully market to the dominant culture in one country may be able to effectively market to that same culture as an immigrant subculture in another country. Kingfisher Beer, the largest brewery in India, sells one of every three beers in the country. In the United Kingdom, with its large and growing Indian immigrant population, Kingfisher has become one of the ten fastest-growing beer brands. The company markets the beer to both Indian immigrants and local consumers (Gerrard, 2017).

Two approaches may be used by a marketing department to assess and adapt to cultural change. Seeking *cultural congruence*, which means products and marketing approaches are designed to meet the needs of the current culture, constitutes the first approach. Only when change occurs will these factors be adjusted or adapted. The second, and less likely method, involves promoting change within the culture. Such an approach may be viewed as including greater risk and features an increased chance of offending members of a society and the government.

When pizza was introduced in China, it was a food form that had never been seen before. Stories emerged of Chinese consumers attempting to eat the pizza with chopsticks. Realizing that there were gaps between the typical pizza the company served in the United States and the cultural expectations in China, Pizza Hut changed its menus so they were more congruent with the local tastes. This meant adding dishes other than pizza, serving wine at some locations, flavoring dishes with flower petals, using local fish in place of typical Western meats, and offering many other adaptations, including one pizza topped with duck meat (Campaign, 2015).

CULTURE AND PURCHASING BEHAVIOR

Cultural influences dictate whether a given region or nation can become a viable target market. Any producer of goods or services first examines culture in order to determine whether those products match the needs and wants of consumers. Culture affects a variety of consumption patterns and purchasing behaviors, including those affected by aesthetics, religious practices, and dietary preferences. The subcultures or countercultures present in a geographic area may also represent an opportunity or an obstacle to expand into the market. In material cultures, for example, shopping facilities in such countries influence the process of looking for and purchasing goods. In many developing countries, traditional street markets are still very popular.

Traditional market in a small Vietnamese village.

Source: Vietnam Stock Images/ Shutterstock.com. Retrieved from https://www.shutterstock.com/image-photo/lao-cai-vietnam-sep-7-2017-1036765303?src=dQFxTc84BpYzAeRra7Haag-1-97

AESTHETICS

aesthetics: concepts
about what
constitutes beauty

Aesthetics, or concepts about what constitutes beauty, affect a vast number of purchases. Items including cosmetics, clothing, and jewelry, spokespersons and models for products, and views of nature are all influenced by cultural views of beauty. In the Caucasus region near Iran, eyebrows that connect across the bridge of the nose are a sign of beauty in women. Views of body weight, muscles, and curves vary widely. Colors, fragrances, and art represent cultural preferences. As a result, target markets are selected, in part, based on concepts of beauty. Products, packages, promotions, websites, and other marketing efforts must also be adapted to fit within a culture.

Differences in aesthetics can lead to marketing opportunities, and these opportunities often center on perceptions of human beauty. Many Japanese consumers believe a thin woman is the physical ideal, which leads to an emphasis on dieting and an attractive market for dieting aids. In 2006, the Japanese dieting scene was buzzing with excitement about the *kanten* plan. *Kanten*, a gelatin made from seaweed, has no calories but does contain fiber, calcium, and iron. The product was promoted as capable of making one feel full, even though no calories were consumed (Itoh, 2014). In other areas of the world, beauty perceptions are quite different. Consumers in many African nations view a heavier person as being more attractive than a slimmer person. Due to the rampant poverty and malnutrition in many African countries, thin people are often viewed as being ill.

Product design can be based on perceptions of aesthetics. Japanese furniture, for example, tends to be relatively austere, with an appreciation for function and straight lines. Tables, chairs, and even beds tend to be short when compared to styles from other countries. In Western cultures, expensive product designs often feature opulence or indulgence.

RELIGION

When a nation or region has one dominant religion, adjusting marketing efforts will be less complicated. The dictates of that religion, including holy days, rituals, foods, gender roles, and other practices, may be examined by a local culturally sensitive partner or employee to determine if a target market exists, and whether the company's product offerings can be tailored, modified, and positioned to match those markets.

When more than one religion is present, marketing decisions become more complex, especially when ideological differences cause conflicts between the religions. The marketing team decides which religion(s) will become the target market(s) and carefully tries to do so in ways that do not agitate or offend members of other religions.

The fast-food restaurant Chicken Cottage first opened in 1994 in London. The company offers *halal* food, catering to Muslim religious dietary requirements. The company also provides products that appeal to non-Muslim customers. The promotional focus accentuates food quality and innovative offerings. The *halal* component, while in the company logo, is not overly emphasized. This promotional approach allowed the company to grow to 140 restaurants by 2010.

International advertisers need to carefully consider the impact religion can have on advertising attitudes. Mistakes are costly and have a negative impact on brand attitudes. Unilever, the parent company of the Lux soap brand, learned that conservative Israelis did not like the image of Sarah Jessica Parker featured in a billboard promoting the product. The original billboards for Lux, one of the leading soap brands in Israel back in 2004, showed the actress in a strappy, backless gown familiar to fans of her role as columnist Carrie Bradshaw from the TV series *Sex and the City*. Within 24 hours of putting up the billboards, a senior rabbi contacted the Israel office of Unilever to threaten a boycott of the company's entire range of products. The company response was immediate and new posters were drawn up, featuring the model covered up in a long sleeved dress (BBC, 2004). Another global brand, IKEA has recently tailored its catalogues distributed in Israel to Orthodox Jews but this religious adaptation was met with criticism. The local branch of IKEA tailored the catalogues to reach this small section of the Israeli market which constitutes 11% of the population (Jewish News, 2017). Cultural adaptation needs to be executed carefully in order to not offend or ignore other groups.

INTERNATIONAL INCIDENT

You are a cross-cultural consultant working for a large multinational company. You were asked to deliver a cultural awareness training to a group of German executives who are relocating to Mexico to head the company's subsidiary based in Mexico City. Prepare a presentation which explains the cultural characteristics of the Mexican culture. Outline the marketing implications of the cultural differences and suggest steps that could help to mitigate the problems arising from the discussed cultural differences.

ETHICS, SOCIAL RESPONSIBILITY, AND CULTURE

Marketing activities of multinational companies often exert unintended pressure on cultural values and behaviors of consumers. The fundamental reason for the activities of multinational businesses in free market economies is to generate a profit for their shareholders. Companies make every effort to increase sales in order to make a profit as long as these activities are within the law. This often means that companies encourage the consumption of products and services where it is not needed, for example by using sales promotion to encourage consumers to buy more than they need, or to offer credit to vulnerable consumers.

Ethics is a system of moral principles which governs a person's behavior.

On the other hand, culture influences the ethical attitudes and behaviors of business managers (Christie et al., 2003). Members of one culture may view a particular behavior as unethical, whilst the same behavior would be acceptable in another culture. For example, nepotism is acceptable in many collectivistic cultures, but frowned upon or often illegal in many Western countries. **Ethical relativists** maintains that ethical values are relative to the norms of one's culture. This approach suggests that there are no universal standards of behavior that can be applied to all people at all times. The only ethical standards against which a society's values and practices can be judged are its own. If ethical relativism is correct, there can be no common framework for resolving moral disputes or for reaching an agreement on ethical matters among members of different societies (Lewis and Unerman, 1999).

Ethical relativism: ethical values are relative to the norms of one's culture

Ethical absolutism argues that there are fundamental values that cross cultures, and companies must uphold them. Such a view is the foundation of many international codes of conduct for businesses and marketers, for example The Federation of European Direct Marketing Code of Practice.[6]

Ethical absolutism: there are fundamental values that cross cultures, and companies must uphold them

Whilst ethics reside in individuals, firms should clearly establish the rules of ethical behavior for their employees and managers. Ethical dilemmas should always be solved having the best interests of consumers and the environment in mind.

CHAPTER 2: REVIEW AND RESOURCES

Strategic Implications

Strategic decisions include deciding whether to position a brand as global or local, or whether to standardize or adapt the marketing mix. Given the importance of culture, decision-makers should ensure that the overall international marketing program considers the cultural similarities and differences between target markets. Analyzing and incorporating cultural knowledge in international marketing decisions should be recognized as an essential component of the overall organizational strategy. In order to identify potential targets for international expansion, as well as viable market segments for products internationally, knowledge of local cultures is needed.

Tactical Implications

Each of the approaches to understanding and describing the cultural characteristics of the societies described in this chapter is important to consider by the firm to achieve its overall international marketing strategy. Tactical decisions for targeting different cultures are rooted in the overall corporate strategy. Following either a standardization or adaptation strategy, for example, requires knowledge and understanding of the material and subjective culture of the target country or region. The overall international strategy of the firm will likely fail in the absence of a deep understanding and appreciation of the cultural similarities and differences and how they impact on the various parts of the marketing mix. For instance, the choice of advertising appeals for specific campaigns will be influenced by the culture of the target market if such direction at the strategic level was suggested.

Operational Implications

Day-to-day international marketing operations are guided by both strategic and tactical decisions. Ongoing research activities are necessary to address cultural differences, regional preferences, and consumer attitudes toward a company's products. Recruiting and training a sales force that is culturally aware may be one example of an operational implication. The mode of communicating with a subsidiary's employees may also be the operational implications of cultural differences. Package labels may have to be printed in the language of the target country, or some other adjustments may be made.

In summary, cross-cultural similarities and differences play a vital role in international marketing. The demand for products and services that are culturally appropriate is greater than ever, and international business decisions require that this information be gathered in the most effective and efficient method available. Cultural differences should always be taken into account when attempting to perform any international market research project. The control of this process is an important issue as well, with many firms opting for a combination of both in-house and field arrangements.

TERMS

culture

material culture

subjective culture

values

monochronic-time orientation

polychronic-time orientation

present-oriented cultures

future-oriented cultures

past-oriented cultures

cultures of honor

cultures of achievement

cultures of joy

consumer culture

global consumer culture

cultural distance

psychic distance

cultural imperatives

cultural electives

cultural exclusives

subcultures

countercultures

aesthetics

ethical relativists

ethical absolutists

REVIEW QUESTIONS

1. Define culture.

2. Define material culture.

3. Define subjective culture.

4. Describe the various models of cultural differences.

5. How could the models of cultural differences be used in marketing?

6. What is the difference between cultural-level values and individual-level values?

7. How do individual-level cultural values affect consumer behavior and marketing?

8. Define cultural imperatives, cultural electives, and cultural exclusives.

9. Define cultures of honor, joy, and achievement.

10. Describe consumer culture and global consumer culture.

11. What is psychic distance?

12. What is cultural distance?

13. What is the main argument behind ethical relativism?

14. What is ethical absolutism?

DISCUSSION QUESTIONS

1. Discuss the importance of material and subjective culture in international marketing.

2. Why is the understanding of culture important in making business-to-business marketing decisions? Discuss the importance of power distance and hierarchy in managing B2B marketing relationships.

3. Culture influences international marketing activities, but marketing activities also influence culture. Describe how global brands influence local cultures and discuss the ethical dilemmas of such influence.

4. Discuss to what extent "Buy National" (e.g., "Buy British") campaigns are effective and for which product categories would they be most successful?

5. Describe global culture. Do you think a truly global culture exists? In what way has technology helped the emergence of global cultural patterns?

ANALYTICAL AND INTERNET EXERCISES

1. Using an Internet search engine, look for advertisements for a global brand that is well known in many different countries. Compare and contrast the advertisements and relate them to cultural aspects of the target cultures.

2. Coffee is a drink consumed in many countries. Using the Internet and library resources, prepare an overview of coffee culture in the following countries. Explain where coffee chains such as Starbucks or Costa Coffee could be or are the least and most successful and why.

   - Italy
   - India
   - Colombia
   - France
   - Finland

3. Visit the website of the World Values Survey and read about the different clusters of cultures proposed by researchers of this project. Think about how this information can be used for international marketing purposes.

4. Organic food consumption has been steadily growing over the past decade but it still varies by countries. Using reliable online sources, find out which countries have the highest organic food consumption and then research the cultures of these countries. Propose explanations for the variations, and discuss the relevance of culture (both material and subjective) in the variations of consumption of organic food.

STUDENT STUDY SITE

Visit **https://study.sagepub.com/baack2e** to access these free additional learning tools:

- Web Quizzes
- eFlashcards
- SAGE Journal Articles
- Country Fact Sheets
- Chapter Outlines
- Interactive Maps

CASE 2

KitKat in Japan: Accidental Success in a Foreign Market

"Sweet tooth" is a term used to describe a liking for foods that are sweet. Most people, regardless of which culture or region they come from, enjoy sweets in one form or another (Bramen, 2010). Sweets are part of material culture, and the type of sweets liked the most and the manner of consuming them vary by region (Michaud, 2013; Krondl, 2016).

In many cultures, a serving of cakes, cookies, biscuits, or wafers is consumed with a cup of tea or coffee. For example, in the UK, the office tea time is considered a cultural experience with its own rituals and includes a biscuit or a cookie (BBC, 2017b). Biscuits in the United Kingdom, the Isle of Man, and Ireland are hard and may be savoury or sweet, such as chocolate biscuits, digestives, ginger nuts, and custard creams. In the United States, a "biscuit" is a quick bread, somewhat similar to a scone, and usually unsweetened. Regardless of differences in definitions, one sweet product found alongside a cup of tea in many countries is a Kit Kat, a chocolate-covered wafer biscuit produced globally by Nestlé.

Kit Kat bars are manufactured in various countries around the globe including: Brazil, Mexico, UK, Canada, Australia, South Africa, Germany, Russia, Japan, United Arab Emirates, and Bulgaria.[7] In the United States The Hershey Company, a Nestlé competitor, produces Kit Kat bars under license, due to a prior licensing agreement with Rowntree.

Rowntree's of York, a British company which was acquired by Nestlé in 1988, originally created the Kit Kat bar. The standard bars consist of two or four fingers composed of three layers of wafer, separated and covered by an outer layer of chocolate. Each finger can be snapped from the bar separately. The first Kit Kat-type bar was sold in the UK by Rowntree in 1935, when it was called Chocolate Crisp, and the shape has changed little since then.

The wafer's name originates from a seventeenth-century literary club which met at a pie shop owned by pastry chef Christopher Catling. The group was called the Kit Kat club and adapted its name from an abbreviated version of the owner's name.[8]

The company started to expand internationally in the 1950s, first into Anglo-Saxon countries: Australia, Canada, New Zealand, and South Africa.[9] The next phase of internationalization included Germany in the 1970s, and a licensing agreement with the American company, The Hershey Corporation, to sell it in the United States. In the same decade, Kit Kat entered the Japanese market, and a decade later a new manufacturing facility in Japan opened. The biggest single retail outlet for Kit Kat is Dubai airport duty-free store. Around 1 tonne of Kit Kats are sold there each day.[10]

Kit Kat's success in Japan is a prime example of how adapting a product to local requirements helps to create a global success. Since the first Kit Kat went on sale there in 1973, the nation has embraced it, making it one of its top-selling chocolate brands. KitKat retail sales in Japan have risen steadily since 2011, in contrast to a decline for the past two years in the UK. Such success is clearly tied to the country's liking for unusual flavours—more than 300 varieties have been created, from wasabi to melon (CNN, 2017; Schanen, 2017b).

Kit Kat's success story in Japan begins with an accidental stroke of luck: the name of the chocolate bar sounds similar to the Japanese phrase *kitto katsu*: "you will surely win." Japanese consumers started buying Kit Kat wafers as good-luck presents for students sitting university entrance exams. In 2009, Nestlé collaborated with Japan Post to launch the postable Kit Kat. The idea was so successful that currently about half of the country's 600,000 annual exam-sitting students now receive this chocolate-covered wafer for good

(Continued)

(Continued)

luck every year. Nestlé has successfully differentiated the brand by understanding how the brand was used in the local cultural context as "Have a break, have a Kit Kat," does not have the same meaning to the Japanese. At present, around 5 million Kit Kat bars are consumed in Japan every day and the demand is growing (Schanen, 2017a).

Japan's KitKat craze.

Source: gnoparus / Shutterstock.com. Retrieved from https://www.shutterstock.com/image-photo/hokkaido-japan-october-16-2013-japanese-366302480?src=dhDgPae68YmayuzgoloNew-1-9

1. The initial success of Kit Kat in Japan was accidental. Discuss how Kit Kat could adapt the product and market it in other countries to appeal to local cultures of its consumers.

2. In Poland, Kit Kat is often bought and included, along other confectionery products, in *sniegust*, a gift of sweets, fruits, money, and clothes given to godchildren at Easter time. In the UK, the product is often consumed with tea during breaks at work. Which cultural traditions and practices could Nestlé relate the consumption of Kit Kat to?

3. Why do you think so many different flavours have been developed for the Japanese market? Why has it not been the case in other countries?

3

GLOBAL TRADE AND INTEGRATION

LEARNING OBJECTIVES

After reading and studying this chapter, you should be able to answer the following questions:

1. How does free trade influence the international marketing context?
2. What are the relationships between free trade, integration, and international marketing?
3. What are the major trade agreements around the world?
4. How does protectionism affect free trade?
5. How do laws and ethical concerns affect trade and international marketing?

IN THIS CHAPTER

KIKKOMAN SOY SAUCE: A TRADITION OF TRADE

People around the world enjoy soy sauce. The salty condiment plays a role similar to ketchup or salsa and adds flavor to more than just traditional Asian foods. Soy sauce with stir-fried vegetables and rice can be found on dinner tables in many countries.

Soy sauce dates back to *jiang*, a fermented-meat condiment used in the Chinese Zhou dynasty (1122–221 BC). While the condiment traces its roots to China, many of the world's leading soy sauce brands originated in Japan. *Shoyu*, the name for Japanese soy sauce, has been a condiment since at least the Muromachi period (1336–1568 AD). *Shoyu* plays a large role in Japanese cooking. To the Japanese, soy sauce contains a fifth taste, called *umami* or "flavor," joining the four traditional tastes of sweet, salty, sour, and bitter.

As Japan developed, the country started exporting *shoyu* in the seventeenth century. Dutch traders shipped barrels from an outpost on an island off the coast of Japan to a Taiwanese trading post in 1647. By 1737, the Dutch East India Company sold soy sauce in all of Southeast Asia, India, Sri Lanka, the Netherlands, and other parts of Europe. By 1866, the Japanese government charged an export tariff on soy sauce. At least 400,000 barrels were exported each year during the 1860s (Tanaka, 2000).

One of the current leading soy sauce producers is Kikkoman Shoyu Co. Ltd. The company traces its roots to *shoyu* production in Noda, Japan, in the mid-seventeenth century. Noda, located on a large plain, served as the breadbasket for nearby Edo (today's Tokyo). By 1917, the region offered soy sauce throughout Japan and East Asia. Kikkoman Shoyu Co. Ltd emerged from a series of organizations of local *shoyu* producers in 1964 to become the dominant local brand.

The company adopted an aggressive exporting focus following World War II. To facilitate exports to the U.S. market, the company opened a base in San Francisco. Kikkoman currently produces and exports soy sauce to most of Europe, to China, to North and South America, and to Southeast Asia.

Facing decreasing demand due a declining population in Japan, the company introduced Saku Saku Shoyu. This flake version of soy sauce acts like a salty sprinkle over rice and salads. More than just salty, the new product adds the taste of smoked vegetables (Koruse, 2017).

Questions for Students

1. What is the role of trade in the spreading popularity of soy sauce?

2. Do the Japanese origins of Kikkoman help or hurt the company's international marketing program?

3. How can a marketing team take advantage of the increasing demand for soy sauce?

CONSUMERS AROUND the world enjoy soy sauce.

Source: https://www.shutterstock.com/image-photo/zagreb-croatia-january-24-2016-kikkoman-366782222?src=qygMgvtoLfenzarvGUbqmw-1-19

OVERVIEW

Consumers purchase many products that originate in other countries. The movement of goods across borders ties countries, businesses, and citizens together. The flow of goods increases the diversity of products for people to enjoy. Trade creates new competition for local companies. Many governments actively monitor and attempt to influence the exchange of goods.

importing: the transfer or shipping of goods into a country

This chapter focuses on the movement of goods, people, and money, including the two main types of trade. *Exporting* takes place when goods are transferred or shipped to a foreign country. When goods are transferred or enter into a country, **importing** occurs. The elements associated with free trade are presented first. The process of lowering barriers between countries, or integration, serves as the main focus of this chapter. Legal and political systems affect the distribution of goods, or the place component of the marketing mix.

Next, a discussion of integration that incorporates broader issues including the reasons for the success of integration activities and the role of the World Trade Organization (WTO). An in-depth review of integrative bodies and trends around the globe follows. Discussion of specific examples highlights the role of integration in influencing marketing activities. Lowering barriers to the movement of goods, people, and money through integration represents a significant part of the international marketing environment.

Protectionism is then introduced with a review of the methods governments use to limit trade, including the recent growth in protectionist activity globally. The theoretical advantages and disadvantages from trade are summarized, followed by methods governments use to stimulate trade. The chapter concludes with a review of laws and ethical considerations in global trade.

LEARNING OBJECTIVE #1:

How does free trade influence the international marketing context?

FREE TRADE

free trade: an economic situation in which goods travel across boundaries with little interference by individual governments

Goods, money, and people move across the borders of countries. The movement of goods forms the foundation of international marketing activities. **Free trade** occurs when products travel across boundaries with little governmental interference.

The role of free trade stirs considerable debate. Basic questions emerge regarding whether it should be encouraged and if it hurts local citizens by leading to the loss of jobs. The essence of the debate focuses on free trade and integration versus protectionism.

GOVERNMENTAL FORMS

When conducting international trade, marketers consider the types of governments in a specified region or country, including democracies, authoritarian states, or anarchies. A *democracy* vests political power in the citizens of a country, either directly or through elected representatives. Many countries have some form of voting or elections. For a country to be truly democratic, however, those votes or the officials who are elected should be able to wield actual political power. Many forms of democracy exist.

Power rests in the hands of a small number of individuals, or even one person in authoritarian governments, such as monarchies, dictatorships, and theocracies. A *monarchy* is a government led by single ruler who inherits the position. Some, such as the one in Great Britain, are constitutional monarchies with a king or queen as a head of state holding only limited political power. Saudi Arabia and Swaziland maintain absolute monarchies in which the hereditary ruler retains control over the political system.

Dictatorship governments are led by a ruling elite or individuals that hold all political power. The power results from control of the military, through wealth, or those factors combined with corruption. Examples of dictatorships include North Korea, and Cuba. When the ruler or ruling body claims political power due to religious reasons and in many cases is ruled by a religious figure, such as in Iran or the Vatican City, the form of government is a *theocracy*.

Anarchism occurs in the absence of any ruling governmental form. Countries experiencing anarchy may revert to tribalism or warlord rule. Somalia from the early 1990s to the mid-2000s offers an example. Businesses tend to avoid entry into a country moving toward or in a state of anarchy.

When researching potential markets, correctly identifying the situation in the country constitutes one of the primary challenges. Citizens in the People's Republic of China elect 2,987 members to the National People's Congress (NPC), and the NPC votes to elect national figures, including the president. While this might appear to be a functioning democracy, upon closer examination a researcher would discover that 70% of the delegates are members of the Communist Party. Nearly all votes in the NPC are unanimous or nearly unanimous, and delegates from dissenting parties are harassed by the police and often arrested.[1] A quality source for realistic, detailed descriptions of government types is the *CIA World Factbook*.[2] Table 3.1 present various government types.

Governmental forms influence choices made with regard to the allocation of resources. Governmental leaders often dictate the distribution of wealth and economy activities. As an extreme example, the government of North Korea, under dictator Kim Jong-un, concentrates a great deal of national resources on the unreported sale of missiles, narcotics, and counterfeit cigarettes and currency, and other illicit activities, to the detriment of many citizens in terms of their standard of living, and the only beneficiary is the government.

TABLE 3.1 Countries and Governmental Type

Country	Type of Government
Afghanistan	Islamic Republic
Argentina	Republic
Botswana	Parliamentary Republic
Cuba	Communist State
Kazakhstan	Republic, Authoritarian Presidential Rule
Morocco	Constitutional Monarchy
Qatar	Emirate
Somalia	No permanent national government
United States of America	Constitution-based Federal Republic

Many assert that free trade merits government intervention, and the government type may influence the form of this intervention. Others argue that free trade represents a fundamentally positive force. International trade theory provides the foundation for this discussion, with two theories that serve as guides: absolute advantage theory and comparative advantage theory.

ABSOLUTE ADVANTAGE

absolute advantage theory: a theory that states a country has the ability to produce a greater amount of a good or service using the same amount of resources used by another country

One international trade theory is associated with the writings of Adam Smith. **Absolute advantage theory** suggests that a country has an advantage when it can produce more of a good or service than another country using the same amount of resources. The theory draws attention to the advantages countries hold in terms of certain activities.

Country-level absolute advantages lead to trade. For example, a country may have a highly skilled group of twenty computer software designers. These designers work hard, apply their training, and produce high-quality computer software. The twenty designers produce one piece or unit of software. The same country does not possess the ability to produce clothing well. It would take fifty computer software designers to produce one piece of clothing.

A second country may have a highly skilled group of twenty clothing designers. The clothing made in this country is the most stylish, is produced more efficiently, and represents the best quality. The twenty designers produce one piece of high-quality clothing. The same group of designers has little to no computer software design skills. It takes seventy-five designers to product one piece of computer software.

For both of these countries, trade allows for a focus on a specialty—computer software or clothing—while letting the experts in the other country concentrate on what they do well. The first country holds an absolute advantage in terms of computer software. The labor input from the twenty computer software designers would produce far more computer software than the same amount of labor input, in this case the twenty clothing designers from the second country. Consequently the first country would be inclined to trade its computer software for clothing and the second would seek to trade clothing for computer software. Table 3.2 models this process.

TABLE 3.2 Absolute Advantage

Country A	Country B
Labor Input = 20 software designers	Labor Input = 75 clothing designers
Output = 1 piece of computer software	Output = 1 piece of computer software
Labor Input = 50 software designers	Labor Input = 20 clothing designers
Output = 1 piece of clothing	Output = 1 piece of clothing

Trade contributes to higher levels of innovation through specialization. Each country focuses on its area of expertise and more domestic competitors emerge to meet the needs of the global market. Each of the countries involved benefit. Eventually, consumers begin to associate the country with a specialty, whether it is Japanese electronics, American movies, or French wine. South Korea increasingly creates a particular kind of music known as K-Pop. As it grows in popularity, the question arises as to whether music can be K-pop even when it no longer comes from South Korea (Liu, 2017).

COMPARATIVE ADVANTAGE

In the modern international trade environment, many nations trade with less-developed or least-developed countries that do not hold advantages in any type of production. Absolute advantage theory suggests that no trade would occur in these circumstances. If one country is better than another at both software design and clothing production, there would be no mechanism for trade between the two countries. Comparative advantage theory explains how trade might still take place.

Comparative advantage theory posits that a country has an ability to produce a good or service at lower levels of *opportunity cost* than other countries. Opportunity costs represent the key component of the theory. A trade-off exists when a country produces two products instead of focusing on just the product that it produces most efficiently.

comparative advantage theory: a theory that states a country has an ability to produce a good or service at lower levels of opportunity cost than that in other countries

In the example above, the first country would require five designers to produce one piece of computer software, and ten designers to produce one piece of new clothing. The country has sixty designers total. A second country is less efficient in conducting either activity (software or clothing). In that country, thirty designers are needed to product one piece of computer software and fifteen designers to produce one piece of clothing. In that situation, when the first country holds an absolute advantage in terms of both computer software and clothing design, it would still be more efficient to focus solely on computer design, because it makes optimal use of the available designers. In terms of total output, as presented in Table 3.3, two separate conditions emerge. In the first, Country A and Country B do not trade and instead split production duties for the designers evenly.

TABLE 3.3   Comparative Advantage Production without Trade

Country A	Country B
Labor Input = 60 designers	Labor Input = 60 designers
Labor Input Computer – 30 designers	Labor Input Computer = 30 designers
Labor Input Clothing = 30 designers	Labor Input Clothing = 30 designers
Total Output =	Total Output =
3 pieces of clothing, 6 pieces of software	2 pieces of clothing, 1 piece of software

In this case, the sixty designers in Country A produce three pieces of clothing (thirty divided by ten) and six pieces of computer software (thirty divided by five). As shown, the total output is nine units. In Country B, the same number of designers produce two pieces of clothing (thirty divided by fifteen) and one piece of software (thirty divided by thirty), resulting in a total output of three units. How might trade change this process? Table 3.4 presents the answer.

TABLE 3.4   Comparative Advantage Production with Trade

Country A	Country B
Labor Input = 60 designers	Labor Input = 60 designers
Labor Input Computer = 60 designers	Labor Input Clothing = 60 designers
Total Output = 12 pieces of software	Total Output = 4 pieces of clothing

By focusing on the comparative advantage, Country A does not waste thirty designers producing clothing less efficiently than they would produce computer software. Instead, all sixty designers produce software, resulting in twelve pieces of software (sixty divided by five). The lost efficiency in the case of no trade, as in Table 3.3, represents the opportunity cost. Country A is better off producing software and then trading some of that software for clothing with Country B. In the case of Country B, the focus on clothing production also increased total output, in this instance to four pieces of clothing (sixty divided by fifteen).

Comparative advantage theory presents a strong argument for country specialization. The advantages that emerge offer the core benefits from trade. Specializing allows both countries to benefit. Production efficiency increases, consumers in both countries are able to purchase more goods, and, over time, the countries become more skilled at their specialties.

THE BENEFITS OF FREE TRADE

Using the economic theories of absolute and comparative advantage, many economists have built arguments that conclude free trade offers several benefits. Table 3.5 presents four of those arguments.

TABLE 3.5   **Benefits of Free Trade**

Free trade restrains the power of the state and empowers individuals
Free trade brings people together across distance and cultures, leading to peace
Free trade makes everyone wealthier
Free trade encourages basic human rights

Individual freedom and empowerment often emerge as benefits of free trade. Consumers enjoy the ability to choose from a range of products from around the world instead of governmental forces leveraging power to reduce choice. Businesses and business owners participate in a fair, open global market. Government does not constrain business activity, which leads to greater freedom.

Trade between countries, at its core, connects people. A salesperson from Italy interacts with a retailer in Tunisia. An Algerian consumer becomes a fan of a German brand. Small connections such as these multiply around the world, drawing people closer together. Interconnectivity increases cultural knowledge, intertwines countries economically, and reduces conflicts between states. Free trade increases the chance for peace. Positive economic consequences of international trade for countries combined with pleasant individual-level purchasing activities and experiences may help reduce conflicts between nations.

The absolute advantage and comparative advantage theories suggest that free trade may be related to greater levels of wealth. The ability to specialize, the drive to innovate, and operational efficiencies increase in free trade situations, which lead to a rise in global market wealth. Consider the success story of Mauritius. Political leaders in this small island country in the Indian Ocean, typically described as African, seek to attract trade through effective governance and political stability. While the government focuses on more growth in trade, the foundation of the country's growth economically rests on the shoulders of increased trade, particularly in the apparel, textile, and offshore financial services (Raji, 2017).

The increase in wealth, particularly in less-developed countries, helps facilitate greater freedom for citizens. Wealth often represents power. Given sufficient wealth, citizens begin to have a voice in their governance. When a strong middle class with a large enough political sway emerges, the citizens of a country can pressure governmental leaders to grant greater political freedoms. The wealth that comes from trade then leads to greater human rights. Slovenia, the crowning success story of the efforts to integrate former Soviet Union Eastern European countries into Western Europe, has experienced rapid economic development. This has led to human rights progress, including the unusual step of voting that citizens hold the right to have access to drinkable water.[3]

GOVERNMENTAL POLICIES SUPPORTING TRADE

Many governments take steps to encourage trade, often in the form of trade agreements. Almost all regions of the world have existing trade agreements designed to ease the movement of goods between countries. Some countries establish **free trade zones**, which are specially designated areas within a country featuring separate laws that encourage trade. These laws may include a reduction or complete removal of tariffs or fees on goods entering or leaving through the free trade zone. Preferential currency exchange rates, reduction of business start-up fees, and preferential access to distribution channels are additional incentives present in free trade zones. When promoted and developed correctly, free trade zones foster rapid growth. The United Arab Emirates focuses on freed trade zones to drive economic growth. Firms in the zones maintain 100% ownership structures and relative freedom to repatriate profits. For those not in the zones, ownership must be at a minority level, with majority ownership for native United Arab Emirates' firms. CNN and Sky News Arabia are first-movers to the zones, and the policy is estimated to lead to at least $200 million in new buildings.[4] Free trade zones feature specially designated areas within a country that have separate laws designed to encourage trade.

free trade zones: specially designated areas within a country that have separate laws designed to encourage trade

INTEGRATION

Integration refers to the process of using agreements between countries to lower limits on the movements of products, capital, and/or labor. Integration allows governments to facilitate trade, and many countries have joined such agreements. These arrangements reduce barriers to trade; however, integration refers to more formal, deeper agreements.

integration: the process of using agreements between countries to lower limits on the movements of products, capital, or labor

---

LEARNING OBJECTIVE #2:

What are the relationships between free trade, integration, and international marketing?

LEVELS OF INTEGRATION

Several degrees of the integration or links between countries exist. Table 3.6 presents various levels.

A free trade area institutes the first level of integration. When a group of countries enters into an agreement to reduce tariffs, quotas, and other barriers to the movement of goods and services, the result becomes a **free trade area**. The North American Free Trade Agreement (NAFTA), consisting of Mexico, Canada, and the United States, established a free trade area.

free trade area: a group of countries that have entered into an agreement to reduce tariffs, quotas, and other barriers to the movement of goods and services

customs union: a group of countries that have entered into an agreement to remove barriers to the movement of goods and services and to have a uniform tariff policy toward non-member countries

common market: a group of countries that have entered into an agreement to remove barriers to the movement of goods and services, to have a common tariff for non-members, and to allow the free movement of capital and labor within the market

economic union: a group of countries seeking to harmonize economic policies among members, and attempting to follow the same economic policy

political union: the complete integration of political and economic policy by a group of countries

TABLE 3.6 Levels of Integration

Levels of Integration	
Free trade area	Least Integrated
Custom union	
Common market	
Economic union	
Political union	Most Integrated

Custom unions produce more integrated agreements between countries. Custom union members agree to remove barriers to the movement of goods and services and consent to a uniform tariff policy toward non-member countries. MERCOSUR (*Mercado Común del Sur*), or the Southern Cone Common Market, is a customs union with the goal of becoming a common market. As a success story for this process, Bolivia joined in 2015 and Paraguay, while suspended for parts of the 2010 due to political instability, has been reinstated as a full member since 2013 (Felter and Renwick, 2017).[5] As a counter-vailing story highlighting the instability in the region, the political and human rights issues in Venezuela led to its suspension from MERCOSUR in the winter of 2016.[6]

Common markets move beyond custom unions by removing barriers to trade within the market, by maintaining a common tariff system for non-members, and by allowing the free movement of capital and labor within the market. The European Community, within the broader European Union (EU) framework, is a common market. A citizen of France may freely move to Italy to work, without barriers. An investor in Frankfurt, Germany, is able to move capital from a German bank to a Spanish bank without restrictions.

As countries integrate, the process moves closer and closer to joining as one country, instead of separate countries within a group. The next level, an **economic union**, occurs when countries agree to an economic policy that seeks to create harmony between members as they attempt to follow the same economic policies. The countries often create a common currency along with a central bank. The EU currently constitutes an economic union.

A **political union** is the complete integration of political and economic policy. It represents the final level before the creation of a new country. Presently, no examples of a political union exist, although some nations in the European Union have expressed the goal of becoming one.

INTEGRATION SUCCESS FACTORS

Many factors influence the successes or failures of integrative efforts. Successful past integration builds skills and commitment to the integrative process. Regions including Western Europe and the Americas trace their integrative traditions to the early 1900s.

A cultural disposition toward trade and connections, even in the face of historical conflict, eased those transitions. Post-World War II Western Germany quickly transitioned to participating as a full member in various European integrative activities.

Some countries have experienced historical events and contain divergent cultures, which makes increasing ties with neighbors more difficult. Regions such as Asia do not have the same tradition of trade agreements and are less inclined to overlook past conflicts. China and Japan still maintain resentment and conflict over activities, including war crimes committed during War World II (Stokes, 2016).

Geographic proximity creates an advantage for the Singapore–Taiwan relationship.

Integration between countries enhances the movement of resources across country borders. Often, complementary resources that fill gaps for the countries involved increase the chance of integration success. NAFTA's member countries have some resource overlaps although each country also brings unique resources to the group as well. Mexico features a large population of lower-wage labor; the United States employs innovative technology coupled with a large, rich market of consumers; and Canada holds an abundance of natural resources. Even with the presence of complementary resources, the rise of anti-integration political forces has led to attacks on NAFTA by candidate and President Donald Trump.

Physical distance also exhibits an influence. Countries in closer proximity to each other encounter a natural trade advantage. Geographic distance increases costs and complicates shipping. Physical distance affects the economic union between Singapore and Taiwan as compared to a union between Singapore and South Africa. The geographic proximity affords an advantage to the Singapore–Taiwan relationship.

INTEGRATION TRENDS

Several trends and global integration processes have recently emerged. The movement in types of products involved represents one of the most significant changes in the past thirty years. Initially, trade deals focused on manufactured goods. The origins of the European Union revolved around coal and steel. Although manufactured goods still play a significant role, as evidenced by the large number of textiles and consumer electronics imported into Western Europe and the United States, increasingly services are traded. Several of the companies involved in the export of services focus on information technology, and many may be found in emerging markets. Predictions regarding the growth of India's software services exports ranged from 10% to 12% for fiscal year 2017; an estimated total value of nearly $121 billion.[7]

offshoring: the movement of a business activity to another country

Instead of exporting, some businesses offshore manufacturing or business processing. **Offshoring**, which has been incorrectly called "outsourcing," refers to the movement of a business activity to another country. Offshoring often involves the use of a third party when entering a foreign country. The process is moved "offshore," to another country. Company leaders establish facilities that remain under the overall organizational umbrella. Kikkoman, the Japanese company in the opening vignette, established sales processes in San Francisco. This is offshoring although the company maintains control.

outsourcing: relinquishing organizational control of a business process and instead hiring a third party external to the company to operate the process

Offshoring is not the same as outsourcing. **Outsourcing** refers to relinquishing organizational control of a business process and hiring an external third party to conduct the process. Companies outsource the software development function when a third party, not a group within the company, designs software for the company. This would be considered outsourcing whether the third party resides in the same or in a different country. When the third party resides in a foreign country, the process is called *offshored outsourcing*.

The past twenty years have witnessed an increase in offshoring, particularly business process outsourcing (BPO) activity. BPO activity focuses on business support services. According to the Cushman & Wakefield "Where in the World?" Report, India generated 56% of the global BPO activity. This reflects the country's early focus on business process outsourcing, including activity with GE and Anderson Consulting as early as 1995, coupled with a global reputation for expertise in this space.[8] The report indicates that the other top countries with mature BPO markers are 1) Romania, 2) the Philippines, 3) Hungary, and 4) Morocco. The top five pioneering, or emerging, countries in the report are 1) Vietnam, 2) Peru, 3) Lithuania, 4) El Salvador, and 5) Indonesia.[9]

Bottom-of-the-Pyramid

Integration poses important implications for bottom-of-the-pyramid marketing. The reduction of barriers to trade and investment presents an opportunity for companies to target bottom-of-the-pyramid consumers and for those consumers to obtain access to additional goods and services. Essilor International, based in France, is one of the world's largest corrective lens makers. Recognizing a need for eye care, company leaders have concentrated on bottom-of-the-pyramid consumers in India since 2004.[10] The access to this new product by Indian consumers resulted from fewer barriers to trade and investment. The draw of these consumers drives business in developing countries to push for integration with less- and in some cases least-developed countries that were not traditionally the focus of trade negotiations.

THE WORLD TRADE ORGANIZATION AND INTEGRATION

The World Trade Organization (WTO) facilitates trade between its 160 member countries, with 20 questions in the process of gaining membership.[11] The WTO traces its roots to the beginning of the United Nations. In 1948, the United Nations Conference on Trade and Employment entered discussions about forming an International Trade Organization (ITO). A compromise structure resulted: the General Agreement on Tariffs and Trade (GATT). For the next forty-seven years, the GATT provided the rules governing trade between signatory countries. The agreement continually evolved. Member countries, including new signatories, met in a series of eight rounds of negotiations (see Table 3.7). The last of the eight rounds of negotiations, the Uruguay Round, ended in 1994 and created the World Trade Organization. On January 1, 1995, the GATT was replaced by the WTO.

The World Trade Organization primarily seeks to open member nations to trade. Member countries utilize the WTO as a forum for the negotiation of trade agreements and as the arbitrator of trade disputes. The WTO is often associated with the removal of trade barriers. At the same time, the organization supports some such barriers, such as those designed to protect consumers, prevent the spread of disease, to serve as punishment for failing to follow WTO trade rules, or to assist developing markets. In cases where barriers exist, the WTO encourages transparency and consistency. Together, these forces increase predictability for outside businesses and investors.

TABLE 3.7   Negotiation Rounds for the GATT

Name	Year	Number of Countries Involved
1. Geneva Round	1947	23
2. Annecy Round	1949	13
3. Torquay Round	1951	38
4. Geneva Round	1956	26
5. Dillon Round	1960–1961	26
6. Kennedy Round	1964–1967	62
7. Tokyo Round	1973–1979	102
8. Uruguay Round	1986–1994	123

Source: Adapted from World Trade Organization. Retrieved from www.wto.org/english/thewto_e/whatis_e/tif_e/fact1_e.htm.

MOST-FAVORED-NATION STATUS

A fundamental component of World Trade Organization membership is most-favored-nation (MFN) status. All member countries with MFN status must be treated equally. The clause is the first article of the original GATT agreement and provides the fundamental benefit from WTO membership. Upon joining the WTO, countries enjoy ensured equal access to all member country markets. Tariffs and other barriers may be in place, but should be applied consistently, resulting in a more level playing field. Free trade agreements and special access for developing countries are the exceptions to this rule. The WTO agreement also calls for equal treatment of local and foreign goods.

TARIFF RATES

The World Trade Organization helps establish tariff rates. The WTO has not led to, and in some cases does not even call for, the abolition of tariffs. While industrial countries have lowered tariffs rated under both the GATT and the WTO to the point that tariffs on industrial goods have fallen to less than 4%, many tariffs remain in place. In those cases, the WTO focuses on transparency. The WTO asks member states to set ceilings on tariffs for specific goods.

DISPUTE RESOLUTION

The World Trade Organization adjudicates trade disputes. It does not have the ability to fine members. The organization can permit the aggrieved party to charge counter tariffs. Japan and India repeatedly dispute tariffs for steel products. In early 2017, Japan requested a formal dispute-settlement panel to resolve a plan instituted by India known as "safeguard duties," which were tariffs, to protect the country's local hot-rolled steel coil industry. Japan claims that these duties were unnecessary and have led to a steep decline in Japanese exports of this specific product to India. After a mandatory sixty-day negotiation period proved unsuccessful, the requested panel continues to try to resolve the dispute.[12]

THE FUTURE

The World Trade Organization has begun the Doha Round of member trade negotiations with the goal of further expanding trade liberalization. Negotiations that started in 2001 stalled and, facing increased global scepticism for free trade remain mostly delayed. The Nairobi Package, passed in 2015, does represent progress in beginning to remove the largest barriers to agricultural trade growth for the least-developed countries, including potential progress on subsidies and tariffs of politically sensitive crops in developed countries.[13]

The WTO has been a target for protesters and often endures the brunt of complaints regarding trade liberalization or the opening of markets. Protestor concerns echo general arguments for protectionism, including the need to defend jobs, to reduce the negative environmental effects from the expansion of international trade, and to thwart the weakening of trade union power due to the lack of an effective global labor organization. Some protestors hold more extreme views regarding the role of corporations and distant government officials in setting economic policies. In cases where individuals feel as though their voices are not being heard, they believe meetings such as those held by the World Trade Organization permit the powerful to make decisions that hurt the weak. In developing countries, individuals sometimes believe that the WTO lacks enforcement power. As an example, for various reasons several developed countries including the United States maintain subsidies on cotton production. While numerous agreements have been made, developed countries have missed implementation deadlines. The group known as the "Cotton Four" (Benin, Burkina Faso, Chad, and Mali) continue to push for stronger agreements and for accountability to meet those agreements.[14]

LEARNING OBJECTIVE #3:

What are the major trade agreements around the world?

INTERNATIONAL MARKETING IN DAILY LIFE

BEEF EXPORTS AND INTEGRATION

The export of beef provides an example of the complications associated with exporting. Beef is a food staple in many countries. The primary factors that influence the international marketing environment are associated with beef products. Culturally, at one extreme, consumption of beef is part of celebrations and social events. Killing a "fatted calf" as part of a family event is noted in the Bible as part of the Judeo/Christian heritage. At the other extreme, Hindus consider cows to be sacred and would never kill or consume them.

Governmental regulations regarding beef production, exportation, and importation are restrictive in many countries. Officials work to make sure diseases do not pass from one country to another by the movement of live cows or of beef products. Several years ago, an outbreak of mad cow disease led to strong restrictions on cattle movements across national boundaries.

Infrastructure dictates the ease with which beef can be moved from one region to another. It may be sold in street markets in one nation and in supercenter grocery stores in others. Beef vendors range from individual farmers and merchants to large beef processing plants.

Language dictates the types of beef to be sold. The term "family steak" appears in grocery stores in the United States but not in other countries. Consumption of raw hamburger as *steak tartare* is a popular delicacy in France. Beef Wellington was first cooked in England.

Economic systems lead to situations in which few can afford high-end beef products, such as steak or roast. Even hamburger may not be purchased, or is rarely purchased, by those at the bottom-of-the-pyramid. Economic systems are often supported by products such as beef. The United States' top partner for beef exports is Japan including $286 million in beef tongue alone.[15]

In this section, while examining integration trends across markets, the implications for the exporting of beef will also be considered. Integration, and the theories that support the positive effects from trade, originated in Western Europe.

EUROPEAN INTEGRATION

Over the past century, governments have focused on decreasing trade barriers and increasing integration between countries. Although these activities take place worldwide, regional differences exist regarding approaches and degrees of integration. The differences affect how businesses export or choose to enter various markets.

THE EUROPEAN UNION

At the conclusion of World War II, the emerging Cold War between a communist Soviet Union and democratic Western Europe raised fears of another continent-wide conflict. To increase economic and political ties, six countries formed the European Coal and Steel Community in 1950. These countries agreed to operate all coal and steel industries under common management. With the central role steel and coal production played in creating military materiel, the joint management reduced the chance of war between the members.

On March 25, 1957, the members of the European Coal and Steel Community signed the Treaty of Rome establishing the European Economic Community. As a common market, the treaty pushed for the removal of barriers to the flow of people, goods, and services between the countries. Table 3.8 traces the progress over the past fifty years.

The 1960s

In the 1960s, conflict between the West and the Soviet Union increased, and the Berlin Wall that separated West and East Germany was built. In response, the European Economic Community took steps to more rapidly increase ties among members. In 1962, the organization established a common agricultural policy that set a standard food price and policy across member countries. Six years later, in 1968, the members removed all custom duties or tariffs between each other and set a common tariff for imports from non-member countries. In effect, the European Economic Community became a customs union.

TABLE 3.8   History of the European Union

1950	European Coal and Steel Community is founded by Belgium, France, Germany, Italy, Luxembourg, and the Netherlands
1957	The Treaty of Rome is signed by Belgium, France, Germany, Italy, Luxembourg, and the Netherlands
1962	A common agricultural policy is introduced
1968	All custom duties are removed
1972	Currency exchange rates for member countries are linked
1973	Denmark, Ireland, and the United Kingdom join the European Economic Community (EEC)
1981	Greece joins the EEC
1982	Spain and Portugal join the EEC
1986	The Single European Act is passed
1992	Treaty on European Union is passed
1993	The European Economic Community is renamed the European Union. The EU agrees on the four freedoms: the free movement of goods, services, people, and capital
1995	Austria, Finland, and Sweden join the EU
2002	Euro coins and notes begin to circulate
2004	The Czech Republic, Cyprus, Estonia, Latvia, Lithuania, Hungary, Malta, Poland, Slovenia, and Slovakia join the EU
	Bulgaria, Romania, and Turkey become candidate countries to join the EU
	A proposed European Constitution is agreed upon by the heads of government of EU member states, but, over the next few years, fails to be ratified by each member state
2007	Bulgaria and Romania join the EU
	Croatia and the Former Yugoslav Republic of Macedonia become candidate countries to join the EU
	The Treaty of Lisbon is passed
2010	Iceland becomes a candidate country to join the EU
2013	Croatia joins the EU
2013	Iceland takes steps to informally withdraw its application

The 1970s

Major changes occurred in the European Economic Community during the 1970s. Member currencies were tied together in 1972. While each country maintained a separate currency, the fluctuations or movements of value between member currencies could move only within a set band, which linked currency values.[16]

Three new countries joined in 1973. Around that time, the organization introduced some environmental protection laws. The European Regional Development Fund was created to facilitate development of impoverished areas. The decade ended with the direct election of leaders of the European Economic Community in 1979.

MAP 3.1   European Union Expansion and Current Membership

The European Union over time has expanded to include most of the countries on the continent.

The 1980s

Greece joined the European Economic Community in 1981. Spain and Portugal followed in 1982. To increase the flow of trade, the Single European Act, passed in 1986, started a program to normalize trade regulations across members. The Erasmus Program, which began in 1987, led to funding for students studying in another member country's universities. The decade ended with the Berlin Wall coming down and the beginning of the collapse of the Soviet Union.

The 1990s

As the political landscape of Europe changed, the European Economic Community took steps to expand and to further integrate. The first was the Treaty on European Union, signed in Maastricht, the Netherlands, in 1992. The treaty established the groundwork for a single currency and increased ties regarding foreign defense policy. It also renamed the European Economic Community the European Union (EU). January 1, 1993, marked six years from the signing of the Single European Act. At that point, the European Union agreed on the four freedoms: the free movement of goods, services, people, and capital.

Austria, Finland, and Sweden joined in 1995, and the Schengen Agreement in the same year allowed for passport-free travel for many EU members. In 1997, the Treaty of Amsterdam was ratified, leading to institutional reforms that further integrated member countries. Also, in that year, ten Central and Eastern European countries began the process of joining the union. The original goal of combating the Soviet Union was met. A common currency, the *euro*, was introduced in eleven member countries for financial and commercial transactions in late 1999.

The 2000s

In 2002, *euro* coins and notes began circulation. The EU moved toward further political union, including sending military units to the former Yugoslavia to assist in peacekeeping. Ten new countries joined and three others became official candidate countries.

The European Constitution in 2004 was designed to reform management of the EU and to create the position of a European foreign minister to speak with one voice for members on foreign affairs. With France and the Netherlands voting against the proposed constitution, the treaty was not unanimously approved. The treaty represented the first major setback toward continual integration. Bulgaria and Romania joined in 2007, with Croatia and the Former Yugoslav Republic of Macedonia becoming candidate countries. With twenty-seven members, the Treaty of Lisbon was ratified in 2007 with the goal of streamlining operations and increasing integration. Table 3.9 and Map 3.1 identify the organization's current members and candidate countries.

ORGANIZATION OF THE EUROPEAN UNION

The European Union continues to be the world's most integrated union of countries. It includes approximately 508 million people and covers a geographic area approximately half the size of the United States. The economy of the EU is the world's second largest.[17] Table 3.10 lists the main institutions and the primary responsibilities of various union institutions.

The European Council serves as the head institution. The European Council has no formal power; however, council leaders normally drive the EU agenda. The European

TABLE 3.9 European Union Member and Candidate Countries, 2017

Member Countries	
Austria	Italy
Belgium	Latvia
Bulgaria	Lithuania
Croatia	Luxembourg
Cyprus	Malta
Czech Republic	Netherlands
Denmark	Poland
Estonia	Portugal
Finland	Romania
France	Slovakia
Germany	Slovenia
Greece	Spain
Hungary	Sweden
Ireland	United Kingdom (in the process of leaving)
Candidate Countries	
Albania	Montenegro
The former Yugoslav Republic of Macedonia	Serbia
Turkey	
Potential Candidates	
Bosnia and Herzegovina	Kosovo

Council is not the same as the Council of the European Union. The Council of the European Union is the main decision-making body. The Council's ministers represent various activities such as foreign affairs, agriculture, and transportation. The European Council passes legislation jointly, called *co-decisions*, with the European Parliament.

The European Parliament consists of 751 democratically elected members. It also has legislative responsibilities, including drafting legislation and, along with the Council, approving the EU budget.[18]

The power to propose legislation rests with the European Commission, the executive body of the European Union. Independent of national governments, the European Commission focuses on enhancing the best interests of the overall union. The Commission serves for five years before a new one forms. To establish a new Commission, the member states propose a Commission president whom the European Parliament then approves. The president then appoints members to the Commission who are then also approved by the European Parliament.

The members of the European Union are bound by treaty and agreement to take certain steps. As a result, the EU established a court of justice. Focusing on legislation implementation, the court ensures that laws are interpreted and applied consistently. The court has the power to settle disputes between members, and also makes sure countries act as the law requires.

The European Union operates two additional institutions. The first, the Court of Auditors, monitors the use of EU funds. The Court of Auditors has twenty-seven members, one from each member state. The second, the European Central Bank, focuses on monetary policy with the goal of price stability.

TABLE 3.10   Major European Union Institutions

European Council	Made up of the heads of state from each member state, it sets the general political direction and priorities of the EU
Council of the European Union	Made up of the national ministers of member states, the Council of the European Union discusses and, together with the Parliament, adopts EU laws
European Parliament	Elected every five years, the members of the European Parliament draft legislation
European Commission	Consists of appointed commissioners and the EU's civil service. The European Commission proposes EU legislation and checks it is properly applied across the EU
Court of Justice	The Court of Justice applies and interprets EU laws and agreements
European Court of Auditors	The European Court of Auditors audits the implementation and financing of EU agreements by member states
European Central Bank	The European Central Bank sets EU monetary policy

Source: Adapted from EUROPA, "EU Institutions and Other Bodies." Retrieved from https://europa.eu/european-union/about-eu/institutions-bodies_en

BEEF EXPORTS IN THE EUROPEAN UNION

In terms of beef and trade, the high level of economic and political integration in Europe affects marketing activity. Beef and other products only deal with administrative barriers at one point of entry to the European Union. Whether the agricultural product enters through Portugal, Germany, or Greece, access through one country represents access to the entire market.

Labor moves freely within the European Union. A salesperson who legally works in Italy may move to a position in France with limited paperwork. The price of a pound or kilogram of meat stays in the same currency, the *euro*, throughout most of the member countries, which reduces transaction costs and makes trade easier.

Agricultural products, as compared to many other commodities that are traded, take on special significance. Agricultural subsidies often become the focus of intense discussions during trade negotiations. The inability to compromise around these products has derailed trade agreements that were otherwise supported. In the case of American beef, the European Union takes a strong stand against certain agricultural practices deemed harmful to consumers. Specifically, the EU views the use of certain hormones to promote cattle growth as potentially harmful to humans, and considers one of the hormones typically used in the United States to be a carcinogen.[19] As a result, U.S. producers find it difficult to export beef to European Union countries. Beef exporting reveals the paradox of the integration of such a large market. While the EU is open to most goods, when the market is closed, outside businesses lose a major exporting opportunity.

OTHER EUROPEAN TRADE ORGANIZATIONS

Other trade organizations are present in Europe. The largest such organization in Western Europe is the European Free Trade Association (EFTA). Current members include Iceland, Liechtenstein, Norway, and Switzerland. The EFTA features limited trade barriers between members and common policies toward non-members. These policies include free trade with the members of the European Union.

The other main trade-related organization in Europe is the Commonwealth of Independent States. Its membership includes many Eastern European or Central Asian countries that have not made steps to join the European Union (see Table 3.11). The stated goals of the Commonwealth are economic integration, including common economic policy and free movement of goods, labor, and capital; however, actual implementation of these practices has been slow.

TABLE 3.11   Members of the Commonwealth of Independent States

Azerbaijan	Moldova
Armenia	Russia
Belarus	Tajikistan
Georgia	Turkmenistan
Kazakhstan	Uzbekistan
Kyrgyzstan	Ukraine

Finally, as part of potential acceptance into the European Union, candidate countries often join the Central European Free Trade Agreement, which was created in 2007. Past members that have then entered the European Union include Bulgaria, the Czech Republic, Hungary, Poland, Romania, Slovakia, and Slovenia. Currently, Albania, Bosnia and Herzegovina, Croatia, Kosovo, Macedonia, Moldova, Montenegro, and Serbia are seeking membership and actively work to reduce barriers to trade both with each other and with the European Union.[20]

BREXIT AND THE EUROPEAN UNION

On June 23, 2016 the United Kingdom held a vote whose outcomes attacked the foundations of political and economic integration in Europe. With 72% of the country voting, 52% of voters cast a ballot for the United Kingdom to leave the European Union. The various regions of the country had different perspectives, with England, particularly northern England, and Wales supporting the change (Hunt and Wheeler, 2017). Northern Ireland and Scotland backed "remain" or to stay in the EU. The vote resulted in the British Prime Minister, David Cameron, resigning with Theresa May replacing him. While against exiting during the campaign around Brexit, Theresa May now supports the move as the will of the people of the United Kingdom. Her government started the official process of leaving the European Union on March 29, 2017 (Hunt and Wheeler, 2017).

The future remains uncertain. Prime Minister May called for an election in the early summer of 2017. Her party ended up losing their majority, and she was forced to cobble together a government by partnering with other parties. This included the Democratic Unionists Party in Northern Ireland. While only holding ten seats, this new actor is sensitive to anything that affects the border with the Republic of Ireland.

Negotiations on leaving the European Union have started, but both the politics and economic implications are still unknown. Even if the political parties involved switch, all major parties have pledged to follow through on Brexit. The real question is what it will look like. And what it means for the world economy moving forward. The coming months, and years, will answer that question (Hunt and Wheeler, 2017).

INTEGRATION IN THE AMERICAS

North and South America have major trade organizations. None of the institutions compares to the European Union but they do ease the movement of goods within the Americas. Table 3.12 identifies some of the key trade areas and agreements.

TABLE 3.12   Key North and South American Trade Areas, 2017

Agreement	Population	Overall GDP
North American Free Trade Association (NAFTA)[a]	441 million	$17.0 trillion
Southern Cone Common Market (MERCOSUR)[b]	286 million	$3.2 trillion
Andean Community[c]	100 million	$580 billion
Dominican Republic–Central America[d]	376 million	$19.0 trillion
United States Free Trade Agreement Caribbean Community[e]	17 million	$107.8 billion

Notes:

[a] North American Free Trade Agreement, www.naftanow.org/facts/default_en.asp;

[b] XLVIII Summit of Heads of State of MERCOSUR and Associated States, July 17, 2015, www.itamaraty.gov.br/images/documents/Documentos/Fact_Sheet_Mercosur_English.pdf;

[c] Andean Community, www.mea.gov.in/Portal/ForeignRelation/Andean_Community_February.2013.pdf;

[d] *The World Factbook*, Central Intelligence Agency, Washington, DC, www.cia.gov/library/publications/the-world-factbook/;

[e] http://caricom.org/.

Source: Adapted from Central Intelligence Agency, *The World Factbook*. Retrieved from CIA.gov World Factbook, www.cia.gov/library/publications/the-world-factbook/index.html.

NORTH AMERICAN FREE TRADE AGREEMENT

NAFTA is the only agreement spanning an entire continent. The United States, Canada, and Mexico entered it in 1994, leading to the world's largest free trade area. As of 2017, the NAFTA region included 441 million people and $17.0 trillion of goods and services. The initial agreement called for the removal of all tariffs and quotas by January 1, 2008. While the majority of these goals were met, the agreement has experienced growing political attacks. President Donald Trump's platform attacked NAFTA repeatedly. Since elected, he has pushed to renegotiate the agreement (Gillespie, 2017).

Trade by NAFTA countries counts for $946.1 billion of goods. Investment in the countries due to the agreement is estimated to be $635.8 billion. Arguably most important, the estimate is 39.7 million jobs created across all partner countries.[21] Although the future of NAFTA remains uncertain, much like Brexit, the agreement became an unexpected political hot topic in the United States during the 2016 election.

MAP 3.2 North American Free Trade Agreement Members, 2011, iStock photo

With the three member states of Mexico, Canada, and the United States, the North American Free Trade Agreement is the only trade agreement spanning an entire continent (see Map 3.2).

Beef Exporting and NAFTA

Although trucking and milk continue to face barriers, trade in beef has been an important component of NAFTA. Forty percent of America's total value of exported beef went to Mexico and Canada between 2002 and 2005. Even with the ban on U.S. beef for a brief period in 2003 due to concerns about mad cow disease, the reduction of barriers to the movement of beef continued. In the case of Canada, the country initially used two separate tariffs rates—one before and one after a set quota was passed. The quota tariffs were removed as NAFTA was implemented, and eventually all U.S. and Mexican beef was excluded from the quota system in Canada. The United States and Mexico followed suit and also removed tariffs on Canadian beef. This allowed each country to focus on the type of beef it produces best—that is, on its comparative advantage. Mexico does not have the domestic production of large feed grain necessary for grain-fed beef. Instead, the country imports this beef from the United States. Grain-fed beef also is preferred by Canadian consumers, allowing for American beef producers to raise beef prices in that market without losing market share (Henneberry and Mutondo, 2009).

SOUTHERN CONE COMMON MARKET

The Southern Cone Common Market, or *Mercado Común del Sur*, was founded in 1991 with the signing of the Treaty of Asunción. MERCOSUR seeks the eventual elimination of barriers to trade, development of joint policies toward non-members, and a common currency. Implementation has not met expectations. Members frequently add barriers to trade, and response mechanisms often have been in-effective. Some member countries elect to use other organizations to resolve trade disputes instead of using MERCOSUR's administrative function. Map 3.3 identifies the members.

The countries within the trading block also have faced extreme economic and political instability. Argentina's currency crisis and a conflict over a pulp mill on the Paraguay–Uruguay border have caused member states to struggle to maintain their commitment to MERCOSUR's principles.[22]

One area of success for MERCOSUR has been in the negotiation of trade agreements.[23] The trading block signed a free trade agreement with Israel in 2008 and with Egypt in 2010.[24] Negotiations are ongoing to create an agreement with the European Union. If the EU agreement is approved, it would represent the largest such agreement ever made; however, disagreements over agricultural subsidies must first be overcome.[25]

Beef Exporting and MERCOSUR

Beef also plays a central role in the diet of consumers in MERCOSUR. In 2010, Uruguay passed Argentina as the world's top meat-eating nation, per capita (Webber, 2010). Beef represents an important component of the economies of Brazil, Argentina, and Uruguay. Local competition, especially from Brazilian, Argentinian, and increasingly Uruguayan beef, would make entering the MERCOSUR market difficult. Consumers trust local producers and, with the central role of beef in the economies of these countries, many MERCOSUR countries use high tariffs to protect local producers.[26]

Trade within MERCOSUR faces barriers. Unlike NAFTA or the European Union, beef exports to Argentina or other member states do not automatically gain entry into other member states. Still, with the size of the market large, the role of beef being highly important to consumers, and the economies of many members growing, MERCOSUR has the potential to gain in influence.

ANDEAN COMMUNITY

The Andean Community has deep historical roots of trade integration and cooperation in South America, as reflected in the 1969 Andean Pact. Initially, the Andean Pact focused on protecting local industries from outside competition through high tariffs, a practice known as *import substitution*. In 1989 a shift toward a model of open trade with both member and non-member states occurred. In 1997, leadership structures were reformed, with a Council of Presidents and of Foreign Ministers being introduced. To reflect these changes, the Andean Pact was renamed the Andean Community. To view the current members of the Andean Community, see Map 3.3.

The Andean Community and MERCOSUR also both joined, along with Guyana and Suriname, the Union of South American Nations (UNASUR), in 2004.[27] The goals of this pan-South America organization are mainly political, although some discussions of economic integration have taken place. UNASUR shares many goals with the Latin American Integration Association. This organization, whose roots trace back to the Latin American Free Trade Association that emerged in the early 1960s, aims to combine Central and South America into one common market.

MAP 3.3   South American Free Trade Areas

For all Latin American attempts at political integration, instability in the region, coupled with emerging resistance to free trade in the United States represent two counter-vailing forces. While pro-trade countries in the region look to deepen ties in response to politics in the USA, recent instability in formally stable countries leads to hesitance, and the future remains uncertain.[28]

OTHER TRADE ORGANIZATIONS OR AGREEMENTS

Central American governments have signed several trade agreements. In 2004, the United States became part of the Dominican Republic–Central America–United States Free Trade Agreement (CAFTA-DR). The agreement slowly entered into force, starting with El Salvador in 2006 and ending with Costa Rica in 2009. Textiles have been an important component of the trade deal, with negotiations focusing on encouraging trade.[29]

The islands in the Caribbean (see Map 3.4) traditionally also focus on removing barriers to trade. In 1965, shortly after many of the islands earned independence, Antigua and Barbuda, Barbados, Guyana, and Trinidad and Tobago formed the Caribbean Free Trade Association (CARIFTA). The initial goals of CARIFTA included economic development and encouragement of trade. In 1973, the group changed the name to the Caribbean Community (CARICOM). In 2001, members signed a revision of the Treaty of Chaguaramas stating a long-term goal of starting a CARICOM Single Market and Economy (CSME). The first step of this process is the CARICOM Single Market, which currently has twelve members.[30] The ten Caribbean countries share a currency, the Eastern Caribbean *dollar*, through the Eastern Caribbean Central Bank (ECCB). The countries involved increasingly integrate, with free movement of citizens, movement of social-security benefits with that movement, and a CARICOM certificate of skills that applies to all member states.[31]

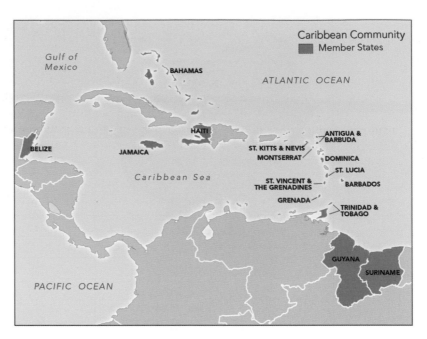

MAP 3.4   Caribbean Community Member States

The islands in the Caribbean traditionally focus on removing barriers to trade.

INTEGRATION IN ASIA, AFRICA, AND THE MIDDLE EAST

Asian, African, and Middle Eastern countries traditionally do not embrace integration to the same degree as European or South and North American countries, but Asia recently has shifted to focusing more on reducing trade barriers. As Table 3.13 indicates, trading agreements exist, but the degree of integration does not match that present in the European Union or NAFTA countries.

TABLE 3.13   Asian Trade-Related Agreements

Association of Southeast Asian Nations Free Trade Area
Asia-Pacific Economic Cooperation
Trans-Pacific Strategic Economic Partnership Agreement
South Asian Association for Regional Cooperation

ASSOCIATION OF SOUTHEAST ASIAN NATIONS FREE TRADE AREA

The oldest trade agreement in Asia, the Association of Southeast Asian Nations (ASEAN), began in 1967. The original member states—Indonesia, Malaysia, Philippines, Singapore, and Thailand—had the goal of banding together to help economic growth and to ensure peace. Over the next thirty-five years, Brunei Darussalam, Vietnam, Laos, Myanmar (Burma), and Cambodia joined. While the ASEAN agreement focused on increasing economic ties, in 1992, the members officially created the Association of Southeast Asian Nations Free Trade Area. All members of ASEAN, including those that joined after 1992 (Vietnam, Laos, Myanmar [Burma], and Cambodia), are part of the free trade area.[32] The members of the ASEAN free trade area (FTA) are shown in Map 3.5.

The Association of Southeast Asian Nations concentrates on political alliances, defense, culture, and education. Economic integration constitutes one of the group's primary goals. In 2015, ASEAN established the ASEAN Economic Community.[33] Meeting in Malaysia, members committed to greater trade partnerships and a reduction in cost for trade. The group also began efforts to smooth the process of immigration with the goal of freer movement of people.[34]

The main barrier to further integration for ASEAN lies in the disparate political and economic features of the members. The government of Myanmar has been tradition- ally at issue. With the democratic elections in 2016, and with potential steps back around transparency and political freedoms in other members, Myanmar has rapidly transitioned to a potential leadership role within the organization.[35]

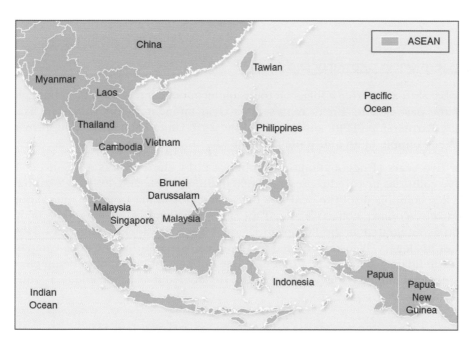

MAP 3.5   The Members of the Association of Southeast Asian Nations Free Trade Area

The oldest trade agreement in Asia, the ASEAN, began in 1967.

ASIA-PACIFIC ECONOMIC COOPERATION

The Asia-Pacific Economic Cooperation (APEC) group currently has twenty-one members (see Table 3.14). Each member borders the Pacific Ocean. The organization accounts for 2.8 billion people, 59% of global gross domestic product (GDP), and 49% of world trade in 2015.[36] The organization launched the "Ease of Doing Business Action Plan" in 2009, and since then the ease of doing business increased by 14.8%, the time for construction permits dropped from 169.7 to 136.9 days, the time to start a business decreased by 13.7 days to 14.8 days, and the cost of doing so fell by 9.8% of per capita income.[37]

TABLE 3.14   Members of the Asia-Pacific Economic Cooperation

Australia	Papua New Guinea
Brunei Darussalam	Peru
Canada	Republic of Korea
Chile	Russia
China	Singapore
Hong Kong	Taiwan
Indonesia	Thailand
Japan	The Philippines
Malaysia	The United States
Mexico	Vietnam
New Zealand	

TRANS-PACIFIC PARTNERSHIP

A global shift away from a focus on trade and economic integration has taken place over the past decade. Brexit represents a clear moment in this shift. The Trans-Pacific Partnership (TPP), and its role in the 2016 United States election, provides another example of an anti-trade moment.

After five years of negotiation, in October of 2014, the TPP was announced. The twelve countries involved represented 800 million people and 40% of global trade. One key component of the deal was the removal of China from the integration.[38] The twelve-country collective stated the ambitious goal of forming an economic union as integrated as the European Union.[39] Then President Obama saw TPP as part of his legacy. It instead turned in a political issue during the 2016 campaign. Both candidates—Trump and Clinton—came out against it, and after being elected President Trump abandoned the program. He labeled it as a "terrible deal" during the campaign.[40]

SOUTH ASIAN ASSOCIATION FOR REGIONAL COOPERATION

The South Asian region, contains few large trade agreements. The largest connecting organization, the South Asian Association for Regional Cooperation (SAARC), consists of eight member countries: Afghanistan, Bangladesh, Bhutan, India, Maldives, Nepal, Pakistan, and Sri Lanka (see Map 3.6). These countries signed the SAARC Preferential Trading Agreement in 1993 and have discussed a potential SAARC free trade area. Political conflicts between the countries in SAARC, particularly between India and Pakistan, present roadblocks to integration. Consequently, many South Asian countries pursue more easily negotiated bilateral trade agreements. The area has much potential, with 21% of the world's population and 3.8% of the world's GDP.[41] The agreement has become increasingly unstable. The most recent meetings of all parties were cancelled due to Afghanistan, Bangladesh, Bhutan, and, most importantly, India stating they would not attend. The main point of contention for all countries appears to arise from complaints about various actions from Pakistan (Roy and Ghimire, 2016).

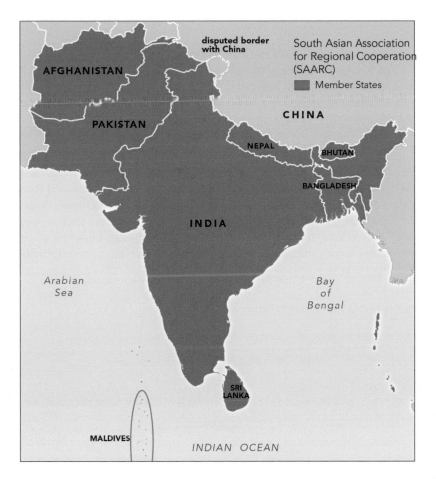

MAP 3.6 Members of the South Asian Association for Regional Cooperation

The South Asian Association for Regional Cooperation (SAARC) includes eight member countries.

BEEF EXPORTS IN ASIA

The exporting of goods to South and East Asia faces many obstacles. A beef exporter to that region would encounter tariffs, regulations, and other barriers when attempting to enter many of the markets. Some of the countries have signed individual trade agreements, yet the region does not have a strong, multi-country trading block to facilitate the movement of goods. Until the political and historical reasons for a reluctance to work together are overcome, exporters of beef and other products will find it easier to navigate other markets rather than trying to enter Asia.

Beef has also been the focus of specific protests in various countries in the region. Taiwanese regulators do not allow the growth drug Paylean in imported beef. Recent imports from the United States have included the banned drug, leading to protests and increased screening. The concerns over beef have slowed down talks on a broader trade agreement.[42]

INTEGRATION IN THE MIDDLE EAST AND AFRICA

The removal of trade barriers has taken place around the globe. The Middle East and Africa have made progress on integration, although both regions have not reached agreements that allow trade to flow freely with each region.

Middle East

The Greater Arab Free Trade Area (GFTA), founded in 1997, includes seventeen members of the Arab League plus Algeria. Table 3.15 displays the members as well as the members of another key Middle East economic agreement, the Cooperation Council for the Arab States of the Gulf (GCC). The GFTA agreement calls for an eventual uniform tariff between members, sharing of standards, and an aggressive 40% reduction of tariffs. The GFTA operates under the broader Council of Arab Economic Unity.

The Cooperation Council for the Arab States of the Gulf, also known as the Gulf Cooperation Council (GCC), founded in 1981, overlaps membership with the GAFTA and Council of Arab Economic Unity (CAEU) (see Map 3.7). The council focuses on many issues beyond trade and to a lesser extent, economic integration. Recent conflicts between Qatar and other GCC members have curtailed any progress on these goals, with Saudi Arabia, Bahrain, Egypt, and the United Arab Emirates all breaking diplomatic relations with the country. Until this broader crisis is solved, further integration will be unlikely (Qiblawi, 2017).

TABLE 3.15   Key Middle East Economic Agreements

Cooperation Council for the Arab States of the Gulf
Bahrain, Kuwait, Oman, Qatar, Saudi Arabia, and the United Arab Emirates
Greater Arab Free Trade Area
Bahrain, Egypt, Iraq, Jordan, Kuwait, Lebanon, Libya, Morocco, Oman, Palestine, Qatar, Saudi Arabia, Sudan, Syria, Tunisia, United Arab Emirates, and Yemen

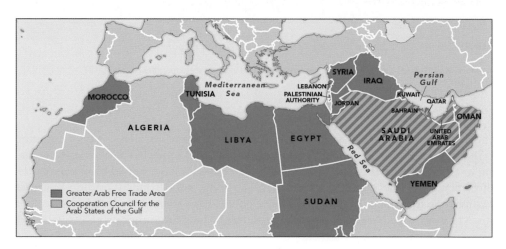

MAP 3.7   Trade Agreements in the Middle East

Countries in the Middle East have signed various trade agreements.

Africa

Countries on the African continent have traditionally expressed interest in integration. The oldest customs union in the world, the Southern African Customs Union (SACU), is located on the continent.[43] The vast majority of the countries on the continent are signatories to one or more economic agreements (see Tables 3.16 and 3.17). The Abuja

Treaty, signed in 1991, has the goal of establishing the African Economic Community, which includes almost every country on the continent. The Abuja Treaty laid out a series of steps to regional free trade areas leading to a common market and finally to an economic union similar to the EU, complete with a continental currency. The first step in this process has been completed at the regional level, with almost all African countries being in a regional bloc. To move forward, African leaders met to celebrate fifty years of the African Union in May 2103, and at that meeting committed to Agenda 2063.[44] Part of this includes a continent with free flow of goods, capital, and people, and the first step in that process is the founding of the Continental Free Trade Area. If completed, it would be the largest free trade area in the world (Warford, 2016). Map 3.8 identifies countries engaged in African Trade Agreements.The objective is to fast track the process to move forward as quickly as possible, and five meetings have already taken place.[45]

TABLE 3.16   Economic Ties in Africa

Arab Maghreb Union
Algeria, Libya, Mauritania, Morocco, Tunisia
Common Market for Eastern and Southern Africa
Burundi, Comoros, Democratic Republic of the Congo, Djibouti, Egypt, Eritrea, Ethiopia, Kenya, Libya, Madagascar, Malawi, Mauritius, Rwanda, Seychelles, Sudan, Swaziland, Uganda, Zambia, and Zimbabwe
Community of Sahel-Saharan States
Benin, Burkina Faso, Central African Republic, Chad, Comoros, Côte d'Ivoire, Djibouti, Egypt, Eritrea, Ghana, Guinea, Guinea-Bissau, Kenya, Liberia, Libya, Mali, Mauritania, Morocco, Niger, Nigeria, Sao Tome and Principe, Senegal, Sierra Leone, Somalia, Sudan, The Gambia, Togo, and Tunisia.
East African Community
Burundi, Kenya, Rwanda, South Sudan, Tanzania, and Uganda
Economic Community of Central African States
Angola, Burundi, Cameroon, Central African Republic, Chad, Democratic Republic of the Congo, Equatorial Guinea, Gabon, Republic of the Congo, Rwanda, and Sao Tomé and Príncipe
Economic Community of West African States
Benin, Burkina Faso, Cape Verde, Côte d'Ivoire, Gambia, Ghana, Guinea, Guinea-Bissau, Liberia, Mali, Niger, Nigeria, Senegal, Sierra Leone, and Togo
Economic Community of the Great Lakes Countries
Burundi, Democratic Republic of the Congo, and Rwanda
Intergovernmental Authority on Development
Djibouti, Eritrea, Ethiopia, Kenya, Somalia, Sudan, South Sudan, and Uganda
Mano River Union
Côte d'Ivoire, Guinea, Liberia, and Sierra Leone
Southern African Customs Union
Botswana, Lesotho, Namibia, South Africa, and Swaziland
Southern African Development Community
Angola, Botswana, Democratic Republic of the Congo, Lesotho, Madagascar, Malawi, Mauritius, Mozambique, Namibia, Seychelles, South Africa, Swaziland, Tanzania, Zambia, and Zimbabwe.

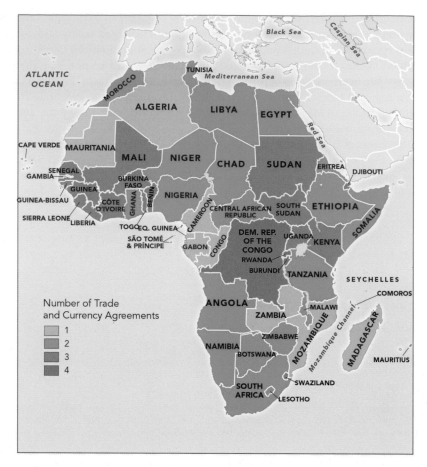

MAP 3.8   African Trade Agreements

Several African countries have signed trade and currency agreements.

TABLE 3.17.   African Currency Agreements

Central African *Franc*
Cameroon, Central African Republic, Chad, Republic of the Congo, Equatorial Guinea, and Gabon
West African *Franc*
Benin, Burkina Faso, Côte d'Ivoire, Guinea-Bissau, Mali, Niger, Senegal, and Togo
West African Monetary Union
Ghana, Guinea, Liberia, Nigeria, Sierra Leone, and The Gambia

Beef Exports in Africa

Those wishing to export either to Africa or to the Middle East encounter several obstacles. The limited and inconsistent trade integration in the region does little to alleviate these barriers. An American beef exporter would be hesitant to attempt to enter either market. Beef consumption remains at low levels across the continent. As countries develop, however, the amount of red meat consumed does increase. In Nigeria, 10 million consumers have become middle class in the last decade. These consumers are more likely to purchase meat. As a result, Nigeria has a $9 million market for red meat, the second largest on the continent. Zambeef, a South African beef producer, has moved aggressively into the Nigerian market. With approximately 1.25 billion people on the continent, further economic development could lead to opportunities for beef exporters globally.[46]

LEARNING OBJECTIVE #4:

How does protectionism affect free trade?

PROTECTIONISM VS. FREE TRADE

Protectionism refers to the desire to protect domestic businesses from the exports of foreign firms through governmental policy. Lobbying by the effective domestic companies often creates pressures on governments to respond.

protectionism: the desire to protect domestic businesses from the exports of foreign firms through governmental policy

GOVERNMENT POLICIES LIMITING TRADE

Governments employ a variety of different tools or devices when trying to reduce imports (see Table 3.18). *Tariffs*, essentially a tax on imports, are the most common. Tariffs can be product or country specific, and are designed to protect local industries. The European Union has targeted tariffs on shoes imported from Vietnam and China to defend the region's footwear industry (Miller, 2010).

A second governmental tactic is an *embargo*. Instead of a fee or tax, embargoes either prevent any goods from entering a country or prevent goods from being exported by a country. Often embargoes are driven by a political conflict, and can be rooted in national security claims. President Trump has considered citing national security to protect steel production in the United States. The linkage between steel and security is controversial. Both Democratic and Republican Presidents have been hesitant to be protectionist. What happens next is an open question, as the Trump Administration weighs options.[47]

TABLE 3.18 Government Policies Limiting Trade

Tariffs
Embargoes
Quotas
Subsidies
Import Licenses
Other Administrative Barriers
Currency Convertibility

In some cases, governments place limits on the amounts of a good that can be either exported or imported. The Chinese government maintains a *quota* on exports of rare earth elements, including seventeen unique elements used in miniature electronics such as those used in the iPhone. After reaching the quota, no more exports of rare earth elements are allowed during that year.[48]

Instead of limiting the ability of foreign companies to export to a market, some governments attempt to support local producers. A *subsidy* represents the payment of money to domestic businesses. India provides subsidies for food grain-based distilleries.[49] By lowering the operation costs of these businesses, the money or subsidy given to these distilleries creates a competitive advantage over foreign companies seeking to export to the Indian market.

Governmental leaders can limit imports by requiring that businesses that wish to import goods purchase an *import license*. By limiting the number of licenses, the amount of overall imports may be reduced. Indonesia requires import licenses for any business wishing to import clothing, footwear, food and beverages, electronics, and toys.[50]

Other administrative barriers can slow the movement of goods. In Indonesia, the use of import licenses is supplemented by governmental regulations limiting imports to five ports: Belawan in Medan, Tanjung Priok in Jakarta, Tanjung Emas in Semarang, Tanjung Perak in Surabaya, and Soekarno-Hatta in Makassar. At those ports, inspections of the goods delay entry, as do paperwork and other administrative procedures.

The final step a government may take to limit imports revolves around *currency*. Money earned in one country often needs to be exchanged for another currency when it is transferred out of the country. Currency convertibility represents the ability to make currency transfers. Governments are able to limit the amounts of currency that can be exchanged or even ban the exchange of certain currencies. This action limits the ability of companies that use the banned or limited currency to conduct business in the country.

ARGUMENTS FOR PROTECTIONISM

When other countries employ methods to limit trade, governments often take protectionist steps. Various reasons exist for these actions and some of the reasons overlap. In general, the arguments for protectionism focus on protecting a country's well-being. Table 3.19 presents a common list of reasons.

The goal of protecting local industries plays a prominent role in many governmental actions. In many countries, defending agriculture spurs protectionism of farm products. Local farmers often represent an iconic component of the country's history. In addition, self-sufficiency for food production may be valued and the agricultural lobby may be strong. Tariffs and other barriers increase the cost of food in Korea and Japan, an estimated 1.7 and 1.9 times the global market price (Richard Katz, 2010).

TABLE 3.19   Arguments for Protectionism

Protect local industry, especially infant industry
Respond to local political and popular pressure
Protect national security
Earn revenue
Promote consumer safety
Discourage immoral business practices
Protect the environment with sustainable practices
Protect culture

Infant industries merit protection. Young or new businesses often lack the experi-ence, economies of scale, and overall support to compete with large multinational corporations. Governments seek to prevent competition from foreign firms until the local infant industry becomes mature enough to compete. Governments in emerging economies often take aggressive steps to protect young, targeted industries. The rationale used is similar to that offered by developed countries in the past. Great Britain used tariffs to protect the infant wool industry in the seventeenth century. In the rapid growth of post-war Japan, protectionism was used. One famous example was the unique properties of Japanese snow that led to a ban on foreign ski equipment. China and India followed a similar path (Pilling, 2010).

Often trade barriers result from local political and popular pressure. Workers who face potential unemployment, business owners with apprehensions about the potential loss of profit or bankruptcy, or local governmental officials who fear the loss of a key local industry may aggressively pressure national governments to put protective barriers in place. In Nigeria and West Africa in general, the importing of chicken is banned. In response, KFC contracted with local chicken farms for supplies (Jargon, 2010).

Protectionism may also be justified based on national security concerns. The trade in military goods, or dependency on other nations for resources associated with national defense, represents common justifications for barriers to trade.

Tariffs, administrative fees, and other trade barriers earn revenues for governments. In cases of corrupt governments, these fees may go directly into the pockets of governmental officials. This situation creates a powerful incentive for revenue-earning barriers.

Trade barriers may be driven by concerns with consumer safety. A government may ban or screen products that potentially could harm consumers. The process of product screening adds time and complications to importing, but concerns about consumer protection outweigh these issues. The European Union safety procedure, under the consumer chief, includes a rapid notification system called RAPEX that lessens delays due to safety concerns. The objective is to balance safety concerns with the desire to keep the European Union as open to trade as possible.[51]

Protectionism may be motivated by moral concerns among citizens, particularly employees, in foreign countries. Severe work conditions, lack of employee rights, and concerns about environmental protections represent reasons to limit trade with a country. In many nations, citizens are hesitant to buy products from foreign com-panies that practice unfair and potentially unethical business practices. Every year at Halloween, U.S. newspapers print articles revealing the use of child labor in West African countries such as Ghana and Côte d'Ivoire to harvest and process cocoa beans, which has led governments to pressure large multinationals to find more ethical sources for cocoa (Castro and Wang, 2010).

Environmental and Sustainability Issues

Trade raises environmental concerns. As sustainability increasingly becomes a focus for governments, citizens, and many businesses, the differences between environmen-tal regulations in various countries draw greater attention. Environmental regulations may result in an increase in costs, at least in the short term; companies producing in countries with less-stringent regulations may be able to lower prices for consumers as a result. Some environmentally conscious consumers and businesses are willing to pay higher prices for such items.

The opening of markets to low-priced products that create pollution generates significant environmental implications. In some cases, the companies producing in the foreign markets are domestic companies moving production to avoid environmental regulations. For many countries, the fines for polluting are smaller than the cost of upgrading the production process, reducing any incentive to make a change (Spencer, 2007). The actual transportation of exports also leads to pollution. The estimated amount of sulfur dioxide, the main pollutant linked to acid rain, that is released by global shipping, surpasses the amount released by all of the world's cars, trucks, and buses combined (Stanley, 2007).

Trade affects the cultural identities of countries. The importing of art, entertainment, music, and other similar items from Western countries influences the culture of a least- or less-developed or a developing country. To protect that local culture and tradition, governments take protectionist steps. In Quebec, to protect the local French traditions, strict laws regulate language usage. The Charter of the French Language requires that all business signs include French, and if English is also used, the French component of the sign must predominate (Rogers, 2010).

LEARNING OBJECTIVE #5:

How do laws and ethical concerns affect trade and international marketing?

THE FUTURE

Arguments regarding free trade and protectionism will likely continue. Many national leaders conclude that regional trade associations are in their country's best national interests, as witnessed by the growth in membership in these organizations. Countries including North Korea that refrain from joining trade associations tend to join when national leaders or dictators need to do so to maintain internal power. Often, the citizens of those countries experience an economic disadvantage as a result.

LEGAL AND ETHICAL ISSUES

Global trade often places marketers in countries where business practices may involve legally and ethically questionable corruption and bribery. U.S. law outlaws bribery. In 1977, the U.S. Congress passed the Foreign Corrupt Practices Act. This applies to the activities of American business people while abroad. More specifically, it outlaws the payment of bribes to any government official in return for any business preference or favors. In 1998, an amendment to the law increased its coverage to any foreign person or firm that, either directly or through a third party, cause the payment of a bribe in the United States. Any company that lists securities in the United States, such as on the New York Stock Exchange, must abide by the Foreign Corrupt Practices Act.[52] The U.S. government prohibits U.S. companies and citizens from participating in any foreign country-sponsored boycott. The regulation is generally referred to as the Anti-Boycott Law. While rooted in concerns regarding potential support of the Arab League boycott of Israel, the law applies to all foreign boycotts.

Governments also commonly regulate businesses to make sure that monopolies do not form. *Antitrust laws* designed to prevent monopolies are common in many countries. In the United States, the primary antitrust laws are the Sherman Act (1890) and the Clayton Act (1914). The Federal Trade Commission and the Justice Department enforce the statutes. Similar enforcement structures are present in other countries. In Indonesia, for example, a local company, Temasek Holdings Pte. Ltd, was found to have violated Indonesian anti-monopoly laws through its ownership of stakes in two local cellular companies (Venkat, 2011).

The application of laws outside of country borders is called *extraterritoriality*. The passage and application of these laws represents the one final issue with regard to legal restrictions and marketing activity covered in this chapter. Many laws apply to U.S. citizens while acting abroad, such as the Foreign Corrupt Practices Act (as amended, 1977). Concerns arise when local laws conflict with U.S. laws. International marketers should be aware of the laws they must follow. They should also engage in only the activities with which they feel ethically and morally comfortable.

CHAPTER 3: REVIEW AND RESOURCES

Strategic Implications

The first step of the strategic management process, analysis, and diagnosis, involves assessments of internal company strengths and weaknesses combined with an analysis of opportunities and threats posed in the external environment. The strategic evaluation of global trade provides the backdrop for numerous international marketing activities. Company leaders examine regions, such as the European Union, MERCOSUR, the Andean Community, or the Pacific Rim, to determine whether a region presents a viable area to target with exports. Then specific countries will be studied to see if the local government favors free trade or engages in protectionism. Local laws and customs will be evaluated as part of this analysis. Many times, protections are aimed at specific products or industries, which makes this information valuable to company leaders prior to implementing any strategic exporting decisions.

Tactical Implications

At the tactical level, brand managers, sales managers, promotions managers, and others investigate the best methods to conduct operations in target areas. A financial officer will know that the *euro* is the common currency in the European Union and will incorporate information regarding exchange rates and other financial instruments as part of an exporting program to countries in that region. In a region that does not use a common currency, the financial situation becomes more complex. Preferred modes of shipping vary by region. Laws affecting the movement of goods will be carefully noted as part of the process. Tariffs are to be understood prior to any trade arrangement. Marketing managers at the tactical level take the information gathered for strategic decision-making and adapt it to the area. A brand manager will need to know about any changes in packaging or labeling that will be required. Promotions managers investigate the media which are most popular with locals. Only when tactical operations mesh smoothly with strategic decisions will the exporting process be successful.

Operational Implications

Operationally, companies entering new markets retain employees and other companies to deal with the administrative processes associated with exporting. Individuals may be needed to shepherd shipments across borders. Experience in the paperwork and other processes may speed the border-crossing process. Understanding local regulations, in a broad sense, should be the responsibility of a key individual of a small group in the exporting company. Perishables or other time-sensitive goods will receive special attention. First-line supervisors and entry-level employees carry out the dictates of middle-level marketing managers, including purchasing media time for advertising, working with local shops and stores, and other host country marketing activities.

TERMS

importing	customs union
free trade	common market
absolute advantage theory	economic union
comparative advantage theory	political union
free trade zones	offshoring
integration	outsourcing
free trade area	protectionism

REVIEW QUESTIONS

1. Define exporting and importing.

2. What does the absolute advantage theory explain?

3. What does the comparative advantage theory explain?

4. What are the potential benefits of free trade?

5. In global trade, what is meant by the term *integration*?

6. Briefly describe free trade zones, custom unions, common markets, economic unions, and political unions.

7. Briefly describe offshoring and outsourcing.

8. What are the primary activities of the World Trade Organization (WTO)?

9. Outline the primary activities of the European Union (EU).

10. What are the three members of the North American Free Trade Agreement (NAFTA)?

11. On what continent is the Southern Cone Common Market (*Mercado Común del Sur*, MERCOSUR) located?

12. What are the names of the Asian trade-related agreements?

13. What is protectionism?

14. What methods can governments use to limit trade?

15. What arguments are made in favor of protectionism practices?

DISCUSSION QUESTIONS

1. Write an argument for free trade and a counterargument for protectionism. Regard-less of your initial perspective on the topic, try equally hard for both arguments. Can you build a legitimate case for both approaches?

2. Trace the history of the European Union, highlighting how each step increased the level of integration. Then consider the organizational structure of the EU. How does the structure reflect the history?

3. Consider the history of integration in the Americas. How do MERCOSUR and the Andean Community compare to NAFTA? How are all three similar and how do all three affect integration in the region?

4. Examine the list of African economic agreements in Table 3.18. What do you learn from looking at this list? What does the list say about what steps governments need to actually begin to integrate?

5. The Federal Corrupt Practices Act outlaws bribery. Does this law give American businesses an unfair advantage or create a disadvantage when working with foreign governments and businesses?

ANALYTICAL AND INTERNET EXERCISES

1. Some economists look at the role of trade in economic development and con-clude that labor standards represent a barrier to economic development. Jeffery Sachs, a famous Harvard economist and a driving force behind the United Nations Millennium Development Goals, was quoted as saying: "My concern is not that there are too many sweatshops but that there are too few." The United Nations also has a standing body focused on labor protection, called the Inter-national Labour Organization (ILO). Visit the ILO website or other websites that argue for protectionism (www.ilo.org). Are these arguments convincing? Why or why not?

2. Calculate the comparative advantage each country will get from trade considering the following case:

Country A	Country B
Labor Input = 15 Workers	Labor Input = 15 Workers
Labor Input Widgets = 10 Workers	Labor Input Widgets = 10 Workers
Labor Input Doodads = 5 Workers	Labor Input Doodads = 5 Workers
Total Output = 30 Widgets, 10 Doodads	Total Output = 10 Widgets, 5 Doodads

What happens in the case of specialization and trade? Calculate the total output. How can trade then result in a higher amount of each good for each country?

3. Using Google and library resources, research the Free Trade Area of the Americas. What was this agreement? Why did negotiations stall and what does that tell you about potential barriers to further integration globally?

4. Research online a recent antitrust or monopoly case. The case may be in the United States or in another country. How does preventing monopolies potentially help consumers? Is there a counterargument to be made for how a monopoly might help consumers?

STUDENT STUDY SITE

Visit **https://study.sagepub.com/baack2e** to access these free additional learning tools:

- Web Quizzes
- eFlashcards
- SAGE Journal Articles
- Country Fact Sheets
- Chapter Outlines
- Interactive Maps

CASE 3

DHL and Facilitating Small Business Trade

DHL began as a small document courier between the West Coast of the United States and Hawai'i. The company has grown into one of the leading logistics and shipping companies in the world. Named for the three businessmen that founded the company in 1969, Adrian Dalsey, Larry Hillblom, and Robert Lynn, DHL has looked for new opportunities from inception. Recognizing a gap in the market, the company started by shipping papers to and from San Francisco and Honolulu.

The company also focused on international growth. The early 1970s witnessed growth in shipping to the Far East and Pacific Rim, including services in Japan, Hong Kong, Singapore, and Australia. The company expanded into Europe in the 1970s, opening an office in London in 1974 and in Frankfurt in 1977. At the same time, DHL expanded shipping into the Middle East, Latin America, and Africa. In 1983 the company began shipping to and from Eastern Europe. In 1986, DHL became the first express shipping company in China.

The 1990s led to more changes. The German company Deutsche Post became a shareholder in 1998, laying the foundation for eventually becoming the 100% owner in 2002.

The company invested aggressively in expansion by opening a $60 million facility in Bahrain in 1993 and by introducing a major information technology center in Kuala Lumpur, Malaysia, in 1998. DHL spent more than $1 billion on a fleet of airplanes for the European and African markets in 1999.

Deutsche Post took over greater operational control in the 2000s and the organization focused more on emerging markets. From 2003 to 2008, DHL invested more than $200 million to improve operations in China. In 2004, the company opened an information technology facility in Prague and in the Czech Republic, and also became majority owner of Blue Dart, an Indian express shipping company. By the end of the decade, DHL was conducting business activities in more than 220 countries and territories, with more than 3,000 customers and 300,000 employees, and was generating revenue of more than 46 billion *euros* per year.

A substantial part of DHL's growth resulted from facilitating trade for small- or medium-sized businesses. These organizations often offer products that consumers in other countries would purchase, if the product could successfully reach that market. DHL offers networking events, website resources, and specialized computer software to support companies that want to trade. A dedicated website (www.DHLsmallbusiness.com) provides additional assistance. The website facilitates the sharing of knowledge between businesses.[53]

1. Consider the expansion pattern of DHL. How might this relate to the integration activities discussed in this chapter?

2. Does the reduction of barriers to trade help or hurt DHL's business? Justify your answer.

3. Visit the DHL small business website (www.DHLsmallbusiness.com). What are four activities on the website that facilitate small business trade?

4. Would a supporter of protectionism view DHL's activities as positive or negative? Do you agree with that perspective?

DHL delivery systems assist many small businesses internationally.

Source: retrieved from https://www.shutterstock.com/image-photo/banska-bystrica-slovakia-september-29-2017-1074363272?src=uEZtZLti_X44KDEMVEk--Q-1-0

4

COUNTRY SELECTION AND ENTRY STRATEGIES

LEARNING OBJECTIVES

After reading and studying this chapter, you should be able to answer the following questions:

1. What two factors drive market economies, and how are these factors different in command economies?

2. How do Rostow's five stages of economic development apply to the concepts of most-, less-, and least-developed economies, emerging markets, newly industrialized countries, and transition economies?

3. Which factors help create a national competitive advantage for an economy?

4. How do the five forces that increase competitive rivalries relate to industry-level competitive advantage?

5. How do the various modes of entry balance a company's level of control with its level of risk?

IN THIS CHAPTER

Opening Vignette: Teens and Jeans: Clothing in Transition

OVERVIEW

Economic Systems

Economic Development

Global Competition and National Competitive Advantage

Industry-Level Competitive Advantage

Economic Forces and International Marketing

Sustainability and International Marketing

Modes of Entry

Theories of Entry Mode Selection

Strategic Implications

Tactical Implications

Operational Implications

Terms

Review Questions

Discussion Questions

Analytical and Internet Exercises

Case 4. Mobile Communications: Entry into Africa

TEENS AND JEANS: CLOTHING IN TRANSITION

Denim continues to be one of the most widely used fabrics in the world. Pants made of denim are sold on most continents. What varies between nations is how the pants are constructed, marketed, and worn. In some countries denim jeans provide protection from the elements as an individual heads off to work in the fields or a factory. At the other extreme, high-end fashion jeans symbolize status, exclusivity, and social connections.

At the nexus of the blue jean industry, teenagers offer a sweeping and diverse target market. In economies where incomes are low and economic development lags behind other nations, teens still want to wear jeans. Years ago, in the former Soviet Union, any individual who could "import" jeans from the Western world had access to a valuable commodity.

Countries experiencing economic development, when combined with certain cultural elements, demonstrate demand for jeans at all price levels. At the high end, Moleton Brazilian-style jeans compete with low-rise and "butt lift" products. An adventuresome tourist might be tempted to try one or more of these local versions. A web surfer could

(Continued)

(Continued)

be enticed to buy a pair online. Nearby countries, and possibly more cutting-edge retailers worldwide, may consider importing these sexy, form-fitting products. Other Brazilian citizens with lower incomes will purchase more standard fare. Brazilian and Spanish textile firms have joined together to sell lower-cost Blue Monster jeans targeting this lower-income market.

Russia features a "hip-hop-style" retailer, G-Style, that markets jeans to eager teens. Brands include CLH, Akademiks, Live Mechanics, and Apple Bottoms. These products mimic those sold in the West but are offered at more affordable prices.

In developed countries, jean-wearing features even greater social stratification. Designer French jeans such as 2Leep sell for hundreds of *euros*. Trewano Jeans are popular with the young and teens in Germany. Lees and Levis compete for customers with more modest means, as do Old Navy products in the United States.

Beyond economic conditions, jean-wearing faces the same cultural, language, political, and legal systems, and infrastructure variations present for other products. Provocative jeans in Brazil may be deemed highly inappropriate in other cultures. Jean brands must adequately translate into other languages to become viable. Jean vendors must adjust to local infrastructure, including delivery of products and the availability of appropriate retail outlets. Size limitations on retailers may limit potential economies of

Jean-wearing faces the same cultural, language, political and legal systems, and infrastructure variations as other international products.

Source: © 101dalmatians/iStockphoto

scale, possibly leading to increased prices or smaller profit margins. Levi Strauss jeans often cost more outside of the United States partially due to these space limitations. Governmental regulations and taxes further influence the marketing of local versus international denim products.

The future of jean-wearing on a global basis includes trends that have evolved in some nations but not in others. The Dockers line in the United States, for example, targets older customers who no longer look or feel good in tight-fitting low-rider products. Currently, many social circles seek worn, faded-looking, and even torn jeans. Manufacturers will need to adjust if this trend ends, much as they did when bell bottom pants went out of style. In any case, the world of jeans presents marketing opportunities to local firms as well as to any international company that can catch the wave of a fashion trend.

Questions for Students

1. How would purchases of jeans be affected by a nation's approach to commerce, such as communism, socialism, or capitalism?

2. How would the marketing of jeans to teens take place in less-developed nations in which people have lower amounts of money but still wish to wear stylish clothes?

3. How should a company export jeans to another country, through local retailers or by using a more elaborate mode of entry?

OVERVIEW

Marketing across borders involves several steps. The process begins with the selection of the country to enter. After choosing the country, the next decision is the specific type of entry mode to employ. Also, the manner in which the organization's overall structure will be modified is considered.

This chapter opens with a presentation of the types of economic systems present in the global environment. Economic systems are one of the guiding factors used to analyze the context of international marketing (see Figure 4.1). The degrees of economic development and modernization affect the potential to sell within a given nation. Economic systems help identify groups of nations when considering market entry. Various methods of grouping countries based on type and level of economic development are explored.

Marketers consider industry-level factors when selecting countries. Two industry-focused frameworks are used. The first explains how nations create national-level advantages within certain industries. The second consists of the forces that increase competitive intensity within one industry.

Following the decision to enter a country, marketers then choose an entry mode. The modes of entry and the factors that influence deployment of one approach over the others are explained next. The dominant theoretical explanations of this strategic international marketing approach are reviewed. The chapter concludes with an example of mode of entry choice.

LEARNING OBJECTIVE #1:

What two factors drive market economies, and how are these factors different in command economies?

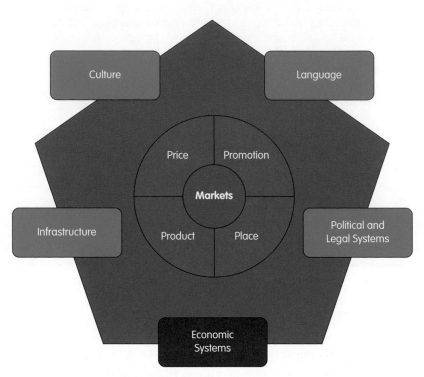

FIGURE 4.1   **The International Marketing Context**

ECONOMIC SYSTEMS

A country's economic system affects marketing strategies. Economic systems dictate the distribution of resources to members of the society, the ability to accumulate wealth, and the levels of purchasing power individual consumers hold. Three economic systems are market economies, planned systems, and mixed systems (see Figure 4.2). The terms *capitalism*, *communism*, and *socialism* apply to these economic systems.

FIGURE 4.2   **Basic Economic Systems**

MARKET ECONOMY

A region in which economic decisions are made in the marketplace is a **market economy.** The marketplace may be found anywhere money changes hands, such as in a **capitalist economic system.** Supply and demand influence purchases. *Supply* is the amount of goods and services that producers provide at various prices. *Demand* is the amount or quantity of goods and services consumers are willing to buy at various prices. The *market price*, or *equilibrium price*, represents the meeting place between supply and demand. A market economy includes one additional force, profit. Companies earn profits for goods and services when the prices charged create revenues that exceed the sum of the costs. Two additional forces drive market economies: private property rights and competitive marketplaces.

market economy: an economy in which most economic decisions are made in the marketplace

capitalist economic system: a marketplace in which transactions take place with limited government regulation or interference

Private Property Rights

Private property rights allow individuals to buy land, machinery, and other goods. Some of these goods are for personal use, such as houses and furniture, while others are used to start businesses. A new owner of a restaurant often begins by purchasing or renting a building and the equipment needed. An entrepreneur wishing to open a clothing shop secures a location and then purchases inventory. Property rights are not universal. In China, for example, individuals own the property on the land but only lease the land through complicated contracts. The leases cover various amounts of time and specific usages. If the owner of a restaurant in China wants to convert a restaurant into a factory, it may violate the terms of the lease.

Competitive Marketplaces

A free and competitive marketplace means the government does not interfere with prices or sales activities. In any market, some items such as illegal drugs cannot be sold without government intervention. Other goods require regulation, including dangerous chemicals. Some countries may set prices for staple items while other countries allow prices to vary. In Venezuela, the prices of bread, milk, and other basic foods are established by the government.[1] In a competitive market economy the government plays a more limited role.

The Heritage Foundation works with the *Wall Street Journal* to publish a yearly ranking of degree of economic freedom for countries worldwide. Table 4.1 lists the ten most and least economically free countries on this index for 2017.

COMMAND ECONOMY

A central authority makes all key economic decisions in a **command economy.** The government, or a national leader, decides what will be produced, how, and for whom. Command economies can be strong and moderate. Countries with command economies feature socialist economic systems. **Socialism** refers to an economic system in which the state owns at least some parts of industry.

Heavy governmental control takes place in a *strong command economy.* Communist states such as Cuba have strong command economies, as do some Latin American and African nations. **Communism** is an extreme form of socialism that bans private ownership of property. Communist states try to reach a goal of full employment, where every citizen who wants a job has one.

command economy: an economy in which a central authority, normally the government, makes all key economic decisions

socialism: an economic system in which the state owns at least some parts of industry

communism: an extreme form of socialism where private ownership of property is outlawed

TABLE 4.1   Heritage Foundation 2017 Index of Economic Freedom

Ten Most Economically Free Countries, with Overall Score	
Hong Kong	89.8
Singapore	88.6
New Zealand	83.7
Switzerland	81.5
Australia	81.0
Estonia	79.1
Canada	78.5
United Arab Emirates	76.9
Ireland	76.7
Chile	76.5
Least Economically Free Countries, with Overall Score	
North Korea	4.9
Venezuela	27.0
Cuba	33.9
Republic of Congo	40.0
Eritrea	42.2
Zimbabwe Myanmar (Burma)	44.0
Equatorial Guinea	45.0
Timor-Leste	46.3
Algeria	46.5

Source. Adapted from "2017 Index of Economic Freedom," The Heritage Foundation, Washington, DC. Retrieved from www.heritage.org/index/ranking.

Cuba maintains one of the last strong command economies in the world. Facing an economic crisis, reforms of the system have been proposed. At present, the majority of the citizens in the country work at state-owned companies. Government officials manage these companies. Governments also regulate land use and permission must be received from officials before idle land can be farmed (Frank, 2010).

In *moderate command economies* a degree of private enterprise operates. The state owns all of the major resources, which may include mining and ores, other national resources, and some industries such as airlines. Governmental leaders seek high levels of employment, and often a strong social support network assists the unemployed.

The distribution of wealth constitutes a primary difference between a command economy and a marketplace economy. In a market economy, only those who contribute to profits in some way find employment. Often, great poverty and great wealth exist in the same country. In a command economy, differences in wealth may be less dramatic for most of the population, but in many command economies those at the bottom-of-the-pyramid are far poorer than in free market economies.

MIXED ECONOMY

When the marketplace guides part of an economic system, and the government runs the other part, the nation features a **mixed economy**. The government typically oversees defense, education, building and repairing roads, fire protection, and other services. The marketplace vends other items, including necessities, sundries, and luxuries.

Most countries have mixed economies. One force, the marketplace or the government, tends to be more dominant than the other. In the United States, the marketplace is more dominant than the government. In many European and Latin American countries the government is more dominant. These types of economic systems will be studied by the marketing team in an international company to help identify potential customers and to better understand the potential economic regulatory forces the business may encounter.

mixed economy: an economic system in which part is guided by the marketplace and part is run by the government

---

LEARNING OBJECTIVE #2:

How do Rostow's five stages of economic development apply to the concepts of most-, less-, and least-developed economies, emerging markets, newly industrialized countries, and transition economies?

ECONOMIC DEVELOPMENT

The degree of economic development present in a region constitutes an important consideration for marketers. In the literature regarding the evaluation of the economic and social status of a nation, many political and ideological controversies arise. At the core, an argument regarding what constitutes "development" and "modernization" continues. Various nations exhibit differing patterns of work activity, product development and sale, levels of employment, and consumption based on some "stage" of development or economic activity. These distinctions are used to assess a country's business potential.

MOST-, LESS-, AND LEAST-DEVELOPED ECONOMIES

Views of economic development have been summarized by the terms *most-*, *less-*, and *least-developed*. The United Nations designates these categories, which have replaced the terms first-, second-, and third-world economies. Table 4.2 displays nations that have been identified in the new categories. Purchases of products and services are affected by the status of each, which in turn affects the ability for international companies to secure new market segments.

The stage of economic development determines the potential to market and sell goods and services in a given region. In a least-developed nation, fewer items may be salable and most would target basic needs. Greater development affords an increased number of potential products to be sold to an expanding number of potential customers. A mobile phone "app" that makes it possible to find a restaurant and place a reservation online would be viable in the most-developed countries, especially Germany and the

United Kingdom, which have the greatest number per capita of mobile phone owners. In least-developed nations, especially Burma (Myanmar) and Niger, the marketing team would expect to find fewer potential consumers for both the app and for restaurants with online booking facilities.

TABLE 4.2 Consumption Rates in Most-, Less-, and Least-Developed Countries

	Population	GDP per Capita (PPP)	Number of Mobile Phones	Mobile Phones per 100 people
Most-Developed Countries (Industrialized with high per capita incomes)				
Canada	33,487,000	$38,400	21,455,000	64.1
Germany	82,329,000	$34,200	107,245,000	130.3
United Kingdom	61,113,000	$35,400	75,565,000	123.6
France	64,057,000	$32,800	59,259,000	92.5
Japan	127,078,000	$32,600	110,395,000	86.9
United States	307,212,000	$46,400	270,000,000	87.9
Less-Developed Countries (Industrially developing with some world trade)				
Colombia	43,677,000	$9,200	41,365,000	94.7
Thailand	65,998,000	$8,100	62,000,000	93.9
Chile	16,601,000	$14,700	14,797,000	89.1
China	1,338,612,000	$6,500	634,000,000	47.36
Brazil	198,739,000	$10,200	150,641,000	75.7
India	1,156,897,000	$3,100	545,000,000	47.1
Least-Developed Countries (Industrially underdeveloped, agrarian, subsistence)				
Niger	15,306,000	$2,400	1,677,000	11.0
Chad	10,329,000	$1,500	1,809,000	17.5
Sudan	41,087,000	$2,300	11,186,000	27.2
Myanmar (Burma)	48,137,000	$1,200	375,000	0.78
Cambodia	14,494,000	$1,900	4,237,000	29.2
Haiti	9,035,000	$1,300	3,200,000	35.4

Source. Adapted from the *CIA World Factbook.*

ROSTOW MODERNIZATION MODEL

One view of the manner in which an economy develops and grows was proposed by Walt Whitman Rostow (1991). The model has the five stages indicated in Table 4.3. A *traditional society* features the first stage of development. In a subsistence economy, farming is the primary occupation and means of production. Limited technology exists and the capital required to purchase raw materials and create services and industries is not widely available. One term used to describe this type of society is *underdeveloped*, and citizens have income levels found at the bottom-of-the-pyramid.

TABLE 4.3   Rostow Stages of Development

Traditional Society
Preconditions for Take-off
Take-off
The Drive to Maturity
The Age of Mass Consumption

The second stage, *preconditions for take-off*, commences when improved technologies within a country emerge. This stage requires the development of a rudimentary transportation system to encourage trade. These two phases signal the earliest signs of a developing economy.

During the third stage, *take-off*, manufacturing industries grow rapidly; airports, roads, and railways are built; and growth expands as investment increases. One of the characteristics of a nation in take-off mode is that a few leading industries can support long-term economic growth. England experienced take-off when the textile industry emerged in the seventeenth century.

In the fourth stage, *the drive to maturity*, growth remains self-sustaining, having spread to all parts of the country, and leads to an increase in the number and types of industries. More sophisticated transportation systems including modern road systems and airports evolve and manufacturing expands, combined with improved electrical systems and increased access to electricity. This leads to rapid urbanization. Some traditional industries (such as textiles in England) decline. Mature countries are also called "industrialized."

In the fifth and final stage, *the age of mass consumption*, rapid expansion of tertiary, third-wave support industries occurs alongside a decline in manufacturing. Citizens in these economic systems enjoy abundance, prosperity, and a variety of purchasing choices (Rostow, 1991).

In each stage the presence and growth of potential target markets change. Development of an economy typically leads to a wider variety of products and services combined with increasing competition. When a government limits free enterprise, consumers have fewer options, with fewer potential target markets.

EMERGING MARKETS

Rapid global economic development has occurred in many countries over the past fifty to sixty years. These nations have passed through most of the Rostow modernization processes. As a result, many regions enjoy improved living circumstances. These nations have emerged as sophisticated markets for foreign businesses. Countries moving through the transformation from developing to developed are **emerging markets**. Such economies offer increased access to global goods and services. Mexico, South Africa, and countries in Asia are emerging markets. The term *EMM* (emerging market multinational) describes multinational corporations operating in emerging markets (Fan, 2008).

emerging markets: economies in countries that have moved through the transformation from developing to developed

A subclass of emerging markets exists: big emerging markets (BEMS). These are countries that have experienced rapid economic development and growth and contain large populations. The four biggest are the BRIC countries: Brazil, Russia, India, and China. Each is a major economic and political force in its geographic region.

BEMS offer international marketers large markets, lower costs relating to production, and opportunities to learn about rapidly changing marketplaces (Enderwick, 2009). Economic developments in these nations improve the economies of neighboring countries that have trade or business ties. The size of each of these markets makes it an appealing location for foreign investment and market entry. The recent focus on China and India provides an example of the influence of emerging market economies (Fu et al., 2009).

NEWLY INDUSTRIALIZED COUNTRIES

The two frameworks (most-, less-, and least-developed countries, and the Rostow modernization model) have been criticized for failing to recognize that some nations have experienced rapid economic expansion and industrialization. This means they are neither less nor more developed. Instead, these nations are characterized **as newly industrialized countries**. Examples include China, Taiwan, South Korea, Hong Kong, Mexico, and Brazil.

newly industrialized countries: nations that have experienced rapid economic expansion and industrialization that are neither less- nor most-developed countries

Newly industrialized countries are always emerging markets, even though not all emerging markets are necessarily newly industrialized countries. Table 4.4 displays characteristics exhibited by newly industrialized countries. These characteristics suggest that governmental forces often dictate the path to development. In contrast, some emerging markets may not exhibit them. Russia offers an example of this type of economy. It remains more dependent on commodities, specifically natural gas and oil, than a typical newly industrialized country (Oakley, 2008). National leaders do not focus on exports and have not undertaken many of the legal or economic reform steps that would be found in a newly industrialized country.

TABLE 4.4   Factors Related to Growth in Newly Industrialized Countries

Political stability
Strong savings rates
Outward orientation to expand into foreign markets
Advantage in one or more factors of production (land, labor, raw materials, technology)
Presence of growth industries
Emphasis on entrepreneurship
Economic and legal reforms

Most newly industrialized countries have created trade relationships with other nations and attract foreign investment. Factors that contribute to rapid growth in newly industrialized countries include those displayed in Figure 4.4 (Issak, 1997). The expansion of trade and increased standard of living present in South Korea, Taiwan, Hong Kong, and Singapore have led to these nations being called the Four Tigers, or the Little Dragons of East Asia.

TRANSITION ECONOMIES

transition economies: rapidly developing economies that occur in what were formally communist countries with centrally planned economies

Transition economies occur in formally communist countries with centrally planned economies. Many countries from Eastern Europe transitioned from centrally planned communist states to free market economies. In some, the conversion occurred rapidly and by design. Examples include Poland and Slovenia from behind the "Iron Curtain." Slovenia was part of Yugoslavia and began the changeover to a separate nation in 1991. Democracy flourished and the nation moved rapidly to transition economically. Helped by political change and its location on important trade routes, the country quickly developed. Slovenia became the first Eastern Europe country to join the European Union and to adopt the *euro*.[2] In other countries, such as China, the economic transition has not been coupled with political change and has been more incremental.

Transition economies offer opportunities for international marketers. Governments in these countries seek to improve the standard of living and quality of life for citizens (Kaynak et al., 2009). The countries often exhibit split consumption patterns. Younger consumers who grow up in a free market system are willing to purchase foreign goods. Older consumers, especially those accustomed to a centrally planned economy, remain resistant to foreign goods and may call for a return to communism, a symptom called "transition fatigue."

Corruption commonly constrains transition to an open market as national leaders cope with the vestiges of the communist regime. New institutions do not necessarily change mindsets. Some governmental leaders worry that a transition that moves too rapidly may lead to democracies without citizens that are ready to participate. Corruption, both at the corporate and consumer levels, then becomes a major obstacle to progress. Table 4.5 presents part of a recent Transparency International survey of corruption in 178 countries. The index ranks countries according to the perception of corruption in the public sector.

TABLE 4.5 Transparency International Corruption Perception Index

Ten Countries with Highest Index Scores	
Denmark	9.3
New Zealand	9.3
Singapore	9.3
Finland	9.2
Sweden	9.2
Canada	8.9
Netherlands	8.8
Australia	8.7
Switzerland	8.7
Norway	8.6
Ten Countries with Lowest Index Scores	
Somalia	1.1
Myanmar (Burma)	1.4
Afghanistan	1.4
Iraq	1.5
Uzbekistan	1.6
Turkmenistan	1.6
Sudan	1.6
Chad	1.7
Burundi	1.8
Equatorial Guinea	1.9

Source: Adapted from "Corruption Perceptions Index 2010 Results," Transparency International, Berlin. Retrieved from www.transparency.org/policy_research/surveys_indices/cpi/2010/results.

In Poland, where a prototypical transition took place, the nation underwent massive changes. On January 1, 1990, the Polish government introduced a set of economic reforms called "shock therapy." While the tactics met with criticism, they led to a rapid transition for the average Polish citizen. Although the transition exacerbated the gap between young and old and rural and urban, it ultimately moved Poland to the point that the country now belongs to the European Union.

Transitions produce opportunities for new companies to fill gaps left by communist systems. For example, bananas were scarce in Poland before its changeover. The introduction of the fruit to the Polish marketplace led one young boy to ask his father, "What are those yellow sausages?" The first marketer to introduce bananas to the country made a large profit.

A dynamic conversion environment generates entrepreneurship opportunities. In countries including China, Poland, and Slovenia, the activities of entrepreneurs have spurred growth and helped allocate resources more efficiently (Johnson and Lovman, 1995). Table 4.6 displays some of the features of transition economies.

TABLE 4.6   Features of Transition Economies

Liberalization	Prices set by supply and demand, removal of trade barriers
Privatization	Previously government-owned industries moved to private ownership
Legal and Institutional	Legal structures set up to allow for ownership of property
Reforms	Contracts enforced, and the rule of law enacted
Budget Reform	Hard budget caps set by governments to help control inflation

EFFECTS ON INTERNATIONAL MARKETING

The economic system and the level of development present in a country directly affect an international marketing program. A command economy does not allow the degree of diversity of products that could be targeted at individual groups, as compared to a market economy. In a mixed system, the marketing team identifies the products that may be produced and differentiated from those controlled by the government.

The nature of competition may be influenced by the economic system. A country producing a single form of a product faces no internal competition. The product will be positioned and sold to target markets in other nations, creating a different type of competition (Baack, 2008).

INTERNATIONAL INCIDENT

An executive from Argentina traveled to finalize a first-time sale of raw materials to a company in Japan. The executive was careful to bow in the appropriate fashion and had memorized a greeting in Japanese. He also had purchased an appropriate gift for the occasion. When negotiations for the final price began, the Argentine executive offered what he felt was an appropriate price. The Japanese management team sat quietly and did not respond. The executive soon began to feel uncomfortable. He offered a lower price just to break the silence. Did he make a good decision, or was he missing something?

The developmental process that countries undergo affects marketing activities. Transition economies do not exhibit the same characteristics as those in newly industrialized countries. This suggests that consumers in these markets differ. Transition economy consumers may be uncomfortable with the pricing process or unaware of basic products and product categories. Higher levels of product and brand awareness are often present in newly industrialized country consumers. At the same time, newly industrialized countries tend to feature governmental protections of local companies, especially in the early stages, which limits the ability of foreign companies to compete.

STAGE OF DEVELOPMENT AND BOTTOM-OF-THE-PYRAMID

Low-income, bottom-of-the-pyramid customers often reside in least-developed economies or in Rostow's traditional societies. When a substantial cluster of low-income individuals lives in a geographic area, the infrastructure may not be as advanced; the culture often revolves around agrarian life and poverty; skill sets tend to be low among the majority of citizens, and the political and legal systems do little to improve living conditions.

In such circumstances consumers may not be inclined to purchase a common item, such as a soft drink. In Kenya, an average citizen consumes thirty-nine servings of Coca-Cola per year. In the developing country Mexico, the average citizen consumes 665 servings per year. Ned Dewees, a major investor in soft drink common stock shares, concludes that Africa offers an "enormous opportunity" for Coke. As nations begin to evolve into the take-off stage, consumption rates should rise dramatically (Stanford, 2010).

Many marketers display interest in least-developed, traditional economies. The potential exists for products to be tailored to consumers in those regions. As an economy moves forward and infrastructure emerges, the opportunities tend to grow and expand (Hill, 2010).

LEARNING OBJECTIVE #3:

What factors help create a national competitive advantage for an economy?

GLOBAL COMPETITION AND NATIONAL COMPETITIVE ADVANTAGE

International marketers choose countries to enter based on specific features. In addition to economic development issues, marketers analyze countries based on what each does well. Some have reputations for technological superiority, such as Japan and Germany. Others including China and India gain attention based on lower labor costs. Certain industries become the basis of global leadership or **national competitive advantage** for countries.

national competitive advantage: a circumstance in which a country has built a reputation with regard to an aspect of producing a product, such as technological superiority or lower labor costs

Michael Porter's theory of national competitive advantage explains the reasons countries succeed in some industries and not in others. Table 4.7 displays Porter's diamond of the five factors that generate national competitive advantage. The factors move beyond the traditional focus on the cost of labor, currency differences, or natural resources, and instead concentrate on what leads a country to innovate.

The ability to innovate helps establish a national competitive advantage. The first four factors drive an overall national competitive advantage. The fifth factor, the government, indicates how an administration can leverage and encourage the development of the first four factors.

TABLE 4.7   National Competitive Advantage Factors

Demand conditions
Related and supporting industries
Firm strategy, structure, and rivalry
Factor conditions
Government

DEMAND CONDITIONS

Consumer, business, and governmental demand make up a country's specific conditions. Some nations are less responsive to consumer needs than other countries, especially when the domestic market is larger or more sophisticated than foreign markets. Consumers who influence global tastes in a category or industry help a nation become the category's global leader. Consider French fashion. French consumer tastes in high fashion affect companies worldwide. Sophisticated consumers have forced French designers to stay on the cutting edge. This provides the nation with an advantage, which has been institutionalized as *haute couture* or "high dressmaking." To qualify for the designation, French law requires each producer to register with the government. Complicated standards must be met to receive the designation.[3]

RELATED AND SUPPORTING INDUSTRIES

Industries need support from the other companies and/or industries that provide inputs, support production, or facilitate various aspects of operations. Nations with this type of network support enjoy one condition required to generate a national competitive advantage.

Finland's Nokia is one of the world's largest mobile phone manufacturers. Within Finland, Nokia has the support from companies in the industries needed to be successful, including Codenomicon, which tests the robustness of software; Navicron, a wireless technology company; and Tracker, which provides navigation software (Harris, 2007). The presence of these companies provides a competitive advantage to Nokia, which by extension leads to innovation and a national competitive advantage in mobile phone production for Finland.

FIRM STRATEGY, STRUCTURE, AND RIVALRY

Nations differ in terms of how the government allows companies to be formed, maintained, and structured, including control of domestic and potentially foreign competitors. Firm strategy, structure, and rivalry apply to these features.

National differences exist between German and Italian systems. In Italy, companies tend to be smaller, family-owned, and privately held. German companies are often larger, highly structured, and employ managers with technical backgrounds. These differences explain the German focus on sophisticated engineering designed to create mass-market products. Italians focus on luxury, high-end products. Multiple companies engage in intense rivalries between German automakers and between Italian leather companies (Porter, 1990).

FACTOR CONDITIONS

Factor conditions include components needed for production of goods or services, such as labor and infrastructure. Each industry exhibits specific factors associated with success. Traditionally, such factors were natural endowments that nations possessed. They included labor, land, or various natural resources such as oil and minerals. Increasingly, national competitive advantage grows from resources that have been created. Trained human resources and/or a strong scientific community provide examples of created resources.

Large labor pools or other natural resources do not always lead to innovation. Japan has been called "an island nation with no natural resources" (Porter, 1990). The lack of resources led the country's leaders to focus on the education required to develop the skilled human resources needed to compete globally. Even a country with an ample supply of petroleum needs the technological knowledge necessary to access that resource.

Factor conditions lead to national competitive advantage when specialization exists. Consider the highly specialized, highly focused skills needed to succeed in the film industry. The American industry maintains a national competitive advantage. The various directors, actors, producers, and cinematographers that create movies are arguably the best in the world. As a result, American films generate revenues globally. Movies made in India in Bollywood have begun to compete in this marketplace through the introduction of similar technologies and skills.

Factor conditions include components needed for production of goods or services, such as labor and infrastructure.

Source: Photo courtesy of Chih-Kuo, Kuo clearspace.tw.

GOVERNMENT

As is the case in a mixed economy, the government and a free market both play roles in creating a national competitive advantage. Industry innovation results from competition; however, governmental activities can establish the infrastructure needed. Governmental support for education, cooperation between related industries, new technologies, emerging industries, and consumer protections enhance an environment that leads to industrial innovation.

Governments that fail to intervene in trade or in competition for resources help expand the foundation for innovation. Laws limiting cooperation between direct industry rivals lead to innovation through competition. In general, policies that increase competition while supporting innovation lead to a national competitive advantage.

Further, governmental actions such as the institution of trade barriers including tariffs and other importing restrictions, as were described in Chapter 3, receive careful consideration by company officials. These factors combine with other elements in determining a company's ultimate decision whether to seek entry into a new country.

When successful, governmental activities guide a nation with one or more clusters of similar industries that together generate a national competitive advantage, such as in London's financial industry. In new industries, nations compete to establish a dominant cluster. Cna's rapid entry into the wind turbine market positions Beijing as the home to the world's leading wind turbine producers, Sinovel and Goldwind (Ford, 2009).

LEARNING OBJECTIVE #4:

How do the five forces that increase competitive rivalries relate to an industry-level competitive advantage?

INDUSTRY-LEVEL COMPETITIVE ADVANTAGE

Industries also compete internally. Michael Porter has identified factors associated with an industry-level competitive advantage. Five competitive forces influence the overall industry competitive intensity (see Table 4.8). The first four forces work together to increase rivalries among competitors, the last force. Analysis of these forces helps specify the level of competitive intensity in an industry within a country. A country with a highly intense competitive environment may be unattractive for potential entry. Such competition lowers potential profits and increases the chance of company failure.

TABLE 4.8   Five Competitive Forces

Threat of new entrants
Threat of substitute products
Bargaining power of suppliers
Bargaining power of consumers
Rivalry among competitors

THREAT OF NEW ENTRANTS

The threat of new entrants affects the nature of local, national, and international competition. High profit margins or large potential markets of consumers attract new entrants. The large size of the markets in big emerging markets alone sparks interest and enhances the chance of new entrants. For industries in those countries, a larger market size increases the potential for new competitors.

Barriers to entry can be used by companies to prevent or limit new entrants. In addition, steps that make it difficult to leave an industry or barriers to exit also limit new entrants. Brand equity, large initial cost requirements, regulations, monopolies over distribution or needed resources, and/or a lack of specific, hard-to-learn knowledge create barriers to entry.

ZTE is a Chinese telecommunications equipment manufacturer that decided to enter the European market. The company's marketing team recognized that several barriers limited the ability to be a successful new entrant in Europe. To gain cultural knowledge, ZTE joined with local partners. Some barriers the company encountered were not controllable. For example, European Union officials, in response to pressures from European business competing with ZTE, considered placing tariffs on ZTE's products (Hunt, 2005; Dalton, 2010).

THREAT OF SUBSTITUTE PRODUCTS

Substitute products increase competitive intensity. When consumers can switch from product to product, companies face stronger competitive pressures to entice consumers to make the switch. To respond, marketers may attempt to increase switching costs or seek to retain customers in some other way.

Brand loyalty, product differentiation, and repeat purchase rewards decrease switching. Increasing brand loyalty is a common marketing goal. A hotel in Cameroon that provides Internet access and attentive concierge services, and tailors a customer's stay to their personal preferences, exceeds expectations and generates loyalty. A restaurant in Spain selling the national dish *paella* might charge a modestly lower price than competitors while offering an equal taste and portion size to compete with other restaurants. Both the hotel in Cameroon and the restaurant in Spain discourage competition, especially when no comparable or substitute services (overnight lodging or local cuisine) are available.

Product differentiation occurs when a product achieves the status of being recognizably different from those of competitors. Korean Airlines made substantial efforts to differentiate from other carriers. While travel substitutes exist, none offers the speed and convenience of the company's jets. An international firm that successfully establishes product differentiation may be able to reduce competition, charge a higher price, and enjoy above-average profits (Lilach and Wymbs, 2005).

Repeat purchases dampen the opportunities to take away market share and to create substitute products. A person accustomed to buying a local flavor of chewing gum will be unlikely to switch to a chewing gum from another country.

BARGAINING POWER OF SUPPLIERS

Companies within an industry typically use the same supplier or a small group of suppliers for the resources needed, including labor and raw materials. Suppliers of these resources with strong bargaining power increase competition within the industry.

Bargaining power increases when only one or a small number of suppliers is present. A resource provided by one or a small number of suppliers results in greater power for the producers of that resource. Prices for the resource rise and suppliers can refuse to provide the resource.

Marketers take steps to lower the bargaining power of suppliers. When necessary, companies buy the supplier or start to supply the resource internally. Companies that find substitutes for the resource or look in other markets, such as in other countries for new suppliers, are able to reduce supplier bargaining power.

Wal-Mart, the global chain of retailers, initially signed an exclusive contract with Toronto-based Cott Corporation in 2002 to supply the company with its store brand Sam's soft drinks. Wal-Mart, having more power than the supplier, made the decision to end that exclusive relationship effective January 2012 and pursued an alternate approach in which multiple companies supply soft drinks for the store brand. If the power had rested with Cott Corporation, Wal-Mart would not have been able to make this change (King, 2009).

BARGAINING POWER OF CONSUMERS

Consumers possess bargaining power. When only a few individuals purchase a product, such as can be the case in business-to-business marketing, those buyers have power. As with supplier power, small numbers of consumers increase competition. Industries with high-cost items face greater consumer power because the companies within the industry are dependent on each sale. Price sensitivity increases consumer power due to the increased likelihood of a customer switching to a lower-priced competitor.

Brand loyalty decreases consumer bargaining power. The same holds true for opening new markets or increasing market share. In general, moving to increase the number of consumers reduces rivalries within an industry. An increase in the numbers of consumers increases the size of the revenue "pie" companies compete for. Brand loyalty and growth in market size shift power from consumers to producer companies.

RIVALRY AMONG COMPETITORS

Together, the four forces above work to increase rivalry among competitors. An industry with high supplier and consumer bargaining power, many substitute products, and a strong threat of new entrants is forced to cope with extreme rivalry among competitors.

Company-specific factors, outside of the four forces discussed in this section, increase rivalries among competitors. Widely accessible knowledge and processes result in more rivalry than does specialized, difficult-to-imitate knowledge. Innovation, especially when legally protected, reduces competition within an industry.

When every company in an industry competes based on similar, duplicable factors, rivalry becomes intensified. Companies can instead compete based on specialized knowledge, which reduces rivalries. In the pharmaceutical industry in many countries, when a single pharmaceutical company introduces a new medicine, that drug is protected from competition for a period of time. During that time period, the legal prohibition of copying the drug drastically reduces the level of competition and rivalry. Once the protection is removed, competing pharmaceutical companies are allowed to introduce versions of the medicine, which greatly increases the level of rivalry.

ECONOMIC FORCES AND INTERNATIONAL MARKETING

Economic forces interact with various additional primary influences on international marketing, as displayed in Figure 4.1. Culture, language, political and legal systems, and infrastructure combine to determine the overall marketing environment in a country.

Economic forces strongly link to *culture*. An agrarian economy often features limited travel, primitive technology, and an emphasis on manual labor. At the extreme, sons in a patriarchal agrarian society are highly valued for their ability to work, whereas daughters are viewed as an expense. In many areas of China, where previous government attempts were designed to limit each family to one child, the number of males born far exceeds the number of females. Culture, consumer behavior, and economic development tend to interact with one another. Recent research suggests that the consumer value *materialism* is on the rise in China, in part due to changing economic forces (Podoshen et al., 2011).

Language is affected by an economy and by economic development. New terminology associated with technology often emerges. Terms such as "tweet" or "QR code" have been introduced globally. In many parts of the world, citizens speak more than one language, which can translate into additional marketing opportunities, but also increases the threat of entry by outside competitors, because multiple languages facilitate the ease of entry.

Political and legal systems are strongly tied to economic systems through laws regulating commerce and by granting or withholding private property rights. Governmental activities often influence the economic system. Governments establish protectionist tax codes, seek to keep out international imports, or enact other policies designed to encourage international trade. Some governments go to the extreme of supporting practices such as *dumping*, the deliberate under-pricing of goods in order to gain entry into another country. Political and legal systems can speed up or slow down progress to a more sophisticated economic environment, as evidenced by levels of economic change in Poland as compared to China.

Economic growth reflects the addition of more-complex *infrastructure*, including communication systems, roads, and other utilities such as electric power and running water. Infrastructure development plays a prominent role in the Rostow modernization model.

In summary, any marketing team considering entry into a new country considers its economic environment before taking any additional steps. Many times the economic system in one country will be similar to that of a nearby nation. Countries in the European Union contain such similarities, as do the Four Asian Tigers. The same holds true for the United States and Canada. Comparable economic systems often make entry into a new country easier. Whether the system is similar or dissimilar, one of the next projects for marketers will be to select the best mode of entry into that nation.

SUSTAINABILITY AND INTERNATIONAL MARKETING

The continuing focus on sustainability is present in international marketing. Consumer demand for green products has grown and marketers realize that serving those needs attracts consumers. As technologies improve, sustainable business practices lead to lower costs and increased profits.

The buy-local movement has reduced the environmental footprints of many businesses. A banana grown in Florida travels a far shorter distance to an American grocer than one grown in Brazil. The reduction in miles results in lower greenhouse gases released into the atmosphere.

Economic development in emerging markets has brought with it large environmental costs. In China, 200 million citizens are projected to move from poverty into the middle class in the coming decade. Significant environmental implications of this growth exist. The building of dams to generate hydroelectric energy to fuel Chinese growth has displaced at least 23 million people and may have caused the Sichuan earthquake that killed 80,000 people in 2008 (Bosshard, 2011).

Use of virtual water offers an example that captures the challenge of sustainability. Production of a product or service requires water. That product or service is then exported. The traded good then represents the transfer of water from one country to another. For example, 1 ton of beef exported from the United States contains approximately 13,193 metric tons of virtual water (Chapagain and Hoekstra, 2004). Map 4.1 identifies the net virtual water resulting from trade for countries globally. Map 4.2 displays water consumption footprints, on average, for various countries.

Balancing economic growth with environmental protection creates a global challenge as more countries develop economically. Sustainable business practices, when properly implemented, have the potential to address these concerns. The greatest amount of attention to sustainability is likely to be paid by companies in least-, less-, and most-developed countries.

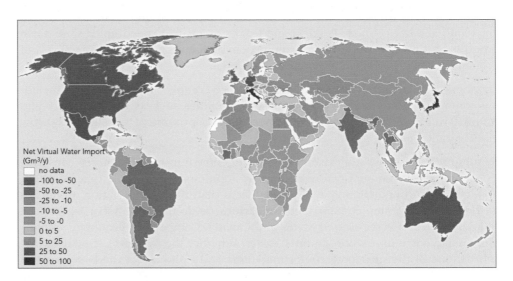

MAP 4.1   Net Virtual Water Globally

Trade also moves "virtual water," or the water used to produce the good or service being traded.

Source: © GWSP Digital Water Atlas. Retrieved from http://atlas.gwsp.org/index.php?option=com_content&task=view&id=93

As countries develop economically, water consumption increases. Sustainability advocates aim to reduce each nation's global water footprint.

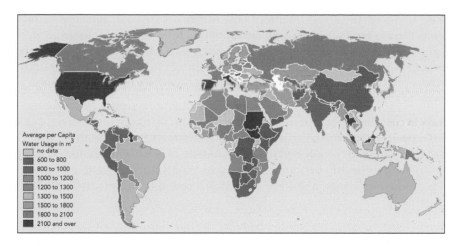

MAP 4.2   Global Water Consumption Footprints

Source: retrieved from http://www.gfk-geomarketing.com/en/press/map_of_the_month/archive.html

---

LEARNING OBJECTIVE #5:

How do the various modes of entry balance a company's level of control with its level of risk?

MODES OF ENTRY

After selecting a country to enter, international marketers take steps to move the product to the market. Several options exist. The various approaches are called entry modes. Table 4.9 provides a list. Each experiences differing levels of corporate control, cost, and risk. International marketers balance these concerns and choose the mode that best fits the internal environment of the country being entered.

TABLE 4.9   Types of Entry Mode

Types of Entry Mode	Concerns
Exporting	Cost
Licensing	Control
Franchising	Risk
Wholly Owned Subsidiary	
Joint Venture	
Strategic Alliance	

EXPORTING

The first option many companies explore will be **exporting** the product. The product is shipped in one manner or another into a foreign market. Companies export in a variety of ways, including:

- direct sales and
- use of an intermediary

exporting: a mode of entry in which the product is shipped in one manner or another into a foreign market

The rise and growth of the Internet make *direct sales* easier. Business-to-business transactions are facilitated by website contacts, followed by visits from personal sales representatives or meetings at events such as trade shows. In some instances, a company shops for resources or finished items from a variety of manufacturers worldwide and then selects the best choice. Spot markets for crude oil often utilize this type of transaction format.

Individual customers surfing the web locate products that will be directly shipped to any nation with infrastructure that has developed to the point in which routine package delivery takes place. A Swedish tourist who visits Hawai'i and enjoys macadamia nut products there can easily locate ABC Stores or Hilo Hatties, make purchases, and have them delivered to her home by FedEx or some other carrier.

Numerous *intermediaries* vend products across networks of countries. Agent wholesalers or retailers represent items without taking title to those goods. These types of intermediaries facilitate transactions in business-to-business and consumer markets. An Italian olive oil company can contract with an intermediary to represent the product in any country where olive oil consumption has begun to rise. A ticket transaction company in Ireland sells tickets to soccer matches to buyers from nearby countries as well as those living farther away. Merchant intermediaries buy and resell items. Silk cloth woven in Japan may be purchased by wholesalers who offer it to fabric stores and clothing manufacturers in other countries.

In these instances, items are exported and sold in other countries without any additional company restructuring or activity. Exporting features a low cost relative to other entry mode forms. With no large purchases made or long-term obligations to local partners, exporting offers the simplest form of market entry. Lack of control will be a concern. In some cases, the company literally ships the good and has no further contact with it. Control over the retailers that buy and/or sell items does not exist. The manufacturer cannot offer input into matters such as product displays or other elements involved in consumer choice. Without this control, the company risks losing the ability to enter the market more aggressively at a later date.

LICENSING

licensing: a contract that grants a company the legal right to use another company's brand, image, and other marketing components

Instead of entering a country, marketers chose **licensing**, or a contract that grants a company the legal right to use another company's brand, image, and other marketing components. Many large and successful global brands use licensing to increase revenues. Several professional basketball and soccer teams have licensing agreements that allow other firms to create jerseys, hats, and other items bearing the team's name, logo, and often the name of the star player. In exchange, the teams receive licensing fees.

Companies license popular press books and textbooks to other countries. Novels written in Spanish in Paraguay that receive international acclaim will be licensed for translation to other countries. Many textbook providers license books for reprint and sale in other countries, including a translation combined with cultural adaptation. For instance, a photo of a woman dressed in provocative clothing that appears in a Canadian textbook will be removed when the book is prepared for a Muslim country such as Saudi Arabia.

Licensing provides a quick, low-cost method to enter a foreign market. Selling the rights to create a product to a local partner generates revenues. Often the licensee holds additional knowledge about the local market that increases the chance for success. Lack of control constitutes the primary concern. A local partner, after signing the contract, can detract from the company's image. Without control over decision-making, the owner of the license has the freedom to make what may be poor marketing choices.

Fast-food chains can create franchising arrangements to expand internationally.

FRANCHISING

To increase the level of control over operations in another country, some organizations move from exporting or licensing to franchising. **Franchising** is a contractual agreement to implement a business model. Companies involved in international franchising include McDonald's restaurants, KFC restaurants, 7–11 convenience stores, Supercuts hair salons, and Jani-King cleaning establishments. While international franchising agreements are common in developed countries, they can also be effective in emerging markets with pent-up demand for high-quality products and services (Welsh et al., 2006; Baena, 2009).

franchising: the contractual agreement to implement a business model

A contract specifies the business model in a franchising relationship. In return for an upfront fee, signees are allowed to use the company's colors, images, and products, which provides greater control over the marketing process by the parent company. The risk to the parent company lies in a poor franchisee. The contract signee might ignore the agreement or make poor decisions. The parent company covers the costs associated with inspecting and maintaining franchise locations at acceptable levels. Those that do not meet standards are warned, and if the units are not of sufficient quality, the relationship will be terminated. Taking such a step includes adjusting to local legal conditions as they relate to franchise contracts.

INTERNATIONAL INCIDENT

The McDonald's global brand has successfully endured the challenges of international markets and changing consumer food preferences. This outcome is partly due to the adaptation and innovation strategy that McDonald's follows: the company comes up with products and services to address the specific needs of a diverse consumer market—as shaped by demographic, economic, and local factors around the world. Another important factor contributing to the international success of this multinational company is its foreign market entry strategy based mainly on the franchise model.

You are a marketing specialist for a highly successful Fish and Chips restaurant chain that operates in the UK. Your supervisor has asked for a report outlining the advantages and disadvantages of the franchise model in general, and what makes this particular entry strategy so successful for McDonald's. Then you are asked to conclude what would be useful as your company seeks to expand into Asia and Australia. What does your report say?

JOINT VENTURES

joint venture: a legal partnership that involves an investment, a division of ownership, and the creation of a new legal entity, or when two companies combine to create a product

Some companies choose to partner with local businesses when entering a country. When these legal partnerships involve an investment, a division of ownership, and the creation of a new legal entity, the newly created business is a **joint venture**. An example is Hindustan-Unilever, a combined India–UK company. Joint ventures take many different forms. The categories of joint ventures include (1) majority owned, where the foreign company owns 51% or more of the joint venture; (2) minority owned, where the foreign company owns 49% or less of the joint venture; and (3) 50% / 50%, or an equal split of ownership.

A second form of joint venture involves two companies combining to create and sell a product. It may be a physical good, such as an automobile, or a service. The partnership between Quantas Airlines, which flies to Australia and New Zealand, with American Express has led to the Quantas American Express Classic Card, a joint venture.

Joint ventures feature several advantages. Partners provide access to local connections and explain the local business environment. Sharing of risk lessens potential losses. Costs are lowered. Joint ventures may evolve into stronger relationships, such as strategic partnerships.

Lost or leaked proprietary knowledge will be a concern with joint ventures, because the partner now has access to the information and may not keep a patent-protected technology secret. Also, joint venture partners may misappropriate company assets or break the joint venture and then use that knowledge to succeed in separate, independent business ventures. Conflicts between joint ventures partners can also sour the relationship and limit the success of the venture.

STRATEGIC ALLIANCES

strategic alliance: a formal agreement between companies to work together to achieve a common goal

Companies may share goals but the leadership team may not want to create a joint venture. In these cases, firms often form strategic alliances. A **strategic alliance** represents a formal agreement between companies to work together to achieve a common goal. Resource sharing, project funding, and knowledge transfer all happen within most strategic alliances. In contrast to joint ventures, a separate legal entity is not created. Instead, an alliance, limited in scope, works toward the overall goal.

Strategic alliances evolve out of other modes of entry. A joint venture arrangement may grow into a more trusting, goal-sharing partnership. Wholly owned subsidiaries, over time, may establish strategic alliances with members of the distribution channel. Many strategic alliances investigate problems that affect all or most members of an industry. Sharing research on a new technological breakthrough or combining resources to enter a new market are two common goals for strategic alliances.

With less financial commitment than either a wholly owned subsidiary, as described next, or a joint venture, and with fewer formal legal ties between companies than a joint venture, strategic alliances present lower risks. The entry mode retains less control by the parent company. This increases exposure to a potential partner leaving or stealing technology. The Chinese car company Chery's (Qirui) first car, built in the city of Wuhu in 1999, was based on Volkswagen manufacturing blueprints. The company paid a financial settlement to Volkswagen, but the model's success enabled Wuhu to grow into one of East Asia's largest car manufacturers (Hessler, 2010).

WHOLLY OWNED SUBSIDIARY

When a company enters a country by establishing a 100% ownership stake in a business in that country, the organization has created a **wholly owned subsidiary**. These units comply with local regulations, adjust to local cultural standards and customs, operate in the native language, fit with local economic conditions, and are supportable through the local infrastructure. At the same time, the company that establishes the subsidiary can feature its own brand, logo, and color scheme, and maintains control over both managerial operations and marketing decisions.

wholly owned subsidiary: a company enters a country by establishing a 100% ownership stake in a business in that country

Control is the primary advantage for the company with a wholly owned subsidiary. The company maintains control of the market entry and does not need to share decision-making or profits with other parties. Although governmental and other external factors influence company success, this success grows from external factors, not from inept partners. The ability to protect proprietary information from potential competitors constitutes another aspect of control.

The time and money needed to enter another country with a wholly owned subsidiary creates risk. A failure is absorbed by the company alone. Without a local partner, the parent company pays the entire cost of entry. Some control may be lost when local expertise is required to help with the transition to the new country. In addition, any learning costs associated with acclimating to the local culture and regulatory environment must be absorbed.

Wholly owned subsidiaries can be divided into acquisitions or Greenfield investments. For *acquisitions*, the company purchases a local business that is then transformed into the subsidiary. In the case of a *Greenfield investment*, the company builds the subsidiary from the ground up.

China allows for a unique form of the wholly owned subsidiary—the wholly foreign-owned enterprise. Entirely foreign, both in terms of ownership and funding, the subsidiary maintains special economic status within China. These businesses typically manufacture goods solely for export to foreign markets. By giving up access to the Chinese market, less governmental regulation and control applies.

ENTRY MODE FAILURE AND EXIT

Before entering a market, company leaders consider the possibility of a failure. A plan will be in place regarding market exit preentry. The plan includes setting clear, measurable goals regarding entry success with set deadlines for assessing the goals. Failure may not reflect poor planning. Instead, it may result from external, unpredictable forces leading to the entry problems. Regardless, understanding the potential for failure allows firms to measure the amount of acceptable risk or losses, which in turn affects the length of contracts, the pace of the market entry, or the entry mode chosen.

When leaving the market, marketers try to maintain the relationships built during the time in the country. Contracts should be settled as fairly as possible, for example. Marketers recognize that a company's reputation in one nation may affect its reputation in neighboring countries. Further, the partner in the country being exited might be a potential partner in a separate country, and those individual relationships may be important to future entry success. Finally, it is always possible that the firm will choose to enter the market again at a later date.

THEORIES OF ENTRY MODE SELECTION

Several factors influence international entry mode selection. Various explanations of these factors have been given. Three dominant theories include internationalization theory, internalization theory, and eclectic or OLI theory.

INTERNATIONALIZATION THEORY

A core question in international marketing involves the reasons companies choose to expand into foreign markets, what steps are taken, and in what order. Internationalization theory provides one theoretical attempt to answer those questions. Internationalization theory is also known as the Uppsala Model. It suggests that companies go through four stages during the move to becoming global organizations: 1) no regular export activities, 2) export via independent representatives, 3) establishment of an overseas sales subsidiary, and 4) foreign production (Johanson and Wiedersheim-Paul, 1975).

The model views global entry as an incremental process. A company begins by exporting to close, familiar markets. These activities enable company leaders to gain the knowledge needed to export to other nearby markets. Then, sufficient market experience and market knowledge accumulate and lead to increased commitments and resources given to expanding internationally. Eventually the company opens overseas sales subsidiaries and starts producing in foreign markets (Johanson and Vahlne, 1977).

Psychic distance plays a key role in country selection under the Uppsala Model. *Psychic distance* refers to the differences between managers from various countries, which include communication, language, legal and political structures, education, and cultural values. Cultural values include those proposed by Hofstede, such as power distance, individualism/collectivism, uncertainty avoidance, and femininity/masculinity. Management styles vary in individual countries (Magnusson et al., 2008). International marketers who are aware of them are able to reduce communication problems and increase trust, leading to an improved chance of entry success.

INTERNALIZATION THEORY

Internalization theory moves beyond the ordered, staged approach of internationaliza-tion theory to focus solely on the reasons a company's leaders select a specific entry mode. The assumption is that there are specific advantages to each entry mode type. These advantages, typically in terms of rent or profit, constitute the reasons a firm's marketing team might choose one approach over another.

Internalization theory argues that exporting is a marketing choice. Supply and demand guide the process, the company requires little control, and exporting costs less than other modes of entry. In cases where the market works efficiently, such as in countries where governments are not involved, where there are no unusual risks or uncertainties, and where trusted partners can be found, the market decision rep-resents the best option. In essence, when the company's managers are familiar with a foreign market, there are no extreme external factors limiting the ability to enter that market, and the company's leaders are not concerned that company knowledge will be copied, it will be best to export due to the lower costs involved. Also, in a pure market situation, the risks will be lower. A company can ship the product to the country, make a profit, and keep costs low.

In reality, a government often plays a role in trade. Further, in many countries high levels of risk are present. The situation may be further complicated by the uncertainty in many markets due to cultural differences and the lack of stability. Overall, for many markets, exporting remains excessively risky. In these cases, company marketing managers choose to internalize—hence the name of the theory.

Internalization refers to taking some degree of ownership of the process of entering a country. Typically, doing so involves opening a wholly owned subsidiary or starting a joint venture. Internalization may also be referred to as the hierarchy choice, by inter-nalizing the entry into the corporate hierarchy. The costs of this approach may be high, but in many cases are offset by the level of control gained from ownership. Greater control allows company leaders to respond to risk and uncertainty. Internalization also enables the company to exploit market power and protect key assets, especially hard-earned knowledge, from being potentially stolen by competitors.

ECLECTIC OR OLI THEORY

Eclectic or OLI theory seeks to integrate a variety of theoretical explanations of market entry decisions into one integrated model. The theory assumes that exporting will be the most efficient and preferred form of entry but that inefficiencies or problems in the market mean that many times the best decision is another form of entry. Decisions are based on three factors:

1. ownership advantages,
2. location advantages,
3. internalization advantages.

Ownership advantages explain the "why" of multinational corporation foreign activi-ties. These advantages include the reasons marketers spend the time and effort to enter a foreign country. Two types of ownership advantages are present: asset and transaction advantages. *Asset advantages* include anything the company does well, similar to the specific assets present in internalization theory. The company can earn money in foreign markets because of its ability to do something that competitors cannot. *Transaction ownership advantages* include the ability to capture transactional benefits, such as lower costs, from the common governance of a network of ownership assets. Apple created an innovative product, the iPad, that was difficult for competitors to copy, which became an ownership advantage.

Eclectic theory explains the "where" of entry location advantages. Some markets are more attractive than others and are entered first. Local resources, natural and human; governmental activities; market potential; and lower political risk make some countries more alluring. Many large corporations have begun entering or considering entering India in the last decade largely because of the 1 billion consumers within the country, which offers a location advantage.

The final advantages suggested by the eclectic or OLI theory are internalization advantages. These are the "how" of market entry, and the advantages that come from making the correct entry decision. While exporting is the default option, when management considers entering an attractive market (location advantages) and the company holds unique assets that will generate sufficient profit (ownership advantages), the correct selection of entry mode type leads to internalization advantages. To select the right type of entry mode, companies need to balance risk, uncertainty, the ability to exploit economies of scale, and cost.

ANALYSIS

Each of the three theories seeks to explain the factors that might affect a strategic marketing manager's reasoning process when selecting a mode of entry. Internationalization theory best applies to what might be termed "concentric" expansion, or moving into close, similar markets first, because they will be easier to enter, and then expanding outward to more-difficult, less-similar markets. Internalization theory suggests processes by which managers balance assessments of risk and costs. The process leads managers to select the most efficient and appropriate entry mode. Eclectic theory combines ideas about ownership, location, and internalization that marketers might use to make judgments about which mode of entry would be best for a given company.

CHAPTER 4: REVIEW AND RESOURCES

Strategic Implications

A commonly used approach to strategic management involves five steps: analysis and diagnosis, strategy generation, strategy evaluation and choice, strategy implementation, and strategic control. The first step, analysis and diagnosis, contains the classic SWOT evaluation, where SW stands for company strengths and weaknesses and OT represents the environmental opportunities and threats.

Assessment of economic conditions takes place as part of the analysis and diagnosis/OT phase. When examining another country's circumstances, the economic system in place may present opportunities or obstacles. Nations engaged in free enterprise and greater degrees of capitalism may offer more open environments for international trade. Societies with closed markets are the least inviting. In most cases, mixed economies contain varying degrees of viability. Assessments of the economic system in place begin the strategic planning process. Then, evaluation of any national competitive advantage informs the marketing team about any impediments that would place the company in a weak competitive position, or identifies the opportunity to enter a market with little resistance.

Considering the modes of entry is part of the second step of the strategic management process, strategy generation. The marketing manager and team evaluate the potential strategic options, such as exporting, licensing, franchising, joint ventures, wholly owned subsidiaries, and strategic alliances across the criteria of cost, risk, and control. Then a strategic mode of entry can be chosen.

Tactical Implications

Each economic system requires differing tactics. Free market capitalism will likely necessitate advertising and promotions in order to stand out and be noticed. Socialist systems often present limits in terms of marketing activities. Tighter controls over matters such as comparative advertising, pricing, and discounting may be present. Communist countries pose the greatest challenges to entry.

Distribution systems vary widely by the level of economic development present in a country. A nation in the most-developed category features distribution networks facilitated by more sophisticated transportation and communication systems. Developing and emerging economies have less-developed systems of distribution, but systems will be constructed over time. A few major industries are present, which may present marketing opportunities in terms of supply materials or supporting companies in those industries in some fashion. In less-developed economies, distribution will be challenging. Consumers at the bottom-of-the-pyramid have less disposable income; however, innovative companies have found ways to reach them with adapted goods and services.

Operational Implications

Economic systems influence the methods used to present products to consumers. The presence or absence of retail chains changes the types of advertising, sales promotions, and pricing systems that will be utilized. In free enterprise systems, selling tactics will vary at the business-to-business and consumer levels due to the presence of competitors.

Pricing and discounting in socialist and communist systems may differ from capitalist economies due to the nature of the competition and of the economic regulatory system. The marketing team studies and adapts to these tactical issues prior to entry into a new market.

Selection of a mode of entry dictates additional operational activities, including the ways in which products are packaged, shipped, and sold. The degree of control present influences how a company moves products from one nation into another.

TERMS

market economy	mixed economy
capitalist economic system	emerging markets
command economy	newly industrialized countries
socialism	transition economies
communism	national competitive advantage

exporting	joint venture
licensing	strategic alliance
franchising	wholly owned subsidiary

REVIEW QUESTIONS

1. Define the terms market economy, planned economic systems, and mixed systems.

2. Explain the concepts of capitalism, socialism, and communism in terms of market economies, planned economic systems, and mixed systems.

3. Describe the concepts of most-developed, less-developed, and least-developed economies.

4. What are the five stages of the Rostow modernization model?

5. How are emerging markets related to the five stages of the Rostow modernization model?

6. What is a newly industrialized country?

7. Describe a transition economy.

8. Define the concept of national competitive advantage and list the factors that support a nation's competitive advantage.

9. What are the five major competitive forces present at the industry level?

10. Describe exporting, and note which factors make exporting the lowest-cost, lowest-risk, and lowest-level of control international marketing option.

11. How is licensing different from exporting?

12. What are the features of a franchising arrangement?

13. Why does a wholly owned subsidiary feature the highest degree of control coupled with the greatest levels of cost and risk?

14. What two types of joint ventures are possible for international marketing organizations?

15. Describe a strategic alliance.

16. Describe internationalization theory.

17. Describe internalization theory.

18. How does eclectic or OLI theory explain the mode of entry selection processes?

DISCUSSION QUESTIONS

1. Explain how private property rights and marketplace competition are different in market economies and command economies. What might be the difference in these two factors between strong command economies and moderate command economies? Do these economic forms influence the rate of development in less- or least-developed countries? Why or why not?

2. What types of marketing opportunities would be present in BRIC countries that would not be available in least-developed economies? Would the number of

bottom-of-the-pyramid consumers in either country influence the ability to move toward becoming most developed? Why or why not? What other factors make it harder or easier for a national economy to grow and expand?

3. Explain how the five main industry-level competitive forces would affect marketing programs for the following products:

    - motorbike manufacturers

    - mobile phone service providers

    - fast food chain restaurants

In each instance, how would a nation's economic system impact the five competitive forces?

4. Choose a mode of entry for the following products and defend your choice using one of the three mode-of-entry theories:

    - a Mexican salsa product exported to Paraguay

    - French automobile batteries exported to Turkey

    - Japanese tennis equipment exported to South Korea

ANALYTICAL AND INTERNET EXERCISES

1. As more countries began the process of economic reform and development, analysts struggle to label these new markets in a way as memorable as BRIC or the Four Tigers. The BRIC acronym, which stands for Brazil, Russia, India, China, is now widely accepted. Using the CIA *World Factbook* at cia.gov, create a table comparing these countries in terms of the role of government in the economy, size of economy (in terms of overall GDP and GDP per capita), population, amount of exports, key products exported, and any other variables that may reveal important similarities or differences. Then, based on the numbers, discuss how the countries in BRIC are similar and different. Does one country seem more attractive to international marketers than the other members of the group? Why or why not?

2. Google now offers public data for consumers at www.google.com/publicdata/home.[4] One of the databases provided is called *World Development Indicators,* which was developed by the World Bank. Use the data there to create three graphs that show the developmental process for at least three transition economies. What variables did you choose? Why? For which question did the resulting graphs provide visual evidence?

3. Countries generate national competitive advantages over long periods of time. In many cases, these advantages then become part of the tourist appeals for these countries. For example, the official French tourism website emphasizes French wine (http://us.franceguide.com/). Make a list of five countries and the product(s) that you associate with those countries. Then, using a search engine, find the official tourism promotion website for that country. If you are unable to find the website, select a different country. Does the website promote the national competitive advantage for the countries? How prominently and in what ways?

4. Internationalization theory presents a set, staged model for international expansion. The automobile manufacturer Toyota represents one of the world's largest and most global brands, but the expansion of the company internationally did not begin until the late 1950s. Using the websites below, track the international expansion of each company. Did each company follow the Uppsala School's model?

"History of Toyota," Toyota, Tokyo, Japan (updated 2011). Retrieved from **www.toyota-global.com/company/history_of_toyota/.**

"Globalizing and Localizing Manufacturing," Toyota, Tokyo, Japan (updated 2011). Retrieved from **www.toyota-global.com/company/vision_philosophy/globalizing_ and_localizing_manufacturing/.**

"Role of the Global Production Center (GPC) Fostering Globally Capable Personnel," Toyota, Tokyo, Japan (updated 2011). Retrieved from **www.toyota-global.com/ company/vision_philosophy/globalizing_and_localizing_manufacturing/role_ of_the_global_production_center.html.**

STUDENT STUDY SITE

Visit **https://study.sagepub.com/baack2e** to access these free additional learning tools:

- Web Quizzes
- eFlashcards
- SAGE Journal Articles
- Country Fact Sheets
- Chapter Outlines
- Interactive Maps

CASE 4

Mobile Communications: Entry into Africa

Africa offers a fast growing and exciting mobile phone market, with more than 50% growth per year since 2002. More than 28% of African consumers own mobile phones; a larger market than North America. One analyst suggested, "This is a market in the making—as the U.S. was 150 years ago and as China was 20 years ago. If you can get in and if you ride this constantly changing market, there are countless fortunes to be made."[5]

Beyond South Africa and possibly Kenya or Uganda, the rest of the African continent is less- or even least-developed economically. Several factors account for the rapid growth in generally poor consumers in these countries. The village of Dertu in Kenya is far removed from quality roads and infrastructure. The village does not have effective fixed landlines for a telephone service. Instead, the leader of the village, Ibrahim Ali Hassan, describes a mobile phone as his "link with the outside world." When a local farmer was outside of town as his wife went into labor, a mobile phone call rushed him back to take her to the hospital. The baby was healthy and named after the phone company—Celtel. When a young child was bitten by a snake, a cell phone call helped the victim's parents identify the correct antidote.

Across Africa outside access to isolated communities is created by mobile phones. Instead of traditional landlines, consumers have moved directly to mobile communication. Ninety percent of phone subscribers in Africa use mobile phones. They often prefer the more accessible pay-as-you-go models, which allow consumers greater flexibility than traditional monthly plans. Payments are linked to usage rates. Consumers keep multiple SIM memory cards, switching to the company providing the best rate for the call being made. Short calls or even flashing—the act of calling and hanging up after one ring so that the person will not be billed for the call—also help keep costs low.

Mobile phones usage in Africa differs from other parts of the world. For many consumers, mobile technology provides a primary source of information. Mobile phones help track the price of crops and send reminders to take medicines. They save wasted trips outside of the village. Due to this focus on function, many mobile phones typically are stripped down to only provide the ability to call and send text messages.

Mobile banking also drives increased usage. As traditional banks struggle to penetrate many parts of the continent, mobile banking fills the gap. Vodafone used its m-Pesa (*pesa* is Swahili for money) mobile banking service to expand into Kenya. In two short years, the product went from introduction to 5 million customers. More than 50% of the Kenyan market uses mobile banking for money transfers. While transactions are small, around 1,500 Kenyan shillings ($20), the lower fees than traditional banks have saved poor Kenyans an estimated $4 million per week.

Africa offers a potentially rich target market for mobile phone providers.

In some areas, mobile minutes are substitutes for actual money. In Uganda, a villager can transfer money to relatives through the village mobile phone representative. A prepaid

(Continued)

(Continued)

card is purchased, which is added to the relative's account, and then, after a fee has been paid, that amount in cash is transferred to the relative.

The African market appears to have given local companies a first-mover advantage. Outside companies entering the highly competitive market have struggled. There are large barriers to entry in terms of cost and governmental approval. Markets tend to be intensely competitive with three, four, five, or even six local providers. The result has been that a large number of the largest companies are local or are from other developing countries.

Various types of ownership structures exist in the African telecommunications industry. Table 4.10 summarizes some of the important players. Ownership varies from state-owned industries to joint ventures to subsidiaries.

TABLE 4.10   Partial List of African Telecommunications Companies

COUNTRY / Countries	FIRM	OWNERSHIP STRUCTURE	ADDITIONAL NOTES
Kenya	Safricom	Private owned	
Mali	Sotelma	State owned	Selling 51% stake
Morocco	Maroc Telecom	Vivdendi subsidiary	
Mozambique	Mcel	State owned	
Mozambique	Vodacom	Subsidiary	
Nigeria	Mtel	State owned	
São Tomé	São Tomé Telecoms	Joint venture	49% state owned 51% Portugal Telecom
Senegal	Sonatel	Joint venture	57% state owned 43% Telecom (France)
Tunisia	Tunisie Télécom	State owned	
Western Africa	Cellcom	Private owned	
Africa	MTN	Private owned	
Africa	Zain	Private owned	

Source: "The Telecommunications Sector," *African Business* (London) no. 349 (January 2009): 27.

In summary, the African cellular phone market's rapid growth exemplifies the potential for all markets, regardless of level of development, to potentially generate profit.

1. Discuss the difference between the use of mobile phones in the African cellular phone market compared with cell phone use in developed-country cellular phone markets.

2. How might the different ownership structures in Africa reflect potential economic systems in the host countries?

3. Would the model for mobile phone expansion apply to other less- or least-developed countries? Why or why not?

4. How do Porter's five factors explain the high level of industry competitive intensity in the African mobile phone market?

5. How might an African government apply Porter's national competitive advantage diamond to further spur mobile phone specialization within a country?

5

INTERNATIONAL MARKETING PLANNING, ORGANIZING, AND CONTROL

LEARNING OBJECTIVES

After reading and studying this chapter, you should be able to answer the following questions:

1. How do planning, organizing, and control activities influence international marketing programs?

2. What activities are involved in international strategic planning?

3. What are the basic components of an international marketing tactical planning program?

4. What forms of organizational structure do international companies use?

5. Which activities are parts of an international marketing control system?

6. How will emerging trends affect international marketing in the future?

IN THIS CHAPTER

THE SYRIAN REFUGEE CRISIS AFFECTS MARKETING IN THE EU

The civil war in Syria has challenged and changed governmental activities, military efforts, and marketing programs, both in that country and in others around the globe. Of note, member countries in the European Union felt strong pressures to adapt to the influx of people seeking a more peaceful place to live and work. The war began in 2011 and continued through 2017. Within the borders of Syria, more than 6 million citizens have been displaced. Another 4.8 million became refugees. Approximately 10% of those fled to Europe.[1]

In Germany, nearly 1 million refugees arrived in 2015, with another 300,000 in 2016. The influx put enormous strain on the country's bureaucracy to process claims and tested confidence in Angela Merkel's right–left coalition government. Many moved via the so-called Balkan migrant trail, which subsequently closed. Prior to that point migrants moved through Turkey into EU nations. The closure halted much of the resettlement in Greece.[2]

France agreed to taking in 30,000 individuals during 2016. Prime Minister Manuel Valls worried that the inflow would destabilize much of Europe. With Turkey experiencing violent terrorist activities and Greece experiencing a major economic crisis, the concerns seemed well founded. Dutch Prime Minister Mark Rutte agreed, worrying that Europe might be close to breaking point and that the international communities would need to come up with a common response or run the risk that one of the European Union's founding principles regarding the free movement of people between nations would start to unravel (Chrisatis et al., 2016).

Backlash against the refugees took the form of economic and political "populism." On June 23, 2016, British balloters voted to leave the EU in the stunning Brexit referendum. Much of the discontent centered on frustration with governmental policies regarding immigration.

The movement of Syrians into Europe was accompanied by cultural and religious clashes, most notably fears of Islamic refugees. Language barriers existed and many EU countries were not in the position to integrate new people into their economies. Businesses within the EU and around the world have experienced the challenges, but also the opportunities presented by a growth in new citizens.

Questions for Students

1. How would the flow of immigrants into a country influence the evaluation of the nation's external environment?

2. How would the Syrian refugee crisis affect strategic (company-wide) and tactical (marketing division) planning processes?

3. How might the refugee crisis change goals and standards set for the purposes of strategical and tactical control systems?

OVERVIEW

A successful international marketing program integrates company strategic planning, organizing, and control processes. The strategic plan guides every element of a marketing program. This chapter commences with a discussion of the strategic planning process as it relates to international marketing.

Next, international marketing tactical plans receive attention. Managers prepare these plans based on overall corporate or strategic-level plans. Tactical marketing plans guide the international marketing program for specific products and markets. As such, they apply to specific strategic business units within the overall international organization.

A description of organizational structure follows, including alternatives for devising an effective and efficient organizational design. Then, marketing control systems at the strategic, tactical, and operational levels are described. This chapter concludes with an analysis of trends that will influence international marketing programs in the future.

Figure 5.1 presents the overall international marketing context within which marketing managers make strategic, operational, and tactical decisions. The components of the international marketing context influence these processes. The emerging trends in international marketing presented at the end of this chapter also affect the overall international marketing context.

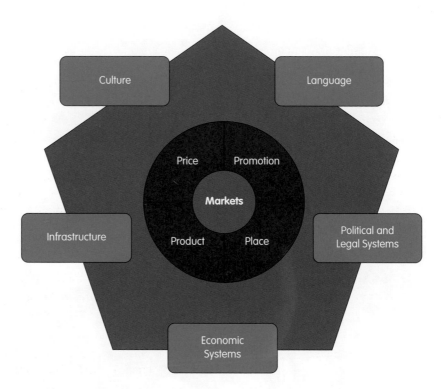

FIGURE 5.1   The International Marketing Context

LEARNING OBJECTIVE #1:

How do planning, organizing, and control activities influence international marketing programs?

planning: the process whereby managers develop goals, strategies, and activities that will best position the firm for success in the international marketplace

INTERNATIONAL MARKETING PROGRAMS

Planning, organizing, and controlling international marketing operations constitute critical elements of international marketing. The **planning** process involves managers developing the goals, strategies, and activities designed to position the firm to succeed in the international marketplace. **Organizing** is the process through which managers design the structure of the organization, assign responsibilities, and work to ensure effective communication. **Control** focuses on measuring progress against what was planned, taking corrective actions as they are needed, and rewarding success. Planning, organizing, and control are interrelated concepts, as well as in all of the aspects of strategic marketing displayed in Figure 5.2.

organizing: the process through which management designs the structure of the organization, assigns responsibilities, and ensures effective communication flows throughout the company

FIGURE 5.2 Planning, Organizing, and Controlling

control: the process of comparing performance to standards, making corrections when needed, and rewarding success

PLANNING LEVELS

A planning process occurs at three levels: strategic, tactical, and operational. **Strategic planning** provides the overall direction of the firm, the development of goals, and the allocation of resources in the pursuit of those goals. Top managers prepare the strategic plans that spell out the company's intended long-term direction and intentions.

strategic planning: plans for the overall direction of the firm, the development of goals, and the allocation of resources in the pursuit of those goals, as prepared by top management

Two important themes emerge at the strategic level: organizational efficiency and effectiveness. *Efficiency* means conducting international marketing activities without wasting time and resources. *Effectiveness* concentrates on conducting international operations in ways that enable the firm to achieve its goals (Clow and Baack, 2010). Efficiency has been described as "doing things right" and effectiveness as "doing the right things." Quality strategic processes enable managers to maximize the efficiencies and effectiveness of the company's operations, including all marketing activities.

tactical planning: plans for specific activities and programs that support the overall direction set at the strategic level

Tactical planning focuses on specific activities and programs that support the direction set at the strategic level. Middle-level marketing managers normally concentrate on specific functions, such as product design, advertising, or distribution as they prepare tactical plans.

Operational plans dictate the day-to-day entry-level activities. Operational plans apply to the efforts of first-level managers. They pertain to short-range activities and duties.

operational plans: plans that dictate the day-to-day entry-level activities that are crucial parts of successful international marketing programs

Each aspect of an international marketing program relates to and is informed by the planning process. The plan dictates markets to be targeted, products to be sold, pricing methods, distribution channels, and promotional activities. Planning specifies an organizational design, communication systems, and strategic goals to be achieved.

LEARNING OBJECTIVE #2:

What activities are involved in international strategic planning?

INTERNATIONAL STRATEGIC PLANNING

international strategic planning: the plan for the overall direction of the firm

International strategic planning identifies the overall direction of the firm. It provides the basis for all marketing activities. Table 5.1 summarizes the key elements in the process. As shown, effective international strategic planning begins with an emphasis on the mission and overall direction of the firm. The process includes scanning the organization's external and internal environments, forecasting future events, and making decisions about which plans to undertake. Managers use the strategic plan to help specify marketing goals and allocate the resources needed to implement and complete the plan.

TABLE 5.1   Elements of Strategic Planning

Mission Statement Formulation
Environmental Assessment
Forecast of Future Events
Selection of Strategies
Determination of Goals
Allocation of Resources in Pursuit of the Plan

Recently, HSBC France presented a new strategic plan. The document listed a series of objectives and activities for the company including, "(1) focusing on wealth management for personal customers, (2) bolstering international connectivity for business customers, (3) further developing the Global Banking and Markets platform in Paris as a strategic hub for the HSBC Group, and (4) strengthening synergies between customer groups." To carry out these initiatives, various steps were established. The activities included increasing training for wealth management staff, establishing twenty-five new branches, hiring more relationship managers focused on business customers, and opening three new regional offices within France.[3]

MISSION STATEMENTS

mission statement: a document that delineates why an organization exists and guides the overall direction of the firm

A **mission statement** declares why the organization exists and guides the direction of the firm. Australia's Woolworths group pursues a mission statement that includes the idea of being "A business built on integrity," and the statement "We are on a mission to deliver the best convenience, value, and quality for our customers." Many mission statements have undergone revisions to incorporate the importance of seeking to serve a global marketplace in a sustainable fashion. Anadarko, a global petroleum company, states in the company's mission statement that it intends to create "a competitive and sustainable rate of return by developing, acquiring, and exploring for oil and gas resources vital to the world's health and welfare."

Other mission statements pay attention to additional visible issues. Sinopec, a Chinese petroleum and chemical company, states "Over the years, Sinopec adheres to the concept of scientific development, and actively explores sustainable development. While creating wealth and energy to the community, the company also fulfils its corporate social responsibility and strives to achieve harmonious development between production and security, energy and environment, enterprises and employees, enterprise and society."

Mission statements form the parameters for major company decisions. The company Google referenced its mission "to organize the world's information and make it universally accessible and useful" when leaving the Chinese market. Facing censorship from the Chinese government, Google's management team believed that it could no longer achieve the company's mission.[4]

At times, corporate-level planning lead to the firm's division into strategic business units, or distinct parts of the overall business. A strategic business unit operates in a specified market area and has specific and separate goals, objectives, and control mechanisms. A strategic business unit for a firm engaged in international marketing may be a division or office in a foreign country.

The Volkswagen Group (Germany) consists of two main divisions including the Automotive Group and the Volkswagen Financial Services Group. The Automotive Group contains twelve brands worldwide, including Audi, Bentley, Bugatti, Lamborghini, SEAT, Škoda, Scania, Volkswagen, and Volkswagen Commercial Vehicles.[5] As international operations expand, the division of an international company into strategic business units grows in importance.

International strategic planning focuses on the overall direction of a firm such as Rolex.

ENVIRONMENTAL ASSESSMENTS

The mission of the firm combined with an assessment of potential market areas, countries to be served, and marketing responsibilities often determine how the firm will be divided into strategic business units. These assessments include an analysis of various internal and external factors present in the environment. External factors include culture, language, political and legal systems, economic systems, and infrastructure. Internal factors consist of human and financial capital, competitive advantage, market knowledge, and responsiveness to market changes and demands.

An analysis of the company's internal environment identifies its strengths and weaknesses. The external environment presents threats and presents opportunities. Managers combine these elements to engage in a SWOT analysis (strengths, weaknesses, opportunities, threats) and to investigate various strategic responses, as depicted in Figure 5.3.

In the first box (Plan to Pursue) shown in Figure 5.3, an opportunity presents itself in an area of company strength. This might lead to a plan designed to take advantage of the situation. In the second box (Decide to Pursue or Not), an opportunity exists in an area where the company is weak. Managers in that circumstance choose whether to commit resources to strengthen the company and pursue the opportunity or to leave it for others. In the third circumstance (Monitor), a threat occurs in an area where the company is strong. Managers monitor this situation and take action as needed. In the fourth box (Plan to Fend off Threat), a threat exists in an area and the company is weak. Failure to respond may lead to the organization's downfall.

As an example, in many emerging markets, particularly China and India, consumers prefer mobile phones with multiple SIM or identification card slots, which allow one phone to be used for multiple phone numbers, a circumstance that creates a threat to mobile phone manufacturers without such features. Facing dropping market share in these markets, Nokia introduced three separate phones, all of which contained multiple SIM card slots (Lawton and Wong, 2011). The new approach provides an example of a company responding to an external factor; the differences in features consumers prefer in their phones.

	Opportunity	Threat
Strength	Plan to Pursue	Monitor
Weakness	Decide to Pursue or Not	Plan to Fend Off Threat

FIGURE 5.3   SWOT Analysis

FORECASTING FUTURE EVENTS

Strategic managers forecast in three main areas: economic conditions, sales projections, and changes in technology. Economic conditions provide part of the framework for future strategic plans. For example, The Conference Board (2017), in describing the prospects for the international economy in 2017 stated, "The looming labour shortage in mature economies and skill deficiencies in emerging markets will add further challenges to global economic prospect. Global growth lacks demand drivers and potential output is likely shrinking while uncertainty is increasing."

A sales forecast predicts the level of revenue a company expects to receive during the upcoming year. These projections influence planning processes and expenditures. When forecasts project sales revenues to increase, company leaders allocate additional funds for raw materials, inventory levels, sales force activities, and other more general projects such as research and development. When managers expect sales revenues to decline, they often cut back on some of the same factors.

Changes in technology also impact the overall marketplace. Continual development of new products as well as improvements to products and the methods to produce them change the nature of competition for firms competing in the global economy.

Important political events such as Brexit affect future international planning and organizing activities. Such drastic changes in the external environment impact on how international marketing is conducted within trading blocks and outside of them.[6] Multinational companies, such as HSBC, may have to rethink and reorganize various marketing activities to adjust to operating outside of the EU (Morris and Partington, 2017).

Managers and forecasting departments cannot predict every event. International managers could not have predicted the massive earthquake and resultant tsunami that devastated Japan in early 2011. Nevertheless, the event drastically affected international businesses. Car makers in particular were hit hard. The tsunami heavily damaged a semiconductor plant in Ibaraki owned by Renesas Electronics Corporation. The plant manufactured chips for the major Japanese automakers, and Toyota and Honda both faced inventory shortages. Honda had just begun using a new type of chip and faced the sharpest shortage as a result. The shortages particularly affected business in China, with Toyota sales declining by 35% and Honda dropping by 32%.[7] Only recently have these firms rebounded from the element of the economic downturn.

SELECTION OF STRATEGIES

Next, the actual strategies will be determined and stated. At the strategic level, many strategies relate to what is called the organization's "portfolio of businesses" or "portfolio of activities." Table 5.2 lists some of the more basic approaches.

TABLE 5.2 Types of Strategies

Types of Strategies	Explanation
Acquisition of or merger with another company—domestic	Join with another domestic company and export goods with that firm
Acquisition of or merger with another company—separate country	Join with foreign company and export goods through that company or make products in the new host country
Development of new product(s) or brand(s)—standardization	New product made and exported with the same name and marketing approach in both countries
Development of new product(s) or brand(s)—adaptation	New product made and exported with unique name and/or features; marketing tailored to new area
Vertical integration	Take over a new aspect of the marketing channel
Horizontal integration or joint venture	Partner relationship with company in host country for the same or similar products
Divestment	Sell off an existing company intact; domestic or foreign
Liquidation	Sell off component parts of an existing company; domestic or foreign

Each strategy presented in Table 5.2 might be chosen based on the outcome of a SWOT analysis at the corporate level. Many of the growth-related strategies correspond with the presence of an opportunity. Mergers, acquisitions, entering a new country, and the development of new products or brands would be undertaken when a potential new market or need has been identified or when combining with another company creates synergies, efficiencies, or the ability to reach a wider market.

A vertical integration strategy may be pursued for a variety of reasons. A SWOT analysis might reveal that doing so would strengthen a company's overall position or that it might fend off an impending threat. Direct marketing programs and ecommerce expansion create a new approach to the marketing channel and might actually achieve both strategic goals (becoming stronger *and* fending off the threat created by competitors).

Divestment and liquidation strategies may also serve more than one purpose. They can help an organization eliminate a weakness and become stronger at the same time by improving an organization's financial position. Doing so may enable expansion or greater concentration on other, more successful products, brands, or activities.

Each of these strategies has major implications for individual departments, including marketing, sales, and public relations. Any time an organization engages in new activities or pursues a new strategy, the effects of the plan ripple through the entire company. Mergers, acquisitions, integration approaches, and product development all affect the manner in which individual departments plan and carry out the strategic dictate. Use of tactics and operational plans helps reach various strategic goals.

DETERMINATION OF STRATEGIC GOALS

At the strategic level, company managers often set goals in numerical terms, such as return on investment, sales figures, market share attained, and overall market penetration. Strategic goals take other forms, such as increased brand recognition, awareness, or an improved company image worldwide. Attainment of these goals can be measured through various forms of market research, as described in Chapter 8. These company-wide standards provide the basis for the strategic control process. They clarify the direction of the company and alert managers when the organization has begun to drift off course from its stated mission.

ALLOCATION OF RESOURCES IN PURSUIT OF THE GOALS

Strategic planners allocate the resources needed to achieve strategic goals. Distributing resources coincides with the development or redesign of the overall organizational structure. Determining the most efficient and most effective organizational structure will be a major component of the organizing element of international strategic marketing planning.

Managers at Ethiopia's Star Soap and Detergent Industries, PLC, which experienced positive growth for more than a decade, have directed company resources in two main strategic areas. First, the producer of laundry soap, toilet soap, liquid detergent, powder, and bar soaps seeks to expand company products offerings to capture a greater market share within the home country. Second, the organization uses funds to deploy agents to new regions in order to enter new markets.[8]

The five components of the strategic planning process set the tone for marketing tactics and operational plans. The mission statement directs overall company operations, including its approach to the marketplace. An environmental assessment provides valuable information to the marketing team regarding potential opportunities and threats that arise in conjunction with company strengths and weaknesses. These, in turn, shape marketing efforts to take advantage of opportunities and fend off threats by employing both strategic and tactical responses. Company leaders forecast future events in the areas of economic conditions, sales projections, and changes in technology. Marketing teams then respond with tactics designed to adapt to changes in the environment. Organizational leaders create strategies and then determine the strategic and tactical goals that spell out what would constitute successful efforts. These goals form the basis of the strategic control process. Finally, managers allocate resources to implement strategic plans and achieve strategic goals. Resources granted to the marketing department should be used efficiently and effectively, as part of the overall international marketing program.

> ## LEARNING OBJECTIVE #3:
>
> What are the basic components of an international marketing tactical planning program?

INTERNATIONAL MARKETING TACTICS

Tactical planning concentrates on specific international marketing activities, guided by the overall strategic-level plan. Tactical-level planning involves management of the segmentation, targeting, and positioning activities for the firm's products or services in specific international markets combined with the other elements of the marketing mix—pricing, promotion, and distribution.

STEPS USED TO CREATE INTERNATIONAL MARKETING TACTICS

Developing tactics as part of an international marketing plan is an essential part of successful international marketing management. Different businesses develop different marketing tactics; the typical steps involved in developing international marketing tactics are presented in Table 5.3.

TABLE 5.3   Steps in Creating the International Marketing Tactical Plans

Executive Summary
Situational Analysis
Analysis of the Internal Environment
Analysis of the External Environment
Target Market Description
Prepare and Present Tactics
Specify International Marketing Goals and Objectives

An executive summary provides a brief overview of the overall marketing plan, including goals and objectives, recommendations, and tactics for all domestic and international activities. The summary will be the last component of the marketing plan to be written, in order to accurately portray the remainder of the document. The summary should clearly link the international marketing plan to the company's broader strategic goals.

A situational analysis at the tactical level includes an analysis of the internal, external, and customer environments, along with the development of a SWOT (strengths, weaknesses, opportunities, and threats) analysis for the marketing department, often for each strategic business unit, product type, or geographic area (nation or region). The information leads to the development of specific marketing goals, objectives, and programs for every targeted international market.

The analysis of the internal environment assesses the factors relevant to the marketing program for a given international market. The analysis includes market knowledge, the success of current marketing programs, and the firm's competitive advantage. The firm's competitive advantage, based on market-relevant capabilities, enables the marketing team to address customer needs more effectively than the competition.

The analysis of the external environment contains the factors that apply to the marketing campaign for a given market. An assessment of economic conditions, political and regulatory forces, language, culture, and other external factors offers insights into any challenges present in a market.

Effective marketing tactical plans contain in-depth descriptions of target markets for the product or service in the to-be-entered country. A target market analysis confirms whether sufficient demand for the product exists, and whether the product can be effectively positioned to attract that demand.

The marketing team confirms that a target market will be large enough to support market entry. After target markets have been chosen the selection of an entry mode can take place. Much of the information for this analysis will be obtained through international marketing research. Issues such as consumer wants and needs, and preferences, cultural influences, and brand loyalty play important roles in the analysis of customers. Most of this information comes from primary research in the target market chosen by management. A target market description and the entry mode selection steps of the marketing tactical plan present crucial information used in identifying viable international market segmentation strategies.

At this point, marketers are able to spell out specific marketing tactics. These actions apply to every aspect of a marketing program. Table 5.4 identifies examples.

TABLE 5.4   International Marketing Tactics

International Marketing Tactics	Explanation
Product improvement—standardization	Product changed for all markets; same product and marketing approach in every country
Product improvement—adaptation	Product tailored to fit needs of target host country's market
Pricing	Pricing system development
Distribution	Channels chosen and developed for domestic and international markets
Promotion—standardization	Same message in all markets
Promotion—adaptation	Message targeted to various host country markets
Public relations	Messages and activities to promote company image domestically and internationally

Based on the analyses of the external environment and the selection of marketing tactics to be deployed in response, company leaders set international marketing goals and objectives for the program. An international marketing goal might be to increase brand awareness and penetration in a particular market over the next five years. Part of that objective would be, for example, to increase sales in the marketplace by 2% annually.

A quality tactical marketing program constitutes one of the most critical elements in an international strategic planning program. Managers make decisions regarding products, pricing methods, promotional approaches, and distribution systems. The international marketing tactical program details the appropriate product positioning for the market and the product's unique selling proposition. Middle and first-level managers devise specific action plans that enable the firm to pursue the overall marketing strategy.

INTERNATIONAL OPERATIONAL PLANS

The operational portion of an international marketing plan includes duties such as job assignments, responsibilities, and support for the various marketing activities. Action plans outline the "on the ground" elements of a marketing program. Examples of plans devised at the operational level include fundamental activities such as recruiting salespeople for international assignments, creating advertisements and promotions for local markets, and designing or seeking to improve inventory control systems.

In summary, many of the activities that are part of developing international marketing tactical plans are similar to those conducted as part of the strategic planning process. Managers construct international marketing plans for specific programs, products, or services, in specific international markets. In most cases, the plans are devised for specific strategic business units SBUs. Strategic plans outline the direction of the overall organization, specifically its structure, direction, and goals. Marketing plans are more narrowly focused, concentrating on individual marketing activities, such as a pricing system or method of distribution.

LEARNING OBJECTIVE #4:

What forms of organizational structure do international companies use?

ORGANIZING AND ORGANIZATIONAL STRUCTURES

The second component of strategic operations involves designing or modifying a company's organizational structure through the organizing process. Many international companies have well-defined structures in place. Changes in the internal or external environment, the decision to expand operations globally, or alterations to existing strategies might create the need for a completely new structure or an adaptation of the existing structure. Regardless of the events that lead to the organizational structure design or re-design, the decisions should be based on designing the most effective and efficient international organization possible.

International businesses employ numerous forms of organizational structure. Company executives base choices on the company strategies to be pursued combined with the intensity of international marketing activities. A company that engages solely in exporting will establish a different structure than one present in a multinational corporation. Managers select and install the organizational structure they believe will most effectively and efficiently enable the firm to efficiently and effectively reach its goals. This section presents alternative forms of structure. No one form of organizational structure will be the best or correct type. Any of the alternatives discussed below, or a combination of approaches, may be suitable in certain international situations.

DIRECT EXPORTING STRUCTURE

A simple structure used by businesses new to international marketing supports direct exporting. In this form of structure, companies ship international orders to customers directly or through an intermediary.

The decision to engage in either direct (home-based or foreign-based) exporting or indirect exporting through agent or merchant middlemen is based on potential operational efficiencies and synergies with existing strategies. The responsibility for the exporting function, along with responsibility for international sales, normally falls to the marketing department. Marketing efforts are largely undifferentiated between domestic and international customers. Top managers treat all markets much the same way. They pay little attention to international differences in customer wants, needs, or requirements.

Company leaders will likely find it difficult for the firm to continue with a direct exporting form of structure when international sales begin to account for a larger portion of revenues. Instead, the company tends to reorganize around international marketing activities. Nevertheless, a simple direct exporting structure, such as the one displayed in Figure 5.4, can work well for a company that starts to engage in international marketing or one that begins to introduce products internationally.

The Indian company Tata recently began to sell the company's low-cost car, the Nano, to consumers in Indonesia, Thailand, Sri Lanka, and potentially parts of Africa through direct exporting. While only approximately 500 units had been exported by May of 2011, the company planned to use exporting to build demand for the product before moving to more expensive methods of getting the Nano to consumers.[9] Company literature now proclaims, "Our marque can be found on and off-road in over 175 countries around the globe."[10]

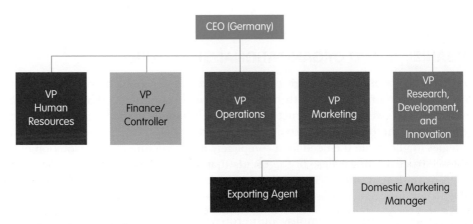

FIGURE 5.4   **Direct Exporting**

INTERNATIONAL DIVISION STRUCTURE

As international activities begin to intensify, company leaders might choose to develop an international department, office, or division to oversee international sales. Depending on the organization's size and complexity, the division may oversee several international offices or salespeople. For smaller organizations, however, all international sales may be managed domestically by the international office or department. This structure resembles a direct exporting structure with one main difference. In an international division, one central control department assumes responsibility for international marketing and sales activities and the division remains distinct from domestic marketing activities (see Figure 5.5). Delegating responsibility and authority for international sales can be a successful approach for firms in this situation.

When firms establish international offices, organizational leaders decide whether to hire home, host, or third-country national employees. International offices create the advantage of establishing a local presence along with better access to market-relevant information. Governmental forces may require a local office in order to conduct business in some countries. The international division structure helps meet these requirements and often gains favor with foreign governments. This form of structure is widely used in international marketing.

South Korean automaker Kia Motors employs international divisions.[11] The company operates international business divisions with sales subsidiaries in Australia, Belgium, Canada, China, France, Germany, New Zealand, Russia, Spain, Sweden, the United Kingdom, the United States, and part of Eastern and Central Europe.[12]

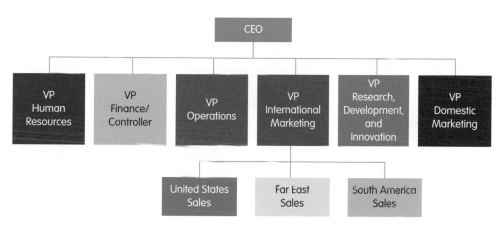

FIGURE 5.5   International Division

DIRECT FUNCTIONAL REPORTING

A combination between the direct exporting and international division structures is a functional structure with direct reporting duties to a home-based marketing manager or vice president (see Figure 5.6). This method allows for the presence of foreign offices, but streamlines the reporting duties directly to the domestic marketing manager. The approach may have limited usefulness because many global companies prefer to develop international divisions or offices.

STRATEGIC ALLIANCE ORGANIZATIONS

Many market entries involve partnering with local companies. Based on common goals between the companies, strategic alliances can be devised in a variety of ways. An example of this approach may be found in the operations of Taiwan's Acer company, which creates a variety of strategic partnerships with firms in Asia and other parts of the world.

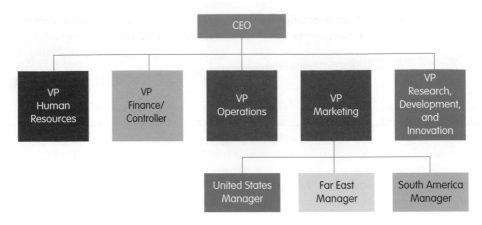

FIGURE 5.6   Direct Functional Reporting

The type of control needed creates one key criterion used when selecting a strategic alliance format. The common control option features a strategic alliance with its own independent management. The alliance becomes an entity with separate goals and decision-making from the partner companies. This may lead the strategic alliance to make choices contrary to the interests of the companies that started the alliance. Collective control represents the other organizational option. This approach allows partners to work together to manage the alliance, with the goal of generating optimal mutual benefits for the partner companies, even at the expense of the alliance (Luo et al., 2008).

Trust represents one of the key factors influencing the type of organization formed and the degree of linkage between alliance partners. In cases of high trust, companies share highly sensitive or important knowledge with partners (Murray, 2001). Trust may be especially important in instances of partner asymmetry, which occurs when one alliance partner is an unequal member of the alliance. Asymmetry results from differences in market position, proprietary knowledge, overall company size, or a variety of other factors. Overall, the asymmetry is rooted in unequal contributions to or benefits from the alliance (Dussauge and Garrette, 1995). Organizational structure, particularly control and structured contributions, can help mitigate the negative effects of asymmetry.

REGION-BASED ORGANIZATION

A truly global organization may choose to have distinct office locations, and strategic business units in each specific region served (see Figure 5.7), which leads to a region-based organizational structure. This structural approach enables the company to be responsive to local market differences utilizing a relatively simple organizational structure with clear lines of authority and responsibility.

As each region grows in importance to the organization's international strategy, the region-based organizational structure may become the most viable. As with the international division or direct functional reporting structure, company leaders may choose from home, host, or third-country nationals for staffing purposes.

As trade areas (such as the European Union or NAFTA) continue to be part of the international marketing landscape, the region-based approach grows in usage. Each region's division employs a marketing staff devoted specifically to the region. The regional structure remains viable as long as low trade barriers stay in place within the targeted regions. When barriers become significant, a different form of structure may become more attractive for international marketing purposes.

The Sage Group, a United Kingdom-based provider of business software, services, and support that targets small and medium-sized business, employs a regional structure. Focused on providing a local-based service, the company serves seven broad regions: Europe, Africa, the Middle East, Asia, Oceania, Latin America, and North America. Within those broad regional markets, the company maintains offices in many countries.[13]

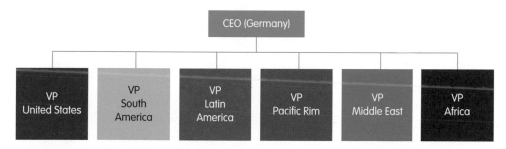

FIGURE 5.7   **Region-Based Organization**

MATRIX ORGANIZATION

Some successful international marketing firms feature organizational designs that are not limited to geographic responsibilities, but instead group employees based on skills and product focus. These groups of employees then report to various broader regional or national managers. The matrix form of structure facilitates flexibility, such as when it facilitates a group of engineers or financing experts providing services to various regions. Of concern, a matrix organization can lead to conflicts when different regions have different needs or pursue differing goals. The engineering team, for example, might find itself being pulled in opposing directions by the various regional operations that have authority over the team's activities.

Honda employs a region-based matrix organization, as presented in Figure 5.8. The company conducts regional operations in North America; Latin America; Europe, the Middle and Near East, Africa; Asia and Oceania; and China. It deploys separate functional operations that serve across each region, such as separate motorcycle operations and purchasing operations. Employees in automobile operations report to the various regions and are responsible for effective automobile production and sales across the regions.[14]

Each of these forms of structure facilitates international marketing programs in different ways. Various internal and external factors lead to the selection of one organizational design over another.

INTERNAL FACTORS AND ORGANIZATIONAL STRUCTURE

Internal and external factors influence the design of organizational structures in ways similar to how they impact overall strategic planning. Some of the more significant internal factors include the company's international orientation, communication and control issues; the intensity of international marketing efforts, the existing

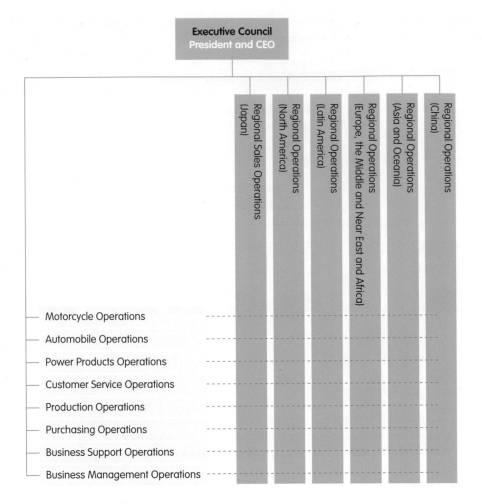

FIGURE 5.8   Organization Structure

Source: Honda, "Organization Structure." Retrieved from https://www.atlashonda.com.pk/organization-chart/

organizational design, and the degree of technology development. An executive makes an important strategic choice involving the best form of structure after considering these and other factors.

Company Orientation

The company's orientation, whether it is an ethnocentric, polycentric, regiocentric, or geocentric orientation, significantly impacts its organizational structure. *Ethnocentric* organizations tend to hire home market employees at home and abroad. When management believes that home country nationals are best able to drive international marketing activities, a home country orientation results. The policies and procedures enacted by the company remain largely unchanged in the host country.

Polycentric companies employ locals in the host country to conduct operations and treat each market as being unique. The skills and local knowledge of host country nationals influence decision-making in these firms.

Regiocentric companies utilize employees from several countries in a region, thereby pooling the expertise of employees from different countries. Geocentric companies focus on hiring the best employees available, regardless of specific country location. These companies maintain a global orientation, without referencing a specific home or host country. The most effective orientation depends, in large part, on the overall strategic direction and mission of the firm.

Communication and Control

Communication and control refer to the degree to which a home office directs activities in various home countries. Companies that require strong, daily involvements tend to develop sophisticated communication and control systems. Some managers prefer to maintain tight controls and frequent contact with overseas markets, whereas others favor a much less rigid approach. These approaches impact organizational design and structure decisions. A direct-reporting, functional approach may work better when managers prefer tighter control and frequent communications; a national or regional approach may fit better when control and communication concerns are less significant.

Intensity of International Marketing Efforts

A company that devotes considerable resources to and derives substantial business from international markets will feature an organizational structure that differs from a firm conducting fewer activities in foreign markets. A company with a small percentage of international business may employ a simple export approach. A truly global organization normally requires an organizational design such as the regional or matrix form of structure. These differences may also be found at the product level. Tata Motors started reaching the foreign markets for the Nano through exporting. As demand continues to grow, the company may need to shift to a new organizational structure. A company such as Honda, with millions of automobiles sold globally, already features a matrix approach to effectively respond to the needs of those markets.

Existing Organizational Structure

For a firm that is relatively new to the international marketplace, the existing organizational design often affects its international structure. A new structure tends to develop slowly and deliberately. An organization that has just begun to enter international marketing may conduct operations with a simple exporting strategy and eventually move to another design. Maruchan, the best-selling ramen noodle brand in the United States, started out as a frozen fish distributor in Japan. The company began to produce ramen noodles in 1961 and export the noodles to neighboring countries in 1972. In 1977 the company entered the American market with the opening of a ramen noodle manufacturing plant in California. At first the company kept a simple organizational structure while exporting, but, as international business grew, it shifted its organizational structure. The unit is now headquartered in Richmond, Virginia.[15]

Technological Investment

Technology increasingly plays an important role in international marketing. The level of technological sophistication and commitment of a company often influences its organizational structure. While technology remains important in all aspects of international marketing, it becomes especially important when establishing international communication and control systems. Communicating with offices in international markets requires efficient and effective technology. Simpler designs require relatively modest technological investments. Synchronizing operations with locations around the globe necessitates more significant investments.

EXTERNAL FACTORS AND ORGANIZATIONAL STRUCTURE

External factors also influence organizational design decisions. These factors include levels of international competition, distances from international customers, customer profiles, and governmental forces. External factors require responses, including how the company will be structured in order to cope with them.

International Competition

The level and intensity of international competition affect an organization's structural design decisions. When few international competitors are present, or if the level of competition stays low, company managers may choose to engage largely in exporting and maintain a functional, direct exporting structure. For more intense levels of competition, a national or regional presence may be more effective. Maintaining close contact with the marketplace enables the firm to monitor competitive actions.

Distance to International Customers

Companies desiring to stay close to international customers often choose the region-based approaches. The local presence afforded by these alternatives helps maintain close relationships with international customers. Close relationships become more likely when there are a number of customers clustered in regions that are far from a firm's world headquarters.

Customer Profiles

Regardless of the distance to international customers, some customers simply demand a local presence, such as a local sales office. The international division alternative works well in these situations. Establishing a presence in a country becomes more important when buyers and sellers make frequent contacts, such as in rebuy or modified rebuy situations. In many industrial buying situations, a matrix organizational structure specific to regions grants an effective level of coordination and control.

Governmental Forces

At times governmental forces dictate organizational structures, most notably when tariffs or other barriers to trade make exporting to markets overly expensive. In those circumstances, company leaders may instead choose to establish subsidiaries within the country, which in turn leads to a different organizational form. Governments may also require that companies find a local partner when setting up a subsidiary. In some cases, the local partner may be required to have a majority stake in the local business. These requirements often lead to different organizational forms.

LEARNING OBJECTIVE #5:

What activities are parts of an international marketing control system?

INTERNATIONAL MARKETING CONTROLS

International marketing control includes assessments of all marketing activities individually and collectively within international markets. These assessments take place at the regional, national, or other appropriate levels. Regardless of level, marketing controls are based on the standards set in the planning process. Control involves more than examining numbers: it requires careful analysis of all the factors that lead to organizational success.

Control in an international marketing environment focuses on measuring progress against what was planned, taking corrective actions when they are needed, and rewarding success. In general, international control consists of four steps:[16]

1.   Restate the standard or objective.

2.   Measure performance as it relates to the standard or objective.

3.   Compare performance to the standard or objective.

4.   Make a decision (make corrections or reward success).

Managers first restate the standards or objectives that were set during the planning function. Many standards are known as **metrics**, another term for performance measures. More recently, the term analytics has arisen in many areas, including analysis of marketing activities. **Analytics** are statistical methods used to evaluate the data and patterns present in those data for the purpose of making more precise judgements regarding which activities have been the most efficient and effective. They assist in the processes of comparing performance to standards. Then corrective actions or rewards to employees will follow.

metrics: performance measures that serve as standards set during the planning process and that are used in the control process

analytics: statistical methods used to evaluate data

STRATEGIC CONTROLS

Strategic controls apply to the CEO and other managers involved in directing the portfolios of businesses held or activities pursued by a single company or corporation. Strategic standards are more encompassing than marketing department goals. They include corporate profitability figures measured by return on investments, the value of a share of common stock, overall company growth in assets, and similar outcomes.

strategic controls: performance measures that apply to the CEO and top-level management team that direct the portfolios of businesses or activities held by a single company or corporation

TACTICAL CONTROLS

The highest-ranking member of the marketing department holds a title such as "vice president of marketing and sales" or "director of marketing." This individual has the ultimate responsibility for the tactical direction of the marketing department, as well as for establishing and evaluating tactical marketing standards. The size of the company and the marketing department dictates the types of controls to be used. In a smaller company, sales, marketing, and public relations may be contained in a single unit. In larger organizations, the three may each be deemed a separate department with its own manager. The typical tactical objectives and goals established for the marketing department's planning and control systems are found in the areas of:

- market share
- sales

- profitability
- customer satisfaction and
- corporate and brand image

These standards will be applied in various ways, including by nation or region, product line, brand name, specific segments, and individual products. This information will then be compiled into an overall assessment of marketing efforts for the entire organization.

OPERATIONAL CONTROLS

Day-to-day operations require specific standards dedicated to highly tangible outcomes. As shown in Table 5.5 some apply to individual employees while others are directed to key activities such as advertising programs or product delivery systems. Supervisors in individual departments help measure these outcomes and assist in developing corrections when outcomes do not match expectations.

TABLE 5.5   Marketing Controls

Strategic Indicators	Tactical Standards	Operational Standards
Profitability (Return on Investment)	New Markets Served	Sales Figures: Individual Salespersons
Market Share Home Country Host Countries	New Product Introductions Home Country Host Countries	Advertising Reach/ Effectiveness
Corporate/Brand Image Brand Awareness Brand Loyalty Brand Equity	Distribution Costs Domestic International	Delivery Efficiency On time percentage Damaged goods Cost per unit
Overall Sales Home Country Host Countries	Distribution Effectiveness Domestic International	Public Relations Positive stories Negative press
	Existing Product Lines/Brands	

When the first three steps of the control process have been completed, the standards have been set, performance has been measured, and a comparison has been made between the established standard and actual performance. The final step of control is to either reward success or make corrections. Corrections take place at the strategic, tactical, and operational levels.

STRATEGIC CORRECTIONS

core competence: the most proficiently performed internal activity that is central to the firm's strategy and competitiveness

Strategic managers focus on either a resource-based approach to strategic direction or a competitive approach. The resource-based approach concentrates on the organization's **core competence**, or the most proficiently performed internal activity that is central to the firm's strategy and competitiveness. Core competencies are based in knowledge and people, not capital and assets. This approach to strategic management seeks the goal of developing a **distinctive competence**, in which a company performs an activity such as production or sales more efficiently and effectively than all its rivals. In marketing terms, this equates to *brand equity* because it means competitive superiority (Wernerfelt, 1984).

At the other extreme, there will be times when strategic managers make corrections designed to deal with various challenges and crises. *Retrenchment* refers to a reduction in spending and investment, with the focus on weathering a downturn. *Divestment* involves selling low-performing assets. Together, these strategies may result in companies leaving the most difficult markets.

distinctive competence: a production activity a company performs at a level that is better than all competitive rivals

TACTICAL CORRECTIONS

Strategic responses constitute the most dramatic and sweeping types of corrections made in control systems, accompanied by various tactical responses. Tactical corrections may be developed for brands, products, and other functions. At the product level, corrections include introducing new products, cutting existing products, or repositioning. Corrections also focus on finding new users or uses, or encouraging more frequent usage. Additional tactical corrections include changing promotional methods and approaches, such as starting a new advertising campaign, or altering the distribution channel or channels.

OPERATIONAL CORRECTIONS

At the entry level, first-line supervisors work with employees to ensure that they correctly carry out the company's marketing directives. Performance appraisal systems and reward systems help ensure that those who make face-to-face contact with the public present the company in a positive fashion. Additional operational corrections include changing methods for conducting daily activities, such as when a cash-based economy begins to shift to the use of debit and credit cards.

INTERNATIONAL INCIDENT

Not all employees are equally comfortable with communicating via electronic media. In fact, some can be nearly hostile toward the use of the media, while others embrace it completely. A complication occurs when an employee who is comfortable with electronic media is stationed in a country with an underdeveloped technological infrastructure. The employee can suffer from a loss of work morale and feelings of isolation. Such an outcome may not be surprising, considering that many consumers have become addicted to media such as the Internet. What could be done to improve communications with the employee and improve his or her morale?

LEARNING OBJECTIVE #6:

How will emerging trends affect international marketing in the future?

EMERGING TRENDS IN INTERNATIONAL MARKETING PLANNING AND CONTROL

Many trends affect international marketing practices. Although it is difficult to predict unforeseen events, it appears likely that the following issues will continue to affect international marketing for the foreseeable future. Major changes center on technological, cultural, and economic issues.

TECHNOLOGICAL ISSUES

The proliferation of mobile phones and smartphones worldwide continues to influence international marketing programs, especially for international service providers. Increased usage of smartphones directly affects cellular phone companies dependent on sales of lower-end, more traditional phones. This represents a strategic opportunity as well as a potential strategic threat, depending on the company's situation and approach.

In emerging or less-developed areas, counterfeit smartphones constitute a growing market. Forty percent of the smartphones manufactured in China are counterfeits. Beyond being less expensive, many offer new product features. Some fake iPhones in China allow the user to install two SIM cards, which makes it possible to maintain two different phone numbers, and such models are popular with consumers in many countries. Chinese counterfeits in Ghana can receive television broadcasts. In Kenya, the phones feature quotes from former President Obama.[17]

Citizens in developing countries typically exhibit higher usage rates of new mobile and digital technologies than many individuals in mature markets. India already has approximately 765 million phones, with 95% of the phones being mobile.[18] Emerging market consumers are more likely to use cell phones. The dependency on the older technology such as conventional computers may prevent developed-market consumers from taking complete advantage of the mobile revolution.[19]

Technology has changed the ways in which employees communicate in international companies. Table 5.6 identifies emerging channels on internal communication in international companies. Table 5.7 notes intranet uses in the same circumstances.

TABLE 5.6   Formal Internal Communication Channels

Traditional Formal Communication Channels	Emerging Formal Communication Channels
Direct messages	Websites
Meetings	Intranet
Memos	Teleconferencing
Letters	Mobile phones
Company manuals/handbooks	Satellite transmissions
Bulletin boards	
Company magazine/newsletter	

CULTURAL ISSUES

Cultural differences can cause international marketing misunderstandings. International marketers that correctly adjust to cultural differences and the interaction between

TABLE 5.7 Intranet Uses

State corporate policies and vision
Provide information to the sales force while making contacts with clients
Maintain human resource records
Facilitate payroll
Pass along employee recognition
Provide information about company events and altruistic causes

culture and technology through effective planning and control systems generate substantial advantages over competitors. Culture's pervasive influence, particularly on consumption, presents a challenge for marketers globally. The future of international marketing will likely be influenced by two forces: cultural convergence and cultural trends.

Increased standardization in strategic and tactical plans and subsequent company activities may be the result of **cultural convergence**, or the growing similarities between consumers globally. These similarities take place in many aspects of life. Areas of convergence include technological, political, and economic trends.

cultural convergence: the increasing similarities between global consumers

Technological similarities and adoption of those technologies help drive increased convergence globally. The practical and societal benefits of many technologies, such as headache medicines or social media, create demand. Consumers transition to these new technologies regardless of any underlying cultural preferences.

Political and economic changes also accelerate convergence. The transition to a more capitalist economy and open, democratic political structure often leads to similar consumption patterns by consumers across those growing economies. Some consumers seek to mimic and, to some degree, also idealize Western, developed-country consumption patterns. Increased wealth and financial stability create the additional discretionary income consumers use to purchase goods.

Businesses also influence the convergence process. The economic development of various countries coupled with more efficient methods to sell goods to all markets lead to global brands. As global companies move into new countries, the employment of local salespeople and distributors, and eventually the establishment of local subsidiaries, result in increased cultural convergence.

Consider the case of Levi Strauss jeans. Founded in 1873, the company created the first blue jeans. During the 1960s the company began to enter Europe (the region of origin for denim) and Japan (Downey, 2010). By 2016, consumers were wearing Levi jeans in 110 countries, and more than half of the company's earnings were generated outside the United States.[20] Changes in levels of convergence led to plans designed to take advantage of this global opportunity.

cultural divergence: persistence of specific values due to sociocultural influences

Consumption exists within the context of a local culture. The persistence of specific values due to sociocultural influences, particularly in the face of outside alternatives, is **cultural divergence**. Product preferences rooted in a culture may cause some people to resist outside goods and new patterns of behavior.

Researchers studied convergence, divergence, and a third term: crossvergence. **Cultural crossvergence** refers to the emergence of a new, global value system

cultural crossvergence: the emergence of a new, global value system as countries become more interconnected

as countries become increasingly interconnected. It represents a melting-pot approach (Ralston et al., 2008). Consumers take the best from various locations and a more global culture emerges. The ubiquity of soy sauce, the rising consumption of salsa as a condiment, the increasing popularity of fruits from all over the world, and the leadership of an Indian company in the global steel market provide examples of crossvergence. It may be that instead of all consumers morphing into "Americans," many increasingly enjoy the benefits of the best goods from a variety of countries.

ECONOMIC ISSUES

Over the past several decades, an increasing global consensus had emerged with regard to lowering barriers to trade, reducing governmental intervention, eliminating business regulations, and adopting the Western model of economic development in which the market is trusted to best serve the interests of citizens. After the fall of the former Soviet Union and the transition toward a more capitalist system for the People's Republic of China, Eastern Europe, and much of Latin America, many nations became increasingly "American" in their business approaches.

The economic recession that began in late 2007 in the United States and grew during the following year for many Western countries changed the economic landscape. The underlying financial crisis at the root of the economic downturn increased skepticism of the traditional, Anglo-Saxon model. The Great Recession also exhibited an uneven impact globally. Developed economies, particularly Western Europe's, faced steep downturns. While France, Germany, and Japan avoided sharp drops, the United Kingdom and much of the remaining developed countries did not. The recession hit Portugal, Ireland, Greece, and Spain (known as the PIGS, although this acronym is offensive to some) particularly hard. Greece and Ireland received assistance from the European Central Bank to prevent the countries from defaulting on loans. Spain and Portugal faced similar problems (Garnham, 2011). The crisis put pressure on maintaining both the *euro* and the connection between countries, but also, to some degree, drew the members of the European Union closer together, leading managers in some countries to look for new business models (Stelzer, 2010).

Of the Western countries, the Nordic countries, with combinations of higher regulation and larger social safety nets, arguably weathered the economic storm better than other European nations. They provided generous support to citizens during the downturn, which meant they faced less unrest and a quicker ability to bounce back. Nicolas Sarkozy claimed that the global recession marked a turning of the page on the traditional, Anglo-Saxon, British, and American economic model (Barker et al., 2009).

By 2016, the influx of Syrian refugees into Europe had made a dramatic impact on economic and political activities within those countries. Company managers made decisions as to whether sufficient numbers of immigrants were present to create more culturally specific products or to modify existing products to meet the needs of immigrants from that country.

Company leaders must consistently respond to economic factors in both planning and control systems. Economic systems as well as economic trends and events influence perceptions of strategic marketing opportunities and threats. They also influence the analysis of organizational marketing outcomes as part of the firm's control system.

Responses to Financial Crises

Companies exhibit differing responses to financial crises, many of which appear in planning and control systems. For many, any collapse in consumer confidence and spending may lead to retrenchment and divestment. During the last major global recession, declining consumer confidence in the United Kingdom led local retailers to retrench and divest by closing more than 250 storefronts (Hughman, 2011). The closures strongly affected companies selling products through those retail outlets.

For other companies, financial crises present opportunities. One typical governmental response to a crisis is extreme movement in lending rates. A company might be able to react to these high or low rates by increasing its amount of lending or borrowing. High rates can lead to increased lending, which results in higher profits, whereas low rates can lead to a less expensive cost of debt. International companies may then use borrowing to expand into new markets or more aggressively pursue new product development.

Many company leaders believe that marketing investments during a recession result in an improved company position when the economy recovers.[21] Some academic research reveals support for this approach, particularly when investments in research and development or advertising are thoughtful and targeted (Quelch and Jocz, 2009; Srinivasan et al., 2011).

Company position before the last global recession affected the ability of firms to respond. Diversified companies, both in terms of the countries or markets in which the company conducts business and in terms of the breadth of products offered, weather financial downturns more effectively than companies selling a limited number of products or single product. The global recession negatively affected General Motors in several ways, leading to the company selling off many brands, closing plants, and laying off employees. The company's struggles led to American government intervention and financial support. One of the few bright spots for GM was its market-leading positions in Brazil and China, two of the fastest growing international markets for sales. Without diversifying into these markets, the company may not have been able to survive the recession.[22] Currently GM enjoys strong growth and profitability following the crises, led by the leadership of CEO Mary Barra (Chew, 2015).

BOTTOM-OF-THE-PYRAMID

The 2008–2009 global recession hurt many bottom-of-the-pyramid consumers. The World Bank estimated that 90 million more people globally moved to earning less than $1.25 a day during the downturn (Atkins, 2009). Even during that time period, many international marketing firms increasingly focused on bottom-of-the-pyramid consumers.

The continent of Africa is home to a billion people, many of which are bottom-of-the-pyramid consumers. Africa has the potential to emerge in the coming decades much as China and India have in the past twenty years. The growth of middle-class Africans, as estimated by the World Bank, is projected to be from 13 million in 2000 to 43 million by 2030 (Connors, 2011a). Many local African firms realize this potential and have taken aggressive steps to meet the needs of the local market. Zambeef, an African meat and produce company, has spent millions of dollars expanding across the continent. The company's export business continues to be active in 2016, especially in southern Africa (Connors, 2011b).

Whether in Africa or in other emerging markets, successful targeting of bottom-of-the-pyramid consumers presents a major challenge for many developing-country firms. Those firms that meet this challenge will build a solid foundation with these consumers. As least- and less-developed countries begin to grow economically, the relationship and brand loyalty with consumers will help drive profits and degrees of long-term success for companies in the regions (Wessel, 2010; Zuckerman, 2010).

EMERGING MARKETS ASCENDING

The decreased dominance of the traditional Western powers due to the recession shifted the focus to the rising powers in Asia and Latin America. During the downturn, China continued to grow, with GDP expansion of 8.3% in 2009 after 9% in 2008. The growth pattern was partially due to aggressive government action, including a large amount of spending. India's economy continued to grow, as did Brazil's. In 2016, the Chinese economy expanded 6.7%, which was lower than the 6.9% experienced in 2015. It was the weakest full-year growth since 1990 but within the government's target range of 6.5–7%, as consumption and investment growth softened. GDP Annual Growth Rate in China averaged 9.76% from 1989 until 2016.[23]

The Shanghai skyline reflects the country's rapid growth.

As a result, emerging market countries have experienced greater political and economic influence. China remains a prime investor in Africa and helped support the eurozone during the bailout of Greece and Ireland (Stelzer, 2010). India continued to increase its role in software offshoring, and Brazil leveraged advantages in terms of natural resources, including offshore oil. Apple's iPhone helps illuminate the role of non-Western countries in the global economy. While designed in California, the product is assembled in China. The parts are made in Taiwan, Japan, South Korea, and six other countries (Prestowitz, 2011). The growing importance of emerging market countries will continue to exert an influence on international marketers in the future.

As the developing world continues to make economic progress, prognosticators have begun to introduce new groupings of countries that move beyond Goldman Sachs' BRIC designation (Brazil, Russia, India, and China). One grouping proposed by the magazine *The Economist* is CIVETS (Colombia, Indonesia, Vietnam, Egypt, Turkey, and South Africa). Another grouping, introduced by the Spanish bank BBVA, is EAGLES (Emerging and Growth-Leading Economies). These include the BRIC countries plus South Korea, Indonesia, Mexico, Turkey, Egypt, and Taiwan (Wassener, 2010). Analysts at Goldman Sachs introduced the MIST countries (Mexico, Indonesia, South Korea, and Turkey) (Gupta, 2011). While it remains to be seen which countries or group of countries successfully develop, these new acronyms highlight the broadening influence of emerging economies.

In summary, planning and control systems that dictate all international marketing activities are being influenced by emerging trends in the marketplace. Changes in technologies, cultures, economic systems and circumstances, financial crises, and emerging markets influence managerial assessments of the factors present in a SWOT analysis, creating new opportunities as well as threats. Companies then consider internal strengths and weaknesses in order to adapt to shifting circumstances so as to remain efficient and effective over time.

CHAPTER 5: REVIEW AND RESOURCES

Strategic Implications

Strategic marketing managers continually assess the effectiveness of overall marketing programs. Companies develop metrics, or the strategic criteria used to analyze the well-being of an international marketing system. In each instance, the marketing leader examines success at the domestic and global levels.

The five forces that affect the international marketing environment continue to exhibit dramatic effects on strategic choices regarding markets, products, pricing tactics, distribution systems, and promotional programs. Top managers consider the influence of infrastructure, economic conditions, political and legal environments, and cultural trends as they make strategic plans and decisions.

Tactical Implications

Tactical managers often oversee product lines, brands, or more specific marketing activities such as distribution. Tactical managers consider larger trends in the international marketing environment but focus on more-tangible, shorter-term considerations. Launching a new product or entering a new market in a host country requires understanding of the current conditions within that nation. The brand leader consults with the firm's cultural assimilator to make sure that a product's name, package, label, price, and promotions all fit with local conditions.

Operational Implications

Individual department managers review outcomes at the day-to-day, operational level. Sales figures are likely to be examined on a monthly basis for each salesperson. Advertising and promotional programs will be assessed within the time frame in which they take place. Operational managers are most likely to hear customer complaints about various activities, from late arrivals of goods to a salesperson's poor service. Local culture dictates how these criticisms will be raised. An expatriate manager adjusts to a new culture in dealing with host country employees as well as with customers and others in the area.

TERMS

planning

organizing

control

strategic planning

tactical planning

operational plans

international strategic planning

mission statement

metrics

analytics

strategic controls

core competence

distinctive competence

cultural divergence

cultural convergence

cultural crossvergence

REVIEW QUESTIONS

1. Define planning, organizing, and controlling.

2. Describe the concepts of efficiency and effectiveness.

3. Define strategic planning, tactical planning, and operational planning.

4. Describe the four elements in a SWOT analysis.

5. Describe a direct exporting structure.

6. Describe an international division structure and a direct functional reporting structure.

7. Describe a region-based organization and a matrix organization structure.

8. Name the internal and external factors that affect the choice of organizational structure.

9. What are the four steps of the control process?

10. Name the strategic, operational, and tactical standards companies use.

11. Describe core competence and distinctive competence.

12. Describe cultural convergence, cultural divergence, and cultural crossvergence.

13. What emerging trends will impact international marketing in the coming years?

DISCUSSION QUESTIONS

1. Relate the elements of the strategic planning process to the concepts of efficiency and effectiveness. Explain how the elements are carried out at the tactical and operational levels.

2. Explain which form of international organizational structure would best match each of the following companies. Explain your reasoning for each choice.

    - Nike

    - Tommy Hilfiger

    - Bank of India

    - Southern African Diamonds

    - A Chinese company that manufacturers chopsticks

3. Create a complete international marking plan for one of the following companies:

    - Japanese company seeking to export rice to other Asian countries

    - Italian automobile company seeking to sell fuel-efficient cars in Africa

    - Information technology software company in India seeking to expand to Australia

    - Spanish winery seeking to enter markets in Central America

4. Make a list of the emerging trends in international marketing identified in this chapter. Explain how they have appeared, or become less relevant in the past decade. What new trends do you believe will affect international marketing? Explain your answer.

ANALYTICAL AND INTERNET EXERCISES

1. Visit coca-cola.com. The website gives the viewer the option to switch to the websites for various countries. This option is typically a tab at the top right. Using the tab, explore websites for various countries. Look at least-developed country websites, websites for countries on each continent, and websites for emerging markets. Based on an in-depth review of at least five websites, discuss how Coca-Cola changes the website content to reflect local technological and cultural preferences.

2. Youtube.com contains videos from throughout the world. Search for consumer-generated videos from various countries. Vary the countries based on factors of your choosing, but be certain to include countries that are different. Examining the videos, do you find evidence of cultural convergence, divergence, and/or crossvergence? Use specific examples to support your claims. After finishing, consider how the target market for youtube.com across these markets may or may not explain finding convergence.

3. Examine the websites of five companies that are not based in the United States. Find the organizations' mission statements. Compare the statements in terms of an emphasis on being a global company, a sustainable company, or an ethical company.

STUDENT STUDY SITE

Visit **https://study.sagepub.com/baack2e** to access these free additional learning tools:

- Web Quizzes
- eFlashcards
- SAGE Journal Articles
- Country Fact Sheets
- Chapter Outlines
- Interactive Maps

CASE 5

Samsung: Overcoming Strategic, Tactical, and Operational Challenges

In 2016, South Korean tech giant Samsung experienced an embarrassing and financially challenging issue. The Galaxy 7 Note mobile phone was connected to dozens of reports of the devices overheating and in some cases bursting into flames (BBC, 2017a). Images and photographs could be found on postings and websites around the globe. The fire hazard led the U.S. Department of Transportation to ban the device from all domestic flights (Jansen, 2016). Company officials responded with an immediate recall and replace program, which many customers ignored (at their peril).

The financial impact was immediate. The company reported a net loss during the financial quarter in which the recall occurred. Image damage from negative publicity occurred worldwide. Eventually company leaders blamed the defect on batteries made by suppliers.

The medium term impact on the marketing department was profound. Marketers had to be concerned with any spill-over effects, wherein the problems with the Galaxy 7 Note could be attributed to other products produced by the company. Advertising, public relations, and promotional programs had to be put on hold and then reconfigured to deal with negative consumer perceptions. The company released several statements indicating how the problem had been solved and would not recur.

Retail outlets and their employees also dealt with various aspects of the product's problems. They were being asked to explain the problem and the remedies offered by Samsung. Decisions were made regarding their willingness to continue to carry the Samsung line in individual stores. Individual salespeople would logically be inclined to steer customers towards other companies and brands.

The saving grace financially was Samsung's diverse line of products. The majority of the company's profits earned during the 2016 calendar year came from selling various components, such as semiconductors, memory chips, and display screens. Oppo, LG, and Dell all use Samsung parts in phones, televisions, and laptops. Consequently, the firm returned to profitability in the fourth quarter of 2016 and enjoyed a profit for the full year as well (Pham, 2017).

1. Using a SWOT analysis, what strategic issues did Samsung's management team face during the product recall crisis period?

2. Using a SWOT analysis, what tactical issues did Samsung's marketing team face during the product recall crisis period?

3. Beyond a reliance on diversification (numerous products and product lines), what strategic responses would you recommend for Samsung going forward?

4. Choose four global regions (Pacific Rim, NAFTA countries, etc.). Explain how marketers of Samsung products would need to respond to consumers (and retailers) in those regions.

PART II
INTERNATIONAL MARKETS AND MARKET RESEARCH

CONTENTS

6

MARKETS AND SEGMENTATION IN AN INTERNATIONAL CONTEXT

LEARNING OBJECTIVES

After reading and studying this chapter, you should be able to answer the following questions.

1. What is market segmentation and how does international market segmentation differ from domestic market segmentation?

2. What are the primary factors used to identify international consumer and business-to-business market segments?

3. Which consumer segments can be found across different countries to be targeted with standardized products and services?

4. How can the marketing team use regional and national segmentation methods to improve a company's global marketing program?

5. How to assess the market potential of a segment?

IN THIS CHAPTER

Opening Vignette: Musical Segmentation

OVERVIEW

MUSICAL SEGMENTATION

One constant that may be found anywhere on the planet is music. The forms vary, the instruments are similar in some cultures and quite different in others, but songs often feature universal themes and emotions, regardless of where they are sung. International marketers are likely to be involved with music in one way or another as products move across international boundaries.

Music reflects culture, and culture changes music. More traditional musical forms have roots that extend far back into history, no matter the home country. In Asia, common traditional instruments include versions of the flute and stringed instruments. The *ruan*, a four-stringed fretted instrument used for opera and other performances, dates back more than 1,600 years in China. The spike fiddle is widespread in the Gobi areas of central

Mongolia and among eastern Mongols; the *khuuchir* and the *dorvon chikhtei khuur* are a two- and a four-stringed spike fiddle, respectively.

In Saudi Arabia and other Middle Eastern countries, the flute-like *ney* (or *nay*) accompanies folk songs; the *bandir* (or *bendir*), a type of small drum, keeps rhythm; and the *qanan*, a stringed instrument, enriches the unique sound. African drums create distinctive rhythms that accompany longstanding musical and cultural traditions.

Over time, musical instruments move across national boundaries, as do musical formats. The piano, violin, oboe, harp, trumpet, and numerous other instruments shape classical music sounds across many cultures. Pioneering classical music composers have emerged from a variety of countries, and the music shared between those nations creates cultural contacts and closeness.

Today, forms of music span the globe, moving more quickly due to communication advancements that make it possible to watch performances as they take place in other nations. Hip-hop artists may be found around the world. Numerous Country and Western fans reside in Japan. Music connects with language, fashion, cultural change, and other elements of local, regional, national, and international environments.

A variety of international marketing opportunities emerge from music. They include the exporting of musical instruments; the sale of music on the Internet, iPod, CD, music video, or on the radio; performances by musical artists touring the globe complete with sponsorships; and the musical backgrounds that accompany advertisements and commercials. Marketing professionals moving into new countries will quickly be exposed to local musical tastes. A quick review of the most popular YouTube artists in the location is a great place to start.

CONSUMERS AROUND the world enjoy music.

(Continued)

(Continued)

Musical acts appeal to consumers across the globe. In 2016, top performing artists who have conducted successful worldwide tours include Adele, Coldplay, Stone Roses (English band), Madonna, The Rolling Stones, and Beyoncé (McIntyre, 2016). Many regions or countries have unique stars for their market. Consider the case of Ronghao Li, a Chinese popstar winner of multiple Golden Melody Awards (the Taiwanese equivalent of the Grammys focused on the region). His popular hit, "King of Comedy" has over 46 million views on YouTube, and he is a huge star in the region with a long series of hit songs since his start in 2013. For his most recent tour, Warner Music Taiwan partnered with Digital Domain to capture the tour in VR for usage in just Greater China.

To effectively incorporate music into an international marketing program, the marketing team examines the cultural context in which music is performed, including its connections to religious life, festivals, popular culture, and other events. Musical preferences link to any number of potential market segments, including distinctions by age, gender, income level, religious affiliation, culture, counterculture, and others. Just as the numbers of songs and musical styles are broad, the international marketing possibilities created by music are nearly as endless.

Questions for Students

1. Do you believe music shapes cultural movements, accompanies cultural movements, or merely reflects cultural movements?

2. What types of market segments are associated with various musical forms?

3. What role does music play in international marketing that may be different from marketing in only one country?

OVERVIEW

Part I of this book explained the essentials of international marketing. A basic framework was established, economic systems and modes of entry were examined, and the nature of global trade and integration was presented. These factors help form the basis for carrying out all other strategic international marketing functions.

Part II concentrates on international markets. This chapter analyses markets and the segmentation process. Chapter 7 analyses strategic international positioning. Chapter 8 reviews market research, which helps the company's leadership understand the context present in a new country of entry. The elements presented in these three chapters combine to assist in an orderly analysis of potential target markets along with the characteristics of persons living in those regions.

Market segmentation represents one key component of success in an international context. In order to successfully target consumers, marketing managers identify groups of people willing to purchase the company's goods and services and who have the means to do so. The market segmentation process begins with answers to basic questions: What do people want? What do people need? Can they afford these items? Are there consumers with similar characteristics that can be targeted with the same products or services? What influences their cravings and choices? The study of the marketing potential in any country relies on an understanding of the cultural context, the type of economy that exists, and other general circumstances within that nation. These factors make it possible for the marketing team to identify the company's target market segments and the characteristics of buyers in those market segments.

The forces that affect market segmentation processes include a number of the factors examined in this chapter, as presented in Figure 6.1. The intricacies of international market segmentation programs are explored. Finally, the chapter identifies the ethical issues that arise in those circumstances.

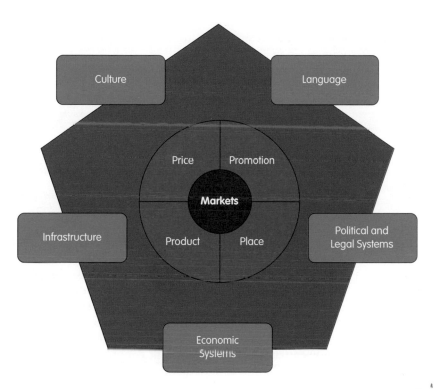

FIGURE 6.1   The International Marketing Context

LEARNING OBJECTIVE #1:

What is market segmentation and how does international market segmentation differ from domestic market segmentation?

MARKETS AND SEGMENTATION

A **market** consists of people with wants and needs, money to spend, and the willingness to spend money on those wants and needs. International markets vary due to several factors. Marketers consider these factors when developing international segmentation approaches. Companies typically sell to two major groups: consumers and other businesses. Both groups experience needs for products in the areas shown in Table 6.1. Governments make up a third major group, which is similar to but unique from businesses.

market: people with wants and needs, money to spend, and the willingness to spend money on those wants and needs

TABLE 6.1   Consumer and Business Market Needs

Consumer Markets	Business Markets
Convenience	Renewable
Shopping	Nonrenewable
Nondurable	
Durable	
Specialty	Finished Goods

In addition, both consumers and businesses want or need various services. Services include the items summarized in Table 6.2.

TABLE 6.2   Types of Services

Services to Consumers	Services to Businesses
Personal	Legal
Financial	Financial
Sundry and Luxury	Rental
	Maintenance
	Specialty

market segmentation: a process that involves identifying specific groups based on their needs, attitudes, and interests; the grouping of consumers based on their needs, attitudes, and interests

International market segmentation: the process of identifying specific segments—whether they are country groups, other businesses, or individual consumer groups—of potential customers with homogeneous attributes across different countries, or within a single foreign market, that exhibit similar responses to a company's marketing mix

Identifying wants and needs of specific sets of groups, including consumers and businesses, is one of a company's primary objectives. **Market segmentation** consists of identifying every viable potential customer group. **International market segmentation** is the process of identifying specific segments—whether they are country groups, other businesses, or individual consumer groups—of potential customers with homogeneous attributes across different countries, or within a single foreign market, that exhibit similar responses to a company's marketing mix. When identifying market segments, marketers seek to understand the cultural factors that exist across marketplaces, as well as all of the other forces in the international marketing context.

THE STP APPROACH

A key marketing activity in both domestic and international markets will be identifying distinct groups of customers that may be interested in a product or service. A company can then create the item and brand that provides customers with a distinct choice in the marketplace. Methods to reach those consumers, based on their unique characteristics, can then be selected.

STP approach: segmentation, targeting, and product positioning processes

The core system used in this process is the **STP approach**, or segmentation, targeting, and positioning. *Segmentation* consists of identifying every viable potential customer group that can be reached through the marketing of a product and/or service. Most companies cannot create enough products, services, distribution channels, and marketing methods to reach every available market segment. Consequently, the *targeting* component of the STP approach involves selecting the market segments the firm will be best able to target or reach. *Positioning* involves the creation of perceptions in the minds of consumers about the nature of a company, its brands, and its products and services.

STP helps the marketing team meet the goal of optimizing sales and profits by reaching the proper audience, both in terms of products served and in the methods used to contact those individuals or companies (Kotler and Armstrong, 2007). For example, the British footwear company Dr. Martens segments consumers based on footwear needs, targeting those attracted to edgy fashion. Footwear positioning emerges from four pillars: creativity, music, fashion, and self expression (Rosandic, 2011).

LEARNING OBJECTIVE #2:

What are the primary factors used to identify international consumer and business-to-business market segments?

INTERNATIONAL MARKET SEGMENTATION

A company or brand's overall market consists of the cumulative total of all persons and organizations with needs or wants that can be satisfied by certain products or services. To more effectively serve such needs, marketers specify various target groups so that the product itself and/or the supporting messages can be tailored to each group. A **market segment** consists of a set of businesses or a group of individual consumers with distinct characteristics (Clow and Baack, 2012). For a market segment to be viable in the eyes of the marketing team, it must pass four tests:

market segment: a set of businesses or a group of individual consumers with distinct characteristics

1. Those within the segment should be homogenous or have similar characteristics.

2. The segment must differ from other groups and the population as a whole.

3. Sufficient demand must be present to make the segment financially feasible.

4. Methods to reach the market must exist, both in terms of physical delivery of the item and in terms of the marketing messages that would entice customers to make purchases.

International marketers spend a great deal of time and money identifying viable market segments (Steenkamp and Ter Hofstede, 2002). Market segmentation processes apply to consumer groups and to the business-to-business arena, in domestic and international markets. The first step in international segmentation is often segmenting and selecting country markets. Figure 6.2 lists the steps of international market segmentation.

Country markets will be selected based on several assumptions. First, company officials discern the degree of heterogeneity *between* countries. The greater the differences, the less likely a standardized approach can be featured. Second, the level of homogeneity *within* a country becomes important, as it suggests an identifiable target market. Third, marketers focus on macro-level cultural differences in order to understand how a good or service should be modified for a region. Fourth, a cluster of similar national markets makes it possible to expand into several countries. In addition other internal factors such as a company's experience with that country or similar countries, as well as the perceptions managers have regarding the degree of similarity to the country of origin. Marketing professionals also look for the emergence of segments that will transcend national boundaries. They examine the existence of within-country differences. They may also seek out smaller micro markets within and between countries.

Step 1: Identify 'macro' segments of countries based on evaluation	Step 2: Establish the profile of each country based on the relevant data	Step 3: Select country markets	Step 4: Identify B2B or B2C customer segments	Step 5: Assess the viability of each segment	Step 6: Select segments to target

FIGURE 6.2   Hierarchy of Steps in International Market Segmentation for a Firm with an Existing Product/Service.

Source: Adapted from Wind and Douglas (1972).

INTERNATIONAL CONSUMER MARKET SEGMENTS

When consumers or end users are the primary target market for a firm's offerings, the consumer market segmentation approaches listed in Table 6.3 are the most common. These groups or categories may be combined in international marketing efforts.

TABLE 6.3   Consumer Market Segmenting Variables

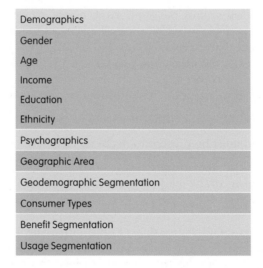

Demographics

Gender

Age

Income

Education

Ethnicity

Psychographics

Geographic Area

Geodemographic Segmentation

Consumer Types

Benefit Segmentation

Usage Segmentation

DEMOGRAPHICS

Demographics are population characteristics. Market segmentation programs often employ demographic variables, especially gender, age, income, education, and ethnicity. International companies create goods and services to meet the needs of these groups and market to them.

Gender

Previous marketing experience indicates that males and females purchase different products, buy similar products with different features (e.g., hair care items), desire products for dissimilar reasons, and purchase the same products after being influenced by different kinds of appeals through diverse media.

In the international arena, genders roles vary greatly. Males and females often enact divergent roles, dependent upon a local culture, including which person in the family is the primary shopper. In many cultures, females may play submissive roles within the family structure. These cultural norms, in turn, influence purchasing processes as well as the items sold.

Cultural concepts regarding attractiveness affect the types of products desired in a nation or region. In some cultures, women shave their legs and armpits, while in others they do not. Consequently, target markets for razors and shaving devices vary depending on the dominant culture. In some cases, subcultures within the country may display the consumption pattern needed to indicate a potential market segment.

Gender roles within a culture also affect the delivery of services. Purchases of life insurance and other forms of financial protection may vary when cultural norms dictate that all inheritances go to male family members. Citizens more frequently utilize child-care services in cultures where greater numbers of females work outside the home. Personal services, including hair care, beautification, and maid services, will be influenced by the dominant culture of the country or region.

Age

Many marketing efforts target persons of a certain age, including children, young adults, middle-age adults, and senior citizens. Age may be combined with another demographic, such as gender, to identify market segments. Senior men and women and their younger counterparts often purchase different items.

Age dictates adjustments to marketing efforts in various ways, due to local circumstances. For example, many populations experience shorter life expectancies, thereby changing the concepts of "old" or "senior citizen." Also, children in affluent, most-developed nations are more likely to have a greater number of wants and needs as compared to those in less- or least-developed nations.

In many collectivist cultures, grandparents play substantial roles in raising children. Consequently, messages targeting parents in one country may be directed at grandparents in others. Also, advanced age may be highly revered in some cultures and perceived as a disadvantage in others. The emphasis on maintaining a youthful appearance will be affected by these circumstances, which in turn affects the products to be sold and the methods used to promote them.

Age affects other purchasing patterns. Younger shoppers in some countries might be more inclined to purchase products from other nations, whereas older consumers resist foreign products. Younger consumers may be more likely to spend rather than save earnings, especially in newly industrialized countries and other emerging markets.

Income

Marketers often use individual or family income as a demographic segmentation variable. Lower-income households primarily purchase necessities, such as food, clothing, and housing needs. In poorer countries, even necessities may be difficult to obtain. As income increases, consumers are able to enjoy some sundry items including vacations, automobiles, more fashionable clothes, and meals at medium-priced or high-end restaurants. In less-developed countries, a trip to a Starbucks coffeehouse can be viewed as a medium-priced, high-status purchase, and Starbucks actively reinforces that image. At the extreme, producers of luxury items such as yachts and private planes target the wealthy.

The distribution of wealth within a nation or region largely dictates the use of income segmentation. In bottom-of-the-pyramid countries, the majority of consumers earn wages so small that companies need to adjust the prices and packages sizes of necessities, such as cleaning products or personal hygiene items. In many countries large segments of consumers earn nearly equal amounts of money, often with a small wealthy upper class.

Economic conditions affect incomes. Recessions lead to families cutting back on discretionary spending. The marketing team examines economic circumstances prior to launching an effort in a new host country. During the economic downturn after 2008, research indicates that U.S. companies that increased spending on marketing relative to market size had a 4.3% return on capital whereas those companies that cut marketing spending lost 0.8%. Expenditures on marketing activities that focused on face-to-face contact and relationship building were especially effective (Wilkinson, 2010).

INTERNATIONAL INCIDENT

You work for a mobile phone manufacturer that has developed a new smartphone. The new device is similar to existing products offered by the company but is much cheaper. Your task is to conduct market segmentation analysis in order to identify suitable market segments in Eastern Europe and to discover the best social media sites to target them. At the end of the process, you need to propose segments that would be interested in this smartphone. Which sources of information would you use in order to help you in this process? Would the proposed segments be similar or different across the different countries in the region?

Education

Income and education are closely related. Educational attainments in populations vary widely. In less-developed countries, a substantial percentage of the population may be illiterate or have completed only the most basic level of education. Consequently, these individuals obtain limited job skills and receive the lowest wages. As the number of high school and college-educated persons rises, and the quality of these institutions improves, new target markets emerge for a variety of products. As a simple example, books may not be widely sought in least-developed economies, whereas popular press books, novels, including digital versions, and printed materials such as special-interest magazines would be desired in emerging economies as well as in most-developed nations.

When advertising returned to Cambodia after decades of war and unrest, outdoor advertising became the primary medium. Local advertisers used images rather than words, or copy, in outdoor promotions. With a high illiteracy rate and low levels of education, the images were more effective than words would have been in promoting various brands (Yeow, 1996).

Ethnicity

Ethnic groups may be present within a given country or nation. These groups often exhibit differing purchasing patterns and product preferences. Ethnicity serves as a segmentation variable in both domestic and international settings. Products and marketing programs can be tailored to individual groups within the area. One method for identifying a market segment would be to seek out a subculture based on ethnicity that is the minority in a country.

According to former German Chancellor Helmut Kohl, more than 3 million Turkish people lived in Germany as of 2011. The number of Turkish people seeking asylum in Germany rose dramatically in 2016, partly due to the increase in terrorism in Turkey. With a spending power of €18 billion, this ethnic population has become an attractive target for marketing activity; however, companies needed to use caution as tensions between immigrants and native Germans began to rise (Noah, 2016). To reach this group in Germany, some companies advertised in local Turkish-language newspapers and explicitly referenced Turkish heritage and culture in promotions (Erdem and Schmidt, 2008).

PSYCHOGRAPHICS

Psychographic profiles emerge from a person's activities, interests, and opinions. Psychographics are influenced by cultural differences and are influenced by numerous factors such as religious beliefs, local customs, language, and even the popularity of local sports (Kahle et al., 1999). Cultures vary with regard to individualism or collectivism, gender equality, humane orientation, and future orientation dimensions. Countries with individualistic tendencies offer opportunities to market personalized products and items that make a person stand out from the crowd. When gender equality is present, fashion and clothing may feature unisex design. Humane orientation may affect the delivery of products and services that assist disadvantaged people and those with disease. Consumers in cultures with short-term orientations may be much less likely to purchase products featuring long-term usage. Short-term orientation may, in part, reflect life expectancy.

GEOGRAPHIC AREA

Some marketing appeals target people in a geographic area or region. Many times differences exist in purchasing patterns in rural versus urban areas, creating unique segments. Geographic details influence product availability, such as when a land-locked region experiences greater difficulty importing and exporting products due to the lack of an ocean port.

Germany can be divided into several distinct regions, including Bavaria, the Black Forest, Germany's East, the North and Baltic Sea area, the Rhine Valley, and Ruhrpott. Each exhibits distinct subcultures shaped by geographic features, economic circumstances, and historical events. The southern and northern regions of Germany are influenced by the presence of a body of water in one but not the other. Economic circumstances vary, in part due to the levels of affluence attained by those who did not live under the communist regime or the government of Turkey. The division between citizens of the former East Germany and West Germany continues, and, as noted, internal tensions increased as immigration rates rose. These differences may dictate the presence of a potential market segment or suggest that one does not exist, even though the regions are part of the same country.

Australia consists of several distinct markets. Wants and needs differ in the Outback area compared to those in the Highlands regions or the cosmopolitan areas of Sydney or Melbourne. Consumers in the major cities have needs that are similar to the needs of consumers in any major city worldwide. Consumers in the Outback and Highlands regions experience needs based heavily on climate, topography, and wildlife.

GEODEMOGRAPHIC SEGMENTATION

A hybrid form of geographic segmentation allows companies to enrich geographic approaches to segmentation by adding demographic and psychographic information.

Geodemographic segmentation may also be useful when various regions feature differences. In addition to the regional distinctions in Germany, differences exist between southern and northern China and between Western and Eastern Europe. Several companies focus specifically on geographic and geodemographic research. The firm ESRI, for example, provides executives with cutting-edge technologies for utilizing data from around the world. Sources such as ESRI help managers to combine geographic and demographic data into useful information for decision-making.[1]

Another useful but local tool is ACORN (acorn.caci.co.uk) described as a consumer classification that segments the UK population based primarily on where they live. By analyzing demographic data, social factors, population, and consumer behavior, it provides precise information and an understanding of different types of people based on the zip code (postcode) of their home address.[2] In the USA, Clarita's lifestyle segmentation provides a similar segmentation tool called MyBestSegments.[3]

BENEFIT SEGMENTATION

Benefit segmentation focuses on the advantages consumers receive from a product or service rather than the characteristics of consumers themselves. This approach features the advantage of focusing on the benefits sought by consumers, which may be the fundamental reason for the existence of true market segments. Benefit segmentation recognizes consumer choices much more accurately than other descriptive variables, such as demographic characteristics. Also, demographic or psychographic information can be combined with benefit information to identify more specific segments.

A given product or service may deliver one benefit in a given country and a separate benefit in another. For example, batteries may offer convenience in some settings but generate a much greater benefit in regions where power supplies are routinely interrupted.

Benefits consumers derive from items or services are affected by religious and cultural circumstances, economic conditions, and personal income variables. This segmentation approach is often used in the international travel and tourism industry because it helps to identify consumer motivations and the satisfaction of what they need and want from their travel trips. In a study about Japanese travelers to North America, researchers identified that there were three main benefit-based segments of travelers: novelty/nature seekers, escape/relaxation seekers, and family/outdoor activity seekers (Jang et al., 2002).

Another important application of benefit-based segmentation in the travel industry is to divide the market of senior consumers; an important global market segment growing in importance (Eusébio et al., 2017). These characteristics may then be used to develop marketing communications materials by the destinations to target the selected segments.

Another example of benefit-based segmentation is the case of clothing (which may be useful when analyzing the UNIQLO case study at the end of this chapter). Recent research sought to discover whether there are market segments for the fashion industry that cut across countries and respond differently to advertising messages. A survey identified four cross-national market segments based on the benefits sought: "information seekers," "sensation seekers," "utilitarian consumers," and "conspicuous consumers" (Ko et al., 2007). The existence of such segments across countries suggests that advertisers may develop standardized campaigns that emphasize the selected benefits to target each group. Table 6.4 presents the characteristics of the discovered segments.

TABLE 6.4 Example of Benefit-Based Segmentation of Clothing Applied to International Markets.

Segment	Characteristics
Information seekers	These consumers like learning about fashions and trying new things, but have little concern for actual product performance. Information about cutting-edge fashion is important to them, they like consulting magazines/books to know what is new. They like to visit a variety of stores even if they have no immediate intention of making a purchase
Sensation seekers	Aesthetic elements in clothing (e.g., taste, color, design, coordinating) are important to this group. They are interested in color coordination and believe they have good taste in choosing clothing products. Aesthetic aspects of clothing are important to them when making purchase decisions
Utilitarian consumers	Members of this segment are highly concerned about comfort and the functionality of the clothing. They primarily choose clothing because it is a necessity, their purchases are planned. These consumers think in utilitarian terms and weigh value and functionality higher than the other segments
Conspicuous consumers	These consumers have a strong belief in the value of prestige or high-priced brands and products. They value clothing that is of high quality and is associated with high social status. They purchase high-priced, high-prestige brands because of the acknowledgment it brings from others

Source: Ko et al. (2007).

LEARNING OBJECTIVE #3:

Which consumer segments can be found across different countries to be targeted with standardized products and services?

CONSUMER TYPES

National boundaries have long served as convenient ways to identify market segments. More recently, companies increasingly target segments across boundaries. A newer method used to identify market segments involves finding concentrations of global, glocal, or local consumers. These individuals have been influenced by cultural circumstances, history, the local political system, and economic conditions.

Global Consumers

Many consumers in different nations earn similar incomes and hold the same social status levels. These individuals often exhibit common purchasing patterns, suggesting the presence of an international market segment consisting of global consumers. These consumers typically live in developed countries; however, this segment also includes wealthy consumers in developing and even less-developed countries, especially when those individuals have access to international media and the Internet (Cleveland and Laroche, 2007).

Global consumers focus less on price and instead buy products that meet global quality standards. They are often located in urban settings and exhibit high levels of **cosmopolitanism**. These **high-cosmopolitanism** consumers consider themselves as members of a larger global community rather than as merely maintaining an allegiance to a local culture and community. Global consumers wear similar clothes, use technology in similar ways, and consume similar entertainment. They watch for the newest American blockbuster movie to appear at the local theater on their iPhones while sipping Cokes and wearing designer jeans (Hannerz, 1990).

cosmopolitanism: the view that a person is a member of a larger global community rather than merely maintaining an allegiance to a local culture and close-by circumstances

High-cosmopolitanism consumers view themselves as members of a larger global community rather than as merely maintaining an allegiance to a local culture and community

GLOBAL CONSUMERS AND INTERNET USAGE SEGMENTATION

Internet usage and e-commerce (including mobile commerce) continue to grow.[4] Table 6.5 presents the top twenty countries according to the number of Internet users. Online shoppers around the world share similar traits and serve as a prime example of global consumers. Internet shoppers worldwide are similar in regard to their desire for convenience, impulsivity, and exhibit more favorable attitudes toward direct marketing and advertising. They tend to be wealthier, younger, and are heavier users of e-mail along with the Internet. At the same time, each part of the world remains unique in social norms, culture, and infrastructure. Such differences may cause the profiles of Internet shoppers and non-shoppers to differ across national boundaries (Brashear et al., 2009). Internet usage may be an important segmentation factor, especially for such e-commerce activities as marketing communications, online shopping, mobile commerce, or health communications.

TABLE 6.5   Number of Internet Users: Top Twenty Countries

No.	Country	Population 2016 Est.	Internet Users June 16	Internet Penetration (%)	Growth (*) 2000–2016 (%)	Facebook Users June 16
1	China	1,378,561,591	721,434,547	52.30	3,106.40	1,800,000
2	India	1,266,883,598	462,124,989	36.50	9,142.50	157,000,000
3	United States	323,995,528	286,942,362	88.60	200.90	201,000,000
4	Brazil	206,050,242	139,111,185	67.50	2,682.20	111,000,000
5	Indonesia	258,316,051	132,700,000	51.40	6,535.00	88,000,000
6	Japan	126,464,583	115,111,595	91.00	144.50	26,000,000
7	Russia	146,358,055	103,147,691	70.50	3,227.30	12,000,000
8	Nigeria	186,879,760	97,210,000	52.00	48,505.00	16,000,000
9	Germany	80,722,792	71,727,551	88.90	198.90	31,000,000
10	Mexico	123,166,749	69,000,000	56.00	2,443.90	69,000,000
11	Bangladesh	162,855,651	63,290,000	38.90	63,190.00	21,000,000
12	United Kingdom	64,430,428	60,273,385	93.50	291.40	39,000,000
13	Iran	82,801,633	56,700,000	68.50	22,580.00	17,200,000
14	France	66,836,154	55,860,330	83.60	557.20	33,000,000
15	Philippines	102,624,209	54,000,000	52.60	2,600.00	54,000,000
16	Vietnam	95,261,021	49,063,762	51.50	24,431.90	40,000,000
17	Turkey	80,274,604	46,196,720	57.50	2,209.80	46,000,000
18	Korea, South	49,180,776	45,314,248	92.10	138.00	17,000,000
19	Thailand	68,200,824	41,000,000	60.10	1,682.60	41,000,000
20	Italy	62,007,540	39,211,518	63.20	197.10	30,000,000
	TOP 20 Countries	4,931,871,789	2,709,419,883	54.90	903.70	1,051,000,000
	Rest of the World	2,408,287,703	966,404,930	40.10	961.40	628,433,530
	Total World Users	7,340,159,492	3,675,824,813	50.10	918.30	1,679,433,530

Source: Internet World Stats. Retrieved from www.internetworldstats.com/top20.htm.

GLOCAL CONSUMERS

The word "glocal" combines the words "global" and "local." It reflects dual consumption patterns. Glocal consumers buy global products, but the purchase represents a special occasion rather than a typical purchase. They may be inclined to seek out products that mimic global products but ones that are priced slightly lower. They may be of a lower socioeconomic status, but their purchasing preferences also reflect strong ties to the local community and local consumption. Glocal consumers are often rural migrants who are relatively new to an urban setting and to the new purchasing opportunities present in that environment.

Glocal consumers tend to shop at the neighborhood corner markets, drink traditional beverages, and enjoy local cultural entertainment. They occasionally go to KFC for a meal or watch an American film. Glocals are more likely to purchase local versions of foreign goods and services, such as staying at a local hotel that mimics a Western chain. International marketers can devise advertisements with glocal themes that appeal to these markets (Hung et al., 2007).

LOCAL CONSUMERS

Local consumers rarely consume foreign products. For either economic or taste reasons, these consumers maintain traditional consumption patterns. Many local consumers live in rural settings where they only infrequently have the opportunity to purchase foreign goods. These consumers often exhibit high levels of **ethnocentrism**, or the strongly held belief that one's culture is superior to others. Ethnocentrism is, in many ways, the opposite of cosmopolitanism. Ethnocentric consumers generally exhibit a tendency to avoid purchasing foreign-produced products (Shankarmahesh, 2006).

ethnocentrism: the strongly held belief that one's culture is superior to others

The country of Uganda has one of the highest rates of alcohol consumption in the world. For many locals, the drink of preference is not foreign but local drafts made from some combination of distilled sorghum, millet, maize, sugar, bananas, and pineapples. Even the local word for any sort of alcoholic drink, *waragi*, is a corruption of the colonialist British "war gin" into a more inclusive, Ugandan word. The preference for local spirits reflects a typical local consumer consumption pattern (Smith, 2009).

GREEN MARKETING AND SUSTAINABILITY-ORIENTED SEGMENTS

Recently, an increasing number of more environmentally friendly products have been developed in the international arena. When conducting a market segmentation program for these items, the distinction may be drawn between consumer preferences for green products when as a matter of choice versus when it becomes a matter of necessity.

CONSUMER PREFERENCES

One of the primary challenges facing green marketers has been consumer unwillingness to spend more for environmentally safe products. In essence, the majority of customers only purchase green products when the item maintains the same level of price, quality, convenience, and performance (Dawkins, 2004).

GREEN BY NECESSITY

In bottom-of-the-pyramid nations, sustainability often becomes a driving force in purchases. Any item that saves or reuses water, runs on solar power or renewable batteries, or helps in some other way to preserve natural resources has a better chance of being accepted and purchased. Part of the reason is that such products also save the consumer money. A growing amount of evidence suggests that sustainable products create one of the largest marketing opportunities in nations where the majority of citizens live below the poverty line.

SC Johnson has focused on developing sustainable agricultural processes for the production of a key ingredient, pyrethrum, for the company's botanical pesticides. The company sources much of this ingredient, which is made from chrysanthemums, from East Africa. Working with farmers in the region, the company established sustainable practices that ensure profits along with the long-term viability of the crop for East African farmers.[5]

In sum, numerous forces influence segmentation processes by influencing what consumers want or need, how much money they have to spend, and subsequently the willingness to spend that money. These factors can be used to develop regional and national segmentation strategies.

USAGE SEGMENTATION

Consumer segmentation can be based on the frequency of usage by groups that purchase the product or service, including the company's best customers, average users, and casual or light users. The objective will be to provide the highest level of service to the best customers while promoting the company to the other two groups, in the attempt to maximize sales to all groups. In the hospitality industry, hotels in some countries offer frequency programs for vacationers and those who travel more often. For other consumers, taking a trip and staying in a hotel may be a once-in-a-lifetime experience.

INTERNATIONAL BUSINESS-TO-BUSINESS MARKET SEGMENTATION

The primary goals of business segmentation efforts are to provide better customer service and to group similar organizations into clusters to enhance marketing efforts. Table 6.6 identifies methods used to segment business-to-business markets.

SEGMENTATION BY INDUSTRY

Many industries extend past national boundaries. Identifying segments by industry, such as health, automotive, financial, or clothing, represents a common approach in international marketing. Marketing employees break segments down into smaller subcomponents. An organization selling small appliances such as radios, mobile devices, or hair dryers accounts for differences in the electricity available, such as alternating versus direct current, when specifying market segments. Major financial and insurance providers, including the Italian provider Generali Group, offer financial products and services that vary by industry need.[6]

TABLE 6.6   Criteria of Segmenting Business-to-Business Markets

Industry
Size
Geographic Location
Product Usage
Customer Value

SEGMENTATION BY SIZE

Market segments may be identified based on the size of a company's sales volume or its number of employees. Large firms with 100,000 employees do not have the same needs as smaller companies with 100 or fewer employees. Typically, selling to a large firm focuses on the company's purchasing department. For smaller firms, the owner or general manager often makes purchase decisions and becomes the target of marketing messages. The marketing team assesses the number of smaller and larger purchasers in a nation or region before developing a program to reach these buyers.

Economic circumstances often dictate the number and types of business organizations of each size (small, medium, large) in a country. Cultural or institutional traditions might also exert influence. Banks in Spain follow a unique organizational structure, called *cajas*, with roots going back to the Middle Ages. Banks are traditionally linked to cities or regions, and some may be controlled by the Catholic Church.[7] Poverty often leads to many small, barely sustainable family businesses. Political-legal conditions favor corporations and multinational firms in countries that lean toward free enterprise, as opposed to communist or state-directed economies.

For years, FedEx did not segment business-to-business customers. In the mid-1990s, realizing that a lack of segmentation was hindering its growth, the company began segmenting based on account size. By 2005, the company transitioned to one of the most complex segmentation processes in the industry. Mark Colombo, vice president of strategic marketing and corporate strategy, noted, "We look at sizes of segments; opportunities with customers; whether a customer is new; whether we're penetrating, growing, or retaining a relationship; what industry they're in; what distribution model they sell products through; and their geographic locations" (Kontzer, 2005).

GEOGRAPHIC LOCATION

As with consumer segmentation, identifying business market segments by geographic location can be a successful tactic. This includes larger distinctions such as the Pacific Rim as well as more specific differences, including those countries that use the *euro* as a form of currency as opposed to those that do not. Within a given nation, regional geographic distinctions are drawn in order to discover target markets, such as the Basque region that spans the border between France and Spain. United States-based global giant General Electric offers numerous business products and services to customers throughout the world and has focused recently on offering infrastructure services to customers in northern and south-eastern Asia, segmenting markets based on the needs of these regions.[8]

PRODUCT USAGE

Business markets may be segmented based on the manner in which companies use the goods and services. Some services, including those in the financial and hospitality industries, offer more than one use to customers. In the automobile rental industry, various nations have differing laws regarding the rental process. Cars may be used for business trips, vacations, or entertaining clients. Car fleets are also rented to various organizations. These product usage factors may be used to distinguish various target markets. Thermocouple Instruments, part of the British Rototherm Group, offers a wide selection of business-to-business products pertaining to temperature assemblies, thermostats, and flow instrumentation.[9] The company bases its marketing mix on the types of product usage present in various target segments.

CUSTOMER VALUE

Marketers locating business-to-business segments often ascribe values to customers. Normally, in-depth data about each business customer will be available. The marketing team assigns a value to each individual business through sales records and other sources of data and information, placing them into low-, medium-, and high-value groups (Clow and Baack, 2010). Customer value ratings may also be assigned within or to regions, such as South America or the eurozone.

The telecommunications industry features customer value segmentation, for both consumers and business markets. With the high amount of brand switching (also known as *churn*) to new carriers in the industry, the value segmentation can be linked to the percentage of consumers who are likely to switch as a guide to company marketing activities. For the high-value, high-churn segment, the focus should be on aggressive incentives to retain the business. For high-value, low-churn businesses or the low-value, high-churn business no action will be required (Bayer, 2010).

Firms that sell virtually the same goods or services to both consumers and businesses, such as laptop computers, engage in dual channel marketing.

dual channel marketing: selling virtually the same goods or services to both consumers and businesses

spin-off sales: sales that occur when individuals who buy a particular brand at work have positive experiences and, as a result, purchase the same brand for personal use

DUAL CHANNEL MARKETING

Firms that sell virtually the same goods or services to both consumers and businesses engage in **dual channel marketing**. The approach fits several situations. One common scenario occurs when a product sold in business markets is then adapted to consumer markets. Products including digital cameras, calculators, computers, fax machines, and cell phones that were first sold to businesses and then later to consumers. Also, when individuals who buy a particular brand at work have positive experiences and, as a result, purchase the same brand for personal use, **spin-off sales** occur.

One marketing decision involves how to represent the product in each channel. Similarities between the two markets may be featured unless there are significant differences. When consumers and business buyers value different product attributes or desire different benefits, the marketing team customizes messages for the separate markets. In most cases, business customers and consumers seek the same basic benefits from products.

Dual channel marketing results from economic development. Emerging economies, newly industrialized countries, and nations with more developed economic systems feature more businesses combined with a larger number of individuals with disposable incomes. An Italian sales representative who travels throughout the Eurozone may discover she enjoys lodging at the Holiday Inn. When it is time for her family to take a vacation, she might seek out that chain when making travel arrangements. The same scenario will be less likely to take place in least-developed nations. Consequently, the economic status of a country affects potential dual channel markets.

Dual channel marketing creates a major competitive advantage because products are sold in both markets, in terms of both domestic operations and international marketing. Adding customers leads to economies of scale in production expenses and synergies in messages delivered to consumers and other businesses (Imber and Toffler, 2000).

LEARNING OBJECTIVE #4:

How can the marketing team use regional and national segmentation methods to improve a company's global marketing program?

REGIONAL AND NATIONAL SEGMENTATION

Based on the methods for identifying marketing segments that have been selected, international market segmentation programs are developed. Some might be created for large regions, such as the three members of NAFTA or the members of the Eurozone. Others target individual nations and regions within individual countries, including the cultural clusters depicted in Figure 6.8. In addition, language and regional differences may be used to separate distinct target markets. Further adjustments are made to account for regional differences. An analysis of the definition of the term "market segment" illuminates some of these nuances.

WANTS AND NEEDS

Individual consumers experience wants and needs in vastly different ways depending on specific circumstances. In earthquake-stricken Nepal in 2015, wants and needs were reduced to the most basic of human survival issues: water, food, clothing, and shelter. Medical care became nearly a luxury that only a select few could find or afford. Many underdeveloped countries have populations where the vast majority live at this subsistence level. A want in one country may not translate to another. While in many countries, ultrasound meets the desire parents have to know a baby's gender, such is not always the case. Many health clinics in poorer sections of India refuse to identify the gender of a baby during an ultrasound. The concern is that men may divorce a woman when the child is female (Crosby, 2011).

MONEY TO SPEND

Per capita income, or the total income in a country divided by its total population, as displayed in Table 6.7, varies widely by nation. Members of a potential market segment may experience wants and needs in sufficient numbers, yet the ability to pay limits the viability of the market. Per capita income, when combined with the degree of income distribution as dictated by the economic system, dramatically affects the presence or absence of potential target markets. The Gini coefficient index (displayed on the right hand side of the Table) indicates the level of income inequality within a country. A higher Gini coefficient indicates a higher degree of income inequality. A coefficient of 1.0 would represent a single individual holding all of the wealth; a 0.0 would represent perfect income equality or distribution.

TABLE 6.7   Selected Per Capita Incomes in Various Countries

Nation	Per Capita Income (2011 PP$ per day)	Life Expectancy from Birth	Gini Coefficient Index
Belgium	$48.90	81.0	27.7
Brazil	$19.30	75.3	51.3
Chile	$21.60	79.3	47.7
Colombia	$14.30	74.4	50.8
Denmark	$51.90	80.7	28.2
Ethiopia	$3.70	65.0	65.5
Greece	$21.70	81.0	36.0
Russian Federation	$22.40	71.2	37.7
Turkey	$18.70	75.8	41.9
United States	$68.90	78.7	41.5

Source: "Key Development Data and Statistics," The World Bank. Retrieved from www.worldbank.org.

The World Bank, Key Development Data and Statistics, www.worldbank.org, 2015 Data except 2016 data for the United States, Colombia, and Turkey (2015 data were incomplete) (http://databank.worldbank.org/data/reports.aspx?source=world-development-indicators)

WILLINGNESS TO SPEND

The figures in Table 6.7 indicate a wide disparity among select nations which in turn affects wants and needs, money to spend, and the willingness to spend money. Consumers in Denmark and the United States are more likely to desire many more items beyond necessities. Sundries and luxuries may be made available to a number of patrons. In Greece and similar nations with less-dramatic differences in wealth, sundries would be desired by many, with a limited number wishing to obtain luxuries. Haiti and Zimbabwe exhibit a far different type of economy, one in which the vast majority of citizens generate incomes at the bottom-of-the-pyramid.

LANGUAGE

Citizens in many parts of the world speak a common language, such as Spanish. The individuals and countries may constitute a large market segment. In other circumstances, an individual country may feature numerous languages. Switzerland features four official languages: German, French, Italian, and Romansch. India recognizes one official language, Hindi, but the number of other languages spoken across the nation may number in the low thousands. The continent of Africa has complex over-laps between languages and countries. Many of the world's complicated languages are found there, including Xhosa, the "click" language of the San, or "bushmen," of the Kalahari Desert (Ahlstrom, 2011). The country of South Africa alone has eleven official languages: IsiZulu, IsiXhosa, Afrikaans, Sepedi, English, Setswana, Sesotho, Xitsonga, isiNdebele, Tshivenda, and siSwati.[10]

Successful marketing to African consumers requires navigating these complicated lan-guages. The goal of the segmentation analysis would be to make sure that the products and messages match with a viable group of people speaking a common language.

REGIONALLY BASED MARKET SEGMENTS

The segmentation variables discussed above can be used to group countries into regions. Countries in several regions of the world have similar cultures, consumption patterns, and languages, which leads to regional groupings. Often these groupings are based on culture. Two versions of the clusters that have been suggested as groupings are displayed in Table 6.8.

TABLE 6.8 Cultural Clusters

GLOBE Societal Clusters	Ronen and Shenkar Clusters
Nordic Europe (three countries)	Near Eastern
Eastern Europe (eight countries)	Nordic
Sub-Saharan Africa (five countries)	Germanic
Southern Asia (six countries)	Anglo
Latin Europe (six countries)	Latin European
Germanic Europe (six countries)	Latin American
Latin America (ten countries)	Far Eastern
Middle East (five countries)	Arab
Confucian Asia (six countries)	Independent

Source: Ronen and Shenkar (1985).

The GLOBE academic study and the research by Ronen and Shenkar (1985) revealed the following cultural clusters.

These groupings allow for regional segmentation based on similarities across markets. Companies introduce products across the regions, knowing that consumption patterns and business processes will be fairly consistent within the region. Success in one coun-try within the region leads to skills that transfer well within that cluster. Expanding within the cluster will be less costly than expanding to countries in another cluster.

SEGMENTATION AND THE BOTTOM-OF-THE-PYRAMID

The final global segment consists of the 4 billion people worldwide that live on $2 per day or less, the bottom-of-the-pyramid consumers (see Figures 6.2 and 6.3) (Prahalad, 2006). These individuals experience wants and needs but with only limited money to spend. Still, opportunities do exist. Even with a small profit margin, the large size and equivalent large potential volume make this segment increasingly attractive. A $0.01

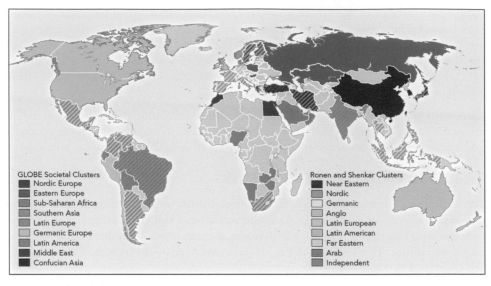

MAP 6.1   Cultural Clusters

margin might result in millions of dollars in profit. To segment this group effectively, companies adjust the marketing mix, including changes in products, prices, and delivery systems, and, in some cases, brands. The goal of these changes becomes to create the capacity to consume by lowering the barriers to purchase.

PRODUCTS

One approach to marketing to bottom-of-the-pyramid consumers involves changing the product, either in terms of the design of the item to meet a slightly different need or by simply lowering the quantity offered per purchase. In India, for example, local companies produce more eco-friendly, single-usage packages or sachets of laundry detergents; foreign multinational corporations now also produce these items.[11] This packaging lowers the price, allowing consumers with limited incomes to purchase the product.

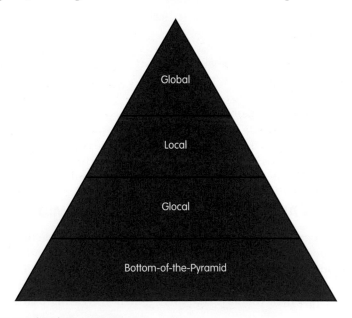

FIGURE 6.3   International Income Segments

PRICING

Pricing may be adjusted to match a market segment. While it may be helpful to lower a price to allow for expression of demand, some evidence suggests that persons at the bottom-of-the-pyramid are also brand conscious. Therefore, pricing based on price–quality relationships remains viable.

Exchange systems, or the methods of facilitating payment, vary within the economics of bottom-of-the-pyramid countries. For example, more extensive use of *barter* whereby an individual trades one good or service for another often takes place. Use of money *or* currency will be limited to the customers who are able to accumulate sufficient amounts to make payments. Further, debit cards rather than actual currency are the norm in many countries. The use of credit may be more dependent on individual relationships than on any company offering such a service (credit cards) to facilitate purchases. Providing credit for purchases that seem relatively small, the equivalent of $10 to $15, can help create the capacity to consume.

exchange systems: the methods of facilitating payment for a product or service

Companies targeting the bottom-of-the-pyramid market often seek to reduce costs to create price reductions. Cost-cutting results from changes in product design. Hindustan Unilever Ltd's marketing team set the goal of lowering the price of ice cream in India in order to reach low-income consumers. Realizing that refrigeration constitutes 40% of the cost, the company introduced a salt-based heat shield that was less expensive to produce, provided more insulation, and contained fewer pollutants, which reduced the costs and the price (Boyer, 2003).

DELIVERY

Reaching target markets involves finding delivery systems that match a local region. This includes identifying traffic systems, the presence of electricity on a routine basis, and more basic elements such as running water. Product modifications match delivery systems when effectively reaching target markets of low-income members of a country. Bottom-of-the-pyramid segments often face problems with electricity access, which necessitates innovations in refrigeration, batteries, and more-efficient energy consumption.

PROMOTION

Promoting products to market segments at the bottom-of-the-pyramid creates distinct challenges. These consumers are less likely to be exposed to mass media and may not be easily reached. Literacy and overall levels of education may be limiting factors. Word-of-mouth endorsements and other less-traditional promotional tactics become valuable tools to contact and persuade these customers to make purchases. At the same time, for many brands, bottom-of-the-pyramid consumers already exhibit brand awareness and demand for the product, making promotion more focused on messages that remind or inform potential customers about a new, lower price.

Even with a small profit margin, the large size and equivalent large potential volume of consumers making less than $1 per day make the bottom-of-the-pyramid segment increasingly attractive.

LEARNING OBJECTIVE #5:

How to assess the market potential of a segment?

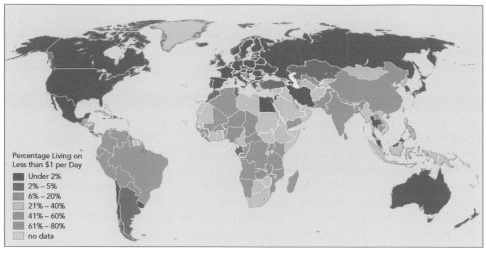

Percentage Living on Less than $1 per Day
- Under 2%
- 2% – 5%
- 6% – 20%
- 21% – 40%
- 41% – 60%
- 61% – 80%
- no data

MAP 6.2 The Percentage of Country Population Living on Less than $1 per Day

A MARKET SEGMENT ANALYSIS

Three terms may be used to help understand the potential of a target market. *Market potential* represents the total number of individuals or businesses that could purchase a product in a given area. *Market demand* consists of the total sales of all brands sold in an area or within a product industry. *Company or brand demand* is the estimated demand for a company's brand. Company demand may also be called *estimated market share*.

The following statistics would emerge from an analysis of the potential sales of solar-powered personal computers in South Africa:

Market potential = 27 million households that might purchase solar personal computers

Market demand = 3 million households that have purchased solar personal computers

Sales of Sony solar computers = 750,000 units

$$Company\ demand = \frac{Sales\ of\ Sony\ computers}{Market\ demand}$$

$$= \frac{750\ thousand}{3\ million}$$

$$= 25\ \%$$

These calculations indicate that Sony's market share, or its company or brand demand, is one-fourth of all computers sold in South Africa. One additional factor may be of interest: the product's *penetration rate*.

$$Penetration = \frac{Market\ demand}{Market\ potential} = \frac{3\ million}{27\ million} = 11.11\%$$

Calculating these statistics may assist the marketing team in making decisions about entering nearby nations or expanding operations within South Africa.

ASSESSING MARKET POTENTIAL

When examining the potential of a region for expansion, five market potential factors should be assessed:

1. availability of financial resources,

2. availability of potential substitutes,

3. ability to offer attractive benefits,

4. current product availability,

5. consumer awareness of the product.

When the marketing team examines the market penetration of South Africa, the firm would either expect to provide the necessary financial resources or would believe access exists to obtain those resources in nearby nations. Based on the Sony market share within South Africa, the company's leaders would assess whether a 25% share would be sufficient to expand into a new country, or if too many potential substitutes are available. Then, Sony's marketers, working with production and other parts of the company, would seek to understand whether the company's products could be differentiated in some way to offer attractive benefits. The competition would be assessed to identify all competitors that could affect current product availability. Finally, consumer awareness in the nation would be examined to determine whether those in the nation are *aware* of the value of a solar-powered personal computer, which continues to work during power outages and in remote regions where electricity is not available.

The target market or market segment for a solar-powered personal computer would be assessed, notably by examining the age, income, and educational level of potential consumers, and possibly by examining geographic factors. If the marketing team determines that sufficient potential exists, then expansion may be justified.

ASSESSMENT CRITERIA

A second method that may be used to study the potential benefits of entering a new market is to examine the segment across four criteria, as follows:

Measurability: Can the segment be quantified and identified?

Accessibility: Can the segment be reached?

Profitability: Is the segment large enough to generate profits?

Actionability: Can a marketing program be designed to stimulate interest and behavioral responses (purchases)?

No matter which method is used to evaluate the potential of a new market segment, the marketing team will consider the context. It may be that, in the short term, a market may not seem viable. The strategic question to be posed in those circumstances is whether entering might elicit benefits in the long range. For example, entering the market may preempt the competition from doing so, thereby gaining a first-mover advantage in a growing or emerging economy. In essence, the final decision to enter a new target market combines an understanding of current circumstances with other judgments.

When an international company is able to capitalize on these opportunities and match them with innovative products, international marketing success often results. Montreal's L'Oréal preempted international competitors by introducing the world's first two-step hair coloring product, L'Oréal Paris' Couleur Experte, by becoming the lead innovator and first-mover in the industry. The development of the patent for the product, along with superb international marketing, led to quick consumer acceptance and marketplace success.[12]

ETHICAL ISSUES IN INTERNATIONAL SEGMENTATION

Many of the ethical issues associated with domestic markets also appear in discussions of international segmentation. For example, one common complaint is that any segmentation program featuring demographics reinforces stereotypes. This tendency might emerge when ethnicity becomes the basis for a market segment, especially when marketing messages play to stereotypical images, both in the dominant culture and in any subculture or counterculture.

A closely related issue occurs in the area of gender discrimination. Females are confined to submissive and subservient roles in many cultures. When a company from a different country, one with opposing views, markets to women, the question arises as to which cultural customs should be observed. For instance, packages and labels for feminine hygiene products may be strongly regulated based on cultural norms; a company may at the same time wish to be able to portray the benefits of the products, however, especially when those benefits include health advantages. The package might also assist less-educated women in identifying exactly what they are buying through the use of a drawing or photo, but the problem remains that any such figure or image might be culturally objectionable to some.

Targeting lower-income segments may be viewed by some critics as being the process of creating overconsumption by people who least can afford to do so. This includes encouraging purchases of less-healthy food products such as fast food, clothes designed to create status rather than to offer functionality, and modes of transportation that are less practical but at the same time are associated with a higher social standing.

Conversely, market segmentation programs may limit access to certain goods or services, especially when the process takes places at the nation level. When only the rich are entitled to educational services or access to a free Internet service, there may be ethical problems associated with a form of discrimination based solely on income or entitlement.

CHAPTER 6: REVIEW AND RESOURCES

Strategic Implications

An international marketing program includes every element of a domestic program. Marketing professionals identify target groups that match with tactics designed to discover the most viable audiences for products and services. Doing so requires an investigation of the regional or national context, in terms of culture, economic conditions, and local customer characteristics and preferences. Completing these processes allows for a program targeted at those who are most likely to welcome a new product or service to a given area.

Effective market segmentation programs, whether domestic, international, or both, require an alignment of the elements in the marketing mix. Marketing professionals match products, prices, distribution systems, and promotional efforts with target markets and position these elements accordingly. At the global level, top managers make strategic decisions with regard to standardization or adaptation. Ford features a standardized international global brand while Proctor & Gamble adapts products to individual nations and cultures.

The strategic direction of the company dictates either a differentiation or a low-cost approach to product development, pricing, and promotional programs. Companies may seek to serve a more general population through differentiation, presenting items as being different and better than competitor products. Others may choose to compete based on low cost to serve the needs of consumers that are price conscious and those that are constrained by their incomes. The local culture has a strong impact on this choice.

Tactical Implications

Numerous tactical efforts are undertaken to support the strategic position dictated by strategies. For example, the product's packaging and label will be altered to fit the legal and cultural dictates of a nation and a target market. Legal requirements vary as to any promise of a product benefit as well as labeling of content. Promotional programs would also be adjusted. This may lead to segmentation approaches based on usage or benefits.

Cultural preferences influence other tactical choices. Beyond the actual products, pricing methods and discounting programs may vary substantially. Some cultures take a dim view of the use of coupons. What may be considered a "sale" price might be determined by local laws and customs. Many cultures inject bargaining into purchase processes. The marketing team accounts for these nuances as well as exchange and payment systems. Further, some cultures and nations strongly discourage comparative advertising. Distribution systems are adjusted to local conditions and the infrastructure present in international markets. Many countries do not have big box super stores. Local small companies dominate instead, which affects order sizes and methods of transportation to be used.

Additional tactics include the selection of sales methods. This would include attending trade shows. When presenting a product to a potential new target market, company employees should first understand that in some international trade shows that executives attend, sales are made on the spot. In others, only information will be collected by lower-level operatives.

In situations where the target market consists of members at the bottom-of-the-pyramid, tactics with regard to packaging may lead to a smaller size and a lower price. As has been noted, many consumers in this market do respond to strong brands, which may at the strategic level indicate that a price–quality relationship focus is viable. The tactics that might succeed would potentially include pricing discounts or offers.

Operational Implications

Day-to-day operations will be influenced by cultural imperatives, electives, and exclusives. Sales force activities, including calling on prospective clients, will be dictated by the culture that is present. This includes greeting prospective clients, engaging in social activities, making the actual sales presentation, dining, and even exchanging business cards. Careful preparation will be made before making contact with potential buyers in a new target market. This includes awareness of differences in language and slang.

Other operational activities associated with target markets include promotions. Consequently, any advertisement, coupon, website posting, sponsorship, public relations event, or alternative marketing tactic such as product placement in a television program or movie should be carefully inspected by a cultural assimilator to make certain the promotion meets the standards of the local culture.

Company activities will be adjusted to meet the norms of a local culture, including understanding, when to close for holidays and adapting to religious preferences and cultural nuances such as whether and when to make eye contact, and the physical distance to maintain between a buyer and seller during the purchasing process.

In summary, market segmentation and target market selection activities in international settings may be viewed as being "distinctively similar" to those in domestic markets. The processes used to identify target markets will be largely the same; differences emerge when segments are assessed to understand how to adapt the marketing mix to meet the needs and wants of a group with money to spend and the willingness to spend that money on a product being sent to a new country or region.

TERMS

market	ethnocentrism
market segmentation	dual channel marketing
STP approach	spin-off sales
market segment	exchange systems
cosmopolitanism	

REVIEW QUESTIONS

1. Define markets.

2. Define market segment and market segmentation.

3. Describe the usual steps in an international market segmentation process.

4. What factors are used to identify consumer market segments?

5. What factors are used to segment business-to-business markets?

6. What do the terms *dual channel marketing* and *spin-off sales* mean?

7. Define the global consumers, local consumers, and glocal consumer concepts.

8. How is cosmopolitanism related to ethnocentrism?

9. How can the marketing mix be adjusted to meet the needs of those at the bottom-of-the-pyramid?

10. What types of consumers are most likely to buy green or sustainable products in industrialized countries?

11. What ethical issues are present in market segmentation processes?

DISCUSSION QUESTIONS

1. Three methods can be used to select employees to sell products or manage marketing operations in foreign markets. *Expatriates* are persons employed by the exporting company who are asked to move or travel to foreign lands. *Locals* are individuals from the target country. *Third-party nationals* are persons who live in neither the home country nor the target country. Which do you think would be best suited to use in an international marketing program focusing on developing new target markets? Why?

2. Think of circumstances (industries or products) that serve as examples of when to use the following types of business segmentation:

   • Industry

   • Size

   • Geographic location

   • Product usage

   • Customer value

ANALYTICAL AND INTERNET EXERCISES

1. Visit the Project GLOBE website (globeproject.com). Write a report about how you believe information from the project can be used to identify market segments, based on the information about market segmentation in this chapter.

2. Choose a country from three of the regions presented in Table 6.7. Using the Internet, collect as much information as you believe is needed to identify the potential for market segments based on age, income, and product usage for the following products:

   • bottled water

   • iPod or similar device

   • frozen pizza to be baked at home

   • life insurance

3. Calculate company demand and the penetration rate using the following statistics:

   Market potential = 130 million

   Market demand = 41 million

   Company sales = 17 million

Explain what the numbers mean and why they are important.

4. Using the Internet, identify consumer market segments in India for two types of music:

    - traditional Indian folk songs

    - music from other countries, including classical, rock, hip-hop, and country and western

    Then, match each of these forms of music using the various forms of consumer market segmentation presented in this chapter.

5. Visit the ACORN website (acorn.caci.co.uk). Using the trial option, find out how ACORN segmentation can be used in designing marketing programs, or localizing marketing offering. Try to find out if similar tools exist in other countries.

STUDENT STUDY SITE

Visit **https://study.sagepub.com/baack2e** to access these free additional learning tools:

- Web Quizzes
- eFlashcards
- SAGE Journal Articles
- Country Fact Sheets
- Chapter Outlines
- Interactive Maps

CASE 6

UNIQLO: Apparel and Segmentation

UNIQLO is a Japanese clothing company, often described as a Japanese version of the GAP, or "the Ikea of clothes." It was originally founded in Yamaguchi, Japan in 1949 as a textiles manufacturer. UNIQLO's first store opened in Japan in 1984. As an SPA (Specialty-store retailer of Private-label Apparel) controlling the entire clothes-making process from design through manufacture and retail, UNIQLO offers high-quality casualwear for men, women, and children at reasonable prices. UNIQLO's name comes from the words "Unique Clothing." It is a distinct brand with a wide competitive set including Gap and Primark at the basics end and Zara at a more premium level. The company operates in a space which is not only crowded in terms of competing retailers, but also in the context of marketing messages trying to target similar consumer segments. As a result, the company's marketing team works hard to get its message across. Marketing innovations such as the Uniqlock and the Loop are useful in helping to build communities and raise the presence of the UNIQLO brand.

The company's vision is to become the world's number one casual clothing brand. One key element of this vision is the establishment of a significant, growing, and profitable overseas business. The first UNIQLO international store opened in the United Kingdom in 2001. By August 2016, UNIQLO International constituted approximately 45% of total UNIQLO sales, with 958 stores (versus 837 stores in Japan). Typical store size is 1,600 square meters, roughly, 16,160 square feet. Flagship stores are larger and these are located in key urban locations. At the beginning of 2017, UNIQLO was present in seventeen countries including Japan, and offered online shopping and shipping to many more, even those where there were no UNIQLO stores.

The founder and Chairman of UNIQLO, Tadash Yanai, and the richest man in Japan, understands that "we cannot win a dominant position in global markets simply by imitating other companies. Instead, true to our unique clothing concept, we seek to create clothes of the future with the potential to change the world."[13] This outsized philosophy is echoed in the company's mission statement: "To create truly great clothing with new and unique value, and to enable people all over the world to experience the joy, happiness and satisfaction of wearing such great clothes."

UNIQLO's global expansion has encountered some failures. In 2001, the first overseas UNIQLO outlets were opened in Shanghai and shortly after, four more in London UK. The retailer set its sights on capturing customers in the United States and the United Kingdom, but a year-and-a-half of poor sales later most of the new stores were closed. Tadashi Yanai told CNN several years later that the number one reason behind such a disappointing international performance was UNIQLO's lack of brand recognition.

At present, UNIQLO has successfully established a unique strategic positioning in the apparel industry in most countries of operation. It provides basic items as "components" to be arranged with other components by the customers, yet offers high-quality items at an extremely low price. The diversity of shoppers attracted to UNIQLO reflects its meticulous engineering. Mass allure permeates UNIQLO's brand, underscored by its tagline, "Made for All." UNIQLO offers colorful, logo-free designs that appeal to a wide range of

(Continued)

(Continued)

consumers but this does not mean that everyone likes UNIQLO's clothing. The brand aims to design low-cost garments with high-fashion sensibility, yielding clothes that can complement both a faded pair of jeans and a designer coat. UNIQLO disguises the limited variety of products it makes by offering them in almost every color imaginable. "We have much fewer styles," says Odake, "especially when you compare us with companies like H&M or Topshop or Zara. That's the secret of why we can get better quality. We try to consolidate the fabric buys as much as possible. H&M sales are bigger, but we have bigger orders. We take huge quantities, and we have negotiation power."[14]

Patrons of UNIQLO often describe its clothing as classic, comfortable, wearable, and high quality sold at reasonable prices. UNIQLO draws people attracted by its specialized products, such as lightweight jackets and T-shirts that are designed to provide extra warmth in winter. However, not everybody buys UNIQLO, and the company needs to carefully select appropriate segments of consumers to target.

1. Discuss how issues of culture, language, climate, and religion would affect marketing programs for UNIQLO clothes in international markets.

2. Which segments should UNQILO target to avoid failure in new markets?

3. How could UNIQLO market its clothes to local and global consumers?

4. What potential market segments can you identify from the information provided in this case?

5. Would there be a market for bottom-of-the-pyramid customers? Why or why not?

7

INTERNATIONAL POSITIONING

LEARNING OBJECTIVES

After reading and studying this chapter, you should be able to answer the following questions:

1. What creates a product's positioning in the global marketplace?
2. What are the main approaches to international product positioning?
3. How can a product's position become an asset in an international marketing effort?
4. What additional challenges affect international product positioning programs?
5. What steps and tactics are used to establish positioning, evaluate positioning, and conduct repositioning in international markets?

IN THIS CHAPTER

Opening Vignette: The Expanding World of Hummus

OVERVIEW

THE EXPANDING WORLD OF HUMMUS

Long ago, consumption of hummus was largely reserved for consumers in the Middle East. In that region, the word translates into "chickpeas" (also known as garbanzo beans), a primary ingredient in the food although several variations also appear including *hummus bitaḥīna* which means "chickpeas with tahini." In one common form, chickpeas are cooked and mashed and then blended with tahini (a paste made from sesame seeds), olive oil, lemon juice, garlic and salt. Although chickpeas are a vegetable that have been cultivated throughout the Middle East and India for thousands of years, arguments arise as to which culture or country first created hummus (or hommos or hummos).

Hummus serves as a dip eaten with pita or flatbread and may be flavored with cumin or other spices. It can be combined with meat and dairy, making it popular in Israel and neighboring nations in the Palestine region. Patrons in Jordan and nearby countries dine on the ingredient for all three daily meals (breakfast, lunch, dinner).[1]

Chickpeas are a complete protein, similar to other combinations of grains and legumes. This makes hummus a food with a high iron and vitamin C content. It also contains beneficial amounts of vitamin B6 and folate and is an excellent source of protein, fiber, and potassium. Hummus is a useful food in vegan, vegetarian, and non-vegetarian diets.

The wide appeal of hummus has led to its distribution spreading worldwide. For example, Syrians in Canada's Arab *diaspora* prepare and consume hummus along with *falafel*, *kibbe*, and *tabbouleh*, even among the third- and fourth-generation offspring of the original immigrants (Magocsi, 1999: 1244). The use of hummus as a snack and dietary item has dramatically grown throughout Europe, aided in part by immigration rates.

At the same time, controversy has arisen. Disputes regarding which nation should have sole rights to the word itself have arisen between Israeli and Lebanese food producers. Proponents note that the term feta (cheese) is reserved for Greece and champagne belongs to a region in France. Boycotts of Israel include efforts to stop other countries from purchasing the country's version of the food (Wheeler, 2008).

Currently, companies including Sabra and Tribe have introduced versions of the product in a variety of countries. In 2016, Sabra faced a recall order in the United States by the Food and Drug Administration due to concerns about listeria contamination (Associated Press, 2016). At the same time, consumption of hummus continues to rise on a worldwide basis.

Hummus is consumed daily worldwide.

Questions for Students

1. How would the time of day influence the consumption of hummus in non-Middle Eastern countries?

2. Should a new company selling hummus emphasize price, taste, or some other feature when establishing international product positioning?

3. Which countries would have a natural advantage or disadvantage when selling hummus to consumers in other nations? Why?

OVERVIEW

The company name "Huawei" may be related to several different perceptions. Some consumers might think of the company and brand as being a high-quality option in the smart phone market, due to its high-quality data card. Others may express fears based on safety problems and recalls of other products manufactured in China. Others still have not formed an opinion. Product positioning, the focus of this chapter, summarizes these attitudes and beliefs. A product, company, or brand's position consists of the general perceptions the public has about it relative to the competition. The marketing goal of satisfying consumer needs with goods or services includes positioning, or how consumer assumptions that they will indeed be satisfied are met. Perceptions form the foundation of positioning.

This chapter starts with a discussion of the basic approaches to positioning in the international marketplace and the considerations involved. The next section describes international positioning efforts to affect consumer feelings and activities about a global business that includes views of the country of origin. Marketers consider culture, language, economic systems, political and legal systems, and infrastructure (see Figure 7.1) when creating approaches to reach international markets through various positioning efforts.

The chapter's next section describes the actual positioning process, including examples of domestic and international positioning maps, along with the incorporation of global competitors. The chapter concludes with a discussion of the ethical issues surrounding international positioning.

LEARNING OBJECTIVE #1:

What creates a product's positioning in the global marketplace?

THE NATURE OF INTERNATIONAL PRODUCT POSITIONING

Chapter 6 introduced the STP (segmentation, targeting, and positioning) process. Market segmentation identifies distinct consumer groups. Targeting selects the groups with which the company intends to engage. Positioning efforts are the final part of the program. Product positioning creates perceptions in consumer minds about the nature of a company and its products relative to those of competitors. Positioning plays a vital role in international marketing by helping a brand stand out among domestic and international competitors (Jaishankar and Oakenfull, 1999).

Product position summarizes consumer opinions regarding the specific features of the product or brand and encapsulates current perceptions of it. **Product positioning** states the intended goal going forward. Marketers design activities to shape or reshape a product's position. Many customers perceived the airline Virgin Blue in Australia as focused on meeting the needs of leisure fliers, which constituted the brand's position. The airline's marketers used the product positioning process to include meeting the needs of business travelers. To help establish this new position, the company introduced a new business cabin class and added flights on key

product position:
what summarizes consumer opinions regarding the specific features of the product

product positioning:
creating a perception in the consumer's mind regarding the nature of a company and its products relative to those of competitors

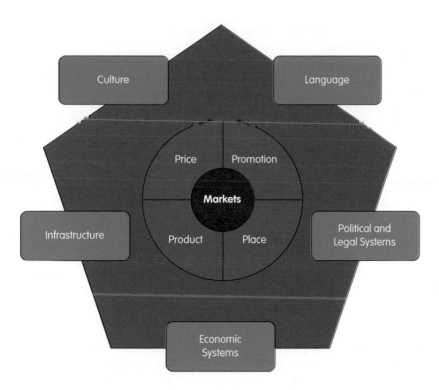

FIGURE 7.1   The International Marketing Context

routes for business travelers. The goal was to shift the company's position through positioning activities.[2]

Numerous variables influence positioning efforts, including product features along with its price, methods of distribution, packaging, support services provided, and consumer interactions with company employees. Two key elements of a product's position are the ways customers view the product or brand and the product or brand's standing relative to those of competitors.

LEARNING OBJECTIVE #2:

What are the main approaches to international product positioning?

POSITIONING STATEMENTS AND APPROACHES

A one- or two-sentence summary of a company's positioning strategy is the **positioning statement**. A positioning statement focuses on the primary benefits the product provides, such as the one made by Huawei: "To focus on our customers' market challenges and needs by providing excellent ICT solutions and services in order to consistently create maximum value for our customers."[3]

Effective positioning can be achieved in at least seven ways (see Table 7.1). In international marketing, emphasizing one of these approaches consistently across markets whenever possible will be the most advisable. This allows for lower

positioning statement: a one- or two-sentence summary of the company's positioning strategy

TABLE 7.1   Product Positioning Approaches

Product Attribute
Competitors
Use or Application
Price–Quality Relationship
Product User
Product Class
Cultural Symbol

production and marketing costs, reduced consumer confusion when visiting other markets, and can lead to increased marketing expertise in enhancing the product's position.

PRODUCT ATTRIBUTES

A trait or characteristic that distinguishes one product from others is a product attribute. The attribute can be used to position a product, such as a "reduced fat" food item or a "no ironing needed" feature for a piece of clothing. Marketing efforts concentrate on the attribute as the key selling point.

Japan's Sony Corporation expanded into foreign markets by emphasizing product features. The company consistently focused on picture quality as the key attribute driving successful international positioning. In 1968, Sony introduced the Trinitron. The television featured what was, for that time, revolutionary "color aperture grille cathode ray rubes" that generated a picture that was clearer than with other technologies. Following this international position based on the attribute of picture quality, Sony offered the Bravia flat screen television in 2005, again positioning the television as offering the best picture. In this case, the company promised "Color like no other."[4]

COMPETITORS

Marketers use competitors to establish position by contrasting the company's product against others. Legal and/or cultural pressures often limit direct contrasts with a competitor, such as through comparison advertising; however, competitor positioning may still be featured in other ways.

Companies in multiple countries face a complex and differing combination of competitors. Competition arises from other international brands or locally produced brands. The country in which the product was manufactured might enter into consumer evaluations. When products ranging from drywall to children's toys made in China reached U.S. markets with major defects, many Chinese brands suffered in various global markets, and some were sued by injured consumers (Chufo, 2010).

The soda market in Turkey provides an example of how local competitors affect positioning. The local soda, Cola Turka, employed the American actor Chevy Chase to position the product as strongly "Turkish." In one spot, Chevy Chase sips the soda and then starts to sing a local song in Turkish. The commercial ends with the actor growing a bushy moustache (Britt, 2003).

USE OR APPLICATION

Use or application positioning involves creating a memorable set of product uses. Bleach may be used as a cleaning product for clothes in one country, as a "germ-killer" in another, and as a way to extend the life of cut flowers in yet another. Use or application positioning requires the identification of the target market customers who might purchase the product and then notes how the product is used in other countries.

PRICE–QUALITY RELATIONSHIP

Companies may highlight a price–quality relationship when competitors offer products at the extremes of the price range. At the high end, the emphasis becomes quality. In the low range, price will be stressed. Price–quality perceptions may be affected by the nation in which an item is produced. Many technological innovations exported from Japan enjoy favorable views about quality due to the country of origin. German-made automobiles often possess the same price–quality status.

New Year celebrations throughout the world often include the consumption of champagne. Many consumers only purchase a bottle once each year. For this product, the price–quality relationship may drive purchase due to the signal of quality. Recently, a food critic survey of champagne in Birmingham, a city in England, revealed that the price of champagne at local groceries ranged from £14.99 to £27.99 per bottle. Even though the critic argued that the most expensive champagne did not merit such a high price, consumers shopping for the beverage assumed that the price positioned the most expensive champagne to contain the highest quality (McComb, 2010).

PRODUCT USER

The product user positioning method identifies a brand or product by clearly specifying who might use it. In transition economies, companies that differentiate by targeting younger consumers as part of a "global" market segment may position products as being universal or worldly. Marketers position services such as hotels, credit cards, and airline travel as favoring business travelers or vacationers. Whereas some product users may drink tea for health benefits, more infrequent users may consume tea for ceremonial reasons.

In the past, marketers of the automobile brand Buick discovered that the cars were typically sold to U.S. consumers who averaged sixty years of age; however, the same brand, when sold to buyers outside the United States, reached a market with an average age of thirty-seven. Consequently, the company started an aggressive promotional campaign targeting younger, Generation X consumers in the United States. The goal was to shift to a newer, younger product user profile.

PRODUCT CLASS

Product class indicates a general category of items within which the good fits. For example, "undergarments for men" include T-shirts and underwear. Other product class groups include "soft drinks" and "energy drinks." Perceptions of product class vary by the culture and the economic circumstances of a country or region. Silk pyjamas target luxury consumers. Those made of cotton are marketed to other buyers.

Tofu offers an example of product class differences. In many parts of East Asia, tofu is a staple food, similar to bread or milk in Western countries. Millions consume it on a daily or weekly basis. In Western countries, tofu does not hold the same status. Instead, it is perceived by many as a foreign product for occasional consumption. Hodo, a Californian company with Asian roots, attempted to move the product class position of tofu to that of a luxury good. The company produces high-end, organic tofu that looks far different from "the white lump" that most find in grocery stores (Weise, 2010).

CULTURAL SYMBOL

Cultural symbol positioning involves an item or brand achieving unique status within a culture or region. Cultural symbols reflect a characteristic of a nation or region and may evolve from popular culture, religion, or other factors that make an area distinct. Any product endorsed by the sports stars Yao Ming in China or Pelé in Brazil may be positioned featuring a cultural symbol.

Consumers often buy a product when it is viewed as a cultural symbol. Many consumers in India consider the spice curry to be a cultural symbol, even though the history of the spice involves several countries. Curry combines several spices, usually including turmeric, coriander, and cumin, among others. It was at least partially created by the British; however, consumers around the world purchase curry when they cook "Indian-flavoured" dishes (Grimes, 2006).

LEARNING OBJECTIVE #3:

How can a product's position become an asset in an international marketing effort?

---

differentiation: emphasis on a unique benefit or component of a product that separates that product from competitors

INTERNATIONAL POSITIONING OBJECTIVES

International positioning seeks to change or create attitudes. Establishing differentiation constitutes one goal of positioning. **Differentiation** results from emphasizing a unique benefit or component of a product that separates it from competitors. Differentiation can be associated with the actual product or an organization's image. Differentiation may develop from perceptions of the product or in terms of support services. Marketers for Casas Bahia, a retailer in Brazil, differentiated the company from competitors by being the first to allow consumers to purchase items using credit (Jordan, 2002).

Differentiation is not the same as the STP process. Segmenting, targeting, and positioning programs seek to identify target market segments containing a homogeneous group of members. Each segment is unique from other segments. Marketers position the product within that target market in terms of various benefits or attributes. In some cases, competitors may share some of these benefits or attributes, such as sugar-free or diet soda.

In contrast, differentiation notes the *specific* benefit or attribute that makes the product unique when compared to competitors. This differentiation typically applies *across* various target markets. When performed correctly, marketers establish a point of difference and value proposition that applies to all market segments, including global target markets.

The search engine Google has achieved differentiation across global markets, even as Bing, Baidu, and other competitors seek to create forms to set themselves apart. Google focuses on the company's position as the top search engine globally. The company's reputation for providing fast searches, for maintaining the innovative edge, and for maintaining vast resources creates differentiation. Many market leaders become synonymous with a product category. Google has achieved this status in online searches: the brand name has become a verb, as in, "I Googled it."

A second goal of positioning programs is to engender brand equity, or the unique benefits that a product enjoys due solely to its brand name.

The Hershey's Kiss is used to represent the brand.

BRAND EQUITY

A second goal of positioning programs is to engender **brand equity**, or the unique benefits that a product enjoys due solely to its brand name. Consistent positioning leads to global brand equity. The benefits of brand equity include the ability to charge a higher price and the presence of increased consumer loyalty. In addition, the company's stock price often will be higher than those of brands without similar levels of equity. These positive outcomes result from the ways consumers view the brand, seeing it as providing a unique benefit. The sources of differentiation or *points of difference* are the strong, favorable, and unique associations consumers have about the brand.

brand equity: the unique outcomes a product enjoys due solely to its brand name

Table 7.2 highlights some strong global brands. Each achieved a level of differentiation based on a point of difference. Mercedes Benz holds a strong position and brand due to perceptions of superior engineering, safety, and customer satisfaction. This point of difference continues around the world. A recent survey revealed it to be Germany's strongest automotive brand. Sony's position begins with perceptions that the company produces superior products across a series of items due to Japan's perceived technological expertise.[5]

TABLE 7.2   Leading Global Brands 2016

Brand	Country of Origin
1. Apple	United States
2. Google	United States
3. Coca-Cola	United States
4. Microsoft	United States
5. Toyota	Japan
6. IBM	United States
7. Samsung	South Korea
8. Amazon	United States
9. Mercedes Benz	Germany
10. General Electric	United States
11. BMW	Germany
12. McDonald's	United States
13. Disney	United States
14. Intel	United States
15. Facebook	United States
16. Cisco	United States
17. Oracle	United States
18. Nike	United States
19. Louis Vuitton	France
20. H&M	Sweden
21. Honda	Japan
22. SAP	Germany
23. Pepsi	United States
24. Gillette	United States
25. American Express	United States
26. Ikea	Sweden
27. Zara	Spain
28. Pampers	United States
29. UPS	United States
30. Budweiser	United States

Source: Adapted from "Interbrand Ranking of the Best Global Brands 2016." Retrieved from http://interbrand.com/best-brands/best-global-brands/2016/ranking/.

BRAND PARITY

brand parity: when brands within one product category are viewed as similar or undifferentiated

Brands without points of difference or unique benefits are more likely to experience perceptions of brand parity. **Brand parity** exists when consumers consider every brand within one product category to be similar or undifferentiated. When consumers deem all products to be basically the same, companies are forced to compete with price or other marketing enticements that reduce revenues per sale, such as coupons, premiums, contests, or bonus packs.

Consider the differences between consumer perceptions of airline travel and of auto-mobile brands. Most airlines suffer from brand parity, because most consumers believe little difference exists between companies. Brands are not differentiated, leading to other marketing tactics. For example, airline carriers often compete based on price. In contrast, some automobile brands are the strongest in the world due to high levels of differentiation. Consumer perceptions of differences in the brands Ferrari, Ford, Bentley, and Hyundai are relatively easy to identify.

INTERNATIONAL PRODUCT POSITIONING CHALLENGES

In attempting to undertake product positioning in an international market, the process will be largely the same as in domestic markets, although differences may arise in response to other factors. The influence of changes in technology, country-of-origin issues, regulations, plus packaging and labeling complications might affect interna-tional product positioning programs. These elements reflect the cultural, language, political and regulatory, economic, and infrastructure influences in the international marketing environment that were displayed in Figure 7.1.

CHANGES IN TECHNOLOGY

The development of new technologies including those designed to improve a nation's infrastructure, strongly influence international positioning efforts. One outcome has been that many consumers see marketing messages transmitted in one country in other nations. Television and radio signals in Italy reach Switzerland, Austria, and France. Consequently, *consistency* becomes a vital element in suc-cessful international product and brand positioning. Positioning statements help maintain consistency.

Conflicting positioning approaches in various countries may damage the brand of a company seeking to make in-roads into a new market. Consequently, company leaders may decide to create new brand names in order to become consistent across markets. The Twix bar is one of the leading candy bars made by Mars. Until the early 1990s, the bar was named Raider in Germany, France, and other parts of Western Europe. Due to increased media bleed across borders and to support more-consistent positioning, Mars changed the brand name to Twix in European markets (Smith, 1998).

LEARNING OBJECTIVE #4:

What additional challenges affect international product positioning programs?

The Digital Divide

Technological differences and comfort levels with new technologies also influence the manner in which a product is positioned in global markets. Less-developed econo-mies suffer from the digital divide, or the gap in technology that limits the ability of countries and regions to develop.

One example comes from personal computer usage. It is estimated that in three-fourths of low-income countries, there are fewer than fifteen personal computers per 1,000 people. In poverty-stricken and remote areas, other issues arise. Cases have been reported in which ants have eaten through hard drives. Oftentimes earthquakes disrupt Internet service for entire regions.[6] Positioning personal computers with these limiting factors changes the methods a marketing team might use.

Consumer Reluctance

Some consumers may be reluctant to try new products and technologies. Mobile phones, sodas, and solar panel arrays are viewed by many of the billions of consumers in emerging or least-developed markets as innovations. Somewhere a consumer just examined a digital camera for the first time. For marketers, this means that these products are automatically viewed as foreign, innovative, and new. For established companies, these perceptions may be contrary to some well-established points of difference and might lead the company to reposition the product.

In contrast, people in more-developed countries take various products for granted, such as mobile phones, Internet access, and computers. Such products play significant economic and social roles. Entering these markets probably means targeting a more sophisticated set of consumers with higher incomes and educational attainments, and should position products accordingly.

In India, the potential market for dental care is large and penetration rates are low. The marketing objective may be to convince reluctant consumers to pay more for value-added product attributes such as gels or teeth whitening. For poorer, bottom-of-the-pyramid consumers, the challenge will be getting consumers to switch to using toothpaste itself instead of the more commonplace toothpowders.[7]

COUNTRY-OF-ORIGIN EFFECTS

country-of-origin effect: the response a consumer has to a product due to the country that is the source, in the consumer's mind, for the product

As companies attempt to establish positioning globally, one common concern will be the product's country of origin. The **country-of-origin effect** summarizes the response a consumer has to a product due to his or her perception of the source country. Depending on the home country and the country being entered, the country-of-origin effect can drastically alter the position of the product. Country-of-origin effects originate in four different areas, as displayed in Table 7.3 (Nebenzahl et al., 1997). Together, these factors work to create the sources of country-of-origin positioning effects.

TABLE 7.3   Sources of Country-of-Origin Positioning Effects

Home country: The influence of a consumer's home country on his or her beliefs
Origin country: The country that the consumer generally associates with a certain product
Made-in country: The country listed on the "made in" label of the product
Designed-in country: The country in which the product was designed

Country-of-origin effects can be positive or negative. Many multinational corporations, such as Coca-Cola, Levi Strauss, and Sony, leverage positive country-of-origin effects to help differentiate products. Some evidence suggests that the country of origin can be more important than the brand name to consumers. One set of consumers may be willing to pay a price premium for goods when they hold positive attitudes toward the country of origin (Han, 2010). Country of origin also affects perceptions of quality, which can be used to reduce feelings of purchase risk, and also to increase the likelihood to buy (Roth and Diamantopoulos, 2009).

Country Image

Country-of-origin effects are often based on stereotyped conceptions consumers have about countries, or the country's image. **Country image** summarizes the attitudes and knowledge consumers have about a nation. Some countries enjoy positive and consistent images globally, including Switzerland's reputation for quality engineering or France's reputation for style. Most-developed countries generally have more positive country images. Less- and least-developed countries often struggle with poor country images. As a result, country of origin may limit the ability of some companies to market products in more-developed countries.

country image: the attitudes and knowledge consumers have about a country

Negative country-of-origin attitudes can be changed over time, as was the case of the South Korean automaker Hyundai. When Hyundai models first entered the American market in 1986, the marketing team faced negative country image problems. Talk show host Jay Leno joked that filling up a Hyundai with gas doubled its value.[8] The automaker's marketers realized consumers were reluctant to buy a car that was "Made in Korea," and was perceived similarly to the Yugo, which was manufactured in the former Yugoslavia. To counter this perception, Hyundai introduced a 100,000 mile, ten-year warranty, the most comprehensive in the industry, in 1998. Finbarr O'Neill, Hyundai Motor's America president and CEO, stated in 2000, "We have to make it OK to drive a Hyundai into the driveway without being apologetic to your neighbours" (Green, 2000). The warranty, coupled with an increase in quality and an aggressive advertising campaign designed to position the company's cars as being highly reliable, led to a major turnaround. While other automobile companies lost market share at the end of the decade, Hyundai increased sales and gained share. The Genesis model was voted 2009 "North American Car of the Year" at the 2009 Detroit Auto Show, suggesting that the negative effects of country image had been largely eliminated (Ingrassia, 2009).

Country image problems emerge in several ways. Table 7.4 lists some common problems. Each influences a company's ability to effectively position products.

TABLE 7.4   Attitudinal Factors Influencing Country Image

Ethnocentrism
Animosity
Nationalism
Religiosity

Ethnocentrism

Cultural values influence international positioning. Country image varies among consumers within a region or nation. While general trends may be present, marketers need to know the specific attitudes of consumers in a target market. Consumers exhibiting high levels of ethnocentrism or the attitude that their country is better than others pay more attention to country-of-origin labels and are more likely to buy products produced in their home countries (Shankarmahesh, 2006).

Animosity

Relationships between countries can confound positioning efforts. Tensions between or within nations arise in many parts of the world, including those between Greece and Turkey, Pakistan and India, and Israel and the Palestinians living in the West Bank and the Gaza Strip. These conflicts influence consumer attitudes and behaviors.

When the United States invaded Iraq in 2002, various countries throughout the world, especially in Western Europe, expressed disapproval. A survey completed in 2004 revealed that nearly 20% of consumers abroad said they would avoid U.S. companies and products such as McDonald's, Starbucks, American Airlines, and Barbie dolls (Mattel's) because of the war. At that time, the more American a product was perceived to be, the more resistance it encountered.[9] Similar responses were to be expected following the 2016 election cycle in the USA, specifically when newly elected President Trump announced a ban on travel by citizens from seven countries from the Middle East (Bomey and Weise, 2017).

animosity: anger toward a country that is rooted in political, economic, or military conflict between countries

Any **animosity** or anger toward a country can be worsened by political, economic, or military conflicts between countries or within a nation, such as has been the case in the Syrian civil war that continued into 2018 which has drawn in nations including Russia, Jordan, Lebanon, and others. A considerable amount of evidence suggests that animosity toward a country strongly influences consumers (Riefler and Diamantopoulos, 2007).

Nationalism

nationalism: the strong pride and devotion consumers have in their country or nation

At times, animosity toward another country couples with **nationalism**, which refers to the strong pride and devotion citizens have in a country or nation. Nationalism can shape responses to a domestic company or engender animosity as consumers examine products from other countries. Nationalism should not be considered as a purely negative or positive attitude. It may be associated with heroic sacrifice, loyalty, and group cohesiveness. From a marketing perspective, it can lead to a preference for purchasing local goods and services (Gineikiene et al., 2017). Conversely, nationalism can precipitate boycotts, protests, and even acts of violence toward another country or a company conducting business in a foreign land. Nationalistic consumers often perceive that buying imported goods is wrong because it negatively impacts the domestic economy (Rawwas et al., 1996).

Earlier this decade, millions of Indonesian farmers threatened to boycott Nestlé products. Angry at a move by Nestlé to stop buying crude palm oil from Indonesian farms, an action that would potentially severely hurt the Indonesian economy, the farmers expressed national pride and attempted to protect their community.[10]

Religiosity

religiosity: the degree to which consumers within a country or region are religious

Attitudes toward countries can be influenced by religion and religious similarities between countries. Increasingly, **religiosity**, or the degree to which consumers within a country or region are religious, has become a factor in international marketing considerations. Religiosity affects shopping behaviors, attitudes toward advertising, purchase information-search processes, and product preferences (Choi et al., 2010). A list of the major religions and percentage of each in select countries is presented in Table 7.5.

Each of these religions practices differing dietary programs, holds religious ceremonies in differing ways, exhibits varying viewpoints regarding the status of women

TABLE 7.5   Religions in Select Countries

Country	Religions
Afghanistan	Sunni Muslim 80%, Shia Muslim 19%, other 1%
Argentina	Roman Catholic 92%, Protestant 2%, Jewish 2%, other 4%
Botswana	Christian 71.6%, Badimo 6%, other 1.4%, none 20.6%
Cuba	85% Roman Catholic prior to communist takeover
France	Roman Catholic 83–88%, Protestant 2%, Jewish 1%, Muslim 5%–10%, unaffiliated 4%
India	Hindu 80.5%, Muslim 13.4%, Christian 2.3%, Sikh 1.9%, other 1.8%
Kazakhstan	Muslim 47%, Russian Orthodox 44%, Protestant 2%, other 7%
Morocco	Muslim 98.7%, Christian 1.1%, Jewish 0.2%
Qatar	Muslim 77.5%, Christian 8.5%, other 14%
Somalia	Sunni Muslim near 100%
Taiwan	Buddhist/Taoist 93%, Christian 4.5%, other 2.5%
United States	Protestant 51.3%, Roman Catholic 23.9%, Mormon 1.7%, other Christian 1.6%, Jewish 1.7%, Buddhist 0.7%, Muslim 0.6%, other or unspecified 2.5%, unaffiliated 12.1%, none 4%

and children, and has unique holy days. Product positioning efforts account for these cultural, language, and daily life variances.

By measuring ethnocentrism, nationalism, animosity, and religiosity, marketers gain a better understanding of the potential effects of country image and country-of-origin image. This information increases the potential to successfully position products ready for export to other countries.

Consumption of simple products, such as drinks, may reflect religious beliefs. American politics, particularly in the Middle East, have led some consumers to want an alternative to Coca-Cola products. Mecca Cola, which is sold in parts of Europe and the Arab world, positions itself in terms of religion. The brand name, Mecca, and the cola's slogan "Don't drink stupid. Drink committed," both reflect targeting of Muslim consumers (Rathwell, 2004).

REGULATIONS

Regulatory environments present an important difference between nations as marketers respond to the international context. Each country's government holds sovereignty over business activities within national boundaries. **Sovereignty** means that the government has authority or control within its state. Foreign businesses must respect it and follow any regulations and rules within the country.

sovereignty: governmental authority or control within its state

At times regulations keep a company from positioning a product in terms of a new benefit or attribute, or in some cases, from entering a market. In Canada, Tropicana orange juice with added calcium is not classified as a food but rather as a drug. Each container is required to have a drug identification number on the label (Condon, 2003). The regulation limits the potential position of this product in the mind of consumers as simply a tasty or healthy beverage. It might be difficult to market the drug "orange juice with calcium," complete with a drug number, to consumers.

PACKAGING AND LABELS

Another difficulty associated with international marketing may be found in packaging and especially labeling regulations. A salmon caught by a fisherman in Canada that is shipped to Thailand for skinning and deboning and ends up on a grocery store shelf in Brazil has three potential points of origin. The question arises as to which country of origin should be printed on the label. A Braun shaver sold in Wal-Mart is made with parts from Germany, Ireland, and Hungary, and was probably assembled in China.

The United States allows differing country-of-origin labels (see Table 7.6). The labels may reflect where the product was produced or where the product was assembled. As is the case in many countries, a product can be labeled "certified made in the USA" even when part of the product was manufactured elsewhere, as long as virtually all parts and processing are of U.S. origin. The "assembled in" label can be used if the last substantial transformation occurred in that country. In general, this means that many product packages, even ones with a "made in the USA" label, were probably partially produced or assembled somewhere else.[11]

TABLE 7.6   Country-of-Origin Label Wordings in the United States

Product of
Made in
Designed in
Packaged in
Assembled in
Certified made in

INTERNATIONAL POSITIONING METHODS

The positioning process, whether international or domestic, includes a series of steps, as summarized by Table 7.7. The company's marketing team first identifies target markets. These targets consist of consumers whose perceptions form the basis for the brand's or the product's position. Members of various target markets may have differing perceptions of the company. A company may be well positioned in one target market but not in another. Next, competitors are identified. Finally, the marketing team conducts an analysis of target market characteristics to identify points of difference. Techniques such as positioning maps help further clarify the position a product or brand holds. Depending on the results of the analysis, efforts to enhance or to reposition the brand may be undertaken.

LEARNING OBJECTIVE #5:

What steps and tactics are used to establish positioning, evaluate positioning, and conduct repositioning in international markets?

TABLE 7.7   The Steps of Product Positioning

1. Identify target markets
2. Analyze competition within the target market
3. Identify points of difference
4. Enhance or reposition, if necessary

IDENTIFY TARGET MARKETS

The second element of the segmentation, targeting, and positioning (STP) approach is target marketing. After identifying a group of market segments, a marketing team chooses the ones to pursue. Market segments are based on demographics, psychographic similarities, geographic area, geodemographics, consumer type, product benefits, or product uses. A set of these segments, typically with a common element, constitutes the target markets that best fit the company.

One concern marketers have about any target market is whether consumers in the group are willing to spend money on the product. Positioning, especially in terms of unique product benefits, often signals a price point. Marketers of Tod's, the Italian leather goods house, position the company's product as high quality with a high price in Japan (Sanchanta, 2005). Japanese members of Tod's target market are affluent, aspiring, global consumers as are those in the United States and China. These individuals spend money on quality products.

A company such as Toyota, with a larger, more price-sensitive target market, becomes more concerned with the price signal that is sent. The price should not signal a level of quality that is higher than members of the target market believe they can afford. This issue becomes particularly important when the marketing team targets local and bottom-of-the-pyramid consumers.

ANALYZE THE COMPETITION WITHIN THE TARGET MARKET

Next, a company's marketing team identifies all potential competitors. Nearly every product or service sold encounters several levels of competition internationally, including product versus product, product line versus product line, brand versus brand, company versus company, and industry versus industry. These perceptions in turn affect positioning efforts.

Product vs. Product

A product first competes with similar products. In the United Kingdom, a variety of home cooking, fast-food, and upscale restaurants offer fish and chips, a standard British fare. More than 8,500 fish and chip shops operate in the United Kingdom; or eight for every one McDonald's outlet. This makes British fish and chips the nation's favorite take-out food.[12] Automobile companies compete at the product versus product level, as a buyer considers a Nissan Altima, Toyota Camry, or Hyundai Sonata. When positioning products globally to compete with other products, careful attention should be paid to issues of quality, product differences, and price at the product level.

Product Line vs. Product Line

A product line consists of similar products within a particular category. Canned fruits may be sold by a company offering a product line that includes mixed fruit, pineapples, peaches, grapes, mandarin oranges, pears, and apples. Typically, a house mark brand represents all of the products in a line. In the United States, Dole's line of canned fruit competes against Del Monte and others. In Thailand, another of Dole's competitors is Bangkok Companies and its subsidiary Thai Fruit Company.

Product lines compete with depth and breadth, both of which affect positioning. The *depth* of a product line is the total number of products in that line. If Thai Fruit Company offers ten varieties of canned fruit, ten becomes the depth of the line. *Breadth* refers to the number of lines offered by the company. The Thai Fruit Company also offers fruit drinks; Dole benefits from a strong association with fresh fruits, especially pineapples from Hawai'i. Dole also offers canned vegetables and packaged salads, creating greater breadth.

Depth and breadth can create a stronger brand image, as the increased number of product offerings leads to the company becoming known to a wider variety of customers. Depth and breadth also contribute to positioning at the product line versus product line level of competition. As depth and breadth expand, customers enjoy more choices and can rely on a brand when shopping, which reduces purchase time and helps quickly eliminate other purchase alternatives. By offering quality salads, Dole increased the odds that those who purchase the salads will also buy its fresh fruit, canned vegetables, or any new company product.

Brand vs. Brand

Well-known companies with powerful brand names have key advantages in positioning efforts. This may be due, in part, to consumer considerations as they compare one company to another. Brand equity contributes to positioning and becomes a major asset in brand versus brand competition. A strong brand makes product diversification processes more manageable. When Sony introduces a new electronic device, consumers are likely to transfer the trust they have in the brand to the new product.

A brand name with negative connotations may experience some difficulties. The Exxon-Mobile Corporation has been vilified by various critics since the 1989 oil spill disaster in Alaska. BP, the British Petroleum brand responsible for the largest oil spill in world history in 2010, undoubtedly has shared the same or a similar fate.

Global brands compete against each other across markets. The toothpaste brands Crest, which is owned by Proctor & Gamble, and Colgate, which is owned by Colgate-Palmolive, battle for the same consumers globally. China represents the largest toothpaste market by volume, and toothpaste marketing activities in the country are particularly aggressive. Consumer reluctance to brush daily continues, and only 20% of bottom-of-the-pyramid rural Chinese consumers do so. Many Chinese view tooth brushing as providing cosmetic rather than health benefits. In response, both toothpaste brands try to establish position in terms of health benefits. Crest had plans to make a television advertisement where half of a white egg is brushed with Crest toothpaste. The egg is then lowered into an acid bath for an hour. After the hour, the side of the egg coated with toothpaste is strong while the other side is brittle and breaks. Colgate's marketing team discovered the potential ad and preempted Crest by making a similar commercial using a seashell instead of an egg (Wentz and Fannin, 1996).

Company vs. Company

When engaging in positioning activities, a foreign company may face an advantage, disadvantage, or relatively neutral outcome when competing with local firms. In some instances, where consumers are more cosmopolitan, a foreign entity may be more readily accepted; in areas where ethnocentrism prevails, a foreign competitor begins with a strategic disadvantage.

Although marketing teams in multinational corporations from developed economies may believe that all they need to do is enter an emerging market to enjoy success, the opposite may be true. Outside companies often encounter difficulties when entering emerging markets and struggle to compete with local competitors (Khanna and Palepu, 2006). This is because local firms meet the needs of home markets. In contrast, multinationals encounter additional costs, in terms of both time and money, to adapt activities in order to address the same needs. Consequently, the costs and risks associated with entering these markets rise and may impede positioning attempts (Khanna and Palepu, 2006).

INTERNATIONAL INCIDENT

As an employee of the 7–11 Convenience Stores company, you travel to Mexico looking for new potential franchisee partners. A meeting is held with a local businessman to gauge his interest. The opportunity seems to be attractive to him, but one concern is raised. A certain amount of animosity exists toward the United States in parts of Mexico, especially following the results of the 2016 election. He is nervous that this partnering will hurt the company's position in the country. This places you in a potentially awkward position. Your company, 7–11, is actually a Japanese company. How do you respond to this issue? Should you correct him? Does the high power distance culture in Mexico, in which status differences have significant meaning, affect how you should respond? More broadly, animosity toward 7–11, even if it is based on a false perception, might constrain moving into the Mexican market. How would you address this problem?

Industry vs. Industry

In any economy, an individual, family, or business has a finite number of dollars. Choices are made on a daily basis. The decision to purchase an expensive cup of coffee in the morning may lead the consumer to skip lunch or to buy only a bag of potato chips at noon.

Understanding the product's industry as well as other industries that take customers away will be part of the positioning process. Recreational activities compete internally (watching a professional soccer match versus going to the movies), and with other businesses where consumers spend money on sundries. During economic slumps, a family may forgo traveling on vacation and instead purchase a new smoker or barbeque grill.

Careful positioning means accounting for all levels of competition. The most powerful influence will be similar products; however, brand names and other factors can change a company's approach. Comparisons with similar brands and products from other industries will include pricing considerations.

IDENTIFY POINTS OF DIFFERENCE

After identifying target markets, evaluating competitors, and reviewing other influences, the marketing team analyzes the company's or product's current position. They conduct market research, normally beginning with consumer surveys concerning attitudes regarding a product. Attitudes are assessed across a variety of features and benefits, both tangible and intangible.

tangible product benefits: the value drawn from the physical components of a product

Tangible product benefits are the value drawn from a product's physical components. The popular Brazilian soda Guarana accounts for more than one-third of Brazilian carbonated drink sales. The bubble-gum-tasting fruit ingredient has a high caffeine content and is also rumored to create romantic benefits. The product provides many tangible benefits including taste and energy.

intangible product benefits: the value drawn from the social, emotional, and nonphysical aspects of consumption

Intangible product benefits are the value drawn from the social, emotional, and nonphysical aspects of consumption. Within the Brazilian market, there are also important intangible benefits to purchasing Guarana, including prestige, patriotic pride, and connections to local communities.

positioning maps: tools used to study a company and its competitors in terms of consumer attitudes or perceptions

Most products offer tangible and intangible benefits to consumers. An analysis of the benefits can become complicated. To organize the process, marketers often employ positioning maps. **Positioning maps** provide tools used to portray the company and its competitors in terms of consumer attitudes or perceptions. Typically the marketing team examines factors that drive purchases and influence purchasing decisions. Positioning maps can help international marketers understand how consumers in other countries perceive a company's products and brands (Jaishankar and Oakenfull, 1999).

Figure 7.2 displays a traditional positioning map featuring price and quality perceptions within the automobile industry. The map indicates that perceptions of quality increase as the price of the product rises. The positioning map also suggests that quality signals price. Most maps that utilize price and quality as the main factors look basically the same across product categories. In the map as shown, Toyota, which in the past decade experienced problems with safety that have been since resolved, may have seemed overpriced at that time, due to quality perceptions. This positioning map is not based on data. It was created by the authors as a sample for illustrative purposes.

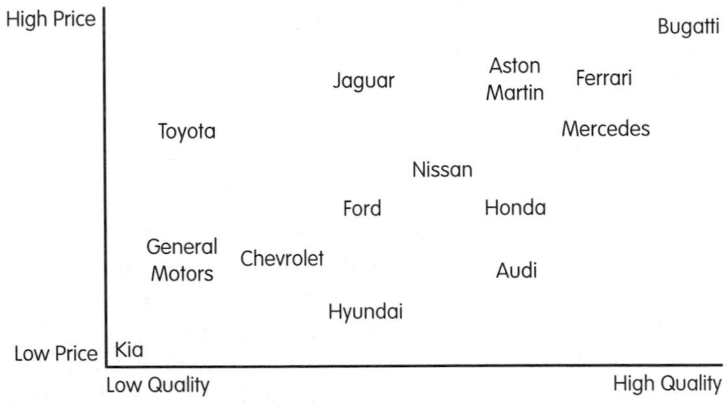

FIGURE 7.2   A Price–Quality Positioning Map

Positioning maps should be designed to identify attitudes related to a company's source of differentiation. Instead of using price, actual product attributes can be examined. The positioning map featured in Figure 7.3 includes the same automobile brands that appear in Figure 7.2, but instead this second map uses consumer impressions of speed and safety as its basis. The map does not display the same relationships as the price–quality map but rather the map suggests clusters of brands. The luxury sports cars cluster together on the high-speed feature but, as a result, produce lower perceptions of safety.

The family car brands such as Ford and Nissan cluster in the middle of the map. Customers perceive these brands as relatively safe but also relatively slow. The brands that do not cluster are differentiated in terms of speed or safety. Audi has the reputation as a safe car, which is how it differentiates from competitors. This position is reflected on the map. When Toyota experienced problems with accelerator pedals that have now been fixed, consumers may have viewed the product more negatively, as shown in this example. This positioning map (Figure 7.3) is not based on data. It was created by the authors as a sample for illustrative purposes.

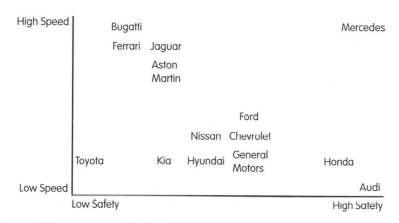

FIGURE 7.3   A Speed–Safety Positioning Map

Share of Mind and Share of Heart

Two additional variables may be used to examine the position of a product or brand: share of mind and share of heart. *Share of mind* refers to the product's position in terms of brand awareness. Consumers considering brands do not readily recall a product with low share of mind, whereas a brand with high share of mind immediately emerges. When consumers are asked to name the top athletic shoe companies, typical responses are likely to include Nike, Reebok, Adidas, and perhaps one or two more brands. These brands enjoy a strong share of mind.

Share of heart focuses more on the emotional components of the consumer attitudes. These include the ways consumers experience the product and its social context. Share of heart suggests that relationships, emotions, and experiences are part of a product's position. Koo Baked Beans have been a popular choice of consumers in South Africa for more than seventy-five years. Strong share of heart arises in citizens from that country who associate the product with positive childhood memories (Koo, 2017).

A product exhibiting high share of mind combined with high share of heart holds a strong marketing advantage. Vegemite, a yeast extract spread, is sold in Australia. Leftover brewer's yeast extract, a by-product of beer manufacture, is combined with various vegetable and spice additives. Vegemite appears dark reddish-brown, almost black, and provides a rich source of Vitamin B. It is thick, similar to peanut butter, very salty, and has achieved nearly cultural icon status. Numerous sources note that Vegemite is to Australian children what peanut butter is to kids in other countries. Vegemite clearly has strong share of mind and share of heart in that market. If a pocket of Australian immigrants were to emigrate, they would undoubtedly constitute a target market for Vegemite based on this strong position. Figure 7.4 displays a share of mind/share of heart example for Vegemite, Sanitarium Peanut Butter, Kraft Jelly, and Philadelphia Cream Cheese in Australia.

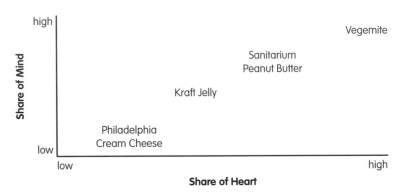

FIGURE 7.4 **Share of Mind and Share of Heart**

As shown, Vegemite enjoys both high share of mind and high share of heart. Marketers dedicate positioning efforts to maintain that standing. Sanitarium Peanut Butter holds nearly as much share of mind, but has less share of heart, because it does not hold cultural icon status. The company maintains a strong position and would likely seek to enhance one or more of the features, perhaps by emphasizing price–quality relationships, product user status, such as children versus adults, or some other positioning approach. Kraft Jelly has a diminished place in terms of both share of mind and share of heart. Should the marketing team discover that share of heart is lower due to perceptions that it is an "American" product with no particular appeal to Australian customers, marketing efforts can be made to improve share of heart and create greater loyalty to the brand by linking the brand to Australia. The marketing team with the biggest challenge would be the one selling Philadelphia Cream Cheese. A logical approach would be to begin with improvements to share of mind, thereby increasing consumer awareness of the product and its many uses. Share of heart and brand loyalty might then grow over time.

The same share of mind and share of heart map, if produced for the United States, would reveal dramatically different results. Most American consumers only know about Vegemite sandwiches due to a line from the Men at Work song from the 1980s ("He just smiled and gave me a *Vegemite* sandwich"). In the United States, Kraft's peanut butter and jelly products would occupy the position held by Vegemite. Consequently, each company's marketing team can use the map to understand a product's position in other countries. Philadelphia Cream Cheese's advertising company recently undertook a massive marketing effort to reinforce the concept that the product could be used in a variety of ways beyond being a spread for crackers, because the marketing team believed the company held a strong share of heart status. The results were a change in share of mind, based on new uses for the product, which in turn increased sales.

ENHANCING POSITION OR REPOSITIONING

Following the analysis of a company's or product's current position, the decision will be made regarding enhancing a current position or seeking to reposition the brand. Most of the time, a position that has been previously established will be reinforced or enhanced. Repositioning normally will be undertaken only when circumstances indicate that a more radical approach is in order.

Tata Motors is an Indian automobile manufacturer. A few years ago, Tata Motors began the process of introducing the Nano in the United Kingdom. In India, the Nano is an austere and simple $2,500 car targeting relatively impoverished consumers. To be successful in the British market, the marketing team understood that the car would require some adjustments. First, it would have to meet more stringent safety standards. In response, the company added extra foam and structures behind parts of the car, reinforced sections of the body, and installed air bags. After passing safety tests, upgrades to the Nano's engine and brakes were created. The modifications were designed to achieve a new position, one in which the same brand name is attached to a radically different and more expensive car. Company leaders believed the car, as adapted, would attract British customers.[13]

Enhancing Position

Enhancing position involves all standard and nontraditional marketing approaches. A brand featuring a *unique product attribute* will be marketed with a strong emphasis on the feature. When targeting a new market in another country, the marketing team ascertains whether those in the market know or value the feature or attribute. Over time, a description or reminder of the attribute might appear in point-of-purchase displays; it may be pointed out on social networking forums; advertisements would highlight the feature; and customer loyalty programs would be designed to encourage repeat purchases. Attempts will be made to build on the unique benefit, especially if a celebrity or well-known company purchases and endorses the item in the target market country.

Positioning based on *competitors*, as part of an international program, likely concentrates on local competitors first. Marketers differentiate the product in some way, typically avoiding denigrating the competition so as not to offend locals. An established product that has achieved a niche may continue to compete by fending off any new entries into the marketplace while seeking to enhance the status of the product relative to that of competitors.

Enhancing *use or application* positioning constitutes a relatively straightforward process. It can be accomplished through the training of salespeople to emphasize various product uses. Advertising then demonstrates those uses. When additional uses for the same product have been identified, the number of potential customers expands. Arm & Hammer baking soda has been successfully marketed in the United States for many years. Growth in sales resulted, in part, from advertising campaigns that touted its many uses. It can be used for cooking, for deodorizing refrigerators, and as a household cleaning agent. Baking soda is viewed differently worldwide. It is not commonly used for baking purposes in France. Rather, *bicarbonate de soude* and the more common *la levure chimique* are used. Promoting alternative uses may be a creative way for the product to gain sales in countries such as France.

Price–quality relationship positioning may be emphasized through various tactics aimed at the position chosen. When a product carries a high price and implies high quality, premium programs allow the marketing team to offer a sales enticement without reducing the price. At the extreme, it may be possible to develop social networks of fans of high-priced items. Conversely, at the low-price extreme, a continuing emphasis on price remains the primary marketing tactic. For those products of medium price and quality, the approach features value as the primary selling point. These methods are highly similar in domestic and international markets.

Product user positioning in international marketing concentrates on psychological, sociological, or spiritual values held by potential consumers. Psychological values include feelings of cosmopolitanism, positive attitudes toward the country of origin, or pleasant feelings associated with the actual use of the product. Products considered to be "everyday" in one country may be perceived quite differently in others. Sociological distinctions include the emphasis on feelings of belonging, social status based on use of the product, or connections to family, such as by purchasing insurance to protect them. Heineken, from Holland, is marketed as a premium product in Canada and is positioned to appeal to the upscale consumer. Religious values are sometimes expressed in the use of some products, such as unleavened bread and kosher meats.

Product class international positioning may rely on a universal endorsement, such as ISO (International Organization for Standardization) 9000 or 14000 standards. These notify buyers that an item contains quality sufficient enough to be considered as competitive with other products in the same class. Retaining ISO distinction maintains a product's position. ISO standards apply to both products and services. Hospitals may seek ISO certification to become known for delivering the highest quality in health care to patients.

Cultural symbol positioning can be an effective international marketing strategy.

Cultural symbol positioning may be based on a local icon, such as Yannick Noah. Noah was a professional tennis player and is a singing sensation in his native France. Cultural symbol positioning may rely on association with a specific national feature, such as the spectacular sunsets on the Greek Isles of Mykonos. As long as the celebrity maintains that status or a national feature remains popular, associating a product with the symbol enhances the status of the product.

Consistency remains the key to enhancing product positioning using any of these methods. Strong brands stand on continual emphasis of the same features. A product's position remains stable unless unforeseen events, competitor actions, or other external forces change it.

Often enhancing a product position involves overlapping concerns. Philips has been successful in the Malaysian kitchen appliance market with three separate brands: Comfort, Cucina, and Essence. Essence is Philips' premium brand. Although both Comfort and Cucina are affordable and positioned as top performers at a reasonable price, Cucina is positioned as the higher-quality, higher-priced brand. Products carrying the brand are high end, with sophisticated technology. For all three brands, Philips balances the price–quality position while emphasizing unique product attributes and use positioning.[14]

Bottom-of-the-Pyramid Positioning

Positioning within the bottom-of-the-pyramid markets is complicated. Consumers often have awareness of the product and its benefits. The challenge is not differentiation; at least no more so than in any other international market segment. The concern becomes shifting the company's focus. For many strongly positioned, premium global brands, the process of creating those brands leads to a high-quality position. The natural concern will be that within the bottom-of-the-pyramid market the position signals a high price. Such a perception may lessen consumer interest because they will believe that they cannot afford the product.

Positioning in the bottom-of-the-pyramid involves educating consumers about the steps the company has taken to adapt to the consumer's level of income. Doing so requires repositioning the product or brand as being attainable in terms of price without losing the differentiation in terms of quality or product features. It may entail the introduction of a new brand that then can be positioned in the minds of consumers.

Ginger Hotels in India are part of the large Indian conglomerate, the Tata Group. Before introducing Ginger Hotels, the company's marketers mainly focused on the luxurious Taj Hotel brand. Ginger Hotels, in contrast, are positioned as "smart basic" hotels that are highly functional but with no frills. The target is bottom-of-the-pyramid consumers (Kazmin, 2009).

INTERNATIONAL INCIDENT

You are visiting Russia as part of an executive exchange program. Upon arrival, you witness two Russian executives engaging in a hug as they greet one another. Assuming this is proper protocol, you hug the two executives and receive a chilly response. Soon after, you offer an apology, explaining that you thought it was the cultural norm to hug as a greeting. The executives laugh and explain that they are old friends. In business settings, a firm handshake is in order. Later, during the meeting, one of the two executives laughs during a light moment and touches you on the arm. What should you conclude?

Every positioning activity will be pursued while looking for the most low-cost approach. Unlike more-developed countries or regions that have more expensive labor, companies seeking to serve the bottom-of-the-pyramid often use local salespeople or contacts in order to minimize selling costs. Beyond the social employment benefits, these individuals can turn into strong advocates for the product or company.

Repositioning

When a product's or brand's position creates an unfavorable circumstance, the company's marketing team may seek an alternative approach. **Repositioning** is the process of changing consumer perceptions of a brand relative to competitors. It requires a sweeping process that must be implemented at the strategic level, thereby affecting every part of the company. It cannot simply be a marketing ploy, which might arouse the suspicions of consumers.

repositioning:
the process of changing consumer perceptions of a brand relative to competitors on key attributes

In the positioning map shown in Figure 7.3, Nissan did not have an advantage with regard to either safety or speed. The marketing department, after seeing the results, might try to reposition Nissan on the variable of safety. Repositioning would involve improvements in the safety features of the automobile (in the design and manufacturing departments), a promotional campaign to inform consumers of these changes (marketing), public relations releases announcing the results of new safety tests when they favor the company, and an overall company focus on safety. Such a strategy includes informing all employees about the new approach and rewarding those who suggest innovations and improvements related to the safety of the automobiles. If successful, a future positioning map would show Nissan moving up on perceptions of safety.

The Hyundai example from earlier in this chapter serves as an example of effective repositioning. The company moved from perceptions of being cheap and low quality to a new position based on improved consumer perceptions of quality. Repositioning cannot be viewed as a quick and easy fix. Some evidence suggests that it can take up to six years for consumer perceptions of quality to shift (Mittra and Golder, 2006).

Findomestic, an Italian bank, began to reposition the service as one that stressed responsibility. Support was provided to consumers that wanted guidance on how to use credit more responsibly. A code of ethics was established for the company and a guide was provided to consumers about financial responsibility. Even with these steps, the company's leaders were disappointed in the results and so, to better communicate with consumers, the first television campaign in the history of the company was rolled out.[15]

SUSTAINABILITY AND INTERNATIONAL POSITIONING

Sustainable business practices differentiate a business from competitors. Positioning a company, business practice, or product as more environmentally conscious allows the organization to occupy a unique space in the minds of consumers. Sustainable business practices are popular around the world.

greenwashing:
a practice in which a company exaggerates or even fabricates the degree of its sustainable or green activities

The benefits created by a sustainable position have led to growing concerns about greenwashing tactics. **Greenwashing** is a practice in which company leaders exaggerate or fabricate the degree of the sustainable or green activities taking place. Treating sustainability as a fad, instead of a core value of the company, leads to greenwashing. Table 7.8 provides examples of greenwashing "sins" (Spaulding, 2009).

Many activities help a marketing department respond to concerns about greenwashing and effectively position brands as genuinely sustainable. When a company appears to be sincere and authentic, and to communicate sustainable practices, consumers tend to believe the message. Truly green programs are accepted and acclaimed in many

TABLE 7.8   Seven Deadly Greenwashing Sins

Greenwashing Sin	Explanation
Hidden Trade-Off	Emphasizing one environmental issue at the expense of another
No Proof	Using assertions not backed by evidence or certification
Vagueness	Using a phrase such as "All Natural" that has no meaning
Worshipping False Labels	Using images that look green but have no meaning
Irrelevance	Emphasizing a green activity unrelated to the product or not allowed by law
Lesser of Two Evils	Being green with a product that by nature is not green (e.g., organic cigarettes)
Fibbing	Making outright false statements or claims

international settings. In future years, going green may become less of a positioning advantage if most companies follow the trend.

ETHICAL ISSUES IN INTERNATIONAL POSITIONING

In the area of positioning, two ethical concerns arise. The first is the role that positioning plays in encouraging consumption. which may drive consumers to purchase things they do not need or to envy those who can afford the product. In essence, positioning appears to lead to envy and greed.

Second, positioning often promises that consumers will become younger, prettier, or more popular. The ethical issue related to body image and self-image is when products are marketed in terms of intangible benefits that are based on social standing. Positioning based on social status has been criticized as a factor in low self-esteem. Instead, critics argue, products should be differentiated in terms of the benefits present or in their use that are not based on social status or unrealistic hopes for improved personal appearance.

CHAPTER 7: REVIEW AND RESOURCES

Strategic Implications

Three basic strategic approaches to the overall direction of a company include cost leadership, differentiation, and focus. These strategies represent the broadest, most strategic perspective on positioning. A business emphasizing differentiation will use the approach to position products, even when the point of difference changes from item to item. In the international marketplace, effective generic strategy positioning will be a primary element in an operation's success.

When entering a new market, establishing an effective position is important. The type of positioning present in one country may not be ideal in others. Strategic positioning focuses on the benefits or value a product or company provides. The most ideal circumstance occurs when this benefit transfers across national boundaries. An important consideration is the role of country-of-origin effects as companies enter new countries. The country image for the company or the brand may hinder the company's ability to position itself in the same way as it does in a domestic market.

Most of the time, a local company will already occupy the position sought by the competitor entering the market. To respond, the marketing team might undertake repositioning based on another attribute, or the company could aggressively compete with the local competitor. Repositioning may injure the company's image, especially when marketing messages are viewed in other markets. Aggressively competing with local competitors risks alienating the exact customers a company intends to pursue.

Tactical Implications

Tactical efforts are undertaken to support the position a company's marketers wish to reach. The product's package and label will be altered to fit the legal and cultural dictates of a nation and a target market. Legal requirements vary as to any promise of a product benefit as well as labeling of content, including statements about country of origin. Promotional programs are also adjusted. Cultural differences dictate more careful wording of advertisements when seeking to position, reposition, or enhance the position of a product.

Various promotional tactics help create and maintain positioning. A promotion such as a contest may be construed as essentially "gambling" in a culture, which would in turn affect the brand's image and position. Promotions represent an opportunity to communicate to consumers a product's attributes and benefits.

The core of product positioning at the strategic and tactical levels rests with the product itself. Effective positioning should be based on what the product itself does well in comparison to competitor products. This lowers barriers to consumer acceptance of promotional activity, and grounds consumer attitudes in product features. Benefits may be intangible or tangible, but attempts to position products in ways incompatible with the actual features of the product will eventually fail.

Operational Implications

Successful positioning is best supported at the operational level through communication and consistency. Individuals working with the company should be aware of the brand's position. Position should be reflected in all operational activities, including distribution, sales, promotion, and all other components of the marketing mix. The focus on positioning ensures a consistent message at all contact points.

Positioning processes become more complicated in international settings. A firm should, whenever possible, present consistent positioning in all markets. With travel and relatively global communications, consumers will eventually be exposed to messages from different countries or regions. These communications should support the overall positioning of the firm.

In summary, international positioning processes should be consistent with those used in domestic markets. The underlying characteristics of the product plus the expertise of the company should drive this consistency. Efficiencies can be gained from consistency and focus; the position that emerges for the company and brand helps lead to long-term success.

TERMS

product position

product positioning

positioning statement

differentiation

brand equity

brand parity

country-of-origin effect

country image

animosity

nationalism

religiosity

sovereignty

tangible product benefits

intangible product benefits

positioning maps

repositioning

greenwashing

REVIEW QUESTIONS

1. Define product positioning.

2. What are the two key elements of product positioning?

3. Define differentiation. What are some examples?

4. How does differentiation help create brand equity?

5. Define brand parity and give an example.

6. In what ways does technology influence global positioning?

7. Define the country-of-origin effect.

8. What do the terms *animosity* and *ethnocentrism* mean?

9. Define nationalism. How is it different from animosity?

10. Define sovereignty.

11. What are the different country-of-origin label options?

12. What are the complicating factors for identifying country of origin?

13. What is product-versus-product positioning?

14. Define product line.

15. What is product line versus product line positioning?

16. What is the difference between brand versus brand positioning, and company versus company positioning?

17. How does positioning relate to price?

18. Describe tangible product benefits and intangible product benefits concepts.

19. How do positioning maps show differentiation?

20. What is the difference between share of mind and share of heart?

21. What are the different ways to enhance a product's position?

22. Define repositioning.

23. Define greenwashing and name the seven deadly sins of greenwashing.

24. What is the change in focus some companies need to make when positioning at the bottom-of-the-pyramid?

25. What ethical concerns does positioning present?

DISCUSSION QUESTIONS

1. There are at least six effective methods for positioning products: (1) competitors, (2) use or application, (3) price–quality relationship, (4) product user, (5) product class, and (6) cultural symbol. Identify two brands associated with the following countries:

   - Mexico
   - United Kingdom
   - Japan
   - Netherlands

Identify the positioning strategy each uses, then suggest an alternative strategy.

2. Choose a product category and make a list of five brands, three of which are not made in the United States. Identify two attributes that are common across these five brands. Using the perspective of a college student (meaning you are part of the target market), create a positioning map for these brands and then interpret the map.

3. Identify two products that compete at each of the following levels, in at least two countries other than the United States. Explain how the competition might influence positioning strategies.

   - Product versus product
   - Product line versus product line
   - Brand versus brand
   - Company versus company
   - Industry versus industry

4. Ethnocentrism, animosity, nationalism, and religiosity all influence consumer perceptions of products. Consider how these factors influence positioning for the following brands when entering France, Thailand, and Saudi Arabia:

   - Royal Dutch Shell
   - Starbucks
   - Haier
   - Carrefour

5. Visit a local retailer and find five products with country-of-origin labels. What countries are they from? How does country of origin relate to product attributes or sophistication? How does it influence the position for the product?

ANALYTICAL AND INTERNET EXERCISES

1. Many companies do not emphasize home country status. As a result, many consumers are unaware of the country or origin for many brands. Research online the home countries for the following companies or brands:

- Firestone
- Smith and Wesson
- Rolls Royce
- Adidas
- Lego
- Burger King
- Huffy Bicycles
- Nokia
- Red Bull
- Volvo

2. Differentiation can be created and/or reinforced by promotional activities. Visit the websites of the following companies and use the home pages to identify how they are differentiated.

   - Sony (sony.com)
   - The Tata Group (tata.com)
   - Hyundai (hyundai.com)
   - Mango (mango.com)
   - The Mandarin Oriental Hotel Bangkok (mandarinoriental.com/Bangkok)

3. One product that has enjoyed international success is Turkish Delight candy. Many companies, including Nestlé, produce versions of the product. In Turkey, firms such as Tatlisumak and Pinar Kuruyemis produce and sell the delicacy both domestically and in other countries. Most Turkish citizens are proud of their local culture and products. Construct individual maps exhibiting share of mind and share of heart for Nestlé, Tatlisumak, Pinar Kuruyemis, a British confectioner that produces "lumps of delight" for Turkey, Great Britain, and Mexico. Explain how differences in status in these countries would affect positioning or the product as well as other international marketing programs for them.

4. Create a share of mind/share of heart positioning map for producers of hummus. Which criteria would be most relevant for international positioning programs? Defend your answer.

STUDENT STUDY SITE

Visit **https://study.sagepub.com/baack2e** to access these free additional learning tools:

- Web Quizzes
- eFlashcards
- SAGE Journal Articles
- Country Fact Sheets
- Chapter Outlines
- Interactive Maps

CASE 7

TOTO: Positioning Plumbing Products Globally

TOTO is the world's largest manufacturer of toilets, producing more than 7 million units each year. The Japanese company was founded in 1917, with "TOTO" being an abbreviation of the two Japanese words forming its full name: Toyo Toki. Although the company manufactures a complete line of plumbing supplies, it is best known for its high-end, innovative toilets.

TOTO enjoys a consistent position across markets, and differentiates from competitors by being the leader in innovation. With 5% of revenues going to research and development (R&D) and an army of 1,500 engineers, the company remains at the cutting edge of toilet technology.

TOTO holds its position based on beliefs about company innovations combined with an emphasis on sustainability. The company began designing water-conserving toilets before many governments began to focus on this improvement. The Aquia model has a 1.6-gallon flush for bulk waste and a 0.9 gallon flush for light or liquid waste. It saves about 20% more water than an ultra-low flow toilet. TOTO also invented and introduced the tankless toilet, which leads to less material waste in manufacturing and a more efficient flush.

TOTO's success has been largely based on its patented invention of the Washlet, an automated, remote-controlled cleaning nozzle. A consumer pushes a button and a nozzle extends to warm-water rinse and then warm-air dry. The nozzle moves back-and-forth resulting in a clean so thorough that the company claims that no toilet paper is needed. This makes the nozzle not only innovative but also green—it eliminates paper waste. The nozzle then retracts and self-cleans before the next usage. The products were first introduced in 1980 and have sold 18 million units worldwide. Washlets are highly popular in Japan and hold 60% of the market share for toilets.

TOTO also features "smart toilets" that offer various luxury features such as a heated-seat, hands-free automatic flushing, tank-less toilets, built-in air-purifying systems, remote control adjustable heated seat temperatures, an energy-saver timer that turns off the toilet during low usage time periods, and even medical sensors to measure blood sugar, pulse, and blood pressure. In Japan, a popular feature in women's restrooms is a set of small speakers that play music to mask any sounds made while the consumer uses the toilet. Two other recent innovations are the automatic closing and opening lid, which the company markets as a "marriage saver," and a rimless design for the bowl, which keeps the bowl cleaner longer.

As TOTO has become increasingly dominant in the Japanese market, with over 70% of households using the company's products, global expansion has become necessary to continue growth. The company currently operates in the following countries:

- China
- Taiwan
- Thailand
- United States
- Indonesia
- Vietnam
- India

TOTO has maintained a consistent position as it has moved into the new markets. Targeting the high-end, "global" market segment, the company emphasizes innovation and sustainability consistently in all of these markets. The newest toilet added to its product line, the Neorest, can cost up to $5,900 in the United States and has been called the world's most expensive toilet.

TOTO enjoys a consistent position across markets, and differentiates from competitors by being the leader in innovation.

TOTO has also attempted to remove American consumer resistance to its innovations, especially the Washlet. The company featured a promotional campaign to encourage Washlet usage. The company used a comparison to dirty dishes at the core of the campaign. It asked the question "Would you use toilet paper to clean dishes?" The company placed a billboard in Times Square in New York with six naked buttocks and the phrase "Clean is happy. No ifs, ands, or..." blocking the more potentially scandalous part of the image.

The company's marketing team realizes that one promotional campaign will not be enough to remove the taboo surrounding its products and use of the Washlet. Instead, a long-term view has been taken. The Washlet faced the same resistance in Japan when TOTO first introduced the product in the early 1980s. TOTO used a similar promotional message "*Oshiri datte arattehoshii*" (Even buttocks want to be cleaned) to promote the product in Japan. Critics respond that the concern is not the taboo, it is the time involved. Americans are not as technology-oriented as the Japanese and focus more on convenience. The Washlet may seem interesting, but consumers in the United States may settle for the convenience and speed of toilet paper.

TOTO continues to be positioned as the global leader in toilet technology. This positioning, across all markets, differentiates the company globally, and provides the foundation for future success (Rilling, 2004; Chantanusornsiri, 2005; Clough, 2005; Lenius, 2005; Terada, 2007; Wongsamuth, 2009).

(Continued)

(Continued)

1. Discuss the challenges TOTO might encounter when seeking to maintain a consistent position globally.

2. How might regulatory activities affect TOTO as it enters markets?

3. Create a positioning map for TOTO using the attributes green and price.

4. TOTO targets high-end consumers in their markets. What are some other potential segmenting factors for the company's target market?

5. It is possible that competitors may follow TOTO's lead by focusing on innovation and green products. What will need to happen before TOTO should consider repositioning? What is a potential attribute that the company could emphasize if repositioning? Would share of mind and share of heart become part of this analysis in some way? Why or why not?

8

MARKET RESEARCH IN THE INTERNATIONAL ENVIRONMENT

LEARNING OBJECTIVES

After reading and studying this chapter, you should be able to answer the following questions:

1. What is an international market research program?
2. What are the steps of the market research process?
3. What roles do primary and secondary data play in the process of designing an international marketing research program?
4. What techniques can be used when developing samples and collecting data for international marketing research?
5. Which factors complicate the analysis and interpretation of data in international marketing research?

IN THIS CHAPTER

Opening Vignette: Tesco Clubcard

OVERVIEW

TESCO CLUBCARD

Tesco, a UK grocery and general merchandise retailer, began 2017 with operations in eleven countries. The company employs 470,000 people, which makes it one of the world's largest retailers. The company created a loyalty program, the Tesco Clubcard, to attract customers and encourage repeat purchases.[1] The card was launched in 1995. It became the foundation of Tesco's rise to dominance in the UK (Winterman, 2013).

Currently, the Clubcard program operates in the UK, Ireland, the Czech Republic, Hungary, Poland and several other countries. In the UK market the system has been highly successful. A Clubcard looks like any other loyalty card goes but beyond the simple promise of rewarding shopper loyalty. Discount vouchers and deals for loyal customers enable Tesco's marketers to use the Clubcard as a data collection tool. The loyalty card, and especially the Dunnhumby database behind it, provide Tesco with an unprecedented level of detail into who its customers are and how they shop.

In order to participate, an individual fills out an application form either online or in-store. The membership application in the UK asks for the person's name, date of birth, postcode, phone number, e-mail address and gender. In Poland, the Czech Republic and other countries similar information is required.

Once a customer receives the card, each transaction is recorded. This provides Tesco's marketing team with information about products purchased, the frequency of shopping, locations, and type of payment. The information can be combined with other data (such as records of customer complaints) and linked to the Clubcard database. As a result, the program yields one of the most detailed customer relationship management (CRM) databases operated by a business organization. A few criticisms have arisen. Some note that the Clubcard has been successful for the company but shoppers have begun to question whether loyalty cards are more helpful to the supermarket or to customers.

TESCO CLUBCARD

Questions for Students

1. What are the ethical issues and privacy considerations with regard to collecting and using data about the shopping behaviors of Tesco customers?

2. How can the data collected via the Clubcard be used? How can they be linked to other items in the company's databases?

3. What cross-cultural issues regarding the use and collection of data might complicate Tesco's loyalty scheme in stores across Eastern Europe?

OVERVIEW

Market research plays a vital role in connecting businesses with customers; however, the information will only be useful when precise information can be attained. Decisions to engage in any international marketing activity become more likely to succeed when they are based on valid and reliable data. Obtaining market information can be challenging. In the international context, differences in language, culture, economic systems, political and regulatory systems, technological development, and marketing infrastructures make data collection more complex (see Figure 8.1). Consequently, what works well in one country might not work at all in another.

International marketing researchers face an additional obstacle: the rapid pace of change. Many global events quickly alter the business landscape. These developments alter the types of information to be gathered as well as the methods used to collect, analyze, and store the data.

This chapter first describes the basic international market research process. It then provides a discussion of primary and secondary data, micro- and macro-level analysis, and qualitative and quantitative research. Various types of research of research programs are assessed. Finally the challenges associated with building successful global marketing research programs are described.

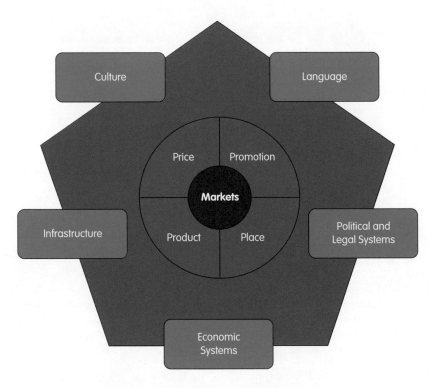

FIGURE 8.1   The International Marketing Context

LEARNING OBJECTIVE #1:

What is an international market research program?

INTERNATIONAL MARKET RESEARCH

Market research is the systematic gathering, storing, and analyzing of marketplace information for use in strategic decision-making.[2] The information collected links the organization with various constituent groups. Companies seeking to meet the wants and needs of customer groups must first understand them. This requires quality marketing information based on an understanding of the research methods that will and will not be useful in a targeted country, culture, or specific market. An effective program often requires the efforts of a research expert from both the home and foreign country so that research results from each country may be more appropriately understood and compared (Douglas and Craig, 1983).

market research: the systematic gathering, storing, and analyzing of marketplace information for use in managerial decision-making

TABLE 8.1 Major Market Research Firms (listed alphabetically)

A. C. Nielsen	United States
Arbitron, Inc.	United States
GfK AG	Germany
IBOPE	Brazil
IMS Health	United States
Information Resources Incorporated	United States
INTAGE Inc.	Japan
Ipsos Group	France
J. D. Power and Associates	United States
The Kantar Group	United Kingdom
Synovate	United Kingdom
Video Research	Japan

An alternative approach for an international company would be to hire an external research firm. By employing an external company, management can draw from the significant expertise of successful research companies. Two benefits of hiring an external firm include convenience and expertise, although hiring one can be costly. Consequently, the decision-maker should consider whether the benefits of convenience and expertise will be greater than the cost of the research. The website www.greenbook.org provides a directory of potential international marketing research firms. Table 8.1 presents a list of major global market research firms.

Market choices, product, pricing, promotion, and distribution decisions are all influenced by international marketing research. Each type of research discussed below is presented in Table 8.2.

MARKET CHOICES

A company considering international expansion considers the markets that will be most accessible and/or easy to enter. Market research assists in discovering the best options. As an example, the concept of psychic distance may be applies to market entry. **Psychic distance** refers to the degree of perceived difference between one culture and another. Some scholars argue that psychic distance is a subjective

psychic distance: the individual's subjective perception of the differences between the home country and the foreign country

TABLE 8.2   Types of International Marketing Research

Type	Sample Issue Addressed
Markets	Which markets would be most accessible for a company?
Product	What product design would be most appropriate?
Pricing	How sensitive are consumers to the price?
Promotion	How do consumers react to advertising campaigns?
Distribution	What is the best method for distributing the product?

perception of the differences between home country and foreign country and therefore cannot be measured with factual indicators such as GDP levels, level of education, or societal development (Sousa and Bradley, 2006). Others propose that the measure of psychic distance is derived from a variety of components that can be identified through market research, such as perceived business-level differences (how business is conducted) as well as the unique features of a culture and economy (O'Grady and Lane, 1996).

Factual indicators often influence how managers perceive foreign countries and affect their decisions of which countries to enter. For instance, the decision by a pharmaceutical company to enter the European marketplace requires understanding several unique standards for medicines and business practices by companies in that region. At the same time, the initial decision to choose markets to consider may be influenced by the management's perception of how similar the country is to the home market. The subsequent market analysis required would include understanding of the methods used by medical practitioners, health care institutions, governmental agencies, and other matters such as pricing systems or the effectiveness of marketing communications.

PRODUCT RESEARCH

Companies that develop products or make alterations to existing offering often utilize product research programs. Product research provides information for international companies that helps the marketing team understand what consumers want. Then, products and services can be tailored to match the needs of those consumers. Cultural differences affect this type of international market research information. Consumer responses to various products change over time. For example, the hamburger was once frowned upon in France. Now, however, the burger has become acceptable in that culture, offering new opportunities (Sigal, 2008). Product research helps marketers remain current on such changing international tastes and trends.

Marketers also consider taste preferences. Coca-Cola introduced a line of drinks in China that included traditional Chinese herbal ingredients (Bokaie, 2001). As a global brand, Coca-Cola took advantage of its international market research program by adapting to the differences in taste revealed by research findings.

International product research also focuses on legal requirements and restrictions. Toyota adapted the engine size of its luxury brand, Lexus, in China by producing a smaller version with a sub-3-liter version. The decision was based on the Chinese government's decision to raise sales taxes on vehicles with engines larger than 3 liters (Shirouzu, 2009). In this instance, the international legal environment changed and research helped to address the problem that arose.

PRICING RESEARCH

Pricing research examines the effects of price on consumer demand and other outcomes. The price of a product often signals its value or worth; however, the meaning of "price" varies across cultures. Marketers routinely consider cultural influences before establishing international pricing policies.

Researchers have discovered that consumers in Poland generally view price as a signal of quality. Consumers are less likely to connect a product's price with quality in other countries. This finding suggests that marketers in some countries might use pricing as a method to entice quick sales. In Poland, however, price changes, especially discounts, would be less useful (Moore et al., 2003).

PROMOTION RESEARCH

Promotion research assesses the effectiveness of marketing communications messages and tactics. In international marketing research, cultural differences dictate that researchers should take steps to ensure the message sent in an advertisement is the one the company intended to deliver. The marketing team at Pizza Hut realized that changes needed to be made in the way the brand was promoted in Hong Kong. Consumers sought not only good food but also more involvement in the process of how the food was delivered. After the advertising messages were adjusted to this cultural nuance, sales for the chain began to rise (Murphy, 2006).

Promotion research relies on cultural sensitivity. Marketing professionals screen messages to make sure they are acceptable in foreign cultures. Given that many advertising campaigns are transmitted on a global scale, market researchers need to assess how consumers in other countries react to them. The use of overtly sexual imagery in television commercials, for example, is generally viewed as being offensive in some East Asian cultures (Prendergast, 2002). Consumers in collectivist cultures such as China react differently to advertisements than would consumers in more individualistic cultures, including Germany. One recent study addressed this issue and revealed that, in general, Chinese consumers more often rated offensive advertisements as uncomfortable, disgusting, and impolite than did their German counterparts (Chan et al., 2007).

DISTRIBUTION RESEARCH

Distribution research seeks out the most effective methods for moving products to consumers. It has special importance because infrastructure development varies greatly around the world. This makes gaining a better understanding of the physical distribution methods available in a target country an important task.

Many countries worldwide suffer from poor transportation capabilities, often due to economic deprivation or topography. Nepal, for example, is largely a mountainous country. The mountains and rugged hills make public transportation difficult. Roads are generally concentrated in the Eastern and central regions of the country. Although air and rail transportation are available, difficulties exist in the physical distribution of goods and services in Nepal and similar countries.

Distribution research identifies the most efficient local systems. One recent study revealed a significant level of cost inefficiency in the retail grocery distribution system in Spain (Barros and Sellers-Rubio, 2008). Consequently, distribution strategies

A nation's topography affects international marketing research programs.

aimed at improving efficiency were developed. Consumer behavior, as it relates to distribution management, should also be considered. In China, many grocery shoppers arrive at supermarkets on foot, thereby limiting the amount of goods they can carry home (Mai and Zhao, 2004). Many forms of shopping, including for groceries, are different in Europe, Africa, and Asia.

LEARNING OBJECTIVE #2:

What are the steps of the market research process?

THE INTERNATIONAL MARKET RESEARCH PROCESS

The market research process often follows the steps highlighted in Table 8.3. The process may take a good deal of time. International marketing decisions require careful deliberation. Samsung Electronics, for example, began market research in India a full year before attempting to enter the marketplace (Kripalani, 2003). In international marketing terms, a single year can be considered to be a relatively short time frame. Ample time should be allowed to ensure that marketing managers capture the best information possible.

DEFINE THE PROBLEM OR SITUATION

Correctly defining the company's key situation or problem will be crucial. An inadequately or hastily defined problem or situation leads to flawed data and

TABLE 8.3   The Market Research Process

Step 1	Define the problem or situation
Step 2	Complete a cost/benefit analysis
Step 3	Develop a research design
Step 4	Develop a sample
Step 5	Collect data
Step 6	Analyze and interpret data
Step 7	Formulate conclusions and write a report

conclusions. Researchers should account for cultural differences early in the process. For example, the marketing team may decide that a sales promotion did not succeed in a domestic market due to declining sales levels across the product category. This may be a non-issue in other areas, however, because sales promotions have never been used as extensively in those countries. The sales promotion problem does not exist in the foreign market, but other marketing issues may be present. Consequently, it may be difficult for managers to communicate the problem effectively across varied markets and stakeholders. Correctly identifying the problem represents a continuing concern for market researchers, complicated by language, behavioral, and cultural differences.

Another roadblock to precisely identifying a problem emerges from the ways individuals evaluate products. Consumers in Portugal may report they are satisfied with a brand of toothpaste whereas consumers in Canada report they are not. Portuguese consumers may base answers about satisfaction on good breath, whereas Canadians respond to perceptions of healthy teeth. In other words, differing criteria regarding the same product have been used. As a result, a research team from Portugal might not understand why the product struggles in Canada. Consequently, the problem statement should take into account the manner in which products are evaluated and work to be certain the evaluation statements are accurate and useful to the culture and country under consideration.

COMPLETE A COST/BENEFIT ANALYSIS

In most business decisions, managers assess the costs and benefits of an activity early in the process. The same holds true for international market research. Some international research projects may be performed at a relatively low cost. Other research techniques involve significant monetary investments.

Making the decision to proceed with research requires the marketing team to compare the importance of obtaining the required information and the time frame within which the information will be collected against the value of the benefits of acquiring the information and the overall difficulty in obtaining the data (Hair et al., 2003). The availability and type of information needed to address the problem can drive up costs. The overall research budget influences these decisions. Sufficient resources should be available to conduct quality research.

LEARNING OBJECTIVE #3:

What roles do primary and secondary data play in the process of designing an international marketing research program?

DEVELOP A RESEARCH DESIGN

Several issues emerge when developing the design of the research, in both domestic and international markets. Decisions will be made regarding the use of primary and/ or secondary research techniques, a micro- or macro-level analysis, and whether to employ quantitative or qualitative methods.

PRIMARY DATA

primary data: data that are gathered by the researcher or research team for a specific project

A researcher or research team gathers **primary data**. They are collected in practically any region of the world. Primary data take many forms, including those displayed in Table 8.4.

In one form of primary research, members of a potential target market complete a questionnaire. The items should be carefully translated to the language of the target market to make certain no confusion emerges. Telephone and Internet surveys serve the same purpose. The data gathered through an interview process will only be as effective as the skill levels of those conducting the interviews. Primary data may be collected by interviewing customers in a store after they have purchased items, a technique known as the mall intercept method, or by questioning members in a focus group. Cultural norms should be carefully followed. For instance, in some nations interrupting someone after the individual purchases an item may be perceived as an aggressive invasion of privacy.

TABLE 8.4   Primary Sources for International Market Research

Questionnaires
Telephone and Internet Surveys
Interviews of Customers
Ethnographic Studies
Observational Studies

Other forms of primary data collection include ethnographic studies and observational studies. An ethnographic study takes place when a researcher studies respondents in their native environment by living with them. Observational studies focus on observing consumers as they shop, as they interact in the marketplace, or as they use products in the home. Researchers can also quietly observe in-store signage and displays, pricing methods, tactics used by members of the sales force, and methods of payment. In a store visit, the researcher makes a purchase in order to observe sales experience in person.

It may be difficult and costly to collect primary data in some regions. Effective programs require a staff of trained and experienced researchers. When the company budgets adequate resources, primary data may prove to be highly useful. The value of primary data is that they are collected in exactly the form that the researcher chooses. Primary data may be especially useful in international marketing because the secondary sources described next often vary dramatically by country and by region.

SECONDARY DATA

Secondary data are collected by an outside agency or other external research sources. The information can be relatively inexpensive to obtain and many sources are available. The U.S. Department of Commerce website (https://data.commerce.gov/) provides a great deal of secondary data. Other outlets include the Department of Commerce International Trade Association (www.trade.gov) and Euromonitor (www.euromonitor.com). Table 8.5 identifies additional secondary sources of international market research information.

secondary data: data that have already been collected by an agency and are made available either free of charge or for a fee

The United States maintains several secondary resource services. Secondary data are accessible in several other developed nations; however, far fewer sources will be available in less-developed countries. Some of the data may not be available for specific regions of a country. Even when they are, these data may not be offered in a useful form, which makes data collection from only secondary sources more challenging.

TABLE 8.5   Secondary Sources for International Market Research

U.S. Department of Commerce, www.commerce.gov/
U.S. Department of Commerce International Trade Association, www.trade.gov
Euromonitor, www.euromonitor.com
Organization of Economic Co-operation and Development, www.oecd.org
International Monetary Fund, www.imf.org
CIA—The World Factbook, https://www.cia.gov/library/publications/the-world-factbook/index.html
World Information, Ltd, www.worldinformation.com
The World Bank, www.worldbank.org
United Nations International Trade Statistics Yearbook, http://unstats.un.org/unsd/trade/default.htm
Europa, www.europa.eu
World Economic Forum, https://www.weforum.org/
GlobalEdge, http://globaledge.msu.edu/
Economist Country Briefings, www.economist.com/topics (search for specific countries within the topics)
The World Bank "Doing Business," http://doingbusiness.org/
Transparency International, http://transparency.org/
Internet World Stats, http://internetworldstats.com

Although secondary data sources offer convenience, these types of data might present problems when used to make many marketing decisions. Although all of the sites listed in Table 8.5 are reputable, secondary information should still be scrutinized carefully. Marketers may struggle to find details regarding the collection of data for government statistics. For instance, the Chinese National Bureau of Statistics keeps many of its data collection methods secret. In response, private research agencies often calculate separate measures of key country-level statistics. In 2011, private researchers found that property prices more than doubled from 2004 to 2010, but the National Bureau of Statistics generated results suggested only a 50% increase.[3]

Outside marketers would want to study both sources of data and consider whether either source would be motivated to skew the figures.

When examining international markets, it can be hard to find ways to compare data and information from one country with another. Consider the problem of accessing market viability. Researchers are able to obtain secondary data about imports and exports in a market; however, simply knowing the level of imports and exports in one country versus another provides limited information regarding the market attractiveness of either nation. Imports may be low in a particular country, but the demand for a specific product may be high. Consequently, the researcher will try to obtain additional information to be able to draw informed conclusions about the market's viability.

MICRO-LEVEL ANALYSIS

A micro-level analysis helps the research team understand the attitudes, preferences, motivations, lifestyles, and intentions of individual consumers. Many companies perform this type of analysis for international market research projects. Micro-level analyses account for language, culture, and other factors that affect or influence individual consumers.

MACRO-LEVEL ANALYSIS

A macro-level analysis often occurs at the national level. The selection of a country to enter requires research devoted to political and legal risk, which, in turn, affects the selection of target markets in various countries. Secondary data can often be collected to examine various macro-level factors, including governmental forms and entry risk.

Marketers consider numerous factors making decisions about entering or serving in other countries. Most research projects that assess other countries require both micro- and macro-level data collection. Macro-level information can often be gathered from secondary sources whereas micro-level information may require a primary data collection program.

INTERNATIONAL MARKETING IN DAILY LIFE

METHODS OF TRANSPORTATION

Traveling is a basic human activity. Modes of transportation vary widely. In many parts of the world, a motorbike offers the most practical and economical choice, which creates a large target market for many companies. The Honda Diamond Blue motorbike recently introduced in Vietnam was an almost perfect replica of the Vespa LX, which is manufactured in Vietnam by the Italian company Piaggio. Some critics argued that Honda was infringing on Piaggio's intellectual property. In fact, Honda had nothing to do with the Honda Diamond Blue. Instead, the motorbike is manufactured by the Vietnam Shipbuilding Industry and Motorbike Corporation (Vinashin Motor) who copied Vespa's design and used Honda's brand name. Vietnam is signatory to international intellectual property treaties with Italy and Japan. Governments in both countries are considering taking legal action. The odds of success in legal actions are low, because Vinashin Motor is a subsidiary of a state-owned company and the Vietnamese government has already signaled that it will support the company's actions (Steinglass, 2010a).

QUALITATIVE AND QUANTITATIVE RESEARCH

Numerous research designs are available to international marketing researchers to collect micro-level information. Researchers begin by choosing to employ qualitative research, quantitative research, or a combination of both. Table 8.6 presents the major types of qualitative and quantitative research methods.

TABLE 8.6   Qualitative and Quantitative Research Methods

Qualitative Methods
Ethnographic Research Design
Observation
Focus Groups
Personal Interviews
Delphi Technique
Quantitative Methods
Survey
Experiments
Test Markets

QUALITATIVE METHODS

Qualitative research designs focus on obtaining information without relying on numbers or measurements. These methods concentrate on understanding the meanings of consumer responses to the researcher's questions. The information gained may be highly valuable in an international context. Qualitative research designs are particularly useful when seeking to understand a given culture (Macnamara, 2004).

Deriving meanings from consumer responses requires the researcher to interpret data from various groups of people. Qualitative methods are *researcher dependent*, which means that the researcher subjectively analyzes the information that has been collected. The use of a qualitative research design typically limits the number of respondents or research subjects included in a sample.

At times cultural norms influence the use of qualitative research designs. In some cultures, consumers are hesitant to express their opinions in front of others, due to factors the researcher did not consider. In China, workers with young children may receive higher salaries than those without. Some workers may lie about having children, which in turn may make them reluctant to reveal the truth when talking to a researcher (Hessler, 2007).

Ethnographic Research Design

Only certain types of qualitative research designs are practical for some regions. An ethnographic research design is one in which the researcher studies respondents in their native environment by living or interacting with them. What emerges

qualitative research design: a research method that focuses on obtaining information without a reliance on numerical expression or measurement

are "thick descriptions" of cultural patterns, shopping habits, and other features of the area. Marketing managers at Unilever's Indian subsidiary, Hindustan Lever, are required to spend two months living in rural villages after being hired. Doing so allows them to see how consumers interact with the company's products (Sanchez, 2006).

Focus Groups

Focus groups are semi-structured or unstructured discussions that generally take place in groups of eight to twelve. A focus group moderator facilitates the discussion and does his or her best to ensure that each member of the focus group has an opportunity to contribute and give opinions. Focus groups are utilized extensively in market research, in both domestic and international contexts. Several issues and challenges emerge when conducting focus groups.

Focus group moderators in international settings adapt to language differences across cultures, nonverbal cues, and cultural customs (Maholtra et al., 1996). A focus group held in China should include a number of younger consumers mixed in with older consumers in order to minimize peer pressure to yield to older consumers' opinions as a sign of respect (Eckhardt, 2004; Watkins-Mathys, 2006).

Eye contact, touching other persons, and posture may all affect a focus group. Staring someone in the eyes may be viewed as aggressive in one culture but essential in another. Raising one's voice may be expected in an African or Latin American focus group but considered rude and boorish in Asia.

Focus groups offer an effective method of obtaining information directly from consumers. When conducting focus groups in other countries, the marketing team includes native speakers to help analyze what has been said in order to ensure the correct meanings are extracted (Watkins-Mathys, 2006). Although the use of these groups in international research presents some difficulties, the benefits of this approach often outweigh the costs. As with other qualitative techniques, additional research approaches are generally needed to supplement the information obtained from focus groups.

Personal Interviews

One-on-one discussions take place between a researcher and a respondent in the **personal interview** method. Cultural nuances often affect the interviews. Consumers in some cultures may be open to expressing their honest opinions whereas subjects in other countries might not be as willing to reveal their feelings. Gender roles create an additional factor; the gender of the actual interviewer should be taken into account. Women in many cultures are hesitant to answer interview questions and may not respond when a male is present. In some countries, women are not allowed to speak with a personal interviewer. A male interviewer may be viewed as intimidating to a female respondent. A female interviewer may be treated harshly by a male respondent in a more misogynistic culture.

Socially Desirable Responses

One complication associated with in-person data collection techniques in international markets is the presence of socially desirable responses. These occur when respondents bias their opinions by what they believe are the most culturally acceptable ways in which to respond to a question or provide an opinion. For example, consumers in collectivist cultures tend to be reluctant to express their true feelings in survey research. This becomes problematic for the researcher seeking to ascertain whether these responses indicate their true feelings, or if they are responding in the ways they feel they should.

INTERNATIONAL INCIDENT

You are performing a market research project in a collectivist culture, Korea. Product sales in the region have been slipping and your supervisor has given you the task of identifying the reasons behind the lagging sales. The research team has decided that a consumer survey is the best method for collecting data from consumers. The team ultimately finds that the majority of the responses on the survey question are quite favorable regarding the satisfaction consumers express toward the company's product. When presenting the results to the supervisor, what would you tell him? What would you suggest?

Delphi Technique

Experts often provide a unique and valuable perspective on a topic. The Delphi technique method taps expert opinions through the use of a panel or group. The members answer a series of questions regarding a topic, often without knowing who else is serving on the panel, as members are stationed in remote locations. The researcher collects responses from all members and circulates them to group members. Typically, the questions are designed to forecast or predict the future. As with any group, disagreements occur. In a second iteration, the researcher then asks the experts to respond once again, after seeing the responses from other panellists, and then make arguments for their perspectives. Eventually the idea is to come to a consensus. The final report presents convergence regarding the underlying agreed-upon answer and strongest prediction. The Delphi technique might be used to help forecast external market concerns such as growth rates in specific markets, potential for economic unrest, or political election outcomes.

Netnography

The netnography research method originated from ethnography. It is applied to understanding social interactions including consumer behaviors. It takes place on online platforms such as newsgroups, blogs, forums, social networking sites, podcasting, videocasting, photosharing communities, and virtual worlds. This method was developed in 1995 by Robert Kozinets as a tool to explore online fan discussions about the Star Trek franchise. Netnography offers a unique and valuable approach to international market research because consumers of global and international brands often "gather" online in order to review products and services or establish brand communities. The availability of online data and ease of access make this a useful tool when exploring selected aspects of consumer behavior cross-culturally (Kozinets, 2002).

Observational Studies

Observational studies involve a researcher watching consumers as they shop and make purchases. One difficulty can be that in some cultures staring at another person is considered to be rude and consumers might be uncomfortable when they discover they are being watched. As with other international decisions, researchers consider the customs of consumers in the targeted countries before proceeding. While there may be difficulties for an obvious foreigner to surreptitiously observe others, observational data can be an effective method to garner rich, in-depth data.

QUANTITATIVE METHODS

quantitative research design: a research design that relies on numerical measurement and analysis

Numerical measurements and analyses are used in **quantitative research design** formats. These methods, including surveys, experiments, and test markets, require skill in designing questions for research subjects and in using statistical techniques to analyze responses and other information.

Surveys

surveys: research instruments that can be administered to large numbers of consumers with relative ease

Surveys are widely used market research tools. Survey instruments can be given to large numbers of consumers with relative ease. Administering surveys may be challenging in international settings. Approximately 760 million people worldwide are illiterate, and two-thirds of those are women (Watkins et al., 2010). Also, some consumers are difficult to reach in more remote locations. Others may be reluctant to record their true opinions or feelings on a survey instrument. Instead, these consumers provide responses biased by cultural norms, which complicates the survey process.

There also may be issues regarding interpretation of figures. Arabs write and read graphics from right to left. A graphic that displays the stages of a process that reads from left to right might cause Arabic survey participants to think the end of the process is the beginning and the beginning is the end.

back translation: a process in which a survey is translated from an original language into a targeted language and then back into the original language in order to check for accuracy and meaning

Conceptual equivalence problems create additional difficulties. These occur when a concept in one country has a different meaning in another. The word "household," for example, has different meanings in various countries. A household may be interpreted as consisting of a father, mother, and children in one country, but may include grandparents, aunts, uncles, and cousins in another.

parallel translation: a process in which two translators are used for the back translation process with the results being discussed and one translation selected

Careful translation of questions is essential when creating an effective international survey. Questions that are misunderstood or deemed offensive in some way may hurt the ability to obtain quality information. To make sure questions are correctly stated, two types of translation techniques are available. **Back translation** is a process in which a survey is translated from an original language into a targeted language—for example, from Italian to Portuguese—and then back into the original language by a different translator. The research team compares the second translated document to the original version to check for accuracy and meaning. Back translation is widely used. **Parallel translation** is a process in which two or more translators are used for each step of the back translation process. When different translations result, the research team discusses the results and selects one final translation. Parallel translation helps to account for the subtle nuances present in each language (Douglas and Craig, 1983).

experiments: research techniques that allow researchers to uncover cause-and-effect relationships by manipulating certain variables and controlling others

Experiments

Experimentation offers another viable quantitative market research option. **Experiments** allow researchers to discover cause-and-effect relationships by manipulating certain variables and controlling others. When utilizing experimentation

Cultural limitations can preclude the use of many qualitative research designs, such as journals.

techniques, researchers seek to identify the effect of one or two independent variables on a dependent variable. In international market research, experiments can be difficult to administer and control, because they may seem too artificial when conducted in a laboratory setting. At other times they provide valuable insights into consumer behaviors.

One experimental technique often used by marketers is the *purchase simulation* method. A room is given the appearance of a retail store. The research team tests certain variables such as color, methods of displaying merchandise, and selling techniques for effectiveness. Researchers also explore how different price levels (an independent variable) affect consumer intentions to buy (the dependent variable).

Advertisements and marketing materials are tested using *portfolio* techniques. Consumers are asked to view a series of commercials dispersed throughout a television program. Next, attitudes and recall are tested in order to see if the ad achieved its desired effect. The same methodology can be used with arrays of newspaper or magazine advertisements. Portfolio experiments assist the marketing team in understanding whether an advertisement that is effective in one country will be equally successful in another.

Test Markets

One form of experimentation that addresses the problems associated with an artificial environment, a **test market**, takes place in realistic marketplace conditions. In essence, results from an experiment in a small area, such as a small township in South Africa, are designed to predict what would happen in a larger area, including all small townships or the entire country.

Marketers employ test markets to better understand cause-and-effect relationships in a marketplace. A company may sell a product at one price in a test market and a

test market: a type of experiment that is constructed within realistic marketplace conditions

higher price in a second market to discover the level of price elasticity that is present. Another marketing team might assess the impact of a coupon program in one area compared to a bonus pack program in another. A third firm can test the effectiveness of an advertising program in a region. In each instance the cause or independent variables (price, promotions, or advertising) are linked to effects or dependent variables (sales figures).

Quantitative research designs are generally considered to be more objective than qualitative research designs. Quantitative research designs tend to work well when the intent is to reach large sample sizes. Surveys can be distributed to large numbers of consumers if the infrastructure of the country allows for such distribution. It is generally more difficult to reach a large number of consumers through focus groups or personal interviews.

Many international marketers combine qualitative and quantitative methods to obtain richer answers to difficult marketing questions. Recently, the British music magazine and website NME (www.NME.com) hired a new editor that wanted to make many changes. Before moving forward, the head of marketing, Tom Pearson, used both a series of focus groups and a survey of customers to gauge the potential effectiveness of those changes.[4]

ONLINE RESEARCH: A HYBRID APPROACH

Online research offers new opportunities for international researchers. Approximately 3 billion consumers had Internet access worldwide as of the end of 2016.[5] Asian countries make up the highest number of Internet users, followed by European countries, and then the Americas. Internet data collection works well in these regions.

Developed regions tend to experience high levels of Internet usage. The latest estimates reveal that countries with almost 100% Internet penetration include Iceland, Norway, and Denmark. Other regions do not have the same adoption rates, especially in less- or least-developed countries. The latest estimates reveal that fewer than 2% of consumers in the African countries of Somalia, Burundi, Eritrea, or Timor-Leste had Internet access at the end of 2016.[6]

Several obstacles must be overcome when conducting Internet market research programs. These include the lack of Internet capabilities and high illiteracy rates in some countries. Also, any Internet survey must be constructed to meet the cultural norms of the target audience. Careful translation and examination of the visual parts of the website will be necessary.

LEARNING OBJECTIVE #4:

What techniques can be used when developing samples and collecting data for international marketing research?

---

sampling: a process wherein only certain members of a population are included in a research study

DEVELOP A SAMPLE

Sampling is a process wherein members of a population are selected for inclusion in a research study because they will be representative of the larger group. Sampling techniques survey a small subgroup rather than the entire population in order to draw inferences about the entire population. Several well-established sampling and quantitative analysis techniques make it possible to have confidence in findings generated by samples.

Deriving the correct type of sample based on the information needed remains a key part of international marketing research. The overall aim of the research project dictates the type of sampling procedure to be used. In general, four types of research considerations should be addressed: descriptive research, comparative research, contextual research, and theoretical research (Reynolds et al., 2003).

The *descriptive research* method allows the researcher to examine attitudes and behaviors that are relevant to one specific country. Descriptive research applies when, for example, a marketing team seeks to understand the attitudes of consumers in South Korea toward automobile makes and models. Researchers focus on describing the attitudes and actions of consumers in that country.

Comparative research takes place when the researchers examine differences between cultures or countries. Comparative research would be used when marketers compare attitudes of consumers in South Korea with attitudes of consumers in India. Efforts focus on ensuring that the results reveal valid differences in attitudes between these two countries.

Contextual research may be performed when the research team attempts to study cross-national groups and how consumers behave in a selected context. The objective of contextual research may not be to discover differences in consumers across different countries but rather to investigate how consumers think or act within a specific context, such as within a certain political system.

Theoretical research examines the extent to which a theory garners support across cultures and national boundaries. The type of research chosen will be based on a specific academic research question. Academic institutions normally perform theoretical research, but the results may be applied to business settings. An international researcher might want to study how various satisfaction theories apply in certain countries or cultures, and the information could ultimately help solve marketing problems.

Next researchers choose between probability and nonprobability sampling methods. A **probability sample** is one in which each element in the population has a known, nonzero probability of being selected for a study. A *random sample* is a type of probability sample in which each element has an equal chance of being selected for study; it involves setting up a process or procedure ensuring that each person in the population has an equal probability of being chosen for the sample.

probability sample: a sample in which each element in the population has a known, nonzero probability of being selected for a study

Random samples are particularly effective when the researcher seeks to make statistical inferences. *Statistical inference* means that the research results obtained from a sample apply to the larger population, which is a common objective in international marketing research projects.

Simple examples of random selection include picking a name out of a hat or choosing the short straw. Researchers may also use computer programs to generate random numbers as the basis of selection (Zikmund and Babin, 2010). A stratified sample process divides the population into different categories and subsamples for further analysis. Using this technique, a researcher would categorize the residents of Great Britain into Labour Party, Conservative Party, or Liberal Democrat Party and then would take a subsample of respondents from within each category. The research team may specify the percentage of final respondents that they prefer in the final sample. For instance, the research team could target a final sample of 40% Labour, 40% Conservative, and 20% Liberal Democrat.

Obtaining a true probability or random sample in most international settings will be difficult, because methods used to reach people create biases. Some citizens do not own telephones, others do not have access to the Internet, and others still are illiterate and cannot read mail. Dispersed populations make selecting a random sample more problematic (Cavusgil and Das, 1997).

nonprobability sample: a sample in which the probability of an element of the population being included in a sample is unknown

A **nonprobability sample** is one in which the probability of an element of the population being included in a sample is unknown, which means a random sample cannot be used. The goal remains to make the sample as representative of the larger population as possible. Various tactics may be used. *Snowball techniques* are nonprobability techniques in which one respondent refers the researcher to the next respondent, and so on. Generating a *convenience sample* is a nonprobability technique in which researchers sample the respondents that are the easiest to reach without regard for how people are selected.

Some results are biased because researchers only reached the most readily available consumers. These individuals may not be representative of the true population being investigated. With international research, two key areas relate to age and education. Young, college-aged consumers in the Middle East may not have the same attitudes as their elders. Older, conservative consumers in Russia may not share similar opinions with younger consumers. Researchers using nonprobability samples should carefully consider these issues.

International sampling introduces several complications. One issue pertains to the lack of availability of accurate demographic information. For many countries, such lists, or sample frames, are not available. Less-developed countries often do not keep valid demographic information. Collection methods can be severely limited or deliberately altered by the ruling government. Identifying the correct sample size will be a key issue. For example, one team was only able to survey 137 randomly selected consumers in Malaysia. In that instance then the marketing team would need to understand how to use these techniques. If the results obtained came from a study of these consumers, the researcher would have an estimate of consumer satisfaction along with a level of confidence with which to gauge the findings.

COLLECT DATA

Marketers adjust data collection methods to fit local customs and the technological infrastructure in place. The proliferation of telephone and Internet communications has changed the landscape of data collection in many countries, but usage rates still vary widely. In 2015, estimates suggested that fewer than 5% of consumers in Arab nations had access to fixed-line broadband.[7] In other parts of the world, fixed-line broadband proliferation is even lower. Africa had less than a 0.5% penetration rate.[8] Internet access also varies. In Latin American countries, only 60% of consumers had access at the end of 2016.[9] This estimate is relatively high when compared to African countries, where only 28% of residents enjoyed Internet access in 2016.[10]

At the same time, the recent growth of mobile phone usage in some countries may lead to new marketing research opportunities. By 2016, more than 60% of individuals in sub-Saharan Africa had access to a mobile phone.[11]

Data collection in international market research may be complicated by levels of literacy, language differences, and cultural barriers. These limitations suggest that international market researchers should be careful to ensure that data collection methods are appropriate for the country, culture, or market under consideration.

Estimates reveal that by 2011 only 29% of consumers in Niger were literate, 39% in Senegal, and 52% in Liberia.[12] These rates are substantially lower than in industrialized countries. Companies often also may have to hide foreign origins. In Iraq, polling companies may need to hide the fact that Americans have employed them to complete the surveys.

Another difficulty occurs when attempting to use maps to find addresses. Some Western cities, such as London, are famous for being difficult to navigate, even with a map. In less-developed countries, maps may be outdated and incorrect. Addresses can create additional complications. A region may not use addresses, *per se*, and other parts of the world may have strikingly different addressing traditions. In East Asia, addresses normally start with the zip code, followed by county or metro area, followed by the city, then the ward or town, then the district, then the block, then the building number, ending with the apartment number if necessary. The order is exactly opposite of that found in most Western countries.[13]

BIG DATA

Big data is a term that describes the large volume of data that an organization receives on a daily basis. Big data is being generated at all times. Data can either be created by people or generated by machines, such as sensors gathering climate information, satellite imagery, digital pictures and videos, purchase transaction records, GPS signals, etc. It covers many sectors, from health care to transport and energy. Systems, sensors, and mobile devices transmit it. Big data arrives from multiple sources at a large velocity, volume, and a wide variety.[14]

The amount of data available may not be the most crucial factor in marketing programs. Instead, what organizations do with the data is what matters. Big data can be analyzed for insights that lead to better decisions. Some international companies have successfully used data to create new products. For example, Nike used data to develop Nike+, the app that is a data-based and data-driven tool for amateur runners to store and compare data about their running activities.[15] Unfortunately, many organizations lack the tools and manpower to analyze such amounts of data (Lazer et al., 2014).

LEARNING OBJECTIVE #5:

What factors complicate the analysis and interpretation of data in international marketing research?

ANALYZE AND INTERPRET DATA

The next phase of international market research involves analyzing and interpreting the data that have been collected. Ensuring that data are actually comparable continues to be an important issue when examining findings across countries and cultures. Two common problems at this point include linguistic difficulties and metric equivalence issues (Okazaki and Mueller, 2007).

LINGUISTIC PROBLEMS

Linguistic problems, or those associated with different meanings for terms, often complicate international market research. Frequently used concepts such as "satisfaction" and "feelings" should be carefully examined to understand how these terms might differ across cultures. The concept of "late" has a variety of meanings, influenced by both language and culture. In French, *en retard* translates as "not on time." The concepts of later and latest roughly translate as "more not on time." Arriving 30 minutes late in Brazil would not be considered rude but rather something approaching normal. Any research questions related to time and punctuality in other countries require consideration and adaptation.

METRIC EQUIVALENCE ISSUES

Metric equivalence issues arise when respondents from different countries systematically score interview or survey questions differently (Mullen, 1995). Cultural differences in response styles can greatly affect research results (Kumar, 2000). In a culture with strong tendencies toward humane orientation, respondents may be much more likely to offer favorable answers to questions, always granting the benefit of the doubt. Countries low on the same cultural characteristics may have respondents who are harsher in their evaluations of items such as product quality, brand loyalty, or other attitudes, feelings, and emotions.

American consumers are willing to express extreme positions on measurement scales, which may not be the case for consumers in other cultures. In collectivist societies, consumers are less willing to express extreme attitudes in either face-to-face or survey research, which affects research results in places such as China, Vietnam, Korea, or Taiwan. One study revealed, for example, that Korean consumers prefer to respond to survey items at the midpoint of a scale (Lee and Green, 1991). Some evidence suggests that cultural patterns, such as individualism or uncertainty avoidance, are related to consumers from various countries being more likely to respond at the extreme end of survey scales (Kumar, 2000). Problems such as these can restrict or alter the range of responses from one culture as compared to those in another culture. Restriction of range of responses can lead to problems with several statistical procedures and affect the required sample size.

FORMULATING CONCLUSIONS AND WRITING REPORTS

The final step in the international market research process is formulating conclusions and writing the research report. Decision-makers reach conclusions regarding whether the firm should expand marketing efforts internationally. If so, they can then choose the best method to enter a country. The research report should be written in a direct and informative way that assists the international marketing team in making decisions (Albaum et al., 2005).

In an international context, this step poses the same communication issues that have been part of the entire process. Often, one of the difficulties is in re-creating an environment that many of the readers of the report will never have visited, which might increase perceived levels of psychic distance. Consequently, those readers may be initially reluctant to accept the findings.

In a recent marketing research project report, the team noted that low-income (bottom-of-the-pyramid) consumers in China used clothes washing machines to clean vegetables. A Western executive might be hesitant to believe this finding. It would be the responsibility of the marketing researcher to present this information in a manner that earns the executive's confidence. When this finding was reported to the Chinese company Haeier, instead of being skeptical, the executives responded by introducing a machine specially designed for cleaning vegetables. The company later introduced a machine that assists in making cheese from goat's milk (Anderson and Markides, 2007). These products were introduced because the marketing team believed research findings and used them to guide strategic decisions.

ISSUES AND CHALLENGES IN INTERNATIONAL MARKETING RESEARCH

The term **scientific method** describes how researchers use observations, empirical evidence, and knowledge to objectively study various phenomena. In international marketing, conducting quality research requires objectivity and the ability to adapt to a changing global environment. Research techniques and conclusions must exhibit reliability and validity to be of use. Other obstacles include political and legal risks that might occur to obstruct research efforts.

scientific method: the use of observations, empirical evidence, and knowledge in order to make objective statements about certain phenomena

OBJECTIVITY

The scientific method requires objectivity. Researchers seek to remain objective as they develop research designs, create the questions featured in data collection, and when arriving at conclusions. An objective approach requires an impersonal viewpoint of a project and the ability to keep personal feelings or emotions from interfering with the process.

When performing international market research, one factor that affects objectivity is the **self-reference criterion**. It occurs when someone applies personal cultural values to the assessment of the behaviors of others (Malhotra et al., 1996). Self-reference leads to stereotyping members of other cultures and to accepting unfounded beliefs about them. A researcher must set aside stereotypes and unfounded beliefs about consumers in other cultures. This includes working to make certain language in questionnaires and other research methods is not biased and does not inflame or artificially influence the subjects in a study.

self-reference criterion: when someone applies his or her own cultural values and background to the assessment of behaviors of others

As an example, many women in Spain do not feel pressured to start careers and are comfortable in making the decision to not work outside the home. This cultural difference might affect the images of women advertisers might use. An emphasis on home and family might be better suited to Spanish women than to those in other countries.[16]

THE PACE OF CHANGE

Marketers consider the pace of change when conducting international research. What was true about a particular culture in the last decade, or even the last year, may not be true today (Tung, 1996). Recently, social media sites such as Twitter have dramatically influenced many consumers through connections between persons from other cultures and countries. Forms of music, world views, and other aspects of daily life continually evolve. Effective market research accounts for these factors.

RELIABILITY AND VALIDITY

In any research design, reliability and validity constitute important standards. Without these two factors, research results become far less useful. Marketing professionals endeavor to make sure both criteria can be met when developing a research project.

Reliability

reliability: the internal consistency of a measure and its ability to be replicated over time

In survey research, **reliability** refers to the degree to which the items used to measure a concept are internally consistent with each other and the extent to which the findings are repeatable over time. Measures are considered to be internally consistent when they appear to measure the same concept.

To demonstrate reliability, a researcher uses more than one measure when assessing marketing concepts. In a situation in which a researcher seeks to measure a consumer's perception of "media accuracy" in her home country, the decision could be to ask the respondent to agree or disagree with research statements, such as

- In general, the media in my country are credible
- I feel a good deal of confidence in the news I read daily
- The newscasters in my country do not attempt to lead their viewers astray

These items appear to be consistent with one another. A scale demonstrates reliability when results are similar across times. In other words, if the survey were given again, answers from the original persons who took the survey should be consistent with persons taking it for the first time.

Validity

validity: the degree to which a concept is accurately measured by survey or research items

In survey research, **validity** refers to the extent to which responses to a measure reflect the actual differences in the concept found across respondents, or the overall level of accuracy of the measure itself. A measure can be internally consistent, or repeatable, but not valid. A scale in a bathroom, for example, could consistently reveal someone's weight to be 210 pounds. If so, it could be said that the scale is reliable. If, however, the person's true weight is 190 pounds, the scale did not indicate a valid finding.

internal validity: when accurate cause-and-effect relationships are identified in a research finding

Reliability and validity constitute important concepts for marketing experiments as well. Two types of validity influence the outcomes of experiments. **Internal validity** results when *cause-and-effect* relationships have been correctly identified by the research. A study that accurately predicts lowering prices by 10% will increase the likelihood a customer in South Korea will immediately buy a new mobile device by 25% is internally valid.

external validity: when cause-and-effect relationships are expected to be found in other situations or settings

External validity means that the statement of cause and effect would apply to other situations or settings. In other words, if a 10% price reduction would also increase the likelihood of a customer purchase by 25% in Paraguay, the study would exhibit external validity. The most powerful external validity emerges if the research indicates that a 10% price reduction of *any item* would result in the same level of change in buyer behavior, regardless of the country involved. The reliability of an experiment is assessed by the degree to which the findings are replicated using subjects drawn from the same population and issues assessed across various groups.

Validity and reliability are more difficult to assess when using secondary data because the researcher does not control the method used to collect the data. Primary data allow the researcher to assess reliability and validity using various statistical techniques.

POLITICAL RISK

Governmental stability and governmental interactions with businesses are topics of concern for international marketers. When entering a market, **political risk**, or the potential for political forces and governmental activities to hamper and harm business activities within a country, should be considered. Political risk reflects the stability of the country being analyzed. Assessing this type of risk involves answering important questions, as displayed in Table 8.7.

political risk: the chance that political forces, such as government activities, will hamper and harm business activities within a country

A complete on-the-ground research effort would be the best method to answer these questions; however, it may be expensive and time-consuming. For preliminary market screening, a variety of sovereign credit rating services are available. Moody's and Standard & Poor's provide information that focuses on currency stability, which can be used as a proxy measure of overall country risk.

When assessing political risk, the marketing team considers how the product relates to the government in question. Alcohol, for example, remains a politically sensitive product and is outlawed in many Islamic countries. Other products are allowed but are likely to be highly regulated. These include children's toys, pharmaceuticals, and birth control products.

Terrorism, or the use of violence and the threat of violence as a means to gain political advantage, runs rampant in several countries. Business leaders consider the potential for a terrorist attack as part of the study of a country. The Pakistani government estimated an economic loss in the billions from 2004 to 2010 due to terrorism. From July 2009 to April 2010 the country experienced a 45% drop in foreign direct investment largely due to security concerns.[17] Many companies avoid countries with elevated levels of terrorist activity.

TABLE 8.7   Assessing Political Risk

What is the chance of a governmental collapse?
What is the potential for a different government to take power through democratic or other means?
What effects would a change in government have on business activities?
What is the role of labor unions in the country?
What are the limits on corporate political activity?
Is the country's currency stable?

LEGAL RISK

Legal risks are those associated with the laws present in a country, and the enforcement of those laws. Legal systems vary dramatically across the globe. Not all countries have well-defined laws and marketers cannot assume that legal infractions will always be pursued by authorities. Further, the extent to which patents, copyrights, and intellectual property rights are protected in various countries remains an important issue for international marketers. Many countries do not offer these protections. Others have such laws but fail to enforce them.

Glodok, a section of Central Jakarta in Indonesia, was the target of high-visibility intellectual property raids in 2010. These raids were touted by the government as signs of enforcement, but many viewed them as only cosmetic. Experts estimate more than 550 million counterfeit CDs and DVDs were sold in 2008. The sales result in 1.4 trillion *rupiah* ($154 million) in lost revenues. The raiding of a small number of vendors selling pirated goods does little to stop the problem, and the legal risk remains for foreign companies entering the country.[18]

ETHICS AND INTERNATIONAL MARKET RESEARCH

International market researchers have an obligation to ensure that their activities are ethical. Ethical responsibilities go beyond simply being objective when performing research. Researchers who are ethical protect the rights and privacy of research participants. They also work to keep confidential information from being leaked to outside parties.

Researchers who engage in experimentation focus on protecting the safety and well-being of research subjects and ensure that no one will be harmed in any way by the research project. While most market research projects are relatively harmless, it would be problematic to manipulate consumers while engaging in a research project. Ethical researchers also make certain that research activities are not misrepresented in any harmful way. One unethical tactic is to engage in "sugging." Sugging is selling under the guise of research. A researcher that suggs begins asking a respondent questions and then attempts to sell the person a product. Practices such as sugging are frowned upon in international market research.

BOTTOM-OF-THE-PYRAMID AND INTERNATIONAL MARKET RESEARCH

International market researchers seek to gather the opinions of bottom-of-the-pyramid consumers so that the findings can be incorporated in various marketing efforts. Bottom-of-the-pyramid consumers make up the largest, but poorest socioeconomic group (Pitta et al., 2008). Many of these consumers may be unable to respond to surveys or Internet research programs, because they do not have access to computers, and many more may be illiterate. Data collection techniques may be adapted, relying more on qualitative methods such as personal interviews or ethnographic methods in order to tap the attitudes and behaviors of this segment.

Pricing research takes on a new meaning when researching bottom-of-the-pyramid consumers. Rather than studying the effect of a pricing change on purchasing behaviors, researchers should instead seek to identify the price consumers are actually able to pay for a particular product or service.

Product research may focus on gauging consumer responses to cost-saving changes to product design, and may explore differences in purchasing frequency. Smaller quantities per purchase may result in more frequent purchasing of the item. Instead of buying a six-month supply of soap, market research may find that bottom-of-the-pyramid consumers prefer buying single-use sachets as needed.

Distribution and promotion research also varies in context for bottom-of-the-pyramid consumers. Many bottom-of-the-pyramid consumers are rural; research should highlight how the consumers access the product. Promotion research in these countries should examine the effectiveness of word-of-mouth efforts rather than advertising, mass media, or Internet marketing campaign approaches.

CHAPTER 8: REVIEW AND RESOURCES

Strategic Implications

Marketing research decision makers should ensure that the overall international marketing program is guided by solid data and information. The market research becomes an essential component of the overall organizational strategy. In order to identify potential targets for international expansion, as well as viable market segments for products internationally, solid research is needed.

To collect quality information for the purposes of international marketing, macro- and micro-level studies are necessary. Undertaking these forms of research requires the commitment of top management. Company executives should allocate the necessary resources to ensure that adequate support is given to international market research. A systematic process of collecting both secondary and primary data should draw support from upper-level managers, who guide the strategic direction of the firm.

Tactical Implications

Each of the four types of international market research described in this chapter regarding products, pricing, distribution, and promotion helps the firm to achieve its overall international marketing strategy. Tactical decisions for international market research are based on the overall corporate strategy. Following either a differentiation or low-cost provider strategy, for example, requires the collection of both pricing and product research in the target country or region. When differentiation is the goal, qualitative methods help researchers understand whether local citizens perceive the differences. The overall international strategy of the firm will likely fail in the absence of valid and reliable international research aimed at the various parts of the marketing mix. International market research tactics play a vital role in ensuring that the overall international marketing strategy is successful.

Operational Implications

Day-to-day international market research operations are guided by both strategic and tactical decisions. Ongoing research activities are necessary to address cultural differences, regional preferences, and consumer attitudes toward a company's products. Researchers can spend a great deal of time each day analyzing international survey or focus group data, as well as drawing conclusions and writing research reports. Researchers also should daily analyze macro-level events that occur in targeted countries or regions.

The pace of global change has increased. Daily events can drastically alter the marketing environment in any given country. This leads researchers to monitor world events on a daily basis.

TERMS

market research

psychic distance

primary data

secondary data

qualitative research designs

focus groups

personal interviews

quantitative research designs

surveys

back translation

parallel translation

experiments

test market

sampling

probability sample

nonprobability sample

scientific method

self-reference criterion

reliability

validity

internal validity

external validity

political risk

REVIEW QUESTIONS

1. Define market research.

2. What are the steps in the market research process?

3. What types of information are revealed in a primary data collection program?

4. What are some of the most commonly used sources of secondary data for international market research?

5. What is the difference between a macro-level and a micro-level analysis?

6. What is the difference between qualitative and quantitative international market research?

7. What are some of the popular quantitative research designs commonly used in the international market research?

8. What are some of the popular qualitative research designs commonly used in international market research?

9. Describe a focus group along with the challenges that come with performing focus groups on an international scale.

10. What are the main differences between back translation and parallel translation?

11. What is the difference between a probability sample and a nonprobability sample?

12. What is the difference between descriptive research and comparative research?

13. What is the difference between contextual research and theoretical research?

14. Describe the four main types of international market research discussed in this chapter.

15. Explain the scientific method.

16. How does the self-reference criterion relate to international market research?

17. Define both validity and reliability and explain how the terms apply to surveys and experiments.

18. What are the major political and legal restraints on performing international market research?

DISCUSSION QUESTIONS

1. Describe the basic market research process. What types of issues should a researcher consider during each phase with regard to international market research? Which phase is most important?

2. Discuss the advantages and disadvantages of secondary and primary research. Which type of research is probably best for micro-level analysis? For a macro-level analysis?

3. Discuss the various types of quantitative research designs. What types of research would be appropriate in developed countries? In lesser-developed countries?

4. How is a desired sample size affected by response characteristics of a particular population?

5. If you had to select between experiments, surveys, personal interviews, or Internet research, which type(s) would be best for research performed in lesser-developed countries?

ANALYTICAL AND INTERNET EXERCISES

1. Using reliable online resources, prepare a critical review of big data.

2. Visit a number of the Internet resources that present secondary data for international market researchers, including the U.S. Department of Commerce (https://data.commerce.gov/, the U.S. Department of Commerce International Trade Association (www.trade.gov), Euromonitor (www.euromonitor.com), Organization of Economic Cooperation and Development (www.occd.org), and the International Monetary Fund (www.imf.org). What type(s) of information do you find? How do you think these sources could be used for international market research?

3. Visit the websites of several market research firms that specialize in international market research such as A. C. Nielsen; Arbitron, Inc.; GfK AG, IBOPE, and INTAGE Inc. Compare the type(s) of research that these firms perform. What are the advantages to using these specialized firms?

4. Enticing consumers to spend more for environmentally friendly products remains one of the primary challenges facing green marketers. International market research can play a key role in identifying potential consumers and market segments for green marketing strategies. Survey techniques can be used to identify segments such as the "true-blue greens," "greenback greens," and "sprouts" (which suggest the levels of commitment consumers have to environmental issues from most to least) that have been identified in most-developed nations. Experiments and test markets can be devised that gauge the effectiveness of offering green products in these cultures. Determining consumer openness to green marketing and sustainability initiatives will be a crucial part of international marketing research for environmentally sensitive companies. Describe the research methods you would use to conduct sustainability research in the following countries:

   - Canada
   - South Africa
   - Morocco
   - South Korea

STUDENT STUDY SITE

Visit **https://study.sagepub.com/baack2e** to access these free additional learning tools:

- Web Quizzes
- eFlashcards
- SAGE Journal Articles
- Country Fact Sheets
- Chapter Outlines
- Interactive Maps

CASE 8

Nestlé: Researching the Confectionary Market

Nestlé is a Swiss transnational food and drink company headquartered in Vevey, Vaud, Switzerland. The company was formed in 1905 by the merger of the Anglo-Swiss Milk Company, established in 1866 by brothers George and Charles Page, and Farine Lactée Henri Nestlé, founded in 1866 by Henri Nestlé (born Heinrich Nestle). It describes itself as the leading Nutrition, Health and Wellness Company that enhances lives with science-based nutrition and health solutions for all stages of life, helping consumers care for themselves and their families. It has been the largest food company in the world, measured by revenues and other metrics, for 2014, 2015, and 2016. It ranked No. 33 on the 2016 edition of the Forbes Global 2000 list of largest public companies.

Nestlé's products include baby food, medical food, bottled water, breakfast cereals, coffee and tea, confectionery, dairy products, ice cream, frozen food, pet foods, and snacks. At the beginning of 2017, Nestlé maintained 436 factories, operated in 189 countries, employed around 335,000 people and owned more than 2,000 brands including Nespresso, Nescafé, Kit Kat, Smarties, Nesquik, Stouffer's, Vittel, and Maggi.

To achieve its mission, Nestlé not only improves existing products but also develops new ones. In order to launch a successful product, consumer preferences have to be anticipated and the product itself should meet their requirements. This makes market research important at Nestlé, especially when consumer tastes change as they do in the case of food products.

Packaged food trends are evolving worldwide. Consumers want food to be tasty and also healthful. The confectionery market is not an exception. Whether it is reduced sugar, smaller portion options, or all-natural flavors; Nestlé works to create tastier and healthier choices. In 2006 Nestlé was one of the first companies in the UK and Ireland to introduce Guideline Daily Amounts (GDAs) on the front of packages. Today over 90% of Nestlé's packs, including catering sized packs, carry GDA information.[19]

Eastern markets, such as Russia, Poland, and Ukraine, have gained importance, because the increasing affluence and evolving consumption of consumers in those countries should compensate for slower prospects in mature markets, such as France, Germany, or the UK. Eastern Europe is one of the world's most intriguing consumer health regions. Anchored by the large Russian market, many are quick to overlook the myriad secondary markets that drive much of the region's spending and whose unique cultural and regulatory environments vary widely. Eastern Europe has seen a slow but steady change in consumers' approach to nutrition. Consumers are not willing to give up the pleasure the sweets give them, however, at the same time they have started to pay attention to what they eat.

With a broad range to choose from, Nestlé chocolate and confectionery products can be enjoyed by almost everyone as a delightful part of a well-balanced diet and active lifestyle.

Preliminary market analysis demonstrated that the fastest growing confectionery category in Eastern Europe is fruit and nut bars. In response to these identified trends, Nestlé would like to launch a new healthy product in the confectionery category. Before making a decision regarding developing and launching a new product, Nestlé wants to deepen the knowledge about consumers' preferences for and current perceptions of healthy fruit and nut bars. Managers would like to find out what consumers are looking for in such products and what type of consumers would be interested in the new product.[20]

1. What issues of confectionery consumption and expectations exactly should be researched at this stage of product development?

2. What secondary data would be helpful in conducting initial market analysis?

3. What type(s) of research would need to be performed in order to establish what products should be developed?

4. Prepare a research proposal for detailing the following: a) research objectives; b) sampling approach and sample structure; c) specific research methods to be used; d) materials needed.

5. What aspects of consumer behavior with regard to conducting market research should be considered when conducting consumer research in Eastern Europe?

PART III
INTERNATIONAL PRODUCT MARKETING

CONTENTS

9

INTERNATIONAL PRODUCT AND BRAND MARKETING

LEARNING OBJECTIVES

After reading and studying this chapter, you should be able to answer the following questions:

1. What product categories are present in domestic and international markets?

2. What product dimensions are considered when making domestic and international marketing decisions?

3. What types of international business products and services are available?

4. What patterns exist as new products move from introduction to eventual decline?

5. What types of decisions must be made with regard to a company's international product mix?

6. What role does brand development and management play in international marketing?

IN THIS CHAPTER

Opening Vignette: A Good Night's Sleep

OVERVIEW

A GOOD NIGHT'S SLEEP

For the 7 billion people currently living, some common denominators exist. For instance, everyone sleeps. Most sleep at night, but the number of variations in resting patterns might seem surprising. The differences also create international marketing possibilities.

Sleeping patterns offer cultural contrasts. Bed times vary widely, often within the same region. A farmer most likely will turn in early and rise possibly before dawn. Many city dwellers stay up later to enjoy nightlife. In hotter regions, taking a siesta or nap in the afternoon is more common. In many cultures, especially those in East Asia, children are likely to sleep in the same beds as their parents. Not surprisingly, then, African Americans and Hispanics are ten times more likely than East Asians to have sex before falling asleep. African Americans are the most inclined to pray prior to turning out the lights. Caucasians are most likely to allow pets in the bedroom.

Numerous marketing opportunities emerge from sleep and rest. Items such as pajamas and nightgowns, night-lights, sheets, pillows, comforters, soothing agents, medications, and more can be sold to those hoping to rest comfortably. Most notably, beds represent a marketplace consisting of billions of people. Beds come in a variety of shapes and sizes. Mattresses are made from many ingredients, including air, water, foam, wool, bamboo, and straw.

The Japanese market a unique form of bed that combines a series of elements. The *shiki* futon is the essential component of the Japanese bed, because it critically influences the overall comfort level of the Japanese sleeping system. A *shiki* futon will be quite different from a Western-style futon filled with foam and wool. The *shiki* futon consists of 100% organic cotton and varies in thickness from two to four inches. In the United States, a *shiki* futon can be expensive. The manufacturing process is meticulous and the materials must be top quality for the futon to hold its shape and firmness.

On top of the *shiki* futon will be a *kakebuton*, which is similar to a comforter. A Japanese *kakebuton* typically will be filled with hand-pulled silk, which makes it extremely lightweight while efficiently retaining body heat throughout the night. It provides a pleasant sleeping experience because it exerts little pressure on the body.

No Japanese sleeping system would be complete without a *soba gara makura*, a buckwheat hull pillow. The pillow helps provide a comfortable night's sleep by perfectly adjusting to the contour of a person's head and neck. *Soba gara makura* materials were used in the original Tempur-Pedic mattresses.

Although not required, many people, especially Westerners, prefer to sleep with a tri-fold mattress underneath the *shiki* futon. The thick foam mattress pad provides a perfect solution for adding an extra layer of comfort to the Japanese sleeping system.

Beds and sleeping habits create new international marketing opportunities.

(Continued)

(Continued)

Finally, many people add a *tatami* (straw mat) or a platform bed to support the entire Japanese bed. The choice between these two elements either makes a portable and foldable sleeping system that can be stored in the closet, or creates a stunning structure in the bedroom radiating with authentic Japanese imagery.

The Japanese bed provides an example of how an everyday experience, sleeping, also presents a major marketing opportunity. With increasing interactions between cultures, the international marketing potential for sleeping products continues to grow.

Questions for Students

1. Which product feature should companies that make beds emphasize the most—price, comfort, health, or a good night's sleep?
2. How would culture influence the sales of beds in international markets?
3. What is the most effective way to build brand loyalty for products, such as beds, that are purchased infrequently?

OVERVIEW

Part I of this textbook presented the backdrop of international marketing. Culture, language, infrastructure, economic systems, and political and legal systems influence domestic or global marketing operations. Part II examined the central core of Figure 9.1: the market. Target market segmentation and product positioning were explained, along with international market research methods to emphasize the starting point for any marketing program: identifying consumer wants and needs.

The third part of international marketing, as shown in Figure 9.1, is the development of the physical goods and intangible services that meet the needs of those in the target market. Companies design and sell within the context of the cultural, linguistic, economic, political, legal, and economic constraints imposed by any country in which a global marketing firm intends to operate.

In this chapter, product and brand management activities are detailed. Chapter 10 expands the discussion by incorporating the concepts of product and service adaptation. Making certain a product fits with a specific country and its culture helps the product compete in the international marketplace.

International product marketing involves understanding the types of products that companies sell and the main dimensions of those products from the viewpoint of the consumer. Companies integrate packaging and labeling concepts into all product decisions, as are choices with regard to the number and types of business-to-business products to be offered. Next, product mix decisions regarding the number of products in a line (depth) and the number of product lines (width or breadth) are made.

International services constitute a growing segment of international marketing efforts. Companies providing financial, insurance, transportation, health care, personal, and tourism services engage in the same marketing activities as those that manufacture and sell physical goods. In addition, marketers carefully evaluate product support services to ensure consumers and business customers receive quality attention during and after the purchasing process.

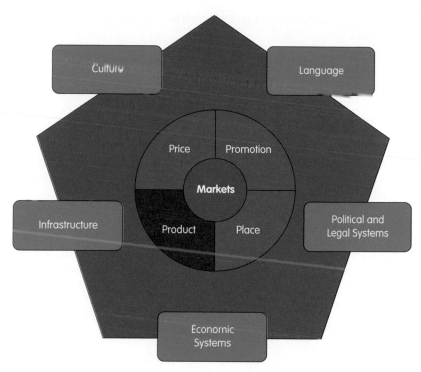

FIGURE 9.1   **The International Marketing Context**

Strategic brand management begins with the designation of a brand, assigning names to individual products and product lines, and decisions regarding how to identify new products. Building powerful global brands involves moving consumers from brand awareness to perceptions of brand equity and feelings of brand loyalty. Brand valuations assist the marketing team in understanding how well consumers view a brand. Product and brand management efforts often determine a company's eventual success or failure.

LEARNING OBJECTIVE #1:

What product categories are present in domestic and international markets?

TYPES OF PRODUCTS

A **product** consists of a bundle of attributes that provide value. Products offer value in many ways. International marketers conceptualize products in terms of tangible, intangible, and symbolic elements. A product as simple as a screwdriver enables consumers to solve a tangible, basic problem (assembling a bicycle) while potentially delivering both intangible benefits (a feeling of safety) and symbolic benefits (the feelings associated with owning a nice set of tools).

A product can be either a good or a service. A **good** is a physical product sold to and used by an individual, household, or business. *Durable goods* are items that are consumed over time. Televisions and household appliances are durable goods.

product: bundle of attributes, including tangible, intangible, and symbolic elements that provide value for exchange partners

good: a physical product sold to and used by an individual, household, or business

Nondurable goods are consumed more quickly. Toothpaste and food items are nondurable goods.

Businesses sell *consumer products* to consumers either directly or through a market channel that employs intermediaries. The buyers, or end users, are individual persons or families. *Business products* are marketed to the other businesses, which are the end users.

A **service** is an intangible product that delivers an act or performance that provides value to individuals, households, and businesses. Services play a major role in the global economy. Consequently, understanding the roles tangible goods and intangible services play in international marketing helps a company operate more effectively.

service: an intangible product that generally centers on an act or performance that delivers value to individuals, households, and businesses

CLASSIFICATIONS OF GOODS

Products consist of convenience, shopping, and specialty items. The factors used to create these categories include how consumers behave regarding products, including purchase frequency, along with the degree of effort consumers expend to make purchases.

CONVENIENCE GOODS

Convenience goods are inexpensive and frequently purchased. Consumers do not devote much time or effort shopping for them. Marketers normally make the items widely available, using intensive distribution methods designed for ease of purchase.

Many convenience products are *impulse products*, or items purchased spontaneously with no preplanning, which contrasts with *unplanned purchases*. Buying toilet paper when a promotional display reminds a consumer about a low household supply is an unplanned purchase; buying ice cream when a promotional display reminds a consumer how much pleasure one receives from eating ice cream is an impulse purchase.

Staple convenience goods are used regularly and tend to be replenished frequently, such as sugar, flour, rice, millet, salt, and soap and are often widely distributed. Staples differ across countries. Chickpeas are a staple part of the diet in India, sorghum and yam are staple foods in parts of Africa, and sweet potatoes and cassavas are staple foods in parts of South America.[1]

Companies sell convenience goods in convenience stores, which have grown in popularity worldwide. East Asian markets have demonstrated a great deal of promise for the convenience store industry. China has witnessed relatively rapid growth in this sector. Popular convenience stores in China include 7–11, Kedi, and FamilyMart, which is one of the largest convenience store chains in Asia. In Japan, *combinis* (the Japanese word for convenience store) offer convenience goods to a large population. Other areas of growth include India, Turkey, Vietnam, and Russia.

INTERNATIONAL MARKETING IN DAILY LIFE
CANDY

A popular convenience good in many countries, candy, presents a contrast in the nature of a product category. What consumers consider to be "candy" varies from country to country. In the United States, most candy contains heavy sugar content, which is not the case in other nations. Instead, candy may be spicy or sour.

In Indonesia, *Ting Ting Jahe* is a spicy candy made from ginger and potato starch. The popular Violet Crumble chocolate bar is sold in Australia. Regional differences such as these will be taken into account when marketing convenience products internationally.

SHOPPING GOODS

Consumers expend more effort searching for and purchasing shopping goods. These products are more expensive than convenience products and consumers purchase them less frequently. Shoppers compare brands and more carefully consider prices. Marketers tend to employ selective distribution strategies for shopping goods. Company leaders select specific retail outlets for each geographic region.

International marketers consider cultural differences and how they affect consumers as they examine shopping goods. Successful marketing programs often offer features and specifications that match distinct countries or regions. For instance, washing machines in many European countries typically use only cold water. Market research plays an important role in discovering a difference such as this.

Department stores and shopping malls carry shopping goods. Stockmann, the largest department store in Nordic countries, has become a well-known source for such items in Finland. Other large destinations include MetroCentre, the largest shopping center in the United Kingdom, and the world's largest mall, the New South China Mall in Dongguan, China. The mall encompasses more than 7 million square feet of retail space. The Mall of America near Minneapolis, Minnesota, attracts over 40 million visitors per year, making it a more popular destination than the Disney theme parks.

Note that shopping "products" include services. Hair care, spa treatments, insurance policies, and numerous other services tend to invite comparisons between providers. Tour guides for various popular locations, such as the Colosseum in Rome, compete with one another for consumer patronage.

SPECIALTY GOODS

Specialty goods are items consumers spend a great deal of time searching for, and generally they will not accept substitutes. These products tend to be expensive and companies market them emphasizing a significant degree of exclusivity. Only a select few retailers offer them in any one country or region, which increases perceptions of exclusivity. Consumers generally do not consider competing brands, as they usually have chosen one particular alternative and expend effort to purchase the preferred brand.

Fender Musical Instruments Corporation, a major musical instrument marketer located in the United States, is the world's leading guitar manufacturer. The company sells instruments worldwide. Consumers are willing to spend much effort, time, and energy in shopping for Fender guitars, although a guitarist may compare prices at various retailers before purchasing a Fender Stratocaster.

Luxuries represent a subcategory of specialty products that are marketed with high prices and a high degree of exclusivity. Hermès scarves and handbags from France are well-known specialty products worldwide. For those consumers in this target market segment, price deserves little consideration. Some Hermès scarves retail for several hundred *euros* and others sell for several thousand *euros*.

Product quality becomes the primary marketing issue for luxuries and specialty products. Consumers pay extra for the quality associated with the goods. Patek Philippe SA, a watch marketer located in Plan-les-Ouates, Switzerland, offers high-quality, world-class timepieces. Customers willingly pay more for the world-class craftsmanship.

The term "specialty" also applies to services as well as physical goods. Lloyd's provides insurance policies for high-end buyers with specific needs, such as when a soccer player has his legs insured in case of injury. Lloyd's insures higher-risk items in more than 200 countries with its 360 Risk Insight program.

LEARNING OBJECTIVE #2:

What product dimensions are considered when making domestic and international marketing decisions?

PRODUCT DIMENSIONS

Products display three key dimensions: the core product, packaging, and auxiliary dimensions (see Figure 9.2). The *core product* satisfies or remedies a basic need. A screwdriver is a core product, as are candy bars and lawn mowers. *Packaging* protects the product and includes features that communicate the brand's name, logo, and trademark.

Auxiliary dimensions include warranties, instructions, company contact information, as well as items designed to promote the brand's image. Marketers differentiate shopping products based on auxiliary dimensions as they present items to potential customers. Every dimension of the product should deliver benefits to the consumer or end user.

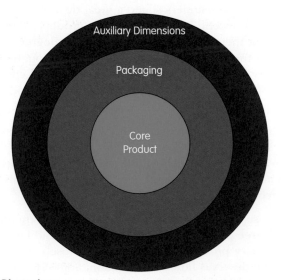

FIGURE 9.2   Product Dimensions

PACKAGING

The product's package protects the item until it arrives safely when exporting or shipping goods from the factory to the consumer. Packaging can become an aspect of a brand's identity, thereby affecting the relationship between the customer and the brand (Underwood, 2003). Companies adapt packages to individual markets based on consumer tastes, preferences, and culture. A match of the package with the market can become the deciding factor in a product's success, because consumers often make purchase decisions at the point of purchase. A study of Thai consumers indicated that the convenience of the package was the most important determinant affecting intentions to buy (Silayoi and Speece, 2007).

Many marketers view packaging as a place for innovation. In the case of wine, the package must protect the contents, because otherwise it might spoil if exposed to air, heat, and light. In the past, wine was packaged in large, air-proof casks. It then moved from the cask or was put into glass bottles to transport home for consumption. The younger the wine, the fresher and more preferred. The invention of cork closures allowed consumers to store wine at home and led to a preference for older, matured wines. The introduction of a screw top reduced the risk of cork contamination, while the use of bags-in-a-box allows European consumers to keep open wine fresh for weeks. The South African packaging company Mondi recently introduced a wine bottle made from PET plastic. The bottles look like glass and the lighter plastic lowers the shipping costs and the carbon footprint associated with delivery. Making plastic requires less energy than glass production. Leveraging the green components of the packaging, the Backsberg winery introduced the Tread Lightly label using the PET plastic bottles (Fridjhon, 2011). Other examples of innovative packing include fridge packs for sodas, liquid soap with a pump, and Apple's innovative iPad2 smart cover.

Packages deliver protective elements, visual elements, symbolic elements, and aesthetic elements. These features plus informational elements are conveyed by the package's shape, label (including color and graphics), layout of product information, as well as via sustainability efforts.

Protective Elements

As is the case with wine, marketers consider the protective elements of packages due to both regional restrictions and sustainability issues. As an example, restrictions in the European Union help reduce unnecessary and hazardous waste, restrict package size, and encourage reusable materials in packages.[2] These restrictions are a part of the Packaging and Packaging Waste Directive of the EU.

Seafood requires special consideration. Producers often distribute seafood over thousands of miles, and product protection becomes crucial. The successful international seafood marketer Royal Greenland A/S delivers high-quality seafood from the farthest reaches of the Earth's oceans to consumers worldwide. The company, headquartered in Nuuk, Greenland, offers high-quality seafood for international delivery while maintaining strict packaging guidelines for sustainability.

Visual Elements

Elements including shape, color, font usage, and pictorials communicate brand meaning to customers and differentiate a product from its competitors. Some of the sensory experiences of consumers come from visual packaging elements. Today's technology permits marketers to incorporate eye-catching colors and shapes that increase purchase likelihood.

Symbolic Elements

Package shapes and features help consumers recognize the brand. The symbolic nature of packaging appeals to a consumer's inner needs and conveys a desired image. Perfume and scent manufacturers, such as Dubai's Al Arabiya Al Swissriya (Arabian–Swiss) fragrance company, spend considerable time and energy creating the proper product bottle and the box that holds the bottle. The company matches symbolic elements with local culture and customs.

Aesthetic Elements

Aesthetics are concepts of beauty. Countries and groups within countries hold diverse views regarding aesthetic attractiveness. What might be considered beautiful in one country may be deemed garish or even ugly in another. Color presents an important aesthetic ingredient in packaging and labeling. Marketers pay close attention to its meaning. Red, for example, symbolizes happiness and good luck in China, whereas it symbolizes caution in the United States and Canada. The color green holds special significance for Muslims.[3] Several Islamic countries feature green as a national color because of the strong association with the Muslim faith. Using green as part of a label should be carefully considered. Marketers should make sure the label does not offend religious sensitivities.

Sustainability

The two major areas of sustainability include product design and packaging. Product designs can become more sustainable by using recycled or recyclable materials, identifying areas where fewer materials can be utilized, and ensuring that production techniques are as efficient as possible.

Many countries and organizations have taken steps to address sustainability issues in packaging. Recently, the Consumer Goods Forum released a report, "A Global Language for Packaging and Sustainability," describing how packaging can be designed holistically with the product to optimize its environmental impact.[4] Focusing on sustainable packaging protects the environment and improves consumer perceptions of the company.

Country-specific sustainability guidelines are available. The Packaging Council of Australia developed a comprehensive program of actions to implement a Toward Sustainable Packaging program about a decade ago. The program seeks to reduce the harmful effects of product packaging.[5] In the United States, organizations such as the Sustainable Packaging Coalition encourage environmentally friendly packaging.[6] Internationally, the ISO 14000 guidelines address various elements of environmental management and provide a general framework for product management as it pertains to sustainability.

Ecology Coatings of the United States provides environmentally friendly standards for coatings and other materials for business buyers.[7] Coatings and resins are important in package design and production. Many companies seek to reduce excessive packaging materials, increase use of biodegradable materials, and incorporate packaging materials that have been produced from energy-efficient operations.

Many consumers prefer green packaging. Demand for environmentally friendly products remained strong even during the 2008 worldwide recession. One study reported that 44% of consumers stated that their green buying habits did not change despite that difficult economic time.[8] In response, some larger businesses have made key changes. KFC serves food in compostable bags in Australia. After six months in a landfill, the bags dissolve into carbon dioxide and water.[9] In the United Kingdom, retailers feature milk containers made almost completely from recycled and recyclable paper. The packaging greatly cuts the amount of plastic in UK landfills.[10]

Labels

A label transmits vital legal information regarding the contents of the package and the product. Marketers ensure that suitable language appears on the package. Some countries have adopted language labeling laws. Canada requires the use of both French and English on packaging. Products marketed in the European Union must be labeled with metric measurements.

Information included on labels helps build valuable brand associations. Labeling serves several communication purposes. Consumers cannot judge the attributes of many products until after the purchase. Labeling assists consumers as they learn about various aspects of the product prior to buying it. Designing a label becomes an important process that becomes magnified when the product ships to another country.

Several cultural factors affect label designs, including the use of art, colors, images, and wording. Marketers respond to these variations in taste by adapting labels. In the United States, a picture or drawing of a squirrel may be used as part of a logo or display with the intent of leading the consumer to believe she is being prudent or thrifty. In other countries, however, locals consider squirrels to be rodents similar to rats. Placing the picture of one on a label would not express the desired image.

Legal Requirements on Labels

Labels provide required information, such as the exact content, weight, size, usage features, warnings about improper product use, and any express warranties. An **express warranty** spells out how the product promises to deliver its value and the remedies available when it does not. For example, tires may be guaranteed to last a certain number of kilometers, under normal conditions and with proper maintenance, and will be replaced or the consumer will receive some form of compensation when they do not.

express warranty: a document that spells out how a product promises to deliver its value and the remedies available when it does not

Other products require more specific warnings. Cigarette manufacturers in the United States must place the surgeon general's warning on each pack. Further, governmental officials proposed that cigarette manufacturers should place graphic images associated with the health effects of smoking on packages. These included images of a corpse, diseased lungs, and children suffering from second-hand smoke. In some countries, the warnings are even more explicit or dire; in others, either no policy exists or the policy in place is not enforced (Neil Katz, 2010).

A label also provides legal information about a product's country of origin. A recent study of Greek wine consumers revealed that information linking a product with a specific place will be one of the top pieces of information that wine consumers seek on a label. The same holds true for region of origin: French wine labels often carry the name of the province or region in which the grapes were grown to assist wine connoisseurs.

One essential part of labeling in the European Union, the "CE Mark" (a French acronym for *Conformité Européenne*), signifies that a product has met EU health, environmental, and safety requirements.[11] The mark allows the product to flow freely throughout the European Union. In the United States, companies must adhere to the Fair Packaging and Labeling Act, which sets mandatory requirements for labeling and encourages voluntary labeling and packaging standards. Labeling standards vary by product type. In many Muslim countries, feminine products cannot display pictures of the item.

LEARNING OBJECTIVE #3:

What types of international business products and services are available?

INTERNATIONAL BUSINESS PRODUCTS

Although consumer products tend to garner more attention in popular press books and magazines; the business-to-business sector plays an equally important role in international marketing. Business products consist of items in the categories presented in Table 9.1.

TABLE 9.1   Categories of International Business Products

Raw Materials
Maintenance, Repair, and Operating Supplies
Component Parts
Accessory Equipment
Process Materials
Installations

RAW MATERIALS

Items used in the manufacture of end products and including natural resources (minerals, ore, chemicals, and fuel) and farm products (beef, cotton, poultry, milk, and soy beans) are raw materials. Mercatto Group of Brazil supplies leather goods from the vast resources of southern Brazil to companies throughout the world.[12] Many global companies use leather in products, which makes it an important raw material in international trade.

MAINTENANCE, REPAIR, AND OPERATING SUPPLIES

Maintenance, repair, and operating supplies are provided to businesses for use in production and other operations. Examples of maintenance, repair, and operating supplies include cleaning products and standard repair tools.

COMPONENT PARTS

Finished products that eventually become parts of other products are component parts. These goods are common in the automotive industry. They include radios, tires, and other essential parts of the vehicle. Comstar in India supplies component parts for several automotive companies including Ford, Mazda, and Volvo.[13] Many consumers are familiar with the brand names of MP3 players and GPS systems that are added to new cars, such Garmin or iPod.

ACCESSORY EQUIPMENT

Products that help facilitate the production of other products but do not become a part of the products themselves are forms of accessory equipment. Examples include office equipment such as the computers designed to help a manufacturer conduct daily operations. The Taiwanese company Anoma Corporation is a worldwide leading manufacturer and supplier of custom power supplies for clients throughout the world such as Siemens (Germany), Samsung (Korea), Philips (Netherlands), and Sony (Japan).

PROCESS MATERIALS

Materials that become a part of other products in an unidentifiable way are process materials, such as food additives and resins. Industrial Resins Sdn Bhd of Malaysia supplies industrial resin products worldwide.[14] Other companies focus on providing coatings and other materials for the manufacture of products. Nearly every manufactured product has some type of coating, which creates a significant international marketing opportunity.

INSTALLATIONS

Major capital equipment products used directly in the manufacturer of other products are installations. Heavy machinery and assembly line equipment are examples. Heavy machinery and other capital installations continue to be mainstays of industrial marketing. Many of the products are automated production machines.

DISTINCTIONS BETWEEN BUSINESS AND CONSUMER PRODUCTS

Although distinctions have been made between business and consumer products, many international marketers offer the same product to both businesses and consumers. The Canadian company Agrium, Inc. markets agricultural products and services through both retail and wholesale channels. The agricultural products help growers worldwide to increase crop yields. The same product can be used as a component process material that is sold to other businesses. The company sells urea, which provides nutrients for plants and can also be used as a resin by lumber companies or to assist in the recycling of aluminium.[15]

Many items are both business products and consumer products. The categorization depends on the use of the product by the customer. A stapler is an example. It may be used at home or in an office. Marketers of products such as this often use multiple distribution channels even though there are no differences in the product itself.

INTERNATIONAL INCIDENT

In Taiwan, purchases, especially large ones, receive thank-you gift rewards. The gifts are branded to serve a promotional benefit. A gasoline purchase may include a box of tissues. Someone who makes a large purchase at a retailer takes the receipt to a special prize section in the store, often near the exit, and gets to choose from a variety of prizes. Rewards are small and simple, such as an alarm clock, house decoration, or a low-cost children's toy. The retail environment in an emerging market often features a high level of personal service, in part due to low labor costs. Stores feature elevator attendants and a large sales force. A shopper may receive assistance from two or three salespeople at one time. What would happen if you took a Taiwanese immigrant or a traveling businessperson to visit an upscale U.S. retailer? The visitor would expect great service and might receive little or no attention from the salesperson in some stores. The shopper would also expect a gift or prize for making a purchase and would not receive one. How would you explain this to your shopping companion?

INTERNATIONAL PRODUCT QUALITY STANDARDS

Offering high-quality products, both physical goods and intangible services, should be a key goal for international marketers. As competition intensifies in many industries, one key to achieving marketing success involves paying close attention to product quality. The term "product quality" refers to many different aspects of a product. Table 9.2 presents dimensions of product quality. The value of each of these dimensions varies by product, country, culture, and individual consumer. To some, durability may be the primary factor influencing a purchase decision, because the product represents a major purchase, and consumers may have limited funds. For others, aesthetics could be the key decision variable, especially for items that become part of a household's decor. A marketing team attempts to identify the most salient features of product quality in the culture of a country.

TABLE 9.2   Product Quality Dimensions

Dimension	Description
Performance	Degree to which the product performs its key functions
Features	Auxiliary dimensions beyond the core product
Conformity	Extent to which the product is produced according to specifications
Reliability	Consistency of product performance over time
Durability	Overall product usefulness over its life
Aesthetics	Appearance and design of high-quality product
Serviceability	Convenience and ease of service of the product

Source: Adapted from Aaker (1991); also Garvin (1987); Keller (1998).

QUALITY STANDARDS

Many buyers look for methods to ensure that products sold across national boundaries are of comparable quality. Demonstrating that a product meets a quality standard will be a key ingredient in international marketing success. Individual companies, countries, and regions seek to meet or exceed quality standards when marketing internationally. The *International Organization for Standardization (ISO)* provides standards that guide management practice as they relate to quality management and assurance. The ISO organization includes more than 160 member nations.

TABLE 9.3   2010 Malcolm Baldrige National Award Winners

Company	Category
MEDRAD	Manufacturing
Nestlé Purina PetCare Co.	Manufacturing
Freese and Nichols Inc.	Small Business
K&N Management	Small Business
Studer Group	Small Business
Montgomery County (Maryland) Public Schools	Education
Advocate Good Samaritan Hospital	Health Care

Source: "Baldridge Performance Excellence Program," National Institute of Standards and Technology, July 19, 2011. Retrieved from www.baldrige.nist.gov/Contacts_Profiles.htm.

The *American Society for Quality (ASQ)*, a global community of experts in quality management, is the sole administrator of the Malcolm Baldrige National Award. The organization presents the annual award in the areas of manufacturing, services, small business, education, healthcare, and non-profit sectors. Table 9.3 lists a recent set of winners. The award pertains to product quality and other areas of management including leadership, strategic planning, customer focus, knowledge management, human resource focus, process management, and business performance.

In the automotive industry, the J. D. Power & Associates Initial Quality Study continues to be considered by many to be the industry benchmark for annual new car quality ratings. Consumers rate their automobiles on both mechanical and design quality. Industry members value the results. Automobile companies operating internationally pay close attention to such ratings.

BOTTOM-OF-THE-PYRAMID INTERNATIONAL PRODUCT MARKETING

Several opportunities are available for products as they pertain to bottom-of-the-pyramid consumers. A central issue will be the price–quality relationship. Traditional marketing logic assumes that consumers will be willing to pay premium prices for high-quality products. Some consumers go out of the way to buy specialty and luxury items.

In bottom-of-the-pyramid circumstances, an effective approach may be to design products offering the basic essentials at minimal prices. Doing so requires that the company carefully consider its obligation to both shareholders and the world community. One concern will be that by offering stripped-down product versions, the company's image will suffer.[16] Marketers weigh slim profits in the short run against the long-term goodwill that may come with serving bottom-of-the-pyramid markets.

Manufacturers analyze product costs carefully. Transaction costs and logistical costs can be higher in less-developed regions. Marketing remanufactured products presents one opportunity to reach these regions. *Remanufactured products* used are goods that have been refurbished through manufacturing processes in order to be restored to acceptable functioning, including those about to be discarded. They often fit with the needs of bottom-of-the-pyramid consumers. The millions of computers, televisions, and cell phones that would have otherwise been thrown away in developed countries each year represent a realistic opportunity for marketing to bottom-of-the-pyramid consumers.

Another international opportunity results from offering smaller package sizes and quantities (Pralahad and Hammond, 2002; Wood et al., 2008). Companies selling items in rural areas of India have achieved success by following adapting package sizes (Rajagopal, 2009). A recent study indicates that easy-to-carry packages with understandable labels influence the buying behaviors of bottom-of-the-pyramid consumers.

INTERNATIONAL SERVICES

The global economy has largely shifted toward a services base. As noted earlier, services are intangible products that are based around an act or performance that delivers value. Effectively marketing them in new countries presents several challenges. Services include those displayed in Table 9.4.

TABLE 9.4   Types of Services

Type of Service	Example
Transportation	Taxi, air travel, bus, rickshaw, boat
Financial Services	Credit/lending, credit/debit card, investment, checking account, savings account
Telecommunication	Landline, cell/mobile phone, Internet connectivity
Insurance	Policies for health, life, property, business, shipping
Health Care	Hospital, family doctor, walk-in clinic, eye care
Personal Services	Hair care, spa, massage, concierge
Recreation/Cultural	Museums, art districts, theater, opera
Business Services	Accounting, consulting
Tourism	Theme parks, tourist attractions, beach, tour guides, destination gambling

A growing interest in the international marketing of services has emerged. Although exports of merchandise still dominate world trade, the marketing of services continues to rise. Many multinational corporations outsource various services to companies offshore in other nations that have expertise in that service (Banerjee and Williams, 2009).

Economies generally progress from agrarian to manufacturing to services over time. Worldwide, services account for an average of approximately 70% of GDP.[17] Services as a percentage of GDP tend to dominate the economies of developed countries. Services often play smaller roles in lesser-developed countries. Table 9.5 presents data for services as expressed as percentage of GDP for several countries.

TABLE 9.5 Services as Percentage of GDP

Country	%
France	77.6
United States	76.9
Belgium	76.1
United Kingdom	75.6
Portugal	73.7
Denmark	72.6
Italy	71.0
Japan	69.3
Germany	69.0
Spain	68.3
Brazil	65.3
Mexico	59.1
El Salvador	58.4
Honduras	55.4
Norway	52.6
Chile	52.3
Ethiopia	42.4
China	40.1
Bhutan	35.2
Angola	25.7
Azerbaijan	23.8
Liberia	21.9

Source: "Services, etc., Value Added (% of GDP)," The World Bank, 2011. Retrieved from ; https://data.worldbank.org/indicator/NV.SRV.TETC.ZS data presented from 2008 indicators.

Tourism can play an important role because it exhibits a major influence on the gross domestic product (GDP) of many countries, which many governmental leaders recognize. Tourism impacts many developed countries. Canada (8.9% of GDP), France (9.7%), Germany (7.5%), Greece (15.5%), Italy (9.3%), Japan (9.1%), Spain (15.3%), the United Kingdom (9.7%), and the United States (9.1%) have major tourism industries (Bowen and Hallowell, 2002).[18] Table 9.6 presents the top tourism economies worldwide. Copenhagen, the capital of Denmark, refocused efforts to increase tourism to its locales through the Wonderful Copenhagen campaign, an attempt to increase the number of tourists to 1 million per year by 2014.[19] The goal was reached.

International marketers consider the *total value concept*, which measures the complete set of values from products customers receive from a service (Babin and Harris, 2009). The Europa Park in Germany provides an example. Guests at the popular German amusement park enjoy rides and entertainment. They experience family fun and create life-long memories. The park features a convenient location with easy-to-find instructions for bicyclists who visit. Value emerges from the many roller-coasters and thrill rides as well as from family bonding and togetherness. Recognizing that

Many governmental leaders recognize the potential importance of tourism to local economies.

TABLE 9.6   Top Tourism Economies

Country	$ billions
United States	1,344.35
Japan	473.74
China	445.47
France	265.77
Germany	259.71
Spain	229.76
United Kingdom	220.48
Italy	204.86
Canada	120.96
Mexico	114.81

Source: "Economic Data Search Tool," World Travel & Tourism Council, 2010. Retrieved from https://www.wttc.org/-/media/files/reports/economic-impact-research/regions-2017/world2017.pdf.

different market segments perceive value differently, the park offers special activities targeting seniors, children, families, and teenagers.[20]

The total value concept applies to retail sales as well. The phrase "service after the sale" often appears in advertisements for shopping goods including automobiles and appliances.

INTERNATIONAL PRODUCT SUPPORT SERVICES

The term "service" might create confusion. Product support services provide added dimensions to the sale of a physical good or intangible service. They accompany a vast number of consumer and business purchases and add an additional element to product marketing. Support services include installation, maintenance, servicing and repair, providing credit, answering questions by telephone or over the Internet, assisting businesses with inventory management, and more general activities such as providing market information.

Many copier and image-reproduction equipment companies offer maintenance and service agreements. Such services build longer-term relationships with customers, making the sale of the next item easier. Other business services assist companies in normal operations, either with the production or maintenance of goods, or with general business operations such as delivery services, telecommunication service, or logistical services. MTU Aero Engines of Germany is a worldwide leader in commercial aero engine maintenance services.

High-quality product support generates goodwill for a variety of domestic and international companies. For example, the German company SMA sells reliable inverters that turn direct current from solar panels into alternating current. Providing effective servicing of the inverters in other countries contributes an important part of SMA's international marketing success.

LEARNING OBJECTIVE #4:

What patterns exist as new products move from introduction to eventual decline?

THE PRODUCT LIFE CYCLE

The product life cycle concept portrays the stages a product undergoes as it progresses, from introduction, to growth, maturity, and decline (see Figure 9.3). The concept applies to physical goods and intangible services, to entire product categories such as mobile phones, and to specific product brands. Individual products may be at different points in the life cycle across different countries and cultures. Digital televisions may be in the maturity phase in France but in the growth stage in developing countries.

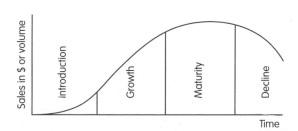

FIGURE 9.3   Product Life Cycle

DEVELOPMENT

Development takes place before the product life cycle commences. Prior to a product's introduction, the development process involves creating and testing the product concept. In most cases, a well-thought-out and executed developmental program will be needed to successfully bring a product to market. Companies do not earn profits at this point because the product is not available to consumers.

pioneering advantage: the advantage that results from being the first mover in a market

A firm can gain a competitive advantage through the development of innovations. The **pioneering advantage** refers to the benefits that result from being the first mover in a market. Haier, a major Chinese manufacturer and worldwide leader in household appliances, achieved a great deal of success by developing processes that enable the firm to respond to market demands quickly and efficiently (Lin, 2009). Responding quickly to market demands helps capture a pioneering advantage. Pioneers carefully monitor investments in research and development and spend a great deal of resources on new product introductions. South Korean giant Samsung pays close attention to its allocation of resources across its new product innovations as well as to its new product success ratio.[21]

INTRODUCTION

The introduction stage commences when the product has been released. Educating the target segment about the new product will be one key activity. Often the goal becomes to establish *primary demand*, or demand for the generic product itself rather than a specific brand. To move consumers, the new product's benefits must be emphasized. Marketing costs tend to be high during this stage due to the expenses associated with promoting the product, acquiring adequate distribution channels, and recouping production and research and development costs. Profits are normally not realized.

International marketers may attempt to introduce products at different periods in different countries and/or regions, thereby staggering demand for the product. The approach is commonly used for products forecasted to have a large demand globally. As an example, Apple's iPad was first released in the United States. The product was introduced to the United Kingdom, Canada, Germany, France, Switzerland, Italy, Spain, Japan, and Australia approximately one month after the U.S. release. Other markets were targeted months later.

GROWTH

When sales begin to increase and profits are realized, the product enters the growth stage. Competition also begins to join the market. Competing firms, or *followers*, enter the industry after pioneering firms have developed and introduced a product.

Firms that introduced the product develop defensive strategies that concentrate on retaining customers. For pioneering companies, retaining customers will be more efficient than obtaining new ones. The iPad drew considerable international competition from Sony (Japan), Samsung (South Korea), and Motorola (United States), pushing the tablet market quickly through the growth stage. During this phase, primary demand ceases to be the focus and market differentiation becomes more important. Competitors in the tablet market quickly developed points of differentiation, including unique operating systems and features.

MATURITY

When sales begin to increase at a decreasing rate and market saturation begins, the product reaches the maturity stage. Due to saturation and intense competition, the only way marketers can obtain new customers will be by taking them from competitors. Companies attempt to hold the market share or entice customers away from competitors. The goal becomes to maintain a company's share in a growing market, thereby increasing sales, or to capture share in a stagnant market in order to increase sales.

Prices generally begin to drop during maturity due to intense competition and expenses related to resulting increased marketing efforts aimed at customer retention. Laptop computers quickly moved from the growth phase of the life cycle to maturity, even as some consumers moved on to tablet models and smartphones. Laptop sales, however, were healthy and they eventually exceeded desktop sales internationally (King, 2011).[22]

Many consumer durables such as appliances have reached the maturity phase in developed countries. Washing machines, clothes dryers, microwave ovens, and televisions are commonly found in most households. Individuals in lesser-developed nations, especially with concentrations of bottom-of-the-pyramid consumers, do not experience the same level of consumption of durables.

Market saturation in one country leads many international marketers to consider introducing a product in other countries. The mobile phone provider industry quickly reached the maturity phase. Statistics indicate that more than 5 billion mobile phone connections exist worldwide, with the penetration rate exceeding 100% in some countries. In other words, there is more than one connection for each person in some nations.[23] Opportunities to market cell phones and provider services are present in developing and bottom-of-the-pyramid regions. Price and technological infrastructure development issues are the most significant obstacles to expansion into these areas.

Firms may attempt to extend the maturity phase in a number of different ways, including increasing the number of users by expanding the overall market, finding new uses for the product, or attempting to increase the frequency of product usage. Companies may also introduce quality improvements, feature improvements, or style improvements in order to prolong this stage.

DECLINE

The decline stage occurs as a gradual or rapid drop in sales takes place. Product sales fall because consumer tastes have changed and new innovations have been introduced. Consequently, the company's marketing team decides how long to remain in the market. A company may discontinue a product, as was the case with film-based cameras. The Eastman Kodak company stopped selling most film cameras in Canada, Europe, and the United States. Kodachrome film, a well-known product from Kodak, was also discontinued in Europe and North America in 2010, and the final processing facility in the United States closed in that year (Bander, 2004). Desktop computers, long thought to represent a growth industry, have begun to show declines in sales worldwide as laptops, tablets, and smartphones earned quick consumer acceptance.

Note that not every product type experiences a life cycle. Some items used in daily living do not appear to ever reach a point of decline or death, including coffee, tea, sugar, and salt; although the companies selling these items may follow the cycle.

PRODUCT CYCLE THEORY

Raymond Vernon first introduced product cycle theory in the field of international economics. The theory explains how products and production move from developed countries to lesser-developed countries (Appleyard et al., 2008). It separates regions into lead innovation nations, developed nations, and developing nations.

The theory suggests that a new product is first developed, produced, and consumed in a *lead innovation nation*, such as Japan. Over time, as the product becomes widely accepted, the manufacturer realizes production efficiencies when foreign demand for the product emerges. The manufacturer then exports the product to other *developed nations* or regions that exhibit sufficient demand, such as the European Union. Production gradually shifts to overseas markets, and eventually the manufacturer exports the product from these markets to both the original market and to lesser-developed countries. Finally, production again shifts, this time to lesser-developed or *developing nations*. Then companies from the original, developed countries devote capabilities to innovations.

Product cycle theory has been criticized for relying on studies of the United States as the lead innovative nation. The research neglects the current trend in which many products are launched simultaneously around the world. Product cycle theory does not appear to fit products introduced by companies that are international in scope from their inception, or born-global firms. In addition, companies often target emerging wealthy customer segments in developing markets early in the product cycle. Later, the company may begin to target other market segments, as predicted by the theory. Even with these criticisms, product cycle theory does explain some patterns of international trade over time (Oviatt and McDougall, 1994).

LEARNING OBJECTIVE #5:

What types of decisions must be made with regard to a company's international product mix?

INTERNATIONAL PRODUCT MIX MANAGEMENT

International marketers face numerous decisions pertaining to brand and product management. Many global companies develop individual products and product lines. Effectively managing portfolios of these products and brands constitutes a key strategic international marketing activity.

PRODUCT LINES AND MIX

product line: groups of similar products within a particular category

product mix: the total number of products that a firm carries

Product lines contain groups of similar products within a particular category, such as the Maddog line of surfboards manufactured in Australia. The **product mix** refers to the total number of products that a firm carries. Maddog also offers an apparel line and scuba accessories. The *depth* of a product line refers to the total number of products in that line. If Maddog sells four types of surfboards, the depth of the surfboard line is four products. The *width* (sometimes called the breadth) of the product mix identifies the total number of product lines a company offers. If Maddog sells surfboards, surfing apparel, and scuba equipment, the width would be three lines.

Bosch International, a leading global supplier of technology and services with head-quarters in Germany, sells products and services to the automotive industry and industrial technology to other firms and to individual consumers. The company also offers products for various building technology industries. The combination of these products across all segments constitutes Bosch's product mix.

MARKET/PRODUCT MATRIX

An important part of international product and brand management will be to strategically match the product portfolio with the various markets a firm serves. A useful tool for conceptualizing the various strategies is the market/product matrix, as presented in Table 9.7. Each of these strategies fits with a unique set of circumstances.

TABLE 9.7 The Market/Product Matrix

Products		Markets	
		Existing	New
	Existing	Market Penetration	Market Development
	New	Product Development	Diversification

MARKET PENETRATION

A firm uses a market penetration strategy when it attempts to increase sales of existing products in existing markets. One market penetration tactic involves developing and promoting new uses for existing products. As has been noted previously in this textbook, baking soda may be used in cooking, to deodorize a refrigerator or freezer, or in toothpaste.

An alternative strategy for successful market penetration, *repositioning*, is the process of changing perceptions of the product in the minds of consumers. Philips, the Dutch multinational electronics marketer, recently repositioned its products under the theme of "health and well-being" from an earlier "sense and simplicity" theme that had been developed for its electronics lines. The idea was to reposition the company away from television and electronics into products that improve everyday living through innovation. Repositioning a company and its product offerings can help the firm to better connect with customers and may lead to higher levels of market penetration.

PRODUCT DEVELOPMENT

Product development strategies take place when a company attempts to introduce new products to existing markets or to enhance existing products with new features or options. Many international firms actively engage in product development. Japan's Sony Corporation develops several new products each year for existing markets. Ford Motor Company developed the Kuga SUV specifically for European markets as part of a product development strategy. Not long ago, Optimal Energy of South Africa began to market the Joule electric car, the first vehicle to be developed and manufactured by a South African company, to the United Kingdom and Commonwealth countries.[24]

DIVERSIFICATION

Firms employ a diversification strategy by marketing new products in new markets. Company leaders choose this strategy as a response to perceived opportunities or as a way to defend against increased competition in existing markets and product lines. Vortex Engineering in India successfully developed a new form of ATM specifically for rural markets. The machines simplified the process of obtaining cash by including fingerprint-reading technologies (Banerjee, 2010).

The Taiwanese corporation Wistron recently announced the move to diversify from its notebook computer business into handheld devices, flat-panel televisions, and three-dimensional televisions. A change such as this allows a company to expand into new products and markets as a response to intense competition in the company's main business.[25]

MARKET DEVELOPMENT

market development: a strategy that focuses on increasing sales of existing products to new customers

A **market development** strategy occurs when a firm attempts to offer existing products in new markets. This international marketing strategy enables a company to minimize problems with local or domestic market saturation by expanding into new countries or regions.

TeaGschwender, a German specialty tea company, grew its business from an original location in Trier, Germany, to more than 130 shops in seven countries.[26] The strategy has proven to be successful in making the company a leader in specialty teas. Starbucks and Harley Davidson have become well known for aggressive market development strategies (Allison, 2010).[27]

International product development requires a marketing team to continually evaluate individual products and product lines, the product mix, packages, labels, and the stage in the life cycle for each product in domestic and international markets. Companies then adjust to economic circumstances, cultural trends, political shifts, and technological innovations within industries and various countries. One tool that can become a major asset in the process is effective management of a company's name and brands.

LEARNING OBJECTIVE #6:

What role does brand development and management play in international marketing?

INTERNATIONAL BRAND MANAGEMENT

brand: a name, sign, symbol, or design, or some combination of these that identifies the products of a firm and distinguishes them from those of the competition

The name, sign, symbol, and/or design that identifies the products of a firm and distinguishes it from competition is the company's **brand**. A *brand name* is the verbal part of a brand that can be spoken (the name Nike), and a *brandmark* is comprised of the nonverbal elements that signify the brand (the name Nike combined with the Nike swoosh). A *trademark* is a legally protected brand name and a *servicemark* is a legally protected service name. Consumers recognize well-known global brands such as Coca-Cola, Sony, and Mercedes-Benz across countries worldwide.

FAMILY AND INDIVIDUAL BRANDING

Family branding means a number of products in a line or mix share the same brand name worldwide. LG, the South Korean electronics giant, features family branding. The LG name appears on televisions, home theater products, washing machines, clothes dryers, and mobile phones. The family brand approach capitalizes on the company's reputation and its trusted, established name. Japan's Toshiba, Inc., employs the family branding strategy for lines of televisions, digital video recorders, laptops, and electronic accessories.

Marketers make sure that the brand name fits the basic product concept to avoid consumer confusion. Family branding holds the advantage of transferring trust in a brand to new products. When Black & Decker offers a new power tool, people who have used other products recognize the name and are more willing to try the new item.

An **individual branding** approach involves creating distinct brand names for each company product or line. The international giant Proctor & Gamble utilizes individual branding for most of the company's products. In the household care line, the company offers Bounce, Bounty, Charmin, Cheer, Dawn, and Downy. Each product carries a unique brand name.

Individual branding works best when the brands do not share common features or uses. In international marketing, companies develop distinctive brands for individual countries. Proctor & Gamble sells many laundry detergents with familiar names; until recently, however, the Ariel brand was only sold in certain markets. Individual branding allows for more-specific targeting of a name that matches a specific geographic region or culture.

BRAND AND PRODUCT LINE EXTENSIONS

Marketers can use two methods to extend brands and product lines. A **brand extension** strategy takes the brand name and adds it to a new product. Britain's Virgin Group Limited has successfully extended the well-respected Virgin brand name across numerous product categories and industries, including airlines, entertainment, and mobile media. The company has recently moved into space travel as an extension of the travel options already offered.

A **product line extension** strategy introduces products that are in a related product category and that respond to specific opportunities in the marketplace. Germany's Adidas Corporation extended its outdoor product line into high-end mountaineering jackets as part of an effort to become a leading brand for performance sports gear. The movement into the jacket product line made it possible for the company to claim that Adidas products increase performance for all types of outdoor activities (Elfes, 2009).

COBRANDING

The practice of placing two or more brand names on the same product is **cobranding**. Recently, the Wendy's/Arby's group announced plans to form an agreement with Al Jammaz Group, a Saudi Arabian franchisee, to open 135 cobranded Wendy's/Arby's restaurants in nine countries in the Middle East and North Africa. The cobranding agreement presented an opportunity for synergies between the established names. Cobranding strategies include ingredient, cooperative, or complementary approaches.

family branding: a strategy wherein a number of products in a line or mix share the same brand name worldwide

individual branding: a strategy in which distinct brand names are used for products

brand extension: a strategy utilized when a brand name is extended from one product to another

product line extension: a strategy that is utilized when new products are introduced that are in the related product category and that respond to specific opportunities in the marketplace

cobranding: placing two or more brand names on the same product

Ingredient Cobranding

Ingredient cobranding occurs when one brand becomes a part of another brand's product, such as when NutraSweet is an ingredient. The Intel processor receives special mention for all the computers that contain it. In some cases, an ingredient brand may be used in a wide range of usage conditions. Kevlar, the synthetic fiber developed by DuPont, is used in armor for soldiers, in musical instruments, in brakes, and as an especially durable type of rope.[28]

Cooperative Cobranding

Cooperative cobranding agreements are reached when two brands receive equal attention and promotion. Team names for professional basketball in Europe are often cobrands, such as Armani Jeans Milano.

Complementary Branding

Brands that enter into complementary cobranding agreements are promoted to suggest they use both brands. Bulgari beauty products are included at Ritz Carlton hotels as part of a cooperative marketing agreement, under the Luxury Division of Marriott International. If one British company sells fish to grocers and another sells chips, it would make sense for the two firms to engage in complementary branding.

BUILDING POWERFUL INTERNATIONAL BRANDS

Developing and maintaining strong brands offers benefits in both domestic and international markets. Marketers recognize that a strong brand can be the key to customer loyalty. Strong brands contribute to higher sales and profits. Powerful international brands extend these benefits to other countries. Building them takes time and careful planning.

BRAND AWARENESS

brand awareness: the strength of a brand's presence in the consumer's mind

A series of steps help lead consumers to favor a brand. First, **brand awareness** results from marketing efforts that place the brand in a consumer's mind. Instilling brand awareness begins by creating recognition. Brand recognition in global markets helps create marketing success. Germany's automobile manufacturer, Audi, worked with its advertising agency to increase brand recognition in the U.S. auto market (Chon, 2007). Although the company had been selling its cars in the United States for years, the marketing team determined that it still needed to increase brand recognition.

Over time, the brand may be recalled with some help, or aided recall. Brand associations assist in building recall. The associations include all of the attributes, images, and symbols that a consumer mentally attaches to a brand. Eventually the brand will be remembered without assistance, or through unaided recall.

BRAND MEANING

brand image: consumer perceptions of a brand

The next step marketers take will be to create the perception that the company's brand represents a product that is different from and better than what the competition offers. The unique benefits a product gains solely due to its brand name create *brand equity*. Much of brand equity results from **brand image**, or the perceptions consumers have of the brand. Brand image includes perceptions of brand quality, which represents the degree to which a product is free from defects and the characteristics of the product that bear on its ability to satisfy targeted needs (Aaker, 1991; also Aaker, 2002; Anselmsson et al., 2008).[29] Brand equity takes time to build. It results from paying consistent attention to product quality, offering excellent customer service, and exceeding consumer expectations. Advertising and promotional efforts can then support the message by providing compelling evidence and testimony that a brand is indeed different and better than the others.

One threat to brand equity, *brand parity*, exists when consumers believe all products in a category are essentially the same, regardless of brand. Brand parity often leads to competition solely based on prices, discounts, and other consumer promotions.

BRAND LOYALTY

When a company's product enjoys the benefits associated with brand equity, it becomes easier to move consumers to a third stage: **brand loyalty**. Brand-loyal customers seek out a specific name and become willing to pay a higher price for the product. They are less inclined to switch brands or cannot be easily enticed to try other brands. Brand-loyal customers become less susceptible to competitor marketing tactics such as coupons, discounts, and bonus packs. Two elements associated with brand loyalty include brand preference and brand insistence.

Brand preference is a mental ranking in which the brand's attractiveness becomes foremost in the consumer's mind; a feeling beyond mere liking. Marketing managers assess brand preference from the target market's perspective. In order to maintain brand loyalty, international marketers seek to instil **brand insistence**, which occurs when the customer will accept no substitutes. Bucchelli is one of the largest U.S. importers of high-quality hair-cutting shears that imports products from Japan, Germany, and Asia. The company encourages its customers to "Insist on the best!" when purchasing hair-cutting products.

DOUBLE JEOPARDY

Double jeopardy occurs when small market-share firms encounter low levels of customer loyalty. Double jeopardy exists because small firms need to build brand loyalty to grow larger, but the very fact of being small makes such growth difficult, if not impossible, to achieve. A study in the United Kingdom sportswear market confirmed the effect: smaller brands experienced lower loyalty than larger brands (Dawes, 2009).

BRAND VALUATION

Brand equity and brand loyalty become part of **brand valuation**; the process of estimating the financial value of a brand. Recently, the ISO (International Standards Organization) produced ISO Standard 10668 as an effort to reach agreement on how to calculate brand valuation. The system requires three types of analysis as part of brand valuation: *legal analysis*, including assessments of the legal protections of the brand; *behavioral analysis*, including the contribution of the brand to purchase decisions as well as the attitudes of all stakeholder groups; and *financial analysis*, including market values, cost, and income figures. International firms with high brand valuations include Nokia, Samsung, BMW, Louis Vuitton, and Honda.[30]

As a cautionary note, although it can take years to build and maintain a strong brand, that brand can quickly be damaged or destroyed. BP undoubtedly experienced a great deal of brand damage due to the 2010 oil spill. Toyota may have suffered as well when

brand loyalty: a consumer's commitment to a product based on positive attitudes that leads to consistent purchase of the brand

brand preference: a mental ranking in which the brand's attractiveness becomes foremost in the consumer's mind

brand insistence: a condition where a customer will accept no substitutes for a specific brand

brand valuation: the process of estimating the financial value of a brand

questions about the safety of the company's automobiles emerged in the same year. The management and marketing teams of both organizations, and others that have endured the same type of damage, have been put into a position that will take concerted effort and careful marketing activities to restore the brand in the minds of consumers.

ETHICAL ISSUES IN INTERNATIONAL PRODUCT MARKETING

As with other areas in international marketing, ethical issues arise in international product management. Companies receive criticism for knowingly selling unsafe or even recalled products in other countries in order to increase international sales or to offset sagging domestic sales. Toys, electrical appliances, motor vehicles, and clothing products have been deliberately dumped in foreign markets. International marketers should obey international rules and regulations to ensure that dumping of unsafe products does not occur.

The unsafe products may not be perceived as unsafe in the market where sold. Problems with tobacco usage by children, even those as young as two years old, have brought international attention to Indonesia. Two of the top tobacco companies in the market are Philip Morris International and British American Tobacco (Damon, 2010).[31] Most agree that it is unethical for the companies to make profits from selling cigarettes to children in any country.

Packaging creates additional ethical concerns. If wasteful or if used to mask the contents, packaging can come under attack. The use of air to make packages seem fuller and the waste associated with plastic bottles of water are two recent examples of ethical concerns about packaging. Using imagery on the package that targets children when the product may not be appropriate for that age group generates another ethical issue.

Treatment of animals in product testing garners attention. Organizations such as People for the Ethical Treatment of Animals (PETA) protest the use of animals to test make-up or other beauty products. Animal suffering should not occur in order to create the personal benefit of looking more attractive.

The product line itself may be an ethical issue. Companies may choose not to sell the full product line in certain markets, denying those consumers access to the benefits from some products. If medicines, healthier foods, or similar products are involved, it may appear that certain managers wrongly select which consumers will have access to health or other positive outcomes. When less-developed countries or certain races do not have access to such life-giving or life-enhancing products, a company's motivation may come into question.

CHAPTER 9: REVIEW AND RESOURCES

Strategic Implications

International product and service decisions require strategic direction. The biggest decisions revolve around the market/product matrix, the product life cycle, and decisions to market to bottom-of-the-pyramid consumers. Many marketers pursue the market development strategy by offering existing products in new and foreign marketplaces. The strategy can be effective particularly in the maturity phase of the product life cycle, because it presents growth opportunities for otherwise stale product sales.

Diversification strategies present viable options for many firms. Strategy makers evaluate the relative advantages of being a market pioneer or follower brand. A pioneering advantage often awaits an innovative company.

Brand strategies begin with the decision to carry one house mark on all products or to feature different names on each product. Then, companies match brand strategies with product line strategies. Extending a product line requires a matching brand approach. When expanding product line breadth or width, a similar branding decision will be made. Decisions to cobrand are also strategic choices, especially those that involve creating relationships with other companies. International cobranding presents a new horizon. Companies with strong global brands enjoy many advantages in the worldwide marketplace.

Tactical Implications

Tactical decisions pertaining to international product marketing follow the overall strategies set by policy makers. Market development, diversification, penetration, and product development strategies will be supported by tactical techniques, including promoting new uses for products or finding new markets to enter. Tactical decisions also focus on the core benefits and auxiliary dimensions that products offer.

Packaging and labeling choices are often tactical decisions. After a product has been developed, marketing leaders carefully consider package design and labeling choices. The decision to create a new package or label constitutes a change in tactics designed to support a modification in strategic direction. A service company that develops a new logo and company mission statement will also modify its letterhead, billing statements, and other components of its operations.

Operational Implications

Much of the work at the operational level focuses on tracking consumer perceptions of quality. These efforts include market research activities. Operational decisions also ensure that the implementation of product plans made at the strategic and operational levels are carried out effectively and efficiently. Consumer reactions to branding strategies receive consideration. Entry-level employees should pay attention to consumer reactions to the firm's brands. First-line supervisors carry the responsibility of making sure the company's brands are presented positively. Managers that train new employees make sure the company's product lines are well understood, so that the ideal item is presented to a business or retail consumer.

TERMS

product	product line
good	product mix
service	market development brand
express warranty	family branding
pioneering advantage	individual branding

brand extension
product line extension
cobranding
brand awareness
brand image

brand loyalty
brand preference
brand insistence
brand valuation

REVIEW QUESTIONS

1. Define the term *product* and name the three elements that are part of a product.

2. What are the three categories of products?

3. What are the three key dimensions of a product?

4. What is meant by the total value concept?

5. What is the difference between a product line and a product mix?

6. How do the main elements of packages affect international marketing programs?

7. What are the main categories of international business products?

8. How can remanufactured products become part of an international marketing program aimed at the bottom-of-the-pyramid?

9. What roles do international product supports play in reaching target markets?

10. What is the role of the service sector in international marketing?

11. Describe the product life theory and explain how the concept applies to international marketing.

12. How are the strategies that make up the market/product matrix used in international marketing?

13. Describe brands, brand names, brand marks, and service marks.

14. Describe the concepts of family branding and individual branding in relation to international brand management.

15. What three forms of cobranding can be used in domestic and international marketing?

16. Describe brand equity and brand parity.

17. Define brand loyalty and name the factors that influence it.

18. How does the concept of brand valuation relate to international marketing?

19. What ethical issues are present in international product marketing?

DISCUSSION QUESTIONS

1. Explain how international marketers can utilize the total value concept in marketing the following products:

   - A theme park in Brazil
   - A rock concert in Ireland

- An online newspaper in the United Arab Emirates
- A bicycle in Japan

2. Discuss how international companies can use market penetration and market development strategies for the following products in developing countries:

- Hand soap
- Paper towels
- Shampoo
- Glass cleaners
- Toothpaste

3. How could the product life cycle be extended internationally for the following products?

- Flip phones

- Coffee percolators

4. Would you use family branding or individual branding for each of the following product categories? Defend your answer.

- Canned foods
- Insurance products
- Mobile phones
- High-end wedding gowns

ANALYTICAL AND INTERNET EXERCISES

1. Visit the websites of several popular shopping malls worldwide. Some examples are below. What differences do you notice in shopping malls across various cultures? What similarities do you see? How do they compare to the malls in your home country?

- West Edmonton Mall (Canada), www.wem.ca/
- The Dubai Mall (Dubai), www.thedubaimall.com/en
- Berjaya Times Square (Malaysia), www.timessquarekl.com/
- Mall of America (United States), http://mallofamerica.com

2. Search tourism websites for various countries or regions. Some examples are below. What are the main selling points for tourism in these countries?

- United Kingdom, www.visitbritain.com/
- France, www.franceguide.com/
- Australia, www.australia.com
- Japan, www.jnto.go.jp/
- India, www.tourismofindia.com/
- Spain, www.spain.info

3. Search the website of major international marketers and find information about the products each offers in various countries. Discuss how each company's product lines vary by country or region for the following:

- Coca-Cola, www.cocacola.com
- Proctor & Gamble, www.pg.com
- Honda, www.honda.com

- LG, www.lg.com
- Samsung, www.samsung.com

4. Visit the J. D. Power & Associates "Initial Quality Study" website (www.jdpower. com/Autos/ratings/Quality-Ratings-by-Brand). Discuss the various aspects of quality that led to the ratings for several of the brands. Are you surprised by the findings? Why or why not?

STUDENT STUDY SITE

Visit **https://study.sagepub.com/baack2e** to access these free additional learning tools:

- Web Quizzes
- eFlashcards
- SAGE Journal Articles
- Country Fact Sheets
- Chapter Outlines
- Interactive Maps

CASE 9

Interface: Prize-Winning, Sustainable Modular Flooring

When the inaugural Sustainability Survey was released by Globescan and SustainAbility, one relatively unknown corporation made the top of the list. Ahead of corporate giants such as General Electric, Toyota, and Wal-Mart was Interface, Inc., a global corporation that markets modular carpet under the FLOR brand. The corporation's website states that the company is "the worldwide leader in design, production and sales of environmentally responsible modular carpet for the commercial, institutional, and residential markets, and a leading designer and manufacturer of commercial broadloom."[32]

Interface conducts operations in numerous countries, including InterfaceFLOR in Europe, InterfaceFLOR in Asia-Pacific, and InterfaceFLOR in the Americas, based in Atlanta, Georgia. In Europe, InterfaceFLOR maintains manufacturing facilities in Craigavon, Northern Ireland; Halifax, West Yorkshire; and Scherpenzeel, the Netherlands. The company runs sales offices in many European cities. InterfaceFLOR Asia operates in China, Hong Kong, Japan, Malaysia, and Singapore.

To be placed at the top of this list of sustainability-focused companies is no easy feat. Interface clearly met the requirements. The survey was distributed to a panel of sustainability experts throughout industry, government, and nongovernmental agencies. It assessed credible commitments to sustainability grounded in the mission of the company.[33]

What is essential to the success of such a "sustainability through innovation" strategy is the connection of the company with its mission and its products. Managers monitor product development programs to ensure that sustainability goals are met. For modular carpet products to remain competitive, the flooring must meet durability standards, must have stain resistance levels present in competitor products, and also must be attractive and marketable to consumers and businesses.

Production processes play an important role. Company leaders examine the entire marketing channel from suppliers of raw materials to final product installation. Methods of delivery of carpet, installation protocols, and inventory control are part of the program. Managers assess the supply chain as well as disposal of the company's core products. Used flooring and carpet to be discarded should be made to be recyclable or at least not damaging to the environment.

Interface is a major manufacturer of a sustainable product: flooring.

Sustainability processes must be continuous. A company cannot simply rest on its laurels. Rather, it requires an ongoing commitment. Interface understands and continues to implement this concept. The commitment dates back many years. Founder and chair Ray Anderson devoted Interface to an effort entitled Mission Zero, which was essentially a mission to only take from the Earth what could be replenished by the Earth. The pledge was powerful, essentially promising that the company would be the first name in industrial ecology worldwide. The results of the effort have been outstanding: the company has decreased greenhouse emissions by more than 80% and lowered the use of fossil fuels by 60%. The Mission Zero initiative carries a promise that the company will eliminate any negative impact it has on the environment by the year 2020. These efforts naturally garnered considerable praise. *Fortune* magazine listed the company as one of the most admired in America.

While many business thinkers assume that the sustainability initiatives ultimately raise overall costs, Interface reports that such may not be the case. The company's sustainability program resulted in dramatic sales increases followed by a major growth in profits (Reiss, 2010).[34] To realize these results also requires an authentic focus on innovation, as the entire business model must be incorporated into the program.

(Continued)

(Continued)

Maintaining a leadership position in sustainability presents an ongoing challenge. With strong leadership and a well-accepted mission statement, Interface appears poised to maintain its position for many years to come. As consumers worldwide continue to demand green products and sustainability-focused business models, the future appears bright for other sustainability leaders as well.

1. What product category best matches carpeting, convenience good, shopping product, or specialty product? Does the company's sustainability program influence your answer? If so, how? If not, why not?

2. Explain how the core product, the packaging, and the auxiliary dimensions of carpeting produced in a sustainable fashion might create a marketing advantage for Interface.

3. Where is carpeting in the product life cycle? Using product cycle theory, where would sustainable modular carpet products fit? (You may visit www.interfaceglobal.com to help prepare an answer.)

4. What product support services would be crucial for Interface?

5. Should the marketing team at Interface seek to build and enhance brand awareness? If so, how? If not, why not?

6. How could Interface's sustainability program generate brand loyalty or brand equity, especially when the brand is less well known than other carpet manufacturers?

10

INTERNATIONAL PRODUCT STANDARDIZATION AND ADAPTATION

LEARNING OBJECTIVES

After reading and studying this chapter, you should be able to answer the following questions:

1. How do legal systems influence international marketing programs, including standardization and adaptation strategies?

2. How are international marketing disputes resolved within various legal systems?

3. When is standardization the most viable international marketing strategy?

4. How can adaptation help a marketing team succeed in reaching target markets in a host country?

5. How can standardization and adaptation programs combine to achieve greater international marketing effectiveness?

6. How can global innovation and patterns of diffusion assist the marketing team in reaching target markets, including those consisting of bottom-of-the-pyramid customers?

IN THIS CHAPTER

Opening Vignette: Costa Coffee Global Expansion: Adaptation and Differences in Taste

OVERVIEW

COSTA COFFEE GLOBAL EXPANSION: ADAPTATION AND DIFFERENCES IN TASTE

Coffee is now the second most demanded commodity in the world. Consumers around the globe enjoy drinking it in many different ways (Bland, 2013). World coffee consumption has been steadily rising and international chains such as Costa have capitalized on this universal global trend.[1] Costa's creators, brothers Sergio and Bruno Costa originally from Italy, first sold their coffee to a handful of local caterers and delicatessens in London, United Kingdom. A few years later in 1978, they opened their first coffee shop in London. Almost twenty years later, the chain was acquired by Whitbread Plc in 1995. The first international Costa Coffee shop was opened in Dubai in 1999.

Today Costa is the largest and fastest growing coffee shop chain in the UK; it overtook Starbucks as the UK's largest coffee shop brand in 2007.[2] Costa is the UK's favorite coffee shop, with over 2,200 locations in the UK, over 1,300 stores in twenty-nine international markets and over 6,800 Costa Express self serve units. The company follows a multichannel strategy, with wholly owned stores, franchise stores and stores operated by joint ventures, as well as a wholesale operation.[3]

As of July 2017, Costa operated in many countries around the world including China (395 stores),[4] Poland (137 stores),[5] the Middle East (fifty-six shops spread across Egypt, Jordan, Lebanon, and Kazakhstan),[6] Cambodia (six stores) and Singapore (eight stores).[7] With such a global network of outlets, Costa has opted to offer a range of products that fall into three product categories to appeal to a wide range of consumers.

Category A products are offered to customers everywhere. Every market will have, for example, a blueberry muffin, a chocolate muffin, a croissant, and a panini. Then Costa offers category B products that are regional such as Haloumi Panini in Cyprus. In China, people like the fact that Costa serves Western food, but some customers prefer familiar flavors such as a Szechuan Chicken Panini. Category C products are adapted to each individual market, such as Chinese *mooncakes*—little cakes that are given as gifts (Mortimer, 2011). In other markets, for example in Poland, Costa sells Blueberry Latte and *jagodzianki* (blueberry filled sweet rolls) which respond to Poles' love for blueberries during summer time, or Polish-style coffee which is served in a tall glass and prepared by placing a teaspoon or two of ground coffee in a cup and then pouring boiling water over it and letting it brew for a few minutes.[8]

In the connected global world, Costa's marketing managers recognize that food preferences are culturally unique. To be profitable in a foreign country, Costa Coffee adapts the menu. It relies on detailed consumer insights to identify local tastes, and then creates menu items to satisfy them (Allchin, 2011).

International expansion is one key to Costa's continuing market success. At present, it plans to expand into China and become the number two coffee shop choice for Chinese consumers (Kollewe, 2016). Further market development in India is also a priority (Jain, 2016).

Questions for Students

1. What parts of Costa Coffee operations are the same across markets, and what parts are changed to meet local tastes?

2. Do you think Costa Coffee should adapt marketing messages such as advertisements and loyalty programs to other countries?

3. Should Costa's executives worry that adapting too many things will dilute the Costa's global brand?

OVERVIEW

Differences between markets occur across and within countries. Consumer needs vary, competitors introduce new products and services, and governmental regulations regarding marketing activities evolve over time. Companies entering new countries as well as those conducting continuing operations in other nations must adjust to these conditions. The forces that shape the international marketing context play a major role in shaping strategic decisions about product standardization and adaptation (see Figure 10.1).

Costa Coffee combines aspects of standardization and adaption to succeed globally.

This chapter begins with a brief review of legal systems, which vary across national boundaries. Legal systems affect patents, copyrights, and other intellectual property protections. Disputes over these and other matters often arise between companies in various countries. Methods to resolve these disputes are presented. Next, an examination of how to balance the goal of being responsive to local needs by changing goods, services, and brand positions against cost savings derived from a standardized approach is provided.

A country's legal system often makes adoptation a necessary part of a marketing program. Changes in the product potentially lead to changes in the communications used to promote the item. These decisions are interrelated. The product and communication model of adaptation can help resolve these issues.

Product changes often result from innovations. The process of new product development is the final topic of the chapter. Differences in consumer acceptance of a new product are examined and related to diffusion of innovations. Finally, strategic, tactical, and operational implications for marketers are reviewed.

LEARNING OBJECTIVE #1:

How do legal systems influence international marketing programs, including standardization and adaptation strategies?

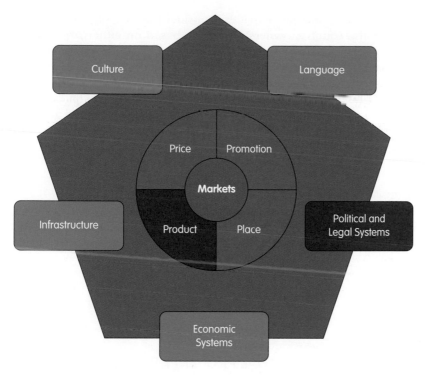

FIGURE 10.1   The International Marketing Context

LEGAL SYSTEMS

Legal systems dictate the methods used when applying and implementing the laws of a country. The systems are rooted in the history of the country and in developing countries are often based on colonial ties. Legal considerations influence a number of international marketing activities, including the decision to enter a country.

A **common law** system relies on legal precedents and usage traditions to form the basis of law. It can be found in the United Kingdom and in former British colonies. The written law applies to disputes and other issues; however, the interpretation by the judicial system coupled with the implementation of the law gives the written law meaning.

common law: a legal system where legal precedent and usage traditions are the basis of law

The most prevalent legal system, **civil law**, utilizes statutes based on written words or a legal code. It can be traced back to its introduction by Justinian, the Byzantine emperor, in Justinian's Code. Laws are written to be comprehensive with clear instructions for how to handle exceptions. Precedent or usage plays no role.

civil law: a legal system in which law is based on written words or a legal code

Legal systems based on religious writings practice **theocratic law**. Islamic law provides an example. Written Islamic law is *Sharia* law. The interpretation of the law or Islamic jurisprudence is called *fiqh*. Theocratic law is the least common legal system worldwide.

theocratic law: a legal system based on religious writings

Table 10.1 provides examples of countries following various legal systems. The systems can be roughly categorized into the three categories, although many countries practice a combination of the systems. Nigeria has a tradition of common law but also uses some components of Islamic law, especially in the northern part of the country. In the United States, common law remains the dominant form, but the state of Louisiana follows a form of civil law.

Legal systems affect marketing activities. Consider the case of property ownership. Depending on the country, ownership can be based on either *prior usage* of the property or official *registration* with legal authorities of the property ownership. In a prior usage context, which is more typically found in common law countries, a person who has used a property is more likely to succeed in an ownership claim over someone who has registered the property. In a registration context, registration becomes more important than usage. To be safe, a company should always register ownership of all property regardless of the legal context in which it operates.

TABLE 10.1   Country Examples of Legal Systems

Legal System	Example Countries
Common Law	United States of America, United Kingdom, India, Australia, Belize, and Malaysia
Civil Law	France, Bolivia, Brazil, Russia, China, Angola, and Chad
Theocratic Law	Iran, Saudi Arabia, The Holy See (Vatican), and Libya

INTERNATIONAL INTELLECTUAL PROPERTY PROTECTION

intellectual property: creations of the mind or the intangible property that result from thought

Protecting intellectual property continues to be a primary challenge to marketers when operating in other countries (Aggarwal, 2010). **Intellectual property** consists of creations of the mind or the intangible property that results from thought. Examples include a song, a new type of electrical plug outlet, or a more efficient process for protecting an individual's identity.

Various tactics are employed to protect intellectual property in international markets. The three major methods include copyrights, trademarks, and patents. These three are all protected under the Agreement on Trade-Related Aspects of Intellectual Property Rights (TRIPS), which is a covenant that all members of the World Trade Organization have signed. While some complaints regarding enforcement continue, especially in some emerging markets, the extension of the TRIPS protections into a greater number of countries reflects the growing focus on intellectual property protection globally.

Copyrights are granted to authors of creative works, such as songs and novels. When a copyright expires, the work enters the public domain. Until then, the work can only be used for profit with the author's or authors' permission. *Trademarks* apply to the symbols, words, phrases, and logos that are attached to brands. These brand marks identify products to consumers and can only be used by the companies that own them. *Patents* apply to inventions, which range from business processes to physical products, or to unique improvements in either one.

One critical form of international protection, the Madrid Protocol (part of the Madrid Union), is an international treaty that allows a company or trademark owner to seek registration and protection in a number of countries by filing a single application. The International Bureau of the World Intellectual Property Organization administers the system. Currently the Madrid Union has ninety-eight members.[9]

Intellectual property protection will be a priority for international marketers. Many companies possess unique assets, such as inimitable technologies or brand equity that requires protection from outsiders. The potential to lose those assets may dissuade a company's executives from entering a market, especially in countries that exhibit poor intellectual property protections.

INTELLECTUAL PROPERTY PIRACY

The unauthorized use or reproduction of intellectual property that has been legally protected is **intellectual property piracy**. Oftentimes piracy takes the form of a close replication of existing products, or *counterfeiting.* A wide range of products are pirated or counterfeited worldwide. Attempts to stop the activity depend largely on the country involved. Many Western nations work vigorously to prevent counterfeiting, whereas China and some other Asian nations do not.

Intellectual property piracy: the unauthorized use or reproduction of intellectual property that has been legally protected

"Blockberry" advertisement from China.

Source: www.gizchina.com/2010/03/10/obama-endorsed-blackberry-clone/.

CORPORATE SPYING

While global travelers may be familiar with seeing knock-off or counterfeit goods in other countries, intellectual property piracy also refers to more serious acts of corporate spying. Corporate spying or espionage involves a company intentionally stealing the designs or business processes of a competitor. Specialists estimate that the cost of such espionage to business is as high as $1.1 trillion annually.[10] In the United States, the corporate espionage phenomenon has led to more FBI investigations of cases, mainly corporate, than were made during World War II.

In response to corporate spying concerns, the U.S. Congress passed the U.S. Economic Espionage Act of 1996.[11] The law makes the theft or misappropriation of a trade secret a federal crime. Penalties include a maximum of fifteen years in prison and/or a fine of $500,000. One of the earliest uses of the law involved prosecuting executives at Four Pillars, a leading Taiwanese adhesive company, for paying an employee at Avery Denison $160,000 to steal $60 million worth of trade secrets. The executives were fined $5 million and ordered to return the materials.[12]

REVERSE-ENGINEERING

Another point of contention can emerge when technical experts reverse-engineer a product or create a replica by breaking down the original and deducing how to manufacturer it. Reverse-engineering has become highly prevalent worldwide. It has reached a point at which reverse-engineering of computer software, such NextEngine's 3-D program, is possible.[13] The process takes place in the entertainment gaming industry, with copies of Xbox 360s and PlayStation 2s prevalent in Latin America (Hall, 2009). Currently, a growing consulting industry that concentrates on preventing reverse-engineering has emerged (Cronin et al., 2009).

COUNTRY DEVELOPMENT

A complicated relationship exists between intellectual property protection and a country's development. Many of the world's emerging markets are known for lax intellectual property protections. Piracy has allowed some nations access to unique assets and has driven innovation within them. On the other hand, a potential link exists between strong intellectual property protection and innovation-driven development. As Table 10.2 indicates, many countries that rank high on industrial technology industry competitiveness have strong intellectual property protections. In contrast, many of the lowest-ranking countries have problems with computer software being stolen.

As countries shift to a more innovation-focused economy, greater intellectual property protection may aid in the process. In theUnited States, the Center for Copyright Information was established as a collaborative project between Internet Service Providers and filmmakers, musicians, and others who may want to protect their content online, to educate consumers about online copyright infringement.[14] At the international level, the World Intellectual Property Organization provides information and support to intellectual property holders.[15]

Some evidence suggests that increased intellectual property protection attracts higher levels of investment from foreign companies and leads to a greater transfer of knowledge between countries (Awokuse and Yin, 2010; Dinopoulos and Segerstrom, 2010). China's current intellectual property protection, which is weaker in practice than its laws would suggest, echoes Japan's intellectual property protections in the 1950s and 1960s. Some expect China to follow the Japanese path and to more strictly enforce intellectual property laws as the country becomes more economically developed (Foster, 2004; Perkowski, 2012).

TABLE 10.2   The Relationship between Intellectual Property Protection, Technology Success, and Innovation Success

Country	Global Innovation Index 2017	Networked Readiness Index 2016	Piracy Rate 2015 (%)	Piracy Rate 2009 (%)
Switzerland	1	7	23	25
Sweden	2	3	21	25
United States	4	5	17	20
United Kingdom	5	8	22	27
Singapore	7	1	30	35
Ireland	10	25	32	35

Country	Global Innovation Index 2017	Networked Readiness Index 2016	Piracy Rate 2015 (%)	Piracy Rate 2009 (%)
South Korea	11	13	35	41
Japan	14	10	18	21
Israel	17	21	33	27
China	22	59	70	79
Australia	23	18	20	25
Poland	38	42	48	54
Vietnam	47	79	78	85
Azerbaijan	82	53	84	88
Sri Lanka	90	63	79	89
Pakistan	113	110	84	84
Nigeria	119	119	80	83

Source: Adapted from "BSA Global Software Survey." Retrieved from http.//globalstudy.bsa.org/2016/downloads/studies/BSA_GSS_US.pdf; "The Global Information Technology Report 2016." Retrieved from www3.weforum.org/docs/GITR2016/WEF_GITR_Full_Report.pdf; and "Global Innovation Index 2017: Switzerland, Sweden, Netherlands, USA, UK Top Annual Ranking." Retrieved from www.wipo.int/pressroom/en/articles/2017/article_0006.html#top.

A contrary opinion regarding intellectual property development has emerged. The *free culture movement*, most strongly associated with Harvard professor Lawrence Lessig, argues that intellectual property protection constrains creativity and limits freedoms. The continual extension of the expiration of copyright, the extension of copyright protection to Internet communication, and the limitations on the ability to copy protected works are all points of contention for the free culture movement (Boynton, 2004)

For large multinational companies, piracy can lead to *brand dilution*. When consumers purchase a counterfeit of poor quality, their negative attitudes toward the knock-off may affect perceptions of the original brand. Over time, this problem can weaken the company's brand equity and dilute the company's brand image.

LEARNING OBJECTIVE #2:

How are international marketing disputes resolved within various legal systems?

INTERNATIONAL DISPUTE RESOLUTION

Legal actions, including those designed to protect a company's intellectual property, are part of doing business. Within one country, disputes can be handled through the local legal system or through professional dispute resolution organizations. As greater numbers of companies enter new countries, the process of dispute resolution becomes more complicated. The process begins with deciding which country's courts should be involved and how court decisions will be enforced. The possible parties involved are citizens, companies, and governments. The interactions between the three entities complicate any dispute resolution process. Issues include those displayed in Table 10.3.

TABLE 10.3   Types of Disputes in International Marketing

Protection of Intellectual Property
Contract Terms/Interpretations
Payment Disputes
Responsibility for Products Damaged in Shipping
Responsibility for Product Liability
Mergers/Acquisitions
Control of a Company

JURISDICTION

jurisdiction: the power to apply law

The first step to dispute resolution, the establishment of **jurisdiction**, defines the power to apply the law or local statutes. In the case of a legal dispute, the laws of the country in which the incident took place hold jurisdiction. Jurisdiction questions can also apply at the state, province, country, or city levels. Some detective television shows touch on the concept of jurisdiction when the lead actor tells the pushy FBI agent, "This happened in New York City. I have jurisdiction here."

Establishment of jurisdiction for legal disagreements can be included in contracts. The setting or location of the jurisdiction may become a point of contention during negotiations. Each company wants to establish jurisdiction in the legal system that gives it the greatest advantage. Typically, it will be in the company's home country, where its legal team has the most experience and comfort, but it can also be in a third country.

Laws also seek to establish jurisdiction. The U.S. Economic Espionage Act of 1996 provided extraterritorial jurisdiction for cases when the offender or the victim is a U.S. citizen. This means that the U.S. legal system would have jurisdiction when a United States citizen is involved. The concern, in both the case of this law and in all cases of jurisdiction, is that when the other party ignores the jurisdiction provisions the only recourse will be legal action in the other party's legal system. In many cases, doing so creates a disadvantage for the party seeking recourse in the foreign system.

METHODS OF DISPUTE RESOLUTION

Companies may use three different methods to resolve disputes: conciliation, arbitration, or litigation. It is not unusual to begin with one process and move to another. In all three cases, the marketing team seeks to balance risk and cost against achievement of the most positive outcome.

Conciliation

conciliation: the various forms of mediation or conflict resolution that companies can pursue before beginning the more formal arbitration process

Many companies prefer conciliation as the first step in resolving a dispute. **Conciliation** applies to the various forms of mediation or conflict resolution that companies can pursue before resorting to a more formal arbitration process. A third party typically mediates between the two companies involved in the dispute. Contracts may include specific wording about how the conciliation process will work. The third party collects information, meets with the two parties involved in the dispute, and presents a possible solution. When the two parties agree, the conflict is resolved and business resumes.

Conciliation offers important advantages over other approaches. The proceedings remain confidential, which protects intellectual property and the privacy of the parties involved. Instead of conflicts being played out in the business press, the media pay little to no attention. Conciliation can be an effective approach in emerging markets where relationships are paramount and where loss of public face can be a major concern.

Some years ago, textile companies in South Africa faced strikes from the 55,000 members of the Southern African Clothing & Textile Workers Union. The strikes shut down production and smaller businesses in South Africa began to close due to the lack of revenue. The employers and the union used conciliation, specifically the Commission for Conciliation, Mediation & Arbitration, to negotiate the dispute and reach an agreement (Wise, 2009). The approach shortened the time period for the strike and kept the negotiations private.

Arbitration

When conciliation does not succeed, the parties typically move to arbitration. The **Arbitration** method is a formal conflict resolution process in which both parties agree to abide by the decision of a third party. The process differs from conciliation in that, instead of making a suggestion, the arbitrator declares a binding decision. Both parties sign a statement, often as part of a contract; that agrees to use arbitration before any conflict emerges. The process has recently received attention from the press due to its use by professional athletes to adjudicate contract disagreements with team owners.

arbitration: a formal conflict resolution process in which both parties agree to abide by the decision of a third-party arbitrator

Arbitration's usage has increased. Numerous arbitration providers are available (see Table 10.4). Providers are located throughout the world and, as with jurisdiction, company leaders typically prefer to arbitrate in their home countries or in countries where they have much experience. Arbitration clauses in contracts can be highly detailed, including the arbitration provider to be used, the number of arbitrators involved, and the place hearings will be held.

Arbitration offers many advantages. Confidential proceedings protect industry secrets and keep the conflict private. The process itself presents both parties with the opportunity to make a case to an impartial third party, much like a legal proceeding, but without the costs associated with going to court. The arbitrator's binding decision will normally be followed by both companies. The one difficulty with arbitration can be that, at its core, the arrangement remains a contractual relationship. When one of the parties disagrees with the arbitrator's finding, the contract can be broken. At that point the only recourse will be litigation.

In the first investor-state dispute brought against the government of Australia, Philip Morris Asia Limited challenged Australia's enactment and enforcement of legislation to require all tobacco products to be sold in Australia in plain packaging. The arbitration was conducted under the United Nations Commission on International Trade Law Arbitration Rules 2010. The tribunal was composed of three arbitrators: Professor Don McRae of the University of Ottawa represented Australia; Professor Gabrielle Kaufmann-Kohler represented Philip Morris Asia. The Secretary-General of the Permanent Court of Arbitration appointed Professor Dr Karl-Heinz Böckstiegel as the presiding arbitrator. The tribunal found that Philip Morris Asia's claim was an abuse of process, because Philip Morris Asia acquired an Australian subsidiary, Philip Morris (Australia) Limited, for the purpose of initiating arbitration under the Hong Kong Agreement challenging Australia's tobacco plain packaging laws. The process of arbitration ended in July 2017 when the Award on Costs was published by the Permanent Court of Arbitration.[16]

TABLE 10.4   Arbitration Providers

International Court of Arbitration Dispute Resolution Services www.iccwbo.org/court/arbitration
European Court of Arbitration http://cour-europe-arbitrage.org/content.php?lang=en&delegation=1&id=1
The Inter-American Commercial Arbitration Commission (IACAC) www.sice.oas.org/dispute/comarb/iacac/iacac2e.asp
The Commercial Arbitration and Mediation Center for the Americas (CAMCA) www.adr.org
World Intellectual Property Organization Arbitration and Mediation Center http://arbiter.wipo.int/center
Association of International Arbitration www.arbitration-adr.org/news/
Hong Kong International Arbitration Centre www.hkiac.org/

Litigation

litigation: a legal proceeding through a judicial system

A legal proceeding through a judicial system, **litigation**, normally will be the course of last resort for companies. Higher risks and costs are associated with litigation. Legal proceedings can last for years and legal fees may reach millions of dollars. Often what becomes even more important than the costs is that the litigation becomes public. Company secrets and "dirty laundry" may be publicly aired, which can hurt a company's image and brand.

Jurisdiction creates a major concern during litigation. Foreign courts follow different norms, which may be confusing to an outsider, giving an advantage to one of the parties. In some cases, the courts themselves may not be fair or unbiased. Even in cases where the findings of litigation are positive, collection of a judgment may not occur. The company can protect itself through bankruptcy by hiding assets in another country, or by leaving the country entirely, thereby removing the jurisdiction needed for collection.

The Russian state-controlled company Rosneft challenged the EU's sanctions against Russia following Russia's involvement in the Crimea conflict; the European Court of Justice which has the right of jurisdiction over the EU's common foreign and security policy ruled that sanctions imposed on Rosneft after Russia's annexation in 2014 of Crimea were valid (Beesley and Foy, 2017).[17]

MARKETING IMPLICATIONS

A key decision to be made when entering a foreign market will be whether to offer a product in its current form or to adapt that product to a nation's unique circumstances. Legal systems contribute a major unique circumstance. As a simple example, beautification products encounter various legal circumstances in nations practicing or being influenced by Islamic law. Islam prohibits the consumption of pork and alcohol, which means many perfumes and lard-based lipsticks are among beauty products that are forbidden to strictly observant Muslims. Turkey's population is mostly Muslim. Still, cosmetics and other beauty products containing the forbidden ingredients are widely available in Turkey even though strict religious practices lead some citizens to reject using such items. Turkey's legal system is not theocratic. In strongly theocratic nations, legal restrictions prohibit or limit the use of many cosmetics and beauty products.

INTERNATIONAL INCIDENT

HiPP is a German international family business which manufactures and sells organic baby food products and baby and mother care products. It is the world's largest processor of organic raw materials. HiPP products are sold in fifty-seven countries worldwide but they are still not available in the United States. Identify and discuss the reasons why HiPP products have not been approved to be sold in the United States.

The marketing and management teams examine the prevailing legal system, including methods of intellectual property protection and conflict resolution, prior to taking any other action with regard to offering standardized or adapted products. Where little protection from counterfeiting exists, careful consideration will be given as to whether a strategic investment in a new country would be worthwhile. Company leaders concerned about conflict resolution give careful thought to any country in which the company might operate at a disadvantage. In essence, standardization and adaptation processes are similar for the product itself as well as for the legal system under which the product will be sold.

LEARNING OBJECTIVE #3:

When is standardization the most viable international marketing strategy?

STANDARDIZATION

One common approach used in international marketing, **standardization**, is the process of applying the same marketing mix to all markets (Erdogmus et al., 2010). A single production process, brand, and appeal are used. While this may seem less responsive to consumer needs in a given country, it decreases costs and increases efficiencies. With standardization, the company can focus on perfecting a single approach. The benefits of this method have been discussed by international marketing writers for many years (Buzzell, 1968). Theodore Levitt (1983) argued that the success for companies comes from concentrating on what everyone wants rather than worrying about the details of what everyone thinks they might like.

standardization: using the same marketing mix in all markets

The cost savings from standardization result from economies of scale and scope. **Economies of scale** refer to a reduction in the cost per unit as the total

economies of scale: the reduction in per unit costs as the total volume produced increases

volume produced increases. A range of efficiencies emerge as a company produces more of a single product. The efficiencies result from increased purchasing power, spreading of fixed costs across a larger volume of units, the potential for managers to be more efficient as they specialize, and the company's ability to use the same promotional materials for a larger market. For companies that standardize, economies of scale reduce costs, which often lead to greater profits (see Table 10.5).

TABLE 10.5   Example of Economies of Scale

Jones Soda	Coca-Cola
Produces 100,000 bottles of soda	Produces 1,000,000 bottles of soda
Cost per soda = $0.50	Cost per soda = $0.25
Price per soda = $1.00	Price per soda = $1.00
Profit for one soda = $0.50	Profit for one soda = $0.75

economies of scope: efficiencies that emerge from producing a variety of similar products

In contrast to economies of scale, **economies of scope** emerge from producing a variety of similar products, which allows for at least parts of the production process and management activities to apply across the product line. For example, the consumer packaged goods company Unilever has a large, sophisticated brand management group. These marketing professionals work on many different Unilever brands at once, creating efficiencies due to economies of scope.

cultural convergence: the increasing similarities between global consumers

Increased standardization may be the result of **cultural convergence**, or the growing similarities between global consumers. Debates occur with regard to the actual degree of convergence present worldwide. Some agreement exists that consumers are becoming more alike in terms of consumption behaviors. Movies, soft drinks, fast-food restaurants, and other products have experienced growing global markets. As potential markets increase in size, the incentive to take advantage of savings that standardization of products offers becomes amplified.

In the case of renewable energy, sustainable sources of energy are sought by countries and companies around the world. Convergence in demand for these resources has risen. The state-owned energy company in Indonesia, PLN, builds solar- and hydro-powered sources of energy. The country's legislature announced plans to spend $84 million on 250 solar power plants.[18] The convergence in demand for solar energy has led to a larger market and greater savings due to economies of scale.

THE GMS: GLOBAL MARKETING STRATEGY

Global marketing strategy: a marketing strategy that encompasses several countries in the world and aims at coordinating a firm's marketing efforts in markets in those countries

A company's approach to the standardization–adaptation dilemma is best described with the use of the **global marketing strategy** (GMS) model. The GMS model describes eight factors that the company must consider when operating in a global marketplace such as: the level of standardization of the marketing mix elements, concentration and coordination of the marketing mix, participation in the global marketplace, and the level of interdependence of international activities (Zou and Cavusgil, 2002). Table 10.6 presents each of the factors considered important in the global marketing strategy. In order to be successful in the global marketplace, international firms must plan and implement marketing strategies that consider all of these factors and are appropriate for the specific product category, industry, and external market conditions.

TABLE 10.6   The Eight Dimensions of Global Marketing Strategy Model

Global Marketing Strategy Dimensions	Description
Product standardization	The degree of product standardization across country markets
Promotion standardization	The degree to which the same promotional mix is employed globally
Standardized channel structure	The degree to which the firm uses the same channel structure globally
Standardized price	The degree to which the firm uses the same pricing strategies globally
Concentration of marketing activities	The extent to which a firm's marketing activities are deliberately performed in a single or a few country locations
Coordination of marketing activities	The extent to which a firm's marketing activities in different country markets are planned and executed interdependently on a global scale
Global market participation	The degree of a firm's market involvement in all major markets in the world
Integration of competitive moves	The degree of interdependence of an organization's competitive marketing efforts in different country markets

Source: Zou and Cavusgil (2002).

The GMS integrates the three popular perspectives of the global marketing strategy: the standardization perspective, the configuration/coordination perspective and the integration perspective.

The eight dimensions of the GMS offer a holistic view of what a firm's global marketing strategy will require. Global marketing strategies do not need to depend solely on standardization to help firms gain competitive advantage in the international market. The specific degree of standardization and integration that the firm should implement depends on both its external and internal environment: marketplace conditions, a firm's management's global orientation, and present international experience (Calantone et al., 2006). A high degree of standardization, concentration and coordination, and integration works well for a company that competes in market sectors where the industry environment supports fast globalization (e.g., mobile phones), and that has a globally orientated organizational culture and management structure. On the other hand, a strategy of adaptation, autonomy, and independence works better in industries where fast globalization is not possible (e.g., food products).

SERVICE STANDARDIZATION

Service providers also need to carefully consider which global marketing strategy is best for their type of service. Many services are offered in a highly standardized form. Airline travel serves as an example. Many international carriers operate under a single brand on a worldwide basis. Other services, such as insurance, financial services, credit and debit cards, and banking often cross national boundaries without major changes. The same holds true for parcel delivery services such as UPS and FedEx.

Standardization, and the efficiencies associated with it, can be a powerful marketing force. Citibank standardizes many components of its credit card business across

The standardization perspective: a firm's marketing mix strategies across different national markets are standardized.

The configuration/coordination perspective: the firm utilizes location-specific advantages, and cross-country coordination captures economies of scale.

The integration perspective: participation in all major world markets and effective integration of the firm's competitive moves across these markets.

markets. As a result, the company has become a leading global financial institution. UAE-Citibank, a subsidiary, has the largest number of credit cards in use in the United Arab Emirates.[19]

LEARNING OBJECTIVE #4:

How can adaptation help a marketing team succeed in reaching target markets in a host country?

ADAPTATION

adaptation: changing a component of the marketing mix to better meet the needs of a local market

When entering new markets, success often hinges on how much goods and services change in response to the differences in those markets. Changing of any component of the marketing mix to better meet the needs of a local market is **adaptation** (Dimitrova and Rosenbloom, 2010). Changes or adaptations can be as minor as adjusting the information about the product to meet local labeling requirements, or as significant as adding new ingredients or creating unique new brand names.

INTERNATIONAL MARKETING IN DAILY LIFE

FOOD PRODUCTS

Responding to local needs as closely as possible constitutes the primary goal of adaptation. Many benefits may emerge. Adaptation can lead to more satisfied consumers, build a stronger and more recognized brand image, and increase sales. Adaptation also incurs costs. Changing the marketing mix may require designing an entirely new advertising campaign or developing an expensive new ingredient. These costs may be higher than the potential return.

Many food products require adaptation. Food is a basic necessity and very few things play a larger role in daily life. Also few product categories are as difficult to sell in a different country or even a different region. In marketing, taboo or forbidden foods are key concerns. The prohibitions on pork for Muslim and Jewish consumers are well known, as is the Hindu prohibition on eating beef. Less well known are Jainist requirements. Jainism is practiced by 4 million people, mainly in India. The religion is strictly vegetarian; in addition, followers typically do not eat tubers or other vegetables that are killed as part of the harvesting process. Some Taoists follow a similar ban on vegetables in the alliaceous family, such as garlic and onion.

Individuals in Western countries also avoid taboo foods. Americans do not eat horsemeat, even though it is common in parts of Europe. Most people in Western cultures do not eat insects or grubs, but the practice is common in Southeast Asia and in the jungles of Latin America. Dogs and cats are pets in part of the world and dinner in others (Harris, 1985).

The examples of taboos show the breadth of differences in food consumption globally. One group's "nasty" food is another's favorite chocolate-covered snack, such as Japanese chocolate-covered grasshoppers and ants. Beyond excluded foods, large differences are present in the role food plays in daily life. Some countries start the day with a large breakfast. Others prefer a light breakfast and a large lunch, followed by a nap (Walloga, 2015). Visitors to Brazil often comment on the country's tradition of eating dinner late in the evening, leading most restaurants to not even open until around 8:00 p.m.

Methods of serving food change from country to country. Traditional Chinese meals are served on a large rotating "Lazy Susan," and each person takes turn serving him or herself. Ethiopian cuisine is also often shared in a communal manner. The dishes are usually served on top of *injera*, a spongy flat bread. Dining involves using the fingers, not utensils. In cases of friendship, individuals may feed someone a bite to indicate closeness. The use of fingers instead of utensils is common throughout Africa, the Middle East, and South Asia.

LAWS AND ADAPTATION

Laws often govern marketing activities. Statutes affect marketing communications, product attributes, green marketing, organizational forms, and interactions between businesses and packaging. The legal system of a country in which the company operates applies to marketing activities as do the laws of the country in which the company is headquartered.

Marketing Communications

Marketing communications present a common legal concern for marketers. Many countries enforce legal restrictions on advertising to children or on advertising potentially unhealthy or addictive substances. False advertising and medicines are also often regulated or prohibited. The 2010 World Cup football tournament in South Africa drew attention to the country's advertising regulations. The country has strict laws, especially regarding health claims. Advertisements are not allowed to claim that a product will help a person slim down or any similar claim.[20] Direct-to-consumer prescription drug advertising is strictly controlled: only two countries in the world – the United States and New Zealand – allow companies to advertise directly to consumers (Ventola, 2011).

Product Attributes

Legal concerns influence product attributes choices. Laws frequently focus on safety and children are a primary group to be protected. Also products that are accepted in one country can be forbidden in others. In strict Islamic countries, this includes a prohibition on alcohol. Brazil has taken an aggressive approach to tobacco regulation. The government limits the tar, nicotine, and carbon monoxide levels allowed in cigarettes, requires a more severe warning on packages, and became the first country in the world to outlaw the use of "descriptors that may induce complacency in consumers regarding the consumption of tobacco products." Descriptors include the words "light," "ultra light," and "mild" (Iglesias et al., 2007).

Organizational Structure

Laws also apply to organizational structures. Governments often express concerns regarding the degree of influence multinational corporations can exert. In these cases, multinational corporations may be required to have local partners, or limits on ownership for foreign companies may be in place. The guidelines often target specific industries, especially those deemed important and in need of protection. India's government deems telecommunications to be such an industry. Foreign ownership of any telecommunications company is limited to 74%. When the U.S. company Qualcomm entered India, a joint venture called Long-Term Evolution was created with two local Indian companies, each of which owned 13% of the new venture.

The other main effect on organizational structure from governmental activity is anti-trust regulation. *Antitrust laws* prevent companies from becoming monopolies. Most countries limit the size of a business to restrain monopolies and preserve competition. The threshold for governmental actions will be different in each region and can even change from case to case. The European Union's approach to antitrust law is often more stringent than that of the United States.[21] The EU fined Intel $1.44 billion for attempting to drive AMD, Intel's main rival, out of the market (Keizer, 2009). In addition, an investigation aimed at Apple sought evidence that the company violated antitrust laws by not allowing Flash to be used in any of its products.[22]

Adapting Packages and Labels

A product rarely enters a new, foreign market without changes being made to packaging. Many of these alterations result from the legal requirements present in a country. Legal requirements regarding product size, materials used, and other components are common. Products are consumed differently in other cultures, necessitating changes to the packaging. Various shapes or materials may be typical in different countries. Glass bottles are more common for soft drinks in some countries. Tall skinny bottles may be associated with energy drinks in one culture and used for different types of drinks in another. Juices may only be sold in glass containers in one country and in aluminum cans in others. Preliminary market research can identify these kinds of cultural nuances and can lead to appropriate adaptation (see Table 10.7).

TABLE 10.7   Packaging and Labeling Adaptation Factors

Legal Requirements
Warranties
Cultural and Aesthetic Factors

Legal stipulations affect product labels. Each country enacts its own labeling requirements. Often these can be complicated and require significant adaptation. The government of South Africa passed a consumer protection law. One provision required retailers to inform consumers of the risk from potentially hazardous products, particularly from those risks that consumers could not "reasonably be expected to be aware of." These risks must be on the labels for the products, and the labels must use "plain and simple language." In response to the law, retailers began updating labels on products, often with legal guidance.[23]

Warranties on product labels differ substantially from one country to another. Warranties are not common in many less-developed or developing countries. In developed countries, especially for high involvement purchases and expensive products, the quality and type of warranty can be a key part of the customer's purchase decision-making process. Regulations regarding warranties are common. In the European Union, consumer protection laws require a two-year warranty for thousands of products. Each must carry understandable instructions.[24]

Cultural and aesthetic factors will be considered as packages and labels are developed for individual countries. Colors, shapes, and sizes are designed to fit local circumstances. They should also mesh with the brand and product name.

Green Marketing and Labels

As consumers increasingly buy products based on environmental or green claims, the need for consumer protection has grown. Greenwashing, or fake green claims, essentially defrauds customers. In response, regulations have been introduced to control this type of labeling. Green marketing regulations are constantly changing as governments struggle to keep up with a rapidly growing industry. For example, the EU introduced the EU Organic logo that should be placed on packaging of organic food produced in the EU. The main objective of this requirement is to make organic products easier to be identified by consumers.[25]

EU Organic farming logo.

Source: © European Union, 1995-2017. Retrieved from https://ec.europa.eu/agriculture/organic/downloads/logo_en

ADAPTATION OF SERVICES

It might be easy to think of services as being nondurable products, but that may not be the case. Several services are durable. Insurance services are consumed year-round, even though premiums and claims are generally paid infrequently. Similarly, business accounting services are usually "consumed" year-round.

Intangibility is not the only product feature that makes services unique. As a general statement, services differ from tangible goods due to intangibility, heterogeneity, simultaneous production and consumption, and perishability elements, as described in Table 10.8.

TABLE 10.8   Characteristics of Services

Characteristic	Description	Example
Intangibility	Services cannot be touched or easily displayed	Manulife Indonesia is a major financial service provider offering intangible services in Indonesia
Heterogeneity	Delivery of service is not standardized and is dependent on social interaction	Bright Ideas Event Coordinators Ltd is a leading event planning company in Vancouver (Canada) that produces unique corporate and special events
Simultaneous Production and Consumption	Customers co-create services along with the provider	AnticaPesa is a top restaurant in Rome, Italy, whose atmosphere is co-created by both staff and guests
Perishability	Services cannot be stored, and they depend heavily on supply and demand	Hemavan is a favorite ski resort in Sweden, where demand is dependent on the geographic surroundings

Service firms utilize several approaches to deal with the unique aspects of company offerings. Malayan Banking Berhad (Maybank) is the largest banking group in Malaysia. The company won the 2009 Promotion Marketing Award of Asia for the development of its Maybank Treats Fair, an event that centered on a four-day shopping extravaganza in a carnival-like setting.[26] By bringing consumers together in a physical location, the company was able to make tangible the intangible.

Ocean Park, a popular tourist water park in Hong Kong, revamped its website by relying largely on interactive technologies to allow the consumer to become more engaged with the company, which allowed customers to co-create the experience with the provider.[27] International airlines often focus on ensuring on-time arrivals of flights to make a brand stand out. Japan Airlines recently won three On-Time Performance Service Awards for delivering a high percentage of on-time flights, adding to the prestige of the brand.[28]

Companies adapt services to meet legal and cultural constraints (Cox and Mason, 2007). For example, in places where theocratic law prevails, charging interest is prohibited, which affects banking and credit card services. Other banking regulations influence how loans may be granted, the definition of usury, and collateral requirements. Further, laws regulating accounting practices vary, causing the need for adaptation of the service.

Strict terrorism laws in Israel substantially affect the nature of air travel into and out of the country. Personal services including grooming are affected by cultural considerations. In some countries, women and men do not visit the same salon for hair care. Tourism services also adjust to local conditions (Thiessen, 2010). Many Spanish hotels decide to make service adjustments in order to attract Chinese travelers. For example, the restaurant menu and other hotel information should be given in Mandarin, guests should never be offered rooms with the number four on it, waiters should remember to serve the eldest person in a group first, and all rooms should have kettles. At the same time, such adaptations to appeal to Chinese tourists may also be driving away other guests as one hotel in Barcelona recently discovered (Burgen, 2015).

In many instances the companies modify the service itself as well as the messages used to market those services. The portrayal of women affects numerous advertisements and marketing for services worldwide. Marketers consider both the product and its communications prior to beginning service provider operations in various countries.

SERVICE QUALITY

Service quality consists of the outcome of an evaluative process in which a consumer compares the service she expected to receive with her perception of the service as provided.[29] A popular approach to measuring service quality is the SERVQUAL method, which measures the concept across various dimensions (Parasuraman et al., 1985). The dimensions can be conceptualized using the "RATER" acronym, which stands for reliability, assurance, tangibles, empathy, and responsiveness, as described in Table 10.9.

TABLE 10.9   Dimensions of Service Quality

Dimension	Description
Reliability	Provider provides service dependably and accurately
Assurance	Provider conveys feelings of trust and knowledge
Tangibles	Provider has appealing facilities, equipment, and personnel
Empathy	Provider conveys a feeling of caring and individual attention
Responsiveness	Provider is willing and able to provide prompt service

Source: Adapted from Parasuraman et al. (1985).

ADAPTATION AND SERVICE QUALITY

Cultural differences influence perceptions of service quality along with perceptions of the relationship between service provider and customer (Ueltschy et al., 2007). In general, reliability constitutes a key element of service quality in the United States, but not necessarily in other cultures (Winsted, 1997).

One recent research effort examined the extent to which each of Hofstede's cultural dimensions relates to the service quality dimensions in various cultures (Furrer et al., 2000). Using this approach, the data suggest that individuals from cultures with large power distance and high collectivism rated the assurance dimension as the most important feature of service, whereas individuals from cultures exhibiting smaller power distance and high collectivism gave equal importance to each dimension. Also, individuals from cultures with smaller power distance and high individualism rated reliability and responsiveness as most important. Tangibles were rated as most important in cultures with large power distance and medium individualism. Small power distance and medium individualism cultures preferred reliability and responsiveness and viewed empathy as moderately important.

In another study, the research revealed that in cultures where openness and frankness are widely accepted, such as in Germany and the United States, consumers feel more comfortable expressing their emotions and openly stating how they feel, hence they are more likely to give customer feedback that reflects experiences. In contrast, in cultures where maintaining group harmony is expected, including Japan, the same behaviors were frowned upon (Ueltschy et al., 2007).

A study of Taiwanese consumers revealed that sincerity, generosity, and courtesy underscored perceptions of service relationships. These consumers were particularly focused on *chin-chieh*, a Mandarin Chinese concept that broadly translates into "warm politeness." These studies indicate that the interpersonal element of service relationships differs across cultures (Imrie et al., 2002).

In summary, the quality of a company's products and services often determines its future success. Quality represents the starting point. From there, other elements, such as advertising, promotion, and other marketing activities, help sell the product and build relationships with customers over time.

MUSIC: LEGAL SYSTEMS, STANDARDIZATION, AND ADAPTATION

Some form of music can be found in nearly every culture. As methods of communication have become more immediate and sophisticated, musical products have begun to regularly move across national borders. Consequently, legal systems, standardization, and adaptation come into play when marketing this global product across borders.

When a music company or performer seeks to sell works in other countries, the actual product itself will first be considered. Sheet music might require translation of the words. Recorded music can be offered in a series of formats, including vinyl albums, cassette, compact disc (CD), or as downloadable music for electronic players such as an iPod or other mobile device. Music can remain in its standardized original language or adapted and recorded to match the language of the host country. Musical performances will be subject to the availability of concert venues, logistical issues, and other local circumstances.

Standardization may be possible in relatively similar cultures. A Canadian musician seeking to break into the British or U.S. market would be able to sing in English, and the format, package, and label could remain the same, assuming French is not the artist's primary language. A Mexican songster might consider rerecording a tune in English in order to reach a wider audience.

Culture also affects the degree to which musical content will be accepted in a country. What may be suitable to people in one region might be offensive to citizens in another. Cultural considerations should be taken into account prior to exporting music in any format.

In addition, the role of radio might influence the music company and the artist. In a country where stations are state owned, it might be difficult to achieve airtime. In a free market economy, access to radio airplay will likely be easier to achieve.

LEGAL ADAPTATION

Following the development of the music format, an additional concern when entering a new country will be the legal system in the host country. Legal nuances affect the degree to which a product or service can be standardized, or whether it must be adapted. When music moves from one country to another in various formats, the overall legal system influences the process. Common law, civil law, and theocratic law treat music in different ways, considering

- content of the music
- restrictions on live performances
- packaging and labeling requirements
- intellectual property protection

Musical Content

The degree to which freedom of expression exists largely depends on two factors: local cultural norms and the legal system. Censorship in some form appears in nearly all legal systems, most notably in the regulation of obscenity. In Europe, music videos can include nudity and other more graphic images. In the United States, obscene words may be heard on a recorded version of a song but will be removed when the song is played on the radio or on television. At the extreme, theocratic law would limit the type of language to be used as well as references to women and religious values.

Restrictions on Live Performances

In 2011, China announced a ban on Western music. Handel's Messiah and other religious songs were not allowed at the country's International Music Festival. In response, the Sinfonica Orchestra di Roma dropped plans to play Mozart's Requiem in the Sichuan earthquake zone in honor of the dead and to raise money for survivors of the 2008 earthquake (Spencer, 2008).

National governments also limit dissent produced in the form of music. Music has a long and storied history of presenting lyrical protests. Oppressive governments work to prevent some music from being performed. In Iran, musical promoter Yaghub Mehrnahad was executed for his role in protest concerts.[30]

Performances are also scrutinized by governments. Highly sexualized musical show performances are popular in Brazil and banned in Libya. A touring band should carefully adapt any musical show to meet governmental restrictions.

Packaging and Labeling Requirements

As is the case with any exported item, local restrictions exist for packages and labels. Portrayals of women and other culturally sensitive figures should be carefully considered. Album covers or CD labels often must be prepared to fit local circumstances.

Intellectual Property Protection

Copying music without paying for it has been a problem in the music industry for many years. Tape recorder technology made it possible to copy songs from the radio or from an album onto a reel-to-reel recorder many years ago. More recently, Internet downloading capabilities have made musical piracy even easier. In the United States, the file-sharing website Napster faced major governmental intervention. The rationale for limiting file sharing is that the intellectual property of the musician and the music company that recorded the song has been taken without compensation.

Today consumers globally are increasingly pirating entertainment goods such as music. In India, the illegal downloading of music to mobile phone chips has become a growing problem. One estimate suggests that the music industry lost *Rs* 300 *crore* in 2009 due to mobile chip piracy (300 million *rupees*, or approximately $6.4 million) (Sharma, 2009).[31]

Music piracy can severely injure a local music industry, which in turn can drastically impact the export of music. France and Spain have been hit hard by music piracy. Local artists from these countries have a difficult time producing new music due to a culture of tolerance toward music piracy. The lack of local music affects international trade in the industry (Pfanner, 2010). In many countries, file-sharing technologies threaten the existence of music production companies.

With Internet access, it is possible for most people around the world to obtain access to music files. Thus, even though legal protection among many countries exists in the form of the Agreement on Trade-Related Aspects of Property Rights (TRIPS), the practicality is that file sharing cannot be stopped on an international basis. No real recourse to collect lost royalties is in place.

Individual countries, however, still take actions for downloading within their borders. Many countries have taken legal steps to reduce music piracy. One relatively new method, the "graduated-response" approach, has been used in South Korea, England, Canada, and France. One or two warnings are given before criminal charges are brought against consumers infringing on intellectual property rights. The laws include pressure on Internet service providers to record information about the individuals or businesses that are using Internet connections inappropriately. These individuals or the businesses themselves face fines or other consequences (Sonne and Colchester, 2010).[32]

In summary, music in all its forms requires decisions regarding standardization and adaptation, both in regard to the actual product as well as to the legal system that governs the marketing of that product in an individual country. Marketing professionals work to make sure any good or service fits with the constraints of the local host nation.

LEARNING OBJECTIVE #5:

How can standardization and adaptation programs combine to achieve greater international marketing effectiveness?

COMBINING STANDARDIZATION AND ADAPTATION

contingency approach: marketers doing what is appropriate for individual markets, which typically leads to a combination of both standardized and adapted components

While the standardization versus adaptation debate may be presented as an either/or situation, in practice marketers often combine the two approaches. The **contingency approach** suggests that marketers should do what is appropriate for each market, which typically leads to a combination of both standardized and adapted components (Jain, 1989). By taking this approach, companies effectively meet the needs of local consumers while still offering some degree of global standardization. Marketers then attend to the factors of the marketing mix that should be adapted or standardized. The default will be standardization because it offers cost savings, although some degree of adaptation often becomes necessary to generate product demand. The conflicting objectives of saving costs versus creating product acceptance are balanced, and the most effective marketing mix will be deployed.

Nestlé utilized a product adaptation approach in Japan by offering a green tea KitKat.

Source: retrieved from https://www.japancentre.com/en/products/5458-nestle-kitkat-mini-share-pack-matcha-green-tea-otona-no-amasa-uji-maccha-kitto-katto?gclid=EAIaIQobChMI2PGHuKG01QIV6LXtCh1fqwZiEAQYASABEgJArfD_BwE&gclsrc=aw

THE PRODUCT AND COMMUNICATION ADAPTATION MODEL

When expanding into new markets, adaptation decisions can be broken down into two separate but related components. First, the same product can be extended into the market—that is, a standardized product may be offered to the new market. Second, communication and promotional materials can be extended into the market. The other options are to adapt the product, communications, or both. These two decisions are coupled and represent four strategic approaches (see Table 10.10).

TABLE 10.10   Product and Communication Extension or Adaptation Model

Product/Communication	Extension	Adaptation
Extension	Dual Extension	Product Adaptation–Communication Extension
Adaptation	Product Extension–Communication Adaptation	Dual Adaptation

Product and Communication Extension

Product and communication extension, or a dual extension, is the strategy in which the same product and communications are extended into the new market. Standardization of everything possible becomes the marketing goal. By using the same product and communications, often not even changing the language, marketing messages focus on the product's attributes. Another by-product of this strategy will be increased consumer interest in a product's country of origin. The dual extension strategy may be found in exporting, which is the process of shipping goods to foreign markets. Exporting companies, especially those beginning the process of entering markets, use a dual extension strategy to lower the costs and risks associated with that market entry.

Clinique and Bacardi are companies that employ product and communication extension strategies (de Mooij, 2010: 283). In some cases, products can meet a global need or be used without change across borders. The Chinese computer power manufacturer Huntkey introduced a universal power strip with a unique plug design that allows it to work in more than 240 different countries.[33] The global appeal of the product allows the company to feature the product and communication extension method.

Product Extension–Communication Adaptation

When marketers keep the same product but make changes to the communication, a product extension–communication adaptation approach has been utilized. Coca-Cola and Pepsi Cola typically apply this strategy. The product remains the same, other than possibly using locally sourced ingredients, but the communication changes. A visit to Coca-Cola's various country-targeting websites reveals how the company adapts communication but keeps the product standardized. The same iconic bottle appears, the color of red is the primary color in most of the websites, and the product is positioned as "happy" and "refreshing" across the majority of markets.

Product Adaptation–Communication Extension

Product adaptation–communication extension involves adapting the product but retaining the same communications program. This often includes maintaining the same basic theme for the advertising, such as testimonials or humor, but changing the product's brand name or adding an additional attribute to the product. Many large consumer companies take advantage of this approach. Some time ago, Unilever in Japan introduced a new brand of Lipton tea. The company adapted the traditional product by adding the amino acid theanine to the tea. The company's communications claim was that the additive allows the consumer both to relax and to focus. The new tea has been branded Lipton *Hirameki*, which means "I've got an idea" in Japanese (Madden, 2007a).

Product–Communication Adaptation

The final approach involves adapting the product and communications, the product–communication adaptation, or the dual adaptation strategy. Large demand and large target markets often are best served by adapting products specifically to individual markets. Cosmetics can be adapted to respond to the demand for unique attributes in new markets. In East Asia, white skin is seen as the beauty ideal. Many cosmetics companies have adapted products to include a whitening version. The market leader is the American brand Oil of Olay, which offers the Olay White Radiance product.

The traditional face cream with a whitening additive effectively reaches the target market. Communication for the product can be adapted to use local models, language, and appeals (Prasso, 2005).

In extreme cases, to be successful in a new market companies invent a new product to meet the needs of new consumers. This can be thought of as an extreme version of dual adaptation. While creating an entirely new product may be difficult, it might be necessary when the firm faces a vastly different but large or strategically important market.

SUSTAINABILITY AND ADAPTATION

Two approaches to sustainability are practiced as part of adaptation. The first, adaptation of the product, includes all of the methods used to design and market items that can be reused or recycled. Electronics, appliances, automobiles, and other durable goods are logical candidates for recycling efforts. Component parts, including ink jets for copiers and printers, can also be manufactured to be reused. Disposable batteries may be replaced with rechargeable forms, and power sources for other products can be adapted to include wind, solar, or other renewable forms of energy.

In many instances, companies adapt packages to more sustainable forms. Chinese companies that were engaged in recycling cardboard products noticed significant declines in orders during the most recent recession. The trend will likely reverse as economic conditions improve.

The second approach to sustainability involves changing the production process. Many firms have designed manufacturing plants and office buildings to save energy through the use of solar panels, new types of roofing, and other innovative energy-savers. Further, by placing plant locations strategically and seeking more efficient forms of transportation, shipping costs can be greatly reduced.

In the future, the movement toward sustainable products and production methods is expected to expand. Companies on the forefront of the trend may realize substantial marketing advantages by becoming the first mover or innovator in sustainability.

GLOBAL INNOVATION

Many companies increasingly emphasize innovation as a source of advantage. The position of innovation manager has been added to many organizations as part of an in-depth innovation strategy. A key component is the process of creating a new product. New product development helps renew a company and assists the marketing team in effectively responding to changes in customer tastes. With estimates as high as nine out of ten new products failing, new product development can be costly and entail a great deal of risk, but creating new products may be necessary for long-term firm success.

The Brazilian Zeebo gaming console product is about the size of a paperback book. It plays online games. The console has been positioned as a gaming console for emerging markets, as a less expensive product when compared to consoles made by Microsoft, Nintendo, and Sony. Fierce competition exists and the risk for failure is high, a typical scenario for new product introductions (Hall, 2009).

LEARNING OBJECTIVE #6:

How can global innovation and patterns of diffusion assist the marketing team in reaching target markets, including those consisting of bottom-of-the-pyramid customers?

Several types of "new" products can be introduced. *New-to-the-world products* are the inventions or discoveries most strongly associated with new product development. The fluorescent light bulb, the personal computer, and the digital music player are all types of new-to-the-world products.

A company may also create a product for an existing product category. These are *new category products*. Microsoft's introduction of the Xbox 360 was a new category product for the company and counts as an example of this kind of new product development.

Another form of extension is an *addition to the product line*. Additions are made to protect a lead brand in the product category from competitors or to fill a gap in the product line. Product lines frequently differ from country to country; an addition to a product line in one country may be an existing product in other. When Samsung introduced two top-of-the-line "beyond smart mobile phones" capable of running thousands of different applications, these were additions to the product line.[34]

In many cases, especially when entering new markets, a producer makes small changes to an existing product. *Product improvements* may be considered a type of new product development. In China, Sprite sells a ginger-flavored product named Sprite on Fire, in reference to the burning sensation from the ginger in the soda.

The final type of new product development, *repositioning*, refers to finding a new use or application for an existing product. This increasingly occurs as companies that sell existing products to bottom-of-the-pyramid consumers offer the items in developed countries. Nestlé repositioned its Maggi brand of dried noodles, which was a top seller in rural India and Pakistan, as an inexpensive but healthy food in Australia and New Zealand (Jana, 2009).

In some cases, an established product in the home market will be considered to be a new product in the country being entered. For established businesses, this means viewing what may be a traditional, old product as something new and innovative. Resistance to the new, especially the foreign, often accompanies the introduction of these products in other markets. The problem will be more likely to occur in certain market segments, such as rural consumers in emerging markets, or older consumers in transition economies. Increasingly, new products become popular in developing countries and are then introduced into developed countries. Fanta, the second-best selling soda in Africa, is a Coca-Cola brand that has not captured a great deal of market share in the United States. The company rolled out an aggressive marketing campaign around a product launch in 2001, but the brand is still only the tenth-best-selling soda in the United States.

TYPES OF ADOPTERS

When entering a market, an effective marketing tool involves targeting the different categories of adopters (see Figure 10.2). Marketers segment consumers based on speeds of new product adoption. *Innovators*, the group of consumers who start using new products first, comprise approximately 2.5% of any market. The next group, *early adopters*, makes up about 13.5% of the market. Marketers often combine efforts aimed at early adopters and innovators when introducing a new product. These two groups represent around 16% of the overall market. Success with these groups often serves as a signal of potential product acceptance.

Companies target early adopters and innovators using promotions designed to ensure adoption. Postpurchase surveys gauge levels of satisfaction with the new product, and, if needed, changes will be made before targeting the overall market. The largest two segments of adopters are the *early majority* and the *late majority*. Each consists of about 34% of the market. Penetration into these groups signals successful product introduction and the movement toward a mature product. The final segment, *laggards*, makes up about 16% of the market. Laggards may never start using the product. In many cases it is cost effective to not target this segment and instead to focus on a successful introduction of a different new product. This begins the cycle of adoption again.

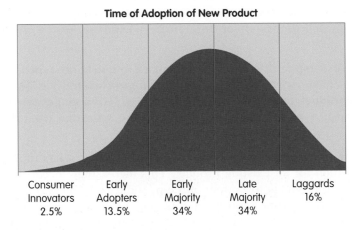

Time of Adoption of New Product

| Consumer Innovators 2.5% | Early Adopters 13.5% | Early Majority 34% | Late Majority 34% | Laggards 16% |

FIGURE 10.2   Types of Adopters in New Product Diffusion

GLOBAL PRODUCT DIFFUSION

diffusion: the process by which an innovation slowly spreads through a culture or group

Diffusion is the process by which an innovation spreads through a culture or group. The process applies to new products and new uses for existing products. The knowledge reaches a few individuals—the innovators and early adopters—and then diffuses, sometimes slowly or sometimes quickly, to the early majority followed by the late majority, ending with laggards.

Marketers consider four factors with regard to diffusion. First is the innovation itself. The marketing team seeks to identify whether the innovation is to existing products or processes. A large difference with existing consumer behaviors leads to a slower rate of diffusion.

The second factor will be the effectiveness of communications about the innovation. Even a quality innovation will sell without effective promotion. Consumers should be exposed to communications designed to encourage trial purchases, and they must understand the message.

Time represents the third key component of diffusion. All innovations take time to spread within a culture. Appropriate marketing mix activities help speed up this process. Poor marketing activity leads to slower diffusion.

The final factor emerges from the members of the society within which the product is introduced. Effectively marketing to them will be particularly challenging in foreign markets. A lack of understanding of consumers and how the product might be used hinders efforts to introduce a new product.

Acceptance of hybrid electric vehicles has gone through the diffusion process. The technology for hybrids can be traced back to the turn of the twentieth century when electric, hybrid, and gasoline cars all fought for acceptance. The second car built by Dr Ferdinand Porsche, the founder of Porsche Vehicles, was an electric–gas hybrid. The modern history of the hybrid begins with the introduction of the Audi Duo III hybrid in 1998. The car was priced out of the mass market and was not a success, but it marked the rebirth of the hybrid category.

At about the same time, Toyota began to mass-produce the Prius, but at that point it was only sold in the Japanese market. The first global mass market hybrid was the Honda Insight, which hit the market in 1999. The car, a three-door hatchback, was a limited success. Consumer innovators and early adopters with a passion for environmental issues purchased the car, and the hybrid innovation began to diffuse throughout society.

In 2000, Toyota released the Prius four-door sedan hybrid in its major global markets. The introduction was successful and the model was declared the 2004 Car of the Year by *Motor Trend* magazine. At that point, the early majority began purchasing the car. By 2009, hybrid technology had diffused across much of society. Ford, Honda, Toyota, Mazda, Nissan, General Motors, BMW, Hyundai, and Mercedes-Benz all manufactured some form of hybrid vehicle.[35] Coming full circle, Porsche announced on January 28, 2010, that it would be manufacturing the Porsche 918 Spider, a plug-in hybrid. Production of the car began in September 2013 and ended in June 2015 (Censky, 2010).[36] Such products may soon become mainstream as countries introduce laws that limit or forbid the use of diesel cars. The UK plans to ban the use of diesel cars and vans from 2040 while half of all new cars in Norway were hybrid or electric at the beginning of 2017 (Asthana and Taylor, 2017; Rodionova, 2017).

NEW PRODUCT DEVELOPMENT AND THE BOTTOM-OF-THE-PYRAMID

New product development is an important part of effective marketing to bottom-of-the-pyramid consumers. Often, creating the capacity to consume necessitates marketers designing a new, less expensive version of an existing product. In many cases the product can then be reintroduced back into developed markets as a less-expensive, downscaled version of the original product. This approach reverses the traditional model of new product development. Companies introduce the product to the masses in the less-developed world and then move it into more economically advanced countries.

GE is the world's leading manufacturer of electro-encephalograph (EEG) machines, with 34% of the global market. The company introduced the MAC 800, a low-cost, stripped-down version of the typical EEG machine used in developed countries. The MAC 800 was developed for emerging markets. To fit the needs of developed country health professionals, a few features were added, such as Ethernet, USB, and telephone ports, but introducing the updated machine was an estimated $1.8 million less expensive than developing a new machine (Jana, 2009).

ETHICAL ISSUES IN STANDARDIZATION AND ADAPTATION

Adaptation of products can lead to ethical concerns. A major concern may be found at the intersection of religion and ethics. Religion often serves as one of the primary sources of ethical values in any culture. When a company enters a new nation, marketers often discover that religious values in the host country conflict with those in the home country. Leaders must decide which values the company should follow. The issue becomes whether marketers should be expected to adapt to controversial or potentially unethical practices. For example, managers of satellite campuses for Western universities in the Middle East wonder if they should require women to wear head coverings and traditional Muslim dress, regardless of their religions. Food providers might examine social norms against eating certain animals or insects before making the decision whether to offer certain products.

ETHICS AND LAWS

Ethics may differ from laws. Some laws (or the lack of a law) conflict with ethical values. When a company operates in many dissimilar legal environments, conflicts arise between the company's values and the laws of the country in which the company conducts business. For example, child labor takes place in many countries. Ethically, a company's management team may feel the need to enforce stricter guidelines than the legal limits in the country. The same may apply to minimum wages, worker safety, and the role of women in the workplace.

CHAPTER 10: REVIEW AND RESOURCES

Strategic Implications

When entering a new country, the marketing team first determines the unique legal requirements of that locale. After studying the legal environment, voluntary adaptation choices are made. Then, the main strategic question for global marketers will be how much of the marketing mix should change. Marketing managers decide on the degree of adaptation that will be necessary to achieve the desired level of local responsiveness, which will be balanced against the efficiency gains from standardization. Regulations and the adaptation necessitated by them are not optional. If the requirements are too stringent, the best strategic choice may be to not enter the country.

International marketers should develop a clear conceptualization of each brand's global position. Decisions are made regarding what should remain constant across borders and what should be changed. The marketing team identifies the brand's meaning and how well it transfers to another culture. Branding decisions are coupled with communication tactics. One of the product/communication strategies will then be chosen.

Tactical Implications

Adaptation and standardization decisions are based on understanding consumers in a market. Market research and local partners help marketers identify local consumer tastes. With this knowledge, product adaptation becomes more likely to succeed. With the global brand's goals in mind, products can be changed and new products can be introduced. Companies must update packaging and modify product labels. Product warranties may or may not be added.

Market research helps identify early adopters and innovators. These consumers can be targeted for the introduction of adapted products, new-to-the-country products, and new-to-the-world products. Understanding these consumers will speed the diffusion of innovative products throughout the country.

Operational Implications

Communication of brand meaning to all employees globally is crucial. Consistent positioning can only be achieved through effective communication. The communication should be two-way. Decisions will be transmitted to employees, bearing in mind that individual workers may discover valuable potential adaptations that can only be seen by individuals with on-the-ground experience.

Local workers should be carefully trained with regard to local laws and statutes. Host country employees can assist in training expatriates. The training should extend beyond legal requirements to include cultural and ethical differences.

Standardized products are often best served by individual training of first-line supervisors and employees, especially those not familiar with an exported product. The benefits of any item that has been adapted to fit the needs of the local community should be carefully explained by those who design advertisements and other communications, as well as the sales force and others making contacts with customers.

TERMS

common law

civil law

theocratic law

intellectual property

intellectual property piracy

jurisdiction

conciliation

arbitration

litigation

standardization

economies of scale

economies of scope

cultural convergence

global marketing strategy

adaptation

contingency approach

diffusion

REVIEW QUESTIONS

1. Describe the three main legal systems: common law, civil law, and theocratic law.

2. Define intellectual property and name the treaty that seeks to protect intellectual property.

3. Describe copyrights, trademarks, and patents.

4. What is counterfeiting?

5. Describe corporate spying and reverse-engineering.

6. What is the relationship between intellectual property protection and economic development?

7. Define jurisdiction and explain how it applies to legal actions.

8. Describe conciliation and arbitration.

9. What are the advantages and disadvantages of arbitration?

10. What are the disadvantages of litigation?

11. Define standardization and name the primary reasons for its use.

12. Describe economies of scale and economies of scope.

13. Define cultural convergence.

14. Define adaptation.

15. Explain how laws affect adaptation and the product areas affected by regulations.

16. How is packaging adapted?

17. How are labels adapted?

18. Describe the contingency approach with regard to standardization and adaptation.

19. What are the four different approaches to the product and communication adaptation or extension model?

20. Define new product development and name the different types.

21. How can adopters of new products be categorized?

22. Define diffusion and explain the factors that influence the speed of diffusion.

DISCUSSION QUESTIONS

1. Explain the differences between the three primary legal systems—common law, civil law, and theocratic law. Is one of these systems more conducive to marketing activity than another? Explain your answer.

2. Many individuals in both developed and developing countries have violated intellectual property protections. Choose a side and make a case as to whether violating intellectual property rights is either wrong or right.

3. Litigation is often the least attractive of the conflict resolution choices. Create a table listing the advantages and disadvantages of conciliation, arbitration, and litigation, then pick the best possible resolution option for a business seeking to protect a patent. Defend your choice.

4. Whether to standardize or adapt a product will be one of the central decisions an international marketer makes. Consider a global product that you recently purchased. What was standardized or adapted? Why did the marketing team make these choices? What was legally required?

5. New products fail at an increasingly high rate. How can the graph of new product adaptation be applied to ensure higher acceptance of a new product?

6. Think of a new product you recently purchased. What factors influenced your decision to purchase the product? Does the product seem to be one that diffuses quickly or slowly across a target market?

ANALYTICAL AND INTERNET EXERCISES

1. Search the Internet for "Coca-Cola virtual vendor." Using this online tool, list at least ten of Coca-Cola's global versus national brands. Why were these choices made? Do you agree or disagree with Coca-Cola's overall brand strategy? Justify your answer.

2. The concept of aesthetics is not easy to explain. Using Google or another online search engine, search for various examples of art and architecture from at least one country from each continent (excluding Antarctica). What does the search reveal about differences in aesthetics and how could it influence the design of packaging for luxury products intended for a global audience?

3. Find a recent example of a case of conciliation or arbitration. Why would the companies involved have preferred this conflict resolution method to litigation? Now find a recent litigation example. What did the companies risk from litigating the dispute?

4. Using the Internet, track the rate of diffusion internationally for the following products:

    *   cell phones

    *   e-readers

    *   professional basketball

    *   online shopping

    *   credit and debit cards

    *   electricity smart meters

    *   organic food

STUDENT STUDY SITE

Visit **https://study.sagepub.com/baack2e** to access these free additional learning tools:

- Web Quizzes
- eFlashcards
- SAGE Journal Articles
- Country Fact Sheets
- Chapter Outlines
- Interactive Maps

CASE 10

Banana Republic in the UK

U.S. clothing and accessories retailer Banana Republic, worn by Olivia Palermo and the Duchess of Cambridge, announced in 2016 that after eight years on British shores it was closing all of its eight UK stores and British consumers would only be able to buy the brand's clothes online. Banana Republic is owned by an American multinational corporation, Gap Inc. It was founded in 1978 by two entrepreneurs and bought by Gap Inc. in 1983. The company offers clothing for men and women in a style described by the company as "versatile, contemporary classics, designed for today with style that endures."[37]

Banana Republic maintains more than 600 stores in North America, ten stores in Europe, seventy stores in Asia, thirteen in the Middle East, seven in South America, and five in Africa.[38] The brand arrived in the UK in 2008 just after the financial crisis, and closed all of its stores by the end of 2016. According to market analysts many external and internal factors contributed to its failure. Consumers became more cost-conscious after the financial crisis and either turned to cheap fashion such as Primark, did not buy clothes for some time, or waited for price discounts. Many consumers moved online to shop for fashion with major competitors offering a wide range of clothes and accessories at competitive prices and convenient and cheap delivery options. The product offering did not live up to the expectations of British consumers who have switched from shopping for clothes to spending money on experiences such as holidays or dining out (Daneshkhu, 2016; Daneshkhu and Vandevelde, 2016).

Analysts suggested that the pricing and promotion strategy did not take into account the nature of the British market and local consumer habits. The brand entered the British market by opening a store on one of the most popular shopping streets in the heart of London, Regent's Street. The company intended to compete with other brands that were present in the crowded clothing market. The promotional and pricing strategy did not however support the intended positioning as a premium brand. Sales promotions damaged the brand's image as consumers were aware of discounts and withheld purchases until the expected discount was offered (Strachan, 2016).

British consumers commented that Banana Republic offered "some good solid styles" but "they tried to bring too much American style here which didn't work" and were overpriced compared to competitors such as Zara. There were almost no stores outside of

London (Table 10.11) which was disappointing to some consumers and did not help to build Banana Republic's brand awareness.[39]

TABLE 10.11   Locations of Banana Republic Stores in the UK

Store location	Neighborhood
King's Road—23 King's Road, Duke of York Square, London SW3 4LY	Chelsea, West London
Bath—24–26 Union Street, Bath BA1 1RS	Shopping district in Central Bath
White City—Unit 2034–2036, Ariel Way, London W12 7GF	Shopping mall in White City, West London
One Way Change—22 Cheapside, London EC2V 6AH	Square Mile in Central London
Covent Garden—132 Long Acre, London WC2E 9AA	Covent Garden, Central London
Canary Wharf—Unit 68, Jubilee Place, London E14 5NY	Shopping mall in the Business/Financial District of London
Kensington—Unit SU2, Barkers Arcade, 63/67 High Street Kensington, London W8 5SE	Shopping street in Kensington, West London
Regent Street—224 Regent Street, London W1B 3BR	Shopping street in Central London

One of Banana Republic's strategic priorities is to further develop an omni-channel shopping experience for customers through the integration of store and digital shopping channels. This could be an opportunity for the brand to raise and maintain brand awareness in international markets, but is also seen as a challenging objective given that competitors are also striving to integrate off-line and online channels.

Banana Republic's current strategies include pursuing selective international expansion in a number of countries around the world through a number of channels. The company intends to open additional stores outside of the United States, and continue to grow online sales internationally. These plans are ambitious and need to be carefully considered and executed because the company has limited experience operating or franchising in some of the intended international locations. In many markets Banana Republic would face major, established competitors. In addition, in many of these locations, the real estate,

(Continued)

(Continued)

employment and labor, transportation and logistics, regulatory, and other operating requirements differ dramatically from those where Banana Republic has more experience. Consumer tastes and trends may differ in many of these locations as well and, as a result, the sales of the products may not be successful or result in the margins the company anticipates. If international expansion plans are unsuccessful or do not deliver an appropriate return on the planned investments, the operations and financial results could be materially, adversely affected.[40]

1. Why did Banana Republic failed in the UK?

2. Compare the product offering of Banana Republic in the UK to the product offering in the United States and Canada. Do you think the brand would have been more successful in the UK with a different product offering?

3. If Banana Republic was to reenter the UK, what should the brand do differently in order to be more successful?

4. If adaptation of the marketing mix is recommended, which aspects of the marketing mix would you recommend Banana Republic to adapt to the British market and in what ways?

5. Do you think that Banana Republic should continue to offer online shopping to British consumers and how should the brand capitalize on this should they wish to reenter the market in the future?

6. What other countries would you recommend for Banana Republic to consider next for their international expansion plans, and what product acceptance challenges would the company face in those countries?

PART IV
INTERNATIONAL PRICING
AND FINANCE

CONTENTS

11

INTERNATIONAL PRICING

LEARNING OBJECTIVES

After reading and studying this chapter, you should be able to answer the following questions:

1. What forms of pricing exist, and how do perceptions influence views of prices?
2. What are the most common strategic objectives associated with prices, and what methods may be used to achieve those objectives?
3. What types of pricing discounts are available to international marketers?
4. What factors influence decisions about price changes in international markets?
5. What ethical concerns are associated with international pricing programs?

IN THIS CHAPTER

WIND TURBINES IN FINLAND: PRICING SUSTAINABILITY AND ECONOMIC INCENTIVES

During the second half of the twentieth century, the Scandinavian nation of Finland transformed from a farm and forest economy to a diversified modern industrial economy. The country's per capita income ranks as one of the highest in Western Europe. The key features of Finland's economy include a high standard of education, equality promotion, and a national social security system. Its challenges include an aging population and the fluctuations of an export-driven economy. The nation has an extensive shoreline with a cold climate featuring long days of sunlight in the summer and long, dark nights in the winter. The population of the country is more than 5 million citizens, with more than two-thirds of the population living in urban areas. Persons living in Finland can expect to reach the age of eighty. Nearly the entire population is literate.

Finland is home to Tuulivoimala Finland Ltd, one of several major corporations devoted to sustainable energy. These efforts address the threats of air pollution, acid rain, and water pollution from power plants and agricultural waste. The company also reaches a lucrative market consisting of neighborhoods wishing to base electric systems on methods other than the national power grid.

A group of Finnish scholars recently made presentations to several regional universities in the United States. The educators described the advantages and challenges associated with setting up neighborhood associations owning their own wind turbines. The advantages included improved property values, because any buyer would know he or she would not have an electric bill to pay each month along with feelings of satisfaction knowing one's home was more environmentally friendly.

One of the primary challenges was pricing. Each turbine costs in excess of 1 million *euros* and would serve approximately fifty homes. While a household would not have to pay an electric bill, it would be required to pay for the system itself, normally financed with a thirty-year bond, plus its share of maintenance and operational costs. Each household would take about twenty years in terms of savings on electric bills to recover the purchase price of the system. Then, however, the household would only pay maintenance costs with all other electricity being free, and at times would receive a stream of revenue from excess electricity sold back to the nation's power grid.

An additional pricing challenge came from negotiating with the government. On the one hand, Finland's government benefits from reduced pollution and not being forced to create additional power supplies for the population and local industries. On the other, revenues from the electricity being sold and taxes on that electricity would be reduced. The question arose as to whether the government of Finland should help subsidize purchases of the wind turbines with tax incentives, since doing so was in the nation's interests.

The final complication arose from making price decisions for homes that were already built versus new construction. How much should the neighborhood association charge existing homes, which required some adaptation to become part of the self-contained grid, as compared to those built with the features included?

The visiting scholars concluded by saying that, whereas pricing issues in these circumstances are complex and require careful calculations incorporating the life of the wind turbine and the houses, they were well worth the effort, for both home buyers and the larger country.[1]

Wind turbines owned by individual citizens create unique pricing challenges.

(Continued)

(Continued)

Questions for Students

1. What should the government of Finland do—provide tax incentives for energy reduction or leave the system as it is?
2. How might the energy savings provided by turbines increase the sale price of a house?
3. Is energy a fixed cost or a variable cost in a household's budget?

OVERVIEW

Part IV of this textbook considers pricing and financial issues in international marketing. Pricing may not seem to be a complicated process. A firm would need to know how much it costs to produce an item, identify the desired amount of profit, and affix a price tag; however, such an approach ignores several factors. Even in domestic-only markets, other influences, including supply and demand, the distribution of wealth, economic conditions, political shifts, and taxation policies affect pricing programs. Figure 11.1 indicates the background for pricing and its connections to the other aspects of international marketing.

Culture affects methods of setting prices, forms of bargaining, and perceptions regarding what price indicates (quality, exclusivity). Pricing language, especially with regard to what constitutes an "established" price or a "discount," varies. Governments regulate prices for domestic and international products. Supply and demand are economic forces that also influence what a company charges for an item. A country's infrastructure affects product costs, delivery charges, and therefore subsequent prices.

Chapter 12 examines international financing, which plays a major role in strategic international marketing decisions. Financing affects decisions to enter countries and the costs of doing business. Financial markets affect profits and subsequent deliberations about whether to expand operations or leave a market.

This chapter considers strategic pricing issues. It first describes the essentials of international pricing, followed by methods of discounting and changing prices. Pricing of new and ongoing products will be examined. Complications that arise when pricing in the international marketplace also are explained. International business-to-business pricing programs receive attention. Finally, quantitative methods for studying pricing as well as aspects of pricing to consumers at the bottom-of-the-pyramid are presented.

LEARNING OBJECTIVE #1:

What forms of pricing exist, and how do perceptions influence views of prices?

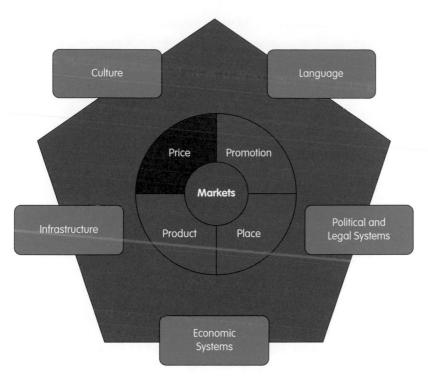

FIGURE 11.1 The International Marketing Context

THE NATURE OF PRICE

Why is the price of milk different in the countries shown in Table 11.1? As shown, a great deal of variation exists. Discovering the reasons for the differences constitutes one of the goals of this chapter, along with explaining how and why prices change.

A **price** is the amount a person, company, or government charges for a good or service. Prices may be established for a single item (a canola), a set of items (a six-pack of Thums Up soda), a combination of products (a six-course meal), a single service (a haircut), a combination of services (air fare and hotel in a one-price package), an event (a performance of Chinese opera), a season or time period (soccer/football tickets for the entire year), and other less common possibilities.

price: the amount a person, company, or government charges for a good or service

As products move through the market channel, the original price will be the one offered by a manufacturer to middlemen, typically wholesalers and distributors. These organizations then resell the item to retailers at the *wholesale price*. Retailers mark up the item, and the final price becomes the *retail price*. Brazilian retailers are allowed to mark up the cost of essential medicines by as much as 30% over the wholesale price to create the retail price (Nobrega Ode et al., 2007). The newest form of pricing, an *Internet price*, may or may not be the same as the retail price. In some circumstances, Internet prices are set lower due to reduced merchandizing and markup costs. In others, the price may be high due to a reduction in the retail price, such as during an after-Christmas sale or one ending the season for summer clothing. Internet prices may be charged by e-commerce operations or on websites of brick-and-mortar stores that also offer items online.

TABLE 11.1   Examples of Prices for One Liter of Milk in Various Countries

Country	Price
Brazil	$0.71[a]
Jamaica	$0.57[b]
Japan	$2.48[c]
South Africa	$1.24[d]
United States	$1.01[e]

(All prices have been converted to U.S. dollars.)

Sources:

a. CLAL, "Brazil: Farm-Gate Milk Prices." Retrieved from www.clal.it/en/index.php?section=latte_brasile;

b. Titus (2010);

d. "Cape Town Cost of Living," www.expatcapetown.com/cape-town-cost-of-living.html;

e. Leonard (2009).

Service prices are charged to other businesses, to the government, and to retail customers. A business may purchase a health insurance program as a service to its employees. The government buys services from vendors for a variety of situations, including the clean-up after a major storm, independent snow plowing operations, and others. Individual customers pay retail service prices for a wide variety of products, from insurance, to personal care, to entertainment.

Another form of pricing is *leasing*. A product, typically a big-ticket item, may be leased for a specified number of years with accompanying servicing, spare parts, and repair agreements. Leasing opens markets for manufacturers and provides foreign companies with the opportunity to use equipment while making level monthly or annual payments. As has been noted in earlier chapters, in China property is not owned: instead, it is leased for a certain amount of time, often seventy years in the city or thirty years in rural areas (Richardson, 2008). A leasing agreement establishes a finite time period, which reduces the purchase risk for the company leasing the equipment. Manufacturers may seek out leases to defend against fluctuations in currencies or political risks.

INTERNATIONAL PRICES

Every form of pricing should be adapted to international operations. When prices are set in other countries the complications of payment systems, discounting programs, types of currencies and currency value fluctuations, methods of payment, and other differences such as negotiation and bartering occur. In essence, marketers spend a great deal of time establishing prices for products sent to other nations.

PRICE AND PERCEPTION

Prices represent a combination of circumstances and perceptions. As depicted in Figure 11.2, three items influence perceptions of price. A consumer may go through complicated considerations of these variables as she considers a price in terms of its fairness or as an incentive to make the purchase. The deliberations can be altered at any time, based on changes in the buyer's level of income, mood, or even the time of day. International marketers seek to find an attractive price for the largest number of consumers.

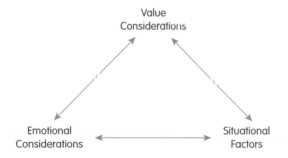

FIGURE 11.2   Price Considerations

VALUE CONSIDERATIONS

Most buyers first consider whether the amount charged represents a reasonable portrayal of the item's value. Perceptions of value normally influence comparisons of an item's price to its quality. Charges for a hotel room with a scenic view of the Dardanelles in Canakkale, Turkey will be substantially higher than for a comparable room without a view, even when the hotels are on the same street. A serving of fish sold in a high-end restaurant in Tokyo carries a higher price, because customers believe it will be prepared by the finest chef cooking with the best ingredients.

Price can convey either that a product is "cheap" or that it is a worthy bargain due to the lower amount being asked. A London tavern selling the exact same ale at a lower price than all competitors expects to make up some of the difference by selling more glasses. Other low-priced items may be viewed as simply trinkets or junk.

Many purchases result from a consumer's conclusion that an item's price matches its level of quality. Rational reasoning often leads to the decision. Consumers also make comparisons with competitor prices, past purchases, and other experiences. One product that has become increasingly popular is the Icelandic-style, *skyr* strained yogurt. The Siggi brand's rapid growth in the United States has not been hindered by its relatively high price—$2.68 for a six-ounce cup at Whole Foods Markets. Many consumers conclude that the unique taste of Siggi *skyr* makes it worth the price.

A Price Perceptual Map

One tool international marketers use to examine a brand's image and market position relative to the competition is a **price perceptual map**, which depicts various companies or products along two dimensions, typically price and quality. Figure 11.3 provides an example of a price perceptual map for hotels in the city of Buenos Aires, Argentina. As shown, three well-known multinational chains offer hotels in the city. These units tend to charge the highest prices per stay. In this city the Hilton does not have the biggest advantage, however, because consumers perceive Caesar Park as being of higher quality and a lower price. A risk exists for Hilton that frequent travelers and locals might conclude Caesar Park offers a better price–quality relationship as they gain experience with the local hotel. Hilton's marketing team might attempt to respond to this perception by highlighting or enhancing the quality of the hotel or by targeting groups that are brand loyal and therefore less inclined to stay at Caesar Park. A loyalty program that offers additional incentives for frequent stays in Hilton properties would assist in this effort.

price perceptual map: a map that depicts various companies or products along two dimensions, typically price and quality

FIGURE 11.3   A Pricing Perceptual Map for Hotels

The marketing team at the Holiday Inn might discover that perceptions of its quality over Loi Suites Esmeralda result primarily from a more well-known brand name. This might lead to similar attempts at improving quality in some way or through other means to strengthen loyalty to Holiday Inn. Marketers for Loi Suites would promote the concept that travelers receive the same quality at a lower price.

A pricing perceptual map creates a visual portrayal of the relationships between price, quality, image, or other variables. Then, the marketing team makes pricing and other strategic marketing decisions based on what it observes. Focus groups and other forms of market research assist in developing pricing perceptual maps. The groups normally consist of travelers to Buenos Aires from other countries, locals, or both.

EMOTIONAL FACTORS

At times reasoning and rational thought do not drive purchase decisions. Many goods and services contain emotional components that affect value judgments and influence purchase decisions. After the British Petroleum (BP) oil spill in the Gulf of Mexico, some angry consumers boycotted the company; 500,000 Facebook users "liked" the Boycott BP page, even though many industry experts pointed out the boycott would hurt local gas station owners, not the large multinational (Lieber, 2010).

Emotional components exist in services, such as hair care, personal finance, and insurance. Hair care may be associated with beauty and sensuality, personal finance with individual success, and insurance purchases with feelings that one has "protected" his or her family.

The same holds true for physical products. Clothes sold in a high-fashion district, such as the *huitième arrondissement* (eighth municipal district) in Paris, likely hold the emotional value related to feelings of being *chic*. An automobile purchase often contains both rational and emotional instincts.

The market leader in Russia, the Lada brand of automobiles (Vladimir Putin drives one), enjoys a cult following in the United Kingdom even though the brand has not been available in that market since 1997. The brand held the reputation of being spartan and inexpensive even though some models were incapable of breaking the speed limit on highways. In spite of many jokes about the car, including the classic "What do you call a Lada at the top of a hill? A miracle!" the low price for the car meant it was often the first car someone in the United Kingdom purchased. Those emotional ties remain strong for some in the United Kingdom and may allow for a successful reintroduction of the brand (McIver, 2010; O'Neill, 2010).

SITUATIONAL FACTORS

Price may reflect an individual's immediate circumstances. A tourist lost in the streets of Budapest, Hungary, might be willing to spend a large amount of money for a taxi to take him back to his hotel. *Impulse buys* are those made on the spot. A unique-looking drink that is red in color being sold in a small establishment on the streets of Sitges, Spain, might cause a thirsty and adventuresome tourist to make a purchase without having any idea about its taste. Common wisdom suggests that money has a different value and is spent differently by vacationers. Other situational factors include the consumer's physical situation, the social setting, the time of day, and the person's mood.

INTERNATIONAL PRICING METHODS

Marketers make pricing decisions following consultations and discussions with several individuals and company departments. Members of the marketing and management teams choose the method to be used in setting the price and eventually determine the price itself. One of the first activities will be to establish strategic pricing goals. Table 11.2 identifies common pricing objectives.[2]

Companies establish pricing goals to fit international operations and may set different goals for various markets. For example, Unilever might pursue the goal of quickly gaining marketing share in Cambodia because the company just began selling products there. To meet this objective, products may feature lower prices and in smaller packages (Hemtasilpa, 2005). In the European market, however, where the company is more established, profitability may be Unilever's goal. In response to recent increases in production costs, the company might raise prices to maintain profit levels, even if their market share goes down slightly (Patrick, 2008).

TABLE 11.2   **Pricing Objectives**

Objective	Measures
Profitability	Total Dollar Profit
	Return on Investment
	Percentage Increase from Previous Year
	Contribution to Overhead
Market Share	Product Market Share
	Product Line or Brand Share
	Company Market Share

(Continued)

TABLE 11.2   (Continued)

Objective	Measures
Enticing New Customers	Number of New Customers
	Percentage of Total Company Customers
Retaining Current Customers	Repurchase Rates
Counter Competitive Actions	Market Share Statistics during a Specific Campaign
	Number of New Competitors Entering the Market
Attract Competitors' Customers	Purchases by New Customers

LEARNING OBJECTIVE #2:

What are the most common strategic objectives associated with prices, and what methods may be used to achieve those objectives?

Following the establishment of pricing objectives, various methods are available for establishing a product's base price. Several pricing methods assist a firm in reaching a pricing goal. They include

- cost-based pricing
- demand-/supply-based pricing
- competition-based pricing
- profit-based pricing

Each serves the purpose of identifying the most viable price.

COST-BASED PRICING

cost-based pricing: pricing based on a careful assessment of all costs associated with producing and selling an item

Cost-based pricing begins with a careful assessment of the costs associated with producing and selling an item. *Fixed costs* remain constant regardless of volume sold. Rent payments, installment payments on machinery purchases, interest on debt, and licensing fees stay the same regardless of the level of production. In addition to total fixed costs, an estimate can be made of the number of units the company seeks to produce and sell. Fixed costs are then allocated to each unit as the fixed cost per unit.

Variable costs are those associated with the production and sale of each item. Raw materials, labor costs, storage, shipping costs, and commissions vary with the number of units produced and sold. *Total costs* constitute the total dollar amount assigned to a product, and are calculated by adding total fixed costs to the sum of all variable costs. Marketers then use various methods to establish a price based on those costs, including break-even analysis, cost-plus pricing, and markup pricing.

break-even analysis: a common method employed to discover the relationships between costs and price

Break-Even Analysis

One common method to identify relationships between costs and price is a **break-even analysis**. The calculations apply equally well to international expansions and other situations. Ray-Ban markets a luxury brand of sunglasses. If upper-middle-class customers in Kenya appear to be a viable market segment, the company's marketing might consider manufacturing and selling sunglasses there. To determine the number of pairs of glasses that would need to be sold to cover the cost of expansion, a break-even analysis such as the one shown in Figure 11.4 would be conducted. Ray-Ban's marketing team would then assess the size of the market segment. If they conclude that 20,000 or more pairs of glasses can be sold in Kenya, the company would break even. Each pair of sunglasses purchased after that number would result in additional revenue that contributes to profit.

$$\text{Break-Even Points (units)} = \frac{\text{Fixed Costs (Total dollars)}}{\text{Price per unit} - \text{Variable costs per unit}}$$

$$= \frac{60,000,000 \text{ KES}}{8,000 - 5,000}$$

$$= 20,000 \text{ units}$$

Where: Fixed Costs = plant rent

Cost of machinery

Interest on debt

Variable Costs = plastic and ingredients to make glasses

shipping cost per unit

packaging cost per unit

increased advertising costs per unit (ads in Kenya)

FIGURE 11.4   A Break-Even Analysis

Note: The Kenyan *shilling* (KES) is the Kenyan currency.

Cost-Plus Pricing

Cost-plus pricing involves setting the product's price based on fixed costs, variable costs, plus the desired profit margin for an item. Experts employ cost plus pricing in cases where costs are unknown or hard to predict, and when leaders want to ensure a certain level of profit regardless of the costs incurred. Contractors, lawyers, and business consultants often employ this method.

cost-plus pricing: setting a product's price based on fixed costs, variable costs, plus the desired profit margin for each item

Cost-plus may be used when pricing chili peppers in Sulawesi, one of the main islands in Indonesia. Much of the island's population is Manadonese who are said to "breathe fire" because 90% of local dishes contain chili as a spice.[3] Although demand stays high, the cost of producing chili peppers can be highly variable because it is influenced by Indonesia's weather. In response to this variability, producers could sign a contract with Starbucks, who uses the peppers for sachets of chili sauce, which prices the peppers at a 15% profit margin. Regardless of the end costs, the producer would be assured a 15% profit. Figure 11.5 provides an example of a cost-plus calculation of price.

Markup Pricing

Markup pricing may apply to cases where costs are known. It offers a straightforward pricing method that adds a standard amount to the costs assigned to a product. The approach may be best suited to retailers stocking large numbers of products

markup pricing: a pricing method that simply adds a standard markup to the costs assigned to a product

Total Fixed Costs = 45,000,000 Rp3

Fixed cost per unit @ 5,000 units (1 kg of chilli)

$$= 45,000,000 \text{ Rp-:- } 5,000 \text{ Rp}$$

$$= 9,000 \text{ Rp}$$

Variable cost per unit for 5,000 kg of chilli = 5,000 Rp

Total Variable Costs = 25,000,000 Rp

Total Costs = 70,000,000 Rp

Desired Profit Margin = Total Costs * Percentage Profit Margin

$$= 70,000,000 * 0.15$$

$$= 10,500,000 \text{ Rp}$$

Profit per Unit = Total Profit -:- Units Produced (5,000 kg of chili)

$$= 10,500,000 \text{ Rp -:- } 5,000$$

$$= 2,100 \text{ Rp}$$

Unit Price = Fixed cost per unit + Variable cost per unit + Desired profit per unit

$$= 9,000 \text{ Rp} + 5,000 \text{ Rp} + 2,100 \text{ Rp}$$

$$= 16,100 \text{ Rp}$$

FIGURE 11.5   Cost-Plus Pricing

Notes: *Rp* stands for Rupiah, the currency of Indonesia; kg stands for kilogram.

and manufacturers that produce large quantities of goods. In those cases, tracking demand per item will be difficult and setting a price for each item would be cumbersome and time consuming. Markup pricing provides a simple, quick method to price many goods. The markup approach typically features a percentage as the margin of profit per good. Note that the percentage profit is taken from the costs and not from the final price, a common error. Table 11.3 presents an example (Braun et al., 2010).

TABLE 11.3   Markup pricing for a 2.5-liter bottle of Guaraná Antarctica soda in Brazil (R# =)

Total Cost per Unit	R$2.00[a]	Final Price
15% Markup	R$0.30	R$2.30
20% Markup	R$0.40	R$2.40
25% Markup	R$0.50	R$2.50

Note: a. R$ stands for Brazilian *reals*.

The markup pricing approach may be most useful when the company's marketing team has determined that consumers are not strongly affected by price. Cost-plus pricing also has value when the company leaders seek to recover start-up or expansion costs first.

The most dramatic price markups reflect more than costs. The primary example appears in the jewelry industry. Diamond prices tend to be set based on the four Cs: cut, clarity, color, and carat weight. At the same time, many retail outlets post prices with huge markups, thereby allowing for negotiation and price reductions for special seasons and with individual customers. Personal preferences and emotional responses to events such as buying a diamond ring to present as part of an engagement strongly influence the amount a consumer will be willing to pay. Large markups allow greater flexibility to the retailer in those circumstances.

DEMAND-/SUPPLY-BASED PRICING

Some marketers criticize cost-based pricing methods for over- or underpricing a product relative to demand. Decreased market share results when an item is overpriced and lost profits occur when it is underpriced. Although it could be more difficult, demand-based pricing can be more precise and efficient.

Demand-based pricing takes advantage of calculations normally associated with economics. It requires an estimation of *demand*, or the amount of items that will be purchased at various price levels, and *supply*, or the amount producers of items are willing to provide or sell at various prices. The *equilibrium point* reflects the intersection of the demand and supply curve, as displayed in Figure 11.6.

To calculate supply and demand, a research format such as a test market will be designed. By pricing an item at various levels in differing markets, it becomes possible to estimate corresponding levels of demand. Thus, in the Asia-Pacific market the average price for beer is approximately $2.20 per liter, whereas in Western Europe it is $4.90 and in the United States it is $3.70. Price differences can be partially linked to the lower demand for beer in Asian countries. The average consumption in China, as one example, is 30 liters per capita per year compared with 80 liters in the United States and Western Europe (McBride, 2010).

Price elasticity of demand measures the impact of price differences on sales and demand. Prices do not strongly affect consumers when *inelastic demand* exists. Instead they make purchases within a price range in which smaller price differences do not affect the willingness to buy. Inelastic demand often exists for staple items. Wheat, a staple item in the United Kingdom, is used to produce many types of food. In 2010 the price of wheat went up 40%, leading to consumer calls for governmental action, because no substitutes were available. This meant that the demand was inelastic even, at a higher price (Inman, 2010). Further, inelastic demand appears in high-end and luxury situations, such as prices for exotic and exclusive hotel rooms rented by the super rich and celebrities seeking privacy as well as for the most costly automobiles.

> **price elasticity of demand:** a measure of the impact of price differences on demand and sales

Highly elastic demand occurs when consumers exhibit extreme price sensitivity. A small price increase drives consumers away, and a small price decrease attracts them. Not long ago, Kirin, the Japanese brewer, introduced the zero-alcohol beer Kirin Zero to the Japanese market. Non- or low-alcohol beers have traditionally struggled in the Japanese market, but the brand has become surprisingly popular. Price created part of the appeal. At around 148 *yen* (about $1.90), a bottle of Kirin Zero is cheaper than regular beer (Inagaki, 2009). Due to the elasticity of demand for a product such as beer that has many substitutes, the low price resulted in increased demand for the new product.

In international markets, local conditions affect demand, supply, and elasticity. Fashionable items experience a different demand curve due to emotional features such as price and status. Demand may be lower because fewer individuals can afford the item, such as an automobile in a less-developed economy, yet the price may be higher, because only the affluent can afford to purchase a car. When coupled with a lower supply and the costs associated with shipping a vehicle to another country, the price changes.

Local customs and traditions often affect elasticity. When a family requires a specific item to perform a religious ceremony, such as a specific type of incense for a Buddhist ritual, that family may be willing to pay more for the product because no substitute exists and the item carries a high emotional value.

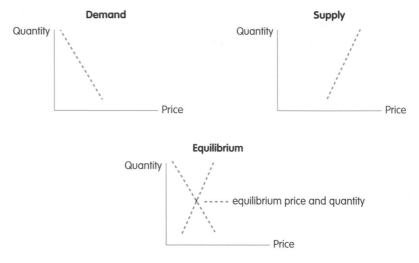

FIGURE 11.6   Demand, Supply, and Equilibrium

INTERNATIONAL MARKETING IN DAILY LIFE
CALCULATING SUPPLY AND DEMAND EQUILIBRIUM

Discovering the exact impact of various prices on supply and demand may not be possible. The marketing team instead attempts to develop estimates of the relationships. This chapter began with a chart of different prices for milk in various countries (Table 11.1). These price variations are due in part to differences in demand and supply. Table 11.4 portrays supply and demand in Brazil, which has a low, inelastic price for milk.

TABLE 11.4   Demand, Price, and Total Revenue for a Liter of Milk in Brasília, Brazil

Price ($)	Demand (liters per week)	Total Revenue ($)
$0.60	1,000,000	$600,000
$0.65	975,000	$617,500
$0.70	800,000	$560,000
$0.75	500,000	$375,000
$0.80	350,000	$280,000

In this instance, the optimal price would be $0.65 per liter of milk, because it yields the highest total revenue.

A second calculation reveals price elasticity. The equation for price elasticity of demand is

$$\text{Price elasticity of demand} = \frac{\text{percentage change in quantity demand}}{\text{percentage change in price}}$$

Table 11.5 was developed for milk in Japan, where dairy milk consumption is not as common as it is in Brazil. Milk substitutes are available, including a traditional preference for soy milk. The market difference leads to differences in price elasticity. As shown, a price of $1.90 per liter results in projected sales (demand) of 1,100,000 liters annually. If the price rises to $2.00, the percentage increase is 5.27% ({$2.00–$1.90} / $1.90). Elasticity in that instance is calculated by examining the decline in sales, from 1,100,000 to 1,000,000, as ({1,000,000–1,100,000} / 1,100,000), which equals –9.09%. When the percentage change in demand (–9.09%) is divided by the percentage change in price (5.27%), the elasticity value becomes –1.72. The absolute value of this number, 1.72, is the elasticity of demand.

An elasticity value of 1.0 represents the point of *unitary* elasticity of demand, because the change in demand is equal to the change in price. Any value below 1.0 represents *inelastic* demand, because the change in demand is lower than the change in price. Any value over 1.0 means *elastic* demand is present, because the change in demand is greater than the change in price.

Most items experience elastic demand to some degree. Consumers at some point become unwilling to purchase the product and seek alternatives. In Table 11.5, when the price is set above $2.00, customers become less willing to pay for the product and look elsewhere.

TABLE 11.5   Price Elasticity of Demand for Milk in Nagoya, Japan

Price ($)	Demand	Percentage Change		Elasticity (%)
		Price (%)	Demand (%)	
$1.90	1,100,000			
$2.00	1,000,000	5.27	–9.09	1.72
$2.10	900,000	5.00	–10.00	2.00
$2.20	800,000	4.76	–11.11	2.33
$2.30	700,000	4.37	–12.50	2.86
$2.40	600,000	4.17	–14.29	3.43
$2.50	500,000	4.00	–16.67	4.17
$2.60	400,000	3.85	–20.00	5.19
$2.70	300,000	3.70	–25.00	6.76

Marketers often discover that elasticity varies by country or by regions within a country. In the case of the Brazilian market, demand for milk will be more inelastic because drinking milk is more culturally the norm and fewer similar substitutes exist than in the Japanese market. For the initial price increase from $0.60 to $0.65, the elasticity was 0.60 (–5.0% drop in demand / 8.3% increase in price), which reflects inelastic demand. Brazilian consumers are less sensitive to changes in the price of milk than are Japanese consumers.

Other factors influence elasticity. Per capita income and income distribution dramatically affect the willingness and ability of consumers to pay within various price ranges. In Paraguay, hair care will be more commonplace in urban areas and elasticity may be lower. In rural areas, hair care prices might be highly elastic and prices will be set at a lower range, due to reduced incomes. When the price rises beyond a certain point, the consumer becomes inclined to have a family member cut his hair rather than paying for it.

International Diversity of Demand

International marketers know that demand curves differ in various countries. Factors such as trade barriers, governmental activities and differences between those activities across markets, and the costs associated with shipping and/or moving into a new market, influence the nature of demand. Also, variances in consumer tastes and preferences between markets due to cultural and environmental influences mean that demand curves do not transfer well across international boundaries. The demand for a product in one country may be totally different from the demand for that product in another. As a result, the strong potential exists that each country exhibits unique equilibrium points between supply and demand and varying levels of elasticity.

In some cases, governments take actions that increase or decrease demand or elasticity. Think City, an electric vehicle designed in Norway, is manufactured in Elkhart, Indiana. The U.S. price for the vehicle, approximately $38,000, is essentially equivalent to the automobile's price in other markets. The U.S. government, seeking to promote cars that do not run on gasoline and, at the same time, create manufacturing jobs, offers incentives that reduce the price to about $30,000. The price drops to $25,000 in California, where the state government offers additional incentives (Motavalli, 2010). These governmental rebates help increase demand.

Global Marginal Analysis

To apply demand differences to a marginal analysis, remember that the demand curve predicts the response to a drop in price. If the curves change from market to market, the marketing team needs to estimate a different curve and conduct a separate marginal analysis for each market. International markets also typically incur different costs, especially if adaptation is required, if there are tariffs that must be paid, or if there are any other potential increased costs. These factors will also change a marginal analysis of supply, demand, and elasticity across various prices (King and King, 2010).

COMPETITION-BASED PRICING

In domestic settings, competition-based pricing remains relatively simple. The marketing team chooses from one of three options:

- below the industry average
- at the industry average, or
- above the industry average

Pricing below the industry average makes price the primary marketing tactic. Big box retail giants, including Vishal Mega Mart in India, Carrefour, and Wal-Mart employ this method. Pricing at the industry average occurs in oligopolistic situations or when brand parity exists. Producers attempt to make the price a less relevant variable and turn the focus to other features, such as convenience or other differentiating product attributes. Pricing above the industry average usually seeks to convey the message of exclusivity and higher quality. Luxury hotels worldwide feature this approach. Other services may be marketed in the same way, as will high-end dining.

In new markets, new layers should be considered when pricing based on competition. The new calculations include

- pricing versus domestic competitors
- pricing versus foreign competitors
- pricing versus domestic and foreign competitors combined

In these circumstances, the marketing team works to identify the types of customers involved. If the majority of customers only purchase domestic products in the product category, then foreign competitors are largely ignored. When Nabisco began exporting Oreo cookies to the United Kingdom to compete with British biscuits (cookies), most locals exhibited low levels of interest in the new items (O'Neill, 2008). As a result, local bakeries could afford to largely ignore the competition.

Pricing against foreign competitors occurs in circumstances in which international bids are being made for a contract. The marketing team tries to identify any incentives given by the government to assist a company in winning the bid. For example, many companies in numerous countries offer water purification products. Should the government of Ghana seek bids for a system, several companies might enter the competition. If a company in Russia receives governmental support to respond to the request for a bid, the company may be able to offer a lower price for a comparable water purification system. At the same time, if relations between Ghana and Russia are strained, then price will not be the only issue involved.

Pricing versus foreign and domestic competitors combined takes place in many markets. Shoe giants Nike and Reebok face both local and foreign competition when trying to place athletic shoes in local stores and when trying to sell the shoes to high school, college, and professional sports teams. In these instances, factors beyond price arise. When some shoes are produced in less-developed nations in factories where workers receive low wages, tariffs may be imposed, trade disputes can arise, and other emotional forces may become involved.

COMPETITION-BASED PRICE SETTING FOR NEW PRODUCTS

Any time a new product launches, the key pricing decisions involve discovering how to position the product using price, capture market share, and recover start-up costs. The same methods apply to entering a new country with ongoing products. The two extreme positions are known as skimming, or skim-the-cream, and penetration pricing.

Skimming

At one end of the new-product–price continuum, **skimming** represents the attempt to recapture start-up costs as quickly as possible. Setting the price as high as the market will bear allows the manufacturer or exporter to generate the most revenue possible in a short period of time. Skimming works for unique products that cannot easily be duplicated. Competitors are discouraged by various barriers to entry, including government regulations, patent protections, and, in the case of international marketing, access to channels of distribution.

skimming: setting a product's initial price as high as the market will bear to allow the manufacturer or exporter to attain as much revenue as possible in a short period of time

Skimming prices tends to invite competition. Other companies observe the high price and higher markup, and some eventually find their way into the marketplace, which drives the price down. Companies may take preemptive action and lower the initial price in staggered steps to maintain market dominance. Sony used a skimming approach to pricing the various PlayStation consoles with the goal of earning a higher profit on brand-loyal, hardcore video game players before dropping the price to attract more casual users (Liu, 2010).

Penetration Pricing

penetration pricing: setting the product's initial price as low as a company can afford, to discourage entry by competition

The other extreme new-product–price approach, **penetration pricing**, occurs when the entrant charges the lowest price it can afford. The method discourages entry by competition, because larger margins do not appear possible. Also, penetration pricing helps a company build sales figures, establish a larger market share, and provides time for consumers to develop brand, product, and company loyalty. The company then can allow the price to drift up, especially if price elasticity remains low.

Penetration pricing makes it more difficult to recover start-up costs. It will take more time due to the smaller margin per product sale. The creators of Zeebo, the low-cost, emerging-market gaming device, selected a price of $240 for its introduction in the Brazilian market. With competitors typically priced up to $1,000, partially due to tariffs, the low price was designed to allow the company to gain market share as quickly as possible. The company experienced losses for the first few years, but the marketing team believed the risk was worth the potential gains in long-term market position (Hall, 2009). Figure 11.7 presents the ways prices tend to move using both skimming and penetration pricing approaches.

Penetration pricing may be used to quickly capture market share for beauty products.

PROFIT-BASED PRICING

profit-based pricing: examining pricing from the perspective of what consumers are willing to pay rather than from the cost of the item

Profit-based pricing examines pricing from the perspective of what consumers are willing to pay rather than the cost of the item. Three situations encourage profit-oriented pricing. The first occurs when an organization operates in a monopolistic competition environment. The second involves pricing to quickly recover start-up costs. The third exists in markets in which prices are set to achieve a balance between demand and supply while generating optimal profits.

In monopolistic competition situations, a form of break-even analysis may be used. Instead of break-even occurring at the point where fixed and variable costs have been covered, profits are added to the formula, as displayed in Figure 11.8.

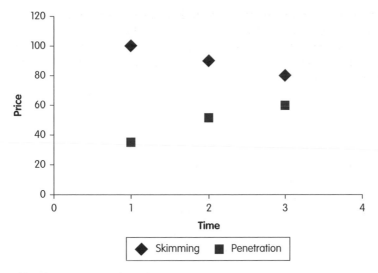

FIGURE 11.7   Skimming vs. Penetration Price

FIGURE 11.8   Profit-Based Pricing Break-Even Analysis

Note: a. £ stands for the pound sterling, the currency in the United Kingdom.

This formula would only apply to circumstances in which the team marketers were certain 60,000 tickets could be sold at the desired price of £600 each.

In the second circumstance, a company may have incurred high start-up costs and might want to recover those expenditures quickly. This might occur when managers believe competitors will quickly enter the marketplace or when the start-up costs have pushed the company to the brink of financial problems. Oftentimes, high start-up costs are associated with moving into a new country. Beyond the development of a physical location such as plant and equipment, various fees and taxes may be present. Costs associated with relocating employees or hiring local workers may be involved. Profit-based pricing becomes viable when demand remains sufficiently inelastic for the company to recover costs by charging a higher price.

Using prices to achieve a balance between demand, supply, and profit becomes an option when demand is elastic. A musical group that plans a concert tour in Europe will first examine the venues for the concerts. When an arena can hold 30,000 patrons, the price can be set high enough to encourage that many purchases. When the price is set too low, many fans wishing to buy tickets are turned away, causing frustration and possibly attempts at gate crashing or scalping. If promoters raise the price, some consumers will decide the event is too costly. Optimal profits are achieved because supply and demand match at the higher price.

When singer Barbra Streisand announced her European tour, demand was high and prices for tickets were as high as $1,200. This price was appropriate for the level of demand in the United Kingdom, and that show sold well. For the Rome concert, the price did not fit demand. Consumer groups protested, sales were slow, and the concert was cancelled (Emling, 2007).

Target ROI Pricing

Another popular method of profit-oriented pricing, **target return on investment (ROI) pricing**, resembles markup pricing because it uses unit costs as a basis for determining the final price. The difference takes place in the markup portion of the formula. With target ROI pricing, information will be required regarding the capital investments associated with production of the product. The goal is to set the price at the proper level to achieve a predetermined ROI. For example, consider the following information from a Swiss manufacturer of designer alarm clocks:

Investment = $500,000

Expected sales = 50,000 units

Unit cost = $15.00

Targeted ROI = 20%

Target ROI price = Unit Cost + [(Target ROI Percentage * Investment) / Expected Sales]

Target ROI price = $15 + [(.20 * $500,000) / 50,000]

$$= \$17.00 \text{ per clock}$$

With sales of 50,000 units, total revenue would equal ($17 * 50,000) = $850,000 and costs would be $750,000. Profit would be $850,000–$750,000 = $100,000, which is a realized return of 20% (0.20 * $500,000 = $100,000). Again, these calculations depend heavily on accurate market research information.

INTERNATIONAL CONSIDERATION IN PRICING GOALS

As has been noted, pricing becomes more complicated when companies sell products across international boundaries. Variable costs rise due to additional shipping, more expensive sales calls, tariffs and taxes, and other items. From a marketing perspective, two concepts deserve consideration as part of international pricing processes. The first requires a balancing of short- and long-term goals. The second, which closely connects, is a consideration of emotional and situational factors. The same product will be priced differently in each market as was shown in the price comparisons for milk in various countries in Table 11.3.

Short-Term vs. Long-Term Goals

Each of the international marketing goals presented earlier in Table 11.2 receives consideration when making pricing decisions. Profitability concerns will naturally emerge. For products that have been sold over a period of time, additional market share objectives may be pursued. Prices may be designed to attract new customers in some circumstances and retain customers in others. Companies set prices to counter competitive actions and/or to attract the competition's customers.

One primary concern will be to balance short-term goals versus longer-term strategic objectives. When entering a new country, profit objectives may include limiting projected losses until the product or company becomes established. Other objectives, such as brand awareness, rise to the forefront. Once an item receives attention, price can become the final element in a decision regarding whether to try the entrant product. Sampling, coupons, and other enticements might be tied to prices to encourage trial purchases. The longer-term strategic objective will be to establish a presence in the new country and to build on that presence over time, with the assumption that profits will eventually accrue due to the establishment of a strong market presence.

Building Relationships vs. Profits

The emotional and situational elements of pricing apply to relationships as well. The Gulf of Mexico area experienced the devastating impact on the BP oil spill in 2010 and the spill affected prices for seafood. In that situation, some international suppliers identified an opportunity to build relationships with restaurants and grocery chains by keeping prices as low as possible. While forgoing some short-term windfall profits, seafood providers could establish relationships and develop bonds that will last for years. In many countries, relationships are more important than profits. Business partners will pay a higher price or take a loss during periods of stress in return for future business contacts or a reciprocal drop in price when the business environment stabilizes (Chen, 2001).

In summary, the four methods used to set prices, based on costs, supply and demand, competition, or profits, apply equally well to domestic and international pricing activities. Each takes place in the context of variables beyond just the amount charged for the item.

The idiosyncrasies of a country or region, combined with the desired objectives displayed in Table 11.2, affect price setting in each situation or market. For example, when a company chooses *profitability* as the primary strategic objective, then the marketing team tends to set prices using costs or profit-based methods. For new products, marketers would be inclined to price to near the ceiling using skimming methods. Enhancing *market share* suggests that pricing will probably be related to or based on competition in some way. Pricing to *retain current customers* may be competition-based or designed to find the supply/demand equilibrium for the volume a company intends to deliver. Should the goal be to *entice new customers* with a new product, then a penetration pricing approach applies. Competition-based pricing or supply and demand approaches would apply to ongoing products and markets. When *countering competitive actions* is the goal, penetration pricing matches new products and competition-based pricing would be the best method for continuing products. To attract competitor customers, pricing would be set using a competition-based method.

In each of these instances, marketers should remember that price represents more than depictions of quality or standing relative to the competition. Prices contain emotional and situational components. Economic conditions change situations. When recessions occur, substitute products become more viable as those challenged by lower incomes look for bargains and other ways of cutting personal expenditures.

Governmental regulations may further complicate pricing decisions for both new and ongoing products. This means that pricing will be an ongoing operation for the marketers and managers in other departments.

PRICING TO BOTTOM-OF-THE-PYRAMID CONSUMERS

When pricing to those with the lowest incomes, new variables become involved. Beyond the price and quality associated with an item, the unit size and payment method contribute important considerations. Effective international marketing to these groups results from a clear understanding of how individuals make purchase decisions.

Capacity to Consume

capacity to consume: the power to use goods and services in the satisfaction of human wants

Capacity to consume refers to the power to use goods and services in the satisfaction of human wants. It consists of wants, goods and services available, time and energy, and purchasing power (Comish, 1936). In the past, the method used to create the capacity to consume among the poor had been to provide the product or service free of charge. Some argue the approach has the feel of philanthropy. While charity may feel good, it may not be the best marketing tactic. Instead, when marketing to consumers with meagre incomes, C. K. Prahalad (2006) suggests that increasing the capacity to consume will be the best approach.

Consumption and choice at the bottom-of-the-pyramid can be encouraged by making small unit packages featuring affordable prices. Many of these consumers experience unpredictable income streams. Consequently, they subsist on daily wages and spend cash cautiously.

Single-serve packages match the needs of this population. Single-serve packages are more common in less-developed economies. In India, where large pockets of low-income consumers live, single-serve sachets have become the norm for a wide variety of products, including shampoo, salt, biscuits (cookies), coffee, tea, ketchup, fruit drink concentrate, mouthwash, skin cream, and even bread.

Marketing smaller units carrying a lower price represents a strategic attempt to reach a large group of consumers. The goal truly is to expand a company's customer base through effective packaging and pricing. Three key elements required by this method are affordability, access (reaching people in their standard shopping places), and availability, or having the product on hand when the individual has money and is ready to buy. Pepsi has started to develop anti-anaemia health drinks targeting bottom-of-the-pyramid consumers in India. To remove price-related barriers, the company plans to charge between Rs1 and Rs2 (1 to 2 *rupees*, or $0.02 to $0.04) per serving.[4]

Credit

A second pricing pillar needed to build sales with bottom-of-the-pyramid consumers, providing credit, may appear to be counterintuitive. It might seem illogical to give credit to persons with uneven and unpredictable income streams; default rates among the poor, however, are lower than they are among their more wealthy counterparts. In Mumbai, some lenders charge 600% to 1,000% interest on loans to low-income customers. A bank charging 25% interest can attract these consumers as customers and cover the costs of potential defaults at the same time. Providing access to credit supports pricing decisions and allows bottom-of-the-pyramid customers to upgrade their living conditions. Many use such credit to improve home lives by financing items such as televisions and mobile phones. Some rent these products to others to help make payments.

Several companies employ creative tactics. In India, small grocers were not able to afford the $440 price for generators as a back up source of power during outages. Unable to get loans, the shopkeepers had few options. A Honda Motor Co. distributor in the state of Uttar Pradesh came up with a unique solution. Twenty shopkeepers formed a group and each of them paid the distributor $22 per month. Every month, enough money was collected to buy one generator, which was awarded to one of the retailers through a lottery. After twenty months, every participant owned a generator (Anderson and Markides, 2007).

Marketing to bottom-of-the-pyramid customers can engender strong feelings of brand loyalty, especially when the company exhibits trust and dignity, and combines those values with appropriate product sizes, features, and prices.

INTERNATIONAL PRICING DISCOUNTS

In the same manner as price setting, price discounting begins with stating a desired objective. Companies do not grant discounts randomly or without careful considera-tion. The amount and type of discount offered will be determined by the rationale for the discount. When a company seeks to defend against the actions of a competitor, it grants price reductions with the competitor in mind. When prices are discounted to build or reward customer loyalty and frequent purchases, other discounts become more effective. Recently the French retailer Carrefour allocated 600 million *euros* to discount prices in France. The objective was clear. Sales in France had declined by 3.4% in the third quarter of one year. In response, the marketing team designed the discounts to increase demand and traffic in the stores (Spencer, 2009). Pricing discounts may be adapted to suit the needs of international marketing. Table 11.6 identifies the main types of pricing discounts.

LEARNING OBJECTIVE #3:

What types of pricing discounts are available to international marketers?

LOSS LEADER

In retail stores, pricing certain items at or below cost in order to build store traffic remains a common marketing tactic. **Loss leader** pricing relies on regular prices for other items in the store in order to generate profits. The loss-leader system also creates sales for other businesses. To attract an order from a wholesaler or retailer, a manufacturer can offer one loss leader designed to encourage a series of purchases of additional products at the regular price.

loss leader: pricing certain items at or below cost in order to build store traffic

At times, companies tie loss leaders with other pricing programs. A *promotional price* takes the form of a price reduction associated with a promotion, such as a pre-Christmas sale. An *introductory price* features a discount for trying something new. A restaurant offering a new menu item may at first sell the product at a discount to lure patrons to try the new food product.

TABLE 11.6   Types of Pricing Discounts

Loss Leaders
Seasonal Discounts
Quantity Discounts
Early-Payment Discounts
Other Channel Discounts

Loss leaders create the advantage of generating interest. Such discounts move consumers to action when they travel to the store and make a special effort to take advantage of the low-price items. Typically other purchases follow. Loss leaders help fend off competitive attacks by appealing to store customers to remain loyal, even as other offers are made. In Canada, a typical approach used by car dealers has been to sell subcompact cars at a loss to attract new customers and to maintain the loyalty of repeat purchasers (Karim, 2007).

The use of loss leaders applies equally well to international marketing. Companies seeking to enter or build share in another country can provide loss leader offers to accompany a catalogue or list of products.

SEASONAL DISCOUNTS

Seasonal discounts are often associated with the tourism and hospitality industries. Vacation resorts, dining establishments, fishing and boat rental services, and entertainment venues including theme parks and music shows often experience peak sales and attendance during warmer months. To entice patrons at other times, companies such as these offer off-season discounts. An international marketing firm can balance seasonal fluctuations by conducting operations in several parts of the world. The summer season in Australia and Brazil takes place during the winter months in North America and Europe, and vice versa.

Seasonal discounts apply to physical products as well. Lawn care and gardening items sell well in warm seasons. Discount offers discourage regular customers from shopping around during peak seasons. When cool weather appears, off-season discounts entice customers to stockpile or purchase items such as a new shovel or hoe for future use.

Sports and entertainment have well-defined seasons. Basketball is played at certain times of the year. Theater productions often shut down during part of the year. Of course, these seasons vary country by country. Offering advance ticket purchases at a discounted price generates cash flow during off seasons.

QUANTITY DISCOUNTS

Organizations provide quantity discounts to retail purchasers and for sales by manufacturers and other suppliers to various channel members. The simplest form of quantity discount, a buy-one-get-one-free offer, encourages retail customers to stockpile items and/or use them more frequently.

Manufacturers offer quantity discounts to wholesalers and retailers. The price per unit declines as the volume of purchases rise. Volume discounts are helpful in some international marketing programs. Rather than a series of sales calls followed by a series of shipments, producers bundle purchases into larger amounts and offer the savings to the wholesaler or retailer.

Quantity discounts appear in advertising programs. Most media companies reduce the price per advertisement as the volume of ads rises. Newspapers allow advertisers to accumulate column inches over time, with the price per inch lowered at various levels of volume. A company ordering 100 column inches pays $5 per inch, whereas an advertiser buying 1,000 column inches during the course of the year may only pay $2 per inch. Television sells sets of commercial packages that reduce the price per spot with increased volume. The same discounting method applies to magazines, billboards, and other venues.

International marketers provide quantity discounts to build relationships. Granting discounts based on volume over time encourages buyers to make repeat purchases. Lines of communication remain open and the sales team may be able to reduce visits to companies, because there is no need to begin a totally new sales approach each time.

EARLY-PAYMENT DISCOUNTS

Another form of discounting, based on early payment, can be offered on an invoice. The term "2/10 net 30" reflects a 2% discount when an invoice is paid in ten days or less. The balance becomes due in thirty days. Early-payment discounts provide buyers with the opportunity to "earn" a lower price through prompt payment. When one firm offers more generous terms (3/20 instead of 2/10) the discount might be the deciding factor in a purchase. Early-payment discounts become more difficult to offer when international shipments are made, due to time differences and more lengthy delivery schedules. Electronic payment systems have reduced some of these complications. A recent survey revealed that a fourth of all U.S. companies offer early-payment discounts, with small businesses being more likely to do so.[5]

CHANNEL DISCOUNTS

Manufacturers provide additional enticements designed to generate sales to middlemen and retailers, known as *trade promotions*. These programs include trade allowances and trade incentives. One form of trade allowance is an *off invoice allowance*, or a per-case rebate paid to retailers for an order. Manufacturers also vend bonus packs with additional merchandise per pack to obtain and retain customers. These approaches reduce the wholesale price per item.

Channel discount offers sometimes include promotions such as free shipping and handling. The total price charged becomes lower. Free shipping discounts are popular in international marketing, where high shipping costs occur.

International marketers can take advantage of zone or region channel discounts. A price discount provided to all countries in the Pacific Rim becomes more attractive when it reduces shipping costs by combining orders on the same mode of transportation. Also, when several countries have similar channels of distribution, such as the Japanese *sogo shosha* (general) trading companies, it becomes possible to send larger orders to a single company or inter-firm risk-sharing organization for further distribution within the country.

LEARNING OBJECTIVE #4:

What factors influence decisions about price changes in international markets?

PRICE CHANGES IN INTERNATIONAL MARKETS

Certain circumstances require companies to change prices permanently rather than temporarily through means such as discounts or surcharges. Prices may be raised or lowered due to a variety of circumstances, including increased costs of raw materials, higher shipping costs, economic changes, and changes in currency exchange rates. Note that prices may at times move lower and at times may rise. Table 11.7 identifies the factors marketers consider when making permanent changes to prices of existing products.

TABLE 11.7   Factors to Consider When Changing Prices

Actions or Reactions of Competitors
– domestic
– foreign
Company Status as Industry Leader or Industry Follower
– domestic
– foreign
Impact on the Brand's Image
Impact on Revenues and Gross Margin
Reactions of Customers
– domestic
– foreign

PRICE REDUCTIONS

A price may be permanently reduced in one or more of three situations. The first occurs when production costs decrease, which results from economies of scale that increase as a firm expands the scope of its operations. It may also take place when start-up costs have been recovered or when the price of a raw material or component part declines.

Price reductions have become common for solar panels. Early in the life cycle of panels, costs per unit were high and the resultant price reflected the expenditures. With the entry of increased competition, growing demand, and governmental incentives for purchases, prices for panels have begun to drop dramatically, with future reductions to be expected in the coming years.

Increased competition can trigger a permanent price reduction. Typically the response takes place when a company begins to lose market share to competitors. Lowering prices as a reaction to competition should not proceed without careful thought. A marketing team may be able to identify ways to maintain share without lowering prices and losing profits.

Telstra, the largest Australian telecommunications company, sells the majority of landlines in the country. Recently, the company faced severe competition from mobile and Internet phone competitors. In response, Telstra's marketing team focused on improved customer service and on negotiating higher fees with the government.[6] These steps were taken before the company considered lowering prices.

When product demand declines, prices sometimes fall. The primary concern will be whether the demand declined due to the entry of a new competitor or the development of a substitute product. Declining demand results in lower revenues. When a product reaches the later stages of its life cycle, the marketing team might look for foreign markets that are not in the same stage as a way to maintain sales rather than lowering price as the only response.

When the Volkswagen Beetle lost popularity in Western markets, the company shifted focus to Latin America, especially Brazil and Mexico. The iconic automobile became popular in those markets, easing the process of removal from other markets. By the time production stopped in Mexico in July of 2003 the automobile was the best-selling automobile in the history of the world (Gunn, 2006).

PRICE INCREASES

Price increases most often result from increases in production costs, including prices of raw materials, labor, and energy. When increasing prices, the company's marketing managers first review the company's pricing objectives and make note of international considerations such as the short- and long-term consequences in foreign markets. Adobe, the software company, charges more in European markets than it does in the United States or in Mexico—as much as 170% higher—due to the cost of maintaining local offices in those countries (Brynildsen, 2007). The price differential in this case is due to labor cost differences.

Companies increase prices incrementally over time or as a single event. Incremental changes may not be announced to customers in the hope they will not notice or become upset due to the gradual nature of the increase. Marketers pay attention to the responses of competitors that may or may not follow suit. Should they not, the company may reconsider the price increase.

When the Volkswagen Beetle lost popularity in Western markets, the company shifted focus to Latin America, especially Brazil and Mexico.

When a price is raised in a single action, customers, especially business-to-business clients, should be notified. Effective explanations should be provided to lessen the impact of the price increase. Contacting business customers in international markets about price increases indicates the company's intentions to be above-board in those relationships, where trust is at a premium. Violating trust damages relationships with other businesses.

Mittal Steel, a company in India, is the largest producer of steel in the world. Not long ago, the company raised the price of steel sold to the government of India three times without an explanation. In response, the Indian government threatened to bring in competitors to bid for the governmental purchases (Njobeni, 2006).

WEBER'S LAW

German physiologist Ernst Heinrich Weber studied the link between a physical stimulus and a desired response. Weber's Law has been transferred to pricing. It suggests that for a price change (a stimulus) to be noticed and to elicit a response, it must be greater than 10%. For those who believe such a relationship is true, the implication would be to try to hold price increases to less than 10% and to make price decreases larger than 10%. The latter often will have a negative impact on the bottom line.

In international marketing, the question arises as to whether Weber's Law applies equally well to every culture. Given that economic systems vary widely, as do personal financial circumstances in a population, the 10% figure may seem arbitrary. At the same time, the general principle, that a threshold exists at which prices go noticed or unnoticed, may be valid.

INTERNATIONAL INCIDENT

You are traveling in Mexico with a very good friend who lives in Japan. Your friend finds a sombrero he likes very much. He asks the vendor the price. The salesperson suggests a number that you know is ridiculous, expecting to bargain down to the amount he actually wishes to receive. You also know that your friend's culture is highly deferent and non-confrontational. How can you suggest to your friend that he needs to look the salesperson right in the eye and demand a lower price? Or, should you tell the vendor that your friend is uncomfortable with bargaining? Or, should you simply do the bargaining yourself on behalf of your friend?

LEARNING OBJECTIVE #5:

What ethical concerns are associated with international pricing programs?

ETHICAL ISSUES IN INTERNATIONAL PRICING

Many of the pricing practices that raise ethical concerns in domestic markets apply to international markets. The more common issues include collusion, predatory pricing, and deceptive pricing (Baack and Baack, 2008). These practices could be legally viable in some countries yet still violate ethical standards within a company or in the mind of the marketing practitioner.

COLLUSION

In oligopolistic markets, a set of major competitors experiences the temptation to set prices at uniform levels either overtly or covertly, through **collusion**. While collusion may be allowed or even expected in countries, the net result can be that prices do not reflect costs or other considerations, yet consumers have no recourse or alternatives. Price collusion continues unless or until new competitors reach the market, which may be difficult due to powerful barriers to entry. Mongolian flour manufacturing companies were accused by governmental regulators in the country of colluding to raise the price of flour in the country and were fined 250,000 tugrik (approximately $190).[7]

collusion: a pricing system in oligopolistic markets in which a set of major competitors sets prices at uniform levels, either overtly or covertly

PREDATORY PRICING

Predatory pricing involves the direct attempt by a major competitor to drive other companies out of business by setting prices unrealistically low. When smaller competitors cannot withstand the loss in sales, the firms eventually become at risk and over time go out of business. Predatory pricing practices are especially harmful when foreign companies compete against domestic firms with fewer resources, especially in less- or least-developed nations.

predatory pricing: the direct attempt by a major competitor to drive other companies out of business by setting prices unrealistically low

DECEPTIVE PRICING

Another ethically questionable practice, **deceptive pricing**, takes place when the marketer promotes one price, yet due to hidden charges, add-ons, or higher prices for products with more than the bare minimum of features, the actual price is much higher. Automobile manufacturers have often used the phrase "starting at" to set prices for models with little or no common accessories, such as a radio or an automatic transmission. Service providers, especially credit card companies, have become notorious for add-on charges and late fees, raising interest rates without notification, ATM usage fees, and other attempts to increase revenues in secretive ways. Each of these issues is present in domestic and international markets. Company standards and individual moral judgments apply to the use or misuse of pricing practices.

deceptive pricing: a pricing system in which the marketer promotes one price, yet charges more using hidden charges, add-ons, or higher prices for products with more than the minimum of features

DUMPING

One more purely international ethical (and legal) pricing issue involves **dumping**, or the practice of selling goods below costs in another country or pricing a product in one country lower than the price of the product in another country. The goal in both cases is to capture the market in the country with the low price. The company may experience a loss on the sales; the goal, however, is to eliminate competitors through the low price. The net result of removing customers will be to be able to eventually charge higher prices and generate higher profit margins.

dumping: the practice of selling goods below costs in another country in order to capture a market

Many governments and the World Trade Organization have outlawed dumping, yet it continues to exist. A great deal of "trade war"-type issues have arisen in cases where one country's leadership believes another practices dumping. These differences often result in complaints to international trade regulation organizations.

Ethical firms refrain from such practices and notify the WTO or the local government when they take place. Dumping accusations are often brought by governments in response to actions of foreign businesses within their borders. Recently, the Chinese Ministry of Commerce found what it believed was evidence of dumping by South Korean and Thai producers of terephthalic acid, a chemical used in clothing and plastic manufacturing.[8]

CHAPTER 11: REVIEW AND RESOURCES

Strategic Implications

Pricing decisions are, at the core, strategic decisions. Three primary competitive forces are price, quality, and the price–quality relationships. These three forces dictate the strategic direction of the organization. Price conveys meaning. It becomes part of a corporation's image and a brand's position. Strategic managers identify relationships between cost and price. A small restaurant owner chooses ingredients that create the best quality for the price she wishes to charge. A microchip manufacturer in Japan is likely to insist on the highest-quality materials in order to create the most durable and efficient product, at which point company leaders would feel comfortable charging a higher price for that item.

At the other extreme, lower costs and prices are vital to success in the discount retail business. Marketing to consumers at the bottom-of-the-pyramid requires pricing strategies that fit the needs of those with the most modest incomes.

Tactical Implications

International pricing tactics take place in three major areas: setting prices, discounting prices, and changing prices. Each is based on the company's primary pricing objectives and strategic position. Pricing based on costs reflects a different tactical approach from one based on demand/supply, competition, or profit motives.

The same holds true for discounting. The marketing team considers not only the objectives for discounts but also the legal and cultural implications in each country. A marketer knows that Islamic countries frown on charging interest, which leads to the use of other charges or fees as part of the price. Many governments regulate what can be termed a "sale" or "discount" as it relates to the "regular" price.

Price changes also begin with a review of pricing objectives. Methods for raising and lowering prices reflect the company's desire to achieve short- and long-term goals as well as to build relationships with other businesses and individual consumers over time.

Operational Implications

Individual storeowners need to understand local customs with regard to pricing items. Should the price be displayed, or only conveyed verbally? Are prices fixed, or is bargaining expected? Methods of advertising discounts and price changes should be studied. A company's image and reputation can be quickly damaged when local norms are ignored.

Sales representatives making presentations to other businesses should be equally aware of pricing protocols. Methods for presenting prices, discounting prices, agreeing to a price, rejecting a price offer, and finalizing the deal should be well understood before the sales call begins. Salespeople that are trained to know and convey the company's strategic and tactical intentions make more effective sales calls. They know when price will be the primary force in the sale, or when it will represent only one smaller element in building markets and creating long-term relationships with businesses in other countries.

TERMS

price

price perceptual map

cost-based pricing

break-even analysis

cost-plus pricing

markup pricing

price elasticity of demand

skimming

penetration pricing

profit-based pricing

target ROI pricing

capacity to consume

loss leader

collusion

predatory pricing

deceptive pricing

dumping

REVIEW QUESTIONS

1. Define price and name the various types of prices described in this chapter.

2. What three main considerations influence perceptions of prices?

3. What are the typical objectives associated with pricing programs?

4. What four factors can become the basis for a pricing program?

5. How can a break-even analysis assist in developing an international pricing program?

6. Define price elasticity of demand, elastic demand, and inelastic demand.

7. When pricing is based on the competition, what three approaches are available?

8. Describe skimming and penetration pricing in international marketing and explain how penetration pricing differs from dumping.

9. What three circumstances match with profit-based pricing?

10. Describe the international considerations in pricing programs noted in this chapter.

11. Define the term *capacity to consume* and explain how it is part of marketing to the bottom-of-the-pyramid.

12. Identify the main types of pricing discounts offered to consumers and businesses.

13. How is a loss leader different from dumping?

14. When making price changes, what factors should the marketing team consider?

15. How does Weber's Law apply to price changes?

16. How do negotiation systems affect business-to-business pricing programs?

17. What four main ethical issues affect international pricing programs?

DISCUSSION QUESTIONS

1. Discuss the value considerations, emotional considerations, and situational factors associated with prices for the following items, specifically as they would relate to international marketing:

    *   accidental death insurance policy

    *   suntan lotion at the beach priced far higher than in local retail stores

    *   tickets to a rock concert featuring a popular band

    *   designer undergarments

2. A pricing perceptual map typically depicts products based on relationships involving price and quality. Describe quality for the following items:

    *   one-night stay in a hotel in Uruguay

    *   fishing tour guide in Cambodia

    *   fish and chips for a British citizen visiting Slovenia

    *   candy for a child in Sudan

3. From the list of pricing objectives stated in Table 11.2, which would be most important for an exporting company in the following situations? Defend your choices.

    *   entering the market with an unknown brand

    *   entering the market with a well-known brand

    *   established company facing new domestic competitors

    *   established company facing new international competitors

    *   product in the take-off stage of the product life cycle in a foreign market

    *   product in the maturity stage of the product life cycle in a foreign market

    *   product in the decline state of the product life cycle in a foreign market

4. Which pricing method (cost, demand/supply, competition, profit-based) would you recommend for the following items to be sold in other countries? Defend your reasoning.

    *   tennis balls by a manufacturer in the Philippines

    *   retail store to open with 20,000 sku (stock-keeping units) in Luxembourg

    *   mobile phone services in Chile

    *   solar panels in Canada

5. Which types of discounts should be given by each of the following companies? Explain your answers.

    *   Hilton International Hotels

    *   AFLAC in Japan

- Perrier bottled water sold in South Africa

- Bulldozers sold by Caterpillar

6. Describe the differences and similarities between dumping, penetration pricing, and predatory pricing. How might Weber's Law be relevant to this discussion?

ANALYTICAL AND INTERNET EXERCISES

1. Draw a pricing perceptual map for these products in international markets, naming the major competitors and placing them on the map. Use the Internet to identify the major competitors, if necessary.

   - automobiles

   - athletic shoes

   - mobile phone service

   - farm tractors

2. Calculate the break-even point in units for the following product:

   Price per unit = $10.00

   Variable cost per unit = $2.75

   Fixed costs = $15,000

3. Using markup pricing, calculate the price for cell phones to be sold in Argentina:

   Total fixed cost = $400,000

   Units to be sold = 50,000

   Variable cost per unit = $50.00

   Markup on price = 20%

4. A company sells packaged cookies in Hungary. The price is €2.50 per package. The company's marketing team believes that in Romania, price elasticity of demand would be €1.67. In contrast, price elasticity of demand in Ukraine would be €0.88. Which country offers the most lucrative market, especially in terms of recapturing start-up costs? Which pricing strategy would be viable in Romania: skimming or penetration pricing? Which would work best in Ukraine?

5. Prepare a report on the advisability of using quantity discounts and early-payment discounts businesses in the following countries, based on cultural norms and governmental regulations:

   - Mexico

   - Niger

   - Saudi Arabia

   - Italy

6. Using the Internet, investigate sales methods, negotiation tactics, and bargaining practices arrangements for the following countries:

- South Korea
- Australia
- Iran
- Brazil

STUDENT STUDY SITE

Visit **https://study.sagepub.com/baack2e** to access these free additional learning tools:

- Web Quizzes
- eFlashcards
- SAGE Journal Articles
- Country Fact Sheets
- Chapter Outlines
- Interactive Maps

CASE 11

Pricing Air Travel

In most of the world, airline travel is available to domestic and international customers. Table 11.8 identifies the top twenty largest airlines in Europe during the year 2016, in terms of passengers. Many of the issues described in this chapter apply to international airline operations. For instance, any competitor in this industry would be subject to the various objectives and pricing methods. Each airline's marketing team could choose from the more common pricing goals, including earning profits, improving market share, retaining current customers, enticing new customers, or countering competitive actions. Selections would be based, in part, on the airline's financial status, country of origin, age, reputation or image, level of governmental protection and investment, and relevant degree of competition.

The pricing methods, based on costs, supply and demand, competition, or profitability, all apply to airlines. The complicating factors are that prices, especially fuel prices, change quickly and dramatically. Supply and demand will be influenced by shifts in economic conditions. Competitors and competitive actions vary widely, as carriers enter and leave the marketplace, while some merge in various types of alliances. Profit targets become difficult to establish in such volatile markets. In addition, issues such as terrorism affect operations and prices, as airlines seek to provide security for flights, passengers, and crew members.

Discounting also affects the international airlines industry. When Ryanair, the low-cost Irish airline, announced plans for flights from the United Kingdom to the United States priced at £10 in the near future, the goal of offering loss leader flights was to gain a foothold in the British market.[9]

Beyond these concerns, ethical issues are germane. For instance, one common practice among airlines has been to label airline fees, which count as revenue for the company, as "taxes." A lawsuit filed against British Airways accuses that airline of the practice and states that the pricing is deceptive.[10]

TABLE 11.8   Top Twenty Largest Airlines Europe, 2016

Position	Airlines	Passengers
1	Ryanair	116.8 million
2	Lufthansa Group (incl. Lufthansa, Austrian, Swiss, Eurowings)	109.7 million
3	IAG (British Airways, Iberia, Vueling, Aer Lingus)	100.7 million
4	Air France-KLM (incl. Air France, KLM, HOP!, Transavia)	93.4 million
5	EasyJet	74.5 million
6	Turkish Airlines	62.8 million
7	Aeroflot Group (incl. Aeroflot, Rossiya, Pobeda)	43.4 million
8	SAS Group (Scandinavian Airlines)	29.4 million
9	Norwegian	29.3 million
10	Air Berlin Group (incl. Air Berlin, NIKI)	28.9 million
11	Alitalia	/
12	Pegasus Airlines	24.1 million
13	Wizz Air	22.8 million
14	Aegean Airlines (and Olympic Air)	/
15	S7 Airlines	13.1 million
16	TAP Portugal	11.7 million
17	Finnair	10.9 million
18	Air Europa	/
19	Flybe	/
20	SunExpress	/

Source: "Largest Airlines Europe," Airports in Europe, September 11, 2017. Retrieved from www.airportsineurope.com/flight-info/largest-airlines-europe/.

(Continued)

(Continued)

1. What should be the primary pricing objectives for the companies at the top of the list in Table 11.8? Would the objectives differ for companies 15–20? Why or why not?

2. Which price setting approach best matches the international airline industry?

3. How might pricing systems vary from Europe among airlines in Asia, the Far East, and the United States, or would they remain basically the same? Explain your answer.

4. Which forms of discounting best match international airline pricing systems?

5. Examine the list of airlines banned in Europe at https://ec.europa.eu/transport/modes/air/safety/air-ban_en.h How would such a ban affect pricing strategies for these companies in other areas where they are not banned?

6. Which of the ethical issues identified in this chapter apply to international airlines? Explain your answer.

12

INTERNATIONAL FINANCE AND PRICING IMPLICATIONS

LEARNING OBJECTIVES

After reading and studying this chapter, you should be able to answer the following questions:

1. How do currencies and currency exchanges affect international business and international marketing programs?
2. What factors affect currency movements in the international marketplace?
3. How do the law of one price and purchasing power parity affect international marketing activities?
4. How do governmental activities influence international finance?
5. What are the relationships between international finance and the elements of the marketing mix?

IN THIS CHAPTER

Opening Vignette: Pricing ArcelorMitall Steel Globally: The Effects of Currency Changes

OVERVIEW

PRICING ARCELORMITALL STEEL GLOBALLY: THE EFFECTS OF CURRENCY CHANGES

Lakshmi Niwas Mitall, owner of ArcelorMittal, founded his company in 1989 in India and it has grown into the world's largest steel manufacturer. With operations in all of the major steel markets plus ever expanding mining activities globally, in more than sixty countries, the firm faces challenging international marketing issues due to international finance complexities.

ArcelorMittal conducts business using a variety of currencies (see Table 12.1). Changes in the value of any of them affect ArcelorMittal's marketing activities, causing the company's leadership attempts to cope with fluctuations in currency exchange rates. The price of steel and other goods moves up or down as currency values change. For example, the company may be paying steel workers in Argentina while selling a large supply of steel in China. If the Argentinean *peso* suddenly changes to be worth far more than the Chinese *yuan*, the costs of production increase and the value of the company's revenue decreases. In sum, currency affects the company's entire marketing strategy.

To cope with this fluid environment the company's financial team hedges or attempts to lessen currency risk. Purchasing various financial instruments makes it possible to offset some of the risk of currency movement. Mitall views the expense of these instruments as necessary to provide currency stability. Without hedging activities, the company's marketing goals would be more difficult to achieve.

TABLE 12.1 Examples of Countries and Currencies in Which ArcelorMittal Operates

Argentina: Argentine *peso*	Morocco: *Moroccan Dirham*
Australia: Australian *dollar*	Oman: *Omani rial*
Bahrain: Bahraini *dinar*	Poland: *Polish zloty*
Canada: Canadian *dollar*	Qatar: *Qatari riyal*
China: *yuan*	Russia: *Russian ruble*
Czech Republic: *Czech crowns*	South Africa: *South African rand*
European Union: *euros*	Thailand: *Thai baht*
Hong Kong: *Hong Kong dollar*	Trinidad and Tobago: *Trinidad and Tobago dollar*
India: *Indian rupee*	Ukraine: *Ukrainian hryvnia*
Israel: *Israeli new sheqel*	United Arab Emirates: *UAE dirham*
Kazakhstan: *Kazakhstani tenge*	United States: *U.S. dollar*
Kuwait: *Kuwaiti dinar*	Venezuela: *strong bolivar*
Mexico: *Mexican peso*	

Note: For details on the *strong bolivar*, see www.economist.com/node/15287355.

Governmental regulations play important roles in limiting or controlling currency movements. ArcelorMittal encounters various currency regulations. The company's managers account for and respond to these regulations. The South African Reserve Bank has strict rules regarding the South African *rand*. The Bank must approve a variety of business activities involving the *rand* while it also monitors payments for trade. The National Bank of Kazakhstan maintains even stricter regulations. To change the local currency, the *tenge*, into a foreign currency, the company must obtain approval for each transaction on a case-by-case basis. The Central Bank of Algeria does not allow cash surpluses to be invested outside of the country. Brazilian law allows currency exchange through only one exchange, and only with a license by the Brazilian bank. Argentina does not permit the country's *pesos* to be converted into any different currency. In some instances domestic companies must even transfer profits from goods shipped from the country back into the *peso* within 360 days.[1]

At the same time, based on Mr Mittal's financial standing, it seems clear his company has effectively responded to the complex marketing and business challenges associated with currency.

(Continued)

(Continued)

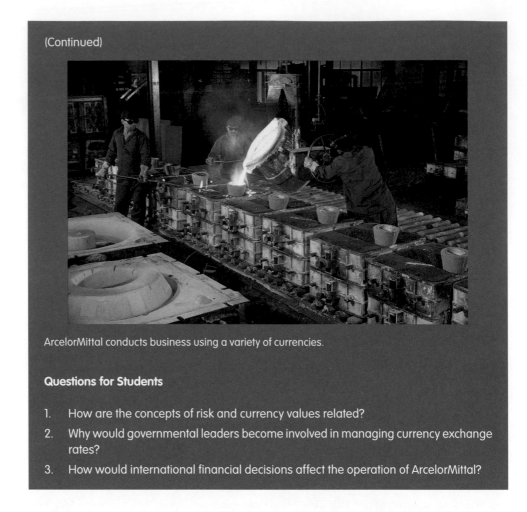

ArcelorMittal conducts business using a variety of currencies.

Questions for Students

1.   How are the concepts of risk and currency values related?

2.   Why would governmental leaders become involved in managing currency exchange rates?

3.   How would international financial decisions affect the operation of ArcelorMittal?

OVERVIEW

Many aspects of pricing programs influence international marketing decisions. The previous chapter examined international pricing from the perspectives of setting prices, discounting, and changing prices. International marketers recognize that outside forces often affect those three activities. One primary influence comes from financial considerations in the home and host countries. This chapter reviews methods for responding to international finance issues in the context of international marketing. Effective financial techniques assist international companies in building effective marketing programs.

This chapter begins with an overview of money and types of currencies. Next, it describes international finance in terms of the basics of capital markets and the financing of transactions. The nature of currency exchange and exchange rates are then reviewed along with the factors that affect currency movement. The factors include individual and business transactions, trade and investment activities, trade deficits or surpluses, inflation, and interest rates.

The role of government in attempting to control the value of a country's currency receives attention. Currency regimes, including floating and fixed exchange rates, constitute one of the primary tools governments can use to manage currencies.

A brief history of currency control as it relates to the gold standard and other methods of currency pegging is presented.

Currency risk and movement often lead to international marketing problems. Methods for predicting currency fluctuations are examined, including hedging and futures contracts. The basics of international finance funding, including acquiring capital, financing ongoing trade operations, methods of countertrade, internal pricing, and shadow pricing, are described.

The conclusion of this chapter applies international finance to international marketing. Financial effects on markets, product, prices, distribution systems (place), and promotional programs are analyzed. The strategic, tactical, and operational implications of the interactions between marketing and finance are noted.

LEARNING OBJECTIVE #1:

How do currencies and currency exchanges affect international business and international marketing programs?

MONEY AND CURRENCY

The basis of international finance and its relationship to international marketing begins with money. *Money* provides the unit of value people accept as a form of payment. The exchange of value stands at the core of international marketing. Money has taken many forms, including salt, stones, seashells, and beads. For something to be considered as money, it demonstrates the five characteristics in Table 12.2. Money serves many purposes, including being used as a measure of value, as a medium of exchange, and as a savings mechanism.

CURRENCY

Currency constitutes the form of money used by a specific country or region. Currencies change and evolve over time. When East and West Germany reunited in 1990, the *deutsche* mark was used instead of the former East German currency, the East German mark. Now, however, German's currency is the *euro*. Various symbols signify a currency. The $ sign represents the U.S. dollar and the Mexican *peso* due to a common origin with the symbol for the Spanish *peso*. In fact, some claim that Mexico used the symbol before the United States (Davies, 2008).

currency: the form of money used by a specific country or region

TABLE 12.2 Properties of Money

Acceptability	It is accepted as payment by a group of people
Scarcity	When a product is scarce, it becomes more valuable and it takes more money to purchase the product, as only a limited supply of money is available
Durability	It will not spoil or become damaged
Divisibility	It can be divided into smaller units
Portability	It is small enough that people can easily carry it around

METHODS OF PAYMENT AND BANKING

Various currencies circulate globally. The use of money represents a constant part of life for most of the people in the world. In most countries, money takes the form of bills and coins. Bills appear in a variety of colors, including pink, blue, purple, and green. Coins are made from multiple alloys and some have striated edges. The United Kingdom features two *pence*, five *pence*, ten *pence*, twenty *pence*, and fifty *pence* coins. Many countries utilize coins corresponding with the value of a dollar. The one-, two-, and five-*pound* coins in the United Kingdom or the one-, two-, and five-*rupee* coins in India serve as examples. The currency names and symbols for the world's ten largest economies can be found in Table 12.3.

TABLE 12.3   Currency Name and Currency Symbol for the Top Ten Largest World Economies

Country	Currency Name	Currency Symbol
China	*renminbi or yuan*	¥
United States	*dollar*	$
India	*rupee*	Rp
Japan	*yen*	¥
Germany	*euro*	€
Russia	*ruble*	руб
Brazil	*real*	R$
Indonesia	*rupiah*	Rp
United Kingdom	*pound*	£
France	*euro*	€

In today's economy, consumers and businesses use physical currency less and less frequently. Instead, many purchases are made electronically. The spending of millions of dollars involves the clicking of buttons, not the physical movement of actual cash.

Businesses use local currencies for incoming revenues (sales to consumers), salaries paid to employees, and payments of company expenses. One currency will often be converted or exchanged for another as part of an international transaction. This may be to bring profits back to the home country, transfer funds to a third country to pay for expansion, or move the money to yet another country to deposit in a bank. Table 12.4 summarizes the ways that business uses currency.

TABLE 12.4   Currency and Business Activity

Bank Deposits and Withdrawals
Conversion to Move across Borders
Employee Salaries
Expenses
Sales
Taxes and Fees

Before entering a new country, the marketing team considers the nature of the currency in the target nation. Decisions regarding methods of payment and forms of investment are made based on the presence of either a hard currency or a soft currency.

HARD CURRENCY

A **hard currency** can be exchanged for other currencies worldwide. Companies trade *euros*, *riyals*, *yen*, dollars, and other foreign hard currencies at set rates in financial centers such as Paris, London, and Tokyo. Hard currencies, also known as *convertible currencies*, help stabilize marketing operations because the partners in a trading or sales relationship can rely on relatively manageable currency risk. Hard currencies allow confidence in the prices and costs of various marketing programs, including the value of a coupon or discount, the amount to be charged for advertising time, and the cost of distributing products through a network of intermediaries.

hard currency: currency that can be exchanged for other currencies worldwide

SOFT CURRENCY

A **soft currency** is unstable and will not be traded at major financial centers. A soft currency can be exchanged or used for purchases within a country, but has limited or no use in other countries. Soft currencies are more commonplace in less- or least-developed nations. Soft currency values fluctuate more and create uncertainty. In order to adapt to a soft currency, the finance department undertakes additional efforts to find methods for managing currency.

soft currency: currency that cannot be traded at major financial centers

After discovering the form of currency to be used in a foreign operation, international marketers examine other international finance factors. Among them, marketers consider exchange rates for money, exchange regimes, and global currency institutions. Soft currency usage for local transactions, coupled with hoarding of hard currency for larger or international transactions, plays a role in limiting international trade growth in various countries throughout Africa, with Zimbabwe often held up as a typical example (Tinashe, 2017).

CRYPTOCURRENCY

The last decade saw the emergence of a new kind of currency, called cryptocurrency. These currencies exist purely in cyber space and are a digital form of money or exchange. Examples include Bitcoin, Ethereum, and Primecoin, with Bitcoin being the most used and well known of the approximately 550 cryptocurrencies in circulation. An emerging technology, countries and banks still struggle to regulate or respond to these currencies. There is some talk of Bitcoin, and others like it, eventually replacing national currencies, but, if true, this is far in the distance. For now, these currencies, and the cryptography protecting them, represent an interesting new phenomenon (Chohan, 2017).

INTERNATIONAL FINANCE

International finance involves the study of currency exchange, investments, and how these processes influence business activities. Actors in global international finance include governments, international organizations, commercial banks, central or government banks, large and small corporations, and individuals. Managing the exchange of currency and gaining access to funds are necessary for international businesses. This includes access to capital to conduct operations as well as the financing of transactions.

international finance: the study of currency exchange, investments, and how these processes influence business activities

CAPITAL MARKETS

capital market: any location, online or physical, where businesses or individuals can raise funds

Any location, online or physical, where businesses or individuals can raise funds becomes a **capital market**. The funds pay for entry into foreign markets, trade with foreign partners, research and development, a physical presence such as an office building or manufacturing plant, and other domestic and foreign expenses.

Companies raise two types of funds in global or local capital markets: debt and equity. *Debt* consists of funds that are borrowed and must be paid back. Debt takes the form of loans, and the structured loans by governments or companies which are called *bonds*. Debt repayment includes the money borrowed plus some interest or fees. The use of fees takes place in Muslim countries, where religious law forbids charging interest. Granting a degree of ownership, typically in the form of stock, in return for an investment of money, results in *equity*. Important international differences exist regarding usage of capital markets. European firms exhibit the tendency to raise funds through debt rather than equity, whereas U.S. firms tend to raise funds more through equity markets.

Companies seek to gain advantages through access to international capital markets. By accessing multiple markets, firms obtain the most efficient and lowest-priced sources of debt and equity. When funding cannot be found in a company home capital market, the firm's leaders may look in other countries.

Company financial officers work to develop the best balance of debt and equity, considering local taxes, regulations, and other variables. The finance department seeks to diversify the degree of risk a company assumes. As more international firms enter global capital markets, greater choice helps reduce some financial risks. Companies operating in several countries often suffer less vulnerability to country-specific economic problems, such as recessions.

THE FINANCING OF TRANSACTIONS

When local customers make purchases, a national currency facilitates the transactions. The use of money within a nation's boundaries normally means a company receives a common currency as payment, and the trade becomes relatively simple. Foreign travelers quickly adjust to local prices, currency values, and other issues such as making correct change when purchasing goods.

Complications emerge when transactions take place across national boundaries. Currency differences affect purchases due to the values of the currencies involved. Transactions between businesses, with governments, and with individual consumers are influenced by the value a currency holds in relation to currencies in other countries.

THE NATURE OF CURRENCY EXCHANGE

exchange rate: the rate at which one country's currency can be traded for another country's currency

A currency's **exchange rate** is the amount at which one country's currency can be traded for another country's currency. Consider a German marketer purchasing advertising time in the British television market. The price of a 30-second commercial on the BBC network will be stated or denominated in British pounds. To purchase the slot, the marketer pays in pounds. Normally, much of a German firm's cash will be held in *euros*; however, the BBC may not accept *euros* as a means of payment. Instead, the German marketer exchanges *euros* for British pounds to complete the transaction. A certain number of pounds will be equal in value to a certain number of *euros*. For example, 1 *euro* may be worth around 85 *pence* (100 *pence* equals 1 *pound* much as 100 cents equals 1 dollar).

Marketers employ a variety of sources to identify the value of an exchange. Typically, the bank or a similar institution that completes the currency exchange provides the rate. Newspapers also post exchange rates physically or online. *Spot rates* are a set amount of exchange for a delivery of currency within two days of the agreement to exchange currencies. Many of these exchanges are immediate, but for large purchases, businesses may need the extra two days to complete transactions. The exchange rates that tourists use are often the spot rates plus a premium to allow for a small profit for the agency facilitating the exchange.

Currency conversion exchange rates take the form of direct and indirect quotes. *Direct quotes* calculate the home currency price per unit against that of the foreign currency. For example, when 1 *euro* is worth around 85 *pence*; 1 *pound* would be the equivalent of 1.17 *euro*. *Indirect quotes* are calculated using the value of the foreign currency. Direct quotes are the more commonly used; however, indirect quotes are used in the eurozone, Australia, and New Zealand.

A potential complication occurs when the currencies involved vary widely in terms of value, because the exchange rate may be confusing. Consider the Japanese *yen*. A kilogram of rice in the country might cost around 225 *yen*.[2] This does not mean that rice is expensive; rather the value of a single *yen* is lower than the value of a single U.S. dollar or a single *euro*. In Japan, the direct quote for the *euro* would be 111.98 *yen* = 1 *euro*. It would require approximately 112 *yen* to purchase 1 *euro*. One kilo of rice would cost about 2 *euros*. In Japan the indirect quote would be 1 *yen* = 0.0089 *euro*, which means that 1 *yen* is not worth 1 *euro* "penny."

The value of the Japanese yen is less than 1 euro penny.

COMPUTING EXCHANGE RATES

A key variable that marketers consider is the percentage change in a currency's value over a period of time. Continuing with the previous example, a marketer may want to know how much the value of the *euro* relative to *yen* has changed over the past month. In other words, a *euro* may be able to purchase more or less *yen*, depending on market movements.

Several formulas must be used to calculate percentage change in the currency depending on whether a direct or indirect quote is used. Figure 12.1 presents the formula for both calculations. Regardless of formula, the same percentage change should result. If the *euro* lost 13% of its value relative to the *pound*, the *pound* would be worth 13% more in *euros* than at the beginning rate.

In international marketing, exchange rates affect prices of goods, values set for promotional items such as coupons and discounts, the use of credit including terms of repayment, and more general issues. A product's positioning often reflects a price/quality relationship. When a currency increases in value due to a shift in the exchange rate, a product may suddenly become more of a bargain or less attractive, not because the product has changed, but because the relationship between the price and the product's quality has been affected.

Beginning Rate: 1 pound = 1.17 euro

Ending Rate: 1 pound = 1.02 euro

$$\text{Direct Quote} = \frac{\text{ending rate} - \text{beginning rate}}{\text{beginning rate}}$$

$$\frac{1.02 - 1.17}{1.17}$$

$$= \frac{-0.15}{1.17}$$

$$= -13\%$$

$$\text{Indirect quote} = \frac{\text{beginning rate} - \text{ending rate}}{\text{ending rate}}$$

Beginning Rate: 1 euro = 85 pence

Ending Rate: 1 euro = 98 pence

$$\frac{85 - 98}{98}$$

$$= \frac{-13}{98}$$

$$= -13\%$$

FIGURE 12.1   Direct Quote and Indirect Quote Percentage Change Formulas

LEARNING OBJECTIVE #2:

What factors affect currency movements in the international marketplace?

FACTORS AFFECTING CURRENCY MOVEMENTS

Currency values move. The exchange rate between two currencies changes over time due to the supply and demand of money. Table 12.5 provides a list of currency movement drivers or factors, excluding the governmental activities that will be described later in this chapter.

In the scenario described earlier in this chapter, a German company exchanged *euros* for pounds to facilitate the purchase of BBC advertising time. Currency movements might influence the transaction. An increase in the demand for the pound changes its value, just as increased demand for a product might cause the product's price to rise. Should the value of the pound relative to the *euro* rise, the cost of purchasing advertising time will be affected.

The typical small daily individual transactions that increase demand for a currency will not move its value; approximately $3.2 billion worth of currency are bought and sold each day.[3] Consequently, the value of a single currency can change greatly depending on these transactions. Several factors affect currency values.

Various forces cause some currencies to be purchased and others to be sold. One side of a transaction consists of those buying a currency. When one group wishes to purchase a currency, the demand for that currency rises. In essence, that activity tends to create a more expensive or valuable exchange rate for the currency. On the other side are those wishing to sell the same currency. The desire to sell may lead to a lower price or a weakening of the currency.

TABLE 12.5   Nongovernmental Factors That Affect Currency Movements

Individual and Business Transactions
Inflation
Interest Rates
Trade and Investment Activity

In currency exchanges, the various actors involved include individuals, companies, and governments. Each entity (buyer to seller) can switch if needed or when a potential benefit arises, which further complicates the process. Someone or some group might switch when they believe money can be made by speculating on a weaker currency. Governments may intervene due to the possible political implications of a change in a currency's value. A follow-the-leader mentality often emerges in which everyone switches to one side when it becomes apparent that it is going to "win." Other external factors also influence currency exchanges and currency valuations, including levels of inflation, interest rates, and trade activities.

Even with those difficulties, understanding currency movement remains as a fundamental element of international marketing. Consider a South Korean automaker exporting to South Africa. Due to the strength of the South African *rand* compared to the South Korean currency, the *won*, the Korean company's exports become priced too high for the South African market. The company's chief financial officer might predict that the *rand* is going to devalue relative to the *won*, which would lower the price of the automobiles. Based on this prediction, the company will continue to export to the market and wait for the currency to devalue. If the company predicts that the *rand* will continue to stay strong, the company may decide to start manufacturing within the country. By manufacturing within the nation's boundaries, the company's costs would be in *rand*, which might make it possible to lower the price of the cars in the market.

INDIVIDUAL AND BUSINESS TRANSACTIONS

General economic health can lead to greater pressure on the "supply" or the "demand" side in a currency tug-of-war. When economies do well, consumers spend more and companies become more likely to make foreign investments as greater transaction demand for currency occurs. *Transaction demand* refers to demand for the currency needed to conduct business activities, such as importing goods or investing in a country's stock market. The opposite is also true. In weak economies, lower demand for the currency exists; there will be lower consumer and business spending, fewer imports, and investors will view domestic companies as less appealing.

While much of the demand for currency results from individual and business transactions, speculators make some currency purchases with the goal of profiting from the transaction itself. They hope to purchase the currency at a low price and to sell it later at a high price. The attempt to make money in the currency market is *currency speculation*, in which investments are made based on predictions of future changes in the currency's value. After the 2008 financial crisis, speculation came under criticism for not providing value and for leading to currency movements based purely on profits for speculators. Others argued that speculators play an important role in balancing out both sides of a currency's valuation.

TRADE AND INVESTMENT ACTIVITY

Business transactions take the forms of trade and investment activities. Governments evaluate them with balance of payment statements. The statements catalogue currency-related activities within a nation. The documents enable international marketers to obtain a broad overview of the trade activity within a country along with the nation's economic ties with other nations.

Trade plays a central role in a country's overall economic position globally. Some countries, such as China or Germany, have a tendency to save, to keep large reserves or savings of currency, and to export. Others, such as the United Kingdom, import many goods and have high consumer spending rates. A balance of payments statement reveals this. Table 12.6 provides an example.

Countries buy and sell goods and services as well as financial assets. A balance of payments statement tracks these activities. The statement contains five components: current account, capital account, financial account, net errors and omissions, and reserves and related items.

The current account catalogues trade in merchandise, services, income, and current transfers. Current transfers refer to any transfers of currency that are not capital-related, such as gifts and grants. The 400 million Saudi *riyals* (*SR* 400 million) given by Saudi Arabia to Pakistan during the 2010 floods would belong under the current account or as a current transfer.[4] Trade balance statements refer to the current account. A surplus or deficit means a trade surplus or deficit. Map 12.1 displays the examples of account balances among various countries.

The accounts shown in Map 12.1 catalogue trades in merchandise, services, income, and current transfers. A capital account contains capital transfers, non-produced assets, and non-financial assets. Typically, little activity takes place in the capital account.

TABLE 12.6   Abbreviated Balance of Payments Statement for the United States

U.S. International Transactions 2009 (in millions of dollars)	
Current Account	
Exports of goods and services and income receipts	2,159,000
Imports of goods and services and income payments	–2,412,000
Unilateral current transfers	–124,943
Capital Account	
Capital account transactions, net	–140
Financial Account	
U.S.-owned assets abroad, excluding financial derivatives	–140,465
Foreign-owned assets in the United States, excluding financial derivatives	305,736
Financial derivatives, net	50,804
Net errors and omissions	162,008

Source. Adapted from Bureau of Economic Analysis, "U.S. International Transactions Accounts Data," September 15, 2011. Retrieved from www.bea.gov/international/bp_web/simple.cfm?anon=71&table_id=1&area_id=3.

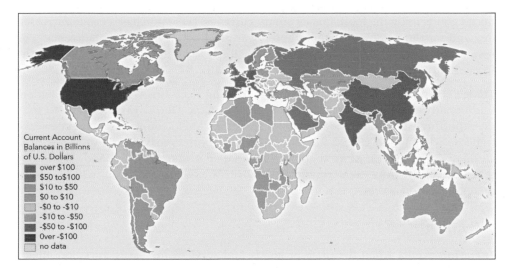

Current Account Balances in Billions of U.S. Dollars

- over $100
- $50 to $100
- $10 to $50
- $0 to $10
- -$0 to -$10
- -$10 to -$50
- -$50 to -$100
- Over -$100
- no data

MAP 12.1   Examples of Account Balances Globally

Source: Wikipedia user Emilfaro. Retrieved from http://en.wikipedia.org/wiki/File:Cumulative_Current_Account_Balance.png

More activity can be identified in the financial account. The account tracks direct investments, portfolio investments, and other financial assets. It includes buying bonds or stocks, and foreign direct investment such as buying a factory or an existing company.

Ideally, a balance of payments document indicates a balance of the activity in the current account with activity in the capital and financial account. Normally, however, compilers of balance of payment statements cannot acquire all of the information needed to finalize the calculations. Incomplete information may be due to unreported activity, timing problems, or simple mistakes in filling out forms. To make sure the statement balances, net errors and omissions are added.

The final item on the balance of statements is reserves and related items, which represents the reserves held by official governmental authorities. The reserve currency refers to the currency most commonly held in reserve accounts. Most commonly, countries hold the U.S. dollar in reserve.

TRADE DEFICITS

Trade consists of exports and imports. *Exports* are goods or services that are shipped from a home country and sold in a foreign market. Goods or services shipped from a foreign country into the home market are *imports*.

trade deficit: the balance of trade that occurs when a country imports more than it exports

Depending on the relationship of exports to imports, a country experiences a trade surplus or a deficit. A **trade deficit** exists when a country imports more than it exports. In that case, local consumers spend the local currency on imported goods. These goods have to be initially purchased in the currency of the country of origin, which leads to increased demand for the foreign currency rather than the domestic currency. Barring activity by one or both of the governments, or possibly other currency influencing factors such as inflation or interest rates, the increase in demand will result in the foreign currency appreciating or rising in value relative to the domestic currency.

trade surplus: the balance of trade that occurs when a country exports more than it imports

A country with more exports than imports enjoys a **trade surplus**, which creates the opposite effect of a trade deficit. Foreign consumers purchase many domestically produced goods using the local, home country currency. Local purchases create increased demand for the domestic currency and lower demand for the foreign currency. The resulting pressure on the domestic currency leads to an appreciation relative to the foreign currency.

Trade relationships affect international marketing decisions. The United Kingdom traditionally experiences a trade deficit with Germany. Germany historically focuses on exporting while the United Kingdom and other Anglo countries often experience trade deficits.[5] In the United Kingdom, British exporters may decide to wait for the German currency (the *euro*) to appreciate relative to the British pound. When this takes place, the price in Germany of the British exports will drop, which in turn increases export levels.

INFLATION

inflation: a situation in which the price of goods and services increases in a country or region

Inflation occurs when the price of goods and services increases. Inflation affects whether a currency will strengthen or weaken. Rates of inflation vary by country and are partly a result of supply and demand for a currency. Price increases within a country are not always accompanied by salary increases in that same country. For consumers, this means that goods and services become more expensive as inflation rises. As a result, governments often take steps including spending and taxation to control inflation by manipulating the currency supply in a country. Officials take steps using these tools when needed.

In other cases, governmental leaders conclude they can help an economy by increasing the supply of money. In these cases, a federal reserve or a national bank introduces more money in the system to increase supply for the domestic currency. Currency values move in response to inflation, both current and predicted. Inflation that is expected in the future weakens the purchasing power of a currency, and the exchange rate reflects that weakness. In India, at one point year-to-year inflation was 10.5%, which meant that, on average, the price of all goods rose 10.5% as compared to the previous year. The price of milk went up approximately 1.8 *rupees* to 29.4 *rupees* per container (Goyal, 2010). The price increase had the most profound effect on bottom-of-the-pyramid consumers. The result was that inflation increased pressure on the *rupee*, which led to concerns about currency weakness.

Inflation concerns international marketers because it influences price. A company in a country with a low inflation rate might encounter difficulties when payments are delayed from a firm in a nation with a higher inflation rate. In essence, the company will be paid with a "cheaper" currency.

INTEREST RATES

Interest rates indicate the percentage rate charged or paid for the use of money. The amount of interest lenders charge relates to currency demand. Rising or lower interest rates influence the weakening or strengthening of a currency's value. Many consumers receive interest on savings and checking accounts. Governmental debt or bonds pay interest, and typically the governmental interest rate determines the rates offered by other lenders within the country. Countries with high interest rates, all else being equal, experience a higher rate of foreign investment in bonds and other instruments linked to the interest rate. The result can be an increased demand for the currency (Kim and Seung, 2006).

interest rates: the percentage rate charged or paid for the use of money

INTERNATIONAL INCIDENT

Your company has started to actively conduct business in Venezuela. The country, while an attractive market in many ways, maintains strict limits on currency conversions. In practical terms, you are unable to transfer your earnings from Venezuelan *strong bolivars* into the *euros* needed to repatriate the money to your Belgian headquarters. Your local partner does not support the Venezuelan government and tells you about a currency black market where you can exchange the money. While the black market operator charges a higher rate to cover the increased risk, it would give you the opportunity to move the revenue out of the country. Do you politely thank your friend for the advice but turn down the offer? Do you consider the offer? The Venezuelan government has begun taking over foreign companies with little to no compensation. Does that affect your decision?

Inflation also affects interest rates. The *Fisher effect* suggests that the nominal or stated interest rate of a country is equal to the actual interest rate plus the rate of inflation. As inflation reduces the value of a currency, interest rates need to reflect both elements. Table 12.7 provides the formula for the Fisher effect.

Overall, interest rates serve an important role in international marketing. When borrowing internationally, interest rates set both the cost of much debt and the return on savings. By influencing currency demand, the difference in interest rates between countries will typically be offset by the differences in exchange rates.

TABLE 12.7   Fisher Effect Formula

Nominal rate = real rate + inflation
Nominal interest rate in Mexico = 5%
Inflation rate in Mexico = 2%
5 = x + 2
3 = x
Real interest rate in Mexico = 3%

LEARNING OBJECTIVE #3:

How do the law of one price and purchasing power parity affect international marketing activities?

THE LAW OF ONE PRICE AND PURCHASING POWER PARITY

Exchange rates do not always link to what can be purchased with a country's currency. Textiles may be relatively less expensive, while electronic goods may be relatively more expensive. These differences are contrary to the law of one price. The law of one price states that identical products should be priced identically in different markets, once the price is converted to the same currency in each market. Consider a staple product such as bread. The price for bread in Poland may be 1.5 *zloty*. In Belarus, the same loaf of bread may cost 1,500 Belarus *rubles*. If the exchange rate is 1 *zloty* equals 1,000 *rubles*, then the products actually have the same price. The apparent difference is due to currency differences. Table 12.8 provides details.

If the price of the bread was 1,500 *rubles* in Belarus and 2 *zloty* in Poland, using the same exchange rate, the price of bread in Poland can be converted to Belarus *rubles*, as shown in Table 12.9. The resulting price is 3,000 *rubles*. This means that the price of bread, once currency differences are accounted for, is higher in Poland than it is in Belarus. In other words, the *zloty* does not go as far in Poland as the *ruble* does in Belarus, at least for a loaf of bread.

TABLE 12.8   Example of Law of One Price

Price of Bread Poland = 1.5 *zloty*

Price of Bread Belarus = 1,500 *rubles*

Exchange rate: 1 zloty = 1,000 *rubles*

Price of bread in Poland converted to Belarus *rubles*

1.5 * 1000 = 1,500 *rubles*

TABLE 12.9   Example of Law of One Price Not Applying

Price of Bread Poland = 2 *zloty*

Price of Bread Belarus = 1,500 *rubles*

Exchange rate: 1 zloty = 1,500 *rubles*

Price of bread in Poland converted to Belarus *rubles*

2 * 1,500 = 3,000 *rubles*

PURCHASING POWER

The law of one price often does not apply. A soda or a candy bar or bus rides are all frequently more or less expensive in other countries due to purchasing power differences. Purchasing power refers to the amount of goods a unit of currency can purchase. If hypothetically 1 *euro* could be exchanged for 1 Japanese *yen*, this would not mean that the currencies would purchase the same amount of a good, a bowl of rice, for example, in the respective home markets. Purchasing power reflects the strengths of different currencies in terms of their abilities to purchase goods.

Marketers consider purchasing power effects because differences influence costs and prices across markets. The Big Mac Index is released periodically by *The Economist* magazine. The index compares the price of the Big Mac (or a comparable sandwich) in all of McDonald's markets. The price of the burger should be relatively the same, but the Big Mac Index indicated otherwise. Price differences may be due to different costs for the various components of the sandwich, unequal labor costs, increased or decreased demand, the cost of transportation of goods, consumer psychology within a country, or governmental activities, particularly taxes on imports.

PURCHASING POWER PARITY

Purchasing power measures featuring a single item or product can be flawed. Specific product features or issues surrounding that product might explain the unique high or low relative cost. Instead, experts examine the price for a basket of goods to identify differences in purchasing power, an approach referred to as purchasing power parity.

The Organisation for Economic Co-operation and Development (OECD) creates a more exhaustive measure of purchasing power using the prices for a basket of more than 1,000 goods and services. Table 12.10 displays the similarities and differences in the ranking for the OECD and Big Mac indices.

Purchasing power drastically influences costs and revenues. Understanding purchasing power leads to more effective methods for comparing costs, prices, and sales across countries. The process at least partially removes the role of currency exchange from the comparison. During the Mexican currency crisis of 1994, the amount of Mexican *pesos* that could be purchased by 1 U.S. dollar dropped 37% from December 20, 1994, to January 5, 1995. The drop in currency value affected consumption, but it did not decline by 37%. By considering the actual purchasing power of the currency instead of its value relative to the U.S. dollar, company leaders held a more realistic perspective of the market.

TABLE 12.10 A Comparison of the Weakest and Strongest Currencies

The OECD and the Big Mac Index		
	OECD PPP[a]	Big Mac Index
Top Five	Japan (1)	Norway (1)
	Switzerland (2)	Switzerland (2)
	France (3)	Brazil (3)
	The Netherlands (4)	Euro Area (4)
	Sweden (5)	Canada (5)
Bottom Five	South Africa (36)	Philippines (21)
	India (37)	Malaysia (22)
	Turkey (38)	Thailand (23)
	Iceland (39)	China (24)
	Russia (40)	Hong Kong (25)

Source: Adapted from "Consumer Prices (MEI)," OECD, October 6, 2011. Retrieved from http://stats.oecd.org/Index.aspx?querytype=view&queryname=221; and "When the Chips Are Down," *The Economist*, July 22, 2010. Retrieved from www.economist.com/node/16646178?story_id=16646178.

Note: a. PPP stands for purchasing power parity.

Marketers employ purchasing power parity scores another way to calculate prices. Instead of focusing on established currency exchange rates, marketers instead use purchasing power parity to convert to an appropriate price for the new market. This allows purchasing power parity scores to be treated as a form of currency conversion.

Consider the example of the price of bread in Poland and Belarus. If 3 *zloty* purchase the same basket of goods in Poland as 3,000 *rubles* do in Belarus, the ratio of 3 *zloty* to 3,000 *rubles* might be used to establish an exchange rate. If bread costs 1,500 *rubles* in Belarus and 2 *zloty* in Poland, the difference in terms of purchasing power parity is 500 *rubles*. Using the exchange rate, as in Table 12.11, the difference is 1,500 *rubles*. A company considering selling bread in Belarus would be well served to consider the purchasing power parity price of bread when entering the market. Setting the price based exclusively on exchange rates might price the bread out of the market.

TABLE 12.11 Purchasing Price Parity Example

Price of Bread Poland = 2 *zloty*

Price of Bread Belarus = 1,500 *rubles*

Purchasing Power Difference: 3 *zloty* = 3,000 *rubles*

1 *zloty* = 1,000 *rubles*

Price of bread in Poland converted to Belarus *rubles* using purchasing power conversion

2 * 1,000 = 2,000 *rubles*

LEARNING OBJECTIVE #4:

How do governmental activities influence international finance?

GOVERNMENTAL ACTIVITY AND INTERNATIONAL FINANCE

Currency and currency exchange are part of the foundation of an economy. Consequently, governments often play active roles in currency management. Almost all global currencies are created and backed by the governments in which they are used. This enables governmental officials to play the most central role in the control of currency value. Through central banks or federal reserves, governments have an almost limitless supply of money. When a government needs more currency, more can be created. This increases the supply of the money and might lead to inflation. Governments are able to purchase large amounts of foreign monies or domestic currencies. These purchasing actions increase demand for the currency.

When the European Central Bank believes that the *euro* has become too strong relative to the pound, it may limit investments in Germany and other European countries from the United Kingdom. A weak pound increases costs for members of the European Union. In an attempt to move the currency value, the European Central Bank could increase the number or supply of *euros*. A higher supply of any good, even currency, should lead to a decrease in price.

Although a government take steps to influence the value of its domestic currency, non-currency-related motives often drive these actions. Governments often increase the supply of money within a country to help spur economic growth. The increased supply of domestic money weakens the currency on the global market. During a recent Irish economic downturn, the government accused the United Kingdom of expanding the money supply in an effort to devalue the pound. The devaluation caused economic problems in the Irish Republic (Garnham, 2009). Marketers in both countries that followed the currency activity were better able to predict the resulting economic issues, which might lessen the effects of the governmental action taken by the UK.

CURRENCY REGIMES

Governments actively set up controlling structures or regimes around domestic currencies. Officials decide which regime to use and then employ governmental instruments to maintain the regime. The type of regime influences the manner in which the currency exchange rate moves and the activities that governments take to maintain that regime. This movement and these actions in turn affect marketing activities. Broadly, the structures lead to two different methods for establishing and monitoring the domestic currency's exchange rate: floating exchange rate and fixed exchange rate regimes.

Floating Exchange Rates

The first type of exchange rate regime, a **flexible** or **floating exchange rate**, occurs in circumstances in which the value of the currency responds freely to market forces. Forces of supply and demand apply. Governmental actions influence the rate and may even have stated goals regarding currency value, but officials do not set hard limits regarding how far they will move.

flexible or floating exchange rate: the rate when the value of the currency is allowed to respond freely to market forces

Float enables a currency to rise or fall in value. When there is increased purchasing of a currency by another currency, such as more *euros* being bought by pounds, the exchange rate changes and the value of the currency that is purchased increases. The rise in the value of one currency relative to another is *appreciation*. In contrast, if the number of purchases of one currency by another decreases, representing a drop in demand, the value of the currency being purchased goes down. The decrease in the value of one currency relative to another is *depreciation*.

Beyond demand, supply also affects currency values in a flexible exchange regime. When the central bank or a similar governmental institution increases the supply of a currency in the world market, the increased supply should result in currency depreciation across the board. If the government instead takes steps to purchase its own currency to remove it from the currency market, supply decreases and the currency appreciates. When Japan increased the supply of *yen* in order to depreciate the currency, the value of the *yen* decreased by 3.1% against the dollar and 3.4% against the *euro* (Halligan, 2010).

Fixed Exchange Rates

The other method governments use to influence currency values is a **pegged** or **fixed regime**. Under this regime, a predetermined band or par value establishes the value of a currency. The government sets limits as to how far the rate can move in either direction. When a country's rate begins to move too far in either direction, the government takes aggressive steps to ensure that the currency does not go outside the designated range.

pegged or fixed regime: the value of a currency when it is set to a predetermined band or par value

Supply and demand forces apply to pegged currencies; however, the governments act more aggressively in response to potential movements in value. The movements may occur in the black markets that typically spring up for controlled currencies due to the appeal of uncontrolled movements. Central banks intervene in the currency market through purchasing of currency or creation of more currency in response to the potential for the currency to no longer maintain par value.

Revaluation and Devaluation

In some cases, the government cannot prevent more dramatic currency valuation changes. Even the largest of governments cannot completely influence market forces. In these cases, the central bank sets a new par value. *Revaluation* refers to a government increase in the par value of a currency under a fixed-rate regime. *Devaluation* refers to a government decrease in the par value. Not long ago, the Vietnam currency, the *dong*, faced aggressive activity in the black market for the currency. In response, the Vietnamese central government devalued the *dong* by 2% against the U.S. dollar setting the new exchange rate at 18,932 *dong* for 1 U.S. dollar, thereby discouraging further speculation (Steinglass, 2010b).

Analysis

Advantages and disadvantages exist for both exchange regimes. For a fixed exchange regime, governments seek to ensure short-term stability. The value of the currency should stay within the prescribed band. The risk with a fixed exchange regime lies in the underlying supply and demand features of currency. If the par value becomes too disconnected from the demand or the supply for the currency, the peg can be "broken." This occurs when the central bank for a government can no longer maintain a peg. When this occurs, the currencies often wildly change in value, leading to drastic losses in value in some cases, which can cause significant economic problems.

Possibly the most famous example of a peg being broken happened on Black Wednesday, September 16, 1992, to the prestigious British pound sterling. The United Kingdom had entered into the European exchange rate mechanism, which pegged the sterling to various other European currencies that also were part of the agreement. Being unable to maintain the peg, the government left the exchange rate mechanism on this date (Whitney, 1993). The rumor at the time was that George Soros, the famous currency speculator, was responsible for breaking the pound sterling. Not only did he potentially break the peg, but also he possibly made $1 billion in personal profit (Woodall, 1995).

For a flexible exchange regime, the opposite concerns exist. The float tends to be protected from extreme fluctuations in value. Instead, daily market forces tend to move the currency up or down. Short-term risks are relatively high, but over the long term the currency should remain relatively stable. Flexible exchange regimes cannot be broken, but tend to be far more difficult to predict in the short term. For example, while the overall trend for the Canadian dollar has been appreciating versus the dollar, with the value of the currency rising by 50% from 2002 to 2008, on any day the value of the Canadian dollar may drop (Gordon, 2010). Predicting the long-term trend is easier than predicting day-to-day changes. Table 12.12 provides some names of fixed and flexible regime countries.

GLOBAL CURRENCY INSTITUTIONS

Many governments place a major emphasis on maintaining currencies and currency values. Throughout history governments have banded together to stabilize them

TABLE 12.12   Sample of Countries with Fixed and Flexible Regimes

Fixed Regimes	Flexible Regimes
Belize	Australia
Bolivia	Brazil
Brunei	Estonia
China	Eurozone
Ecuador	India
Hong Kong	Japan
Iran	Kenya
Lebanon	Mexico
Lesotho	Netherlands
Malawi	Philippines
Panama	South Africa
Rwanda	Switzerland
Syria	Thailand
Turkmenistan	United Kingdom
Uzbekistan	United States

Source: Adapted from "Annual Report on Exchange Arrangements and Exchange Restrictions 2016," International Monetary Fund.

(Fineman, 2009). Marketers who understand the modern system use the information to help predict potential future changes and trends.

After World War II, steps were taken to ensure currency stability. Many governments met in Breton Woods, New Hampshire, in 1944 to deal with the issue. The meeting created the International Monetary Fund and the International Bank for Reconstruction and Development, which is also known as the World Bank. These institutions established separate but related missions.

The primary responsibility of the International Monetary Fund is currency stability. The organization provides short-term loans in response to currency crises and works diligently to monitor currency activities. Loans from the International Monetary Fund may be denominated in *special drawing rights*, the value of which reflects a basket of the member country currencies. The World Bank concentrates on long-term development. Initially, the Bank gave loans and grants to European countries to fund reconstruction. More recently, the Bank's focus has shifted to less- and least-developed countries.

The Bretton Woods agreement established a global currency system. The signatories agreed to fix the value of their currencies in terms of either the U.S. dollar or a certain weight of gold. In turn, the U.S. dollar was always convertible to $35 per one ounce of gold (the "gold standard" that politicians refer to). This American gold standard stayed in place until the early 1970s, when forces put pressure on the peg. The American government had to pay out gold and other reserves to protect the peg but eventually was unable to continue this activity broadly because of an insufficient amount of gold being held in U.S. reserves. The system collapsed and the U.S. dollar and many other countries moved to a flexible exchange regime.

The International Monetary Fund continues to actively monitor currency activities. In 2010, Greece faced country-level economic concerns. The currency for Greece is the

The United States does not rely on the gold standard for currency valuation.

euro. A disconnect ensued between the unique economic events within Greece and the value of the *euro*. The resulting stress on the *euro* threatened the viability of the currency and led many to suggest that Greece should leave the eurozone.

In response, the International Monetary Fund took steps to stabilize both the Greek economy and the value of the *euro*. A loan of €110 billion ($143 billion) plus strong recommendations for governmental actions together helped to stabilize the situation. Tourism makes up almost one-fifth of the Greek economy.[6] Marketers in this industry would be concerned with currency and overall financial stability in the country. In this case, marketers carefully watch International Monetary Fund actions before determining whether to leave the country or to hope to ride out the instability and maintain a position in the market.

The last half-decade has seen relative global economic stability and growth. Instead of active interventions in cases of crises, the majority of International Monetary Fund activity has focused on monitoring and improving on existing activites.[7]

MANAGING CURRENCY RISK

Effective strategic international marketing management leads to revenues and in most cases profits. Currency fluctuations might dramatically reduce profits. When costs increase within a country, or the costs of manufacturing the good are in a separate currency, those expenditures may increase as the value of the currency goes down. Consequently, when a company's activity in a country increases, the exposure to currency risk also rises. A 10% drop in the value of a currency causes problems when a company has revenues of $200,000 in the country. A 10% drop in the value of a currency is a catastrophe when revenues are $20 million (a $20,000 loss versus a $2 million loss). In response, many international marketers take steps to limit monetary risks.

PREDICTING CURRENCY RISK

The best international marketing strategies fail due to uncontrollable currency changes. Successful prediction of currency risk in itself helps increase firm profits. One common way to predict currency risk involves consideration of how the currency market perceives different currencies. The *Wall Street Journal* and the *Financial Times* typically publish two different exchange rates. The first rate listed is the spot rate, or the exchange rate with a guarantee of two-day delivery. The second rate or set of rates are forward rates. Forward rates are the exchange rates for the delivery of the currency at a specific time in the future, which is typically 30, 90, and 180 days using what are called *forward contracts*.

forward rates: the exchange rates for the delivery of the currency at a specific time in the future

Usually differences exist between the spot and the forward rates. The differences result from market predictions of future currency movement. When a forward rate is lower than the spot rate, it indicates the presence of a *discount*. A forward rate that is larger than the spot rate is called a *premium*. The efficient market theory posits that in cases of complete openness and knowledge, exchange rates would reflect this knowledge, market predictions would be accurate, and speculation would not lead to profit. A thirty-day forward contract, according to this theory, would perfectly predict the actual exchange rate in thirty days. Research on the topic fails to provide evidence of this effect (Park and Rhee, 2001). Instead, speculators attempt to make money in exchange markets by taking advantage of a misalignment between the spot rate and the forward rate.

Debt ratings offer a second country-specific predictor of currency risk. **Sovereignty debt ratings** assign a score that represents the potential that a country will default on governmental debt. The ratings assess the overall fiscal stability of a country, which directly ties into currency stability. Moody's and Standard & Poor's publish two of the most commonly used sovereignty ratings. Much like ratings for corporate debt, a country with an AAA sovereignty rating poses less risk than a country with a lower rating such as AA or BBB. A drop in rating can change the behavior of the global currency market and lead to more selling of the country's currency on the global market. Table 12.13 provides the sovereignty ratings for select countries.

sovereignty debt ratings: a rating that represents the chance that a country will default on governmental debt

International marketers assess the importance of sovereignty ratings to guide decisions regarding whether to enter new markets. The lower the probability that a currency will devalue the lower the risk of conducting business in that country becomes. Currency values affect sales prices, valuations assigned to inventories, the costs of marketing activities such as advertising and promotions, and eventual bottom-line profits.

TABLE 12.13 Examples of Standard & Poor's Sovereignty Ratings

Country	Rating
Argentina	B
Belgium	AA
Canada	AAA
Colombia	BBB
Fiji	B+
Honduras	BB–
Malaysia	A–
Pakistan	B
Qatar	AA–
Singapore	AAA
Uganda	B

(Continued)

TABLE 12.13   (Continued)

Country	Rating
United Kingdom	AA
United States	AA+
Venezuela	B–
Zambia	B

Source. Adapted from "Sovereign Ratings List." Retrieved from https://countryeconomy.com/ratings.

HEDGING CURRENCY RISK

hedging: any financial process that lessens financial risk

Currency risk may be lessened through various hedging techniques. **Hedging** refers to any financial process that reduces financial risk. In the context of currency risk, hedging involves purchasing various financial instruments. Forward contracts lock in an exchange rate for thirty, sixty, or ninety days. When a company has a set amount of profit it wishes to convert within a set period, the firm purchases a forward contract for that amount, one that guarantees the exchange rate.

futures contracts: contracts that allow the company to sell or buy a certain amount of a foreign currency at a set exchange rate on a specific date

Company leaders also enter into **futures contracts** that allow the company to sell or buy a certain amount of a foreign currency at a set exchange rate on a specific date. Futures and forward contracts are similar but differ in two important ways. Forward contracts pertain to specific transactions; which means they are customized to specific amounts. Futures contracts specify standardized amounts. Forward contracts, while listed for thirty-, sixty-, and ninety-day contracts, can be purchased for a set date. Futures contracts have a small number of maturation dates, four typically, in a given year. The advantage of futures contracts is that only a percentage of the contract needs to be presented to purchase it. This allows the money that would be needed to purchase a forward contract to be used for other business needs.

International marketers use hedging and futures contracts to ensure the success of company efforts. Should a Thai company ship 1,000 units of a product to Saudi Arabia to be sold at a value of 40 Thai *baht* per unit, these contracts help guarantee that payment in the Saudi Arabian *riyal* will equal those 40 *baht*.

THE BASICS OF INTERNATIONAL FINANCE FUNDING

To enter new markets, companies require capital. Capital will be needed to purchase office space, establish distribution channels, generate warehouse inventory, and fund any other long-term purchases designed to support activities in a new country. Often capital originates from internal sources of funds. When the new business is structured as a subsidiary, the funding comes from the parent company in the form of loans or transfers of funds.

Several additional sources of financing may be used. When the source of expansion capital will be equity, companies seek investors at the three dominant exchanges in London, Tokyo, and New York. Frankfurt and Hong Kong are also hubs for financial activity. In each of these centers, shares of stock are sold to raise capital for the venture.

When the company uses debt to expand operations, bonds may be sold in a variety of markets. Two types of international bonds may be issued. Bonds issued outside of a country but are denominated in a currency different from the country of purchase are called *Eurobonds*. A bond for a company or country that is sold outside the home country and that is denominated in the currency of the country of issue is a *foreign bond*.

When internal funding through internal company loans or sales of common stock is not sufficient for the expansion, external sources of funds may be sought. Debt may be local, which permits the parent company to provide a guarantee in order to achieve approval for the loan. Developmental banks may also be a source of funding. The World Bank provides funding to various organizations. Regional and national developmental banks such as the Inter-American Development Bank, the African Development Bank, or the U.S. Export–Import Bank can also provide funding. Table 12.14 lists regional and national developmental banks.

TABLE 12.14   **Partial List of Regional Developmental and National Banks**

U.S. Agency for International Development
Asian Development Bank
African Development Bank
European Bank of Reconstruction and Development
European Investment Bank
Inter-American Development Bank
Overseas Private Investment Corporations
U.S. Export–Import Bank

Source: Adapted from Suk Kim and Seung (2006).

FINANCING ONGOING TRADE OPERATIONS

The transfer of either goods or currency is at the core of foreign trading. **Terms of payment** refers to the agreed-upon payment in return for the goods or services. Use of currency is the dominant payment form, although other methods are available. A cash payment can be COD (cash on delivery of the goods) or it can be CBD (cash before delivery of the goods). In many cases, the seller provides credit to facilitate transactions. Negotiating credit terms is an important part of international pricing.

terms of payment: the agreed-upon payment in return for the goods or services

A unique aspect of international pricing occurs when two companies and countries engage in **countertrade**, where goods are traded or exchanged without the use of hard currency. The four forms of countertrade include

- barter
- buy-back
- compensation deals
- counter-purchases

Barter involves the direct exchange of goods between two companies involved in a transaction. If Honest Tea were to trade finished tea products made in the United States for raw ingredients from an African nation without cash changing hands, a barter arrangement has been reached.

countertrade: when goods are traded or exchanged without the use of hard currency

Buy-back countertrades are agreements to sell one set of goods and services used in the production of products for another set of goods and services. A price for each will first be negotiated. The seller agrees to buy some of the goods and services being produced as part of the payment system. Should a South Korean DVD manufacturer sell production equipment to Thailand and agree to buy finished DVD systems from the company in Thailand as part of the payment price, a buy-back agreement exists.

Compensation deals include both cash payments and exchanges of materials. A Chinese company requires lithium cobalt oxide to manufacture lithium batteries. The company could purchase the ingredient from a supplier and make payment in the form of finished batteries and cash.

Counter-purchases require two contracts. The first specifies the selling price for the item. The second spells out a period during which the buyer is able to resell the item in combination with other goods and then repay the original seller with the proceeds. Counter-purchases are also called offset trades and are often made with firms in less- or least-developed nations.

Countertrade benefits various countries by allowing countries with lower levels of foreign exchange to attain improved technologies. When Russia trades oil for automobiles; the Russian economy benefits from the technologies in the vehicles being exchanged for an abundant resource.[8]

The challenges of pricing in countertrade arrangements include finding common ground on the prices of the items to be exchanged, the exchange rate or monetary value assigned to the goods, and the volume of goods sent to each party. Individual company leaders, such as the automobile manufacturers selling to Russia, may feel constrained by the terms of the countertrade.

INTERNAL PRICING

Due to the wide variety of companies engaged in partnerships, joint ventures, integrated distribution systems, licensure arrangements, and other intra- or intercompany connections, managers in these organizations seek to reduce costs and lower the impact of governmental restrictions. *Transfer prices* help achieve these goals. In intracompany pricing, a commodity sold by one subsidiary of a company to another section in a second country features a set price that bypasses taxes and tariffs by simply shifting funds internally. Many governments have become aware of these programs and have introduced methods to collect revenues by claiming that unreported profits created by transfer prices should be taxed.

Sustainability advocates increasingly push for shadow pricing for internal financing. *Shadow pricing* means that the opportunity and environmental costs are included in prices, such as water or air pollution. Developing country officials might complain that the environmental costs, especially in terms of carbon output, of foreign manufacturing should be included in assessing price.

Companies also may move money to certain countries that have low to no tax. Called *tax havens*, increased international attention focuses on stopping corporations from avoiding taxes.

LEARNING OBJECTIVE #5:

What are the relationships between international finance and the elements of the marketing mix?

INTERNATIONAL FINANCE AND INTERNATIONAL MARKETING

As the world of commerce becomes increasingly based on global interactions, the role finance plays in international marketing grows in importance. Any company seeking to sell goods in other countries looks for ways to integrate a financial system with the marketing program. Failure to do so may lead to the frustration of identifying customers, contacting them, successfully generating sales, but then not making profits due to financial problems rather than marketing program failures.

To fully develop an international marketing program that accounts for financial concerns involves adjustments to all parts of the marketing mix. Financial issues affect markets, products, prices, places (distribution systems), and promotions.

MARKETS

Target markets in other countries may be skewed due to currency changes. Weaker purchasing power shifts the price–value relationship and might result in a need to target a different segment. For example, inflation in a country would limit the ability of consumers to purchase houses. Suppliers of building materials would be noticeably affected by increasing costs and prices. Inflation in Brazil during the 1990s was severe. Those seeking to build homes purchased materials as soon as they could afford them, because waiting results in a higher price for each item. The net result might be sets of neighborhoods with partially built houses.

Currency values influence the selection of market segments to target in foreign markets. Rapid changes in currency values often lead to a reconsideration of market segmentation. Marketers of necessities are more likely to adjust package sizes in response to fluctuating currencies. Companies offering sundries tend to shift sales to more stable currency markets or use other means to ensure profits.

Price sensitivity defines bottom-of-the-pyramid consumers, which makes this segment particularly vulnerable to currency fluctuations. Marketers may be hesitant to increase prices, because the capacity to consume largely drives demand for bottom-of-the-pyramid consumers. With small margins, currency changes lead some marketers to stop targeting the bottom-of-the-pyramid segments.

International financial issues influence access to debt and capital markets. In many cases, limits are placed on the amount of foreign currency that can be exchanged in a country. In those cases, local sources of financing become necessary. The lack of sophistication in local financial markets and the inability of foreign companies to access those markets may reduce the feasibility of entering a market or cause struggles after entering.

PRODUCTS

Price and quality drive perceptions of products. Positioning relative to competitors depends on effective management of such perceptions. Purchasing power differences make positioning difficult to manage when entering a market. To maintain sufficient profits, company leaders raise prices. A new price often leads to repositioning, which must be reflected in the rest of the marketing mix, including promotional activities.

Access to financing constrains the ability of marketers to research new products within a country. New product development may be expensive and often requires an injection of capital. In essence, it might not be possible to develop and sell some products in foreign markets due to financial constraints. An investigation of financial circumstances should precede any market entry decision.

PRICES

Financial conditions strongly affect international pricing programs. Currency exchange and credit influence the product prices and the resources needed to produce and distribute various items. The marketing team works in concert with financial experts to make sure prices are set to achieve company goals.

Fluctuations in currency create one marketing challenge. Currencies change in value unpredictably and quickly. Argentina recently experienced a major currency crisis. When that occurred, the government devalued the country's currency, the Argentine *peso*, by 29% (Wallin and Moffett, 2002). The *peso* continued to devalue in world markets for the rest of the year. Any company conducting business in Argentina needed to make adjustments to try to maintain profits. Firms that positioned products based on price were strongly affected.

Inflation creates another of the major threats to international pricing programs, especially when the currency for the exporter's country has a manageable rate of inflation but the host country's rate is high. When this situation occurs, a product may be sold at a price that does reflect the item's true value. In addition, the basic components of international finance and the effects of these factors on international pricing, as displayed in Table 12.15, deserve additional consideration.

TABLE 12.15   International Finance Factors That Affect Pricing

Exchange Rate Fluctuations
Price Escalations
Administered Prices

Exchange Rate Fluctuations

In the early part of the 2000s, the value of the dollar against the *euro* made purchases in eurozone countries more expensive. When the trade rate was at nearly $1.30 for 1 *euro*, dollar buying power was substantially reduced. American tourists traveling to popular destinations noticed their dollars would not buy as much. For some, this led to travel to other places. Others purchased fewer items while visiting places such as Spain, France, or Italy.

By the end of the decade, economic circumstances in Europe resulted in an exchange rate of less than $1.00 for 1 *euro*, thereby increasing dollar buying power in eurozone countries. American travelers were enticed by marketing campaigns noting that going to Europe could be visited at "bargain" prices. When pricing items, exchange rates affect what people buy and the methods marketers use to reach them.

Price Escalations

As a product moves from one country to another, the costs of transportation, middlemen charges and markups, tariffs, and other expenses cause the price of the item to rise (Table 12.16). A bottle of Spanish wine might sell in Madrid for the equivalent of $5, yet be priced at $10 or more in other countries due to these uncontrollable factors. Price escalations make competing in foreign markets more difficult for many exporters. Many countries seeking to support more open trade establish foreign trade zones or fee ports in which various tariffs and taxes are not charged, which helps control price escalation in those zones. When a market is large enough to justify the risk and expense, a company might begin manufacturing within the country to avoid some of these costs. Price escalation becomes particularly problematic when targeting bottom-of-the-pyramid consumers. Increased costs often put marketers in a position where either the profit margin must be greatly reduced or the product price becomes too high for consumers to afford.

TABLE 12.16   Causes of Price Escalations

Transportation Costs	Cost of Transporting to the Market
Tariffs	Governmental Fees
Importer Margins	Profit to Cover Process of Importing
Wholesaler Margins	Cost Associated with Inventory Management and Distribution
Retailer Margins	Mark-Up in the Retail Store
Taxes	Value-Added or Other Government Taxes

Administered Prices

Administered prices are set by individual governments, often in an attempt to weaken foreign competitors by setting prices for an entire market. Critics argue administered prices are a form of price fixing with governmental approval. Some international agreements allow for administered prices, which tends to stabilize trade relationships between countries, even though the lowest prices may not be offered to consumers in any of the nations involved.

Administered prices may also be used for sensitive, high-demand, or essential products. Governments set the price for rents in densely populated areas or for staple foods such as milk or rice to ensure appropriate access. In some instances, governments do not set the prices. Instead, when a government is the largest purchaser of the item, it will be able to influence the product's price. By being a large purchaser, the government can negotiate a lower price. For instance, the Russian government asked for a 15% reduction in HIV drug prices from the pharmaceutical company GlaxoSmithKline (Whalen and Osborn, 2009).

PLACE (DISTRIBUTION)

Variances in purchasing power lead to different distribution costs. One type of transportation may be more expensive than another in a foreign market. Packaging may also cost more in one market than another.

The ability to distribute or move currency in and out of a country may also be different in various markets. The ability to change the local currency for a foreign currency is called *currency convertibility*. As noted in the opening ArcelorMitall vignette, many governments limit currency convertibility and some completely forbid it.

PROMOTIONS

Consumer promotions depend on stable costs and prices. The success of coupons and other similar discounts results from the perception of increased value due to decreased price. Currency fluctuations during a consumer promotion may alter this relationship and decrease the effectiveness of the promotion.

The same applies to trade promotions. Trade promotions aimed at distributors typically consist of discounts. With larger purchases being made, trade promotions could become even more vulnerable to shifts in value due to shifts in exchange rates.

In sum, international finance directly relates to the marketing process. It influences the entire marketing mix and affects the firm's bottom line. Profit, a core component of business activity, can be drastically impacted by international finance issues, especially currency movements. Careful planning and coordination between the marketing team and those in finance are required in order to manage these issues.

CHAPTER 12: REVIEW AND RESOURCES

Strategic Implications

International marketers face international finance concerns when entering or maintaining a presence in a market. The stability of the local currency influences initial decisions to enter the market. Unstable currencies may defer entry. Once in the market, currency control measures become an important strategic consideration for company leaders. These hedges incur costs. The marketing and finance teams decide whether the currency risk is extreme enough to warrant hedging, or if the company's exposure is large enough to justify the additional costs.

Effectively finding sources of financing as well as balancing debt and equity remain as key strategic issues for international marketers. Equity gained by selling shares of stock relinquishes ownership and some degree of control. Debt has a specific cost. While activity in global markets provides for access to more sources of capital, it does not remove the need to select the best combination of financial instruments.

Tactical Implications

Hedging currency risk can be complicated. The tactical choices include the types of contracts to buy, the size of the contracts, and timing the maturity of the contracts with the need for the currency. These short-term transactions can become a juggling act. International marketers work with the finance department to ensure effective timing of the flow of money to support marketing transactions.

When the financial instruments are in place, marketing activities can be undertaken. Establishing distribution systems, creating supportive programs such as coupons or premiums, and preparing advertising campaigns will proceed with greater confidence. Understanding when monetary transactions will take place helps the marketing manager understand when the company can expect to receive revenues and when it will render payments to suppliers and others in the target market country.

Product positioning efforts are affected by international finance. The price/quality relationship can be altered by inflation, devaluations of currency, and other shifts in monetary markets. Consequently, the marketing team remains in constant contact with the finance team in order to be able to adjust to monetary differences and maintain the desired position in the marketplace.

Operational Implications

Individual employees deal with currency issues on practically a daily basis. International marketers responsible for a specific country or region will normally know the approximate exchange rate without needing to look it up. The exchange rate is used to calculate sales, costs, and profit.

Individual salespeople should be trained in the basics of international finance. Potential customers in other countries are likely to ask about methods of payment and how each side will be protected from currency risk. In essence, these financial concerns represent part of the price to a foreign buyer.

Expatriate employees require training in the areas of exchange rates and currency fluctuations. These employees need to adjust to the monetary system in the country to which they are sent. They will be affected by other issues such as the currency in which they receive their salaries and expense reimbursements, and will also be influenced by transaction fees charged to move money back to their home countries.

In essence, every person, from the CEO to the first-line person serving in a foreign country, will be better served by having a working understanding of how international finance affects them and their companies.

TERMS

currency	interest rates
hard currency	flexible or floating exchange rate
soft currency	pegged or fixed regime
international finance	forward rates
capital market	sovereignty debt ratings
exchange rate	hedging
trade deficit	futures contracts
trade surplus	terms of payment
inflation	countertrade

REVIEW QUESTIONS

1. What are the five properties of money?

2. What is the relationship between money and currency?

3. Define hard currency and soft currency and note how the two types of currency are dissimilar.

4. Define capital market, and explain the roles debt and equity play in capital markets.

5. Define direct currency exchange rate quotes and indirect currency exchange rate quotes.

6. What are the four factors that affect currency movement?

7. How do transaction demand and currency speculation affect currency values?

8. What are the five components of the balance of payments statement?

9. Define inflation and explain how it affects currency values.

10. How does the government influence currency value?

11. Describe a fixed or pegged currency exchange and contrast it with a flexible or floating regime.

12. What were the outcomes from the Bretton Woods agreement?

13. What does a low or high sovereign debt rating mean?

14. Define futures contracts and forward contracts.

15. Define hedging and note how it is used in international marketing.

16. Where can companies find capital?

17. What are common forms for the capital?

18. Define terms of payment and list examples.

19. Name the types of countertrade.

20. Define internal pricing, shadow pricing, and explain how they are different from one another.

21. How does international financing affect markets?

22. How does international financing affect products, prices, distribution systems, and promotional programs?

DISCUSSION QUESTIONS

1. Brainstorm and list all of the various ways that businesses use currencies. Is there any part of international marketing that is not affected by currency?

2. The Indonesian *rupiah* has recently weakened. Explain how each of the following is related to the weakening in value: (1) individual and business transactions, (2) inflation, (3) interest rates, and (4) trade and investment activity.

3. Examine the U.S. balance of payments statement in Table 12.6. Using those numbers, calculate the American trade deficit. How does this trade deficit then influence the value of the U.S. dollar? If other forces do not prevent this change, what should the long-term value of the trade deficit be?

4. What are the advantages and disadvantages of a fixed or flexible currency exchange regime? How can international marketers use the type of exchange regime to predict potential currency movements?

5. Trace the history of the global currency exchange controls from 1900 to the present. The movement in general has been from fixed systems to flexible systems. Study Table 12.12. The majority of countries that are classified as "developed" have what kind of exchange regime? Why might that be?

6. As the brand manager for a large Brazilian company, you are concerned about exposure to currency fluctuations hurting your profit in Mexico. What steps could you take to hedge this risk?

7. There are three international finance factors that affect pricing (see Table 12.15). Discuss them and steps international marketers can take to limit these effects.

ANALYTICAL AND INTERNET EXERCISES

1. You are an Australian marketer whose company is entering the Indian market. One Australian dollar is worth 43.34 Indian *rupees*. Is this an indirect or direct quote? Calculate whichever quote it is not. When the company first entered the Indian market, the exchange rate was 1 Australian dollar = 44.56 Indian *rupees*. Calculate the percentage change in the rate.

2. One of the most significant currency events of the past twenty years was the Asian currency crisis of 1997. Complete online research regarding the crisis. Were fixed or flexible regimes involved? What was the role of the International Monetary Fund in responding to the crisis?

3. The CIA World Factbook (www.cia.gov/library/publications/the-world-factbook/index.html) includes current account balances for countries. It also lists top exporting and importing trading partners. Look up a country of your choosing. Find out whether it has a trade deficit or trade surplus and then find the country's top trading partners. Finally, look up exchange rates for the country of interest, and its trading partners. How well does the exchange rate reflect the trading relationships between the countries?

4. Using Google, find a currency that has weakened or strengthened relative to the *euro* in the past year. How would this change in value affect international marketers interested in doing business in the European Union? How would it affect the marketing mix, particularly price?

5. Currency values can become political issues. The value of the Chinese *yuan* or *renminbi* is historically a source of conflict between the country and its trading partners. Research the conflict and provide an update on recent steps regarding the value of the Chinese currency.

CASE 12

Microfinance and Bottom-of-the-Pyramid Consumers

For most consumers in developing countries, credit is an afterthought, an easily accessible component of making a purchase. Credit scores are tracked and access to credit can be limited for individuals with a bankruptcy or foreclosure. Still, for the majority of consumers access to credit is relatively easy.

Obtaining credit is a major barrier for bottom-of-the-pyramid consumers in developing markets. As much as two-thirds of the world's population cannot obtain credit from banks. Instead, credit, if available at all, can only be accessed through loan sharks and other forms of organized crime. This debt comes with a hefty cost. Interest rates can be extremely high (Woodward, 2009).[9]

The lack of reasonably priced credit has implications for international marketers. It keeps many consumers stuck in poverty. It limits purchasing power, constrains development, and is a key component of bottom-of-the-pyramid markets.

For years, individuals and groups have looked for ways to respond to the global credit access problem. In 1976, Nobel Prize winner Muhammad Yunus came up with a solution—microfinance. On a trip to his home country, Bangladesh, Professor Yunus conducted an informal survey of the loan shark loans to local villagers. The total amount of the average loan was a small $27. The pain associated with this debt in terms of the amount of interest charged was unequal to the value. The banks in the country would not lend to the villagers because they were not "credit worthy." They had no collateral and low earnings. The profit on a $27 loan also seemed too small for them.

Stepping into the void in the market, Professor Yunus loaned the $27 himself. From there microfinance was born. The concept of microfinance is simple. By fixing the institutional gap, credit can be made available to impoverished individuals. This provides them the funding needed to start businesses and earn their way out of poverty. Women are more likely to repay loans, which makes them the target market for the majority of microfinance loans.

Obtaining credit is difficult for bottom-of-the-pyramid consumers in developing markets.

Mallamma, a forty-two-year-old entrepreneur in Hyderabad, India, used a microfinance loan of 10,000 *rupees* to start a fish business. In one year she grew the business to the point that she sought a second loan of *Rs* 50,000 to hire an employee and continue expanding. In Hyderabad, another borrower, Geetawuli, used an *Rs* 10,000 loan to buy a sewing machine after her husband passed away. In one year, she grew the business to the point that she earns *Rs* 100 per day and has an employee. Both women repaid their initial loans.

Professor Yunus founded the Grameen Bank, which now lends more than $1 billion each year. Ninety-seven percent of their borrowers are women, and all of the loans are self-financed, making the bank highly stable. The company also keeps costs very low. Advertising or other promotions are not used. The simple product coupled with the social goal of helping the disadvantaged allows them to be highly efficient. This efficiency has allowed the Grameen Bank to start loaning to poor consumers in many developed countries.

Microfinance has boomed in the past decade. In India alone, the sector grew at a 50% to 70% annual rate from 2006 to 2009. More than 800 microfinance institutions now operate in the country. There are 183 members of Sa-Dhan, a network of microfinance lenders, and for this group the amount of loans grew from *Rs* 3,456 *crore* to *Rs* 11,734 *crore*. Microfinance is a key component of the Indian economy. It has led to some migration from cities to rural areas to take advantage of the jobs created by microfinance (Gardner, 2008; Karlan, 2008; Bhattacharya, 2009; Foroohar, 2010; May, 2010; Sharma, 2010).[10]

TABLE 12.17   Top Fifteen Microfinance Institutions

Name	Country
ASA	Bangladesh
Bundhan (Society and NBFC)	India
Banco do Nordeste	Brazil
Fundación Mundial de la Mujer Bucaramanga	Colombia
FONDEP Micro-Crédit	Morocco
Amhara Credit and Savings Institution	Ethiopia
Banco Compartamos, S.A., Institución de Banca Múltiple	Mexico
Association Al Amana for the Promotion of Micro-Enterprises Morocco	Morocco
Fundación Mundo Mujer Popayán	Colombia
Fundación WWB Colombia—Cali	Colombia
Consumer Credit Union "Economic Partnership"	Russia
Fondation Banque Populaire pour le Micro-Credit	Morocco
Microcredit Foundation of India	India
EKI	Bosnia and Herzegovina
Saadhana Microfin Society	India

Source: Adapted from Swibel (2007).

Professor Yunus started a global movement. More than 150 million bottom-of-the-pyramid consumers have borrowed money from a microfinance institution. The average microfinance loan is $1,026 and only 3.1% of loans default. The default rate is better than

(Continued)

(Continued)

that for many banks lending to developed market consumers. The amount of finance tripled between 2004 and 2006 to $4 billion globally. The majority of lending goes to women and 85% of lending is conducted in Asia where the movement originated. Growth is fast in other regions, especially Latin America. Even with this growth, it is estimated that 95% of the potential market for microfinance has borrowed money. In markets where microfinance has deep roots, such as Bangladesh, 60% to 75% of the market borrows, which suggests that there is great potential for growth. Table 12.17 lists the top fifteen microfinance institutions globally.

Microfinance has been criticized. As global banks move into the market, many worry that the social roots of the process will be lost. For example, CompartamosBanco, a Mexican microfinance-focused bank, was criticized for using an initial public offering to raise $1 billion in credit. Professor Yunus started microfinance by doing the opposite of what banks do. CompartamosBanco instead acts more like a bank, including charging high interest rates of up to 80% per year. Other critics point out that many microfinance borrowers may have been successful without the loan. The loan is not the root of their success. Instead, their success resulted from successful business and marketing strategies coupled with a great deal of hard work.

Even accounting for the criticisms and changing nature of microfinance, Professor Yunus started a significant social and financial movement. Providing access to credit has the potential to help pull least-developed countries out of poverty and increase purchasing power for billions of consumers. The vast implications for international businesses and marketers continue.

1. Is the goal of microfinance profit or a social benefit? Can it be both?

2. Consider how you use credit on a daily basis. How would your life be different without this credit?

3. Conduct an online search of the world's poorest countries. Do you think microfinance will be effective in these markets?

4. What business benefits are there from increased wealth in least-developed countries?

5. Do you agree with the criticisms regarding banks moving into the microfinance market? Why or why not?

PART V
INTERNATIONAL PLACE OR DISTRIBUTION

CONTENTS

13

INTERNATIONAL MARKETING CHANNEL MANAGEMENT

LEARNING OBJECTIVES

After reading and studying this chapter, you should be able to answer the following questions:

1. What are the essential elements of an international marketing channel?
2. What key marketing channel decisions must be made in order to efficiently and effectively reach customers in other countries?
3. What types of international marketing distribution channels are available?
4. How can the marketing team effectively manage international channels of distribution?
5. How do marketing managers utilize channel power and oversee negotiation processes?

IN THIS CHAPTER

Opening Vignette: Mercedes-Benz: Distributing Luxury

OVERVIEW

MERCEDES-BENZ: DISTRIBUTING LUXURY

What began as a high-end luxury car in Germany has become a worldwide leader across a series of product lines. Sales of Mercedes-Benz automobiles take place in Europe, Russia, the Middle East, the Far East, South America (especially Brazil), as well as in the United States and Canada. To achieve success in each of these areas requires adaptation and "flexible channels and formats" designed to create effective customer contacts (Schmidt, 2012). To create continuous growth, the company increased its emphasis on finding strong investors in international markets, identifying ideal locations for new dealerships, and hiring quality sales personnel to serve in every part of the distribution chain.

The Mercedes-Benz brand operates under the Daimler umbrella of automotive lines. The Mercedes approach is unique however, due to the strong emphasis on the exclusivity of products. Dealerships must pass stringent tests designed to ensure that any customer and owner will feel differently from others. The sales experience combines with a unique servicing approach in which pleasant and comfortable accommodations await any individual who remains at the dealership while repairs or maintenance programs are provided. Others are given high-quality loan cars to use (which also serves as a sales enticement for future purchases). Each sales force will be trained to respond to local conditions, such as those relating to gender (selling cars to women versus men), methods of negotiation (the manner in which sales contracts are finalized, and financing (charging interest versus other methods of granting credit and terms of repayment).

The Mercedes-Benz distribution channel is carefully managed and adapted to the requisites of each nation. Company executives adapt programs to account for customs, duties, regulations, modes of transportation, and any other factor that demands attention, such as the appearance of models in local advertising programs. Each of these elements combines with other aspects of the Mercedes marketing program, with the objective of presenting a consistent message about the uniqueness of the entire purchasing process.

The continuing goal within the Mercedes organization is to provide a high-quality experience for every member of the channel while maintaining positive relationships with local authorities and citizens. Careful development of all documents associated with the transfer of ownership as well as the physical delivery of vehicles helps reduce potential conflicts with organizations in the distribution channel, and any disagreement is resolved as quietly and carefully as possible.

Just as the distribution channel necessitates adaptation for each geographic area and country, the line of products offered receives similar attention and development. The Mercedes-Benz line includes cars with the titles of A to E, each with a specific set of features and advantages. The consistent theme remains an excellent interaction with high-end purchasers around the world.

Questions for Students

1. What is the role of distribution in the sale of high-end luxury products as opposed to other goods?

2. How might perceptions of quality in the retail experience be affected by local cultural customs and mores?

3. What challenges would Mercedes-Benz face in creating dealerships in countries with higher levels of poverty and lower levels of economic development?

OVERVIEW

Strategic international marketing channel management plays a critical role in global marketing programs. International marketing strategies succeed when companies establish and maintain efficient and effective distribution channels.

Part V of this textbook examines the place or distribution aspect of strategic international marketing (see Figure 13.1). This chapter considers international marketing channel management. Chapter 14 concentrates on exporting, physical distribution, and retailing. International marketing channel decisions are influenced by culture, language, political and legal systems, and economic conditions; however, the *infrastructure* present in a target country or market may exert most profound effects on distribution systems. Marketing managers consider these ingredients as they design distribution programs.

The extent to which a company intends to distribute products worldwide constitutes an important decision. Methods include intensive, selective, and exclusive distribution systems. The chapter includes a review of the functions performed by intermediaries and of the 5 Cs used when selecting channel members. It identifies types of international marketing channel partners. International marketing managers consider power issues in preparation for negotiation processes with channel partners.

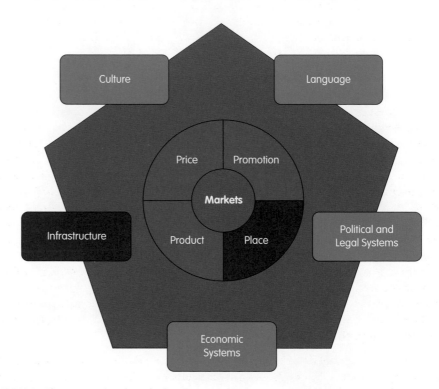

FIGURE 13.1   The International Marketing Context

LEARNING OBJECTIVE #1:

What are the essential elements of an international marketing channel?

---

international marketing channel: a marketing system that promotes the physical flow and ownership of products and services from producer to consumer, including producers, wholesalers, and retailers

INTERNATIONAL MARKETING CHANNELS

The distribution of products to other nations helps spur the global economy. Individual products require various methods to reach international customers. An **international marketing channel** is the system that facilitates the physical flow and ownership of products and services from producer to consumer.

Marketing channel management integrates two key activities: distribution and logistics. **International distribution** systems include the process by which products and services flow between producers, the use of intermediaries, and the transfer of ownership. International **logistics** refers to the strategic management of the flow of products among marketing channel members, including both upstream and downstream activities. *Upstream activities* focus on bringing a product or supplies into a company, while *downstream* activities concentrate on sending a product or supplies to another channel member, usually for resale. The tendency may be to devote the greatest amount of thought to downstream efforts of a marketing channel; however, upstream activities such as ordering raw materials and inbound delivery contribute equally to an effective strategic marketing channel management program.

Distribution system selection results from the evaluation of the marketing channel's structure combined with logistical decisions. Once an organization's marketing team concludes that the company can distribute a product in new areas; decisions regarding the rest of the marketing mix follow. Choices of channels are affected by and affect other marketing decisions. For example, promotional efforts related to distribution may utilize a standardized message in all markets or be adapted to each individual area. Also, price increases may be required in order to cover distribution costs.

DISTRIBUTION INTENSITY

One of the first choices to be made will be the product's **distribution intensity**, which reflects the extent to which products are distributed throughout a country combined with the number of intermediaries contracted to carry the good. Marketers make decisions pertaining to level of distribution intensity on a country-by-country basis because demand for products often varies. Marketing infrastructures also differ. In developing countries, some products can only be made available in limited locations. Open street markets are common for many goods, including grocery items. In open markets, consumers come to a place, often in the middle of a town, to buy necessities. Many times consumers haggle over prices with vendors. In some markets distribution infrastructure is well developed and supports many distribution options. For example, in the UK, online grocery shopping is well established and popular amongst consumers; retailers have efficient delivery services in place. In other countries such distribution has not been as well received. For example, Tesco had to reorganize its offer of online grocery shopping in Poland because of slow adaptation to the service.[1]

In every stage of channel development, international marketers consider the demand for company products, which in turn influences the distribution strategy a firm employs. Table 13.1 displays three distribution intensity approaches.

TABLE 13.1 International Marketing Distribution Intensity

Intensive Distribution
Selective Distribution
Exclusive Distribution

Intensive distribution occurs when a company distributes products through as many wholesalers and retailers as possible in an area or region. This approach matches items that appeal to a large number of consumers. Soft drink manufacturers such as Coca-Cola or Pepsi Cola feature intensive distribution systems worldwide, with the goal of making the product widely available. As was first noted in Chapter 9, intensively

international distribution: the process by which products and services flow between producers, intermediaries, and consumers, including the transfer of ownership

logistics: the management of the flow of products and services among marketing channel members

distribution intensity: the extent to which products are distributed throughout a country and the number of intermediaries that are utilized to carry the product

intensive distribution: an international marketing strategy in which a product is distributed through several wholesalers or retailers in a particular market

distributed items such as convenience goods are low-priced products that retailers sell with a relatively high volume. Examples include products, such as candy, soft drinks, cigarettes, chips, pain medications, cough drops, and packaged doughnuts or pastries.

selective distribution: an international marketing strategy of using only a limited number of channel intermediaries to sell products

A strategy of using a limited number of channel intermediaries in the international marketing program is a selective distribution system. Producers normally exert fairly strong control over channels that utilize selective distribution, because closer relationships develop among channel members. *Shopping goods* are often marketed through selective distribution methods. Products such as appliances tend to rely on this approach. When the international cosmetic dentistry company REMI entered Saudi Arabia, the company partnered with a local health care company, Thimar Al Jarzirah, to access the selective distribution networks necessary to successfully enter the market.[2]

Exclusive distribution systems offer products through only one wholesaler or retailer per market area. Many prestigious product manufacturers, such as Mercedes-Benz, utilize exclusive distribution. French luxury-goods manufacturer LVMH offers several prestige products worldwide utilizing exclusive distribution networks. The French firms Louis Vuitton, Céline, and Guerlain market clothing and accessory products at exclusive upscale retail establishments worldwide.[3]

exclusive distribution: an international marketing strategy that focuses on offering products at only one wholesaler or retailer in a particular market area

A variety of factors influence the development of international distribution channels. Nearly every country contains an established distribution model or structure. For instance, Japan features a complex distribution system. International marketers seeking to conduct business in Japan must first become familiar with that pattern in order to succeed.

Strategic distribution intensity decisions will be based on price, quality, and competition. Marketers match these factors with exclusive, selective, or intensive options. In international markets, selection of a distribution strategy may also be influenced by the infrastructure of the host country and any mitigating factors, such as legal restrictions on imports.

LEARNING OBJECTIVE #2:

What key marketing channel decisions must be made in order to efficiently and effectively reach customers in other countries?

INTERNATIONAL MARKETING CHANNEL DECISIONS

As noted, the type of product and its price affect the choice of an intensive, exclusive, or selective distribution approach. For selective and exclusive products, competitors and brand image become more salient variables. These all influence and are influenced by the desired product position and target market. The relationship between price and quality receives consideration when making distribution channel choices.

Several additional variables arise in international markets. Figure 13.2 lists other factors that affect distribution channel choices. Marketers seek to identify the available intermediaries. Retailers hold lesser and greater levels of prestige and consumer confidence, depending on the host country. The same holds true for wholesale

Type of Product

Price

Competition

Brand Image

Desired Product Position

Target Market

International Considerations

    Available Intermediaries

    Image of Distributors

    Domestic vs. Foreign Issue

    Legal Restrictions

    Taxes on Transportation and Delievery

FIGURE 13.2 International Distribution System Selection Factors

companies. Legal restrictions influence the ability to market products in various countries, including any current quotas or embargoes. Taxes on transportation and delivery systems affect costs and prices.

Marketing professionals consider local circumstances and the effects on distribution before going forward with other activities, such as establishing channels of distribution. Vendors of agricultural goods sold in the United Kingdom deal with the strong negotiating power of the four major supermarkets that dominate the market: Tesco, Asda, Sainsbury's, and Morrisons. Recent statistics indicate that these companies sold 75% of the groceries consumers purchased in a single year.[4]

THE 5 CS OF CHANNEL SELECTION

Several concerns influence international marketers as they select and interact with other organizations in a distribution network. Issues pertaining to the financial *costs* of the system, the *coordination* of marketing efforts, distribution *coverage*, channel member *cooperation*, and channel control are considered. These components are the 5 Cs of selecting channel members (see Table 13.2).

TABLE 13.2 Issues Pertaining to Marketing Channel Structure

Cost
Coordination
Coverage
Cooperation
Control

Cost

Two types of costs become relevant when determining an international marketing channel structure. First, some expenses are incurred when *establishing* the channel as well as choosing members. Then, there are additional payments associated with *maintaining* the system.

International distribution expenses consist of more than just the costs associated with moving products from country to country. The money needed to store, package, prepare, and document product sales is included in distribution costing totals.

The task of transporting goods between countries can present additional difficulties. International distribution systems are often more expensive than those found in purely domestic settings due to the costly nature of moving products between countries or continents. As much as 30% of the price of a product may be directly attributed to funds paid for the distribution of products shipped between continents (Stock and Lambert, 2000). Dispensing products in geographically dispersed countries such as Nepal adds to the overall cost of products. Marketing infrastructure influences the potential for success in creating international marketing channels.

Coordination

Company leaders coordinate the marketing efforts that take place at each level of an international distribution system. Decisions are made as to which promotional and logistical activities each member will perform. Marketing channel coordination requires efficient coordination of the international distribution process.

Coverage

Marketers examine questions pertaining to the extent to which channel members cover certain territories. Channel member roles differ in each country being served. As a result, distribution strategies vary from country to country. When addressing coverage, international marketers consider intensive, selective, and exclusive distribution strategies. For instance, an intensive distribution system means channel members will be expected to cover a wider and more intense territory than would be the case for exclusive distribution.

Cooperation

Although it is difficult, channel leaders attempt to assess the level of cooperation to expect of potential channel members prior to the formation of a formalized marketing channel. The reputations of potential members, along with evidence of previous marketing success in targeted regions or countries become critical. The extent to which marketing channel members trust one another often determines the level of cooperation between parties in a marketing channel (Kumar, 1996).

Control

The degree to which channel members seek to exert marketing channel control constitutes another issue. International marketers lose some control over the physical movement of goods when goods are shipped domestically. Monitoring the movement of goods and ensuring their safe delivery creates additional expenses.

Channel members work together to create an efficient distribution system. Unfortunately, some members are apt to protect their own interests rather than the well-being of the marketing channel. *Opportunism* reflects the tendency for channel members to pursue self-interests rather than those of other members. Consequently, producers monitor the activities of these organizations. Monitoring and controlling the activities of channel members helps the producer to ensure that marketing activities are carried out as planned. A producer can create some control over an international marketing channel by exerting the forms of channel power discussed later in this chapter.

Channel leaders can also consolidate international distribution systems in order to maintain better control and cooperation among channel members. Sony consolidated its distribution efforts in the UK market by selecting two specific distributors, Imago and Midwich, with the goal of improving customer service while increasing channel efficiency (Micheno, 2008).

LEARNING OBJECTIVE #3:

What types of international marketing distribution channels are available?

TYPES OF DISTRIBUTION CHANNELS

Distribution channels dictate the flow of products from the manufacturer or producer to the final end user. Often, the end user will be a retail customer who purchases the product for personal consumption. End users also include businesses and governmental entities. Company leaders designate channels of distribution based on several factors, including business precedent, local conditions, the availability of intermediaries, and managerial preference. Figure 13.3 identifies standard types of direct and indirect distribution.

Consumer Channels				
Direct Channel	Producer	Consumer		
Indirect Channel	Producer	Retailer	Consumer	
	Producer	Wholesaler	Retailer	Consumer
Business-to-Business Channels				
Direct Channel	Producer	End user		
Indirect Channel	Producer	Industrial agent	End user	
	Producer	Industrial merchant	End user	

FIGURE 13.3   Direct and Indirect International Channels of Distribution

DIRECT MARKETING

A direct marketing channel offers a product or service to consumers or end users without the inclusion of wholesalers, retailers, industrial agents, or industrial merchants. Many international marketers believe this approach provides the best option, especially those entering a new host country. In domestic markets, direct channel programs include mailing systems and catalogues. Telemarketing provides another direct marketing tactic. In international operations, the Internet assists companies in reaching consumers through email and by social media.

Many global consumers purchase from direct marketing systems. In Germany, more than 80% of companies feature some form of direct marketing.[5] Telemarketing, email, and direct marketing programs are common in Brazil. Many companies distribute business-to-business goods via direct marketing channels. China's Agri-Business, Inc. focused on direct sales channels in an effort to strengthen relationships with farmers and to increase market share of the company's organic agricultural application products in China. The effort reportedly amounted to 84% of the company's sales during one recent sales period.[6]

Direct marketing channels grant a firm greater control of a brand's image. Wineries, for example seek to control brand identification through direct marketing efforts (Coppla, 2000). A study of French wineries revealed that, particularly for small producers, direct marketing enabled firms to control both costs and quality while nurturing mutually beneficial relationships with individual customers (Gurau and Duquesnois, 2008).

INDIRECT CHANNELS

intermediaries:
organizations that move products from producers to consumers and end users

agent middlemen:
marketing channel members that do not take title or ownership of the products that they market

merchant middlemen:
marketing channel members that take title and ownership of the products being marketed

Goods and services travel through one or more intermediaries in indirect channels. Intermediaries are organizations that move products for producers to consumers and end users, as shown in Figure 13.3. Two types of intermediaries may be employed: agent middlemen and merchant middlemen. Agent middlemen do not take title or ownership of the products. Agents, or brokers, bring buyers and sellers together. These channel members generally work on a commission basis and facilitate international sales. Agent wholesalers may or may not take physical possession of the products that they market. Agent retailers represent services, such as insurance policies, travel tickets (airlines, cruises), and tickets to entertainment events. These retailers do not hold ownership of the services. Instead, a travel agency such as Destination Europe collects fees for reservations of flights and hotels.

Merchant middlemen assume title and ownership of products. These organizations often take possession of the products. When a merchant wholesaler assumes the title and possession of a product, it becomes more difficult for producers or manufacturers to influence or control them. One type of merchant wholesaler, an *import jobber*, purchases products from producers in one country and sells them to established distribution system members in another nation. Merchant retailers purchase goods for resale and then market those products to consumers. Merchant middlemen play a large role in the diamond industry. The luxury diamond company Tiffany & Co. purchases about 50% of the diamonds sold in Tiffany's retail outlets from merchant middlemen (O'Connell, 2009).

Consumer Channels

Many larger international companies ship products directly to retail outlets. This approach bypasses local wholesale operations. The benefits of this method include greater control and reduced costs. Wholesalers mark up items provided to retailers, which raises the final price to consumers. Eliminating the wholesaler enables the manufacturer or producer to charge less, because shipping to a wide array of retail outlets likely will increase transportation costs, as items are not sent in bulk to a single wholesaler location. A manufacturer that negotiates directly with retail outlets retains greater control over company products marketed in host country stores. In contrast, some wholesalers provide goods from more than one manufacturer, which further lessens the degree of control one producer can exhibit.

Trading companies are common in the Pacific Rim. These organizations provide information to clients and offer intermediary activities such as financial and marketing assistance. The Japanese *keiretsus* trading companies act as a family of firms with close relationships and often shared ownership. The *keiretsus* constitute an important part of the Japanese business culture. ITOCHU, Maruberi, Mittsui, and Mitsubishi are four of the largest. These organizations also serve as intermediaries for Japan's exports and have expanded operations to include operations in the areas of mining, oil, and gas exploration, and information technology.[7] The *chaebols* of South Korea feature many similarities. They play key roles in South Korean politics and in the business culture. International marketers targeting these countries carefully consider these organizations when making mode of entry choices and other strategic marketing decisions.

Other marketing teams select the *traditional international marketing channel*, which consists of producers, wholesalers, and retailers. In developed countries, distribution systems tend to be more institutionalized and contain traditional channels. Prices are generally set by the marketing channel with little negotiation involved. Use of international and domestic channels may begin to decline, especially in most-developed nations, as Internet companies emerge in new places.

Business-to-Business Channels

Many countries house large industrial agent and merchant companies. The manufacturer's marketing team selects those that reach the company's target market most effectively. Local conditions and considerations, including legal restrictions, the availability of delivery systems, and the potential to create quality partnerships, affect these decisions.

International marketing channels may include a series of different wholesalers and retailers. Also, several types of firms assist in the physical flow of products through the channel. These firms, known as *facilitating agencies*, assist in various aspects of negotiation, financing, documentation, physical distribution, and warehousing of products internationally. Table 13.3 displays examples.

Marketers examine the various options when making distribution channel decisions. A balance between what has traditionally been the marketing channel in a given country with new possibilities created by improved infrastructure and emerging technologies will be desirable. Then, products are directed to consumers and business-to-business end users through the best available format.

TABLE 13.3　Types of Facilitating Agencies

Freight forwarders	Provide shipping, documentation, customs clearance and brokerage, consolidation, storage, and insurance
Transportation companies	Specialize in moving products through various modes of transportation
Customs brokers	Represent importers/exporters in dealings with customs, including obtaining and submitting all documents for clearing merchandise through customs, arranging inland transport, and paying all charges related to these functions

CHANNEL LENGTH

Marketing channel length reflects the number of intermediaries a product goes through before reaching the consumer. A traditional channel utilizes two intermediaries: a wholesaler and a retailer. Direct marketing has the shortest channel length because the product moves directly from the manufacturer to the customer.

International marketing channels differ significantly in length and complexity. The intricate Japanese distribution system features a number of wholesalers. Further, Japanese consumers tend to make many trips to retailers, and as a result, numerous small retail stores continue to operate in that country. In lesser-developed countries it may not be practical for consumers to make several trips to a store. In those areas, consumers either produce necessities themselves, especially in poorer regions, or stock up on goods when they visit a retailer. Bottom-of-the-pyramid consumers in struggling countries such as Niger, Bangladesh, and Ethiopia offer examples.

Intensively distributed products tend to have longer international marketing channels. When a company distributes a product in several outlets, longer channels may be more effective than shorter channels. In situations such as these, it often takes several marketing channel members to ensure that a product will be available in numerous retail outlets.

Exclusively distributed products often have shorter channels because retailers order directly from producers. The exclusive nature of these channels shortens the length. When supermodel Gisele Bündchen introduced her own cosmetics brand, Sejaa, in Brazil, the Droga Raia chain of drugstores and the Internet retailer Sacks were its exclusive distributors.[8]

STANDARDIZATION OF CHANNEL STRUCTURE

As the global economy becomes increasingly integrated, distribution channels in each country are likely to become similar. At the same time, not all distribution channels will become standardized. Differences will remain across distribution channel types. Nevertheless, as multinational companies continue to expand worldwide, distribution channels will also likely evolve.

ENVIRONMENTAL FACTORS AND MARKETING CHANNEL CONSIDERATIONS

Political, geographical, economic, and cultural differences influence international distribution decisions. Governmental instability often creates a major environmental dilemma. Many countries rely on state-owned distribution networks. For example, the privatization of the distribution network in Russia after the fall of the former Soviet Union led to major changes in the system, with many firms now involved with international marketing channels in the region.

Circumstances in China present an example of the ways geography affects international marketing channels and distribution programs. Mainland China's mountainous regions create physical distribution challenges. India faces a similar situation. Motor carrier and railroad transportation systems do not reach many citizens. Countries such as those in the Middle East include large areas of desert. Vehicles moving goods through those regions must be able to endure higher temperatures. Further, air transportation is limited in many countries, leaving international marketers with fewer distribution alternatives. As a result, the costs and availability of functioning channels influence the selection of a distribution system.

In some countries, geographic hurdles such as mountains are removed or, in the case of Switzerland, tunneled through. To ease the transportation of goods that pass through its boundaries between southern and northern Europe, Switzerland's government launched an aggressive tunnel-building project through the Alps. When it was finished in 2016, it enabled more than 300 trains daily to travel through the tunnels, including the 35.4 mile Gotthard Base Tunnel, the longest in the world (Schmutz, 2011).

EXISTING CHANNELS

Managing international distribution networks requires development of an individual distribution structure for each country. A channel structure that works well in one nation or region may not in another. Understanding the distribution systems present in target countries constitutes a crucial element in developing a successful international distribution system (Lorentz et al., 2007). In some situations, a company establishes an entirely new system. The Swiss pharmaceutical company Novartis developed a cherry-flavored malaria drug called Coartem Dispersible for children in developing countries. The company encountered several challenges when seeking to distribute the drug. Many children in rural areas are not part of the network of national medical facilities that the company would traditionally use to introduce a new medicine. Consequently, the marketing team worked directly with local sellers in rural areas, establishing relationships and using subsidies to encourage drug availability (Guth, 2009).

International marketing professionals seek to ensure that the international distribution channel meets the needs of all parties. The system should effectively serve producers, wholesalers, retailers, and consumers. Analyzing the distribution channel from the perspective of the various constituent groups will be the first step. Channel members use market research to understand distribution patterns in target markets.

FUTURE CHANNELS

Infrastructure choices in international marketing often include consideration of the availability of road, rail, and air transport systems; water, electricity, and natural gas as well as other physical features. Deliveries of products and the availability of those products are influenced by the presence or absence of highways and railroad cars along with other modes of transportation. Map 13.1 presents the major roadways linking countries across the Western Hemisphere. As these types of infrastructure increase in number and quality, trade between countries becomes easier.

The future of physical delivery systems contains promise and problems. In terms of promise, high-speed rail systems, more-elaborate ground transportation companies, GPS tracking devices, and other innovations make it possible to distribute a greater number of products to an increasing number of customers in a wider variety of countries. When accompanied by improved refrigeration systems and better access to electricity and other power sources, the potential to find new markets and develop products that fit continues to grow. This may be especially true in areas of the world inhabited by bottom-of-the-pyramid customers.

The future of physical delivery systems contains promise and problems.

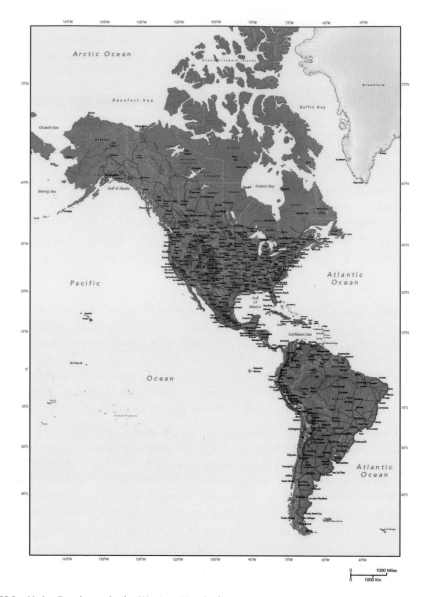

MAP 13.1   Major Roadways in the Western Hemisphere

The increasing number of roadways linking countries together eases trade between countries in the Western Hemisphere.

The problems associated with physical infrastructure result from political and legal systems as well as economic downturns. Although better methods of delivery continue to evolve, many governments limit access to some citizens. For example, the election of President Trump in the United States resulted in changes to the level of access to the nation of Cuba in 2017. Hotel and restaurant chains detected fewer incentives to establish operations in the country when terms on the expansion of trade between Cuba and the USA were altered.

Also economic recessions reduce the ability to take advantage of technological improvements. International marketers continue to assess conditions in various target host countries, seeking opportunities associated with more sophisticated infrastructure systems while also finding ways to overcome obstacles to the movement of goods.

MANAGING INTERNATIONAL DISTRIBUTION CHANNELS

Managing the supply channel involves a series of strategic decisions and activities. Each concentrates on the ultimate goal, which is reaching the target market effectively and efficiently. The key elements involved are

- establishing international channel strategies
- selecting intermediary arrangements
- making channel arrangements and choosing channel partners
- managing international marketing channel functions

ESTABLISHING INTERNATIONAL CHANNEL STRATEGIES

A manufacturer or producer of a service faces a series of issues when marketing an existing product in an existing area, vending a new product in an existing marketing, or when entering a new country or market. Employing a pull or push strategy constitutes the primary choice.

A *pull strategy* means that the producer concentrates on stimulating consumer demand through extensive advertising and consumer promotions. Building demand leads others in the marketing channel to carry additional stock, because customers ask for the product. When this occurs, the item has been pulled through the channel by the end users.

A *push strategy* focuses on providing intermediaries with incentives that lead them to cooperate in marketing the product. Discounts, sales contests, training programs, and other methods entice the wholesaler or retailer to order in greater quantities, thereby pushing the product through the channel to the consumer. When customers find the product in the store with an enthusiastic salesperson recommending the item, the chances of generating greater sales improve.

Individual companies feature both push and pull strategies when distributing items in international markets. Push strategies assist in overcoming intermediary resistance to foreign products. Pull strategies increase consumer demand by making an item seem desirable, easy to use, exotic, or in limited supply. Television advertising remains a popular method for stimulating consumer demand. Television advertising laws vary widely around the world, and international marketers work to ensure that they are followed. Recently, Taiwan moved to become the first country in the world to ban junk food advertisements during children's television programming. The move was motivated by the desire to combat consumer obesity.[9]

INTERMEDIARY ARRANGEMENTS

The second strategic choice is whether to use traditional intermediaries or to create an in-house distribution channel. Several possible intermediary arrangements exist. Three of the most common are

- vertical integration
- horizontal integration
- vertical marketing systems or international strategic alliances

Vertical Integration

vertical integration: a marketing strategy in which one member of the market channel merges with or acquires another intermediary

Vertical integration means that one member of the market channel merges with or acquires another intermediary. Backward vertical integration occurs when a retail chain develops or acquires its own wholesale distribution system. Forward vertical integration strategies involve manufacturers establishing wholesale distribution systems or company-owned retail outlets. For example, the Spanish clothing retail chain Zara produces more than half of its clothing products in-house. Zara clothes are created in a manufacturing center and then completed by seamstresses from 400 local cooperatives. A constant flow of information between the cooperatives and the marketing team ensures the most desired fashions reach the stores. While Gap and H&M may take up to nine months to introduce a new line of clothing, Zara can present items in two to three weeks. The firm is able to respond quickly to any market contingency. The company maintains more than 1,000 outlets worldwide.[10]

horizontal integration: a marketing strategy in which a company acquires or merges with another company

The Italian company Luxottica offers brands and subsidiaries including Ray-Ban, Oakley, Sunglass Hut, and LensCrafters. The company grew vertically by acquiring other firms as it expanded internationally. For instance, in 1995 it bought U.S. Shoe Company to gain access to the LensCrafters subsidiary. Other acquisitions then followed. From manufacture to distribution to retail outlets, Luxottica has become a global vertically integrated giant.[11]

Horizontal Integration

When a company acquires or merges with another company at the same level of the distribution channel, the strategy is horizontal integration. These efforts include manufacturers joining with other manufacturers, wholesalers acquiring other wholesalers, or retailers merging with or acquiring other retailers. Not long ago, the retail chain Best Buy acquired Chinese giant Five Star. One decision was whether to retain the two brand names and operate independently or to merge the brands. The Best Buy brand was unknown in China and Five Star was well known. Strategic choices such as these accompany horizontal integration efforts (Clow and Baack, 2011).

vertical marketing system: a distribution arrangement in which the producer, wholesaler, and retailer perform marketing activities as a unified system

Vertical Marketing Systems and International Strategic Alliances

A **vertical marketing system** distribution arrangement involves the producer, wholesaler, and retailer performing marketing activities acting as a unified system. These systems determine the extent to which various functions will be integrated into the distribution system. Often vertical marketing systems include partial ownership shared by the cooperating companies.

International strategic alliances create enduring cooperative arrangements between firms that utilize resources from distinct firms headquartered in two or more countries; much in the same way as vertical marketing systems. Utilizing international strategic alliances in a distribution channel enables firms to establish a more effective method to deliver products (Mehta et al., 2006). As firms continue to build longer-term relationships with international channel members, this type of alliance will continue to grow. Such was the case when Siemens Worldwide, located in Germany, partnered with China's Huawei to form an alliance aimed at competing in China's 3G mobile technology market (Parkhe, 1991).

GRAY MARKETS

A **gray market** involves distributing products through channels not authorized by the marketer of the product.[12] In international marketing, the process is often referred to as *parallel importing*, or the use of gray market (or grey market) tactics across international borders (Inman, 1993).

gray market: the practice of distributing products through distribution channels that are not authorized by the marketer of the product

With parallel importing, international distributors begin to sell a product in either unauthorized countries or through unauthorized retailers. Wholesalers buy a product in one country at a low price and resell it at a marked up price in other markets or to unauthorized retailers. A gray market creates a problem when a producer markets products in a home country and in foreign countries. The producer ends up competing domestically against its own brands that were imported into the country by overseas distributors.

In general, gray marketing is legal. It does, however, violate almost all marketing channel agreements. Marketers lose control over key parts of products, such as a manufacturer's warranty, in those markets. While consumers and retailers selling gray market goods may obtain lower prices and access to goods, the manufacturer and the retailer with exclusive rights both suffer. Responses to gray market challenges take the form of contractual and legal responses.

Contractual approaches include both proactive and reactive approaches. Proactively, exporting companies can clearly spell out terms that indicate gray marketing violates the agreement and can lead to termination of the arrangement. The reactive contractual response will be to dissolve the arrangement with the distributors that violate agreements. Then, either new distributors are found or the organization may stop shipping items to distributors selling via gray market tactics.

Legal responses take place with local courts. Sony Corporation of Japan filed and won a lawsuit that claimed that the company Nuplayer of United Kingdom was utilizing parallel exporting tactics with its distribution of the game consoles. Nuplayer was ordered by the High Court of Justice in London to discontinue selling the consoles (Smith, 2005).

INTERNATIONAL INCIDENT

While working for an international company that conducts business in Ethiopia, you discover that a major wholesaler is selling your products to retailers that your company does not authorize. Also, the prices are lower than those charged to the authorized retailers.

(Continued)

(Continued)

The wholesaler plays a major role in distributing your products in the region and is one of your biggest channel members worldwide. A small authorized retailer hears about the practice and has threatened to stop carrying your product until the problem is resolved. Your company has experienced problems with the wholesaler in the past, but you badly need its business due to its size and expertise in the region. You must balance the needs of the small, authorized retailer with the unauthorized actions of the wholesaler. What do you do? How do you address the power imbalance between the two intermediaries? What types of power do you think your firm can exert? Would it be wise to do so?

INTERNATIONAL MARKETING IN DAILY LIFE

MANAGING INTERNATIONAL MARKETING CHANNEL FUNCTIONS

International marketing channel members perform many value-added activities. Overall, marketing channel members bring efficiency and a level of continuity to what would otherwise be a chaotic process of delivering goods from producers to consumers. Table 13.4 presents the various functions of international marketing channel members.

To illustrate the management of various channel functions, consider the export and sale of electric toothbrushes to international consumers. Many dentists agree that an electric toothbrush advances oral hygiene significantly. Patients suffer lower levels of gum disease and removing plaque is easier. In addition, increasing evidence suggests that quality dental care is strongly related to overall health. The Proctor & Gamble toothbrush brand, Oral-B, is a worldwide leader in electric toothbrush technology. The brand has successfully penetrated markets globally, including Central and South America, Europe, and the Asia Pacific region. The company is currently making in-roads in the Middle East by overcoming the various cultural, technological, promotional, and distribution challenges.[13] Every factor that influences international marketing was involved in the process.

TABLE 13.4   Functions of International Marketing Channel Members

Research market needs	Determine buyer needs and ability to purchase
Promote products to end users and channel members	Use financial and marketing incentives to increase purchases
Fulfill order-taking duties	Includes order entry, order fulfillment, and order delivery
Communicate with other channel members	Share information about customer buying patterns and preferences along with local market research information
Warehousing, inventory control, and materials handling	Store products until they are sold, keep track of items, move products within both the manufacturing and the warehousing systems
Address discrepancies of assortment	Manage demand for a wide array of products by consumers with producers' desire to manufacture a limited array
Secure payment and extend credit	Provide reassurance that payment will be made, and follow through with actual payment
Transport products to channel members and end users	Select method of transportation

RESEARCH MARKET NEEDS

Intermediaries helped Proctor & Gamble export the Oral-B line of products by providing information about the degree of dental care in a region and the availability of retail outlets willing to place the product prominently before potential consumers. The intermediaries identified the number and type of individuals that might be convinced to try this new form of dental care. In less-developed economies, questions pertaining to infrastructure would be addressed as part of such an analysis.

The emphasis on dental hygiene and care can be influenced by cultural trends, particularly with reference to the importance of having bright shiny teeth and a white smile. Language barriers come into play in explaining the nature of an "electric" toothbrush. Political and legal forces define whether the product is considered to be a medicinal item, making it subject to local medical laws and statutes. The economic status of a target nation affects the number of citizens that could afford the item. Infrastructure influences the sale and delivery of items, in terms of getting the product into the hands of consumers, the type of electric currency delivered to homes, as well as its availability on a daily basis. Battery technology is often placed into electric toothbrushes so they may be charged and used when needed.

PROMOTE PRODUCTS

When promoting the product to other channel members at the retail level and to end users, intermediaries can offer a great deal of assistance. Proctor & Gamble promotes products to both wholesalers and retailers. Assistance to intermediaries might take the form of volume purchase incentives, cooperative advertising, and other methods designed to convince them to carry the product. In some countries, wholesalers are willing to help promote the toothbrushes to retailers. Retailers would then promote products to the ultimate consumer by use of discounts, coupons, premiums (free item given with the purchase of a toothbrush), contests (best smile), sweepstakes (drawings for free products), bonus packs (toothbrushes in combination with toothpaste), and perhaps even free samples, such as in-store demonstrations of using the product. These types of promotional activities are a large part of marketing channel responsibilities.

ORDER PROCESSING

Order processing consists of all the activities associated with fulfilling a customer's order, including order entry, order fulfilment, and order delivery. Technological developments, including Internet and mobile technologies, have influenced this area of distribution. In many contexts, order processing technologies have significantly influenced order-time-to-delivery cycles. This may be particularly relevant if small initial purchases are made by intermediaries, to be followed up with larger orders should the toothbrush achieve market penetration.

The group of people involved with order processing, termed the *operational network*, also plays a vital role in order fulfilment (Welker and Wijngaard, 2009). Although technology rapidly changes the international marketing landscape, people continue to play a vital role in international marketing success.

COMMUNICATE WITH CHANNEL MEMBERS

Channel members communicate frequently with other members of the international marketing channel. Sharing information about customer buying patterns and preferences would be one key part of marketing electric toothbrush products.

Some consumers might experience the purchase risk associated with buying an item that totally changes their dental care and morning or evening grooming routines. Local market research information would also be helpful. Should the number of local dentists be limited, it might be helpful for Proctor & Gamble's marketing team to find additional ways to transmit information to local customers about the health benefits of the products, possibly through physicians or small medical clinics. Information on local markets becomes a crucial part of revising current marketing strategies.

WAREHOUSING, INVENTORY CONTROL, AND MATERIALS HANDLING

Warehousing involves storing products until they are sold. Electric toothbrushes would not require a great deal of storage space, which would mean a warehouse may not be needed. Marketing channel members also focus on inventory control. Maintaining an optimal inventory of products that will meet consumer demand without burdening the system with excessive stock constitutes a challenge for logistics managers. In the case of electric toothbrushes, identifying the amount needed in order to always have products in stock without an excess would be the key. Materials handling includes all activities associated with moving products within the manufacturing and warehousing systems.

ADDRESS DISCREPANCIES OF ASSORTMENT

One fundamental concern in all domestic and international marketing channels is the discrepancy of assortment problem. The problem results from the simple idea that producers generally desire to produce a large number of a limited variety of products, while consumers usually desire limited quantities of a wide variety of products.[14] To remedy this discrepancy, channel members engage in what is known as the *sorting function*. The sorting function includes sorting out, accumulating, allocating, and assorting, as described in Table 13.5.

By performing these functions, channel members are able to ensure that the needs of all parties, including producers, wholesalers, and retailers, are met by the channel structure. Intermediaries sort electric toothbrushes in combination with other small electronic consumer products, such as electric razors and hair-cutting devices. They also sort them to be combined with other dental products, including pre-rinse, mouthwash, toothpaste, and dental floss. Wholesalers divide larger inventories of electric toothbrushes into smaller units to be purchased within the local retail distribution system, such as drug stores, department stores, and possibly grocery stores or other outlets. Retailers are able to accumulate these personal care items to provide an assortment of products to consumers.

TABLE 13.5   Revolving Discrepancies of Assortment

Sorting Out	Channel members break heterogeneous deliveries into relatively homogeneous stocks of products
Accumulating	Channel members accumulate products for retailers and retailers accumulate products for consumers
Allocating	Channel members break down large inventories into smaller units that are demanded by downstream members
Assorting	Channel members build assortments of various goods for distribution throughout the marketing channel

SECURE PAYMENT AND EXTEND CREDIT

Documentation plays an important role in order processing. In particular, a bill of exchange is used to facilitate order processing and payments. The bill of exchange represents an agreement between parties in which one party, a *drawer*, directs a second party, a *drawee*, to issue a payment to yet another party, a *payee*. A bill of exchange creates a secure transaction for both parties.

Another instrument that facilitates order fulfilment and payment, a letter of credit, is a document issued by a bank to signal the creditworthiness of a buyer to a seller. The letter of credit ensures the seller of the buyer's creditworthiness by stating that the bank backs the buyer's credit. These agreements are made between the electric toothbrush manufacturer and all intermediaries (wholesalers and retailers) that purchase and resell the product.

TRANSPORTATION

The global transportation of products will be an important part of international marketing channels. Products must be delivered reliably and effectively. Deliveries are reliable when they are on time. They are effective when the shipments arrive undamaged by the mode of transportation. Several transportation modes are available to international companies. The Oral-B toothbrush might be delivered in larger quantities using delivery trucks or possibly even the mail system in smaller packages.

MAKING CHANNEL ARRANGEMENTS AND CHOOSING CHANNEL PARTNERS

A *channel arrangement* guides the administration of the marketing functions to be performed in the distribution system. *Channel partners* are organizations with relationships that help move products from producers to consumers. Three forms of channel partner systems are contractual, administered, and partnership. Each results in unique relationships between organizations in the channel arrangement.

A *contractual channel arrangement* consists of a binding contract that identifies the tasks to be performed by each channel member with regard to production, delivery, sorting, pricing, and promotional support. International contractual arrangements specify legal elements of the relationship, including the country holding jurisdiction over disputes. These types of contracts tend to include well-defined details with little room for interpretation. The agreements assist companies of all sizes with international marketing campaigns and are particularly useful for smaller companies attempting to expand internationally. Phoenix Footwear Group (U.S.) entered into a contractual channel agreement with the Canada Shoe Corporation for an exclusive footwear distribution arrangement for the Canadian marketplace.[15]

An *administered channel arrangement* includes one dominant member in the distribution channel. *Channel captains* coordinate the marketing tasks provided by the channel members. Powerful manufacturers often become channel captains. Many vertical marketing systems feature channel captain arrangements, such as those created by South Korea's Samsung in its distribution system.

A *partnership channel arrangement* permits members of the channel to work cooperatively for the benefit of all firms involved. Sharing information will be one key element of an effective partnership. Developing these arrangements in international markets can be complicated by factors in the global environment, including differences in technology and infrastructure, legal restrictions, and cultural nuances.

bill of exchange: an agreement between parties in which one party, a drawer, directs a second party, the drawee, to issue a payment to another party, the payee

letter of credit: a document issued by a bank to signal the creditworthiness of a buyer to a seller

INTERNATIONAL INCIDENT

As a student in college, you took four years of Spanish and believed you were fluent in the language. You travel to Brazil on a business junket, exploring opportunities to market your company's product to various distributors. Upon arrival, you notice that most of the Brazilians are speaking Portuguese, a language that is similar enough to Spanish that you can follow much of the conversation. In an attempt to break the ice, you offer a phrase in Spanish meant to compliment them. Instead, they seem miffed. What did you do that was culturally inappropriate?

LEARNING OBJECTIVE #5:

How do marketing managers utilize channel power and oversee negotiation processes?

MANAGING CHANNEL POWER AND NEGOTIATION PROCESSES

horizontal channel conflict: conflict that occurs between members of a marketing channel at the same level

vertical channel conflict: conflict that occurs when there are disputes between channel members at different levels in the system

marketing channel power: the ability of one channel member to control or influence the marketing decisions of another channel member

Two major types of channel conflict occur in international distribution channels, horizontal conflict and vertical conflict. **Horizontal channel conflict** emerges when disputes occur between members of a channel at the same level, for example, between retailers carrying the same product. One retailer may be upset about the unfair pricing of the other company. **Vertical channel conflict** occurs when disagreements arise between channel members at different levels in the system, such as between a wholesaler and a producer, or between a producer and a retailer.

MANAGING CHANNEL POWER

Channel members seek to gain or maintain control and manage channel conflict through the use of various power bases. **Marketing channel power** is the ability of one channel member to control the marketing decisions of another channel member.[16] Table 13.6 displays five sources of marketing channel power.

TABLE 13.6   Power Bases in International Marketing Channels

Legitimate
Referent
Expert
Reward
Coercive

Legitimate

Legitimate power results from contractual channel arrangements. It may be created through contracts and formal agreements in which channel members agree to certain conditions of distribution and yield to the legitimate power of other channel partners. M4 Science Corporation of the United States recently signed an international distribution agreement with Fukuda Corporation of Japan to establish distribution channels in the Japanese market.[17] Legitimate channel power for M4 Science resulted from the specifics of the distribution contract.

Referent

Referent power rises when channel members desire to be associated or identified with a particular producer or product. Marketers of prestigious products hold referent power. This form emerges when several potential channel members wish to carry and promote a product. Any retailer wishing to carry Sony products might defer to the referent power held by the Sony Corporation.

Expert

Channel leaders are able to exert influence when other members perceive the organization to be specialists in the marketing of the product or service. Expert power can reside with any marketing channel member. In international settings, expertise results from having the best understanding of local conditions. Local intermediaries in host countries often enjoy power based on expertise. The successful children's apparel chain Mamas & Papas of the United Kingdom entered into a franchising arrangement with Al Tayer Group of the United Arab Emirates.[18] The expert knowledge that the Al Tayer Group has in the Middle East region was a valuable asset in the relationship.

Reward

One straightforward type of power in the international marketing channel comes from the ability to reward other members. Producers reward international marketing channel members by offering better profit margins, providing product incentives, and signing exclusive channel member agreements. Rewards in the marketing channel are often based on perceptions of equity, which suggests rewards in the marketing system in the form of some type of compensation should be based on a channel member's contribution to overall channel success (Stern et al., 1996). Celplas Industries Nigeria Limited, a leading household products company in Lagos, recently rewarded its distributors in the country for exceptional performance by giving items including automobiles, motorcycles, appliances, and televisions to them. Rewards including these can help foster improved relations throughout the marketing channel (Abdulaziz, 2010).

Coercive

Companies demonstrate coercive power when they sanction other channel members for the failure to perform various marketing duties. Quite commonly, reductions in discounts, allowances, or profit margins may be instituted by channel leaders as forms of marketing channel coercion.

The retailer Wal-Mart plays a significant role in the Mexican economy and business environment. The company sells almost 30% of all supermarket food in Mexico, and overall sales make up 2% of the Mexican gross domestic product. As such, the company leverages its size and importance to coerce other channel members to give the company favorable terms.[19]

The disadvantage of using coercion comes from the potential for a decline in trust, which would be particularly damaging for a company trying to establish a positive relationship in a host country. Further, coercive tactics can injure the status of an organization with various companies and governments in other countries.

TRUST AND COMMITMENT IN INTERNATIONAL MARKETING CHANNELS

Power struggles and imbalance lead to instability in the marketing channel. Effective marketing channels are based on mutual trust and commitment rather than on the displays of channel power. *Marketing channel trust* refers to the willingness to rely on other marketing channel members, and *marketing channel commitment* reflects the desire of channel members to continue channel relationships (Morgan and Hunt, 1994). Trust and commitment lead to improved cooperation and coordination of marketing channel activities.

CROSS-CULTURAL NEGOTIATION AND INTERNATIONAL MARKETING CHANNELS

International marketing involves negotiation. Consequently, the successful management of international marketing channels requires close attention (Phatak and Habib, 1996). Cultural differences often impact negotiations. International marketers work to control or limit the potentially negative effects of cultural differences.

In Japan, South Korea, and Mexico, the buyer is king. In negotiations, the cultural expectation will be that the buyer should receive a more beneficial deal solely because that individual makes the purchase. Negotiation simulations across countries suggest the presence of this bargaining advantage (Requejo and Graham, 2008).

STAGES IN THE NEGOTIATION PROCESS

Negotiations typically follow the process displayed in Table 13.7. While stages in the process can be longer or shorter or can have varying importance depending on the countries or marketers involved, in general the same stages apply to any negotiation (Greenhalgh, 2001).

Negotiations commence before the involved parties meet. The preparation stage marks the beginning. In the first stage, marketers prepare for the interactions and look for the negotiating tactics that might succeed. This involves role playing or practicing the negotiation, collecting information regarding the company and country involved in the negotiation, or setting written guidelines regarding the outcome. Successful negotiations result from detailed, thoughtful preparation.

TABLE 13.7   Stages of Negotiation

Preparation
Relationship Building
Information Gathering
Information Using
Bidding
Closing the Deal
Implementing the Agreement

After marketers complete preparations, relationship building follows. Cultural variables influence the tactics to be used. Managers in collectivist cultures such as Ecuador, Venezuela, Indonesia, and Guatemala normally focus heavily on relationship building prior to any discussion of bargaining issues. Conversations about families, countries, or key contacts within either company that both negotiators know may occur. In many settings, the relationship building stage of the negotiation process lasts a long time and over multiple meetings. Negotiations should typically be between members of a company holding the same status level, particularly in high power distance countries, where status differences are more influential. If one partner sends its chief marketing officer, the counterpart's representative should hold the rank of chief marketing officer or a similar title.

As relationships form, marketers attempt to gain information about the other party through continual research or discussions with the negotiation partner through information gathering. One goal of this process is to collect insights regarding the agreement the other party seeks. The information can then be used by the negotiator.

To reach that final agreement, the negotiation involves bidding. In this stage, the negotiating parties make gradual steps from their most preferred positions or desired outcomes to an actual, or final, agreed-upon outcome. Negotiations often plan for a BATNA or *best alternative to a negotiated agreement*. BATNA signifies the option that can be used if an optimal agreement cannot be reached. As such, it becomes a source of power for a negotiating party. Negotiating parties have a great deal to gain by understanding each other's BATNA position (Lewicki et al., 2010).

BATNA: best alternative to a negotiated agreement

When the bidding stage ends successfully, the negotiators can close the deal. Here, the parties formalize an agreement in a culturally recognized or legal fashion. For some cultures, a handshake represents a finalized deal. In others, the deal is not complete until contracts are signed. Arriving at a successful outcome results from leveraging the preparation, the relationship built, and information gathered.

The final step of the negotiation will be the implementation of the agreement. As with other aspects of international marketing, the implementation of agreements for international marketing channels or other marketing components requires that actions be undertaken in accordance with the contract or settlement. Both parties in the negotiation ensure that they perform the agreed-upon actions. In some cases, the negotiated terms will not be successfully implemented. In those cases, the sides try to graciously break the agreement. In cultures that focus on relationships, maintaining a relationship when implementation fails may lead to more beneficial terms in later interactions.

CULTURAL INFLUENCES ON NEGOTIATIONS

Cultural variables influence international negotiations. Key areas of concern include interests, behaviors, and desired outcomes; relationships, communication, and perceptions; negotiation context; Hofstede's dimensions; managerial thought processes; and the overall negotiation culture.

Interests, Behaviors, and Desired Outcomes

Culture affects negotiations in many ways, including the interests and priorities of the negotiating parties, the strategic behaviors of the parties, and the patterns of interactions between them (Brett, 2007). All individuals have interests and priorities, as will the organizations involved in the negotiation process. Specific behaviors and patterns of interaction, such as choice of direct/confrontational or indirect/cooperative interactions follow. Negotiating parties choose tactics based on the cultural context. As an example, collectivist and high-context cultures including India and Hungary lead to interaction processes that differ from individualist and/or low-context cultures, such as Australia, Switzerland, or Finland.

Relationships, Communication, and Perceptions

Four key areas receive attention when dealing with cross-cultural interactions (Hall, 1960). These areas can dramatically influence the negotiation process:

- relationships
- communication
- time perceptions
- space perceptions

In terms of relationships, negotiators need to know whether long-term connections are desirable in the other culture.

Time perceptions, the third area, include whether the culture is polychronic (polychromatic) or monochronic (monochromatic). A monochronic culture is one in which negotiations and operations occur in a one-at-a-time fashion. A polychonic culture involves multi-tasking, or more than one activity taking place with disruptions, stoppages, and restarts as a common feature. An individual who is used to a monochronic pace and method of operation may be disturbed and upset when interactions are constantly interrupted.

Space perceptions involve the role of personal space, or the physical distance between individuals in interpersonal interactions and negotiations. Closeness might signal aggressiveness or intrusion in Romania but trust in another country, such as Saudi Arabia.

Negotiation Context

The overall negotiation context or climate affects each of the four key areas. Research suggests that both the environmental context and the immediate context significantly influence negotiations (Phatak and Habib, 1996). The environmental context includes variables that cannot be easily controlled. These include issues such as legal and political developments, international economics, ideological differences, and culture. Factors in the immediate context include those things that are easier to control, such as the bargaining power of the participants, relationships, and the processes by which potential conflicts are resolved.

Hofstede's Dimensions

Cross-cultural negotiation research provides some guidelines that can be used for successful international negotiations. Hofstede's cultural dimensions, as previously noted in Chapter 2, may provide useful insights.[20] Regarding power distance, negotiators carefully consider the social class of potential customers and show proper respect. Negotiators work to convince partners that a person of equal status attends the bargaining sessions. Some cultures, such as those found in China and Japan, are high in uncertainty avoidance, and as a result, buyers or channel partners from these cultures will likely demand rules and procedures for dealing with uncertain events if they should arise.

Further, Chinese and Japanese employees operate in collectivist cultures. Consequently they prefer negotiating teams rather than one-on-one negotiations. The inclusion of a marketing team, rather than a reliance on individual salespeople, helps form solid business relationships.

Gender roles are also considered. Although the role of women in business is evolving and many women have assumed roles with greater power, members of some cultures still prefer to conduct business with men.

Thought Processes

People from various cultures perceive the world and think in different ways (Nisbett, 2003). Thought processes are shaped heavily by culture, tradition, and the educational system in play in the specific country, and are critical to negotiations. Western cultures tend to rely more heavily on logic when arriving at conclusions than do Eastern cultures. Eastern cultures tend to view negotiations holistically, whereas Westerners tend to focus on specific parts of a problem or negotiation issue.

Significant time, resources, and attention will be given to the entire international negotiation process. Negotiating teams are carefully selected and given appropriate training. The negotiation process will be monitored very carefully to ensure that agreements that are reached are beneficial for all parties involved.

Overall Negotiation Culture

Two different approaches to culture exist. Information-oriented cultures view the negotiation process in one way; marketers from relationship-oriented cultures perceive negotiations differently. Table 13.8 identifies features common to these two types of cultures. The two approaches lead to different behaviors during negotiation. Israeli and United Kingdom negotiators are more likely to promise something during negotiations, while Brazilian and Korean negotiators are less likely to do so. French and Taiwanese negotiators are more inclined to reveal personal details about themselves; whereas Japanese negotiators tend to reveal little personal information. German negotiators typically give commands during negotiations. Brazilians are likely to use the word "no" while the Japanese and Chinese almost never use the word during a negotiation. American negotiators also avoid using the word no, and are likely to refer to the opposing negotiator as "you," whereas negotiators in other countries will not.

TABLE 13.8   Information-Oriented and Relationship-Oriented Negotiation Cultures

Information Oriented	Relationship Oriented
Focus on Competition	Focus on Increasing Trust
Low Context	High Context
Less Respect for Authority	Authority and Position Play Key Roles
Individualism	Collectivism
Impatient	Less Focused on Time

Source: Adapted from Requejo and Graham (2008).

As this summary of negotiation suggests, effective bargaining in an international context requires attention to detail. Negotiators should be chosen based on personality characteristics that indicate they enjoy working with people who are different from themselves, and that they are intrigued by cultural differences. Ethnocentrism likely will stall nearly any bargaining session.

CHAPTER 13: REVIEW AND RESOURCES

Strategic Implications

Choosing and managing channels of distribution and retail outlet formats constitute strategic decisions. The executive team matches products, prices, and other variables with target markets in other countries. International market research information becomes especially important in this effort. Then, decisions can be made regarding how the international marketing channel will be integrated into the company's existing channel structure.

One major decision for policy makers pertains to the appropriate level of distribution intensity in each country. The match between the firm's existing channel structures and the structures required in the targeted country is also considered. Company leaders make decisions regarding the methods to be used in managing distribution channels, including push and pull strategies, and channel arrangements, such as vertical integration, horizontal integration, or a vertical marketing system, in advance of entering a new host country. They also examine issues related to physical distribution to make sure customers can be efficiently and effectively reached.

Tactical Implications

Marketing managers are designated to make arrangements with international marketing channel members. The issues present in the 5 Cs are considered—cost, coordination, coverage, cooperation, and control. Managers may work with existing channel members, if possible, or attempt to find new members to handle the international exchange. Managers also consider the appropriate match of international retailers to the international strategy set forth during the formation of the overall marketing strategy. Many varieties of international retailers operate in various countries and the choice of retailer is important. Managers at the tactical level are also instrumental in assessing channel member performance and, when necessary, discontinuing channel relationships and contracts.

Operational Implications

Entry-level employees and first-line supervisors work constantly to ensure that the product flows efficiently through the marketing channel. Managers monitor the daily operations of the system, with a particular focus on maintaining positive relationships with international wholesalers and retailers. Managers also inform those at higher ranks about issues pertaining to maintaining control of the channel, performing channel leader duties, dealing with channel conflict, and exerting channel power when necessary. First-line supervisors work to ensure that valid information is shared among channel members, with special attention paid to local market conditions.

TERMS

international marketing channel	international logistics
international distribution	distribution intensity

intensive distribution	vertical marketing system
selective distribution	gray market
exclusive distribution	bill of exchange
Intermediaries	letter of credit
agent middlemen	horizontal channel conflict
merchant middlemen	vertical channel conflict
vertical integration	marketing channel power
horizontal integration	BATNA

REVIEW QUESTIONS

1. Define the term international marketing channel.

2. Describe international distribution and international logistics.

3. What three distribution intensity strategies can marketers employ?

4. What are the 5 Cs of marketing channel structure?

5. Describe the direct and indirect international channels of distribution.

6. How is an agent middleman different from a merchant middleman?

7. Describe the concept of channel length.

8. What factors influence the choice of international distribution systems?

9. Describe the natures of vertical integration, horizontal integration, and vertical marketing systems.

10. What is a gray market?

11. Describe a push strategy and a pull strategy.

12. What functions are performed by marketing channel members?

13. What power bases are found in international marketing channels?

14. What are the stages of negotiation in an international marketing channel dispute?

DISCUSSION QUESTIONS

1. What type of distribution tactic, intensive, selective, or exclusive, do you think should be used for the following products?

    - milk in the United Kingdom

    - luxury jewelry in France

    - high-end automobiles in Germany

    - cigarettes in Mexico

2. The 5 Cs of channel member selection represent key components in the strategic distribution process. Apply the 5 Cs to the following products:

- school supplies

- sports equipment

- fast food

- perfume

3. Table 13.4 provides a list of the functions of international marketing channel members. Apply the list to the following companies, industries, or situations:

    - automobile manufacturers

    - disposable pens and cigarette lighters

    - exclusively distributed goods

    - selectively distributed goods

4. Describe how channel leaders can exert each of the power bases—legitimate, referent, expert, reward, and coercive—on marketing channel members who market televisions in selected retail outlets in Europe.

ANALYTICAL AND INTERNET EXERCISES

1. Search the Internet for websites of major international marketers, such as Carrefour from France. What can you learn about the international marketing channels for these companies and countries? Suggested websites include:

    - Carrefour, www.carrefour.com

    - General Electric, www.ge.com

    - Samsung, www.samsung.com

    - Hyundai, www.hyundai.com/kr

2. Find a product that is intensively distributed in a country of your choice. Look for this information on the Internet. What can you say about its distribution channels in that country?

3. Using the Internet, go to a search engine and find three international marketing channel logistics providers. Examine the websites and note the services these companies offer.

4. Using websites such as www.cia.gov and other resources that explain cultural components, examine the following countries. Explain how the 5 Cs of channel selection would be affected by what you find.

    - Pakistan

    - Sweden

    - Japan

    - South Africa

STUDENT STUDY SITE

Visit **https://study.sagepub.com/banrk2e** to access these free additional learning tools:

- Web Quizzes
- eFlashcards
- SAGE Journal Articles
- Country Fact Sheets
- Chapter Outlines
- Interactive Maps

CASE 13

JDA Software Services

In 1978, James D. Anderson founded JDA Software Services in Canada. The initial goal of the company was to provide software solutions for the retailing industry, but the company rapidly expanded into a full-service, global supply chain management company. By 2010, the company had transformed the distribution processes of more than 6,000 companies in industries including manufacturing, wholesale distribution, third-party logistics, retail, passenger travel, and cargo and freight. Global in scope, the company maintains offices throughout North America, Latin America, Asia, Australia, and Europe, including locations in Brazil, Mexico, Chile, Singapore, Taiwan, India, China, and the Philippines.[21]

One of the main factors leading to the company's success has been an aggressive acquisition strategy. The company has acquired many of the leading brands in the logistics field including i2 Technologies, Manugistics, E3, Intactix, and Arthur. With these services, the company can assist clients in almost all distribution-related problems.

The company focuses on providing services to mid-sized companies. Often these companies face costs or infrastructure barriers to adopted complicated logistics-related software. To overcome them, JDA offers its branded Supply Chain Now solution. The software, hosted via the JDA Private Cloud, leverages cloud computing to avoid the costs and time consumed by onsite technology set-up.[22]

The company recently won the Green Supply Chain Award from the magazine *Supply & Demand Chain Executive*. The award was based on the company's supply chain strategist solution. The process optimizes a company logistics while accounting for carbon emissions, carbon taxes, cap and trade structures, and other sustainability-related components of the process. Compared to competing tools, the JDA approach enables companies to actively monitor these various issues to find the best possible solution.[23]

The use of this software then gives JDA clients a competitive advantage. More channel captains, such as Wal-Mart, require suppliers plus the companies supplying those companies to meet a sustainability code of conduct. Without meeting these guidelines, Wal-Mart will stop ordering. The overall industry trend is the same. One estimate claims

(Continued)

(Continued)

that 6% of leading companies deselected suppliers failing to account for carbon in 2010, while more than 50% of companies are committed to do so in the future (Reese, 2011).

Photo 13.3 displays the opening web page for JDA. The use of a blue background provides a sense of calm and order in what is a turbulent environment. The web page notes a tie-in with OfficeMax, which creates credibility through the name recognition attached to the company. The credibility angle is further reinforced through the reference to JDA granting an award to OfficeMax, which places JDA in a position of authority. Among the many services offered in the banner, "thought leadership" jumps out and invites viewer inquiry. A language option is available for international customers.

JDA Software Services is a full-service, global supply chain management company.

Facing a rapidly changing environment, JDA Software has made aggressive moves in terms of both acquisitions and sustainability leadership. Together these efforts led to first quarter 2011 revenues of $163.6 million, a 24% increase from the previous year, and to the company generating approximately $260 million in cash to fund future actions. With more than 6,000 current customers, the company has a global customer satisfaction rating of 95%, and has become a global leader in channel management technology.[24]

1. Sustainable distribution practices, particularly the management of carbon emissions, have become increasingly important. What role have channel captains such as Wal-Mart played in this process?

2. JDA Software provides services to a broad range of industries. Why do the company's services apply to such a large range of companies?

3. JDA operates on nearly every continent, and in many different countries within those regions. How would the company need to adapt its market channel strategies, dependent on the nation involved?

14

INTERNATIONAL DISTRIBUTION: EXPORTING AND RETAILING

LEARNING OBJECTIVES

After reading and studying this chapter, you should be able to answer the following questions:

1. Why do companies export?
2. What methods of entry into foreign markets can companies use?
3. What are the documents needed for exporting?
4. How can the marketing team effectively operate the five tasks associated with the physical distribution of goods?
5. What factors influence the choice of retail outlets in host countries?

IN THIS CHAPTER

Opening Vignette: Exporting and the Business-to-Business Market: Alibaba.com

OVERVIEW

EXPORTING AND THE BUSINESS-TO-BUSINESS MARKET: ALIBABA.COM

Yahoo.com once was the online company many organizations wanted to copy. Currently, nearly three-fourths of the company's value comes from an investment made in the online Chinese trading website Alibaba.com. The site earned more than *renminbi* 6 billion in 2017, and *China Economic Review* recently named it the top company in China.

The company's roots are in Hangzhou, south-west of Shanghai. Jeffrey Ma , a former schoolteacher, founded the company in 1999 after searching for "Chinese beer" on a U.S. search engine. Recognizing a gap in the marketplace, Jeffrey started an online platform to connect U.S. importers with Chinese suppliers. Over the next decade, the company grew to employ 8,000 people. In 2007, Alibaba.com was listed on the Hong Kong Stock Exchange for $1.7 billion, the largest initial public offering since Google.com.

Alibaba.com achieved success by targeting small- to medium-sized Chinese businesses needing assistance in exporting to the larger global market. Instead of focusing on advertising revenues, the company charges a membership fee and a fee for value-added services. With more than 200 million registered users across 240 countries and regions, Alibaba.com has become the leading online export company.

Distribution plays a key role in the company's success. Alibaba.com headquarters include its famous monitoring room in which maps and moving charts track, in real time, transactions, with larger orders making a larger "ripple." The company maintains its own logistics system and shipping service called Fulfillment. Multiple orders are combined into one international shipment, and buyers can track the orders. The savings to small- and medium-businesses are as high as 30%.

With a majority share of the Chinese business-to-business e-commerce market, Alibaba.com's focus shifted to expanding into new businesses. The company offers China's largest online shopping website (Taobao.com) and an online version of Paypal. com (Alipay.com), and hosts classified ads (Koubei.com). Jeffrey Ma suggested that the company wants to be Google, eBay, Amazon, and Craigslist all at the same time.[1]

Questions for Students

1. How has Alibaba.com leveraged innovations from other companies?

2. Why would Alibaba.com invest in software to assist with the distribution of products for suppliers?

3. Alibaba.com focuses on small- and medium-sized businesses. Why would this be a particularly effective strategy in emerging markets?

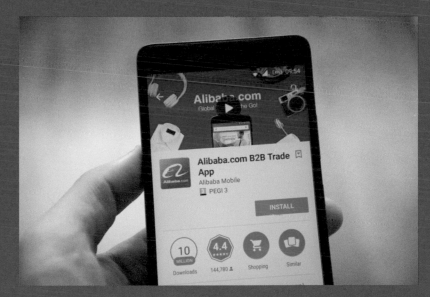

The online Chinese trading website Alibaba.com provides exporting assistance to small- and medium-size Chinese businesses.

OVERVIEW

Many products consumers purchase enter the country through exporting processes. Exporting involves the shipment of the finished product from a foreign country to the country of final purchase. This chapter begins with a review of the exporting process.

It notes the reasons for exporting along with the process of selecting markets to enter. The type of export system used, including direct or indirect, and the different types of intermediaries involved are discussed next. Once in the market, setting of export price takes place. This chapter continues by comparing an export price to a domestic price. A review of the documentation needed to export follows.

The chapter explains the process by which companies ship products and supplies to foreign buyers. The five tasks of physical distribution are noted. The final home for the exported good is often a retail store. A review of international retailing concludes the chapter.

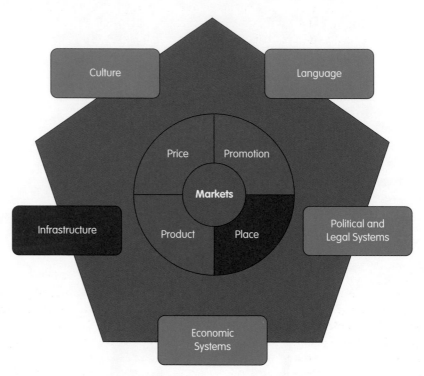

FIGURE 14.1   The International Marketing Context

LEARNING OBJECTIVE #1:

Why do companies export?

EXPORTING CHOICES

Marketers employ various approaches as a company enters a foreign market. To limit risk and cost, in many cases company leaders select *exporting* or shipping a product to a foreign market, regardless of the method of delivery. In 2016, global exporting totalled more than $18 trillion in value.[2] Bringing a foreign product into a market is *importing*.

Relationships between exporting and importing can be complicated. Many of the items shipped across boundaries are the parts or resources businesses need to produce products. The completed products may then be exported. Winget Limited (Seddon

Group, UK) is a major international supplier and exporter of the heavy equipment and mixing products used in the production of other products. The company offers products to be used in the manufacture of artificial and architectural stone products.[3]

Whether business to business, business-to-consumer, or the growing consumer-to-consumer market, exports result from demand in a foreign market. The desire for the product may be relatively latent or is the type of demand in which consumers have a need for an item but are unaware that a product which will meet that need exists.

INTERNAL MOTIVES FOR EXPORTING

Companies export for a variety of reasons. At the most general level, managers decide to export when they believe a company's products can meet a consumer demand while making a profit. Within that general rationale, several more specific explanations for beginning to export exist. Internal reasons often drive a company to export, including those provided in Table 14.1.

TABLE 14.1   Internal Motives for Exporting

Managerial Urge
Unique Product Characteristics
Economies of Scale
Extension of Sales
Lower Risk
Overcapacity

Managerial Urge

The first rationale for exporting noted in Table 14.1, managerial urge, suggests that a managerial champion begins an exporting effort. Often a single person makes the decision. The individual may have experience in the foreign market being targeted or with exporting from a previous position at a separate business. The person simply has a strong motive to expand into new areas. Red Bull creator Dietrich Mateschitz, from Austria, expressed the drive to enter the European and U.S. markets with his high-energy drink. In a few years sales exceeded $140 million annually in the United States, and the company held a 70% share of the market for similar energy drinks by 2001.[4]

Unique Product Characteristics

At times certain product features lead to exporting. A unique asset that consumers will purchase increases the potential to expand a business through exporting. When competitors cannot copy the product easily or when consumers demonstrate low levels of brand awareness that can be increased, the potential to increase sales and profits rises. Other business skills, such as a talented sales force or a leading distribution approach, add further protection from competition and may spur exporting. In the film industry, 3-D movie players are becoming available. The players possess hard-to-copy, unique features, thereby providing an exporting advantage to companies that manufacture them.

Economies of Scale

Exporting to foreign markets increases the size and scope of the business. Economies of scale occur as an increase in the number of units manufactured results in a decrease in the cost per unit. Consequently, company profits often rise by exporting to foreign markets. An international confectionary company producing chocolate, such as the Swiss company Chocoladefabriken Lindt & Sprüngli AG, can increase sales and the margin per item by spreading the fixed costs of making high-quality candy by selling goods in other countries. The company leverages the reputation of Swiss chocolates to reach a wider, global audience.

Extension of Sales

Products experiencing on- and off-seasons may achieve positive results through exporting. Many products including textiles, sports equipment, and tourism go through peak and low sales seasons each calendar year. Exporting to a foreign market helps overcome drops in demand. Ski equipment can be sold in North America during fall and winter and then exported to markets in South America during the North American off season. Wide and Tall Plastic Company, from Hong Kong, exports snow rings, snow ski equipment and tools, and inflatable sports equipment to countries around the world, relying on its website and placement on the Alibaba.com search engine to locate individual customers and distributors in various countries. The organization also serves a trading company in the Asian region. The same would be true for any company manufacturing swimming pools, pool equipment, and swimwear, only during opposite times of the year.

Lower Risk

Exporting products to multiple countries and regions lessens the impacts of economic downturns, government unrest, and various other external risks. Dependency on one market creates greater risk; a decline in that area leads to decreased company sales. Exporting dilutes such a risk by operating in several markets. For example, a recent decline in sales for Coca-Cola, specifically in the areas of diet soda sales and an increased effort to reduce consumption of sugar-based products in Mexico was partially offset by expansion into other markets through products such as Coke Life, which was available in Argentina and Chile and featured an in-between level of calories per serving (64, rather than 1 or zero in diet products and more than 120 in sugar-based drinks) (Trefas Team, 2014).

Numerous internal and external advantages lead companies to export.

Overcapacity

Overcapacity or market saturation in one country often makes exporting to other countries more attractive. Domestic demand for a product may decline in a country. Instead of taking a loss, a firm with warehouses full of products often turns to exporting to sell excess inventory. Examples include firms that manufactured flip phones, laptop computers, and analogue televisions, which became obsolete in more technologically advanced countries but were viable options for consumers in countries with less-developed economies.

EXTERNAL EXPLANATIONS FOR EXPORTING

While internal forces may drive firms to export, factors external to the firm can influence the decision to do so. The global business environment and other forces influence the choice to export. Table 14.2 presents four external factors.

TABLE 14.2   External to the Firm Reasons for Exporting

Change Agents
Foreign Market Features
Domestic Market Features
Unsolicited Orders

Change Agents

Outside change agents may pursue the goal of increasing exports. Trade associations, governmental agencies, port authorities, and many others contact various businesses with the objective of inducing them to export. Often these organizations play key roles by providing the information a firm needs to consider entering a market. In the case of visiting trade delegations, key business decision makers meet with governmental representatives from the foreign market. A face-to-face meeting builds bridges and helps establish the relationships needed to feel comfortable about exporting to a market. One such delegation from Bangladesh visited the Philippines as an attempt to increase trade between the countries, particularly in certain industries. Some of the main industries targeted included plastics, garments, chemical products, and seafood.[5]

Foreign Market Features

The features of potential foreign markets also drive exporting. A foreign country might contain a large group of consumers clamoring for the product. In some instances foreign market similarities with a domestic market increase company confidence regarding the potential to succeed. In other circumstances, features of the country lead to a desire to export. The country may have a large population or have considerable wealth or may be a newly available venue, such as Cuba over the past few years, especially with regard to U.S. and Canadian companies.

The Saudi Arabian market serves as another example. Wealthy oil merchants in that nation crave many of the luxuries enjoyed in the rest of the world. Consequently, producers from a variety of countries export expensive automobiles to Saudi Arabia. More recently, horse racing has grown dramatically in popularity. The Equestrian Club Riyadh lists races, horses, trainers, jockeys, and other information for enthusiasts around the world on its Facebook page. Tourists now travel to the country to participate in the sport in the luxurious racing venues in major cities.

Domestic Market Features

Features of the domestic market may be inviting. A small or limited means of exporting could present the only viable expansion opportunity. A domestic market might be stagnant, saturated, or experience declining demand. Facing difficult domestic conditions or limited opportunities for growth in such a market might lead executives in some companies to look to exporting to increase sales. The National Basketball Association in the United States has targeted China due to its immense population, the popularity of the sport, and market saturation in the domestic market. Other sports such as American football and baseball have followed a similar path, playing games in Mexico each year.

Unsolicited Orders

With the increased availability of communication across national boundaries, many marketers receive unsolicited orders for products. These orders commonly start with the company's website or through promotional activities that reach foreign markets. Unsolicited orders are one common reason for a firm to begin exporting. Having received the request for the product, concerns regarding demand and risk lessen, and business leaders become more confident of success in the to-be-entered market.

Additional Factors

In addition to the motives summarized in Tables 14.1 and 14.2 managers may consider other factors. Among them, various transaction costs will be analyzed. These would include transportation expenses, local taxes, storage costs, and others. Managers also note the role competition plays. When strong competition is present, the motive to export declines as entry becomes more difficult. Conversely, an open market with weak or no competition serves as an inviting opportunity.

MARKET SELECTION

Once company leaders commit to exporting, they move on to select markets to be entered. Often, the process of committing to exporting dictates the countries chosen to be entered, such as in the cases of unsolicited orders or change agents or managerial connections to the market. When a marketing team seeks to enter multiple countries, each option requires screening. Countries can be categorized using the various segmentation processes discussed in Chapter 6. Market research examines the size of the potential market and demand for the product. Such information often results in more effective market screening. Exporting to countries that are culturally and geographically close or similar reduces risk and lowers shipping costs. Consequently, many companies start by first exporting to neighboring countries.

market concentration: the strategy a company uses when it exports to a small number of markets or just one key market and then slowly expands to export to new countries

market spreading: a marketing strategy of growing exports in many different markets simultaneously and rapidly expanding to new markets

A choice also exists between market concentration and market spreading. Market concentration occurs when a company exports to a small number of markets or one key market and then slowly expands into additional countries. Market spreading involves growing exports in many different markets simultaneously and rapid expansion to new markets.

Market concentration and spreading represent two extreme approaches. Typically companies use a method somewhere in between the two. One key consideration will be any first-mover advantage that is present. When barriers keep competitors from exporting to the market, market spreading may be the best approach. In contrast, when many competitors already exist, market concentration will lead to higher market share, which will then give the company a stronger competitive position.

LEARNING OBJECTIVE #2:

What methods of entry into foreign markets can companies use?

EXPORT ENTRY MODES

Companies take advantage of two general modes of exporting, direct and indirect. **Direct exporting**, or *export marketing*, involves the producer or supplier being in charge of marketing to foreign buyers. **Indirect exporting**, or *export selling*, occurs when the manufacturer sells the product to intermediaries that then handle the foreign selling of the product. The choice of form will be based on specific company features, the characteristics of the target market country, and the quality of potential intermediaries in that market. Marketers compare the costs associated with direct exporting against the loss of control with indirect exporting.

direct exporting: also called *export marketing*, a system in which the producer or supplier is responsible for marketing to foreign buyers

HOME-BASED DIRECT EXPORTING

Figure 14.2 identifies methods for direct exporting. Each will be presented individually, although marketers often combine the approaches. Many companies establish a home country-based department to oversee an exporting program. These are *built-in departments*, the simplest of structures. The department contains salespeople responsible for selling the product to buyers in the foreign market, often retailers, but many of the other marketing functions are handled by preexisting, domestic-focused departments. A built-in department approach works well for small firms, firms new to exporting, firms with low exporting volume, or firms with a low commitment to exporting.

indirect exporting: also called *export selling*, a system in which the manufacturer sells the product to intermediaries who then handle the foreign selling of the product

Home Country-Based Activities

Built-in Department

Separate Export Department

Export Sales Subsidiary

Foreign Country-Based Activity

Foreign Sales Branch

Foreign Sales Subsidiary

Foreign-Based Distributors and Agents/Representatives

FIGURE 14.2 Methods of Direct Exporting

A second home country-based option relies on a *separate export department*. Such a department carries out the marketing functions needed to successfully export to the foreign country, including promotional activities, pricing, distribution, and adaptation of the product. For complex firms exporting to a large number of markets, many of which are different from the domestic market, this approach may be best.

Firms with a strong export focus and a large amount of export business often establish *export sales subsidiaries*. This type of subsidiary operates independently from the parent company, almost as a separate firm. It maintains complete control over profit and costs, which in some cases can be more efficient.

FOREIGN-BASED DIRECT EXPORTING

Some company leaders prefer one of the foreign country-based direct exporting structures shown in Figure 14.2. The most common of these involves direct exporting through a *foreign sales branch*. These units typically cover a set area with responsibility for the marketing mix within that area. Opening a branch in the region facilitates buyer visits, builds stronger relationships, and in some cases may circumvent government regulations on foreign company activities.

In cases of a large amount of exporting business, company leaders may make the decision to change the foreign sales branch into a *foreign sales subsidiary*. The organization will be more autonomous than a foreign sales branch. The approach grants more authority and independence to the foreign exporting activities.

The final foreign-based direct exporting method features *foreign-based distributors and agents/representatives*. The distinction between distributors and agents revolves around possession of the title or ownership. Distributors take ownership or represent customers for the exporter while agents do not and instead work to connect the exporter to buyers. In both cases, the foreign location of the distributors or agents means that using these intermediaries counts as direct exporting. The use of domestic-based intermediaries, on the other hand, is classified as indirect exporting.

INTERNATIONAL MARKETING IN DAILY LIFE

EXPORTING CHOPSTICKS

People use chopsticks as utensils worldwide. Companies that manufacture them invest in forests and other wooded areas. Wood or bamboo is cut and honed into the final product. In Indonesia, the PT Multisentral Gemilang company produces square-head chopsticks. Should the firm decide to export on a wider basis to restaurants and other customers, the home country-based approaches would be most viable. Company executives could authorize some members of the sales department to seek out Asian restaurants in other countries. Multisentral might also create a separate export department for that purpose. The company would employ export sales subsidiaries until it establishes a stronghold in a region, such as Europe.

Larger-scale operations selling chopsticks might include the use of a foreign sales branch, possibly located in a major metropolitan area, such as New York or Quebec. It is unlikely that Multisentral would expand beyond such an approach to a foreign sales subsidiary or use sales agents or merchants, unless the company also expanded the scope of products offered.

INDIRECT EXPORTING

When exporting indirectly, marketers choose between either merchants or agents. Merchants take ownership or title to the product while agents do not. Figure 14.3 lists the common types of merchants and agents.

Merchants
Export Merchant
Trading Company
Agents
Export Commission House
Resident Buyer
Broker

FIGURE 14.3   Types of Merchants and Agents

Merchants

The marketing team selects from between two main types of merchants. The first, *export merchants*, buy from multiple companies, often from several countries. While called "export" merchants, these merchants typically both import and export products. With operations in many countries, these merchants often maintain relationships globally and choose from multiple companies when buying. Export merchants often purchase commodities or products where the brand plays a limited role and those that are easily sold.

Trading companies operate in many different countries, particularly in emerging markets and in Japan and Korea. The key concern for exporters will be making sure that trading companies do not hold a monopoly on exporting to a country. When such a situation exists, the exporting company will work to establish a relationship with individuals at the trading company.

Agents

The three main types of agents are listed in Figure 14.3. *Export commission houses* represent foreign buyers in the domestic market. These organizations act as purchasing agents when contacted by foreign companies. Commission houses offer a simple and often efficient method of exporting products to foreign markets.

An exporter may also choose to employ *resident buyers*. These firms resemble export commission houses except they become permanent employees of the buyers, instead of the temporary, purchase-oriented export commission employees. This creates the opportunity to build relationships between the manufacturer and the resident buyer, which increases the potential for repeat business and the reduction of any cultural differences that might create difficulties.

Brokers play a different indirect exporting role. These agents work to bring a buyer and seller together. Brokers focus on introductions and facilitation of contractual arrangements rather than on handling the product.[6] Typically, brokers receive a commission on each sale they facilitate. An overarching organization such as the Australian Institute of Business Brokers, which was established in 1989, helps to ensure that quality, legal, and ethical services are provided by member organizations. Services such as these are valuable for international marketers.[7]

INTERNATIONAL INCIDENT

A Danish construction engineer took on a major building project in India. He hired three local engineers to assist in the development and oversight of the endeavor. After a few weeks, the Dane, thinking he was building rapport with the engineers, used some mild profanity while talking with them. His idea was to help them relax while working. Later in the same week, he was trying to attract the attention of one of the engineers on site. He snapped his fingers to signal the person and then beckoned him with a curled forefinger. The engineer stormed over, and said, "I am tired of being treated like a dog. I quit." How could a cultural assimilator have prevented this unfortunate event from taking place?

PRICING EXPORTS

When entering a foreign market, pricing the product presents unique challenges. Companies may choose to set export prices that are lower than domestic prices, higher than domestic prices, or on a par with domestic prices. Each approach presents advantages and disadvantages. Consequently, a company may use different pricing approaches in various markets.

Prices that are lower than domestic prices best match cases in which low consumer awareness of the brand or product category exists. The lower price encourages product trials to help gain initial market share. They may also be necessary when local competitors leverage local, low-cost resources to offer a less expensive version of the product being exported. Entering a market with low prices is similar to penetration pricing for new products.

Charging higher prices than domestic companies often results from the costs associated with exporting. Governmental duties, transportation expenses, market research in the foreign country, and various other expenses all lead to higher exporting costs. The higher price helps to cover the expenses. A higher price also may lessen the additional risk from exporting to new markets. Charging higher prices when entering a new market is similar to skimming pricing for new products.

Keeping the prices the same in the domestic and foreign market will be the simplest pricing choice. When a company initially enters a market, using a par price often allows for the use of the same overall positioning and marketing approach. Matching competitor prices can be especially helpful when the company does not have the ability or time to learn about the market before entering, such as in the case of unsolicited orders.

LEARNING OBJECTIVE #3:

What are the documents needed for exporting?

EXPORTING DOCUMENTATION

The exporting process requires various types of paperwork. Some satisfy government regulations; others finalize the actual business transaction. Effective international marketing programs include paying careful attention to making sure shipments are not held up due to poorly filled-out or missing documents.

REGULATIONS AND DOCUMENTATION

Governments require documentation before they allow goods to enter a country. Ports-of-entry customs officials expect proper documentation and selectively search some containers entering a country. One advantage of using indirect exporting is that the intermediary assumes the responsibility and has the expertise needed to manage customs entry requirements.

Governments have the power to limit imports and exports. Such restrictions may be for national security reasons, economic concerns, or to protect political constituencies. Maintaining strict restrictions on the import of drugs across national boundaries is a major international concern. As an example, the importation of prescription drugs into the United States from unapproved foreign sources is generally against the law. Recently drug purchases from Canada gained public attention because many Canadian drugs are less expensive than the same drugs in the United States. Companies also may face paying custom duties or taxes on the product before being allowed to bring them into the country.

EXPORT AND IMPORT LICENSES

One of the primary documents required for exporting from a country is an export license. For many countries these may be general or validated licenses. The differences between the two licenses are driven by the type of product, the final destination for the product, and the use or user. General licenses apply to products which are not highly regulated. The licenses typically declare the product, its value, and final destination. Validated licenses are more complicated and contain far more information pertaining to the various regulations that apply to the product being exported. Most countries also require import licenses, which also vary in type and regulation.

Understanding that companies seeking to export often feel overwhelmed by the various licensing requirements, various electronic services provide the assistance needed to deal with the process. Systems include the Electronic Request for Item Classification (ERIC), System for Tracking Export License Applications (STELA), the Export License Application and Information Network (ELAIN), and the Simplified Network Application Process (SNAP).

FINANCING

Financing poses another documentary concern for exporters. In some cases, exporters receive payment through an open account. Open accounts operate in a manner similar to an exchange in the domestic market. The exporter trusts the creditworthiness of the buyer and ships the goods without worrying about receiving payment. The exporter may also ship the products on consignment, which involves simply sending a demand for payment, basically an invoice, with the expectation of payment.

Many transportation companies assist in the financing of exporting by using cash on delivery or COD. For this process, the buyer pays for the goods when the carrier delivers them. The carrier provides systems to accept the payment and transfer it to the manufacturer. No official title of ownership or bill of lading is part of this process. Similar to a COD, a cash-with-order system involves the official documentation of ownership transfer. The buyer makes a payment, sometimes a partial payment, before the order ships. Often the payment covers the cost of transporting the product both to and from the buyer, should it be returned for some reason.

With open accounts, COD payments, and cash-with-order systems, the manufacturer assumes the payment risk. In other cases, the exporter does not have sufficient information to be confident about the creditworthiness of the buyer. The concern exporters have is that the buyer may not pay for the shipment, may not be willing to take ownership if the goods are damaged in transit, or may not be willing to take responsibility for other increases in costs, such as currency movement or increased custom duties. At this point, a third party, typically a bank, becomes involved to ensure payment. The various documents and processes that may be used are displayed in Figure 14.4.

Drafts
Documents against Acceptance
Documents against Payment
Credits
Letter of Credit

FIGURE 14.4 Exporting Payment Documents

The core document for many exporters is a draft for payment. Often, this documentation is sent to both the buyer's bank and to the buyer. Drafts vary based on the unique needs of the buying situation. In general, drafts serve as documentation of the order being placed. Holding a draft does not represent the guarantee of payment by the bank, but it does provide proof of an agreement when a dispute occurs.

Documents against acceptance drafts certify that the buyer agrees to pay the exporter by a certain time. The agreement must be signed before the buyer receives title to the goods. Drafts may also be *documents against payment*, where the buyer must pay for the goods before receiving title. For many countries, customs officials will not release goods to the buyer without a signed draft. The buyer can refuse to sign the draft, which results in the exporter having to pay to ship the goods back.

A *letter of credit* provides the most secure option for exporters. For this documentation, the bank receives payment in return for providing credit guaranteeing the purchase. The buyer applies for the credit by providing specifics regarding how the payment will be made to the exporter. The exporter bank reviews the agreement and then, if no problems exist, extends payment to the exporter. The advantage of letters of credit lies in the agreement between the two banks. Both institutions are backing the payment. Table 14.3 presents some of the unique features of letters of credit.

TABLE 14.3 Features of Letters of Credit

Revocable vs. Irrevocable	Refers to whether the importer bank can cancel or change the terms of the agreement without getting approval from all parties
Confirmed vs. Unconfirmed	Refers to whether the bank explicitly confirms the credit in writing on the letter of credit
Transferrable vs. Nontransferable	Refers to whether the letter of credit may be transferred to another party
Revolving	Refers to a letter of credit that applies to regular, ongoing shipments
Deferred Payment	Refers to a letter of credit where payment to the exporter is paid at a specified date or dates after the shipment is received

> **LEARNING OBJECTIVE #4:**
>
> How can the marketing team effectively operate the five tasks associated with the physical distribution of goods?

PHYSICAL DISTRIBUTION

The term logistics applies to all of the activities in the physical movement and storage of goods from the producer to the consumer. The ultimate objective of a logistics program will be to meet the needs of customers in a convenient and timely fashion at the lowest possible cost. Five tasks (see Table 14.4) are associated with logistics and the physical distribution of products.

logistics: the management of the flow of products and services among marketing channel members

TABLE 14.4   The Five Tasks of Physical Distribution

Materials Handling
Inventory Location
Inventory Control
Order Processing
Methods of Transportation

MATERIALS HANDLING

Part of physical distribution involves handling the in-flow of raw materials. Company leaders balance the costs of holding raw materials against the problems associated with running out. In global markets, materials handling becomes a major part of the decision to use a mode of entry that involves manufacturing items in different countries, such as franchising, wholly owned subsidiaries, and joint ventures. A nation's infrastructure constitutes the primary factor in this analysis. As is the case with other aspects of physical distribution, materials handling has largely been automated in many industries, although humans still play key roles in materials-handling activities (Chakravorty, 2009).

The manager of a company's receiving department will be responsible for raw material orders, counting them and preparing them for use. A *bill of lading* specifies the exact amount of raw materials present in a shipment. The exporter must take care of bills of lading prepared in different languages.

INVENTORY LOCATION

The production team identifies the most efficient and effective methods for storing finished goods before shipping to other businesses and customers. A *warehouse* facility stores products before they are placed into the distribution channel. Three alternatives include a private warehouse, a public warehouse, and a third-party warehouse (Barry, 2008).

Private warehouses are owned or leased and operated by firms storing products. In some countries, where real estate prices remain low, a private warehouse offers a cost-effective method of inventory storage.

Public warehouses are independent facilities that provide storage rental and related services for companies. When these are available in a host country, the costs tend to remain low. Also, when a company runs with lower levels of inventory, storage space may be rented only when needed.

Third-party warehouses involve a firm outsourcing the warehousing function. A company specializing in inventory and warehousing can provide the service, thereby relieving the manufacturer of the task. This option matches with a variety of exporting operations. Van Bon Cold Stores Beneden-Leeuwen BV of the Netherlands offers customers a number of warehousing and logistical services for customers shipping products to Europe.[8]

Distribution Centers

Distribution centers are not warehouses, because they are not designed to store products. Instead, a flow of goods moves through the system. Delivery costs from distribution centers usually comprise a large portion of overall distribution costs. The physical location of a distribution center will be important. Most are located near major transportation routes, ports, or terminals. Many international marketers maintain distribution centers worldwide.[9] Some of these centers are wholly owned by the producing firm, while others are public warehouses. Small-sized products are often sent through distribution centers.

In general, distribution center activities are focused on receiving products, storing them, preparing them for delivery, and shipping. One growing trend is the use of *3PL* (*Third Party Logistics*) for inclusion in warehousing activities. 3PL firms provide warehousing and other logistics activities for firms without taking ownership of the products.[10] Examples include Deutsche Post DHL (in Germany), Kuehne Nagel (based in Switzerland), and SNCF (in France), which maintain larger market shares of distribution centers in the European Union.

Warehousing and inventory control activities have been significantly impacted by improved technologies. New technologies such as automated warehousing systems have drastically changed these activities. Automated warehousing systems vary greatly, but often expedite the loading process of products from storage locations to delivery docks. In this way, automated warehousing systems also assist in the materials handling function of physical distribution. Polish footwear marketer New Gate Group (NG2) recently built one of the largest automated warehousing facilities in Eastern Europe. The facility allows for distribution efficiency for Poland's leading footwear company.

INVENTORY CONTROL

The process of determining the appropriate level of inventory to be manufactured, shipped, and stored at a reasonable cost is the task of inventory control. A balance must be achieved between carrying too little inventory, which leads to *stock-outs* and lost sales, and carrying an excess of inventory. Stocks-outs are especially troublesome for international marketers, because reorders take additional time for shipment. Customers may become impatient and withdraw orders. On the other hand, holding excess inventory increases *carrying costs*, or the monies needed to finance the inventory and warehouse the product.

Stock Turnover

The number of times per year in which the average inventory on hand is sold is the stock turnover figure. A high stock turnover rate allows a company to be more efficient, unless it creates stock-outs and the lost sales that result. Stock turnover is calculated by dividing net sales by average inventory in retail currency, or by dividing the cost of goods sold by average inventory in a country's currency. Table 14.5 provides an example of stock turnover calculations. When managing stock turnover, the goal will be to identify the optimal turnover rate that allows for the timely delivery or products without creating excess carrying costs.

TABLE 14.5 Calculating Stock Turnover

Net Sales (*euros*)	3,200,000
Cost of Goods Sold (60%) (*euros*)	1,920,000
Average Inventory (retail *euros*)	800,000
Average Inventory Costs (*euros*)	480,000
Inventory Turnover	4 times
Net Sales -:- Average Inventory = 3,200,000 -:- 800,000	= 4 times
Cost of Goods Sold -:- Average Inventory = 1,920,000 -:- 480,000	= 4 times

Inventory Management Systems

To achieve the objective of finding the correct amount of inventory to carry, a producer may employ various inventory management system protocols. The traditional approach involves calculation of the *economic ordering quantity*, which identifies the point at which merchandise should be reordered along with the amount or volume to reorder. Unfortunately, the formula assumes zero *lead time*—the time from which merchandise is ordered until the time it is received. In international marketing, this assumption would almost always be false or inaccurate.

Instead, many marketers employ the *just-in-time* inventory control system. Just-in-time systems serve two purposes. The first is to order raw materials efficiently, but having them arrive at the precise time they are needed. The second goal is to reduce inventories of finished goods by anticipating future needs, which includes identifying times when sales will be low or at their peak. Just-in-time systems rely on dependable transportation systems, which can be problematic in many countries. The just-in-time method also counts on the marketing team's ability to accurately forecast future sales and future raw material needs, which may be harder to calculate in less stable international markets (Gartenstein, 2018).

The retail equivalent of just-in-time systems is the *quick response* inventory system. It creates a flow that approximates consumer purchasing patterns. An electronic data interchange system will be required to link the supplier's inventory system with the retailer's system. Technological constraints may limit the use of such a system. Trust will be required to establish the link (Songini, 2001).

INTERNATIONAL INCIDENT

A recent graduate of a Canadian university was thrilled to land a position as a sales representative with a major technology company seeking to export into new countries. His first international sales call was to Britain. He studied the differences between British use of language as compared to American terminology, recognizing that a "lift" is an elevator, a "mate" was a term of endearment, and that a detour is called a "diversion." At his first meeting with a set of potential customers, the Canadian ordered a glass of red wine with dinner. Later, he ordered white wine with dessert. The British prospects seemed quite upset with his choice. What social *faux pas* had he committed?

ORDER PROCESSING

Order processing involves completion of the paperwork associated with shipping orders as well as oversight of the physical movement of the goods. Bills of lading and other documents should be inspected to make certain an order contains all items. Then, payment for the shipment can be authorized by the importing company.

METHODS OF TRANSPORTATION

Reducing shipping costs offers one method to make products more affordable in foreign markets. Inbound transportation costs represent 6% to 12% of the gross sales of imported products.[11] The choice of transportation method also determines the speed with which goods will arrive at foreign destinations. The primary modes of transportation are displayed in Table 14.6.

TABLE 14.6   Major Transportation Modes in International Distribution

Air
Water
Railroad
Motor Carrier
Pipeline
Intermodal

Air

Air transportation has grown in usage by international marketers. Air transportation moves products that require overnight shipping. Two important issues regarding air transportation in international distribution include cost considerations and size constraints. Air transportation can be relatively expensive. Also, the size of product generally directly affects its distribution costs. International air transportation relies on adequate airports in or near destination regions. Air transportation in mountainous countries such as Bhutan will be especially limited. For these reasons, some international marketers look for other options.

Water transportation remains the most extensively used method of distributing products internationally.

Water

Water transportation remains the most extensively used method of distributing products internationally. Ocean transportation, in particular, is normally the most cost effective. Ocean going vessels, such as container ships, play key roles in international distribution.

Barges provide an important role in international distribution. In Africa, the organization Common Market for Eastern and Southern Africa, COMESA, seeks to bring various nations together for creating quality shipping routes along the Congo and Nile Rivers.[12] *Containerization* allows international marketers to save significant costs associated with overseas distribution. Water transportation is relatively slow when compared to air transportation, and shipping schedules constrain marketers from the availability of utilizing frequent shipping. Despite this, international companies continue to use it as evidenced in Table 14.7 which presents container port traffic for selected countries for years 2010 and 2014.

TABLE 14.7   Container Port Traffic 2010 and 2014 (in 20-foot equivalent units).

Country	2010	2014
Argentina	1,997,000	2,141,000
Australia	6,143,000	7,524,000
Brazil	6,879,000	10,679,000
Chile	3,123,000	3,743,000
China	115,061,000	181,635,000
France	4,619,000	6,646,000
Germany	14,177,000	19,685,000
Italy	10,520,000	11,313,000
Japan	18,795,000	20,744,000
Mexico	3,161,000	5,274,000
United Kingdom	7,081,000	9,348,000
United States	40,645,000	46,489,000

Source: Adapted from "Container Port Traffic," World Bank (no date). Retrieved from http://data.worldbank.org/indicator/IS.SHP.GOOD.TU/countries.

Railroad

Railroad transportation provides another useful transportation method in international marketing. Although railroad infrastructures vary greatly by country, this method is utilized widely in several industries and countries. Railroad transportation remains popular in developed countries and is the major form of inland transportation in countries such as China, Russia, and Poland. The total rail lines in kilometers in selected countries are shown in Table 14.8.

TABLE 14.8   Rail Line Availability in Selected Countries.

Country	Land Area (in sq km)	2014 (in km)
Argentina	2,736,690	25,023
Australia	7,682,300	9,674*
Brazil	8,358,140	29,817

(Continued)

TABLE 14.8   (Continued)

Country	Land Area (in sq km)	2014 (in km)
Chile	743,532	5,529
China	9,388,211	66,989
France	547,557	30,013
Germany	348,900	33,426
Italy	294,140	16,722
Japan	364,560	16,703
Mexico	1,943,950	26,704
Russia	16,376,870	85,266
United Kingdom	241,930	16,530
United States	9,147,420	228,218

Note: *data from 2009.

Source. Adapted from "Rail Lines: Total Route Km," World Bank (no date). Retrieved from http://data.worldbank.org/indicator/IS.RRS.TOTL.KM.

Motor Carrier

Trucks and other smaller vehicles provide another important international distribution venue. The utility of trucking as a mode of transportation depends directly on the availability of well-maintained highway systems. India, which remains an important emerging market for many international companies, is well known for its challenges with its highway and local street system. Motor carrier transportation is the primary method of domestic distribution in several developed countries, including France, Germany, and Spain.[13]

Pipeline

Pipelines work very well for liquid and gas-based products. Oil is transported through vast arrays of pipelines in many countries worldwide. Natural gas can also be transported by pipeline. Although this form can be inexpensive, it is generally slow. Pipelines are used extensively throughout the world, and are especially prevalent in the oil fields found in the Middle East.

Intermodal

Intermodal transportation combines various transportation modes. Containerization has enabled international marketing firms to reap the efficiencies that result from intermodal transportation. Products may be loaded into containers at the factory, shipped via rail transportation to a port, transported across an ocean, and then loaded onto trucks in the destination country. Other forms of intermodal transportation include *piggybacking*, the practice of loading flatbed trailers on rail cars for delivery on part of a distribution route, at which point they are transferred back to trucks for the balance of the delivery. Intermodal techniques also include *birdybacking* (combining motor carriers and air carriers in a delivery effort) and *fishybacking* (combining water carriers and motor carriers in a delivery effort). FedEx often combines both motor carrier and air carrier deliveries on international shipments.

The choice of transportation method affects the efficiencies and costs of delivery systems. Maps 14.1 and 14.2 display the global movements of beef and dairy products. Exporters would choose transportation systems that would avoid spoilage while keeping shipping costs as low as possible.

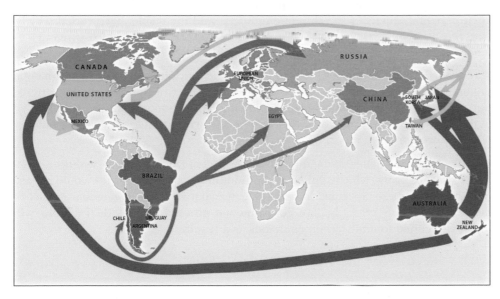

MAP 14.1 Beef Exports Globally

Beef exports reflect both the importance of geographic proximity and the growth of emerging markets.

Source: retrieved from http://www.thebeefsite.com/news/24602/us-lose-billions-to-global-beef-safety-measures

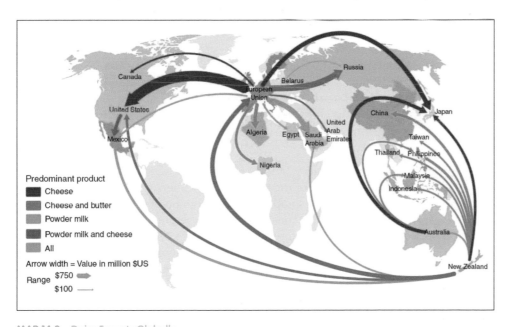

MAP 14.2 Dairy Exports Globally

Cultural preferences for dairy products in Europe influence the methods of distribution used to reach consumers.

Source: retrieved from https://www.ers.usda.gov/data-products/chart-gallery/gallery/chart-detail/?chartId=59833

SUSTAINABILITY AND INTERNATIONAL DISTRIBUTION SYSTEMS

International marketing channels contribute significantly to pollution problems, particularly in the area of international distribution. Airplane emissions, including carbon dioxide and nitrogen oxide, significantly contribute to global warming and climate change.

Shipping also poses environmental problems. Several studies have investigated the environmental impact of the shipping industry, and the results have varied widely. One recent study revealed that the world's fleet of ocean-going ships generates as much air pollution as half of the world's automobiles (Nolin, 2009).

Trains powered by diesel engines also generate significant sources of environmental pollutants. International marketers consider the impact of these methods of transportation in the delivery of products worldwide. Though most marketers are limited in their ability to improve efforts, they can select carriers that focus on sustainability of transportation.

In 2017, the United States, at the direction of President Donald Trump, withdrew from the Paris Agreement, which applied to the amount of carbon countries would release into the atmosphere. Speculation persists as to what will be the eventual impact of the decision. Many critics believe governmental officials in individual nations will feel less inclined to limit carbon emissions as a result.

RADIO FREQUENCY IDENTIFICATION DEVELOPMENT AND INTERNATIONAL TRANSPORTATION

Technology plays an important role in international transportation. Radio frequency identification development (RFID) technology has become a new feature in the international transportation of products as well as in warehousing systems. RFID allows for real-time identification and tracking of products over long distances, which offers advantages to international marketers. Unfortunately, many challenges currently exist with the technology. A lack of international standards for RFID operation, environmental limitations pertaining to the distribution of liquids, information security, and RFID tag failures are problems associated with the global adoption and use of these technologies (Ngai and Gunasekaran, 2009). Some international marketers continue to adopt this technology regardless of these complications. Dutch-based SmartTrac Technology is a leader in RFID applications worldwide.

INTERNATIONAL DISTRIBUTION AND THE BOTTOM-OF-THE-PYRAMID

Reaching the millions of bottom-of-the-pyramid consumers worldwide creates challenges. Rural areas tend to have disproportionately high numbers of consumers living on meager incomes. Most of these consumers purchase only the barest of essentials and shop out of necessity. In many of these countries, agricultural products are not available in sufficient quantity to satisfy demand. In some cases, monopolization occurs because there is only one supplier for the most basic necessities, which can lead to artificially high prices.

Two challenges are associated with reaching bottom-of-the-pyramid customers: cost and access. With regard to cost, transportation can be difficult given the primitive infrastructures that exist, which adds to the expense associated with distributing products to the poor. International distribution channels are adjusted to account for these challenges.

In terms of access, international marketers focus on developing the simplest of product solutions for these consumers at the lowest prices possible. Distribution channels are often relatively primitive, with products having to be transported great distances through sometimes highly challenging conditions. Issues such as refrigeration create additional complexities. Firms that succeed in finding methods to reach such consumers often develop strong levels of loyalty.

TERRORISM AND INTERNATIONAL MARKETING CHANNELS

The increased occurrence of global terrorism has exhibited a significant impact on international distribution activities. Due to tighter security restrictions worldwide, delays in shipments of products to international destinations have become more common. Many international marketers now consider the impact of terrorist activities when formulating strategic plans (Suder, 2006).

In general, terrorism constitutes an external risk that directly impacts product flow. It affects every form of transportation. A recent concern for the transportation of products has been the increase in piracy, particularly in the Gulf of Aden, the Indian Ocean, and the Arabian Sea near Somalia. While piracy levels have dropped due to the global recession, pirates still take hostages. Many ship owners find it less expensive to pay the hostage demands than to pay for the delay in transporting the products to buyers.

The United States Customs Service adopted the Container Security Initiative (CSI) as a response to the terrorist events of September 11, 2001. The initiative addresses the need for greater scrutiny of containers that are shipped into the United States and works to, among other things, identify high-risk containers, and to prescreen and evaluate containers before they are shipped to final destinations. The U.S. Customs and Border Protection developed the Customs–Trade Partnership Against Terrorism (C-TPAT), which also focuses on securing supply chains from terrorist activity (Herman, 2010).[14]

INTERNATIONAL MARKETING CHANNELS AND UTILITY

International marketing channels work to create various forms of utility for customers. *Utility* refers to the needs-satisfying ability of a product or service. In general, four types of utility are provided by international marketing channels, as shown in Table 14.9.

TABLE 14.9   Types of Utility Associated with Distribution Channels

Place utility	Making a product available at a place that is convenient for buyers
Time utility	Ensuring that a product is available when a consumer needs it
Possession utility	Transferring ownership of products to customers
Communication or information utility	Providing information to other channel members and customers

As an example, mobile phones are manufactured in several countries. Companies deliver them through many types of distribution channels to a final destination, providing *place* utility. They can be made available in many different retail locations daily, providing *time* utility. They are also relatively easy to buy, assuming one has the resources, providing *possession* utility. Finally, marketing channel members share information up and down the distribution channel, providing *communication or information* utility to channel members. Retailers and manufacturers alike typically keep in contact with consumers about product upgrades and innovations, providing communication utility to the end users.

INTERNATIONAL RETAILING

The final destination for many products will be a retail store or retail outlet. Retailing activities occur in the smallest villages to the largest cities. Retail commerce plays a significant role in the everyday lives of consumers. International retailers Tesco, Carrefour, Wal-Mart, Costco, and Stockmann are well known in many areas. At the same time, thousands of small, independent retailers operate around the world. These retailers play an important part in international marketing.

international retailing: the retail activities that occur across and inside national boundaries

Retailing includes all marketing activities that are aimed at selling a product or service to a consumer, or end user. International retailing refers to retail activities that occur across national boundaries. One way to approach the topic is from the perspective of an international marketing channel that utilizes small retail firms located in targeted countries that are outside the producer's home country. These retailers play key roles by offering the product directly to the consumer.

International marketers exercise great care when selecting retail outlets. An issue such as store image plays an important role in the selection process for high-end products. Boutique Dos Relógios Plus is an international retailer in Portugal for International Watch Company of Switzerland. Image is vital in this industry and the fit between retailer and manufacturer must be appropriate. The agreement between Mamas & Papas of the UK and the Al Tayer Group of the United Arab Emirates for retail distribution provides an example of how local companies help international marketers through their knowledge of the local business climate. Local businesses can be great assets for companies considering international retailing arrangements.

TYPES OF INTERNATIONAL RETAIL OUTLETS

Many forms of retailing are present worldwide. Many major international retailing firms operate across retail sectors. The Rewe Group, located in Germany, operates nearly 11,000 retail stores internationally that range from supermarkets to hypermarkets to specialty stores.[15] South African retailer Shoprite operates more than seventy supermarkets and hypermarkets throughout South Africa and in other African nations.[16] Many international retailers, such as the Netherlands' Ahold, feature several different brand names internationally. Ahold operates under the names Peapod, Giant, and Martin's in the United States, and Gall & Gall, Etos, and Albert throughout Europe. Table 14.10 presents several types of international retail outlets.

TABLE 14.10   Types of International Retail Outlets

Convenience Stores
Supermarkets
Hypermarkets
Open Air Markets
Department Stores
Discount Stores
Specialty Stores
Online Retailing

CONVENIENCE STORES

Convenience stores offer widely available, intensively distributed products to consumers. Prices at these stores tend to be higher than at discount stores or supermarkets; however, consumers are generally willing to pay slightly more in exchange for easy access. 7–11 is the largest convenience store chain in the world, with approximately 32,000 locations in countries such as Canada, Denmark, Indonesia, Japan, Malaysia, Mexico, and the United States.[17] Convenience outlets are usually smaller than their supermarket counterparts; the store size varies from country to country and from town to town. Japanese *conbinis* operate throughout the country and are especially prevalent in large cities such as Tokyo.

SUPERMARKETS

Supermarkets vary in form around the world. Several international retailers operate grocery stores in more than one country, most often in developed economies. The stores often carry more than food. Utensils, paper products, cleaning supplies, and other items make the inventory more appealing. Sainsbury's, headquartered in London, is the second-largest supermarket chain in the United Kingdom.

HYPERMARKETS

Hypermarkets, or *hypermarts*, are large retail outlets that combine elements of supermarkets and discount clubs. They provide a greater variety of product items. Hypermarts can be as large as several hundred thousand square feet. Auchan Group, a major retailing company headquartered in France, operates numerous hypermarkets throughout Europe and Asia, including China, Dubai, France, Luxembourg, Poland, Spain, and Taiwan. Hyper Panda is the largest hypermarket chain in Saudi Arabia.[18] Hypermarkets offer consumers worldwide the advantages of convenient shopping, large product selection, and low prices.

OPEN AIR MARKETS AND BAZAARS

Open air markets may be found in many regions of the world. Merchants in these markets often vend items such as fruit, vegetables, grocery products, and other items. *Tianguis* are open air markets in Mexico. Bazaars, which may not be open air, remain popular worldwide. These marketplaces bring consumers and retailers together for many types of products. The Grand Bazaar in Istanbul provides an example. The market is one of the oldest in the world. It includes more than 1,000 shops and attracts thousands of consumers every day.

DEPARTMENT STORES

Department stores present distinct product lines in numerous sections, or departments, throughout the retail establishment. Department stores have long been major players in the retail sector and several large companies operate locations worldwide. Shinsegae Centum City, located in Korea, is currently the largest department store in the world, surpassing U.S. giant Macy's, which experienced a major decline in 2017 in the U.S. market. A Shinsegae Centum City store occupies more than 500,000 square meters.[19] Department stores offer consumers the advantages of carrying a large number of products in carefully organized sections under one roof.

In 2017, other retail chains besides Macy's in the United States continued to experience dramatic declines in sales. Numerous organizations closed stores. The presence of online shopping was the primary cause of the downturn (Thau, 2017). Industry analysts have begun to speculate as to whether this trend will take place on a more global scale (Isidore, 2017).

DISCOUNT STORES

Discount stores sell many different product lines at discounted prices. Wal-Mart, the world's largest retailer, is a well-known discount chain that operates more than 11,000 stores in twenty-eight countries worldwide.[20] Discount stores have grown in usage worldwide due in large part to the low prices combined with high product selection. *Outlet centers* or *outlet malls* are also popular in international retailing. The Barcelona Roca Village Outlet and Las Rozas Village Madrid are popular outlet centers in Spain.

SPECIALTY STORES

Specialty retailers focus on relatively narrow product lines. Many variations of specialty stores exist worldwide. United States-based Starbucks is a well-known international specialty store that focuses on premium coffee and related products. The chain currently operates stores in more than fifty countries and sought to open 500 units in China in 2016 (Trefas Team, 2016).[21] Another example of a major international specialty store chain is Footlocker, which sells athletic footwear. Footlocker is based in the United States, and operates 3,500 retail stores throughout Australia, Europe, and North America. The company expected greater revenues and profits from the European market beginning in 2016 (Soni, 2016).[22]

Specialty stores offer consumers a limited selection of very specific products, and are popular in developed countries such as Japan, the United Kingdom, and the United States. One advantage for consumers is that retail employees in these outlets tend to be knowledgeable about the limited lines. Quite often, prices in these stores are higher than in discount or hypermarkets; however the quality of the products also tends to be higher.

ONLINE PURCHASING

Purchases of many products have increasingly moved online. Consumers in more-developed countries increasingly use outlets such as Amazon.com and eBay.com and the trend has spread to emerging markets as well. Responding to these purchases represents a challenge for marketers entering or operating in these markets.

The Chinese online retailer Taobao.com uses local e-commerce websites to reach emerging market consumers. Taobao.com operates a consumer auction website similar to eBay.com, and the Taobao Mall retail portal, where merchants can set up online storefronts, which is similar to Amazon.com. The company's growth has been rapid. In 2010 Taobao experienced a 100% increase in gross merchandise volume, to nearly $60 billion, which surpassed eBay's $53 billion (Orlik, 2011). By 2010, Taobao.com held 70% of China's online retail market with sales of more than $60 billion. Payments on the site are run through Alipay, similar to PayPal, and the service processes around $382.7 million in sales daily. Overall, Taobao has more than 800 million product listings, serves more than 370 million registered users, and is one of the top twenty most-visited websites in the world.[23]

Advertising drives much of the company's revenue, with the company being the second-largest drawer of online advertising revenue, behind Baidu.com but ahead of Google.com's Chinese earnings. Facing competitors such as 360Buy.com, Dangdang.com, and Amazon's Joyo.com, Taobao.com must constantly innovate to keep consumers satisfied.

Distribution represents a key component of an online retailer's success. With almost 70% of domestic mail in China being a Taobao shipment, the company faces a bottleneck. In response, Taobao.com invested nearly $4.5 billion to build a network of warehouses and distribution outlets to better distribute purchased products including building distribution centers in fifty two Chinese cities. The company also has a Taobao supply-chain management platform, and provides value-added services to assist suppliers with logistics. The company's goal is to ship any product ordered online to the customer within eight hours.

THE FUTURE

The future of retailing will be influenced by improvements in distribution systems and other technologies. As more roads are built and more companies become involved in middleman activities, product access will increase in many developing nations. Growth in all of the forms of retailing, including supermarkets, hypermarts, convenience stores, and specialty stores as well as online retailing, can be expected, assisted by the availability of data (big data) and new technologies such as RFID or social networking.

At the same time, the engine of many economies continues to be small, independent companies. This holds true in retailing segments as well as other industries. In less-developed countries, the local bazaar remains the primary retail outlet for the majority of customers.

CHAPTER 14: REVIEW AND RESOURCES

Strategic Implications

The decision to export constitutes a major strategic activity. Internal motives that can guide such a strategic response include managerial urges, the development of unique product characteristics, motives to increase economies of scale in operations, the choice to extend sales or lower risk, or mere overcapacity. External factors that lead to exporting include the influence of change agents, unique features in foreign markets, changes in domestic markets, and unsolicited orders.

A second strategic choice involves use of a market concentration or market spreading approach to exporting. Market concentration focuses on expanding to a small number of markets. Market spreading involves exporting in several different markets simultaneously.

The third strategic decision involves the selection of retail outlets. Top managers choose the types of retail stores to be contacted. Then, the same managers complete agreements with those retail outlets.

These strategic choices will be made following an analysis of the target country or countries. The marketing management teams examine the potential of the market to support profitable exporting arrangements. When the decision has been made, tactical plans are devised and implemented.

Tactical Implications

Selection of export entry modes will be part of a tactical plan. Choices include home country-based activities, including utilizing the current marketing department, a separate exporting department, or an export sale subsidiary. In other instances, a foreign country-based approach will be deployed, taking advantage of the services provided by a foreign sales branch, a foreign sales subsidiary, or foreign-based distributor agents and representatives. When a company uses indirect exporting as the primary method, agents and merchants direct exporting activities on behalf of the company.

A second tactical plan involves price setting. The marketing team may decide to price items lower than domestic products, higher than domestic products, or on a par with those products. The choice will be most influenced by the nature of the competition present.

The third area of tactical activity will be designing and carrying out the tasks associated with the physical distribution of products. These include materials handling, inventory location, inventory control, order processing, and choosing methods of transportation. Specialists in each of those areas guide decisions and choices.

Operational Implications

Operational managers carry out the daily activities associated with exporting. Most notably, this involves completing the exporting documentation. Marketers must make sure the proper documentation needed to satisfy the government accompanies shipments. Operational managers also finalize drafts, documents against acceptance, documents against payment, and letters of credit.

Operational managers complete the paperwork associated with the tasks of physical distribution. They look to make sure bills of lading are in order as shipments arrive. They manage actual warehouse and inventory location facilities and activities. Finally, operational managers retain and reimburse various carriers that physically deliver products.

TERMS

market concentration	indirect exporting
market spreading	logistics
direct exporting	international retailing

REVIEW QUESTIONS

1. Define exporting and importing.

2. What internal motives lead to exporting?

3. What external factors lead to exporting?

4. Define market concentration and market spreading.

5. What are the home country-based methods of direct exporting?

6. What are the foreign country-based methods of direct exporting?

7. What are the major types of merchants and agents used in indirect exporting?

8. What three approaches can be used to price exported products?

9. What are the two main kinds of documents that accompany exports?

10. What are the five tasks of physical distribution?

11. What modes of transportation are used in international marketing?

12. What forms of utility are created by international distribution systems?

13. Define international retailing.

14. What are the major types of international retail outlets?

DISCUSSION QUESTIONS

1. Compare the internal and external reasons for exporting. Can you think of a situation in which one contradicts the other? In other words, are internal reasons compelling to export but external reasons not, or vice versa?

2. Explain which approach, market concentration or market spreading, should be the primary strategy used in the following situations:

    - a new type of sports energy drink

    - 3-D digital video players

    - wines made in Africa

    - tennis equipment by a manufacturer in Brazil

3. Discuss the transportation modes that would work best for the following products that are to be shipped overseas:

    - personal computers

    - industrial equipment

    - mobile phones

    - petroleum products

4. Discuss how place, time, possession, and communication utilities can be created for each of the following:

    - motorcycles in Spain

    - video games in Japan

    - soft drinks in Portugal

    - cereal in Australia

5. Discuss how well you think online retailing would work for the following products:

    • groceries

    • appliances

    • fast food

    • business products

ANALYTICAL AND INTERNET EXERCISES

1. Visit the website of a major international marketer of fruit, such as United States-based Chiquita (www.chiquita.com). What can you learn about the worldwide distribution of fruit from these websites? What logistical activities are critical for the company's success? Search the Internet for information on open air markets and bazaars. In what countries are they popular? Why do you think this is so?

2. Using the Internet, identify three major international export merchants. What services do the companies offer? What regions do they serve?

3. For the following products and countries, identify the type of warehouse that should be used as well as the method of transportation that should deliver the product to end users. Using the Internet, identify a company that offers the type of warehouse you have chosen and the name of the transportation service.

    • tires manufactured in South Korea and sold in Indonesia

    • golf clubs manufactured in Japan and sold in Australia

    • fruit products grown in Australia and sold in New Zealand

    • high-end dresses and fashions sewn in France and sold in South Africa

STUDENT STUDY SITE

Visit **https://study.sagepub.com/baack2e** to access these free additional learning tools:

• Web Quizzes

• eFlashcards

• SAGE Journal Articles

• Country Fact Sheets

• Chapter Outlines

• Interactive Maps

CASE 14

Marks and Spencer's International Expansion Problems

Marks and Spencer (M&S) is one of the UK's leading retailers and is no stranger to international marketing success. Founded in England in 1884 by Michael Marks and Thomas Spencer, the company has steadily grown to become a major power in the UK and in several other international markets. M&S sells products in international stores across Europe, the Middle East and Asia and it continues to grow its international presence through a multi-channel approach.

M&S is committed to delivering sustainable value for its customers and making every moment special through the high-quality, branded food, clothing, and home products, and financial services available in M&S stores and online. M&S products are available through more than 900 UK and more than 450 international stores—in diverse locations across high streets and out of town retail centers. International revenue totalled £1.2bn in 2016 constituting 10% of the total company revenue.[24]

Internationally, the retailer operates through three different business models—owned, franchise, and joint venture—to bring Clothing & Home collections and Food ranges to its international customers. M&S also has a growing international online business delivered through localized owned and franchise websites and through partnerships with leading marketplaces.[25] The M&S website launched in February 2014 and acts as a window to its products and stores and an online store. As shopping habits change, the retailer combines the best of the web and store to extend its reach and drive more spend from customers. In addition to shopping online via the localized websites, international customers can order through the UK site as M&S delivers to countries including Hong Kong, Italy, Israel, Portugal, Albania, Brunei, Japan, and Finland.

The company has been able to thrive over the years by offering high-quality products and services along with great value for consumers, but has recently been experiencing

(Continued)

(Continued)

serious challenges in some of its foreign markets. M&S strategy in international markets focused mainly on large stores in shopping centers offering Clothing and Home products. M&S operates forty-eight stores in India, and almost as many in Turkey (Rigby, 2016). In 2016, M&S began closing some foreign stores including all ten in China, half of its stores in France and all its shops in Belgium, Estonia, Hungary, Lithuania, the Netherlands, Poland, Romania, and Slovakia (Macadam, 2016). Fifty-three stores have been closed in these ten countries after turnover and profit analysis revealed losses in those markets.[26] This was not the first time that M&S did not succeed overseas. In the 1990s, the company closed stores in Canada, and it is the second time that the company did not succeed in France.[27] Steve Rowe, the Chief Executive of M&S, announced that M&S is not giving up on international markets, but merely restructuring its business and plans to be present in other countries mainly via the option of franchising its Simply Food stores.[28]

1.   M&S has been successful in several foreign markets but failed in others. Analyze the possible causes of M&S international market failure and propose solutions.

2.   If M&S chooses to return to some of the unsuccessful foreign locations, what factors should they consider before reentering them?

3.   Is franchising the right market entry mode for this retailer?

4.   How can M&S build brand awareness in international markets and drive traffic to its international and UK online stores?

PART VI
INTERNATIONAL PROMOTION

15

GLOBALLY INTEGRATED MARKETING COMMUNICATIONS

LEARNING OBJECTIVES

After reading and studying this chapter, you should be able to answer the following questions:

1. How can the individual communications model be used to describe international marketing communications processes?

2. What steps are taken to develop an effective international advertising program?

3. What traditional and culturally based types of advertising appeals do marketing professionals use?

4. How are the traditional executional frameworks adapted to international advertising programs?

5. What types of alternative marketing communications programs are available to international firms?

IN THIS CHAPTER

Opening Vignette: Advertising Jewelry

OVERVIEW

ADVERTISING JEWELRY

Jewelry adorns citizens of countries around the world. Its rich history dates back centuries. People wear jewelry as part of religious ceremonies, dating, engagements, marriages, anniversaries, making fashion statements and political statements, and in other contexts. Both men and women wear small items such as an earring or a stud. One maritime tradition includes having an ear pierced after crossing the equator by ship. Couples exchange rings in wedding ceremonies around the world. Necklaces are worn by men and women for a variety of reasons, including the expression of personal religion. Nose rings can be found in some countries. A recent global fad involved toe rings. Friendship bracelets are exchanged in many countries.

The marketing of jewelry requires adaptation to every element that affects the international business environment. Culture dictates various aspects of jewelry wearing, including the designation of a "ring finger" to signify that one is married. The language of jewelry continues to evolve. The term "bling" has been assigned to gaudy displays of jewelry in some cultures. The term "junk jewelry" has been used to disparage other products. Legal restrictions include the taxation of jewelry exports and other limitations. Infrastructure dictates the distribution of jewelry in less-developed countries. Economic conditions have a major impact on the price and availability of jewelry. In 2011 and 2012, with record-setting gold prices, the cost of an engagement or wedding ring rose dramatically.

Stores as small as convenience marts and as large as high-end specialized retail outlets sell jewelry. Jewelry may be bargain priced in big box retail outlets and marketed as a luxury item in other stores. Turquoise jewelry made by Navajo and Zuni tribes can be found in worldwide markets. In some countries, street vendors offer various types of jewelry. Religious jewelry items are sold in the Vatican and in many nearby shops as well as on dedicated Internet websites.

Advertising for jewelry appears in practically every venue, from traditional media such as television, radio, magazines, newspapers, and billboards to nontraditional locations, including trade shows, country fairs, religious festivals, and cultural events. Jewelry has been marketed on television infomercials, on the Internet, and by direct mail. The endless variety of jewelry uses dictates the large number of advertising programs.

Making commercials to sell jewelry can take the traditional format of selecting an advertising appeal and matching it with an executional framework. Marketers create advertising appeals based on sex, fantasy, rational information, and scarcity for rings, necklaces, or bracelets. Executions including slice-of-life, dramatization, demonstration, testimonial, and even animation are possible.

Marketing and advertising jewelry in international markets requires careful consideration by the foreign company. Culture, shopping habits including bargaining, and methods of payment should be considered first. Marketing messages and advertisements incorporate gender roles, religious constraints, popular culture, and other local considerations as the marketing team attempts to match these elements with the level of quality and price of various items.

Experts predict that the jewelry brands will continue to internationalize. As the global market continues to expand, the possibilities for making and selling jewelry rise (Dauriz et al., 2014). The blending of cultures and concepts of beauty and art will continue to create a rich world of personal ornamentation.

Jewelry adorns citizens of countries around the world.

(Continued)

(Continued)

Questions for Students

1.   How does culture affect the purchase and display of jewelry?
2.   Which advertising media would be most effective for advertising low- and high-end jewelry?
3.   Which advertising approaches best match selling jewelry for romantic purposes, religious purposes, and popular culture purposes?

OVERVIEW

globally integrated marketing communications program: a program that consists of a carefully designed combination of all communications with the company's internal and external publics

One of the key strategic international marketing activities, coordinating a firm's **globally integrated marketing communications program**, consists of a carefully designed combination of all messages sent to a company's internal and external publics. Internal publics include the company's employees, board of directors, and affiliates. External publics include customers, suppliers, wholesale and retail intermediaries, members of the media, the public, and the government. An effective globally integrated marketing communications system speaks to these groups with a clear and consistent voice that represents the firm's image, positioning, brand status, and approach to business.

Part VI of this book focuses on a globally integrated marketing communications program. This chapter examines advertising and other alternative marketing methods of making contact with customers, potential customers, and others. Chapter 16 covers international sales promotions and public relations. Figure 15.1 portrays promotions in relation to other activities associated with a firm's overall international marketing system.

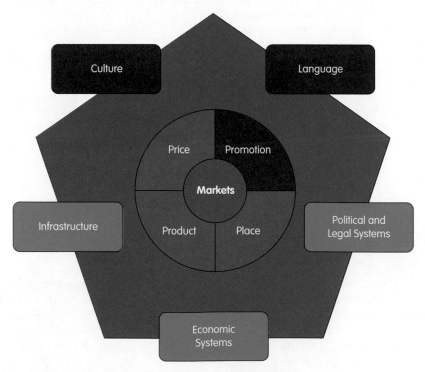

FIGURE 15.1   The International Marketing Context

A globally integrated marketing communications program requires the strategic management of the firm's **promotions mix** (see Figure 15.2). The mix consists of the traditional advertising, personal selling, sales promotion, and public relations efforts. This newer conceptualization of the promotions mix includes digital communication due to its worldwide success and rapid adoption. These tools and activities serve the basic purpose of promoting a firm's products and services to end user customers as well as intermediaries such as wholesale distributors and retail outlets. The optimal promotional mix depends on customer and channel partner needs in order to achieve the company's marketing goals.

promotions mix: a company's combination of advertising, personal selling, sales promotion, and public relations efforts

FIGURE 15.2 The Marketing Mix and the Promotions Mix

This chapter begins with a brief review of a communications model featuring the primary challenges related to communication. Next, advertising programs are presented, including the tasks involved as well as the complications that arise in international marketing programs. One of the strategic decisions to be made when creating an advertising campaign will be in regard to standardization or adaptation of the marketing messages that will be delivered to customers and potential customers.

Advertising appeals, positioning strategies, and executional frameworks receive attention next, including international differences and nuances that affect these programs. The chapter concludes with a presentation of nontraditional marketing programs that have become increasingly utilized in many international settings.

LEARNING OBJECTIVE #1:

How can the individual communications model be used to describe international marketing communications processes?

THE COMMUNICATION PROCESS

International advertising and promotional activities are profoundly influenced by communication issues. **Communication** is the process of sending, receiving, and interpreting information. Two levels of communication exist in organizations. The first, *individual interpersonal communication*, involves the transmission of a message from one person to another, such as when a sales representative makes a presentation to a prospective client or customer. The individual model also applies to a person speaking to a group of people, such as when an advertising manager begins a

communication: the process of sending, receiving, and interpreting information

meeting with a short speech. Further, the individual communications model applies to marketing messages sent via various media, including advertising venues. The second level, *communication systems*, includes the transmission and movement of information throughout an organization. Organization-wide communication systems are described in Chapter 5 of this book.

INDIVIDUAL INTERPERSONAL COMMUNICATIONS

Figure 15.3 models communication between individuals. As shown, the *sender* is the person signaling a message or idea. *Encoding* is the process of forming verbal and nonverbal cues. Verbal cues include anything than can be spoken as language, including print on a page or a text message. Nonverbal cues are the other methods by which messages are sent, including gestures, facial expression, posture, eye contact, and physical distance between the sender and the receiver.

The *transmission device* will be any medium that carries a message. Devices include a vast variety of modes, beginning with light and sound waves but extending to cell phone signals, radio waves, Internet transmissions, physical sensations of touch, paper with writing on it, and numerous others.

Decoding occurs as the receiver processes the message using his or her various senses. One can hear, see, feel, and sometimes taste or smell a transmission. Most of the time more than one sense is involved. A person engaged in a conversation both hears and sees the other individual, who may touch him on the arm or poke his ribs when making a joke. All of these signals are decoded. When a salesperson (the sender) speaks to a customer (the receiver), the customer decodes the information as he listens to the message and seeks to understand its meaning.

The *receiver* is the person or group of persons for whom the message was intended. In a one-on-one setting, there will be one sender and one receiver. During a speech at a meeting, one sender transmits the message to all of the receivers in the audience. An advertising message will be transmitted from the sender (the company) via a transmission device (television signal) to receivers, or members of the television audience.

Feedback consists of the perceived evaluation of the message. In essence, feedback is the response given by the receiver to the sender, verbally or nonverbally. A receiver may convey "I understand," "I disagree," or "That's funny" by how she reacts to the message, using laughter, eye contact, or a nod.[1]

As shown in Figure 15.3, noise can prevent the effective transmission of a message. *Noise* is the name given to all of the potential barriers to communication.

FIGURE 15.3   An Individual Communications Model

BARRIERS TO COMMUNICATION

Anything that can distort or disrupt a message constitutes noise or barriers to communication between individuals. As shown in Table 15.1 numerous types of noise may be present in any conversation or presentation. For effective communication to take place, the individuals involved in the conversation must overcome the barriers. International marketing research can be designed to help reduce or eliminate the barriers that emerge during an interaction with a person from another country.

TABLE 15.1 Barriers to Communication

Individual Differences	Situational Factors	Mechanical Problems
Age	Emotions	Language and Slang
Gender	Context	Technical Terminology
Level of Education	Distractions	Physical Disabilities
Status		Transmission Device Issues
Personality		Nonverbal Contradiction of the Verbal Message

Individual Differences

Each category of barriers presents obstacles to effective communication. An older person may intimidate a young person when speaking to him. Gender differences in communication have been described in many formats, including use of Mars to represent males and Venus to represent females. Educational attainments introduce more complex thinking and a wider vocabulary, which can hinder communication between someone with a graduate degree and someone who is nearly illiterate. Differences in status appear when someone of high rank in an organization encounters a first-level employee or when a celebrity runs into a fan. Personality problems exist when either the sender or the receiver is bombastic and outgoing when the other person is shy and retiring. In an international context, differences between individuals may be due to different cultural backgrounds, traditions, and histories. Understanding how to respond to these differences increases the likelihood of successful communication.

An interesting translation.

Situational Factors

Two major emotions that disrupt communication include anger and depression. Careful listening becomes less likely when either emotion is present. Context consists of emotionally charged settings, such as a funeral or announcement of a death, or when management announces layoffs at a company meeting. After the initial shock, little quality communication transpires. Distractions include noisy settings or meetings in which violent weather is taking place nearby. Senders and receivers become more involved with the distraction than with the conversation. Also, a lack of cultural understanding can lead to anger or frustration.

Mechanical Problems

Language and slang may interfere with communication even in domestic settings. A person who speaks two languages may be less fluent in one, causing difficulty when conversing in the second language. Slang varies by age, culture, and other variables. Technical terminology exists when someone who is well versed in an area, such as information technology, uses words only those in the field would understand when nontechnical individuals are present. These mechanical issues become intensified in an international marketing context. A great deal of communication in this context includes at least one non-native speaker who must cope with both the technical terminology and the unfamiliar language.

Physical disabilities can be a problem for the sender when she has a speech impairment. A physical disability can cause difficulties for any receiver who is hard of hearing, deaf, or blind. Transmission device problems include poor mobile phone signals, trying to shout over wind and rain from a distance, and any other problem with the medium carrying the message. Nonverbal contradictions occur when the sender's verbal cues do not match his gestures, facial expression, or posture.

International Barriers

Each of the individual barriers listed in Table 15.1 may become more extreme in international settings and can greatly influence international marketing programs. For example, older persons may be highly respected in one culture and disrespected in another. Even asking questions about a person's age can make the receiver uncomfortable in some cultures. Gender equality and inequality strongly affects patterns of communication between males and females. Percentages of a population that are educated vary widely across countries, thereby affecting status levels. Personalities may be influenced by cultural surroundings as well. The most commonly cited barriers to communication in international marketing and promotions include:

- language and slang
- directness of address
- eye contact
- ethnocentrism
- stereotyping
- differences in the meanings of nonverbal cues
- use of symbols and cultural icons

Language and slang create initial barriers to communication. An individual who only speaks Mandarin will have difficulties when a business partner only speaks Spanish, even when a translator is present. Slang within both languages can further complicate communication. Mandarin is written using characters rather than letters, which adds further potential disruptions.

Directness of address is culturally based. In some countries, such as Japan, language and conversation are highly deferent. Disagreement would be expressed in the most modest terms possible. Often, Japanese business people will go to extreme lengths to avoid telling a business partner "no." In other nations, such as the Netherlands, the opposite will be true. Unless strong, direct language is used, others may view the speaker as weak or not reliable.

Eye contact may be closely related to directness of address. In some cultures, such as Canada, the failure to make eye contact makes a person seem suspicious and untrustworthy. In others, such as South Korea, looking away displays deference and respect.

Ethnocentrism, the belief that one's culture is inherently superior, may cause either the sender or receiver to convey a sense of feeling superior. Not surprisingly, misunderstandings may result and conflicts or confrontation may emerge.

Stereotyping exists when a person assumes things about another based on that person's race or national heritage. Believing all Germans are rigid, structured, rational thinkers lumps them into a group that undoubtedly does not truly exist. Corresponding methods of speaking would be affected by such an assumption.

Nonverbal cues vary widely by culture. Nodding "yes" in one country is nodding "no" in others. In many Arab nations, the act of crossing one's legs is a sign of disrespect and males holding hands as part of a business relationship indicates trust. Gestures also vary widely. What may have a benign meaning in one country may be an obscene gesture in another. Examples include the "V for victory" with two fingers, and use of the middle finger to point.

High- and Low-Context Cultures

A final communication barrier results from the methods used to communicate. Use of symbols and cultural icons also affects patterns of communication. Religious symbols are major components of many cultures. Failing to recognize them may place a person in an embarrassing situation. The terms *high-* and *low-context* have been applied to culture differences in language usage. Misunderstanding these elements may lead to poorly designed advertising and marketing programs (Hall, 1984, 1994: 85–128).

Low-context cultures are characterized by explicit verbal or written messages. **Low-context cultures** demonstrate high values toward and positive attitudes regarding words. The meaning of a message is mainly contained in the words used. Much of the Western world is historically rich with rhetoric. This, in turn, continues to emphasize the importance of verbal messages. Germany, Switzerland, and the United States are examples of low-context cultures.

low-context cultures: cultures that demonstrate high values toward and positive attitudes regarding words

High-context cultures rely more on symbols and language with less-explicit or spelled-out codes. The meaning of the message is mainly contained in the nonverbal components of the message. This includes facial expressions, body language, the person presenting the message, and the context in which the message is transmitted. High-context communication moves quickly and efficiently. Unfortunately, often the verbal messages are less complete, and for those not familiar with the symbols in a given area, the information becomes difficult to accurately decipher. High-context societies are less accessible to outsiders. Many Asian cultures are high context. Table 15.2 presents differences in high- and low-context cultures.

high-context cultures: cultures that rely more on symbols and language with less explicit or spelled-out codes

TABLE 15.2 High- and Low-Context Cultures

	High Context	Low Context
Meaning of Words	Meaning derived largely by context	Meaning derived from verbage
Nonverbal Communication	Strong emphasis on nonverbals	Smaller emphasis on nonverbals
Symbolism	Important role in communication	Smaller role in communication
Use of Data	Smaller role in communication	Important role in communication
Descriptions	Often incomplete	Fully explained
Status of Speaker	Major role in communication	Smaller role in communication

In advertising and marketing, messages are more explicit, clear, and complete in low-context cultures (e.g., Germany). Selling points are articulated and spelled out. Consumers expect this precision in messages. In essence, numbers, figures, and concise language guide message development. Advertising will be more verbally oriented in many instances.

For high-context cultures, marketing messages and commercials rely more on symbolism and indirect verbal messages. The importance of logos combined with local cultural icons including colors rises. The color red symbolizes celebration in Asian culture. Its use in an advertisement sends a widely understood signal in that region. Visual variables play important roles in high-context cultures (Miracle et al., 1992; Bu et al., 2009).

Complications arise when a company fails to recognize the cultural context. Unless the advertising team can explain why context matters, marketing messages may become misinterpreted or misunderstood. At the same time, a well-designed symbolic message can succeed in a low-context culture. Many persons in low-context countries are able to interpret the Nike swoosh, McDonald's arches, and other logos; religious symbols; and numerous jingles or musical taglines. Also, a well-written advertisement can succeed in a high-context culture, especially when accompanied by appropriate symbols. Focus groups and pretesting of advertisements can help the marketing team predict the effects of a marketing message.

OVERCOMING BARRIERS TO COMMUNICATION

Quality communication results from careful preparation by a sender and receiver in any context, and plays a major role in designing quality international market research. Both senders and receivers have responsibilities that can overcome the barriers that are present. Table 15.3 summarizes these duties.

TABLE 15.3 Creating Quality Individual Communication

Sender Duties	Receiver Duties
Awareness of Barriers	Active Listening
Empathy	Seeking Clarification of the Message
Careful Attention to Nonverbal Cues	
Confirmation of the Message	

Senders are charged with making sure they understand the barriers that might be present. In international settings, speakers should pay even greater care to these issues. Empathy means attempting to understand the receiver's background and point of view. Knowing about nonverbal cues and their usage in other cultures can help avoid many potential conflicts and misunderstandings in a research project. Confirmation of the message may be summarized by the phrase, "Do you understand?" At the same time, the use of such a "yes" or "no" question can be frustrating in high-context cultures, because consumers rarely are comfortable giving such direct answers. Consequently, extra attention is given to make sure the message was received as intended.

Receiver duties include listening carefully and not allowing distractions to interfere with a conversation or presentation. Multi-tasking during long distance phone calls overseas is a bad idea. Clarification of a message means saying, "I don't understand" at the appropriate times. Otherwise a receiver may overreact to what was meant to be a noncontroversial comment.

In international settings, translators and cultural assimilators are key individuals. *Translators* should speak the native language of the host country. Many times the best choice for a translator will be someone who lives in the host country, and uses its language as a first language. *Cultural assimilators* are employees who examine messages and prepare individuals for interactions with members of other countries. They can help a person avoid any uncomfortable lapses in manners as well as explain how to show friendliness and respect in that country. Both of these individuals play vital roles in preparing, interpreting, analyzing, and presenting the findings of an international marketing research effort.

COMMUNICATING MARKETING MESSAGES

The individual communications model can be adapted to advertising programs. Sender companies are advised to understand how media are used and perceived in various cultures. State-owned television stations may cause distrust or even disdain by the public. Commercials and other advertising messages should be translated and back translated to make sure they do not violate local cultural norms. Marketers should monitor the use of visual images and examine photos, especially of women, to make sure an image does not insult local patrons. Even the use of animals or animated characters as brand characters deserves attention. In the United States, a squirrel is viewed as a "thrifty saver." In Latin America, squirrels are in the same category as rats. Feedback may be solicited in the form of focus groups or other methods of market research to make certain advertisements are understood in the manner that they were intended.

Noise and Clutter

In the individual communications model, noise represents all of the elements that can distort or disrupt a message. In advertising, noise would be all of the factors that prevent advertising messages from reaching the intended audience. Clutter presents the predominant form of advertising noise. **Clutter** describes the abundance of marketing messages that consumers routinely encounter. In a developed nation such as France or the United States, a typical citizen will be bombarded with 600 commercial messages each day. The messages are delivered by a variety of traditional and nontraditional media. Those who ride the rapid-transit system in Paris, the Métro, view advertisements as they enter the station, on the walls of the waiting area, and inside the subway trains. The same is true of airports, bus terminals, and other locations. Radio, television, newspaper, magazine, and outdoor ads become a constant part of the day. Outdoor advertising is growing in usage in developing markets also.

clutter: the abundance of marketing messages that consumers routinely encounter

The typical consumer has become adept at tuning out clutter. Digital video recorder technology makes it possible to skip over television commercials. Satellite radio and iPods allow music to be enjoyed commercial free. Internet surfers have become increasing skilled at ignoring advertisements on various websites. Most people look past billboards and advertisements on buses or taxis.

Finding ways to cut through clutter and reach the intended audience represents the marketing challenge for international advertisers. This effort has become increasing difficult as the number of media outlets expands in a wider set of countries. In each culture, what consumers will view and what they will ignore varies by country, age, gender, and other demographics.

The most traditional approach to overcoming clutter, the *three-exposure hypothesis*, suggests that it takes three encounters with a message before a viewer will notice and recall it. To make sure a message will be effective, advertising programs and campaigns must continue to send the message in a series of venues in order to reach potential customers (Krugman, 1972). A contrasting approach, the *recency theory*, argues that a message need only be viewed once, *if* the consumer or business is ready to buy (Freeman, 2003). Either way, continual messaging is required to overcome the barrage of commercials customers come across each day (Ephron and McDonald, 2002).

LEARNING OBJECTIVE #2:

What steps are taken to develop an effective international advertising program?

INTERNATIONAL ADVERTISING MANAGEMENT

advertising management: the process of developing and overseeing a company's advertising program

Advertising management is the process of developing and overseeing a company's advertising program (Clow and Baack, 2012). In an international context, the forces that shape the global marketing environment have a substantial impact on the entire advertising program. Political, legal, language, culture, economic, and infrastructure issues receive attention as a company and its marketing and advertising teams prepare messages for customers and potential customers. Table 15.4 displays the steps involved in advertising management (Clow and Baack, 2010: 167).

TABLE 15.4   Steps of International Advertising Management Programs

1.	Establish international advertising objectives
2.	Create an international advertising budget
3.	Choose an advertising agency
4.	Oversee the advertising program
5.	Assess advertising effectiveness

ESTABLISH INTERNATIONAL ADVERTISING OBJECTIVES

Above all other advertising objectives, presenting a clear and consistent message regarding a company's image and theme constitutes a key international marketing priority. In many parts of the world, advertisements bleed across national borders via television, the Internet, and other media, which means it would be nearly impossible to adapt completely to each individual nation. Even when language differences exist, the goal will be to create a somewhat universal image of the company. In Table 15.5, standard international advertising objectives are presented.

Objectives are chosen based on multiple variables. Creating brand and product awareness becomes the primary goal when a company enters a new host country. Soon after, persuading customers to try a product and encouraging action become logical objectives. Both goals may be accompanied by the drive to provide information. Information may also be the primary objective when company circumstances change, through a disaster or hardship, a merger or acquisition, or when negative publicity arises. Increasing sales and market share serve as objectives during the growth and maturity stages of the product life cycle and later into a company's entry into a host country.

TABLE 15.5 International Advertising Objectives

Create brand and product awareness
Build or improve a brand's image
Increase sales/market share
Persuade customers to try a product
Provide information
Support other marketing efforts
Encourage action

CREATE AN INTERNATIONAL ADVERTISING BUDGET

Achieving one or more of the advertising objectives noted in Table 15.5 requires funding. Company leaders allocate funds to achieve marketing goals in various ways. The primary budgeting methods include:

- percentage of sales
- match the competition
- arbitrary allocation
- objective and task

In international advertising programs, the *percentage of sales* method can refer to overall company sales, sales in one market or country, or percentage of sales in a region. Should the overall company sales figure be used, funds may be distributed equally across all countries in which the company operates or divided according to various priorities. If Nestlé's marketing team decides to increase marketing efforts for Perrier bottled water products in South Korea, additional funds may be devoted to expanding product awareness.

When *matching the competition* is the method chosen, the advertising team seeks to identify the amount a key competitor spends in a given market. An *arbitrary allocation* allows the marketing team to set the budget at the level members believe will be best, or at the amount they believe the company can afford.

The most complicated method—*objective and task*—assigns a monetary amount to the advertising objective chosen. In the case of Nestlé and South Korea, the funds might be set in terms of Swiss *francs* or South Korean *won*. The objective of increasing product awareness would likely require a different amount than increasing market share and other goals.

CHOOSE AN ADVERTISING AGENCY

The first decision made by a company's marketing leaders will be between using members of the company's marketing department to create advertisements, the in-house method, or selecting an external advertising agency. The choice becomes more complex when designing commercials for other countries. One advantage to in-house advertising is that locals will be acquainted with host country circumstances and will be the most familiar with the company's products. Most of the time, the in-house option is less expensive. Companies can complete the entire advertising program or retain boutique agencies for certain activities, including:

- purchasing media time or space (media buyers)
- conducting market research regarding media availability or target audience preferences
- writing copy
- filming or printing the commercial or advertisement
- preparing additional marketing materials such as coupons, contests, sweepstakes, and premium programs
- assisting in designing company logos, letterhead, and signage

Outside Advertising Agencies

When the company's marketing department concludes that an external agency would be most advisable, a local agency provides one option. A globally based advertising agency (Table 15.6), such as Dentsu Worldwide, may have a subsidiary located in the target country. Major agencies often provide the full range of advertising services; other agencies offer some of the functions and outsource others to boutiques. When an outside agency will be chosen, the most common criteria for selection are shown in Table 15.7.

TABLE 15.6   The Biggest International Media Companies

WPP Group	www.wpp.com	Agencies: Addison Group, Ogilvy & Mather Worldwide, Bates CHI&Partners
Omnicom Group	www.omnicomgroup.com	Agencies: BBDO, DDB, TBWA
Publicis Groupe	www.publicisgroupe.com/en	Agencies: Saatchi & Saatchi, Leo Burnett, BBH
Interpublic	www.interpublic.com	Agencies: McCann Worldgroup, Weber Shandwick
Dentsu	www.dentsu.com	Agencies: McGarry Bowen
Havas	http://havas.com	Agencies: Havas Worldwide

TABLE 15.7   Selection Criteria for International Advertising Agencies

Familiarity with local circumstances
Familiarity with the company or industry
Size of the agency
Relevant experience
No conflicts of interest
Creative ability
Services provided
Chemistry with the client

In international advertising programs, the first two criteria are primary considerations. Whether an advertising approach will be standardized or adapted, knowing local circumstances, including cultural constraints, legal restrictions, language, slang, and other nuances, makes it possible to develop the best possible set of messages. Familiarity with the company helps the advertising team match the message to the specific product as well as how it might be used in the local culture.

Matching the size of the agency to the size of the company involved helps make certain the account receives the proper attention. When the advertising agency is far bigger than the client, the account may become lost or ignored. When the advertising agency is too small, the account may overwhelm it.

Relevant experience means that an agency has been engaged in something similar. An agency that has represented a tire manufacturer has relevant experience in the automobile industry and could effectively serve a firm wishing to advertise windshield wipers or batteries. At the same time, the agency would have a conflict of interest if it tried to capture the account from a second tire manufacturer.

Creative abilities and a company's creative reputation may be assessed by the number of awards a firm has earned or by observing the agency's work with other clients. The company examining various agencies will seek out the types of services the agency provides that it desires. Finally, intangibles such as the chemistry between the agency and potential client may become the deciding factor.

OVERSEE THE ADVERTISING PROGRAM

A creative brief normally serves as a template for an advertising program (see Table 15.8). The advertising agency or in-house advertising director will use the components of the brief in making other decisions.

TABLE 15.8 Elements of a Creative Brief

Advertising objective
Target audience
Advertising message
Message support (facts, research findings, endorsements)
Constraints (legal restrictions)

International advertising objectives should be carefully selected before the agency and client company move forward with any type of advertising program. Marketers identify the target audience from the list of methods used to define market segments, including demographics, psychographics, geographic area, geodemographics, product use, and product user variables. The advertising message should be clearly stated with a single sentence. Typically only one message will be delivered in an advertisement. The message generally focuses on the product's unique selling proposition. Trying to send a series of messages in the same commercial will create confusion. Message support will be used to convince potential buyers that the message claim is true and verifiable. Constraints include any local conditions, such as those imposed by theocratic law, along with any warnings or warranties that must be included in an advertisement. The creative brief serves as a guide for the selection of traditional and nontraditional media to be used in the advertising program.

Traditional Media Advertising

In international advertising programs, media selection may be more complicated than in some domestic settings. The agency or advertising manager will become familiar with local preferences and local availability. The most common choices of traditional advertising media include:

- television
- radio
- magazines
- newspapers
- billboard/outdoor
- direct mail

It is commonplace for a nation's government to control some or all media. State-owned television, radio stations, and newspapers may restrict or bar various advertisements. An advertisement for Unilever's skin-care brand, Pond's, was pulled from the air by Chinese authorities due to the use of an actress, Tang Wei, who was banned from all mainland Chinese media (Fitzsimmons, 2008). Other legal restrictions include the prohibition of billboards or the use of direct mail. Cultural nuances will also be considered. For example, in nations with low levels of literacy, the use of newspaper, magazine, and direct mail advertising would be unlikely. In others, use of traditional media such as newspaper advertising may be more effective than use of nontraditional media. In India, newspaper readership has increased over recent years suggesting that print advertising may indeed be a viable option in that country.[2]

Nontraditional Media

In the past decade, many new forms of advertising have arisen. These media may be used to accompany traditional media or as methods to reach customers in unique new ways. Nontraditional media include:

- video game advertising
- movie trailers
- subway tunnels
- in-flight airline magazines
- carry-home and take-out bags
- clothing bearing company names or logos
- mall signs
- kiosks
- posters

The more developed the local economy has become, the greater the number of nontraditional media alternatives. Nontraditional media assist in overcoming clutter. Someone wearing a t-shirt with a Nike swoosh on it advertises to friends and acquaintances who may not even watch television. Many nations feature numerous kiosks dispersed to metropolitan areas. Consumers in those regions are accustomed to finding information on them. Video game advertising has shown great promise in reaching younger males who are not inclined to watch television or spend time searching the web.

Digital Marketing Communications

Technology has changed the way consumers shop, interact with brands, interact with other consumers, and make restaurant reservations or book holidays. International marketers must consider how to use digital technologies (Table 15.9) to communicate with consumers around the world. Digital marketing communications are essentially the digital marketing equivalent of the traditional marketing communications mix adapted to the online marketing environment. Traditional offline and digital marketing efforts must deliver an integrated message across all channels which may be even more challenging if delivered across borders. Global marketers need to consider the usage and access to digital technologies and devise communications plans accordingly. For example, households in rural areas in the EU countries have slightly lower Internet access rates than households in urban and sub-urban areas.[3]

New digital platforms appear, such as for example the Amazon Spark social network initially available only in the USA. Its main purpose is to showcase products to potential customers (Ghosh, 2017). Current trends suggest that some tools become more popular than others, for example mobile advertising is overtaking desktop-based Internet advertising ad revenues (Johnson, 2016). The global growth in mobile phones usage looks promising for brands intending to communicate with consumers across the world. Brands need to be careful not to alienate consumers by inundating them with digital messages.

TABLE 15.9   Examples of Digital Marketing Communications Tools

Search Engine Optimization Advertising	Targeted advertising by search term
Online Advertising	Advertising on websites Programmatic display advertising
Social Media Advertising & Communications	Advertising on Facebook, Twitter, Linkedin, YouTube Consumer–company interactions on social media sites Electronic Word-of-Mouth (EWOM)
Text Message Advertising/Mobile Advertising	Click-to-download ads Click-to-call ads Image text and banner ads
E-mail Marketing	Direct e-mail marketing
Product Review Blogs Customer Review Sites	Trip Advisor website and app Amazon customer reviews

Social media advertising has exploded over the past decade. Facebook and Twitter advertising occurs worldwide. Many traditional advertisements encourage viewers to visit the company's Facebook, Twitter, or Digg page for additional information. While Facebook and Twitter are leading social networking sites, international advertisers often utilize other sites that are found in various regions. The use of these sites and other digital platforms for international marketing campaigns will continue as they grow in popularity.[4] One of the more important ways to reach consumers via social media is to generate electronic word-of-mouth (EWOM) that can be an effective way of reaching consumers in various geographical locations (Chu and Choi, 2011). Programmatic advertising, an automated way of buying and displaying online advertisements, is also predicted to grow globally (Rogers, 2017).

MEDIA SELECTION FACTORS

In choosing from the vast variety of potential advertising venues, international marketers consider three main factors. The nature of the product, the size of the market, and its location are related to choices of advertising media. The primary elements marketers consider include costs, availability, and coverage.

Costs

Two phenomena have influenced media selection in major ways during the past decade. The first is the growing price tag for traditional media advertising time. In many markets worldwide, time on a television or radio station, space in a magazine or newspaper, and even billboard rental fees have risen dramatically. With the explosion of potential media outlets, including the vast number of television stations available worldwide, choosing those that fit in a budget becomes more problematic.

The second issue is an increasing demand by companies that advertise for evidence that an advertising campaign or program produces tangible results. The increasing emphasis on accountability places major pressure on advertising agencies to create messages that lead to more immediate responses (Clow and Baack, 2012: 5). A company's marketing team considers the cost of an advertising program and balances that cost with the potential to achieve the desired objective.

Availability

Oftentimes a company's marketing team would prefer to use an advertising medium only to find out that the medium is not available in a specific nation or region. The Internet is the most common example of a medium that cannot be used in certain countries. Many Internet websites are banned in China, including Facebook, Gmail, Twitter, and YouTube.

Coverage

Even when media are available, sufficient coverage of potential customers may not be possible, especially when those customers are geographically disbursed. Coverage can be affected by infrastructure, such as when television and radio signals do not reach all parts of a country. Magazines and newspapers may not be distributed throughout an entire area. Billboards may not be legal on certain roads, or it may be that so few people pass by them that the signs are not effective. The Australian government in 2010 considered banning many billboard advertisements as offensive and as an attempt to reclaim public spaces.[5]

The marketing team examines the available and viable media and seeks to purchase time and space in a manner that optimizes coverage to potential customers. To achieve this goal, marketers develop a clear understanding of the members of a target market, the media usage habits within that group, and the costs of using those media to run commercials.

ASSESS ADVERTISING EFFECTIVENESS

International advertisements may be presented in three formats. A *continuous* format means commercials will run consistently throughout the year. A *pulsating* format features advertisements throughout the year, with bursts during key seasons, such as New Year's Day or May Day. A *discontinuous* format includes periods where no advertisements are run and heavy amounts are run during key seasons, such as the period surrounding the Cannes Film Festival. Each of the three formats will be evaluated in two areas: attitudinal effects and behavioral effects. The criteria used to assess the effectiveness of international advertising programs include the items displayed in Table 15.10.

TABLE 15.10   Attitudinal and Behavioral Effects

Attitudinal	Behavioral
Brand recognition	Inquiries
Brand recall	Website visits
Recall of the advertisement	Store traffic
Perceptions of position	Direct marketing responses
Brand loyalty	Redemptions of marketing offers (coupons, premiums, contest entries)
Brand equity	Sales by unit changes in sales volume

Some attitudinal changes may take time to instill. An effective advertising program can quickly achieve recognition and recall, especially in the short term. Developing the desired perception of position, brand loyalty, and brand equity normally takes more time, especially when a company enters a new host country. During the 2010 World Cup in South Africa, the low-cost South African airline Kulula.com ran a series of ads that purposely walked the line regarding using World Cup images without permission. One advertisement included the copy "the Unofficial National Carrier of You-Know-What." The governing body of the World Cup, FIFA, responded by taking legal action seeking to remove the ads. The company enjoyed the free publicity and added to the already existing brand position as an irreverent, fun brand (Dardagan, 2010).

Behavioral effects also experience varying results. Inquiries often occur quickly. Changes in other variables, such as sales of big-ticket items, may take longer. Also, competitive reactions and even the weather can delay responses to various promotions and offers. Shopping patterns vary widely. In countries where living spaces are small and storage of any kind is limited, it becomes more difficult to encourage customers to stock up on items. In countries where shopping, especially for convenience items, is a more daily occurrence, advertisements often stress the need for immediate or habitual purchase.

STANDARDIZATION OR ADAPTATION

A marketer seeking to advertise across national boundaries confronts several key decisions as part of the process. The first will be in regard to the standardization or adaptation of marketing messages. As has been noted in an earlier chapter, both products and messages are considered in this process.

Recently, the trend appears to be increasing standardization of messages as media usage becomes more widely available. When a product remains unchanged regardless of the country in which it is sold, messages are often consistent across borders, except for language translation when needed. The Bhalaria Metal Forming Company in India markets cutlery internationally. It would likely market basic knife, fork, and spoon sets, combined with more specialized tableware, with a standardized marketing approach emphasizing quality and value.[6]

雄獅飛躍添喜氣　步步高陞福滿門
皇家銀行財務金融集團祝大家心想事成
欲知我們如何以您為先，請瀏覽www.rbc.com/chinesenewyear

以　為先

RBC

Royal Bank of Canada's advertisement targeting the Chinese community in Canada.

Standardized messages are also designed when products are adapted. Food products may be adapted to local tastes, yet marketing messages remain consistent, as is the case with Knorr soups and sauces. Knorr packages are standardized with the same brand name and logo, and the company promotes the same image, even though products are tailored to individual countries, including the company's goulash soup in Hungary and chicken noodle soup in Singapore ((de Mooij, 2010: 30). The same would be true when appliances are adapted to meet local conditions, including differences in electrical current, or the amount of space devoted to a product such as a refrigerator. Larger products including automobiles will be adapted to meet local legal requirements and consumer needs, yet the basic message sent by a giant such as Audi remains consistent.[7]

When a company such as Proctor & Gamble creates individual brands for various nations or regions, P & G marketing messages are often adapted more significantly. For example, the washing detergent Tide is available in Poland under the name Vizir, and as Daz in the United Kingdom. Packaging of the detergent bears different names in those countries, but the packaging design is the same. Consequently, marketing communications needs to take these differences into account.

VIZIR AND Daz packaging.

INTERNATIONAL LAW AND GLOBALLY INTEGRATED MARKETING COMMUNICATIONS

The use of globally integrated marketing communications must also follow the various laws that pertain to advertising and promotion. Many differences pertaining to advertising and international promotion activities are present across country borders. The Unfair Commercial Practices Directive of the European Union (Directive 2005/29/EC), passed in 2005, outlines a number of marketing and promotional activities that are prohibited in the EU. Other directives set out specific regulations considering promotion of certain products. For example, alcohol promotion regulations differ between the different member states of the EU. Sweden introduced a complete ban on alcohol advertising whilst other countries allow it under certain conditions.[8]

India, a country of growing importance, has a number of laws that pertain to advertising. The Indecent Representation of Women Act of 1986 covers what were deemed to be inappropriate depictions of women in advertising, promotions, and product or labeling designs. The advertising or promotion of cigarettes, tobacco products, and liquor in India is covered under the Prohibition of Advertisement and Regulation of Trade and Commerce, Production, Supply and Distribution Act of 2003.

While laws are established and enforced internationally, most marketers prefer some degree of self-regulation over governmental intervention, and as a result, many self-regulatory bodies exist. The European Advertising Standards Alliance (EASA) is a self-regulatory association useful for learning about advertising and promotion standards throughout the European Union. Similar standards exist in India through the Advertising Standard Council of India. Self-regulation codes also were adopted recently for marketers in China. The China Association of National Advertisers, the China Advertising Association, and the China Advertising Association of Commerce adopted these codes. As China continues to grow in importance in the world's economy, codes such as these assist international marketers to ensure that promotional practices are within established guidelines. International marketers that pay close attention to international advertising and promotions laws, as well as the codes established by self-regulatory entities, encounter fewer problems with governments over time. Table 15.11 lists information about tobacco and alcohol advertising regulations in selected countries.

TABLE 15.11   Alcohol and Tobacco Promotion Regulations in Selected Countries

Product	Country			
	Norway	Guatemala	Pakistan	Russia
Tobacco	There is a ban on direct and indirect forms of tobacco advertising. All forms of tobacco sponsorship are prohibited	Tobacco advertising, promotion and sponsorship is generally allowed, with a few restrictions	Many forms of tobacco advertising and promotion are prohibited, including advertising on domestic TV, radio, billboards, and in print media	All forms of domestic and cross-border tobacco advertising, promotion, and sponsorship are prohibited, with extremely limited exceptions. All forms of financial or other tobacco sponsorship are prohibited
Alcohol	Alcohol advertising is banned	Alcohol advertising, promotion and sponsorship is generally allowed, with a few restrictions	Alcohol advertising is banned	Advertising alcohol products is banned from almost all media

Innovative promotion of beer in Guatemala.

LEARNING OBJECTIVE #3:

What traditional and culturally based types of advertising appeals do marketing professionals use?

MESSAGE DESIGN: TYPES OF APPEALS

Traditional advertising theory suggests that products can be marketed using a method from a set of basic types of advertising appeals. The goal will be to match the message's objective to the medium selected and the appeal format. For many markets, the choice would be made from one or more of the following set of advertising appeals:

- fear
- humor
- sex/sensuality
- music
- rationality
- emotions
- scarcity

A fear appeal walks a fine line. When the amount of fear becomes too great, the viewer tends to turn away from the message. When the degree of fear is too low, the viewer might ignore the message or not take it seriously. Cultural adaption will be required when assessing the degree to which citizens in a region are sensitive to danger. In Western culture, bad breath and body odor can be made to seem catastrophic. In other nations, these issues may be less important. Fear may be generated by a number of sources, including being viewed as a social outcast, worries about financial issues, the desire to protect one's family, concerns about personal health, and other issues.

Humor appeals may be difficult to design due to cultural and legal problems. What people think is funny varies widely across and within each country. Various countries may restrict the use of humor with religion or other values. A cultural assimilator may be able to assist with some aspects of humor, but the assimilator's opinion will only represent one point of view regarding whether the commercial was actually funny.

Academic research investigating humor in advertising reveals that the foundation of humor is incongruity. An unexpected, implausible, or nonactual event forms the roots of humor, regardless of country. The following joke uses the unexpected: A doctor tells a man, "Your wife must have absolute rest. Here is a sleeping tablet." "When do I give it to her?" the man asks. "You don't," explains the doctor, "you take it yourself." The mild humor in this joke is due to the unexpected nature of the punchline. Some research suggests that this type of incongruity is funny globally. Research also indicates that cultures vary in terms of the roles of groups, equality, and other aspects of advertising humor based on the cultural background of the country. Basically, whereas the unexpected typically makes consumers laugh, what is considered unexpected differs from country to country (Alden et al., 1993).

A perfume product may have the objective of increasing brand loyalty by suggesting the scent will make the user feel more feminine. The choice of advertising appeal would likely be a sensual sexual appeal coupled with a medium where romantic music could be played in a quiet, soft setting, and an attractive model would use the perfume. Careful thought will be given to what is legally and culturally acceptable when sexual messages are framed. In Chile, one advertising campaign featured nude celebrities drinking milk, and authorities allowed it to air. In many Middle Eastern countries, sex and gender-related issues are prohibited to the point that sexual appeals in any form are not used (Joelson, 2004; Clow and Baack, 2012: 161).

The use of music occurs in several ways in advertising. It can serve as a background for some other type of appeal, such as dramatic music supporting a fear appeal or a light-hearted tune in a humorous ad. A musical appeal makes the tune the primary element in the advertisement. Music will be tailored to local tastes and the product being marketed.

Cultural matches dictate the most viable moments to feature rational appeals. Many business-to-business advertisements take advantage of a rational presentation of a product's benefits or the endorsement of a professional. The most expensive advertisement in Indian history, costing near *Rs* 4.5 *crore* (approximately $1 million), was a 2010 television commercial for the leading Indian soda Thums Up. The commercial stars the popular Bollywood actor Akshay Kumar and features a rational appeal to attach the popularity and style of the actor to the soda.[9]

Emotional advertising is favored in some nations over others. Western Union recently ran emotional advertising in El Salvador. The message presented a mother talking about her son who had left the country to move to the United States and each month he sent her money using Western Union. Many Latin American citizens have relatives they have not seen for years. The emotional approach worked. Emotions used in advertising include friendships, trust, happiness, security, serenity, anger, family bonds, and passion (Dietrich, 1999).

Scarcity appeals are effective when a product is offered only for a limited time. Often these advertisements focus on a specific event, such as the World Cup or the Olympics. They are used during holiday seasons, including red and green candy wrappers during the Christmas season. Scarcity approaches also fit with marketing to bottom-of-the-pyramid customers, who seek out special deals when they have money available to make purchases.

INTERNATIONAL MARKETING IN DAILY LIFE

CULTURE, GENDER, AND ADVERTISING

Advertising constitutes one of the most visual marketing elements in everyday life. Consumers worldwide are continually bombarded with thousands of advertising messages. The communications often reflect cultural variables. One important variable is gender roles. Gender roles are reflected in advertisements and differ greatly across cultures. In Western cultures, women have historically been portrayed as inferior to men and, quite often, as sex objects. In the United States in particular, women have historically been depicted in housewife roles or in sexually provocative ways. These depictions have evolved over time. Ironically, men are often portrayed in sexually suggestive ways in today's commercials.

Attitudes toward sex and gender roles in advertising tend to be much more liberal in Europe, especially in France where overtly sexual imagery in advertising is commonplace. The European Advertising Standards Alliance (EASA) acts as the main body for advertising self-regulation in the region and works to foster positive depictions of women in advertisements as well as high ethical standards in all advertising campaigns. The body passed guidance principles for the industry regarding sex role depictions in 2009.[10] The principles promote the belief that advertisements should respect human dignity and should not discriminate against either males or females.

In Eastern cultures, advertising practices are much more conservative. The depiction of women has traditionally been based on the stereotype that the place for the woman is in the home. The phrase *danson johi*, a Chinese term that means respect for men and contempt for women, has often emerged in advertising campaigns (Ford et al., 1998). In Eastern cultures, women have often been associated with lower-priced products while men have been associated with higher-priced items. The difference originates from a stereotypical view that men are valued more highly than are women. Some of the tactics appear to have begun to change, but gender stereotypes still persist in advertising around the globe and responsible advertising professionals should consider the cultural influence advertising images have on societal culture (Matthes et al., 2016).

Religious beliefs continue to play an important role in the depiction of women in advertising. In Muslim countries, sexually explicit or inappropriate advertisements are strongly rejected (Clow and Baack, 2012). International marketers carefully consider religious beliefs when constructing advertisements in these regions. Core cultural beliefs vary greatly across countries, and advertisers have much to gain by observing these differences.

CULTURAL PARADOXES

Marketers trained in Western culture and settings would be tempted to rely on traditional appeals. In international marketing programs, however, cultural differences create differing environments. To meet the challenges, overcoming various paradoxes takes precedence. Three often receive the most attention: the equality paradox, the dependence and freedom paradox, and the success paradox (de Mooij, 2010: 218–220).

Equality Paradox

In much of Europe, equality conceptually suggests that income distribution should be relatively uniform. In contrast, those in New Zealand and Great Britain view equality in terms of opportunity rather than income distribution. The net result would be much more dramatic differences in what would be perceived as income disparity. Therefore, advertisers would need to account for host country perceptions of equality when designing commercials.

Dependence and Freedom Paradox

Dependence and independence are opposing values related to power distance and individualism/collectivism. In a collectivist culture such as Japan with greater power distance, children depend on their parents for much longer periods of time. Where power distance is lower and the culture is more independent, children are often encouraged to become self-reliant and go out on their own at a much earlier age. Again, advertisers would need to be aware of these factors when creating messages.

Success Paradox

In masculine cultures, a male may be more likely to knowingly display personal success, or "show off." British culture, which tends to be more masculine, would feature advertisements containing terms such as "best" or "better." In contrast, more feminine cultures, including those in Sweden and Denmark, would refrain from such claims.

Instead more subtle messages are presented, such as "True refinement comes from within," the tagline for a recent Volvo commercial in Sweden.

INTERNATIONAL INCIDENT

United Colors of Benneton's advertisements are often controversial. The company's aim has always been to challenge social norms and break taboos by using shocking advertisements. However, in recent years the brand decided to change its creative advertising strategy and soften the brand image by using advertising that is "never shocking." Social issues are still at the center of the brand's promotional strategy, for example the "United by Half" campaign debuted in India and received very positive response from consumers. Discuss the company's decision to dramatically change its advertising strategy. What are the ethical dilemmas the company faces around the world with campaigns that are socially and politically charged?

INTERNATIONAL ADVERTISING APPEALS

Due to these paradoxes and other cultural differences, appeal formats are often based in other factors in international advertising. Advertisers account for cultural nuances when selecting the dimension to be used. The most common formats include advertisements that reflect the cultural values displayed in Table 15.12.

TABLE 15.12   International Advertising Appeals and Values

Power distance
Individualism/collectivism
Masculinity/femininity
Uncertainty avoidance
Long- or short-term orientation

Power Distance

Cultures with high degrees of power distance often experience advertising with verbal and direct power claims. Feeling of status and prestige may be associated with products. In Portugal, the Alfa 33 automobile has been advertised featuring a reference to feelings of royalty (de Mooij, 2010).

Power distance will be displayed in relationships (young/old) between persons featured in advertisements and how those relationships are demonstrated. In a low power distance culture, advertisements may be designed with a mother and daughter sharing an experience as "friends," whereas in a high power distance culture the same two will be viewed with the elder advising, counseling, or teaching the younger person. High power distance cultures normally exhibit greater degrees of respect and deference to older persons.

Power distance is related to perceptions of independence. Advertisements featuring a child standing on his own would be more appreciated in a low power distance culture where independence is valued. A recent print ad in the Netherlands shows a young boy by himself and references Blue Band margarine, emphasizing his ability to make his own choices. At the opposite extreme, high power distance would lead to commercials featuring dependent relationships between children and parents (Mitchell and Oneal, 1994).

Individualism/Collectivism

When the advertising team knows that messages are being constructed for members of an individualistic culture, the language in the copy will be more direct and personalized, such as the "Treat yourself right" tagline for Crystal Light. Direct references to "I," "we," and "you" become more likely (Han and Shavitt, 1994). A recent Nike advertisement in Spain featured the headline, "The energy I get." The Nike tagline "Just do it" reflects the same direct, individualized message.

Visual elements of commercials focused on individualistic cultures tend to feature a person enjoying the product alone. In the individualistic German culture, a woman takes pleasure in a container of Magnum ice cream by herself, and the copy states, "I share many things, but not everything."

In collectivist cultures, sharing and being part of a group become important elements of the message strategy. The Portuguese product food sweetener Hermesetas is advertised with the comment, "It is so good, you want to share it with others." A person experiencing a product alone may be more pitied than envied. Any advertisement for a restaurant, automobile, or clothing item would need to find a way to be presented in a social setting, enjoyed by the purchaser and his or her friends. Restaurants would have an abundance of food to share with an unexpected guest. Automobiles would be driven with several passengers onboard. Clothing would be enjoyed and shared with others. One estimate suggests that 70% of the world's population is collectivist, which suggests that many individualistic commercials do not fit with the target audience (de Mooij, 2002: 226).

As an example of adaptation of the message for the same product in differing cultures, Jever beer was recently marketed in the individualistic climate of Germany with a photograph of a man standing alone on the beach holding a bottle of the product. In Spain, where the culture is more collectivist, a group party setting portrays the enjoyment of the beer in one advertisement and by a couple close together in another.

As marketing messages travel across international boundaries, it becomes more difficult to structure a message to one sole culture. Media selection can help. Local magazines and newspapers can be utilized for culture-specific messages; television and radio are more likely to bleed into other countries or be sent by Internet messages (Zhang and Gelb, 1996).

Another new development may be found when global brands appear alongside local brands in the same market. In China, consumers often view global brands as being sophisticated and modern. Western-style individualistic advertising of those products would be expected. Local Chinese brands would continue to be advertised with messages and images that reflect local values, and would therefore contain more collectivist elements (Bowman, 2002: 8).

Masculinity/Femininity

Masculinity often connects with individualism. The net result becomes an emphasis on aggression, competitiveness, and winning. An advertisement for the Japanese Nikon camera suggests, "More winners per second," which reflects this perspective. Beyond winning, size becomes an issue in masculine cultures, where bigger is better.[11]

Gender portrayals differ in masculine as opposed to feminine cultures. Often, men are depicted as being incompetent in domestic settings in masculine cultures; the kitchen is the woman's domain and she has the greater expertise. Also, however, women can be portrayed as stronger and more aggressive. A Japanese television commercial for Hitachi features a woman in a battle with flies. Women may be shown winning and being successful in masculine cultures.

Feminine cultures are more caring, appreciate softness, and favor small over large. Sweden's Volvo tagline "True refinement comes from within" expresses the value that you do not have to show off, win, or make sure everyone knows your car is bigger and better. The company often advertises safety and protection over power and performance.

In a feminine culture, an advertisement for a pain reliever would likely carry the message that you can relieve the suffering of someone you love by using the product. The same medicine in a masculine culture would likely be marketed as, "The number one pain reliever," or "The medicine doctors recommend most."

Gender role portrayal will be different in feminine cultures. In Denmark, a product sold in Matas drugstore has been advertised with a male model wearing an apron. In Spain, a man may be shown shopping with his children and nurturing them. In Sweden, one advertisement for Ajax cleaner features a man swinging a mop as if it were a golf club.

Uncertainty Avoidance

Advertisements in countries with high levels of uncertainty avoidance tend to be highly structured and contain a great deal of information and detail. Strong uncertainty avoidance is connected to the desire for explanation, testing, proof, advice, and testimonials by experts. An advertisement for the Russian facial cream Purity Line contains a substantial amount of discussion of the company's laboratory methods, including scientific proof that the product will work. Demonstrating competence becomes important in strong uncertainty avoidance cultures. Automobiles manufactured in Germany can be portrayed as containing superior engineering. Facts and figures reinforce these claims. Using the standard fear appeal is an effective strategy in high uncertainty avoidance cultures (Reardon et al., 2006).

Where uncertainty avoidance is less of a driving force within a culture, advertisers are able to construct messages that are less precise, because they do not need to reduce anxiety or tension. At the extreme, an advertisement for Jamaican tourism portrays, "One love, one life" as the musical theme with the tagline "Welcome to Jamaica," which does not require proof.

Long- or Short-Term Orientation

Customers in countries with a short-term orientation may often view advertisements featuring a scarcity appeal. The approach matches the sense of urgency present in the culture, and leads to phrases such as "Buy now!" Short-term orientation is related to immediate gratification. In the United Kingdom, one advertising headline created by Häagen-Dazs ice cream entices the consumer to enjoy "instant pleasure." Investments in the long-term future, through saving or insurance policies, are hard to advertise in short-term orientation situations. Instead, the advertiser would need to find a way to convince the individual to act immediately, such as through a teaser rate for savings or a gift or premium to accompany the purchase of an insurance policy.

Long-term orientation advertisements are associated with symbols and words regarding the future, stability, and future generations. Mountains, trees, and other long-lasting natural phenomena are displayed in advertisements aimed at long-term cultures, especially in high-context cultures. LG International has advertised in Korea with an elderly man surrounded by the harmony of nature, a message directed to long-term orientation.

Combinations

As is the case in traditional advertising, various combinations of appeals can be devised to match a product, target market, culture, or specific message objective. Traditional approaches are often developed, including humor with fear, humor with sex, rationality with scarcity, and music with practically any other approach. A wide variety of combinations is possible. Those same traditional appeal formats may also be connected to the international appeals. As noted, fear appeals effectively reach those with higher levels of uncertainty avoidance. Scarcity appeals match with short-term orientation. Creative advertisers can develop many combinations of traditional methodologies with these international formats.

Cultural experts also note combinations of the international approaches. Often, masculine cultures are also individualistic. Feminine cultures may be more collectivist. The advertising team can examine other combinations of cultural characteristics in order to construct the best possible advertising program.

The Value Paradox

The value paradox, also known as deprivation hypothesis (Javidan et al., 2006), proposes that advertising often appeals to what is lacking in society to show "the perfect life," hence cultural dimensions and scores for particular cultures should be used with caution when deciding which advertising appeals to use. Cultural dimensions such as Hofstede's, or GLOBE dimensions, offer general guidance but cultures are more complex than a set of scores.

The value paradox is demonstrated by the GLOBE study which showed that cultures which reported high practices for many of the cultural phenomena actually valued them less than those who reported less practices for a particular cultural phenomenon. Cultures which scored very low on the performance orientation dimension indicated that they would like to have more of performance orientation; those that scored high on performance orientation practices indicated that they would like to have less of it. It is often the case that we have to learn the skills that we do not have, and desire the things we do not possess. Cultures are full of such value paradoxes—and this often applies to marketing communications. For example, in American individualistic culture advertising often shows happy families but such images appear less frequent in Japanese advertising. It is the combination of paradoxes that makes advertising to global audiences challenging. Young consumers from the high power distance cultures of Korea and Thailand preferred low power distance appeals to high power distance appeals; American consumers evaluated high power distance appeals more favorably than Asian consumers (Jung et al., 2009). International advertisers need to be aware of and cautious toward the cultural complexities of target countries.

GLOBAL, LOCAL, AND FOREIGN CONSUMER CULTURE POSITIONING STRATEGIES

Global brands need to decide how they want to position their brands in terms of the consumer culture they represent. Several options exist; brands may be positioned as global, or as local or as foreign. The same brand may be positioned as foreign in one country but as local in another depending on the context and brand objectives.

Global Consumer Culture Positioning

Global consumer culture positioning strategy associates the brand with a widely understood and recognized set of symbols and values believed to constitute global consumer culture. Such symbols may include advertising appeals, shapes, colors, images, or brand name calligraphy that are associated with global consumer culture. The brand is defined as a symbol of a global culture which consumers may purchase to reinforce their membership in that segment. This positioning strategy should resonate with increasingly global segments of consumers who associate similar meanings with certain places, people, and things, and who regard a product, service, or brand in essentially the same way regardless of their culture or country (Cleveland and Laroche, 2007). Such consumers are usually younger and cosmopolitan, and are open to new experiences (Carpenter et al., 2012; Westjohn et al., 2012). Appeals that could express this positioning strategy may include performance-oriented appeals, or soft-sell appeals (Okazaki et al., 2010; Czarnecka and Keles, 2014). For example, positioning the product as a "time saver" which represents the value of "saving time" is one specific example of global consumer culture positioning (Alden et al., 1999).

Local Consumer Culture Positioning

This strategy is expressed by positioning the brand as local by using local culture symbols, norms, identities, and images to advertise the brand. This positioning may work well with consumers who are ethnocentric and traditional, or with products for which it is important to emphasize the local origin. Depicting the brand as locally produced, for example by using tags such as "Buy British," "Buy Polish," is also part of this positioning strategy.

Foreign Consumer Culture Positioning

This strategy is very similar to country of origin in which a brand is positioned as foreign. For example, advertising perfumes as French in the United States or Swiss watches in England represents foreign consumer culture positioning.

Some brands use a combination of positioning strategies, for example HSBC uses the tagline "The world's local bank" and uses both global and local cultural symbols in its advertising messages.

LEARNING OBJECTIVE #4:

How are the traditional executional frameworks adapted to international advertising programs?

ADVERTISING EXECUTIONAL FRAMEWORKS

message strategy: the primary tactic or approach used to deliver the key idea to be delivered in an advertisement

When creating an advertising program, a key element to consider will be the campaign's creative message strategy. A **message strategy** is the primary tactic or approach used to deliver the key idea in an advertisement. International message strategies are carefully matched with the company, product, target market, local

HSBC's advertisement appealing to both local and global audiences.

culture, and other conditions in the host country. Three major types of message strategies are cognitive, affective, and conative (Laskey et al., 1989).

Cognitive message strategies present rational arguments or pieces of information to consumers. The key idea will be in regard to a product's attributes and benefits. Consumers can enjoy these benefits by purchasing the product (Asker and Norris, 1982). Cognitive message strategies fit with more rational cultures and those with higher levels of uncertainty avoidance. They also can spell out the extended benefits of a product in a culture with a long-term orientation. In a high power distance culture, a cognitive message strategy can be used showing a parent or teacher explaining a product's benefits to a child or student.

Affective message strategies invoke feelings or emotions and match those feelings with a product, service, or company. A resonance approach connects the product with the consumer's experiences to develop stronger ties between the product and the individual. Emotional advertising elicits emotions related to product recall and choice by developing positive feelings toward the brand. Affective advertising is more emotive and matches with feminine cultures and low power distance cultures. Collectivism also fits with the affective approach, appealing to family, friends, and social connectedness.

Conative message strategies are designed to lead directly to a consumer response, such as a store visit or purchase. Such an approach connects well with short-term orientation cultures. In more masculine cultures, where direct messages are delivered, the advertisement can encourage a "Take action now" response. Individualism can be emphasized with a "Do this for yourself" communication.

cognitive message strategies: advertising messages that present rational arguments or pieces of information to consumers

affective message strategies: advertising messages that invoke feelings or emotions and match those feelings with a product, service, or company

conative message strategies: advertising messages designed to lead directly to a consumer response, such as a store visit or purchase

TRADITIONAL EXECUTIONAL FRAMEWORKS

executional framework:
the manner in which an advertising appeal and message strategy are delivered

In order to deliver cognitive, affective, or conative messages, a delivery system will be employed. The **executional framework** is the manner in which an advertising appeal and message strategy are delivered. Table 15.13 lists the standard methods of sending messages to consumers.

TABLE 15.13   Traditional Executional Frameworks

Animation
Slice-of-life
Dramatization
Testimonial
Authoritative
Demonstration
Fantasy
Informative

The growing sophistication of computer graphics programs has led to greater use of *animation* to present commercials. Animation appears in television spots, on the Internet, and in print media when cartoon characters or other figures pitch products. Animation captures attention, especially when it portrays things that are physically impossible. Many countries are experiencing growth in Internet usage, leading to consumers viewing animation as a cutting-edge, modern method of advertising.

Slice-of-life executions involve four stages: encounter, problem, interaction, and solution. Two or more people meet. They discover they experience a common dilemma, such as a dirty shirt. In the interaction, one explains to another how a product provides a solution. Using the good or service resolves the quandary, making everyone happy. Slice-of-life executions match with high-context cultures, where symbols and rituals supplant lengthy explanations. Collectivist and feminine cultures often feature slice-of-life executions. Japan's collectivism and Norway's feminism fit with this approach.

When a slice-of-life ad contains additional intensity, it becomes a *dramatization*. Expressive cultures in which more extreme circumstances are needed to capture attention relate to dramatization. *Dramatization* meshes with high-context cultures, because less attention to in-depth explanation is given; instead, the problem is simply resolved by the product.

Satisfied customers provide *testimonials*. In collectivist cultures, the recommendation of friends or endorsement by a group of peers will be persuasive. Testimonials of family members or friends giving out advice work well in feminine cultures.

Authoritative messages are delivered by experts, such as doctors, lawyers, and those who use a product in some technical manner. These individuals explain a product's benefits. Experts take on additional status in high power distance countries and those in which low-context communication prevails. For countries with greater degrees of uncertainty avoidance, expertise provides key purchase reassurance. Authoritative messages appear in business-to-business advertisements, where an expert gives a product greater credibility.

Demonstration executions gain value in high-context cultures, where visual images portray a product's benefits. Demonstration also reduces uncertainty for those who require such information. A demonstration in a masculine culture will be designed to show a product's superiority. In feminine cultures, the use of a product to help a loved one, such as a disinfectant being applied to a cut to make it hurt less and heal faster, creates a powerful image of caring.

For those with a short-term orientation, a *fantasy* offers a "get away from it all" option involving sex, love, romance, or self-indulgence. Fantasies are not as well accepted in logical, rational cultures, but a fantasy can be constructed to show someone gaining status and power by using a product in a high power distance culture. Another fantasy could show a high-status person being embarrassed or moved to a lower level in a low power distance country, thereby emphasizing common humanity.

Informative executions deliver straightforward presentations. They work better in low-context cultures and with those seeking to avoid uncertainty. Many business-to-business advertisements are informative, regardless of cultural differences, due to the nature of the message and the audience, which expects more rational and clear-cut information.

INTERNATIONAL EXECUTIONAL FRAMEWORKS

The traditional executional frameworks can be adapted to local conditions for a variety of marketing messages. In a global marketing context, however, other forms of executions are popular. Seven basic forms of advertising in global markets are:

- announcement
- association transfer
- lesson
- drama
- entertainment
- imagination
- special effects

Announcements

Announcements are presentations of facts without the use of people. Visuals portray the message. A *pure display* appears in a shop window. A *product message* transmits information about product attributes in a factual, logical manner. These messages are used in low-context cultures that desire fuller explanations. The *corporate presentation* form of announcement describes the overall corporation with a voice-over or a song. A voice-over presents facts, and a song provides additional context. Each announcement method achieves the goal of providing information to customers and potential customers regarding products, product improvements, releases and offers, and other basic information. Announcements often match the traditional informative executional framework.

announcements: advertising presentations of facts without the use of people

Association Transfers

Association transfers offer a format in which a product is combined with another object, person, situation, or environment. One form of transfer, the *lifestyle* method, associates people with a culture or counterculture of a country. A standard lifestyle presentation connects a product to a youthful approach to life. Germany's Beck's beer often presents commercials depicting young people engaged in active hobbies

association transfers: an advertising format in which a product is combined with another object, person, situation, or environment

or events. With the *metaphor* form of association transfer, the characteristics of an animal or idea are connected with the product. Visual metaphors, often found in high-context cultures, can be concrete or abstract images. Verbal metaphors will be placed in low-context cultures. The *metonymy* approach transfers the meaning of an original object into the brand, such as when a flower blossoms into a bottle of perfume. *Celebrity transfers* associate other persons with a celebrity, who does not demonstrate, endorse, or provide a direct testimonial about the product. Hong Kong actor Jackie Chan has appeared in celebrity transfer commercials.

Lessons, Demonstrations, and Comparative Advertising

lesson: a form of advertising presentation that applies facts and arguments to the audience

The **lesson** form of presentation applies facts and arguments to the audience in the form of a lecture. In low-context cultures, straightforward presentations of facts are welcome. The viewer learns how a product solves a problem or improves her life. In one format, a *presenter* is the dominant present in the advertisement speaking directly and sending the main message. The presenter can use the demonstration format to explain the product's benefits. For collectivist cultures, a set of presenters may appear in the commercial.

A second form of lesson takes the form of *endorsement and testimonial*, which is highly similar to the testimonial and authoritative executional frameworks. A third version, the *vignette*, uses a series of independent sketches or visual situations with no continuity in the action. The product is displayed as the focus of the vignette with a voice-over or song suggesting how it is connected to the story being portrayed. The fourth version of the lesson format, the *demonstration*, is the same as that used in the traditional framework.

comparative advertising: product comparisons where two items are shown in use side by side

Product comparisons may be part of a demonstration presentation, where two items are shown in use side by side. The marketing team should be aware of cultural sensitivities to these types of advertisements as well as any legal restrictions. Argentina, China, El Salvador, Italy, and South Africa do not allow using competitors as part of **comparative advertising**. Other countries, such as the Philippines, have strong restrictions on how advertising can be conducted. Many cultures frown on such comparisons as well, including most of the Scandinavian countries (Durschlag, 1999).

Entertainment

entertainment: when theatrical drama, musicals, shows, comedies, slapstick, humor, horror, or satire provide the primary advertising format

When theatrical drama, musicals, shows, comedies, slapstick, humor, horror, or satire provides the primary advertising format the mode is called **entertainment**. The use of *humor* as an advertising appeal has been presented previously, with the caution that humor is subjective and difficult to create. Humor may not translate well across cultures. A British commercial for Hamlet cigars may be difficult to understand for consumers from other cultures. The concept was to attract attention in a unique way.

Imagination

imagination: an advertising format that utilizes cartoon or other visual techniques to make unrealistic presentations of a make-believe world

The **imagination** format utilizes cartoon or other visual techniques to make unrealistic presentations of a make-believe world. Imagination essentially combines the traditional animation and fantasy executional frameworks. An animated bear has been used across national boundaries to promote the cleaning brand Cif, a French product. The bear's name is *Cajoline* in Greece, *Bamseline* in Denmark, *Coccolino* in Italy, and *Kuschelweich* in Germany.

Special Effects

The **special effects** format delivers a variety of messages by combining animation, cartoon, camera effects (camera motion), recording techniques, music, and other sounds in commercials. MTV takes advantage of special effects to promote the channel globally. Special effects can highlight a dramatization, fantasy, or animation executional framework.[12]

special effects: an advertising format used to deliver a wide variety of commercials by combining animation, cartoon, camera effects (camera motion), recording techniques, music, and other sounds

Combinations

These international advertising executional frameworks do not stand alone. Special effects can be part of an imagination or part of a demonstration. Imagination can be combined with entertainment. The international frameworks also are utilized in conjunction with traditional frameworks. Animation and fantasy can be part of imagination, entertainment, demonstration, and special effects. The role of the advertising agency or in-house marketer will be to discover the most important cultural characteristics and then combine that knowledge with the selection of the advertising appeal(s) and executional framework(s) that best match the product and brand image. The additional challenge is to make the commercial or advertising interesting enough to cut through clutter and be remembered by the target audience.

LEARNING OBJECTIVE #5:

What types of alternative marketing communications programs are available to international firms?

ALTERNATIVE MARKETING COMMUNICATIONS

In addition to the alternative media choices marketers employ to present advertisements, a series of new approaches to reaching consumers has evolved. Alternative marketing communications programs take advantage of the creativity and imagination of the company's marketing professionals. Effective alternative marketing programs overcome clutter and reach consumers in comfortable settings. They allow the company to present a message to an interested audience. Four of the alternative marketing programs that have achieved success are:

- buzz marketing
- guerrilla marketing
- product placements and branded entertainment
- lifestyle marketing

BUZZ MARKETING

One of the fastest growing areas in alternative media marketing is buzz marketing, which is also known as word-of-mouth marketing. The system emphasizes consumers passing along information about a product. Three approaches to buzz include:

- consumers who like a brand and tell others
- consumers who like a brand and are sponsored by a company to tell others
- company or agency employees telling others about the brand

Consumers Who Tell Family and Friends

Consumers who like a brand can be encouraged to tell family and friends. The emergence of social media facilitates this type of buzz. A clever song or video can quickly go viral, leading to greater interest in a product. This type of buzz is the opposite of negative word-of-mouth, which can quickly damage a brand's image. Prior to the Internet, a disenchanted customer was likely to tell around eleven people about a negative experience but only five or six people about a positive encounter. Currently both numbers can quickly rise to dramatic figures. Many international companies monitor what is being said on Facebook and Twitter, seeking to take advantage of positive buzz and to combat any negative comments.

A common tactic for technology companies is to hire advertising agencies to help create buzz around a new product release. Typically, this includes a fake leak of the new product. The company acts as if the leak was unintentional, and sends cease-and-desist letters, but the actual goal is to get bloggers and technology writers to begin writing about the product pre-release. This creates buzz and increases initial sales (Rocha, 2006).

Sponsored Consumers

When a person enjoys a product and the company becomes aware of the individual, marketers can develop *brand advocate* or *brand ambassador* relationships. Recently, Sony employed brand advocates to help launch the GPS camera. One ambassador was paid to travel to Australia and send back photos of the trip, complete with a map showing where various beaches were located. Another variation of the sponsored consumer approach employs *customer evangelists* who are paid to spread the word about products in various social circles, including family, friends, reference groups, and work associates. These enthusiasts host parties and other events featuring the product. Red Bull has employed customer evangelists to host parties, especially on college campuses, in a variety of countries.

Company or Agency Employees

Two methods of using company employees to spread word-of-mouth are possible. The first occurs when the employee openly notes he or she works for the company but feels strongly about its products and brands. This type of positive endorsement occurs in organizations with satisfied and committed employees who are proud to work in the company. Individuals with strong bonds to a firm solicit use of the product, and encourage family and friends to seek employment in the company.

The second method of buzz marketing involves an employee passing along positive word-of-mouth but poses as a "regular person," not revealing her employment status. As an example, a female could stop tourists in front of the Colosseum in Rome, and ask them to take her picture. She can then demonstrate the camera, emphasizing the brand name and its features to the tourists, without ever saying that she works for the company that manufactures the camera. The Word of Mouth Marketing Association frowns on this type of activity, but others believe it is ethical and does not violate any laws (Fernando, 2007).

Buzz Marketing Stages

International word-of-mouth marketing has been compared to a virus going through three states: inoculation, incubation, and infection. *Inoculation* occurs when a product is introduced to a new host country. *Incubation* represents the point at which brand advocates can create the greatest amount of buzz. *Infection* represents a successful program in which brand awareness has been greatly enhanced by positive endorsements.

GUERRILLA MARKETING

Guerrilla marketing offers an aggressive, grassroots approach to marketing. The program emphasizes one-on-one relationships with consumers through innovative alternative means. Typically, a successful guerrilla marketing approach takes advantage of a combination of media, advertising, public relations, and surprise tactics that create buzz.

In Shanghai, only 10% of the population is wealthy enough to ride in a taxi. Passengers are often between the ages of twenty-one and forty-nine. They tend to be white-collar workers. An advertising agency identified the group as a viable market and created contracts in which video-streaming screens were placed in taxis for customers to watch. Estée Lauder, Procter & Gamble, KFC, and Volkswagen took advantage of the opportunity. When Christina Aguilera agreed to perform in Shanghai, nearly 50% of tickets were reserved by persons calling the concert phone number displayed on the taxi screens (Madden, 2007b).

Effective guerrilla marketing programs rely on the energy and imaginations of employees. Success is achieved through profits rather than sales, and by targeting individuals and small groups with marketing messages rather than with mass media advertising. Guerrilla marketers seek cooperative arrangements with other companies. The customer base grows through referrals and through return business.

In 2008, Skoda asked British Facebook users to prove just how "mean" or "lovely" they were. The winners at each personality extreme won a new car. Havas-agency-owned Archibald Ingall Stretton created the social-media campaign for Skoda. The first version was the "made of lovely stuff" campaign that ran in 2007. The entrant deemed most lovely received the prize. Then, a "made of meaner stuff" TV and print campaign created by Fallon, London, followed. It was, in essence, a dark reworking of the made of lovely stuff campaign, in which the meanest participant won the car. Both contests created considerable buzz for Skoda (Hall, 2010).

International guerrilla marketing programs begin with the identification of *touch points*, where customers eat, drink, shop, socialize, and sleep. Connecting with consumers in logical places where the product can become part of their lives will be the goal. The marketing team then looks for creative and imaginative ways to enhance the connection.

PRODUCT PLACEMENTS AND BRANDED ENTERTAINMENT

Movie presentations and television programs offer quality venues to reach customers in ways other than traditional advertising. A *product placement* is the planned insertion of a brand or product into a movie or television show with the goal of influencing viewers. The international appeal of films makes it possible to influence consumers in a more subtle way.

Many international television programs include product placements. *Britain's Got Talent*, the British version of *America's Got Talent*, began featuring placements in 2011. The high-profile American program has a longstanding relationship with Coca-Cola. Television critics worried that placements in British programs would affect their credibility, calling them "stealth advertising," while others believed they would generate much needed revenues.[13] The impact of product placements on sales is difficult to establish but advertisers continue to use it as it increases brand awareness (Kamleitner and Khair Jyote, 2013).

Branded entertainment weaves a product or brand into the storyline of a movie or television show. In the CTC drama *The Eleventh Hour*, Nicorette gum was integrated into a story about a character trying to quit smoking. The George Clooney film *Up in the Air* prominently featured American Airlines as part of the storyline.

Program Success

To achieve success in product placements and branded entertainment programs, marketers follow some basic principles. First, the product or brand should plausibly fit with the program. A sports program logically matches with sports or energy drinks. Placements flow sensibly in those venues. In the case of Nicorette gum and American Airlines, the products wove seamlessly into the stories. Second, the brand must be prominently featured. In the U.S. version of *American Idol*, more than 4,000 placements were made during the 2006–2007 season. Only a few will actually become noticed, such as the glass of Coca-Cola on the judges' table. For other products, payments to place products probably did not yield positive results. Third, the attempt should be made to create an emotional connection between the product and the audience. This feature will be the most difficult to achieve. Any time a product can be given as both a prize with a corresponding gift to a charity, the potential to increase an emotional attachment rises. If the product can in some way assist or comfort a character in a story, it also becomes more likely that viewers will see the brand in a more favorable light.

Product placements and branded entertainment are growing in use worldwide. The programs benefit advertising companies seeking to gain exposure in ways other than traditional media advertising. From the perspective of movie and television studios, charging money to use brands in shows generates much-needed revenues.

LIFESTYLE MARKETING

In many countries, lifestyle marketing practically occurs as a natural event. Lifestyle marketing involves making contact with customers in comfortable settings, including where they take part in hobbies, at entertainment venues, and at shopping locations. In many nations, the majority of shopping takes place in central locations where vendors meet to sell their goods on nearly a daily basis. Festivals featuring religious holidays or cultural events are common. A marketer can look for a logical tie to an event and set up a booth or table to take advantage of the connection.

Musical performances offer lifestyle marketing opportunities. An opera or symphony will attract one type of company, such as a high-end fashion designer. A rock concert or hip-hop event attracts other types of clothing companies, energy drinks, and other products. A country and western or bluegrass-type festival may be linked to farm equipment and products.

Effective lifestyle marketing goes beyond simply finding the right venue. The marketer looks for a special enticement that will attract attention, such as a giveaway or free sample. Those who make contacts with potential customers become key company representatives. They should be trained to be engaging, polite, and upbeat about the brand.

Bottom-of-the-Pyramid

Of all the alternative marketing and media programs available, lifestyle marketing best matches with reaching bottom-of-the-pyramid customers. These individuals have less access to traditional media. They may not even own television sets. They may encounter people wearing clothing with company endorsements, but they often cannot afford such clothing. Kiosks and outdoor/billboard advertisements might attract their attention, but these customers must view the product as being within their financial reach in order to achieve any effect.

Lifestyle marketing reaches bottom-of-the-pyramid customers in the most comfortable settings, such as where they shop. Products that have been adapted to smaller packages with lower prices can easily be presented in farmers' markets, local street markets, and in places such as outdoor markets in rural areas.

ETHICAL ISSUES IN INTERNATIONAL ADVERTISING

Advertising professions receive a great deal of criticism from social commentators. The complaints typically center on the role advertising plays in a country, with arguments suggesting that many advertising activities are, or can be, unethical or influence consumers behavior in a way that leads to problems. Some of the most common objections include these:

- advertising overemphasizes materialism
- advertising increases prices
- advertising perpetuates stereotypes
- advertising unfairly focuses on children
- advertisements are often offensive
- advertising dangerous products is unethical

The first criticism, that advertising overemphasizes materialism, takes on additional significance in the case of bottom-of-the-pyramid consumers. The argument is that these individuals, who may be less savvy with money, are encouraged to purchase items that they want but do not need. For example, soft drink products may be sold at a low cost ($0.025), but that price may represent one-fourth to one-eighth of a person's daily income. Should advertising target such individuals?

A longstanding complaint has been that advertising increases prices. The counterargument is that advertising lowers prices by increasing competition and that, without advertising, fewer items are sold, thus raising the price. Both sides of the argument provide statistics favoring their point of view.

Some critics suggest that advertising perpetuates stereotypes. A narrow distinction may be made between stereotyping and market segmentation. At the same time, many protests center on the ways in which advertisers portray older people, minorities, and citizens of other countries. In the 2011 Super Bowl, an advertising attempt at humor using doddering senior citizens drew complaints, as did an effort at humor featuring citizens of Tibet. In international marketing, careful attention should be paid to unpopular stereotyping.

Many products consumed by children are advertised in ways that social critics deem unacceptable, arguing that advertising unfairly focuses on children. The use of cartoon characters and small premiums such as children's toys combined with food products advertising unfairly influences those who are unable to form mature judgments. Some governments restrict the amount of commercials that may be targeted at young people, or do not allow them at all.

Advertising can be offensive in a number of contexts. Beyond stereotyping, messages may offend the audience, which may perceive that they violate cultural norms or are mean-spirited toward a group of people. Negative reactions to ads have long-lasting effects. Advertisers are advised to carefully screen commercials before their release.

Some object that advertising dangerous products is unethical. Many unsafe products have been advertised for years, including smoking products, alcohol, and others. Governments in various nations create laws regarding what may be advertised and in which venues. International advertising accounts for these legal restrictions prior to beginning an advertising program.

Digital advertising and the use of "big data" may result in unethical approaches. For example, Facebook allowed advertisers to buy data that could identify consumers who used particular search terms and target them with unethical messages (Maheshwari and Stevenson, 2017).

Common wisdom suggests that advertising must be handled carefully in order to be both ethical and effective. The use of cultural assimilators, focus groups, and even local attorneys can help a marketing organization make sure that company messages will be well received and not violate any local customs, religious practices, or notions of fairness.

CHAPTER 15: REVIEW AND RESOURCES

Strategic Implications

Effective international advertising programs require the combination of three variables: the message, the media, and the audience. Many of the advertising elements described in this chapter represent strategic choices. Advertising management programs include the steps of establishing objectives, creating an advertising budget, choosing an advertising agency, overseeing the advertising program, and assessing advertising effectiveness. Advertising objectives are strategically selected, depending on the situation. A company entering a new market will seek different objectives as compared to one with a longstanding operation in another nation. Managers choose which form of advertising budget to employ. Options include the percentage of sales, match the competition, arbitrary allocation, and objective and task methods. The choice between an in-house advertising program and a relationship with an advertising agency will be a strategic decision.

Further selection of a standardization or adaptation format for advertising will be made by top-level managers. The overall direction of the advertising program takes place under the guiding hand of the company's top marketers. The strategic direction of a company's advertising program carefully accounts for cultural factors, legal restrictions, infrastructure concerns, economic conditions, and communications issues.

The advertising agency will present choices, including the use of fear, humor, sex/sensuality, music, rationality, emotions, and scarcity to the marketing management team, who will then make the decision as to which approach to feature. In international settings, additional choices will include considerations of power distance, individualism/collectivism, masculinity/femininity, uncertainty avoidance, and long- or short-term orientation.

Choices of nontraditional marketing programs, including buzz marketing, guerrilla marketing, product placements and branded entertainment, and lifestyle marketing, are also strategic in nature.

Tactical Implications

Media choices are normally tactical decisions made by the advertising agency in conjunction with marketing managers. The advertising team selects logical combinations of traditional media, including television, radio, magazines, newspapers, billboard/outdoor, and direct mail. These choices are supplemented by the use of nontraditional media such as video game advertising, movie trailers, subway tunnels, in-flight airline magazines, carry-home and take-out bags, clothing bearing company names or logos, mall signs, kiosks, and posters and digital marketing communications.

Tactical-level marketers implement nontraditional marketing programs. They will select specific buzz marketing formats. They develop and implement guerrilla marketing programs. They negotiate product placements and branded entertainment packages with movie and television studios. They select lifestyle marketing locations and establish operations in those locations.

Operational Implications

First-line supervisors carry key responsibilities associated with effective advertising and nontraditional marketing programs. In the area of advertising, these managers should make certain that entry-level employees are aware of company advertisements, especially those making special offers. When extra merchandise will be required as part of a heavily advertised promotion or special offer, the first-line supervisor makes sure the merchandise is ordered, received, and then placed in attractive and convenient ways.

Entry-level employees and first-line supervisors will be on the front lines of lifestyle marketing, guerrilla marketing, and buzz marketing programs. They will be at the booths and will directly interact with customers. An advertising program cannot succeed unless the efforts of those in contact with the public implement all levels of an advertising program.

TERMS

globally integrated marketing communications program

promotions mix

communication

low-context cultures

high-context cultures

clutter

advertising management

message strategy

cognitive message strategies

affective message strategies

conative message strategies

executical framework	comparative advertising
announcements	entertainment
association transfers	imagination
lesson	special effects

REVIEW QUESTIONS

1. Define globally integrated marketing communications.

2. What elements make up the promotions mix?

3. Define communication.

4. What elements are included in a model of individual interpersonal communication?

5. What are the primary barriers to effective international communication and marketing programs?

6. Describe low- and high-context cultures.

7. Outline the sender and receiver duties in creating effective individual interpersonal communication.

8. What are the steps of an international advertising management program?

9. What four methods can be used to create international advertising budgets?

10. Name the traditional media advertising venues.

11. Name the nontraditional advertising media venues.

12. Name the most common attitudinal and behavioral measures of advertising effectiveness.

13. Briefly describe the traditional advertising appeal formats.

14. Explain the cultural paradoxes that complicate international advertising.

15. Briefly describe the international advertising appeal formats.

16. Describe the three most common message strategies.

17. Briefly describe the traditional advertising executional frameworks.

18. Briefly describe the seven most common international executional frameworks.

19. What are the four most common alternative marketing programs?

DISCUSSION QUESTIONS

1. Make a list of the most common barriers to individual interpersonal communication. Explain how these factors become more complicated in international marketing. Explain how each of these variables also constitutes a barrier to communication throughout an organization.

2. For each of the international advertising objectives displayed in Table 15.5, explain how each of the traditional advertising appeals could (or should not) be used to achieve the objective. For each of the international advertising appeals and values

noted in Table 15.12, explain how each could (or should not) be used to achieve the objective.

3. Explain how each of the traditional executional frameworks noted in Table 15.13 is or is not related to the international advertising executional frameworks.

4. Discuss how the four nontraditional marketing methods would fare in low-context cultures. Explain how the methods match or do not match such a culture. Explain how each would be different in high-context cultures.

ANALYTICAL AND INTERNET EXERCISES

1. Find examples of advertisements for the same brand in different countries. Compare and contrast the selected advertisements and try to assess their fit to the target cultures.

2. Prepare a report on the application and future of programmatic advertising in global advertising campaigns.

3. Write down the selection criteria used when choosing international advertising agencies. Explain how each criterion would affect the selection of an agency for the following products and situations:

    • Britannia biscuits in India

    • Boden clothing sold in Denmark

    • Kia automobiles sold in the UK

    • Beliani furniture sold in Canada

4. Using an Internet search engine, look up five international advertising agencies. Write a report on how each conducts operations in global markets, including differences and similarities.

5. Develop a creative brief for international advertising campaigns for the following products. Specify which countries would be targeted. Make sure you match the advertising objectives with a message strategy, type of international advertising appeal, and type of international advertising executional framework to be used in advertising the following products:

    • Croove app

    • Huawei smart phones

    • Black & Decker lawn mowers

    • Jarritos drinks

6. Go to the website of the Word of Mouth Marketing Association (www.womma.org). Find its ethical statement regarding stealth marketing and company employees as brand advocates. Write a report about what the organization believes is and is not ethical.

STUDENT STUDY SITE

Visit **https://study.sagepub.com/baack2e** to access these free additional learning tools:

- Web Quizzes
- eFlashcards
- SAGE Journal Articles
- Country Fact Sheets
- Chapter Outlines
- Interactive Maps

CASE 15

Smart Phone Apps: MyBabyBio and MyLifeBio—Born Global Firms in a Crowded App Market

International competition in the smart phone applications market can be described as intense. With the vast number of companies and individuals that design smart phone apps on the rise, and with an increasing number of smart phone users worldwide, the number of potential individual and business customers continues to grow. Reaching this vast marketplace in a manner that cuts through clutter constitutes the primary challenge for many app designers and marketers. Two smartphone applications, MyBabyBio and MyLifeBio, have recently been introduced into this competitive market. The founder of the company and developer of the apps, Chris Bianca, had previously worked for a major British online grocery retailer but decided to establish his own company in 2016. He is an international entrepreneur following a business strategy approach that could be described as born global.

MyBabyBio and MyLifeBio apps were developed with an intention of responding to consumers' fears over online privacy. Recent research shows that social media users share less personal information now as Facebook has recently discovered (Griffin, 2016). Users move to other social media sites such as Snapchat or Instagram that offer stricter security. Some parents decide to not share photos of their children online altogether (Kelion, 2017). The creator of the apps intends to capture this sceptical audience of parents who are very concerned about sharing their family images online. The company intends to promote the apps in an international market, initially in English-speaking countries and later expanding into other markets after implementing necessary changes.

The founder has carried out some market research in the UK, and learnt that consumers generally liked the idea of MyBabyBio as it provided better security for sharing photos and videos of children with other users of the application. MyLifeBio has not attracted as positive reviews because it has been seen as very similar to already existing apps and websites such as Facebook. The founder of MyBabyBio hopes that his idea will attract enough users to generate substantial income mainly from in-app purchases such as personalized family photo albums, photo frames or tote bags. His hopes are supported by the evidence that app users are more willing to pay for in-app purchases than for downloading the apps themselves.[14]

Born global firms undertake international business at or near their founding. They are a type of highly international small and medium-sized enterprise. Born globals have emerged in substantial numbers worldwide, in conjunction with globalization and development of advanced information and communications technologies.

Promoting and convincing individuals to use new apps may be challenging because although users are concerned about their digital privacy, they do very little to change their online behaviors (Chamorro-Premuzic and Nahai, 2017). Hence, persuading potential consumers to use an app such as MyBabyBio may be difficult, especially when they have to pay for it. Although some consumers are willing to pay for apps that matter to them, the majority of mobile apps that make profit are gaming apps.

MyBabyBio has been so far advertised on Facebook and in local parenting magazines in the UK. These efforts raised some product awareness and led to 300 consumer registrations and application downloads. Research shows that many consumers install applications on their phones but in most cases very few use them (Tiongson, 2015). The founder is hopeful that further promotional activities in the UK and abroad will attract more users and the app will start generating income.

No, these do not need to be made public...
I need to get a job one day!

https://mybabybio.com

MyBabyBio Twitter Image.

Source: https://twitter.com/mylifebiography.

1. Conduct an analysis of competitors and assess the international market feasibility of the two apps mentioned in this story.

2. Prepare a marketing communications brief for a global marketing communications agency detailing the problem, aims and objectives, and prepare a budget for a promotional campaign for one or more target countries.

3. Prepare a globally integrated marketing communications plan to promote the two apps. Which countries would you target?

4. How would you use traditional advertising with nontraditional marketing? Which nontraditional marketing communications program would you employ?

5. Propose a set of advertising appeals that you would use in a standardized advertising campaign for the MyBabyBio app.

16

INTERNATIONAL SALES PROMOTIONS AND PUBLIC RELATIONS

LEARNING OBJECTIVES

After reading and studying this chapter, you should be able to answer the following questions:

1. What are the relationships between international consumer promotions and trade promotions?

2. How do international consumer promotions help a company achieve its marketing goals?

3. When are international trade promotions incentives used?

4. How does the public relations team or department handle negative publicity or image-damaging events?

5. How can the public relations function help build a positive image of a company and its brands?

IN THIS CHAPTER

Opening Vignette: Marketing Herbal Remedies

OVERVIEW

MARKETING HERBAL REMEDIES

The practice of medicine varies greatly around the world. Among the more divergent aspects of health care is the use of herbal remedies. In a nation such as Nigeria, limited access to even rudimentary medical care exists, mostly notably to citizens in remote areas. One response has been to integrate what may be termed "traditional" medical care with the longstanding usage of indigenous herbal remedies. The result has been a marketing opportunity for local companies willing to "professionalize" the production and distribution of herbal products to local consumers.[1] Part of the program has been to create positive publicity regarding the potential benefits of traditional remedies and to push for the incorporation of these items into the traditional medical system.

In China, herbal medicine usage dates back more than 5,000 years. More than 450 substances are available to local citizens and are increasingly sold in other nations. Organizations such as the Australian Acupuncture and Chinese Medical Association Ltd promote the benefits of herbs for treatment of a wide variety of maladies, ranging from simple sinus pressure to impotence.

In Europe and the United States, herbal approaches are lauded and treated with caution. Companies marketing herbal remedies must comply with local regulations with regard to both product ingredients and to how items can be represented in advertising.

In every circumstance, the prevalence of sales promotion tactics continues to rise. The use of coupons, samples, bonus packs, and other incentives seeks to pull products through to retailer shelves via customer demand, as they stand alongside other medicines such as aspirin and cough syrup. Trade promotion incentives help push items onto shelves

(Continued)

(Continued)

through their appeal to members of the market channel through programs including trade incentives, trade shows, and cooperative marketing.

At the same time, scrutiny of this highly lucrative collection of products continues. Critics argue that many items have never been tested through scientific evaluation. The Food and Drug Administration in the United States does not regulate or oversee herbal products, which results in considerable latitude in the types of claims made about products as well as the content of the herbs themselves.

The European Union states that traditional herbal medicines should be considered as "acceptably safe, albeit not having a recognized level of efficacy" (Moreira et al., 2014: 248). A major decision placed herbs into a special category of drugs in which less rigorous requirements are imposed on non-clinical and clinical studies of them. A similar regulation proposal was made by the Brazilian National Health Surveillance (Anvisa). Concerned scientists worry about three problems. First, less proof of actual drug efficacy is required in many countries. Second, some herbal products are suspected of creating carcinogenic and/or hepatotoxic effects. Third, the use of herbs may change or inhibit the effectiveness of traditional drugs.

Consequently, an uncertain future accompanies the production and marketing of herbal products. Individual national standards tend to have the greatest impact on how items are created and sold (Moreira et al., 2014).

International marketing means that herbal remedies can be made available to the vast number of individuals experiencing various medical problems.

Questions for Students

1. How might companies use coupons, price-off discounts, bonus packs, free samples, contests or sweepstakes, and premium prizes to sell herbal remedies in international markets?

2. What types of offers could herbal medicine manufacturers offer to retailers to increase sales?

3. How should the public relations department in an herbal medicine manufacturing company communicate with various publics and critics?

OVERVIEW

Promotional activities play an important role in international marketing, both during boom economic times and periods of recession. As noted in the previous chapter, a firm's promotions mix consists of advertising, personal selling, sales promotion, and public relations. The promotions mix includes social media in today's global marketplace. This chapter continues the description of international promotions.

Sales promotions provide an additional venue to reach consumers and move them toward purchases. Marketers integrate promotional programs with a firm's other communications. This chapter describes the nature of sales promotions in the international context and makes a distinction between a push strategy and a pull strategy. It continues with evaluations of the types of consumer promotions offered to individual buyers. Consumers react to promotions in different ways, which means the international marketing team examines how they tend to respond to promotions in various regions and countries.

Trade promotions seek to push products onto retail shelves and create positive relationships between manufacturers and intermediaries. Some incentives are financial while others involve cooperative efforts and manufacturer-generated training programs. Trade shows offer venues in which buyers and sellers can meet. Company leaders consider international differences in these programs when seeking to market products.

This chapter concludes with a description of public relations activities. The public relations team facilitates communications between the company and all internal and external publics. Public relations involve responding to negative events and publicity as well as highlighting a company's positive contributions to a local community and the larger society.

The communication process plays an important part in promotional programs and all other elements of marketing. Personal and impersonal forms of communication take place in sales promotions. Personal communication includes face-to-face visits between a salesperson and a customer. In these meetings, coupons are redeemed, discounts are given, and other promotional items change hands. Impersonal communication takes place over various media, such as television, radio, and mobile phones. The media deliver the message to be sent, including electronic coupons and other sales promotion offers. In international marketing, additional potential barriers to communication emerge, including differences in language, use of slang, forms of technical terminology, and cultural nuances. Effective communication facilitates the development and delivery of quality sales promotions.

LEARNING OBJECTIVE #1:

What are the relationships between international consumer promotions and trade promotions?

INTERNATIONAL SALES PROMOTIONS

sales promotions:
marketing activities
that are designed to
stimulate consumer
and marketing
channel demand for
a product or service

consumer promotions:
sales promotions
directed at
retail customers

trade promotions:
sales promotions
targeted at
intermediaries, most
notably wholesalers
and retail outlets

Sales promotions are marketing activities designed to stimulate consumer and marketing channel demand for a product or service. They take two forms: consumer promotions and trade promotions. **Consumer promotions** are directed to retail customers. Consumer promotions include coupons, sweepstakes, refunds and rebates, premiums, bonus packs, price-off programs, and samples. Companies provide **trade promotions** to intermediates, most notably wholesalers and retail outlets. Trade promotions consist of trade allowances, trade contests, trade shows, and point-of-purchase materials. Social media efforts target both consumer and trade groups.

International sales promotion efforts focus on stimulating demand across national or cultural boundaries. Some of these efforts concentrate on short-term goals, such as when marketers design sales promotions programs to stimulate immediate purchases. Effective strategic international sales promotions programs also work to achieve longer-term objectives including building brand loyalty or strengthening a company's image. Marketers design advertising campaigns in concert with sales promotions to boost sales in the short term and increase consumer loyalty over time.

International marketers consider cultural differences when preparing sales promotions programs. They analyze differences in motivators, consumer behaviors, and decision-making processes before a company markets products across national boundaries (Foxman et al., 1988). Market research activities become part of developing quality international promotions. As a simple example, offering product samples in some cultures might be discouraged or even considered as inappropriate by some consumers. In others the use of sampling is commonplace.

PUSH VS. PULL STRATEGIES

As first mentioned in Chapter 13, one key decision facing international marketers in both distribution channels and the promotions mix involves the inclusion of push or pull promotional strategies. A *push strategy* occurs when a marketer promotes a product to intermediaries. These efforts reach wholesalers first, who then promote the product to the retailers that promote the product to consumers.

Trade promotions are push strategies. They focus on building intermediary demand and support. English brewing company SABMiller utilized a push strategy for the introduction of Kozel, a Czech lager, to the United Kingdom (Charles, 2010). SABMiller and other firms developed sales contests, training programs, and point-of-purchase materials specifically for marketing channel members. The activities became an important part in international marketing success because of the critical role that intermediary support plays.

A *pull strategy* focuses on stimulating product demand at the consumer level. When a consumer expresses interest in a product at the retail store, it encourages the retailer to carry the item. The product will be ordered from wholesalers who purchase the product from the manufacturer. Consequently, demand for the product is "pulled" upward through the marketing channel by the consumer from the intermediary and then the manufacturer. Consumer promotions support pull strategies, because the individual buyer receives the incentive.

International marketing giant McDonald's employed a pull strategy with the introduction of *kazasu* coupons in Japan. The mobile marketing pieces enabled consumers to redeem coupons, choose meals, and pay for purchases using mobile phones (Keferl, 2008). The company provided the promotion to retail consumers in the hope that demand would pull products through the marketing channel.

LEARNING OBJECTIVE #2:

How do international consumer promotions help a company achieve its marketing goals?

INTERNATIONAL CONSUMER PROMOTIONS

Consumer promotions target consumers. The use of international consumer promotion tactics has grown dramatically. Several explanations for the growth in popularity of these techniques exist. Decreasing mass media advertising budgets, the fragmentation of media audiences, difficulties with measuring mass media effectiveness, the increasing power of retailers, and advertising clutter have contributed to this growth.

Many international consumers either tune out mass media advertising or have cynical attitudes about advertising on television, radio, in newspapers, and other traditional media. For these individuals, making a more intimate connection becomes important. Many consumers enjoy direct personal contacts. Consumer promotion efforts facilitate such interactions because they enable companies to more intimately reach consumers. The incentives help achieve a variety of additional goals, including the following:

- obtaining initial trial usage of a product by consumers
- increasing consumption of an existing brand
- building brand loyalty
- maintaining or building market share in mature markets
- preempting competitive efforts, including competitor consumer promotions
- supplementing advertising and personal selling activities

Table 16.1 displays common types of consumer promotions.

TABLE 16.1 International Consumer Promotions

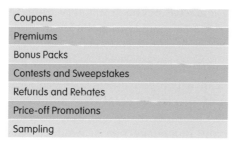

Coupons
Premiums
Bonus Packs
Contests and Sweepstakes
Refunds and Rebates
Price-off Promotions
Sampling

COUPONS

Coupons enable consumers to save money on specific products or services. The types of coupons companies offer include those displayed in Table 16.2. Each form helps stimulate product purchases including situations in which a new product is being marketed.

Historically firms placed coupons in newspapers as inserts (print media) or mailed directly to consumers. In European nations, many couponing strategies focus on direct mail delivery. European consumers tend to be receptive to couponing, but less than

American consumers.[2] Some European retailers rely more heavily on couponing and in-store promotions than on other promotions. Other types of coupons will be placed on retail store shelves or delivered at check-out counters with merchandise receipts by an electronic scanner and printer.

TABLE 16.2   Types of Coupons

Print Media
Direct Mail
In- or on-Package
In-Store (display)
In-Store (Scanner Delivered at Check-out)
Response Offer
Internet Delivered (Electronic Coupons)

Many international companies distribute coupons on popular social networking sites and via email. Electronic coupon distribution techniques have become common and a proliferation of mobile couponing has taken place. Companies transmit mobile coupons through various mobile devices. The format enjoys a great deal of popularity in Japan and Korea. Consumers in these countries tend to be receptive to mobile delivery of coupons because individuals in many Asian are more technologically advanced than individuals in other parts of the world (Brassington, 2010). The Japanese market research firm Netasia estimates that 76% of Japanese consumers have scanned a QR coupon bar code using a mobile device (Harding, 2010).

Mobile couponing use continues to grow. The United States-based marketer Groupon offers daily deals on products through the Internet and recently established operations in Europe. Groupon purchased international competitors including Germany's CityDeal as part of the effort to expand internationally (Axon, 2010).[3]

Mobile coupons are not popular everywhere. Reactions vary greatly by region and by culture and are strongly impacted by the availability and cost of these technologies. International marketing research should be conducted in order to gain an understanding of consumer reactions to electronic coupons.

Couponing can be part of a larger marketing effort. Kellogg's Canada recently ran a "resolution" campaign in which consumers received an on-package coupon on specially marked boxes of Special K cereal. The promotion granted consumers a price break and promoted healthier living and weight loss.[4] These types of promotions work to stimulate the immediate sale of product and can then become part of achieving strategic marketing objectives such as building brand loyalty. In this instance, Kellogg's achieved the goal of promoting better living while encouraging an immediate purchase response.

PREMIUMS

A premium is an item offered as a reward for purchasing another item. Premiums take the form of gifts or prizes. A reward item might be given free of charge or it can sometimes be priced modestly, sometimes under the guise of a shipping and handling fee. A premium represents an additional incentive for a consumer to buy a product. Figure 16.1 identifies various types of premiums.

Free-in-the-mail	Consumer mails in proof of purchase to receive gift
In- or on-package	Gifts contained in packages of products or attached to package
Store or manufacturer	Gift accompanies purchase at a store; given by retailer or manufacturer
Self-liquidating	Consumer pays small amount of money (handling/postage charge) to receive gift

FIGURE 16.1 Types of Premiums

Premiums may be incorporated into an international marketing program. Consumer acceptance of premiums varies by culture. A recent study of grocery shoppers in Hong Kong revealed that premium programs were more effective than either contests or sweepstakes (Shi et al., 2005).

Many consumers enjoy receiving extra products, and, as a result, premium-type promotions have become increasingly common. Not long ago, Kellogg's gave away free packets of cereal to consumers in the United Kingdom as part of its "Wake Up to Breakfast" campaign. To obtain the free product, consumers had to collect coupons placed on various cereal boxes. After the consumer collected three coupons, they were entitled to a free box (Quilter, 2009).

The TLC Marketing Worldwide company creates premium programs for companies operating in Africa. Two recently successful programs offered movie tickets as premiums for those who purchased personal services such as hair care and also to consumers who signed up for mobile phone services.

Premiums incur the costs associated with developing the prize or reward. Often, a package will be altered to accommodate the prize. Gifts that consumers view as cheap trinkets may harm a firm's image. Consequently, marketers give consideration to matching the nature and value of the premium to the product and its target audience.

BONUS PACKS

A bonus pack offers additional merchandise in a package for the same price, such as a "buy three, get one free" package of bar soap. A bonus pack may also take the form of a bottle that is larger than the product's standard size and is marked "25% more, free." By purchasing the pack, consumers receive additional merchandise at the standard price. Bonus packs assist in combatting increased international competition.

SUP Warehouse in Australia offers bonus packs on items connected to surfing and paddle-boarding. The company specializes in accessories enthusiasts use, such as board bags, caps, and many other items. Bonus packs such as these may lead to brand- or vendor-switching, and encourage consumer loyalty, thereby preventing switches to other brands or vendors.

Marketers employ bonus packs to entice consumers to stockpile an item. This decreases the chance that the consumer will switch to a competitor and offers a proactive method of protecting a product's market share. For example, in response to losing customers to store brands, Proctor & Gamble offered bonus packs for Duracell batteries with the goal of maintaining market share. The program's costs were offset by a reduction in traditional advertising spending (Cordeiro, 2010).

Bonus packs incur the additional expense of providing extra merchandise. Also, shipping expenses may rise because the packs will be bulkier and heavier. Cost increases become more dramatic when products are shipped long distances or across international borders. Marketers weigh the expense of providing the free additional item(s) against the benefits of maintaining customer loyalty and/or fending off competitive efforts. In many countries, living quarters are often relatively small. Bonus packs that take up additional storage space may not be as attractive in those circumstances. In the case of SUP Warehouse, the company relies on Internet sales rather than retail space, which makes the use of bonus packs less costly and more attractive to the company and to consumers.

CONTESTS AND SWEEPSTAKES

Contests are promotions with game-like qualities that reward a consumer's skill at some activity. The contest winner receives a prize in the form of a product or money. A contest occurs when consumers compete to develop a new advertising slogan for a company or when individuals compete to predict the winners of a sports event, such as the World Cup. These activities require a degree of skill or knowledge.

Contests provide value in many international markets because they generate consumer interest and excitement. Walkers, a UK-based potato chip marketer, held a successful skill-based contest in which customers were invited to compete by developing a new flavor of potato chip. The winner won £50,000 in prize money and a percentage of product sales revenues.

Prizes in contests contain the *intrinsic value* associated with demonstrating skill or knowledge. They also carry *extrinsic value* based on the actual value of the prize (additional food item versus curved HD television set). Effective contests create both forms of value as motives.

Sweepstakes rely on chance drawings of consumer names in order to select the winner of a promotion. Sweepstakes take a form similar to a lottery or random drawing. If a certain number or name is selected, the consumer wins a prize. Both contests and sweepstakes are present in international marketing programs. A recent sweepstakes was held by Dubai's City Center Mall. The Mall rewarded consumers who spent at least 300 United Arab Emirates *Dirhams* (*AED*) with lottery numbers that could be redeemed online for chances to win prizes of up to 100,000 *AED*.[5]

Although contests and sweepstakes often lead to immediate consumer responses, they may not influence long-term sales. Consumers can quickly lose interest in a product or brand after the contest or sweepstake ends. At that point, marketers should design a new form of promotion to help sustain consumer involvement.

Cultural norms as well as political and legal systems strongly influence participation rates and interest in this form of sales promotion. For example, the Swedish government prohibits games of chance (sweepstakes/instant wins) but allows games of skill (contests). Therefore, preliminary research will be necessary to understand the type of contest or prize that the targeted segment of consumers will value. It must also be acceptable to the local community and government.

REBATES

Rebates require consumers to mail a form or certificate to a marketer along with a receipt or proof of purchase in order to receive money back from the manufacturer or retail outlet. This type of sales promotion tends to work well at generating consumer interest in an item as long as consumers value the amount of the rebate. It should generate sufficient desire to lead to the effort to receive the money.

Not every consumer will take the time or expend the effort needed to receive a rebate. Research suggests that a large percentage of consumers do not complete the steps necessary in order to claim them. One side effect of unclaimed rebates is additional program profitability, because the money is not paid out. Rebates tend to be effective methods for generating consumer attention and interest. They can also be useful tools for salespeople who attempt to sell products to end users, especially in international markets. Utilizing rebates can therefore be effective for gaining entry into new markets globally.

A recent study of Chinese consumers indicated that they highly value rebates and view them positively. The results also revealed that consumers with higher incomes were particularly pleased with rebates (McNeill et al., 2008). Although this may seem like an unexpected result, it may be that higher-income consumers do not rely on rebates for cost savings but rather view them as pleasant surprises.

PRICE-OFF PROMOTIONS

Price-off promotions present the consumer with an immediate price break, expressed as a percentage of the price or an absolute amount, at the time of purchase. The manufacturer might emphasize this type of promotion by printing the price on a product's package, or a retailer might offer the price on a shelf tag signage. Price-off promotions are widely used in international marketing. Capcom Europe, a leading international developer and marketer of videogames with worldwide headquarters in Japan, utilized this approach as a means of promoting popular video game titles throughout Europe (Kev, 2010).

Price-off programs and other discounting tactics may be effective tactics in countries with emerging market economies. As part of an overall strategic approach, price flexibility can support efforts to build share and create consumer loyalty, thereby creating a competitive advantage (Bozadzhieva, 2016).

Consumer responses to price-off promotions tend to be generally favorable. Marketers run the risk, however, of teaching consumers to wait for special pricing deals before buying the products if they use this technique too often. Price-off reductions also reduce revenues and often cut into bottom line profits. Only when sufficient additional volume offsets the price cut is the program cost effective. At the same time, many international marketers believe price offs help to fend off competitive offers, thereby sacrificing short-term revenues for longer-range customer loyalty. The marketing team first studies the local laws pertaining to granting discounts as they relate to "standard" prices.

SAMPLING

A consumer tries a product free of charge in a sampling program. Sampling stimulates consumer interest in a product as it reduces purchase risk. The consumer takes advantage of testing the product without paying any money. Samples are often mailed to consumers or are given out in retail outlets. Retailers around the world often offer free samples to consumers. A description of various forms of sample distribution is provided in Figure 16.2.

One example of a new approach to sampling was designed by Japan's Sample Lab, Ltd. The company offers retail outlets that specialize in giving away product samples from dozens of companies. The firm also operates the Lcafe in Tokyo's Shibuya district, a well-known, popular destination for young consumers in Tokyo. When customers

In-store	Given in a retail outlet
Direct sampling	Items delivered to consumer homes or business locations
Media sampling	Sample contained in a media piece (e.g., perfume insert in magazine)
Selective sampling	Provided to patrons at an event (concert, sports event)
Response sampling	Consumer asks for sample to receive it (e.g., Internet response)
Cross-ruffing sample	Sample attached to another product (e.g., syrup sample with pancake mix)
Professional sample	Items given to doctors, hospitals, other professionals passed along to consumers

FIGURE 16.2 **Methods of Sample Distribution**

purchase food items or drinks at the café, they receive tokens they can exchange for sample products (Noorbakhsh, 2008). The sampled products become strong enticements for eventual purchases.

Consumers often exhibit positive attitudes toward sampling and these attitudes influence decisions to seek out samples, a finding that was confirmed by a study of Hong Kong consumers. The study revealed that the more positive that consumer attitudes were about sampling, the greater the likelihood that consumers would seek out samples, especially when consumers stated they were the types of individuals who would engage in such behaviors (Prendergast et al., 2008).

Sampling may boost short-term sales, because the majority of consumers who try a product will purchase it at least once. Sampling provides an effective method of enticing an immediate sale in the grocery industry, where it becomes relatively easy to persuade consumers to sample an item. Sampling succeeds when the consumer requests the sample either in writing or via the Internet. Social networking sites also offer consumers an efficient method of requesting product samples. Vaseline recently distributed free samples of products to consumers who requested them in the United Kingdom.[6] The expense of sampling is one disadvantage. International marketers calculate the trade-offs between the benefits and costs of sampling.

Many marketers couple sampling programs with other consumer promotions. Once a free sample has been given, the consumer is presented with a coupon redeemable at the first purchase. Companies pass samples out during sponsored events, such as an energy bar given to spectators as they enter a stadium to see a soccer match.

INTERNATIONAL INCIDENT

In certain cultures, gift-giving and what may be considered bribery remains a standard way of conducting business. It is considered to be unethical in other cultures. Imagine that you are meeting with a prospective buyer who requests a "sample" of one of your products. The problem is that the sample she requests is not one of the ones that you are attempting to sell. Also, you are restricted by company policy from offering samples that may not result in an immediate sale. The buyer is adamant that you must give her a sample of the other product if you intend to do business with her. What do you do? How would you approach this subject with the prospective buyer? How might you communicate the problem to your boss?

SOCIAL MEDIA AND CONSUMER PROMOTIONS

Social media and social networking sites have become important marketing avenues. The majority of international Internet users visit social networking sites regularly. International marketers increasingly focus on these sites and include them in consumer promotion campaigns. One estimate revealed that the international use of social media promotions will soon exceed $3.3 billion annually (Balasubramanyam, 2009). Some international marketing firms employ search engine optimization managers to assist in online international marketing campaigns. Japanese marketers have taken advantage of social networking sites longer than firms in most other countries.

International marketers access social networking sites for advertising and send promotional materials such as coupons and contest entries directly to consumers. Consumers register for contests and request print coupons directly from these sites. Consumers often become fans of companies and brands by joining their social networking pages.

Facebook and Twitter are often targets of international marketing efforts, but firms also pay attention to foreign sites because the popularity of these media varies by country (Ward, 2008). International marketers work to ensure that they are present on the appropriate sites. Renren is a popular social networking site in China, while Gree and Mixi are widely visited in Japan. One popular French site, Viadeo, has millions of visitors worldwide. The Google-owned site Orkut is well received in India and Brazil. Citizens in Poland tend to go to Nasza Klasa. One of the first decisions for the international marketer will be selecting the most effective social networking site to feature in a sales promotion campaign.

Although social media sites tend to appeal to younger segments, the use of the media cuts across demographics. For individuals in some countries Internet access is available to only those with higher incomes. In other countries, social media and the Internet reach a much broader audience. The rapid penetration of the technologies creates access to various sites across national boundaries.

To achieve success in social media programs, the marketing team matches messages with other content and consumer promotion offers as well as a country's language and culture. International marketers make sure that bloggers are either from the local country or, at the very least, are familiar with the language, dialect, and customs of that country.

One often-overlooked reason for including social media in international marketing campaigns is to reveal to consumers that a company and its products are adapting to the changing times. The Ford Motor Company has used social media internationally, at least in part for that specific purpose. International customers tend to view brands as more relevant when they make connections through the Internet, which means social media programs play an important role in consumer promotions campaigns.

TYPES OF CONSUMERS AND INTERNATIONAL CONSUMER PROMOTIONS

Four groups summarize individual reactions to consumer promotions. Figure 16.3 identifies the potential value of each type. *Promotion-prone consumers* take advantage of coupons, price-off programs, and premiums. They are not loyal to any given brand and look for the best deal. Consequently, targeting consumer promotions in this group does not lead to the best results, because they will simply move on after a deal ceases to be offered.

Promotion-prone	Moderate (will use, but does not create loyalty)
Price-sensitive	Low to moderate (will use, but only to get the best price; does not create loyalty; may encourage stockpiling)
Brand-loyal	Low to moderate (does not increase consumption; serves as a reward)
Preferred-brand	High (encourages brand-switching and point of purchase decisions)

FIGURE 16.3   Values of Consumer Promotion Types

Price-sensitive consumers use price as the only purchase criterion. They take advantage of consumer promotions that reduce the price or increase a purchase value, such as a bonus pack. Once again, the consumer promotion being offered does not truly succeed with this group; it may increase sales in one instance, but these individuals continue to look for the best price.

Brand-loyal consumers purchase only a favored brand and do not look for, nor do they often buy, substitutes. Promotions targeted at this group should work toward maintaining loyalty and increasing consumption. When loyal consumers perceive the promotion as a "reward," it has succeeded.

Consumer promotions can be highly useful in targeting *preferred-brand consumers*. These individuals select from a set of brands they favor most. The right consumer promotion can make the difference in a purchase decision, causing the consumer to select a brand due to the additional incentive offered.

Few customers consistently remain in one category. A person may be price sensitive for some items and brand loyal when it comes to others. The ideal promotions program targets individuals that respond to the promotion and may be moved toward greater loyalty over time. Should Coca-Cola wish to build loyalty in Argentina, coupons, bonus packs, and sweepstakes may be used over time with the shorter-term goal of building interest and immediate purchases, combined with the longer-term objective of increasing the preference for Coke over Pepsi or a local competitor such as Chola de Oro.

International consumer promotions managers examine a country or region to discover the most prevalent types of consumer promotions. Consumer research takes the form of surveys and interviews or test markets. When people in a region tend to be price sensitive, coupons and price-offs work more effectively. For brand-loyal consumers in a region, premiums and contests that allow them to express loyalty in some way are advisable. For areas with larger pockets of promotion-prone consumers, the marketing pieces should attempt to inspire loyalty in some way.

CONSUMER PROMOTIONS AND BOTTOM-OF-THE-PYRAMID CONSUMERS

Marketers often target bottom-of-the-pyramid consumers with promotions emphasizing price. Couponing and bonus packs, as well as special price-off promotions, effectively promote items to these consumers. Many bottom-of-the-pyramid consumers do not live close to any traditional retail outlets. In many cases products are transported to the remote areas or villages where such consumers live. This can be expensive for the international marketer, but the goodwill associated with the effort can outweigh the short-term monetary costs. The concern is that bottom-of-the-pyramid consumers may wait for the next promotion, instead of transitioning to buying the product at a higher price. Promotions that cause a loss may be ineffective to penetrate this market. Promotions that generate a small profit margin provide a better method for encouraging bottom-of-the-pyramid consumption.

ADDITIONAL ISSUES IN CONSUMER PROMOTIONS

International marketers often find that consumer promotion techniques that are ineffective in one market or country will succeed in another market or country. Direct mail serves as an example. Direct mail programs that deliver coupons and premium prizes have waned in effectiveness in the United States; however, the tactic continues to be effective in other parts of the world. International marketers monitor developments in direct mail marketing to ensure that it does not become inefficient or wasteful.

In many countries, sales promotion decisions depend, at least in part, on social class. Premiums and couponing may work well for one social class but not another. Redeeming coupons in some societies presents the impression that the buyer is poor and from a lower social class.

Several legal concerns must be addressed when offering sales promotions internationally. As noted, contests and sweepstakes face legal restrictions. In Canada, a contest cannot offer money solely as a prize and the contest must test some type of skill. The marketing team would wish to know if coupons can be copied and redeemed by retailers that do not actually receive them from customers. Counterfeiting coupons by retailers creates an unnecessary expense. Premium programs encounter restrictions with regard to charging shipping fees in some countries.

Many countries regulate what is a standard price and how often prices can be reduced through techniques such as price-off programs. Germany, for example, did not allow sales discount prices until 2004. For several years, consumers were unaware of the concept unless the English word "sale" was included in marketing materials.

Similar laws regulate bonus packs. Offers, such as "three for the price of two," are illegal in some European countries. Consequently, the European Union has begun the process of trying to standardize regulations regarding sales promotions (Eaglesham and Solman, 2001).

Sampling programs face legal restrictions as to where they can be distributed, or require a permit to give them in various parts of a city. The marketing team first investigates the local legal system before trying any consumer promotions tactic.

LEARNING OBJECTIVE #3:

When are international trade promotions incentives used?

INTERNATIONAL TRADE PROMOTIONS

Trade promotions are provided to marketing channel intermediaries. They often play an important roles in the success of products worldwide. Trade promotions have gained a great deal of international marketing attention and tend to be used extensively. The promotions help establish initial support for new brands, encourage intermediaries to promote existing brands, and assist in building and maintaining strong working relationships with marketing channel members. Intermediary cooperation is essential to the success of international marketing campaigns. Trade-oriented promotions help ensure cooperation from channel members. Producers use some techniques, such as sampling, as both consumer and trade promotions. Table 16.3 summarizes various international trade promotion techniques.

TABLE 16.3   International Trade Promotions

Trade Shows
Trade Allowances
Cooperative Advertising
Trade Contests
Training Programs
Point of-Purchase Materials

TRADE SHOWS

A trade show gathers industry representatives to examine products and services presented to prospective buyers. Trade shows generally focus on generating buyer interest. Shows make it possible to establish contacts with industry representatives. When many companies and representatives attend trade shows, this method of trade promotion becomes both effective and efficient.

One advantage of utilizing trade shows is the ability to demonstrate a product. Trade shows are well attended in European nations. In general, companies allocate a greater percentage of promotional expenditures to trade shows in Europe than in other regions of the world (Gopalakrishna et al., 1995).

Tecno Bebida is the largest beverage industry trade show in Latin America.[7] Exhibitors from food, drink, hotel, restaurant, and packaging companies attend the show held annually in Brazil. RetailTech, held in Tokyo, is Japan's largest trade show. It specializes in retail information technologies. Participants make valuable contacts and learn about the latest developments in areas such as retail information systems, warehouse efficiencies, and digital marketing.[8] Events such as these can be effective when a firm tries to reach new prospects, learn about new technologies, or study industry developments. Marketing teams examine the cultural context surrounding a trade show. Figure 16.4 describes various types of trade show participants.

Power Buyers	Individuals empowered to make purchases (often top managers)
Buying Teams	Sets of employees looking for the best vendor to possibly make purchase
Education Seekers	Seek information and make contact but do not normally make purchases
Reinforcement Seekers	Company officials seeking reassurance that previous purchases were the best decisions

FIGURE 16.4   Types of Trade Show Participants

In many parts of the world, the trade show attendees are the corporate officers authorized to finalize purchases. In these circumstances, the manufacturer goes beyond demonstrating a product to trying to finalize the sale. In the United States, attendees tend to be information seekers who are not authorized to buy merchandise. Further, effective marketing efforts involve making certain those attending trade shows follow the cultural norms of the region. In Asian shows, gifts are often given to those who visit a booth. Also, the use of female decorative models to adorn products may be routine in one country and inappropriate in another. A trade show strategy can often by combined with sponsorships in international markets.

TRADE ALLOWANCES

A **trade allowance** is a price reduction or other consideration paid by a company to intermediaries as an incentive to purchase or promote a specific product. Many types of trade allowances are available to international marketers, including those presented in Table 16.4.

trade allowance: a price reduction or other consideration paid by a company to intermediaries as an incentive to purchase or promote a specific product

TABLE 16.4 Trade Allowances

Off-Invoice Allowances
Bill-Back Programs
Slotting Fees and Slotting Allowances
Display Allowances

Off-Invoice Allowances

Invoice allowances, which are often referred to as "off-invoice" allowances, grant price reductions on orders (literally off the invoice for the order) based on agreements between the manufacturer and the retailer. These invoices identify a predetermined purchase quantity that triggers the discount. They also apply to other agreements. The price incentives directly increase the margins that retailers realize. An example of an off-invoice allowance occurs when an international marketer such as Samsung grants a price break to wholesalers who distribute a certain volume of Samsung products internationally.

Bill-Back Allowances

A bill-back allowance takes the form of a monetary allowance presented to the retailer or intermediary at the end of a promotional period. In order to qualify for the allowance, the intermediary must perform one or more promotional activities, such as putting up displays, providing free samples, redeeming consumer coupons, or offering price cuts.

Bill-back programs increase the manufacturer's reach by creating incentives for additional marketing activities. Merchandise sold as a result of those marketing activities will be at full price. Only the actual marketing activity creates additional costs. These programs create more positive relationships between manufacturers and intermediaries, which will be crucial to the success of international marketing campaigns.

Large international beverage marketers, including Pepsi and Coca-Cola, utilize these allowances for retailers who perform important marketing functions. The retailer initially pays for the activity, and then submits an invoice to the manufacturer for the cost, thus leading to the term "bill back."

Slotting Fees and Slotting Allowances

A slotting fee or slotting allowance is a payment made by a manufacturer to a retailer in order to secure shelf space in the store. Retailers set fees based on the amount of space allotted to a product, such as a 12-inch space on an eye-level shelf, or an 18-inch space on a ground-level shelf. Retailers claim that, as the proliferation of brands in each category increases over time, competition for shelf space rises as well. Slotting fees help to spread the risk of new product introductions between the retailer and

Coca-Cola utilizes trade allowances for retailers that perform important marketing functions.

manufacturer. Consequently, manufacturers will be inclined to only pay slotting fees when they have a great deal of confidence about a new product's potential.

Slotting allowances are common in European countries, where they are generally referred to as *listing fees* (Stanton and Herbst, 2006). They are also prevalent in the United States and in all parts of the world. The practice has recently drawn attention in China where major retailers such as Wal-Mart and Carrefour utilize them.[9] International marketers seeking to conduct business in Europe may expect to pay slotting allowances at the retail level, especially in larger stores and big box chains.

Display Allowances

A display allowance promotion involves a retailer contracting with a manufacturer to place a product display in a prominent location in the retail outlet for a predetermined amount of time. When the retailer agrees to the terms of the allowance and performs the activities as agreed, the company earns an incentive in the form of a rebate at the end of the promotional period. The incentive takes various forms. Display allowances are common in the grocery market where large manufacturers encourage retailers to help promote products. Proctor & Gamble pays Nucare, a British pharmacy, display allowances to receive key shelf locations and prominent displays.[10]

COOPERATIVE ADVERTISING

Cooperative advertising, or co-op advertising, results from an agreement between a manufacturer and an intermediary. In a co-op advertising arrangement, a manufacturer agrees to pay for part of the advertising expenses of a retailer when the retailer promotes a product in a local market. Co-op advertising agreements are widely used. It appears in an advertisement that states, "Our products are found in finer stores, including ABC retailers." The expense of the promotion would be split based on an agreement between marketer and retailer. Co-op advertising continues to grow in usage, much like slotting fees, when the risks and marketing costs of products are split between international marketer and retailer.

TRADE CONTESTS

Manufacturers develop trade contests to provide rewards or incentives for intermediaries that either reach certain sales goals or outsell other intermediaries. These contests have proven to be effective in some international markets. In general, the reward or incentive takes a monetary form. Companies offer other things of value, ranging from special event tickets to merchandise as incentives in trade contests. From the retailer's perspective, it will be necessary to balance winning a given sales contest with providing information and service about products not in the contest. When retail salespeople become overly focused on one marketer's contest, other products may be neglected. This often occurs in the case of electronics retailers, where one brand receives greater attention and effort as the outlet or salesperson seeks to win the prize, thereby paying less attention to other, more potentially profitable brands that may be of more value to the customer as well.

TRAINING PROGRAMS

Manufacturers deliver training programs to marketing intermediaries as part of a trade promotions effort. Although training does not necessarily apply to every industry, it provides a beneficial form of trade promotion for complex products. IBM Business Solutions offers a number of trade promotions and training opportunities for retail customers.[11] Training retail sales personnel in an international context creates value. Training programs often increase sales and productivity levels of salespersons. General Electric has gained attention for its high-quality training program. The company recently focused on training customers in the Southeast Asia region, a region that continues to grow in importance for international marketers (Barcala et al., 1999; Malone, 2007).

POINT-OF-PURCHASE MATERIALS

Point-of-purchase materials take a variety of forms, but the goal remains the same: to encourage the immediate sale of the product by the end user. Point-of-purchase materials assist intermediaries, most generally retailers, in promoting a product to end users. The materials are effective because many items consumers purchase in retail stores are chosen on impulse with little or no preplanning. Marketers understand that making contact with consumers at the point of purchase increases the probability of a product being selected.

point-of-purchase materials: displays and materials that take a variety of forms, with the goal of encouraging the immediate sale of a product by the end user

Retailers and other intermediaries consider point-of-purchase support from manufacturers to be worthwhile. They do, however, often require an incentive for allowing point-of-purchase displays in an outlet. For this reason, manufacturers frequently provide trade allowances in exchange for the placement of point-of-purchase materials.

Retailers recognize the value of display space on retail floors and often charge for the use of the space.

Many countries contain few big box stores. When designing point-of-purchase displays to be sent to an international customer, the marketing team first examines the amount of retail space available for displays. The display's size can then be adapted to that space. Then, marketing professionals address other factors, including the most popular and symbolic colors, proper language, and other local circumstances as part of the design of the display.

CHALLENGES

Varying levels of access to new technologies continue to present a major challenge to international sales promotions programs. In lesser-developed regions of the world, sales promotions, such as sampling, take on additional importance. Other challenges include varying consumer responses to the individual sales promotion techniques. Couponing and in-store promotions are well received in Europe, as are direct mail campaigns. Mobile couponing is especially popular in Japan and Korea. The international marketer carefully considers differences such as these when entering a new country or market. International marketers also consider legal differences and all restrictions placed on sales promotion activities worldwide. Language differences pose a serious challenge for international marketers, as does the appropriate selection of social networking sites.

Large retailers, including chains such as Tesco (United Kingdom), Carrefour (France), and Wal-Mart (United States), as well as regionally based chains, hold increasing channel power, due to the number of choices available for each product line. Big box retailers carry thousands of products, presenting consumers with numerous options. As a result, manufacturers feel compelled to offer trade promotions to gain favor with retailers and achieve placements in stores. Many suppliers believe trade promotions are the only effective tool available to keep other companies from capturing space on retail shelves. This may be especially true for international companies attempting to gain shelf space in foreign countries in the face of rapidly growing global competition.

INTERNATIONAL SALES PROMOTIONS CAMPAIGN MANAGEMENT

One continuing issue in international sales promotion is the decision to establish local offices, regional offices, or a world headquarters to manage the promotions. Ultimately the decision might boil down to standardization versus adaptation. Although adaptation offers the advantage of catering to local market needs, it might dilute the image of a brand globally due to contradictory messages being delivered. Significant research will be required when considering this choice.

In many instances sales promotions must change country by country due to a variance in technological availability. Consumer promotions play an important role in countries where mass media advertising possibilities do not exist due either to technological limitations or consumer poverty. Some countries are geographically diverse. In many areas, rugged terrain makes access to traditional television or the Internet difficult or impossible. International marketers look for creative methods to reach these consumers with sales promotions.

Regardless of whether a standardization or adaptation strategy is chosen, international marketers seek to ensure that sales promotions are managed strategically. To ensure continuity of communication and message, each promotion should fit within the overall strategic direction set by marketing managers, which constitutes a critical part of the success of a promotional campaign (Mullin and Cummins, 2008).

LEARNING OBJECTIVE #4:

How does the public relations team or department handle negative publicity or image-damaging events?

INTERNATIONAL PUBLIC RELATIONS

The promotions mix contains other key elements and activities. Many of these link consumer and trade promotions with other marketing tactics. Public relations efforts then combine with other promotional efforts to present a more fully integrated image to customers and others.

Public relations involve the management of communication with all organizational stakeholders. The public relations function is handled by the department or unit in a firm that manages publicity and other marketing communications programs. The public relations team may be part of the marketing department or a stand-alone unit in the organization. Public relations include developing quality contacts with all publics and stakeholders. Internal stakeholders are the employees who work in a company. External stakeholders include all others who have contact with the organization. Table 16.5 provides a list of external stakeholders.

public relations: the management of communication with all organizational stakeholders

TABLE 16.5   External Stakeholders

Unions	Customers
Shareholders	Local Community
Government	Financial Community
Media	Special Interest Groups

CHANNEL MEMBERS

These stakeholders will be informed about company activities and responses to events using various media and communication methods. The standard tools available to the public relations department include

- public relations releases
- correspondence with shareholders
- company newsletters
- annual reports
- the public relations section of the organization's website
- special messages and special events

The two primary activities conducted by the public relations department include addressing negative publicity and events and promoting positive publicity and image-enhancing activities.

ADDRESSING NEGATIVE PUBLICITY AND EVENTS

damage control: reacting to negative events caused by a company's mistake, consumer grievances, or unjustified or false claims made by the press or others seeking to injure a company

Damage control takes place when the public relations team responds to negative events. Such events may be caused by a company's mistake, consumer grievances, or unjustified or false claims made by the press or others seeking to injure a company. When the company is in the wrong, company executives ask the public relations team to repair the damage to whatever degree possible. Two of the more common methods used to address company-created problems are crisis management programs and apology strategies.

Crisis Management

Crisis management involves refuting a false claim in a forceful manner. Company leaders make public statements explaining why the charges are not valid. They also provide evidence proving that the negative publicity is unjustified. The next element of crisis management will be promoting the positive aspects of a company's operations that also refute the negative claim. A company accused of using child labor in dangerous working conditions, when innocent, disputes the basic premise, provides evidence that child labor has not been employed, and then may continue with employee endorsements of the company's safety and overall method of operation.

A recent example appeared in the situation encountered by the Nestlé company in India. The worldwide giant had enjoyed a dominant market share with its Maggi brand of noodles. Unfortunately, a local governmental agency claimed that its research identified a highly unsafe level of lead in the product. The company quickly responded that its own testing produced quite different results. The crisis exploded when the national government sought to impose a national ban on the product, even in spite of the voluminous evidence provided by Nestlé that the noodles were well within safety limits.

The failure to effectively respond created a longer-term negative environment for Nestlé. As CEO Paul Bulcke stated, "This is a case where you can be so right and yet so wrong. We were right on factual arguments and yet so wrong on arguing. It's not a matter of being right. It's a matter of engaging the right way and finding a solution." He added: "We live in an ambiguous world. We have to be able to cope with that" (Fry, 2016). The event provides strong evidence of the need for effective and immediate crisis control when unexpected negative events occur. In this case for Nestlé, the impact and recovery time is likely to exceed three years (Bhushan, 2016).

Apology Strategies

An apology strategy consists of four elements. First, the company's leader offers an expression of guilt, embarrassment, or regret. Second, a statement acknowledging the inappropriate activity and accepting any sanctions imposed should be provided. Third, the company's leader publicly rejects the inappropriate behavior and approves of the proper action. Finally, the company offers and/or provides compensation or penance to correct the wrong.

In international circumstances, ceremonies and methods for offering apologies vary. In Asia, an apology would be finalized with a bow to an individual consumer or to a representative of an organization or consumer group. In other countries, a handshake might finalize the apology. For example, Toyota's chief executive officer promised a "fresh start" after a series of incidents involving vehicles that included rapid, unexplained acceleration and other defects. The move was made quickly to limit damage to the firm's reputation for building high-quality cars (Reed, 2010).

Partial Guilt

When a company is connected to a negative event and is partially responsible, leaders may offer excuses, explanations, or justifications. An *excuse* will be a pronouncement that the firm and its leaders cannot be held fully responsible for the predicament because it could not be foreseen. An *explanation* may be created to explain that the negative publicity has been disproportionate to the act. In essence, the public relations response will be, "This was a singular incident and is not how we typically conduct business."

A *justification* involves using logic to diminish the degree of negativity associated with the event, such as, "It wasn't that bad," or "If we don't pollute, we will be out of business and people will lose jobs." Many oil companies make this argument with regard to offshore drilling; in essence that the consequences of not drilling are greater than the problems (oil spills and accidents) that are part of the process.

LEARNING OBJECTIVE #5:

How can the public relations function help build a positive image of a company and its brands?

POSITIVE PUBLICITY AND IMAGE-ENHANCING ACTIVITIES

The other aspect of public relations programs includes all of the actions that support the generation of positive publicity along with programs that enhance an organization's image. Company employees deploy various public relations tools to optimize these programs. An *entitling* occurs when the company takes credit for a positive outcome, such as when a pharmaceutical company suggests that its efforts help reduce illness and mortality rates by making products available in a less-developed nation.

An *enhancement* emphasizes the value of an outcome. A firm dedicated to lessening carbon emissions will likely note that it "helps to save the planet for the next generation." At times, entitlings and enhancements result from less-concrete linkages, such as when a sports drink takes credit for an athlete's success or a team's performance.

Several marketing programs can be coupled to the goal of creating positive publicity and enhancing a firm's image. These include

- sponsorships
- event marketing
- cause-related marketing
- green marketing and sustainability

Sponsorships

A **sponsorship** creates an agreement between a marketing organization and an individual, team, or a landmark. International car racing, such as the twenty-four

sponsorship: an agreement between a marketing organization and an individual, team, or a landmark hours of Le Mans (*24 heures du Mans*), in France, features sponsors for drivers and cars. Both the racer and the vehicle are covered with patches and decals endorsing a wide variety of products. Additional sponsor advertisements line the racetrack. In the same country, bicycle-racing teams in the *Tour de France* receive compensation and support from sponsors.

A building or sports stadium may be the basis for a sponsorship. Reebok Stadium houses the English Premier Football Club, the Bolton Wanderers. In Yorkshire, England, the former Huddersfield Stadium has been renamed McAlpine Stadium.

Sponsorships assist in brand recall and help build brand loyalty. Fan allegiance to a participant or team should transfer to the sponsor. Stadium sponsors believe naming rights grant an organization greater credibility and enhance brand recall. Sponsors are expected to invest a sum of money in exchange for some type of promotional consideration on the part of the person or team.

Event Marketing

event marketing: using marketing techniques to connect with buyers through specific live events including concerts, performances, or festivals to promote a product or brand

A promotional tactic closely related to sponsorships is **event marketing**. Event marketing uses marketing techniques to connect with buyers through specific live events including concerts, performances, or festivals to promote a product or brand. Event marketers employ these techniques to connect with both consumers and trade channel members, which makes these programs a form of both consumer and trade-oriented sales promotions. An example of event marketing includes the efforts by Chinese company Yingli Green Energy. In the past decade the company became the first renewable energy company to sponsor the FIFA World Cup.[12]

Sponsorships programs and event marketing have grown rapidly in international marketing over the past several years. The programs often accompany other consumer promotions efforts. At an event in which a sponsored participant is involved, a company can set up a booth, offer free samples and coupons, run a contest or sweepstakes, and employ social media to make on-site connections as part of the program.

Cause-Related Marketing

Opportunities exist for firms to support social causes that are important to consumer values. Swedish giant Ericsson continues to support and sponsor the Swedish Paralympic Team. The sponsorship reflects the company's desire to break down walls of prejudice against persons with disabilities.[13] Sagami Rubber Industries of Japan sponsors music events, which not only helps promote the company's products but also heightens consumer awareness of contagious diseases such as AIDS. The company's sponsorship of the music event "Protected" promoted the safe sex message as well as condom products. The event also allowed Japanese hip-hop artists to advertise the products with free samples.[14]

Cause-related marketing can be an effective activity for a company seeking to promote and publicize its mission and core values. When the cause does not appear to fit with the organization or its activities, consumers quickly become cynical and often develop negative attitudes toward the company. Consequently, care should be given to the selection of proper causes for a firm to engage with, noting that customers and the public often comment on such programs on various social media outlets.

Green Marketing and Sustainability

An increasing number of international companies have become engaged in sustainable marketing practices. For some, the opportunity to publicize these efforts creates more favorable consumer attitudes. Other firms undertake green programs but do not emphasize them in marketing or public relations activities. The reasoning is that consumers may not believe the claim that the company has become more environmentally friendly, instead concluding that only a token effort has been made. Other consumers think that green products and production methods have higher costs that lead to price increases.

The public relations team faces the challenge of highlighting green efforts in a manner that does not overemphasize what has been done. Often the goal will be to add a layer of positive thought about a company and its brands, and no more.

SOCIAL MEDIA AND PUBLIC RELATIONS

The international growth of social media usage presents an additional set of tasks for the public relations team. Large organizations in particular monitor what bloggers and others engaged in social media connections say and write about the company. A negative event often quickly goes viral and causes the company embarrassment or creates a bad impression of the organization.

Internet interventions involve identifying false statements about a company and then responding to the allegations. A member of the public relations team will self-identify and present the organization's perspective. At times, the public relations employee can correct false information or present alternative interpretations of an event that has transpired.

Internet interventions: identifying false statements about a company and then responding to the allegations in the same communication channel

MARKETING IMPLICATIONS

In the international arena, public relations programs have become vital links between companies and various stakeholders. The public relations team remains vigilant to identify any negative publicity and to respond to it in a culturally appropriate fashion. Reactions may be sent out through traditional public relations tools such as press releases or via social media outlets.

Positive publicity and image-enhancing marketing programs receive support from the public relations team. The goals are to inform, persuade, and remind the public that the company seeks to do the right thing and contribute positively to the local community and all constituents.

Public relations efforts are influenced by the major factors affecting international business. Employees tailor public relations releases to each individual country's language, culture, legal and political systems, economic conditions, and infrastructure. The marketing team works to ensure the language is correct and does not offend, and that the cultural implications of both negative and positive events are clearly understood. In some countries, the media are owned or controlled by the government, which influences how messages are designed and delivered. Economic conditions and infrastructure influence media choices and method of delivering messages as well.

CHAPTER 16: REVIEW AND RESOURCES

Strategic Implications

Outlining the direction of the promotions mix and sales promotions programs generates a series of key strategic decisions. The promotional mix facilitates the direction of the overall marketing program. The promotions mix also supports the desired company image and product position globally. International marketing managers seek to identify the correct mix of consumer and trade promotions, with carefully chosen marketing objectives in mind. Normally, companies utilize both forms of sales promotions.

As international marketers consider a brand's global position, they select a standardization or adaptation approach to sales promotions. Language and cultural differences influence these decisions, as do legal restrictions. Leaders ask questions regarding whether promotional efforts will translate effectively across borders. International marketing managers then decide whether these promotional decisions should be made at the corporate or regional offices. The ultimate strategic objective remains to present a consistent message that accentuates the firm's image and position across all boundaries.

Tactical Implications

Middle-level managers implement the various consumer and trade promotions chosen at the strategic level. Should a company's marketing team decide to use coupons, marketers study the methods of delivery and select those most likely to succeed. Premium programs require understanding of the most efficient method for delivering prizes to customers. Contests and sweepstakes must meet any local legal requirements as well as cultural expectations. Price-off programs account for regulations regarding what constitutes the standard price and how often a discount can be granted. Refund and rebate programs comply with regulations and meet with cultural understanding of the promotions.

Trade promotions are adapted to meet standard business practices of a region or country. Company leaders carefully choose which trade shows to attend and how to conduct business at those shows. Trade allowances will be granted to companies with managers that understand and appreciate them. Cooperative advertising programs must fit with local laws and customers. The same will be true for trade contests and training programs. Point-of-purchase materials are distributed to retailers that will use them.

International marketing managers work to ensure that the tactics that are selected match the overall promotional strategy. By following the overall marketing strategy, continuity and consistency of communications will result.

Operational Implications

At the operational level, marketing employees at the entry level are the ones who actually deliver consumer and trade promotions. Consumer promotions must be managed so that entry-level employees know how to redeem coupons, present premium prizes, and grant price-off discounts. Employees should be trained to understand the overall marketing goals of the consumer and trade promotions, and how these factors apply to the individual contest, sweepstake, coupon, bonus pack, or free samples they will handle. Employees play a critical role in the success of international promotional campaigns, and their training is crucial. For trade-oriented promotions, supervisors monitor the activities of employees who interact with wholesalers and retailers to ensure that these channel members are carrying out their promotional duties by following up on offers that are accepted.

TERMS

sales promotions

consumer promotions

trade promotions

trade allowance

point-of-purchase materials

public relations

damage control

sponsorship

event marketing

Internet interventions

REVIEW QUESTIONS

1. What elements comprise a firm's promotional mix?

2. Define sales promotion and name its two primary activities.

3. Describe a push strategy and a pull strategy in international marketing.

4. Define consumer promotions and name the major types of consumer promotions.

5. Name the forms of coupons and how they are offered in international markets.

6. Describe a premium and a bonus pack.

7. What is the difference between an international contest and an international sweepstakes?

8. How can international marketers use social networking sites in marketing campaigns?

9. What three types of consumer reactions are present when individuals encounter international consumer promotions?

10. Describe trade promotions and the forms they take.

11. What are the major forms of trade allowances?

12. What is cooperative advertising?

13. Define public relations and name the types of internal and external stakeholders reached by public relations programs.

14. What is damage control?

15. What methods can a company use for damage control?

16. Define entitling and enhancement.

17. What positive publicity and image-enhancement programs are used in international public relations efforts?

DISCUSSION QUESTIONS

1. Which do you think is more important for an international marketer who is introducing a new product: a push strategy or a pull strategy? Why? What specific types of tactics do you think are most important in introducing new products?

2. What consumer promotion technique or techniques would work best in a country that does not have wide-scale access to mass media technologies such as television or the Internet? Defend your answer.

3. What role do social media play in international consumer promotions? How will the use of social networking grow in the future?

4. How do trade promotions differ in developed versus developing nations? In what ways could an international marketer use this information when developing sales promotions in these countries?

5. Explain how a public relations program would be different in a country in which the media are owned and operated by the government, as opposed to those that operate freely.

6. Describe an incident that occurred in another country that caused a company negative publicity. How did the company respond? Was the response appropriate? Why or why not?

ANALYTICAL AND INTERNET EXERCISES

1. Visit the website of a major international marketer such as Coca-Cola. What do you learn about the company's worldwide sales promotions? What tactics do you like? Are you surprised by any of them? Compare them to the sales promotion tactics used by a direct competitor. Are they similar, or very different? Explain your answer.

2. Visit the website of the international promotions company DDB (www.ddb.com). What sales promotion techniques are highlighted? What clients does the company list? How many of these clients can be considered to be international marketers? Go to one of the DDB international subsidiaries. What differences are present on those sites?

3. Visit the website of the major European retailer Tesco (www.tesco.com). What consumer-oriented sales promotions are highlighted? If you were shopping at one of the stores, which promotion would interest you the most?

4. Visit Facebook.com. What international companies do you see using the site for sales promotion? What types of promotion do you see? Do you think that these are effective or ineffective? What could the company do better to improve its use of social networking?

5. Using Google or Bing, identify an international public relations firm. Write a report describing the organization's activities and programs.

STUDENT STUDY SITE

Visit **https://study.sagepub.com/baack2e** to access these free additional learning tools:

- Web Quizzes
- eFlashcards
- SAGE Journal Articles
- Country Fact Sheets
- Chapter Outlines
- Interactive Maps

CASE 16

Marketing Facial Tissues

Sooner or later, everyone sneezes. In many parts of the world, the response will be to reach for a facial tissue. Numerous international marketing opportunities accompany the manufacture, distribution, and sale of facial tissues.

When marketing facial tissues products, each of the elements present in the international marketing context should be addressed. With regard to culture, facial tissue is used in a variety of ways, dependent on the country or region where it is sold. In Taiwan, paper towel products are not widely available. Spills are cleaned up with facial tissue. In other nations, citizens use facial tissue as toilet paper, even though technically the two are different. Toilet paper should be designed to decompose in a sewer system or septic tank, but some nations such as Iraq often do not have such systems. In Western culture, facial tissue may be for more than sniffles; women employ it to remove make-up. In less-developed countries, bottom-of-the-pyramid customers may not even be acquainted with the product.

The language of facial tissue also varies. The French call them *mouchoirs*. The Swedish version is *ansiksservetter*. At the same time, the term "Kleenex" remains the same in France or Sweden. A person in China might be confused by the concept of a facial tissue, even though the person has purchased an equivalent product, but for alternate uses.

Governments often regulate the ingredients used to create facial tissue. As greater environmental concerns emerge regarding deforestation, an impact on harvesting trees to produce facial tissues may occur. Some facial tissues carry ingredients such as lotions or perfumes, which might subject them to additional regulations, including those associated with medical and cosmetic products.

Economic conditions influence the patterns of the distribution of facial tissue. In developed and Western cultures, such products are widely distributed convenience items made available in a variety of packages. For bottom-of-the-pyramid markets or for least-developed economies, the same product may receive limited or no distribution support.

Infrastructure affects the delivery and price of facial tissue. The products are light, but packages do take up some space. Modes of transportation as well as the information technology that might be used to market facial tissue will be tailored to individual countries.

(Continued)

(Continued)

Numerous international marketing opportunities accompany the manufacture, distribution, and sale of facial tissues.

1. Describe how the use of sales promotions would vary in terms of the actual use of facial tissues, depending on the nation and region involved.

2. Describe how the type of sales promotion would change for facial tissues, based on local cultural differences in international markets.

3. Describe the manner in which local conditions such as distribution channels and types of retail outlets would affect the selection of sales promotion tactics.

4. Describe the manner in which local conditions (culture and governmental forces in particular) would influence the selection of trade promotion tactics.

NOTES

CHAPTER 1

1. Proven Models, "Howard V. Perlmutter." Retrieved from www.provenmodels. com/578/ep%5Br%5Dg/howard-v.-perlmutter/.

2. "Business: Exit the Dragon? Carrefour in Emerging Markets," *The Economist*, 393 no. 8652 (2009, October 10): 68; "Carrefour UAE Donates Food Supplies Worth AED 625,000 to People in Need," Al Bawaba (London), October 12, 2009; Berton (2009); Jitpleecheep (2009); Sinha (2009); "All Carrefour Outlets in Japan to Be Renamed Aeon Wed," Jiji Press English News Service (Tokyo), March 8, 2010; Pignal (2010); Vijayraghavan and Chakravarty (2010).

CHAPTER 2

1. "Japanese style rooms." Retrieved from www.japan-guide.com/e/e2007.html.

2. www.kfc.ca/?aspxerrorpath=/.

3. "Surfing 1: Tahitian Origins," Hickok Sports. Retrieved from www.hickoksports. com/history/surfing01.shtml.

4. "Surf History: Remember When....," Santa Cruz Surfing Museum.org, 2015 (Santa Cruz, CA). Retrieved from http://www.santacruzwaves.com/2015/09/remember-when-three-hawaiian-princes-introduced-surfing-to-santa-cruz-now-130-years-later-their-historic-redwood-surfboards-have-returned-home/.

5. Slow Food, 2017. Retrieved from www.slowfood.com/about-us/.

6. FEDMA, European Code of Practice 2017. Retrieved from http://ec.europa.eu/justice/policies/privacy/docs/wpdocs/2003/wp77-annex_en.pdf.

7. "Nestlé Celebrates the 75th Year of Kit Kat," October 11, 2010. Retrieved from www.nestle.co.uk/media/pressreleases/NestleCelebratesThe75thYearOfKITKAT.

8. "Kit Kat." Retrieved from www.nestle.com/investors/brand-focus/kitkat.

9. "Kit Kat." Retrieved from www.nestle.com/investors/brand-focus/kitkat.

10. www.nestle.com/asset-library/documents/investors/fact-sheets/kit-kat-fact-sheet.pdf.

CHAPTER 3

1. "Asia: Democracy in Action: China's National People's Congress," *The Economist* 394 no. 8671 (2010): 51.

2. The World Factbook, Central Intelligence Agency, Washington, DC. Retrieved from www.cia.gov/library/publications/the-world-factbook/index.html.

3. "Slovenia Adds Water to Constitution as Fundamental Right for All," *Guardian*, November 18, 2017. Retrieved from www.theguardian.com/environment/2016/nov/18/slovenia-adds-water-to-constitution-as-fundamental-right-for-all.

4. "Aldar to Build New Site for Abu Dhabi's Free Trade Zone for Media," Reuters (Online), May 22, 2017. Retrieved from www.reuters.com/article/aldar-abudhabi-contract-idUSL8N1IO2MD.

5. "Bolivia to Join MERCOSUR as Full Member," Reuters (Online), July 17, 2015. Retrieved from www.reuters.com/article/brazil-mercosur-bolivia-idUSE5N0V801 V20150717.

6. "Mercosur Suspends Venezuala over Trade and Human Rights," BBC.com, December 2, 2016. Retrieved from www.bbc.com/news/world-latin-america-38181198.

7. "India's IT Exports Seen Growing 10–12 Percent in Fiscal 2017," Reuters (Online), February 4, 2016. Retrieved from www.reuters.com/article/india-outsourcing-out-look-idUSI3N15J2RS.

8. Cushman & Wakefield Company Report, "Where in the World? Business Process Outsourcing and Shared Service Location Index 2016," November 29, 2016. Retrieved from www.cushmanwakefield.com/en/research-and-insight/2016/business-process-outsourcing-location-index-2016/.

9. Cushman & Wakefield Company Report, "Where in the World? Business Process Outsourcing and Shared Service Location Index 2016," November 29, 2016. Retrieved from www.cushmanwakefield.com/en/research-and-insight/2016/business-process-outsourcing-location-index-2016/.

10. "Social Innovation: Creating Products for Those at the Bottom-of-the-Pyramid," INSEAD Knowledge, December 12, 2017. Retrieved from https://knowledge.insead.edu/responsibility/creating-products-for-those-at-the-bottom-of-the-pyramid-1957.

11. The WTO. Retrieved from www.wto.org/english/thewto_e/thewto_e.htm.

12. "India Prepared to Counter Japan on Steel Dispute in WTO," *Financial Express* (India), March 14, 2017. Retrieved from www.financialexpress.com/economy/india-prepared-to-counter-japan-on-steel-dispute-in-wto/586801/.

13. The WTO. Retrieved from www.wto.org/english/thewto_e/minist_e/mc10_e/nairobipackage_e.htm.

14. The WTO. Retrieved from www.wto.org/english/tratop_e/agric_e/cotton_e.htm.

15. "U.S. Beef Exports Post Strong First-Quarter Results," *The Mapleton Press*, July 2, 2017. Retrieved from www.enterprisepub.com/mapleton/news/u-s-beef-exports-post-strong-first-quarter-results/article_783bd338-5ed5-11e7-bbeb-d7a7b6eb6992.html.

16. The World Factbook, Central Intelligence Agency, Washington, DC. Retrieved from www.cia.gov/library/publications/the-world-factbook/geos/us.html.

17. The World Factbook, Central Intelligence Agency, Washington, DC. Retrieved from www.cia.gov/library/publications/the-world-factbook/geos/ee.html.

18. "The European Parliament: The Citizen's Voice in the EU. A Short Guide to the European Parliament," Publications Office of the European Union, Luxemburg, October 2015. Retrieved from www.europarl.europa.eu/pdf/divers/EN_EP%20 brochure.pdf.

19. "US Renews Fight against EU Ban on Hormone-Treated Beef," EURACTIV.com with Reuters, December 22, 2016. Retrieved from www.euractiv.com/section/trade-society/news/us-renews-fight-against-eu-ban-on-hormone-treated-beef/.

20. http://cefta.int/.

21. North American Free Trade Agreement. Retrieved from https://www.nafta-sec-alena.org/Home/Welcome

22. "The Americas: A Turning Point?; Mercosur," *The Economist* 384 no. 8536 (2007): 52.

23. "The Americas: A Turning Point?; Mercosur," *The Economist* 384 no. 8536 (2007): 52.

24. "Chemical Business NewsBase: Oils and Fats International: In Brief: Egypt, Mercosur Sign Free-Trade Pact," Chemical Business Newsbase (Cambridge), November 1, 2010.

25. "Countries and Regions: Mercosur," European Commission (Online). Retrieved from http://ec.europa.eu/trade/policy/countries-and-regions/regions/mercosur/.

26. "Uruguay: Terry Johnson Wants Quality Beef," *El Observador Económico* (3ADI English Language Abstracts) (Montevideo), October 15, 2006.

27. "UNASUR: Union of South American Nations," Comunidad Andina. Retrieved from http://www.internationaldemocracywatch.org/index.php/union-of-south-american-nations

28. "Colombia, Peru Lift Bans, Open Markets to U.S. Beef," *Western Farm Press* (Clarksdale), 28 no. 27 (2006); "Pushing for Peru Beef," *Minneapolis* 44 no. 4 (2007): 54.

29. "CAFTA-DR (Dominican Republic–Central America FTA)," Office of the United States Trade Representative (Washington, DC). Retrieved from www.ustr.gov/trade-agreements/free-trade-agreements/cafta-dr-dominican-republic-central-america-fta.

30. "Caribbean Single Market and Economy," csmett.com. Retrieved from www.csmett.com/content2/csme/history/caricom_organisation.shtml.

31. "CARICOM Single Market and Economy (CSME): Overview," Caricom.org. Retrieved from http://caricom.org/work-areas/overview/caricom-single-marke-and-economy.

32. Association of Southeast Asian Nations. Retrieved from http://www.asean.org/asean/about-asean/

33. ASEAN Economic Community, ASEAN.org. Retrieved from http://asean.org/asean-economic-community/

34. ASEAN Economic Integration Brief, The ASEAN Secratariat, Jakarta, Indonesia, June 2017. Retrieved from http://asean.org/storage/2017/06/AEIB_No.01-June-2017_rev.pdf.

35. "Myanmar and ASEAN Build Their Relationship," Oxford Business Group. Retrieved from www.oxfordbusinessgroup.com/analysis/myanmar-and-asean-building-relationships-new-friends-and-old.

36. "Achievement and Benefits," APEC.org. Retrieved from www.apec.org/About-Us/About-APEC/Achievements%20and%20Benefits.

37. "Achievement and Benefits," APEC.org. Retrieved from www.apec.org/About-Us/About-APEC/Achievements%20and%20Benefits.

38. "Trans-Pacific Free Trade Deal Agreed Creating Vast Partnership," BBC.com, October 6, 2015. Retrieved from www.bbc.com/news/business-34444799.

39. "TPP: What Is It and Why Does It Matter?," BBC.com, January 23, 2017. Retrieved from www.bbc.com/news/business-32498715.

40. "TPP: What Is It and Why Does It Matter?," BBC.com, January 23, 2017. Retrieved from www.bbc.com/news/business-32498715.

41. The World Factbook, Central Intelligence Agency, Washington, DC. Retrieved from www.cia.gov/library/publications/the-world-factbook/.

42. "Taiwan to Boost Screening of US, Canadian Beef over Banned Drug," *McClatchy–Tribune Business News* (Washington), January 20, 2011.

43. "Continued Economic Reforms Would Attract More Foreign Investment," World Trade Organization, April 23, 2003. Retrieved from www.wto.org/English/tratop_e/tpr_e/tp213_e.htm.

44. "Agenda 2063," africanunionfoundation.com. Retrieved from http://aufoundation.africa/african-economic-platform/

45. "Continental Free Trade Area (CFTA) Legal Texts and Policy Documents," tralac.org. Retrieved from www.tralac.org/resources/by-region/cfta.html.

46. "Africa Population." Retrieved from www.worldometers.info/world-population/africa-population/.

47. "Trade War Risks from National Security Tariffs Outlook," FoxBusiness.com, June 18, 2017. Retrieved from https://www.wsj.com/articles/trade-war-risks-from-national-security-tariffs-14978000378.

48. China's Rare-Earth Exports Slide, Still Bust Quota," *Wall Street Journal* (Online), January 19, 2011.

49. "Budget to Have Subsidies for Food Grain-Based Distilleries," *Hindustan Times* (New Delhi), February 2, 2011.

50. "Government Revokes 1,104 Import Licenses," *The Jakarta Post* (Jakarta), February 10, 2010.

51. "EU Says China Making 'Considerable Progress' in Product Safety," BBC Monitoring Asia Pacific (London), November 23, 2007.

52. "Foreign Corrupt Practices Act: An Overview," The United States Department of Justice (Washington, DC). Retrieved from www.justice.gov/criminal/fraud/fcpa/.

53. "DHL Launches International Trade Initiative for Small and Medium-Sized Enterprises," *Insurance Business Weekly* (Atlanta), August 8, 2010; "DHL Launches Next Generation Shipping Software Designed for Small Businesses," *Computer Business Week* (Atlanta), July 21, 2008; "DHL Provides Express Delivery for Stretchy Shapes," *Manufacturing Close-Up* (Jacksonville), September 3, 2010.

CHAPTER 4

1. "Daily Bread Caracas," Economist.com/Global Agenda (London), March 17, 2008.

2. "The Official Travel Guide by Slovenian Tourist Board," Slovenian Tourist Board (2010). Retrieved from www.slovenia.info/en/zgodovina-in-kultura.htm?zgodovina_in_kultura=0&lng=2.

3. "What Is Couture?," Wisegeek.com (2011). Retrieved from www.wisegeek.com/what-is-couture.htm.

4. "Data Visualizations for a Changing World," Google Public Data Explorer (2011). Retrieved from www.google.com/publicdata/home.

5. Ewing (2007); Ford (2008); Versi (2008); Kennedy (2009); Magada (2009); Morgan (2009); "The Telecommunications Sector," *African Business* (London) no. 349 (January 2009): 27–30; "A Doctor in Your Pocket," *The Economist* 391 no. 8627 (April 18, 2009); "Mobile Phone Growth Biggest in Africa," *African Business* (London) no. 352 (April 2009): 8; Hujsak (2010).

CHAPTER 5

1. Syrian Refugee Crisis: Fast Facts, World Vision. Retrieved from www.worldvision.org/refugees-news-stories/syria-refugee-crisis-faq-war-affecting-children.

2. "Germany expects up to 300,000 refugees in 2016," *Guardian*. Retrieved from www.theguardian.com/world/2016/aug/28/germany-300000-refugees-2016-bamf.

3. "HSBC France Unveils Strategic Plan," The Pak Banker (Lahore), July 8, 2011.

4. "Google Stands Up to China's Censors; Search Engine Bravely Fulfils Its Mission Statement," *Financial Times* (London), January 14, 2010.

5. "The Volkswagon Group in Summary," Volkswagon Group. Retrieved from https://www.volkswagenag.com/en/group.html.

6. "How 'Brexit' Could Change Business in Britain," *The New York Times* (Online). Retrieved from www.nytimes.com/interactive/2016/business/international/brexit-uk-what-happens-business.html?_r=0.

7. "Nissan Sees Less Impact from Disaster Than Toyota, Honda," *Asia Pulse* (Rhodes), June 24, 2011.

8. Star Soap and Detergent Industries, PLC, 2017. Midroc Ethiopia. Retrieved from http://ethioasia.com/about.html

9. "Tata Exporting Nano," *Wall Street Journal* (Online), May 9, 2011.

10. Tata Motors, 2017. Retrieved from www.tatamotors.com/about-us/company-profile/.

11. "Kia Expects to Increase Market Share," *Wall Street Journal* (Online), May 6, 2011.

12. Kia, "Home Page." Retrieved from https://www.kia.com/us/en/homeSagee, "About Us." Retrieved from http://sage.com/ourbusiness.

13. "A Rich History of Product Innovation," Maruchan, accessed at www.maruchan.com/about_maruchan.html.

14. Honda, "Organization Structure." http://world.honda.com/RandD/fandf/.

15. Maruchan, "A A Taste of History." Retrieved from https://www.maruchan.com/about/.

16. Maruchan, "A A Taste of History." Retrieved from https://www.maruchan.com/about/.

17. "Talk Is Cheap; Counterfeit Handsets Proliferate in China," *The Economist* 393 no. 8658 (2009): 68.

18. "Conference on Mobile Revolution in South Asia," *The Business Times* (Singapore), February 17, 2011.

19. "Canada Trailing Developing World in 'Mobile Revolution,'" *Dawson Creek Daily News* (British Columbia), October 13, 2010.

20. Levi Strauss & Co., "Global Workplaces." Retrieved from www.levistrauss.com/about/global-workplaces.

21. "Finance Heads Believe Marketing Investment Is Needed in Recession," *Marketing Week* (London), March 19, 2009.

22. "Kicking GM's New-Stock Tires," *Wall Street Journal* (Online), November 12, 2010.

23. www.tradingeconomics.com/china/gdp-growth-annual. Retrieved January 24, 2017.

CHAPTER 6

1. Esri, "About Esri." Retrieved from www.esri.com/about-esri/index.html.

2. ACORN, "Understanding Consumers and Communities." Retrieved from http://www.acorncommunity.org/about/.

3. Claritas. Retrieved from www.claritas.com/; Claritas, "MyBestSegments." Retrieved from https://segmentationsolutions.nielsen.com/mybestsegments/.

4. "Pitney Bowes Survey Finds Majority of Global Consumers Shop Cross-Border," October 12, 2016. Retrieved from www.businesswire.com/news/

home/20161011006722/en/Pitney-Bowes-Survey-Finds-Majority-Global-Consumers; "APAC Leads Cross-Border e-Commerce," October 13, 2016. Retrieved from www.warc.com/LatestNews/News/APAC_leads_crossborder_ecommerce.news?ID=37565; "E-commerce Statistics for Individuals," December 2017. Retrieved from http://ec.europa.eu/eurostat/statistics-explained/index.php/E-commerce_statistics_for_individuals.

5. "SC Johnson Grows Sustainability Around the World; New Ad Stems from a Flower," PR Newswire (New York), April 2, 2010.

6. www.generali.com.

7. "Finance and Economics: Roll Up, Roll Up; Spain's Savings Banks," *The Economist* 398 no. 8719 (2011): 87.

8. General Electric, "Worldwide Activities." Retrieved from www.ge.com/company/worldwide_activities/index.html.

9. Thermocouples, https://www.peaksensors.co.uk/thermocouples/

10. "South Africa," The World Factbook, Central Intelligence Agency (Washington, DC). Retrieved from www.cia.gov/library/publications/the-world-factbook/geos/sf.html.

11. "Sustainability for Sound Business," *Industrial Management* 49 no. 4 (2007): 11.

12. "Pre-Empting the Competition," *Strategyonline* (Canada). Retrieved from www.strategyonline.ca/articles/magazine/20031006/handb.html?page=3.

13. "About Us." Retrieved from www.fastretailing.com/eng/about/; Talk Asia. Retrieved from http://transcripts.cnn.com/TRANSCRIPTS/1203/03/ta.01.html; "Japan's King of Casual Smartens Up." Retrieved from www.ft.com/content/afae506a-cb51-11e1-b896-00144feabdc0.

14. "About Us." Retrieved from www.fastretailing.com/eng/about/; Talk Asia. Retrieved from http://transcripts.cnn.com/TRANSCRIPTS/1203/03/ta.01.html; "Japan's King of Casual Smartens Up." Retrieved from www.ft.com/content/afae506a-cb51-11e1-b896-00144feabdc0.

CHAPTER 7

1. Top Food Facts, "The History of Hummus," March 20, 2013. Retrieved from http://topfoodfacts.com/the-history-of-hummus/.

2. "Australia's Virgin Blue Casts Net to Catch More Biz-Class Flyers," *Asia Pulse* (Rhodes), February 23, 2011.

3. http://www.huawei.com/en/about-huawei

4. "Sony to Close Symbol of TV Business," *Knight Ridder Tribune Business News* (Washington), February 1, 2007.

5. "Automotive; ADAC-Automarx: Mercedes-Benz Is Germany's Strongest Brand," *Journal of Transportation* (Atlanta), December 18, 2010.

6. "Of Internet Cafes and Power Cuts: Technology in Emerging Economies," *The Economist* 386 no. 8566 (2008): 90.

7. "Analyse the Oral Care Market in India Where Low Penetration Offers Growth Opportunities," *Business Wire* (New York), May 1, 2008.

8. "Business: Three-Point Turn; Hyundai in America," *The Economist* 383 no. 8534 (2007): 79.

9. "The Decline and Decline of Brand America," *BusinessLine* (Chennai), February 4, 2005.

10. "Indonesian Farmers Threaten to Boycott Nestlé Products," *Indonesia Government News* (New Delhi), March 24, 2010.

11. "Made in the USA? The Truth Behind the Labels," *Consumer Reports* 73 no. 3 (2008): 12–14.

12. "The Nation's Favourite Dish: Fish and Chips," Historic-UK.com, www.historic-uk. com/CultureUK/FishandChips.htm.

13. "Modified Nano Meets EU Crash Regulations," *Automotive Engineer* 34 no. 7 (2009): 6

14. "Philips to Enhance Position as a Top-Notch Brand in Kitchen Appliances," *Bernama* (Kuala Lumpur), August 6, 2003.

15. "Italy: Findomestic Launches Brand Repositioning Campaign Based on 'Co-Responsibility,'" *The Pak Banker* (Lahore): June 19, 2010.

CHAPTER 8

1. "About Clubcard." Retrieved from https://secure.tesco.com/clubcard/about/.

2. This definition is based on the American Marketing Association's definition of the concept found at www.marketingpower.com.

3. "China's Statistics Are Private Property," *Wall Street Journal* (Online), February 17, 2011.

4. "Market Research: Digging Deep to Find the Right Insight," *Marketing Week* (London), September 23, 2010.

5. "Internet World Stats," Internet World Statistics: Usage and Population Statistics. Retrieved from www.internetworldstats.com.

6. "Internet Users by Country (2016)." Retrieved from www.internetlivestats.com/ internet-users-by-country/.

7. ICT Facts & Figures. Retrieved from www.itu.int/en/ITU-D/Statistics/Documents/ facts/ICTFactsFigures2015.pdf.

8. ICT Facts & Figures. Retrieved from www.itu.int/en/ITU-D/Statistics/Documents/ facts/ICTFactsFigures2015.pdf.

9. "Latin American Internet Usage Statistics," Internet World Stats: Usage and Population Statistics. Retrieved from www.internetworldstats.com/stats10.htm.

10. "Internet Usage Statistics for Africa." Retrieved from www.internetworldstats. com/stats1.htm.

11. "World Bank Blogs: Mobile Phone Penetration." Retrieved from http://blogs. worldbank.org/category/tags/mobile-phone-penetration.

12. "Liberia at a Glance," Development Economic LDB (February 25, 2011). Retrieved from https://www.google.com/search?client=firefox-b-1-ab&ci=ty8tW4GSDtLG sQXpgoKYBQ&q=world+bank+liberia+overview&oq=world+bank+liberia&gs_ l=psy-ab.1.0.0i71k1l8.0.0.0.14267.0.0.0.0.0.0.0..0.0....0...1..64.psy-ab..0.0.0.... 0.YBxTXhPh6sE.

13. "How Does the Japanese Addressing System Work?" Retrieved from www.sljfaq. org/afaq/addresses.html.

14. "Big Data Europe." Retrieved from www.big-data-europe.eu/; "Digital Single Market." Retrieved from https://ec.europa.eu/digital-single-market/en/ big-data.

15. WPP, "The power of big data to unlock new brand experiences." Retrieved from www.wpp.com/wpp/marketing/branding/the-power-of-big-data-to-unlock-new- brand-experiences/.

16. "Marketing to Women: Femininity, Roles and Pigeonholes," *Brand Strategy* (London), September 14, 2007: 40–41.

17. "Growing Terrorism to Hamper Economic Growth: Acting President ICCI," *The Balochistan Times* (Quetta), July 5, 2010.

18. "Indonesia Objects US Move to Include Country on Copyright Watch List," *BBC Monitoring Asia Pacific* (London), March 19, 2010.

19. "Chocolate and Confectionery." Retrieved from www.nestle.co.uk/brands/chocolate_and_confectionery.

20. This case study was written based on a case study issued by Nestlé Poland for their Nestlé Forum 2007 recruitment initiative (www.forum.nestle.pl/). The website is no longer active.

CHAPTER 9

1. "Staple Foods: What Do People Eat?," FAO Corporate Document Repository. Retrieved from www.fao.org/docrep/u8480e/u8480e07.htm.

2. "Packaging and Packaging Waste," Europa. Retrieved from http://europa.eu/legislation_summaries/environment/waste_management/121207_en.htm.

3. "Towards a 'Green' Ramadan," *Gulf News* (Dubai), August 28, 2009.

4. "A Global Language for Packaging and Sustainability," Consumer Goods Forum, July 8, 2010. Retrieved from http://ec.europa.eu/environment/waste/packaging/legis.htm.

5. "Towards Sustainable Packaging," Packaging Council of Australia, 2007. Retrieved from http://www.pca.org.au/sustainability.

6. Sustainable Packaging Coalition (n.d.). Retrieved from https://sustainablepackaging.org/.

7. Ecology Coatings (n.d.). Retrieved from www.ecologycoatings.com/profiles/investor/fullpage.asp?f=1&BzID=1672&to=cp&Nav=0&LangID=1&s=0&ID=8935.

8. "Study: Consumers' Demand for Sustainable Products Remains Strong," Dupont Tate and Lyle BioProducts, May 21, 2009. Retrieved from https://www.prweb.com/releases/dupont/sorona/prweb2448384.htm

9. "KFC Bags Go Green," *Townsville Bulletin* (Townsville, Qld), February 2, 2010.

10. "Introducing the Green Bottle That's Made from Paper," *Sunday Times*, July 5, 2009.

11. "CE Marking-Home," International Trade Administration. Retrieved from https://2016.export.gov/cemark/eg_main_017267.asp .

12. Mercatto Group (n.d.). Retrieved from http://localemercatto.ca/ .

13. Comstar Corporate (n.d.). Retrieved from http://comstarauto.com/comstar_company_history.html.

14. Industrial Resin Sdn Bhd (n.d.). Retrieved from https://malaysia.exportersindia.com/industrial-resins-company1769622/.

15. Agrium, Inc. (n.d.). Retrieved from https://agrium.com/user/login?destination=node/2402 .

16. This section is based on Habib and Zurawicki (2010).

17. "Key Development Data and Statistics," The World Bank, 2011. Retrieved from http://databank.worldbank.org/data/reports.aspx?source=world-development-indicators

18. "Economic Data Search Tool," World Trade and Tourism Council (n.d.). Retrieved from https://tool.wttc.org/ .

19. "Copenhagen in New Drive for Tourists," *The Copenhagen Post* (Online), May 17, 2010. Retrieved from www.cphpost.dk/business/business/119-business/48989-copenhagen-in-new-drive-for-tourists.html.

20. Europa Park (Rust, Germany). Retrieved from https://www.europapark.de/en.

21. "The World's Most Innovative Companies," *Bloomberg Businessweek* (Online). Retrieved from https://www.bloomberg.com/news/articles/2008-04-16/the-worlds-most-innovative-companies

22. "Laptop Sales Exceed Desktop Sales Globally," Laptop Logic.com, December 26, 2008.

23. "Over Five Billion Mobile Phone Connections Worldwide," European Journalism Centre, 2010. Retrieved from https://www.bbc.com/news/.

24. "SA's Joule Car Aims to Electrify Car Market," BusinessDay.co.za, July 27, 2010. Retrieved from www.businessday.co.za/Articles/Content.aspx?id=116064.

25. "Taiwan's High-Tech Firms Diversify to Survive," *Taipei Times*, February 11, 2010. Retrieved from www.taipeitimes.com/News/biz/archives/2010/02/11/2003465735.

26. TeaGschwendner, 2010. Retrieved from https://www.teegschwendner.de/tee-shop/?gclid=Cj0KCQjwvLLZBRDrARIsADU6ojAhl0CHrn_qyiu_trsCbPDD6W6pjJxfK29F4dy5Lc6kkP8KZVIvDU4aAu3WEALw_wcB .

27. "Harley Davidson Reports First Quarter 2010 Results," Harley Davidson (April 20, 2010). Retrieved from http://investor.harley-davidson.com/news-releases/news-release-details/harley-davidson-reports-first-quarter-2010-results.

28. Kevlar, 2011. Retrieved from www2.dupont.com/Kevlar/en_US/index.html.

29. The definition based on the conceptualization by the American Society for Quality (www.asq.org).

30. "Best Global Brands 2011," Interbrand. Retrieved from http://interbrand.com/best-brands/best-global-brands/2011/ranking/.

31. "Indonesia: Overview," International Resource Center, March 2011. Retrieved from https://www.idrc.ca/en/what-we-do/regions and countries/asia/indonesia.

32. Interface, 2008. Retrieved from www.interfaceglobal.com/default.aspx.

33. "Sustainability Leaders: Celebrating 20 years of leadership. Retrieved from https://globescan.com/wp-content/uploads/2017/07/GSS-Leaders-2017-Survey-Report.pdf.

34. "Toward a More Sustainable Way of Business," Interface (Online), 2008. Retrieved from http://interfaceglobal.com/Sustainability.aspx. Craig Reiss, "Why You Need to Know TED," Entrepreneur (Online) (2010), www.entrepreneur.com/article/217243.

CHAPTER 10

1. "World Coffee Consumption." Retrieved from www.ico.org/prices/new-consumption-table.pdf.

2. "Our Brands: Costa." Retrieved from www.whitbread.co.uk/our-brands/costa.html.

3. "Whitbread PLC Results, Reports and Presentations." Retrieved from https://www.whitbread.co.uk/investors/results-reports-and-presentations.

4. "Whitbread Capital Market Day 2016." Retrieved from https://markets.ft.com/data/announce/full?dockey=1323-13050191-3AIN9F3FG2NJQB3KI30R5O0LUS.

5. "Costa Coffee dziala juz w 20 miastach Polski." Retrieved from https://costa coffee.pl/aktualnosci/pokaz/uid/costa-coffee-dziala-juz-w-20-miastach-polski; "Costa Pays £163.36m for Coffeeheaven," *Independent*, December 16, 2009. Retrieved from www.independent.co.uk/news/business/news/costa-pays-1633 6m-for-coffeeheaven-1841930.html.

6. "Costa Coffee." Retrieved from https://www.youtube.com/watch?v=rjutjQwJCmw.

7. "Costa." Retrieved from https://www.costa.co.uk/business/.

8. "Letnie nowosci dla koneserow kawy w Costa Coffee." Retrieved from www.costa coffee.pl/aktualnosci/pokaz/uid/letnie-nowosci-dla-koneserow-kawy-w-costa-coffee; "Kawy." Retrieved from www.cafecosta.pl/menu-kawy.

9. "Madrid—The International Trademark System." Retrieved from www.wipo.int/madrid/en/.

10. "Cyber Espionage is Reaching Crisis Levels" Retrieved from http://fortune.com/2015/12/12/cybersecruity-amsc-cyber-espionage/ .

11. "Introduction to the Economic Espionage Act." Retrieved from www.justice.gov/usam/criminal-resource-manual-1122-introduction-economic-espionage-act.

12. "2 Taiwanese Convicted in Economic Spy Case," *Los Angeles Times*, April 29, 1999. Retrieved from http://articles.latimes.com/1999/apr/29/business/fi-32206.

13. "New 3-D Scanners Speed Reverse-Engineering," *Manufacturing Engineering* (Dearborn) 141 no. 5 (2008): 28–31.

14. "About the Center for Copyright Information." Retrieved from www.copyright information.org/about-cci/.

15. "The World Intellectual Property Organization." Retrieved from www.wipo.int/portal/en/index.html.

16. "Tobacco Plain Packaging—Investor-State Arbitration." Retrieved from https://www.ag.gov.au/Internationalrelations/InternationalLaw/Pages/Tobaccoplain packaging.aspx.

17. "InfoCuria—Case-Law of the Court of Justice." Retrieved from http://curia.europa. eu/juris/liste.jsf?pro=&nat=or&oqp=&dates=&lg=&language=en&jur=C%2CT%2CF &cit=none%252CC%252CCJ%252CR%252C2008E%252C%252C%252C%252C%252C %252C%252C%252C%252C%252Ctrue%252Cfalse%252Cfalse&td=%3BALL&pcs=O or&avg=&page=1&mat=or&parties=rosneft&jge=&for=&cid=67329#.

18. "Accelerating the Market for Renewable Energy in Indonesia,"February 7, 2017, https://www.renewableenergyworld.com/articles/2017/02/accelerating-the-market-for-renewable-energy-in-indonesia.html.

19. "Citibank No. 1 Credit Card Issuer in the UAE, First in Retail Spending," *Al Bawaba* (London), October 5, 2005; "Which Are the 10 Most Popular Credit Cards in the UAE?" Retrieved from www.emiratesnews247.com/10-popular-credit-cards-uae/.

20. "Foodstuffs, Cosmetics and Disinfectants Act, 1972 (Act 54 of 1972): Regulations Relating to the Labeling and Advertising of Foodstuffs," Department of Health Government Gazette no. 30075 (July 20, 2007). Retrieved from http://www. nda.agric.za/doaDev/sideMenu/fisheries/03_areasofwork/Aquaculture/Aqua PolGuidLeg/Legislation/FoodstuffsCosmeticsDisinfectantsAct54of1972.pdf.

21. "Antitrust." Retrieved from http://ec.europa.eu/competition/antitrust/overview_en.html.

22. "Apple Adds the European Union to Its Antitrust Woes," 9TO5Mac, July 6, 2010. Retrieved from http://9to5mac.com/2010/07/06/apple-adds-the-european-union-to-its-antitrust-woes/.

23. "S. Africa: On High-Risk Products, Retailers Have New Obligations," *The Pak Banker* (Lahore), April 13, 2010.

24. "Guarantees and Returns." Retrieved from http://europa.eu/youreurope/citizens/consumers/shopping/guarantees-returns/index_en.htm.

25. "EU Law on Organic Production: An Overview." Retrieved from https://ec.europa.eu/agriculture/organic/eu-policy/eu-legislation/brief-overview_en.

26. Promotion Marketing Awards of Asia (n.d.). Retrieved from www.pmaa-awards.net/documents/11.%20Best%20Effective%20Long%20Term%20Mkt%20Campaign.pdf.

27. "Ocean Park Settles Social Media Pitch," *New Media Power*, May 11, 2015. Retrieved from http://www.marketing-interactive.com/ocean-park-settles-social-media-pitch/ .

28. Flightstats.com (n.d.). Retrieved from https://www.flightstats.com/v2/.

29. This definition based on Gronroos (1982).

30. "Organiser of Music Concerts Executed," *Freemuse*, August 21, 2008. Retrieved from https://freemuse.org/news/iran-organiser-of-music-concerts-executed/.

31. A *crore* is a unit of measurement in South Asia equal to 10 million.

32. "Notice and Notice Regime." Retrieved from www.ic.gc.ca/eic/site/oca-bc.nsf/eng/ca02920.html.

33. "Huntkey Launches 'Universal' Power Strips; Compatibility, Safety, Functionality—Three in One 'Housekeeper,'" *PR Newswire* (New York), March 19, 2010.

34. "Samsung Introduces Two New Mobile Sets in Bangladesh," *Bangladesh Business News*, July 29, 2010. Retrieved from https://economictimes.indiatimes.com/magazines/panache/samsung-launches-galaxy-j6-j8-a6-and-a6-with-chat-over-video-feature-from-rs-13990-onwards/articleshow/64255798.cms

35. "History of Hybrid Vehicles," Hybrid Cars, June 13, 2011. Retrieved from https://www.hybridcars.com/history-of-hybrid-vehicles/.

36. "Number 918 Comes Off the Line." Retrieved from https://newsroom.porsche.com/en/products/porsche-918-spyder-manufaktory-end-of-production-11123.html.

37. "Banana Republic." Retrieved from www.gapinc.com/content/gapinc/html/aboutus/ourbrands/BananaRepublic.html.

38. "Gap Inc.'s Global Footprint." Retrieved from www.gapinc.com/content/attachments/gapinc/GPSEarnings/Global%20Footprint.pdf.

39. "Gap to Shut all Banana Republic Shops in the UK," *Guardian*, October 18, 2016. Retrieved from www.theguardian.com/uk-news/2016/oct/18/gap-to-shut-all-banana-republic-shops-in-the-uk.

40. "Annual Reports and Proxy." Retrieved from http://investors.gapinc.com/phoenix.zhtml?c=111302&p=irol-reportsAnnual.

CHAPTER 11

1. Finland, *The World Factbook*, Central Intelligence Agency, 2011. Retrieved from www.cia.gov/library/publications/the-world-factbook/geos/fi.html; Small Wind Turbine Businesses in Finland, Momentum Technologies, LLC. Retrieved from http://energy.sourceguides.com/businesses/byP/wRP/swindturbine/byGeo/byC/Finland/Finland.shtml#29417; www.Tuulivoimala.com.

2. "What are Supply and Demand Curves?" Retrieved from www.mindtools.com/pages/article/newSTR_69.htm.

3. "Indonesia Sweats High Chili Prices," *Global Post* (Chatham), August 5, 2010.

4. "Pepsi Plans Low-Cost Beverages, Snacks to Fight Anemia," *Businessline* (Chennai), June 30, 2009.

5. "A Quarter of Firms Offer an Early Payment Discount," *Credit Control* (Hutton) 26 no. 8 (2005): 36–38.

6. "Telstra Profits Decline," *Lateline Business* (Ultimo), February 11, 2010.

7. "Mongolian Firms Fined for 'Collusion' on Flour Prices," BBC Monitoring Newsfile (London), August 17, 2010.

8. "Mofcom Released the Final Ruling for Anti-Dumping Investigation into Imported Purified Terephthalic Acid," Info: Prod Research (Middle East) Ramat-Gan, August 16, 2010.

9. "US for £ 7 Is a Loss Leader," *Travel Weekly* (UK), May 4, 2007.

10. "Lawsuit Claims British Airways Guilty of Illegal, Deliberately Deceptive Pricing," Canada NewsWire (Ottawa), May 14, 2010.

CHAPTER 12

1. ArcelorMittal, September 27, 2017. Retrieved from www.arcelormittal.com.

2. "Market Price in Japan," Rice Databank Co., Ltd, July 27, 2011. Retrieved from https://www.ft.com/content/f4db3b26-6045-11e5-a28b-50226830d644.

3. Triennial Central Bank Survey (December 2007), Bank for International Settlements.

4. "Saudi Arabia Tops in Flood Aid to Pakistan," *McClatchy–Tribune Business News* (Washington) September 2, 2010.

5. "UK Goods Trade Surplus with US Widens," February 10, 2017. Retrieved from https://www.marketwatch.com/story/uk-goods-trade-surplus-with-us-widens-2017-02-10.

6. "IMF Would Consider Extending Greece More Aid," *Wall Street Journal* (Online), September 16, 2010; "Greek Tourism Outlook Less Grim, China to Be Wooed," *Financial Mirror* (Nicosia), June 22, 2010.

7. World Economic Outlook Update, July 2017, "A Firming Recovery," International Monetary Fund. Retrieved from www.imf.org/en/Publications/WEO/Issues/2017/07/07/world-economic-outlook-update-july-2017.

8. "Countertrade," American Heritage Dictionary. Retrieved from www.answers.com/topic/countertrade-1.

9. "Finance and Economics: Poor People, Rich Returns; Microfinance," *The Economist* 387 no. 8580 (2008): 98.

10. "Doing Good by Doing Very Nicely Indeed: Microfinance," *The Economist* 387 no. 8586 (2008).

CHAPTER 13

1. "Grocery e-Shopping in Poland Does Not Pan Out: Tesco Partially Withdraws from This Market" [E-zakupy spożywcze w Polsce to niewypał? Tesco częściowo wycofuje się z tego rynku]. Retrieved from http://antyweb.pl/tesco-tnie-ezakupy/.

2. "Remedent, Inc. Announces Exclusive Marketing and Distribution Agreement for Glamsmile(TM) Veneers into Saudi Arabia," *Business Wire* (New York), April 24, 2008.

3. Louis Vuitton. Retrieved from www.lvmh.com.

4. "Germany: Selling U.S. Products and Services," U.S. Commercial Service, United States Department of Commerce. Retrieved from https://2016.export.gov/ccg/germany090798.asp

5. "Germany: Selling U.S. Products and Services," U.S. Commercial Service, United States Department of Commerce. Retrieved from https://2016.export.gov/ccg/germany090798.asp

6. "China Agri-Business's New Direct Sales Channel Continues to Grow," PR Newswire, August 13, 2010. Retrieved from http://stocks.energyreportnews.com/energyreport/news/read/19305944/china_agri

7. "Japanese Trading Companies: The Giants That Refused to Die," *The Economist* 319 no. 7709 (1991): 72–73.

8. "Brazil: Classy Brands to Distribute Gisele Bündchen Cosmetics Sejaa," *Brasil Econômico* (SABI English Language Abstracts) (São Paulo)", January 17, 2011.

9. "DOH Bans Junk Food Ads on Children's Television," *China Post* (Online edition), January, 29, 2010. Retrieved from https://chinapost.nownews.com/20100129-132695

10. "Business Floating on Air," *The Economist* 359, no. 8222 (2001): 8.

11. "Vertical Integration: Luxottica, SCRIBD". Retrieved from www.scribd.com/doc/305305445/Vertical-Integration-Luxottica.

12. This definition based on Duhan and Sheffet (1988).

13. Oral-B. Retrieved from www.oralb.com/international/.

14. This section based on Stern et al. (1996).

15. "Distribution Agreement," RealDealDocs. Retrieved from http://agreements.realdealdocs.com/Distribution-Agreement/DISTRIBUTION-AGREEMENT-2835241/.

16. Definition based on El-Ansary and Stern (1972).

17. "M4 Sciences Signs International Distribution Agreement with Fukuda Corp." Retrieved from https://www.businesswire.com/news/home/20100721006583/en/M4-Sciences-Signs-International-Distribution-Agreement.

18. "Mamas and Papas Launches Eighth International Store in the Kingdom of Bahrain." Retrieved from http://www.tradearabia.com/news/RET_145240.html Franchiseek.com.

19. "Wal-Mart Altering Culture of Mexico/Retailer's Power Similar to That in U.S.," *Houston Chronicle* (Texas), December 6, 2003.

20. These assertions are based on the work of Chang (2005).

21. JDA Software, "About JDA." Retrieved from www.jda.com/company/company-index/.

22 "MEBC, Inc. Expands Partnership with JDA Software," *The Pak Banker* (Lahore): May 11, 2011.

23 "2010 Green Supply Chain Awards 'Sustainability Becomes Strategic,'". Retrieved from https://trove.nla.gov.au/work/117587358?q&versionId=131061438.

24. "JDA Software Announces First Quarter 2011 Results," *The Pak Banker* (Lahore), May 4, 2011. Also, JDA Software, "About JDA." Retrieved from www.jda.com/company/company-index/.

CHAPTER 14

1. "Alipay Spat Leaves Alibaba Group, Yahoo Relationship Fraying," *Interfax: China Business Newswire* (Hong Kong), June 8, 2011; "Alibaba Overtakes Google in Mainland Ad Sales," *China Economic Review Daily Briefings* (Shanghai), December 10, 2010; "Alibaba: China's Sourcing Trailblazer Reaches a Turning Point," *China Economic Review* (Shanghai), April 6, 2011; "Alibaba Makes It Easier for U.S. Retailers to Acquire Top-Quality Chinese-Designed Products," *Business Wire* (New York), April 26, 2011; "Alibaba Has New Express Delivery System," *China Economic Review Daily Briefings* (Shanghai), January 19, 2011; "Alibaba and the 2,236 Thieves: An Online Scandal in China," *The Economist* 398 no. 8722 (2011): 73.

2. World Trade Organization, "International Trade Statistics, 2015." Retrieved from www.wto.org/english/res_e/statis_e/its2015_e/its2015_e.pdf.

3. "Our Locations," Winget Limited. Retrieved from www.winget.co.uk/our Locations.aspx?Continent=Middle%20East.

4. "Red Bull's Good Buzz," *Newsweek*, May 14, 2001.

5. "DFA: Bangladeshi Trade Delegation to Visit PHL Late January," gmanews.tv, January 14, 2011. Retrieved from www.gmanews.tv/story/210592/nation/dfa-bangladeshi-trade-delegation-to-visit-phl-late-january.

6. Export Broker Services, Export Trade Brokers. Retrieved from www.exporttrade brokers.com/exportbrokerservices.html.

7. Australian Institute of Business Brokers. Retrieved from www.aibb.org.au/.

8. Van Bon Stores, "H&S Group." Retrieved from www.vanbon.nl/.

9. "Global Distribution Centers," FlashGlobal. Retrieved from http://flashglobal.com/global-supply-chain/global-distribution-centers/.

10. "3PL Solutions," Victory Packaging. Retrieved from http://info.victorypackaging.com/3pl-solutions?utm_campaign=3PL%2FE-commerce%20&utm_source=ppc&utm_medium=text%20ad&gclid=CjwKEAjwm7jKBRDE2_H_t8DVxzISJACwS9Wb3avEIgK JajzGT4xaEQSc6pO6UnJd8UkNns40VoX_dRoCpRfw_wcB.

11. "Transportation Services Overview," *U.S. Industry Quarterly Review: Transportation & Logistics*, 2nd Quarter (2006): 135–137.

12. COMESA (n.d.). Retrieved from www.comesa.int/.

13. "Transportation Services Overview," *U.S. Industry Quarterly Review: Transportation & Logistics*, 2nd Quarter (2006): 135–137.

14. "CSI in Brief," U.S. Department of Homeland Security (n.d.). Retrieved from https://www.globalsecurity.org/security/ops/csi.htm "C-TPAT Overview," U.S. Department of Homeland Security (n.d.). Retrieved from https://www.cbp.gov/border-security/ports-entry/cargo-security/ctpat

15. Rewe Group. Retrieved from https://www.rewe-group.com/en/company.

16. Shoprite. Retrieved from https://www.shoprite.com/.

17. "International Licensing," 7–11 (n.d.). Retrieved from http://corp.7-eleven.com/AboutUs/InternationalLicensing/tabid/115/Default.aspx.

18. HyperPanda. Retrieved from www.panda.com.sa/english/index.php/about-us.html.

19. "Shinsegae Centum City: World's Largest Department Store," Bukisa.com. Retrieved from http://busan.for91days.com/shinsegae-the-worlds-largest-department-store/.

20. Wal-Mart. Retrieved from http://walmartstores.com/AboutUs/.

21. "Starbucks Coffee International," Starbucks. Retrieved from www.starbucks.com/business/international-stores.

22. "Annual Report 2010," Footlocker. Retrieved from www.footlocker-inc.com/investors.cfm?page=annual-reports.

23. Taobao's Gross Merchandising Volume, Statista, 2016. Retrieved from www.statista.com/statistics/323075/taobao-quarterly-gross-merchandise-volume-gmv/; "Alibaba Group to Drive Major Investment in Logistics in China to Allow Merchants to Meet Growing Domestic Consumption," *Business Wire* (New York), January 19, 2011.

24. "M&S Today." Retrieved from http://corporate.marksandspencer.com/aboutus/mands-today.

25. "Marks & Spencer Sets Out New Vision of 'Sustainable' Multichannel Retail." Retrieved from http://internetretailing.net/2016/11/marks-spencer-sets-out-new-vision-of-sustainable-multichannel-retail/.

26. "M&S Retreats from Poland: Report," *Radio Poland*, November 8, 2016. Retrieved from www.thenews.pl/1/12/Artykul/279059,MandS-retreats-from-Poland-report.

27. "Marks & Spencer Closing Ahead of Schedule." July 14, 1999. Retrieved from https://www.cbc.ca/news/business/marks-spencer-closing-ahead-of-schedule-1.184100.

28. "Marks & Spencer (UK) Restructure International Operations." Retrieved from www.worldfranchiseassociates.com/franchise-news-article.php?nid=3628; "Plan A 2025 Commitments." Retrieved from https://corporate.marksandspencer.com/documents/plan-a/plan-a-2025-commitments.pdf.

CHAPTER 15

1. Adapted from de Mooij (2010: 164).

2. "Why India's Newspaper Business Is Booming," *The Economist* (Online), February 22, 2016.

3. Eurostat Statistics Explained (n.d.). Retrieved from http://ec.europa.eu/eurostat/statistics-explained/index.php/Digital_economy_and_society_statistics_-_households_and_individuals.

4. "Global Media Report," McKinsey & Company, December 2016. Retrieved from www.mckinsey.com/industries/media-and-entertainment/our-insights/global-media-report-2016.

5. "Aust Parliamentary Committee to Review Billboard Advertisements," *Asia Pulse* (Rhodes), December 14, 2010.

6. Bhalaria. Retrieved from www.bhalariametal.net/profile.html.

7. Audi. Retrieved from www.audi.com.

8. Eurocare. Retrieved from www.eurocare.org/library/updates/revision_of_the_eu_audio_visual_media_services_directive_avmsd.

9. "India: New Thums Up Ad Most Expensive," *The Pak Banker* (Lahore), January 8, 2010.

10. "Issue Brief Portrayal of Gender," EASA. Retrieved from http://www.easa-alliance.org/issues/gender.

11. "Land of the Big," *The Economist*, December 21, 1996.

12. For a more complete description of these formats, see de Mooij (2010: ch. 10).

13. "How Product Placement Will Transform British TV," ThisIsMoney.co.uk, January 24, 2011. Retrieved from www.thisismoney.co.uk/news/article.html?in_article_id=521679&in_page_id=2.

14. "Gartner Mobile App Survey Reveals 24 Percent More Spending on In-App Transactions Than on Upfront App Payments," *Gartner*, May 26, 2016. Retrieved from www.gartner.com/newsroom/id/3331117.

CHAPTER 16

1. "Modern African Remedies: Herbal Medicine and Community Development in Nigeria," *Policy Voice: African Research Institute*, April 21, 2015. Retrieved from www.africaresearchinstitute.org/newsite/publications/modern-african-remedies/.

2. "A Coupon Nation: Americans Proudly Use Coupons More Than Shoppers in Great Britain, India and China, Among Others," August 21, 2013. Retrieved from www.prnewswire.com/news-releases/a-coupon-nation-americans-proudly-use-coupons-more-than-shoppers-in-great-britain-india-and-china-among-others-220485721.html.

3. "Coupon Site Groupon Expands to Europe," Boston.com, May 17, 2010. Retrieved from www.boston.com/business/technology/articles/2010/05/17/coupon_site_groupon_expands_to_europe/.

4. Kellogg's Canada. Retrieved from www2.kelloggs.ca/Promotion/PromotionDetail.aspx?PID=21157.

5. "Dubai's Cite Centre Mall Takes Its Sales Promotion Online," Menafn.com, accessed at www.menafn.com/qn_news_story_s.asp?StoryID=1093279166

6. Vaseline. Retrieved from https://www.youtube.com/user/VaselineUK.

7. Tecno Bediba. Retrieved from www.biztradeshows.com/trade-events/tecno-bediba.html.

8. "Overview," Shopbiz.com. Retrieved from www.shopbiz.jp/en/rt/.

9. "Walmart Follows Carrefour on Raising Fees," *The Economic Times*, February 21, 2008. Retrieved from https://economictimes.indiatimes.com/news/international/carrefour-wal-mart-battle-for-market-share-in-china/articleshow/2800198.cms.

10. "Nucare Encourages Pharmacies to Build Haircare Category," *Chemist & Druggist* (London), October 13, 2001.

11. "Digital Media for Retail Solution from IBM and Cisco," IBM Business Solutions. Retrieved from www.ibm.com/solutions/cisco/us/en/solution/H186213N23135Z95.html.

12. "Yingli Green Energy Announces Global Sponsorship of 2010 FIFA World Cup," Yingli Solar corporate, February 3, 2010. Retrieved from http://ir.yinglisolar.com/phoenix.zhtml?c=213018&p=irol-newsArticle&ID=1382290 &highlight=.

13. "Company Facts: Sponsorships," Ericsson. Retrieved from www.ericsson.com/thecompany/company_facts/sponsorships.

14. "Welcome to Sagami's Website," Sagami Rubber Industries. Retrieved from www.sagami-gomu.co.jp/en/index.html.

BIBLIOGRAPHY

Aaker, David A., *Managing Brand Equity: Capitalizing on the Value of a Brand Name* (New York: Free Press, 1991).

Aaker, David A., *Building Strong Brands* (London: Simon & Schuster, 2002)

Abdulaziz, Abdulaziz, "Nigeria: Cleplas Rewards Distributors in Kano," *All Africa*, January 29, 2010. Retrieved from http://allafrica.com/stories/201001290662.html.

Aggarwal, Raj, "Business Strategies for Multinational Intellectual Property Protection," *Thunderbird International Business Review 52* no. 6 (2010): 541–551.

Ahlstrom, Dick, "Language Complexity Declined in Move Out of Africa," *Irish Times*, April 21, 2011.

Albaum, Gerald, Edwin Duerr, and Jesper Strandskov, *International Marketing and Export Management* (Harlow: Prentice Hall Financial Times, 2005).

Alden, Dana L., Wayne D. Hoyer, and Chol Lee, "Identifying Global and Culture-Specific Dimensions of Humor," *Journal of Marketing 57* no. 2 (1993): 64–76.

Alden, D. L., J.-B. E. M. Steenkamp, and R. Batra, "Brand Positioning through Advertising in Asia, North America, and Europe: The Role of Global Consumer Culture," *Journal of Marketing 63* no. 1 (1999): 75–87.

Allchin, Josie, "Caroline Harris, Head of Insight at Costa," *Marketing Week*, October 5, 2011. Retrieved from www.marketingweek.com/2011/10/05/caroline-harris-head-of-insight-at-costa/.

Allison, Melissa, "Starbucks Reports Strong First Quarter Results as Via, International Sales Take Off," *The Seattle Times* (Online), January 21, 2010. Retrieved from http://seattletimes.nwsource.com/html/businesstechnology/2010846852_starbucks21.html.

Anderson, Jamie and Costas Markides, "Strategic Innovation at the Base of the Pyramid," *MIT Sloan Management Review 49* no. 1 (2007): 83–88.

Anselmsson, Johan, Ulf Johansson, and Niklas Persson, "The Battle of Brands in the Swedish Market for Consumer Packaged Food: A Cross-Category Examination of Brand Preference and Liking," *Journal of Brand Management 16* no. 1/2 (2008): 63–79.

Appleyard, Dennis R., Alfred J. Field, Jr, and Steven L. Cobb, *International Economics* (Boston, MA: McGraw-Hill, 2008).

Arvind, Phatak and Mohammed Habib, "How Should Managers Treat Ethics in International Business?," *Thunderbird International Business Review 40* no. 2 (1998): 101–118.

Asker, David and Donald Norris, "Characteristics of TV Commercials Perceived as Informative," *Journal of Advertising Research 22* no. 2 (1982): 61–70.

Associated Press, "Sabra Recalls Hummus amid Listeria Contamination Fears," November 21, 2016, *USA Today* reprint. Retrieved from www.usatoday.com/story/money/business/2016/11/21/sabra-recalls-hummus-amid-listeria-contamination-fears/94236298/.

Asthana, A. and M. Taylor, "Britain to Ban Sale of All Diesel and Petrol Cars and Vans from 2040," *Guardian*, July 25, 2017. Retrieved from www.theguardian.com/politics/2017/jul/25/britain-to-ban-sale-of-all-diesel-and-petrol-cars-and-vans-from-2040.

Atkins, Ralph, "Global Strengths and Weaknesses Are Exposed," *Financial Times*, October 6, 2009.

Aubrey, A., "Why We Got Fatter During the Fat-Free Food Boom," March 28, 2014. Retrieved from www.npr.org/sections/thesalt/2014/03/28/295332576/why-we-got-fatter-during-the-fat-free-food-boom.

Awokuse, Titus O. and Hong Yin, "Intellectual Property Rights Protection and the Surge in FDI in China," *Journal of Comparative Economics 38* no. 2 (2010): 217–224.

Axon, Samuel, "Going Global: Groupon Buys European Clone CityDeal," *Mashable. com*, 2010. Retrieved from http://mashable.com/2010/05/16/groupon-citydeal-europe/.

Baack, Donald, *International Business* (New York: Glencoe-McGraw-Hill, 2008).

Baack, Donald and Daniel Baack, *Ethics and Marketing* (Upper Saddle River, NJ: Pearson Custom Publishing, 2008).

Babin, Barry J. and Eric G. Harris, *CB – Consumer Behavior* (Mason, OH: Cengage, 2009).

Baena, Veronica, "Modeling Global Franchising in Emerging Markets: An Entry Mode Analysis," *Journal of East–West Business 15* no. 3/4 (2009): 164–188.

Balasubramanyam, Seshan, "Is Future of Social Media Global?," *International Business Times* (Online), 2009. Retrieved from www.ibtimes.com/articles/44646/20100823/emarketer-united-states-facebook-nielsen-brazil-italy-new-zealand-hong-kong-canada-singapore-experia.htm.

Bander, James, "Ending Era, Kodak Will Stop Selling Most Film Cameras," *Wall Street Journal*, January 14, 2004.

Banerjee, Arindam and Scott A. Williams, "International Service Outsourcing: Using Offshore Analytics to Identify Determinants of Value-Added Outsourcing," *Strategic Outsourcing: An International Journal 2* no. 1 (2009): 68–79.

Banerjee, Devin, "Expanding Banking in India," *Wall Street Journal* (Online), July 28, 2010. Retrieved from http://online.wsj.com/article/SB1000142405274870370090457539 1460677186520.html?mod=WSJ_latestheadlines.

Barcala, M. F., M. J. S. Perez, and J. A. T. Gutierrez, "Training in Small Business Retailing: Testing Human Capital Theory," *Journal of European Industrial Training 23* no. 7 (1999): 335–352.

Barker, Alex, Chris Bryant, and Ben Hall, "Sarkozy Claims Credit for Regulation Plans," *Financial Times*, April 3, 2009.

Barros, Carlos Pestana and Ricardo Sellers-Rubio, "Analysing Cost Efficiency in Spanish Retailers with a Random Frontier Model," *International Journal of Retail & Distribution Management 36* no. 11 (2008): 883–900.

Barry, Curt, "Keeping DC Costs at Bay," *Multichannel Merchant 4* no. 4 (2008): *1*, 45.

Basanez, M. E., *A World of Three Cultures* (Oxford: Oxford University Press, 2016).

Bayer, Judy, "Customer Segmentation in the Telecommunications Industry," *Journal of Database Marketing & Customer Strategy Management 17* no. 3/4 (2010): 247–256.

BBC, "Rabbis Clean up Spicy Soap Advertisements," November 24, 2004. Retrieved from http://news.bbc.co.uk/1/hi/world/middle_east/4039461.stm.

BBC, "Galaxy 7 Note Recall Refuseniks Face New Action," January 17, 2017a. Retrieved from www.bbc.com/news/technology-38664325.

BBC, "The Politics of the Office Tea Round," March 14, 2017b. Retrieved from www.bbc.co.uk/news/business-39155646.

Bear, Jacci Howard, "Red," 2010. Retrieved from http://desktoppub.about.com/cs/colorselection/p/red.htm.

Beesley, Arthur and Henry Foy, "European Court Upholds Russia Sanctions after Rosneft Challenge," *Financial Times*, March 28, 2017. Retrieved from www.ft.com/content/ef1c271e-6528-31b1-8426-feeb75e77d19.

Benady, D., "Concern about the Effects of Global Brands," 2008. Retrieved from www.marketingweek.com/2008/07/04/concern-about-the-effects-of-global-brands/.

Berton, Elena, "Carrefour Seeks to Overturn Antitrust Ruling in Indonesia," *WWD* *198* no. 95 (2009, November 5): 15.

Bhattacharya, Saumya, "Want a Job, Go Rural: At a Time When Urban Jobs Are Dwindling, Microfinance Is Creating Jobs in Rural India Provided You Have the Right Skills and Aptitude," *Business Today* (New Delhi), March 8, 2009.

Bhushan, Ratna, "Maggi Ban Impact: Nestle India May Take 3 Years to Recover," *The Economic Times*, February 24, 2016. Retrieved from https://economictimes.indiatimes.com/industry/cons-products/food/maggi-ban-impact-nestle-india-may-take-3-years-to-recover/articleshow/51114562.cms.

Bicheno, Scott, "Sony Consolidates Distribution Network to Ensure Highest Levels of Service and Expertise," *Hexus.channel*, 2008. Retrieved from http://channel.hexus.net/content/itcm.php?item=16029.

Bilsky, W. and S. H. Schwartz, "Values and Personality," *European Journal of Personality 8* (1994): 163–181.

Bland, Alastair, "Coffee Here, and Coffee There: How Different People Serve the World's Favorite Hot Drink," March 15, 2013. Retrieved from www.smithsonianmag.com/travel/coffee-here-and-coffee-there-how-different-people-serve-the-worlds-favorite-hot-drink-3214272/#1OU5XxCKEoq05acC.99.

Bokaie, Jemima, "Coca-Cola Plans 'Chinese' Drinks," *Marketing*, October 17, 2001.

Bomcy, Nathan and Elizabeth Weise, "Travel Ban Effect? 'World Is Going to Start Closing the Door," *USA Today*, January 30, 2017. Retrieved from www.usatoday.com/story/money/2017/01/30/donald-trump-immigration-muslim-travel/97247774/.

Bosshard, Peter, "Dam Nation," *Foreign Policy*, March 8, 2011. Retrieved from www.foreignpolicy.com/articles/2011/03/08/dam_nation.

Bourne, Joel K., "Inside the Curl: Surfing's Surprising History," 2013. Retrieved October 13, 2017, from http://news.nationalgeographic.com/news/2013/08/130803-surfing-surprising-history-hawaiian-culture-extreme-sports/.

Bowen, D. E. and R. Hallowell, "Suppose We Took Services Seriously? An Introduction to the Special Issue," *Academy of Management Executive 16* no. 4 (2002): 1–5.

Bowman, J., "Commercials Rise in the East," *M&M Europe: Pocket Guide to Asian TV* (London: Emap Media, 2002).

Boyer, Nicole, "The Base of the Pyramid: Reperceiving Business from the Bottom Up," *Global Business Network*, May 2003. Retrieved from www.visionspring.org/downloads/docs/GBN_BOP_Paper.pdf.

Boynton, Robert S., "The Tyranny of Copyright," *New York Times*, January 25, 2004.

Boyte, H., "How Consumer Culture Is Killing Citizenship," 2016. Retrieved from http://billmoyers.com/story/consumer-culture-killing-citizenship/.

Bozadzhieva, Martina, "Global Companies Need to Adopt Agile Pricing in Emerging Markets," *Harvard Business Review*, September 19, 2016. Retrieved from https://hbr.org/2016/09/global-companies-need-to-adopt-agile-pricing-in-emerging-markets.

Brady, Diane, "Pepsi: Repairing a Poisoned Reputation in India," *Business Week*, June 11, 2007.

Bramen, L., "The Evolution of the Sweet Tooth," 2010. Retrieved from www.smithsonianmag.com/arts-culture/the-evolution-of-the-sweet-tooth-79895734/.

Brashear, T. G., V. Kashyap, M. D. Musante, and N. Donthu, "A Profile of the Internet Shopper: Evidence from Six Countries," *Journal of Marketing Theory and Practice* 17 no. 3 (2009): 267–282.

Brassington, Chris, "Mobile Coupons Are Failing to Catch On, Why?," *The Huffington Post*, July 21, 2010. Retrieved from www.huffingtonpost.com/chris-brassington/mobile-coupons-are-failin_b_654714.html?ref=twitter.

Braun, Karen, Wendy M. Tietz, and Walter T. Harrison, *Managerial Accounting* (2 ed.) (Upper Saddle River, NJ: Prentice Hall, 2010).

Brett, Jeanne M., *Negotiating Globally: How to Negotiate Deals, Resolve Disputes, and Make Decisions across Cultural Boundaries* (2 ed.) (San Francisco: Jossey-Bass, 2007).

Britt, Bill, "Chevy Chase Does Turkish Cola Ads Aimed at Coke and Pepsi: Spots Air as Anti-American Feeling in Turkey Runs High," *Adage.com* (London), August 1, 2003. Retrieved from www.cenktolunay.com/articles/cola_turka.htm.

Broderick, Amanda J., Gordon E. Greenlet, and Rene Dentiste Mueller, "The Behavioural Homogeneity Evaluation Framework: Multi-Level Evaluations of Consumer Involvement in International Segmentation," *Journal of International Business Studies* 38 no. 5 (2007): 746–763.

Brynildsen, Jen C., "The International Pricing of CS3 Is Insane," *FlashMagazine.com*, April 18, 2007. Retrieved from www.flashmagazine.com/news/detail/the_international_pricing_of_cs3_is_insane/1421.htm.

Bu, Kyunghee, Donghoon Kim, and Seung-yon Lee, "Determinants of Visual Forms Used in Print Advertising: A Cross-Cultural Comparison," *International Journal of Advertising 28* no. 1 (2009): 13–47.

Burgen, S., "Mandarin Menus and No Rooms with a 4: Spain's Hotels Adapt for Chinese Tourists," *Guardian*, June 7, 2015. Retrieved from www.theguardian.com/world/2015/jun/07/spain-hotels-adapt-chinese-tourists.

Buzzell, Robert D., "Can You Standardize Multinational Marketing?," *Harvard Business Review 46* no. 6 (1968): 102–113.

Calantone, R. J., D. Kim, J. B. Schmidt, and S. T. Cavusgil, "The Influence of Internal and External Firm Factors on International Product Adaptation Strategy and Export Performance: A Three-Country Comparison," *Journal of Business Research 59* no. 2 (2006): 176–185.

Campaign, "Pizza Hut Delivering Poorly in China," 2015. Retrieved October 20, 2017, from www.campaignlive.co.uk/article/pizza-hut-delivering-poorly-china/1351372.

Carpenter, J., M. Moore, A. M. Doherty, and N. Alexander, "Acculturation to the Global Consumer Culture: A Generational Cohort Comparison," *Journal of Strategic Marketing 20* no. 5 (2012): 411–423.

Castro, Charita L. and Jialan Wang, "Don't Be Tricked by Treats; Halloween; Say 'Boo' to Chocolate Companies That Use Cocoa Made from Exploiting Child Labor," *St. Louis Post—Dispatch* (Missouri), October 28, 2010.

Cavusgil, S. T. and A. Das, "Methodological Issues in Empirical Cross-Cultural Research: A Survey of the Management Literature and a Framework," *Management International Review 37* no. 1 (1997): 71–96.

CBC News, "Big Retailers Taking French Sign Battle to Quebec Court," 2012. Retrieved from www.cbc.ca/news/canada/montreal/big-retailers-taking-french-sign-battle-to-quebec-court-1.1287036.

Censky, Annalyn, "Porsche to Produce Plug-In Sports Car," *cnnmoney.com,* July 28, 2010. Retrieved from http://money.cnn.com/2010/07/28/autos/porsche_hybrid/index.htm?hpt=T2.

Chakravorty, Satya S., "Improving Distribution Operations: Implementation of Material Handling Systems," *International Journal of Production Economics 122* no. 1 (2009): 89–103.

Chamorro-Premuzic, T. and N. Nahai, "Why We're so Hypocritical about Online Privacy," *Harvard Business Review,* May 1, 2017. Retrieved from https://hbr.org/2017/05/why-were-so-hypocritical-about-online-privacy.

Chan, Kara, Lyann Li, Sandra Diehl, and Ralf Terluttee, "Consumers Response to Offensive Advertising: A Cross Cultural Study," *International Marketing Review 24* no. 5 (2007): 606–628.

Chang, Lieh-Ching, "An Examination of Cross-Cultural Negotiation: Using Hofstede Framework," *Journal of American Academy of Business* (March 2003): 567–570.

Chantanusornsiri, Wichit, "Bowled Over: TOTO of Japan Elevates Mundane Bathroom Fixtures," *Knight Ridder Tribune Business News* (Washington), May 27, 2005.

Chapagain, A. K. and A. Y. Hoekstra, "Water Footprints of Nations," *UNESCO-IHE: Institute for Water Education 16* no. 1 (2004). Retrieved from www.waterfootprint.org/Reports/Report16Vol1.pdf.

Charles, Gemma, "SABMiller Introduces Kozel Beer to UK," Brand Republic, September 20, 2010. Retrieved from www.brandrepublic.com/news/1029404/sabmiller-introduces-kozel-beer-uk/.

Chen, Ming-jer, *Inside Chinese Business: A Guide for Managers Worldwide* (Cambridge, MA: Harvard Business School Press, 2001).

Chew, Jonathan, "What Volkswagen's Next CEO Can Learn from GM's Mary Barra," *Fortune,* September 23, 2015. Retrieved from http://fortune.com/2015/09/23/volkswagen-ceo-mary-barra-gm/.

Chohan, Usman W., "Cryptocurrencies: A Brief Thematic Review," *Discussion Paper Series: Notes on the 21st Century, University of New South Wales,* August 4, 2017.

Choi, A. S., "What Americans Can Learn from Other Food Cultures," 2014. Retrieved from https://ideas.ted.com/what-americans-can-learn-from-other-food-cultures/.

Choi, Youngtae, Rahul Kale, and Jongkuk Shin, "Religiosity and Consumers' Use of Product Information Sources among Korean Consumers: An Exploratory Study," *International Journal of Consumer Studies 34* (2010): 61–68.

Chon, Gina, "Audi Pursues Brand Recognition in U.S.," *Wall Street Journal* (Online), May 8, 2007.

Chrisafis, Angelique, Larry Elliott, and Jill Treanor, "French PM Manuel Valls Says Refugee Crisis Is Destabilizing Europe," *Guardian,* January 22, 2016. Retrieved from www.theguardian.com/world/2016/jan/22/french-pm-manuel-valls-says-refugee-crisis-is-destabilising-europe.

Christie, P. M. J., I.-W. G. Kwon, P. A. Stoeberl, and R. Baumhart, "A Cross-Cultural Comparison of Ethical Attitudes of Business Managers: India Korea and the United States," *Journal of Business Ethics 46*, no. 3 (2003): 263–287.

Chu, S.-C. and S. M. Choi, "Electronic Word-of-Mouth in Social Networking Sites: A Cross-Cultural Study of the United States and China," *Journal of Global Marketing 24* no. 3 (2011): 263–281.

Chu, S.-C. and S.-C. Huang, "College-Educated Youths' Attitudes toward Global Brands: Implications for Global Marketing Strategies," *Journal of International Consumer Marketing 22* no. 2 (2010): 129–145.

Chufo, Veronica, "Chinese Drywall: Judge Awards $2.6 M to 7 Local Homeowners," *McClatchy–Tribune Business News* (Washington), April 8, 2010.

Cleveland, M. and M. Laroche, "Acculturation to the Global Consumer Culture: Scale Development and Research Paradigm," *Journal of Business Research 60* (2007): 249–259.

Clough, Alexandra, "Luxury Toilet Maker TOTO USA Opens in Wellington Mall," *Knight Ridder Tribune Business News* (Washington), March 14, 2005.

Clow, Kenneth E. and Donald Baack, *Marketing Management: A Customer Oriented Approach* (Los Angeles, CA: SAGE, 2010).

Clow, Kenneth E. and Donald Baack, *Cases in Marketing Management* (Los Angeles, CA: SAGE, 2011).

Clow, Kenneth E. and Donald Baack, *Integrated Advertising, Promotion, and Marketing Communications* (5 ed.) (Upper Saddle River, NJ: Prentice Hall, 2012).

CNN, "Japan's KitKat Craze: It's Gone Gourmet, with over 300 Flavors," 2017. Retrieved from http://edition.cnn.com/travel/article/japan-kitkats-chocolate/index.html.

Comish, Alison, "Capacity to Consume," *The American Economic Review 26* no. 2 (1936): 291–295.

Condon, George H., "Why Can't Canadians Buy Red Bull and Pro-Activ?," *Canadian Grocer 117* no. 2 (2003): 82.

Conference Board, "What Is the Global Economic Outlook for 2017?," 2017. Retrieved from www.conference-board.org/economic-outlook2017/.

Connors, Will, "Africa Rising: In Nigeria, Used Cars Are a Road to Status; Growing Middle Class Makes Bumpy Transition from Perilous Buses; Taking 'Baby Boy' Home," *Wall Street Journal* (Online), January 18, 2011a.

Connors, Will, "Africa Rising: Catering to New Tastes as Incomes Climb; Zambian Beef Processor Expands to Nigeria with Aim of Spreading out across the Continent," *Wall Street Journal* (Online), February 10, 2011b.

Coppla, C. J., "Direct Marketing Sales Boom with the Proliferation of Wine Clubs," *Wine Business Monthly* 7 no. 6 (2000): 20–23.

Cordeiro, Anjali, "Battery Makers Recharge War: Procter & Gamble to Continue to Offer Bonus Packs of Its Duracell Brand," *Wall Street Journal* (Eastern edition), January 27, 2010.

Corus, "La Chaîne Disney: New TV Offer for the Whole Family Starting September 1!," 2015. Retrieved from www.corusent.com/news/la-cha%C2%94ne-disney-new-tv-offer-for-the-whole-family-starting-september-1/.

Cox, Juliet and Colin Mason, "Standardisation versus Adaptation: Geographical Pressure to Deviate from Franchise Formats," *The Services Industries Journal 27* no. 8 (2007): 1053–1072.

Cronin, John, Jed Cahill, and Mike McLean, "Prep Patents with Reverse Engineering in Mind," *Electronic Engineering Times*, June 8, 2009: 3–32.

Crosby, Jackie, "A Glimpse of Health Care in India: An Edina Doctor Says a Trip to India Showed Her the Need to Improve Health Care in Other Parts of the World," *Star Tribune* (Minneapolis), May 8, 2011.

Czarnecka, B. and S. Keles, "Global Consumer Culture Positioning: The Use of Global Consumer Culture Positioning Appeals across Four European Countries," *Journal of Euromarketing 23* no. 3 (2014): 59–67.

Dalton, Matthew, "World News: Europe Raises Cry over Chinese Technology," *Wall Street Journal*, October 6, 2010.

Damon, Arwa, "Mom of Toddler Smoker in Indonesia Seeks Help for Him," *CNN World*, May 31, 2010. Retrieved from www.cnn.com/2010/WORLD/asiapcf/05/31/indonesia.smoking.baby/index.html.

Daneshkhu, Scheherazade, "UK Fashion Market Suffers Steepest Decline since 2009," *Financial Times*, October 17, 2016. Retrieved from www.ft.com/content/c55cd612-945f-11e6-a1dc-bdf38d484582.

Daneshkhu, Scheherazade and Mark Vandevelde, "Clothes Buying Goes Out of Fashion in the UK," *Financial Times*, September 24, 2016. Retrieved from www.ft.com/content/5c274b28-7f3d-11e6-8e50-8ec15fb462f4.

Dardagan, Colleen, "Airline Flies Again with a New Advertising Campaign," *The Mercury* (Durban), March 22, 2010.

Dauriz, L., N. Remy, and T. Tochtermann, "A Multifaceted Future: The Jewelry Industry in 2020," McKinsey & Company Retail, February 2014.

Davies, Roy, "From Thalers to Dollars," *University of Exeter*, 2008. Retrieved from http://projects.exeter.ac.uk/RDavies/arian/dollar.html.

Dawes, John, "Brand Loyalty in the U.K. Sportswear Market," *International Journal of Market Research 51* no. 4 (2009): 449–463.

Dawkins, Jenny, "Corporate Responsibility: The Communication Challenge," *Journal of Communication Management 9* no. 2 (2004): 106–117.

De Mooij, Marieke, *Global Marketing and Advertising: Understanding Cultural Paradoxes* (3 ed.) (Los Angeles, CA: SAGE, 2010).

Dietrich, Joy, "Western Union Retraces Roots: The Emotions of Money Transfers," *Advertising Age International* (October 1999): 24–25.

Dimitrova, Boryana and Bert Rosenbloom, "Standardization versus Adaptation in Global Markets: Is Channel Strategy Different?," *Journal of Marketing Channels 17* no. 2 (2010): 157–176.

Dinopoulos, Elias and Paul Segerstrom, "Intellectual Property Rights, Multinational Firms and Economic Growth," *Journal of Development Economics 92* no. 1 (2010): 13–27.

Douglas, Susan P. and C. Samuel Craig, *International Marketing Research* (Englewood Cliffs, NJ: Prentice Hall, 1983).

Downey, Lynn, "A Short History of Denim," *Levi Strauss & Co.* Retrieved from http://www.levistrauss.com/wp-content/uploads/2014/01/A-Short-History-of-Denim2.pdf.

Downie, Andrew, "7 Cool Ideas: A Sweet Ride in Brazil (The Future of Energy)," *Time* (Canadian edition), *166* no. 18 (2005): 40.

Dubey, J. and R. P. Patel, "Small Wonders of the Indian Market," *Journal of Consumer Behaviour 4* no. 2 (2004): 145–151.

Duhan, D. and M. Sheffet, "Gray Markets and the Legal Status of Parallel Importation," *Journal of Marketing 52* no. 3 (1988): 75–83.

Durschlag, Stephen P., "Comparative Advertising Doesn't Always Work Overseas," *Promo*, January 1, 1999. Retrieved from http://promomagazine.com/mag/marketing_comparative_advertising_doesnt/#.

Dussauge, Pierre and Bernard Garrette, "Determinants of Success in International Strategic Alliances: Evidence from the Global Aerospace Industry," *Journal of International Business Studies 26* no. 3 (1995): 505–531.

Eaglesham, Jean and Paul Solman, "EU Standard for Sales Promotions," *Financial Times*, December 10, 2001.

Eckhardt, G., "The Role of Culture in Conducting Trustworthy and Credible Qualitative Business Research in China," in *Handbook of Qualitative Methods for International Business Research*, edited by R. Marschan-Piekkari and C. Welch, 402–420 (Cheltenham: Edward Elgar, 2004).

El-Ansary, Adel I. and Louis W. Stern, "Power Measurement in the Distribution Channel," *Journal of Marketing Research* 9 (February 1972): 47–52.

Elfes, Holger, "Adidas Leaps from Hot Sneakers to Warm Jackets," *Bloomberg BusinessWeek* (Online), December 9, 2009. Retrieved from www.businessweek.com/innovate/content/dec2009/id2009129_588770.htm.

Emling, Shelley, "That Ticket Cost How Much?," *The Atlanta Journal–Constitution* (Atlanta, GA), July 11, 2007.

Enderwick, Peter, "Large Emerging Markets (LEMs) and International Strategy," *International Marketing Review 26* no. 1 (2009): 7–16.

Ephron, Erwin and Colin McDonald, "Media Scheduling and Carry-Over Effects: Is Adstock a Useful Planning Tool?," *Journal of Advertising Research 42* no. 4 (2002): 66–70.

Erdem, Kutay and Ruth A. Schmidt, "Ethnic Marketing for Turks in Germany," *International Journal of Retail & Distribution Management 36* no. 3 (2008): 212–223.

Erdogmus, Irem Eren, Muzaffer Bodur, and Cengiz Yilmaz, "International Strategies of Emerging Market Firms: Standardization in Brand Management Revisited," *European Journal of Marketing 44* no. 9/10 (2010): 1410–1436.

Eusébio, C., M. J. Carneiro, E. Kastenholz, and H. Alvelos, "Social Tourism Programmes for the Senior Market: A Benefit Segmentation Analysis," *Journal of Tourism and Cultural Change 15* no.1 (2017): 59–79.

Ewing, Jack, "Upwardly Mobile in Africa: How Basic Cell Phones Are Sparking Economic Hope and Growth in Emerging—and Even Non-Emerging—Nations," *Business Week*, September 24, 2007.

Fan, Ying, "The Rise of Emerging Market Multinationals and the Impact on Marketing," *Marketing Planning & Intelligence 26* no. 4 (2008): 353–358.

Felter, Claire and Danielle Renwick, "MERCOSUR: South America's Fractious Trade Bloc," *Council on Foreign Relations* (Online), September 13, 2017. Retrieved from www.cfr.org/backgrounder/mercosur-south-americas-fractious-trade-bloc.

Fernando, Angelo, "Transparency under Attack," *Communication World 24* no. 2 (2007): 9–11.

Fineman, Howard, "Is There a Doctor in the House? Ron Paul, the GOP's Unlikely Savior," *Newsweek* (New York) *154* no. 24 (2009).

Fitzsimmons, Ella, "Ban Exposes China's Ad Censorship Anomalies," *Campaign* (Teddington), May 16, 2008.

Ford, Jocelyn, "Chinese Windmills Blowing Your Way," *Science Friday*, December 10, 2009. Retrieved from www.sciencefriday.com/blog/2009/12/chinese-windmills-blowing-your-way/.

Ford, John B., Patricia Kramer Voli, Earl D. Honeycutt, Jr, and Susan L. Casey, "Gender Role Portrayals in Japanese Advertising: A Magazine Content Analysis," *Journal of Advertising 27* no. 1 (1998): 113–124.

Ford, Neil, "Jumping the Technology Gap," *African Business* (London) no. 347 (November 2008): 62–63.

Foroohar, Rana, "It's Payback Time: How a Bangladeshi Bank Is Growing in the U.S. by Making Tiny Loans to Groups of Poor Women with Entrepreneurial Dreams," *Newsweek* (New York) *156* no. 4 (2010).

Foster, Scott, "Reverse Engineering Firm Ready for Asian Expansion," *Ottawa Business Journal* no. *44* (2004): 9.

Foxman, E., P. Tansuhaj, and J. Wong, "Evaluating Cross-National Sales Promotion Strategy: An Audit Approach," *International Marketing Review 5* no. 4 (1988): 7–15.

Frank, Marc, "Cuba Bows to Pressure to Reform Its Economy," *FT.com* (London), December 13, 2010.

Freeman, Laurie, "Added Theories Drive Need for Client Solutions," *Advertising Age* no. *31* (2003): 18.

Fridjhon, Michael, "Wine," *Business Day* (South Africa), April 8, 2011.

Fry, Erika, "Nestlé's Half-Billion-Dollar Noodle Debacle in India," *Fortune*, April 26, 2016. Retrieved from http://fortune.com/nestle-maggi-noodle-crisis/.

Fu, Guogun, John Saunders, and Riliang Qu, "Brand Extensions in Emerging Markets: Theory Development and Testing in China," *Journal of Global Marketing 22* no. 3 (2009): 217–228.

Furrer, Olivier, B. Shaw-Ching Liu, and D. Sudharshan, "The Relationships between Culture and Service Quality Perceptions: Basis for Cross-Cultural Market Segmentation and Resource Allocation," *Journal of Service Research 2* no. 4 (2000): 355–371.

Gardner, Gary, "Microfinance Surging," *World Watch* (Washington) *21* no. 6 (2008): 30.

Garnham, Peter, "Ireland Points Finger at UK over Pound," *Financial Times*, January 13, 2009.

Garnham, Peter, "Sovereign Debt Fears Hit Euro," *Financial Times*, February 11, 2011.

Gartenstein, Devra, "Advantages & Disadvantages of Just-in-Time Inventory," *Chron*, April 20, 2018. Retrieved from http://smallbusiness.chron.com/advantages-disadvantages-justintime-inventory-21407.html.

Garvin, David, "Competing on the Eight Dimensions of Quality," *Harvard Business Review* (Nov.–Dec. 1987): 101–108.

Gera A. Welker and Jacob Wijngaard, "The Role of the Operational Network in Responsive Order Processing," *International Journal of Manufacturing Technology and Management 16* no. 3 (2009): 181–194.

Gerrard, B., "Kingfisher Beer Boss Looks to a New Brew to Pep Up Sales," 2017. Retrieved from www.telegraph.co.uk/business/2017/09/25/kingfisher-beer-boss-looks-new-brew-pep-sales/.

Ghosh, S., "Amazon Has Launched a Shoppable Social Network Called Spark—Here's How It Works," *Business Insider*, July 19, 2017. Retrieved from http://uk.businessinsider.com/how-amazon-spark-social-network-works-2017-7/#to-open-spark-from-the-amazon-app-click-the-menu-from-the-homescreen-scroll-down-to-programs-and-features-and-you-should-find-spark-listed-1.

Gillespie, Patrick, "Trumps Spells Out His Wish List for a New NAFTA," *cnn.com*, July 17, 2017. Retrieved from http://money.cnn.com/2017/07/17/news/economy/nafta-objectives-trump-trade/index.html.

Gineikiene, J., B. B. Schlegelmilch, and V. Auruskeviciene, "'Ours' or 'Theirs'? Psychological Ownership and Domestic Products Preferences," *Journal of Business Research 72* (2017): 93–103.

Gopalakrishna, Srinath, Gary L. Lilien, Jerome D. Williams, and Ian K. Sequeria, "Do Trade Shows Pay Off?," *Journal of Marketing 59* no. 3 (1995): 75–83.

Gordon, Stephen, "Time to Stop Fretting over the Canadian Dollar," *Canadian Business* (Toronto) *83* no. 2 (2010): 9.

Goyal, Kartik, "It's India's Year of Inflation," *Business Week*, July 26, 2010.

Green, Jeff, "We Got You Covered: Kia, Isuzu Add Warranties as Hyundai Learns," *Brandweek 41* no. 29 (2000): 11.

Greenhalgh, Leonard, *Managing Strategic Relationships: The Key to Business Success* (New York: The Free Press/Simon & Schuster, 2001).

Gregory, May, "Globalisation: How China and India Are Changing the Debate," *Teaching Business & Economics 10* no. 2 (2006): 8–12.

Griffin, A., "Facebook Posts Becoming Less Personal as Site Looks to Encourage People to Post about Their Lives," *Independent*, April 9, 2016. Retrieved from www.independent.co.uk/life-style/gadgets-and-tech/news/facebook-posts-becoming-less-personal-as-site-looks-to-encourage-people-to-post-about-their-lives-a6976551.html.

Grimes, William, "How Curry, Stirred in India, Became a World Conqueror," *New York Times* (Eastern edition), February 1, 2006.

Gronroos, C., "A Service Quality Model and Its Marketing Implications," *European Journal of Marketing 18* no. 4 (1982): 35–42.

Gunn, Malcolm, "Volkswagen Beetle: Fine Lines Six Decades of Beetle: Originally Scoffed at and Called Cheap, More Than 21 Million Cars Later, the Beetle Truly Is the 'People's Car,'" *Prince George Citizen* (British Columbia), December 29, 2006.

Gupta, Udayan, "MIST: The Next Tier of Large Emerging Economies," *Institutional Investor*, February 7, 2011. Retrieved from www.institutionalinvestor.com/banking_and_capital_markets/Articles/2762464/MIST-The-Next-Tier-of-Large-Emerging-Economies.html.

Gurau, Calin and Franck Duquesnois, "Direct Marketing Channels in the French Wine Industry," *International Journal of Wine Business Research 20* no. 1 (2008): 38–52.

Guth, Robert A., "New Child-Friendly Malaria Drug Presents Distribution Challenge," *Wall Street Journal* (Eastern edition), January 27, 2009.

Habib, Mohsin and Leon Zurawicki, "The Bottom-of-the-Pyramid: Key Roles for Businesses," *Journal of Business & Economics Research 8* no. 5 (2010): 23–32.

Hair, Jr, Joseph F., Robert P. Bush, and David J. Ortinau, *Marketing Research within a Changing Environment* (2 ed.) (New York: McGraw-Hill, 2003).

Hall, Edward T., "The Silent Language in Overseas Business," *Harvard Business Review* (May–June 1960): 87–96.

Hall, Edward T., *Beyond Culture* (New York: Doubleday, 1984).

Hall, Edward T., *The Dance of Life* (New York: Doubleday, 1994).

Hall, Emma, "Skoda Offers Cars to Nicest and Meanest Brits on Facebook," *AdAge Global*, November 17, 2010. Retrieved from http://adage.com/globalnews/article?article_id=147156.

Hall, Kenji, "Zeebo Takes Wireless Gaming to Emerging Markets," *Business Week* (Online), May 29, 2009.

Halligan, Liam, "The Real Lesson We Can Learn rrom Japan's Dramatic Currency Sell-Off," *Telegraph*, September 18, 2010. Retrieved from www.telegraph.co.uk/finance/comment/liamhalligan/8010951/The-real-lesson-we-can-learn-from-Japans-dramatic-currency-sell-off.html.

Hamm, Steve and Nandini Laksman, "The Trouble with India," *Business Week*, April 26, 2007.

Han, Hsin-Tien, "The Investigation of Country-of-Origin Effect-Using Taiwanese Consumers' Perceptions of Luxury Handbags as Example," *Journal of American Academy of Business* (Cambridge) *15* no. 2 (2010): 66–73.

Han, S. P. and S. Shavitt, "Persuasion and Culture: Advertising Appeals in Individualistic and Collectivistic Societies," *Journal of Experimental and Social Psychology 30* (1994): 326–350.

Hannerz, Ulf, "Cosmopolitans and Locals in World Culture," *Theory, Culture, and Society* 7 no. 2–3 (1990): 237–251.

Hansen, V., "The Legacy of the Silk Road," 2013. Retrieved from http://yaleglobal.yale.edu/content/legacy-silk-road.

Harding, Robin, "Japan Leads Way with Coupons," *Financial Times*, May 18, 2010.

Harris, Marvin, *The Sacred Cow and the Abominable Pig: Riddles of Food and Culture* (New York: Simon and Schuster, 1985).

Harris, Scott Duke, "Nokia Finds Research Edge in Silicon Valley," *McClatchy–Tribune Business News* (Washington), November 25, 2007.

Hemtasilpa, Sujintana, "Thinking Small Pays Off for Unilever: Cambodia and Laos Strategy Fits Market," *Knight Ridder Tribune Business News* (Washington), January 29, 2005.

Henneberry, Shida Rastegari and Joao E. Mutondo, "Agricultural Trade among NAFTA Countries: A Case Study of U.S. Meat Exports," *Review of Agricultural Economics 31* no. 3 (2009): 424–445.

Herman, Arthur, "Modern-Day Blackbeards: There Is Nothing New about Menace on the High Seas—or about the Solutions That Would Make It Disappear," *Wall Street Journal* (Online), April 9, 2010.

Hessler, Peter, "China's Boomtowns," *National Geographic Magazine 211* no. 6 (2007): 88–111.

Hessler, Peter, *Country Driving: A Journey through China from Farm to Factory* (New York: HarperCollins, 2010).

Hill, Ronald Paul, "A Naturological Approach to Marketing Exchanges: Implications for Bottom-of-the-Pyramid," *Journal of Business Research 63* no. 6 (2010): 602–607.

Holt, D., J. Quelch, and E. L. Taylor, "How Global Brands Compete," *Harvard Business Review 82* no. 9 (2004): 68–75, 136.

Hughman, John, "Retail Retrenchment Continues," *Investors Chronicle* (London), June 29, 2011.

Hujsak, Jonathan, "The Transformative Effect of Cellular Communications on Emerging Economies," *Cost Management 24* no. 4 (July/August 2010): 5–20.

Hummels, David, "Transportation Costs and International Trade in the Second Era of Globalization," *Journal of Economic Perspectives 21* no. 3 (2007): 131–154.

Hung, Kineta H., Stella Yiyan Li, and Russell W. Belk, "Glocal Understandings: Female Readers' Perceptions of the New Woman in Chinese Advertising," *Journal of International Business Studies 38* no. 6 (2007): 1034–1052.

Hunt, Alex and Brian Wheeler, "Brexit: All You Need to Know about the UK Leaving the EU," *BBC.com*, September 5, 2017. Retrieved from www.bbc.com/news/uk-politics-32810887.

Hunt, Ben, "Juggernaut Has Arrived: Chinese Telecoms: New Entrant Tours Europe," *Financial Times*, July 27, 2005.

Iglesias, Roberto, Prabhat Jha, Márcia Pinto, Vera Luiza da Costa e Silva, and Joana Godinho, "Tobacco Control in Brazil," *Discussion Paper, Human Development Department Latin America and the Caribbean Region, The World Bank, and Health, Nutrition, and Population Department Human Development Network The World Bank,* August, 2007. Retrieved from http://siteresources.worldbank.org/BRAZILEXTN/Resources/TobaccoControlinBrazilenglishFinal.pdf?resourceurlname=TobaccoControlinBrazilenglishFinal.pdf.

Imber, Jane and Betsy-Ann Toffler, *Dictionary of Marketing Terms* (Hauppauge, NY: Barron's Educational Series, 2008).

Imrie, B., J. W. Cadogan, and R. McNaughton, "The Service Quality Construct on a Global Stage," *Managing Service Quality 12* no. 1 (2002): 10–18.

Inagaki, Kana, "Alcohol-Free Beer Makes Smashing Debut in Japan's Shrinking Market," *McClatchy–Tribune Business News* (Washington), July 12, 2009.

Inglehart, R. and C. Welzel, *Modernization, Cultural Change, and Democracy* (New York: Cambridge University Press, 2007).

Ingrassia, Paul, "Why Hyundai Is an American Hit: What GM and Chrysler Can Learn from Its Success," *Wall Street Journal* (Online), September 13, 2009. Retrieved from http://online.wsj.com/article/SB10001424052970203917304574410692912072328.html.

Inman, J. E., "Gray Marketing of Imported Trademarked Goods: Tariffs and Trademark Issues," *American Business Law Journal 31* (1993): 18–23.

Inman, Phillip, "Food Inflation: Snack Attack: Price Increases About to Take a Big Bite Out of Your Office Sandwich: Speculation and Rumour Could Be the Driving Force Behind Sudden Market Rise," *Guardian*, August 7, 2010.

Isidore, Chris, "Store Closings Have Tripled So Far This Year," *CNN Money*, June 23, 2017. Retrieved from http://money.cnn.com/2017/06/23/news/companies/store-closings/index.html.

Issak, Robert, "Making 'Economic Miracles': Explaining Extraordinary National Economic Achievement," *American Economist 49*, no. 1 (1997): 59–69.

Itoh, M., "Traditional Jelly Noodles Are Cooling as Well as Healthy," 2014. Retrieved from www.japantimes.co.jp/life/2014/06/17/food/traditional-jelly-noodles-cooling-well-healthy/#.WepMvLWJjIU.

Jahoda, G., "Critical Reflections on Some Recent Definitions of 'Culture,'" *Culture & Psychology 18* no. 3 (2012): 289–303.

Jain, S. C., "Standardization of International Marketing Strategy: Some Research Hypotheses," *Journal of Marketing 53* (1989): 70–79.

Jain, Varun, "Costa Coffee to Focus on Making India Outlets Profitable," *Economic Times*, February 19, 2016. Retrieved from http://economictimes.indiatimes.com/industry/cons-products/food/costa-coffee-to-focus-on-making-india-outlets-profitable/articleshow/51048689.cms.

Jaishankar, Ganesh and Gillian Oakenfull, "International Product Positioning: An Illustration Using Perceptual Mapping Techniques," *Journal of Global Marketing 13* no. 2 (1999): 85–111.

Jana, Reena, "Inspiration from Emerging Economies," *Business Week* (New York), March 23, 2009.

Jang, S. C., A. M. Morrison, and J. T. O'Leary, "Benefit Segmentation of Japanese Pleasure Travelers to the USA and Canada: Selecting Target Markets Based on the Profitability and Risk of Individual Market Segments," *Tourism Management 23* (2002): 367–378.

Jansen, Bart, "Samsung Galaxy 7 Note Banned on All U.S. Flights Due to Fire Hazard," *USA Today*, October 14, 2016. Retrieved from www.usatoday.com/story/news/2016/10/14/dot-bans-samsung-galaxy-note-7-flights/92066322/.

Jargon, Julie, "Corporate News: KFC Intends to Double Its Restaurants in Africa," *Wall Street Journal Asia* (Hong Kong), December 9, 2010.

Javidan, M., R. J. House, P. W. Dorfman, P. J. Hanges, and M. Sully de Luque, "Conceptualizing and Measuring Cultures and Their Consequences: A Comparative Review of GLOBE's and Hofstede's Approaches," *Journal of International Business Studies 37* no. 6 (2006): 897–914.

Jewish News, "Ikea Apologises for Women-Free Catalogue for Strictly-Orthodox Jews," 2017. Retrieved from http://jewishnews.timesofisrael.com/ikea-apologises-for-women-free-catalogue-for-strictly-orthodox-jews/.

Jitpleecheep, Pitsinee, "Carrefour Launches Mini Format: Reflects Commitment to Thai Market," *McClatchy–Tribune Business News* (Washington), October 13, 2009.

Joelson, Daniel A., "Rebel Sell," *Latin Trade 12* no. 8 (August 2004): 16.

Johanson, J. and J.-E. Vahlne, "The Internationalization Process of the Firm: A Model of Knowledge Development and Increasing Foreign Market Commitments," *Journal of International Business Studies 8* no. 1 (1977): 23–32.

Johanson, J. and F. Wiedersheim-Paul, "The Internationalization of the Firm—Four Swedish Cases," *Journal of Management Studies 12* no. 3 (1975): 305–323.

Johnson, L., "7 Big Trends That Are Shaping the Future of Digital Advertising," 2016. Retrieved from www.adweek.com/digital/7-big-trends-are-shaping-future-digital-advertising-171773/.

Johnson, Simon and Gary Lovman, "Starting Over: Poland after Communism," *Harvard Business Review* (March–April 1995): 44–56.

Jordan, Miriam, "Down Market: A Retailer in Brazil Has Become Rich by Courting Poor—Payments of $14 a Month Add Up for Samuel Klein, Sao Paulo's Sam Walton—Self-Esteem for the Masses," *Wall Street Journal*, June 11, 2002.

Jung, J. M., K. Polyorat, and J. J. Kellaris, "A Cultural Paradox in Authority-Based Advertising," *International Marketing Review 26* no. 6 (2009): 601–632.

Kaasa, A., M. Vadi, and U. Varblane, "A New Dataset of Cultural Distances for European Countries and Regions," *Research in International Business and Finance 37* supp. C (2016): 231–241.

Kahle, Lynn R., Gregory Rose, and Aviv Shoham, "Findings of LOV throughout the World, and Other Evidence of Cross-National Consumer Psychographics," *Journal of Euromarketing 8* no. 1/2 (1999): 1–14.

Kamleitner, B. and A. Khair Jyote, "How Using versus Showing Interaction between Characters and Products Boosts Product Placement Effectiveness," *International Journal of Advertising 32* no. 4 (2013): 633–653.

Kannan, S., "How McDonald's Conquered India," 2014. Retrieved from www.bbc.co.uk/news/business-30115555.

Karim, Mike, "Most Subcompacts Are Loss Leaders for Dealers," *Toronto Star* (Toronto), August 4, 2007.

Karlan, Dean, "Measuring Microfinance," *Stanford Social Innovation Review 6* no. 3 (2008).

Katz, Neil, "Cigarette Warning Label Pictures," *Cbsnews.com Health Blog*, November 11, 2010. Retrieved from https://www.cbsnews.com/news/cigarette-warning-label-pictures-slide-show/ .

Katz, Richard, "Japanese Farmers Sow Protectionism," *Wall Street Journal Asia* (Hong Kong) December 13, 2010.

Kaynak, Erdener, Ali Riza Apil, and Serkan Yalcin, "Marketing and Advertising Practices of Turkish Entrepreneurs in Transition Economies: Evidence From Georgia," *Journal of International Entrepreneurship 7* no. 3 (2009): 190–214.

Kazmin, Amy, "India Exchanges Pools for Price; a Market Is Growing for Budget Hotels Aimed at Travellers Who Cannot Afford Luxury but Will Not Settle for Dilapidated, Socialist-Era State Tourist Bungalows," *Financial Times*, August 25, 2009.

Keferl, Michael, "McDonalds Testing IC Card 'Kazau Coupon,'" *Japan Trends*, May 21, 2008. Retrieved from www.japantrends.com/mcdonalds-testing-ic-card-kazasu-coupon/.

Keizer, Gregg, "EU Rejects Intel's Example of Apple in Antitrust Dispute," *Computerworld*, September 22, 2009. Retrieved from www.computerworld.com/s/article/9138374/EU_rejects_Intel_s_example_of_Apple_in_antitrust_dispute.

Kelion, L., "Posting Children's Photos on Social Media Divides Nation," *BBC News*, 2017. Retrieved from www.bbc.co.uk/news/technology-40804041.

Keller, Kevin L., *Strategic Brand Management* (Upper Saddle River, NJ: Prentice-Hall, 1998).

Kelly, Nataly, "The Most Common Mistakes Companies Make with Global Marketing," *Harvard Business Review*, September 7, 2015. Retrieved https://hbr.org/2015/09/the-most-common-mistakes-companies-make-with-global-marketing.

Kennedy, Christina, "Cheap and Cheerful: Economy Handsets Enter the Market," *African Business* (London) no. 353 (May 2009): 52–53.

Kenny, Caitlin, "What Is a Direct Quote?," Conjecture Corporation (n.d.). Retrieved from www.wisegeek.com/what-is-a-direct-quote.htm.

Kev, J., "Capcom Reveal Playstation Network Price Promotion," *Electronic Theatre*, February 8, 2010. Retrieved from http://electronictheatre.co.uk/playstation3/playstation3-news/4105/capcom-reveal-playstation-network-price-promotion.

Khanna, Tarun and Krishna Palepu, "Emerging Giants: Building World-Class Companies in Developing Countries," *Harvard Business Review* (October 1, 2006): 60–69.

Kim, Suk H. and H. Kim Seung, *Global Corporate Finance* (6 ed.) (Maden, MA: Blackwell Publishing, 2006).

King, Carolyn, "Cott Says Wal-Mart Will End Supply Pact," *Wall Street Journal*, January 28, 2009.

King, Danny, "Tablets and Smartphones Slow Laptop Sales," *Dailyfinance.com*, 2011. Retrieved from www.dailyfinance.com/2011/03/03/tablets-and-smartphones-slow-laptop-sales-growth/.

King, Philip G. and Sharmila King, *International Economics: Globalization and Policy* (New York: McGraw-Hill, 2010).

Ko, E., E. Kim, C. R. Taylor, K. H. Kim, and I. J. Kang, "Cross-National Market Segmentation in the Fashion Industry: A Study of European, Korean, and US Consumers," *International Marketing Review 24* no. 5 (2007): 629–651.

Koo, "Only the Best Will Do," February 17, 2017. Retrieved from www.koo.co.za/.

Koruse, Taito, "Japanese Maker's New Take on a Classic Seasoning," *Nikkei, Asian Review*, May 23, 2017. Retrieved from https://asia.nikkei.com/Business/Trends/Japanese-maker-s-new-take-on-a-classic-seasoning.

Kollewe, Julia, "China Expansion Brewing for Costa Coffee Owner," *Guardian*, April 26, 2016. Retrieved from www.theguardian.com/business/2016/apr/26/costa-coffee-whitbread-china-expansion-sales.

Kontzer, Tony, "Wide-Angle View of Customers," *Information Week* (Manhasset), June 6, 2005.

Kotler, Philip and Gary Armstrong, *Principles of Marketing* (12 ed.) (Upper Saddle River, NJ: Prentice-Hall, 2007).

Kozinets, Robert V., "The Field Behind the Screen: Using Netnography for Marketing Research in Online Communities," *Journal of Marketing Research 39* no. 1 (2002): 61–72.

Kripalani, Manjeet, "A Profitable Passage to India: Armed with Market Research, Korean Companies Succeed," *Business Week*, May 12, 2003: 50.

Krondl, M., *Sweet Invention: A History of Dessert* (Chicago, IL: Chicago Review Press, 2016).

Krugman, Herbert E., "Why Three Exposures May Be Enough," *Journal of Advertising Research 1* no. 6 (1972): 11–14.

Kumar, N., "The Power of Trust in Manufacturer–Retailer Relationships," *Harvard Business Review* 74 (November–December, 1996): 92–106.

Kumar, V., *International Marketing Research* (Upper Saddle River, NJ: Prentice Hall, 2000).

Laskey, Henry A., Ellen Day, and Melvin R. Crask, "Typology of Main Message Strategies for Television Commercials," *Journal of Advertising 18* no. 1 (1989): 36–41.

Lawton, Christopher and Chun Han Wong, "Nokia Shows Off New Phones; Cellphone Maker Unveils Devices as It Prepares for Microsoft Software Transition," *Wall Street Journal* (Online), June 22, 2011.

Lazer, D., R. Kennedy, G. King, and A. Vespignani, "The Parable of Google Flu: Traps in Big Data Analysis," *Science 343* no. 6176 (2014): 1203–1205.

Lee, Chol and Robert T. Green, "Cross-Cultural Examination of the Fishbein Behavioral Intentions Model," *Journal of International Business Studies 22* no. 2 (1991): 289–305.

Lenius, Pat, "TOTO Adds Aquia Toilet to Its Green Products Line," *Supply House Times, 48* no. 8 (2005).

Leonard, Christopher, "Global Milk Glut Squeezes Dairy Farmers, Consumers," *The Missourian* (Columbia, MO), May 25, 2009. Retrieved from www.columbiamissourian.com/stories/2009/05/25/global-milk-glut-squeezes-dairy-farmers-consumers/.

Levitt, Theodore, "The Globalization of Markets," *Harvard Business Review 61* no. 3 (1983): 92–102.

Lewicki, Roy J., Bruce Barry, and David M. Saunders, *Essentials of Negotiation* (New York: McGraw-Hill/Irwin, 2010).

Lewis, L. and J. Unerman, "Ethical Relativism: A Reason for Differences in Corporate Social Reporting?," *Critical Perspectives on Accounting 10*, no. 4 (1999): 521–547.

Lieber, Ron, "BP Boycott Won't Do Much," *The Ledger* (Lakeland, FL), June 14, 2010.

Lilach, Nachum and Cliff Wymbs, "Product Differentiation, External Economies, and MNE Location Choices: M&As in Global Cities," *Journal of International Business Studies 36* no. 4 (2005): 415–434.

Lin, Thomas W., "Haier Is Higher," *Strategic Finance* (December 2009): 41–49.

Liu, Hongju, "Dynamics of Pricing in the Video Game Console Market: Skimming or Penetration?," *Journal of Marketing Research 47* no. 3 (2010): 428–443.

Liu, Mariana, "Do You Need to Be Korean to Be K-Pop?," *cnn.com*, June 12, 2017. Retrieved from www.cnn.com/2017/06/12/asia/exp-edition-non-korean-k-pop-band/index.html.

Lorentz, Harri, Chew Yew Wong, and Olli-Pekka Hilmola, "Emerging Distribution Systems in Central and Eastern Europe," *International Journal of Physical Distribution & Logistics Management 37* no. 8 (2007): 670–697.

Luo, Yadong, Oded Shenkar, and Haresh Gurnani, "Control-Cooperation Interfaces in Global Strategic Alliances: A Situational Typology and Strategic Responses," *Journal of International Business Studies 39* no. 3 (2008): 428–454.

Lury, C., *Consumer Culture* (Cambridge: Polity Press, 1996).

Macadam, Dan, "M&S to Close Clothing and Home Stores in Turnaround Plan," *BBC News*, November 8, 2016. Retrieved from www.bbc.co.uk/news/business-37906466.

McBride, Sarah, "Beer-Drinking Trends in Emerging Markets Bode Well for Big Brewers," *NPR Planet Money blog*, August 18, 2010. Retrieved from www.npr.org/blogs/money/2010/08/18/129275835/beer-drinking-trends-in-emerging-markets-bode-well-for-big-brewers.

McComb, Richard, "Put Some Fizz into the New Year: We Road Test the Champagnes on Offer... So You Don't Have To," *Sunday Mercury* (Birmingham), December 26, 2010.

McIntyre, Hugh, "These Are the Highest-Grossing Tours and Concerts of 2016 (So Far)," *Forbes*, July 21, 2016. Retrieved from www.forbes.com/sites/hughmcintyre/2016/07/21/13578/#b9421fc34d20.

McIver, Brian, "Up the Lada; Soviet 'Skip' Back on Road: To Celebrate Its Unlikely Return, We Toast World's Best 'Worst Car,'" *Daily Record* (Glasgow), May 13, 2010.

Macnamara, Lim R., "The Crucial Role of Research in Multicultural and Cross-Cultural Communication," *Journal of Communication Management 8* no. 3 (2004): 322–334.

McNeill, L., K. Fam, and K. Chung, "Chinese Consumer Preference for Price-Based Sales Promotion Techniques—the Impact of Gender, Income and Product Type," *ANZMAC* (Sydney) (2008): 1–7.

Madden, Normandy, "Unilever's Lipton Hirameki," *Advertising Age*, July 11, 2007a.

Madden, Normandy, "Upstart's Taxi Play Helps Brands Flag Down Rich Chinese," *Advertising Age*, October 29, 2007b.

Magada, Dominique, "Esoko: The New Market Info System for African Farmers," *African Business* (London) no. 353 (May 2009): 46–47.

Magnusson, P., D. W. Baack, S. Zdradkovic, K. Staub, and L. S. Amine, "Meta-Analysis of Cultural Differences: Another Slice at the Apple," *International Business Review* 17 no. 5 (2008): 520–532.

Magocsi, Paul R., *Encyclopedia of Canada's Peoples* (Toronto: University of Toronto Press, 1999).

Maheshwari, Sapna and Alexandra Stevenson, "Google and Facebook Face Criticism for Ads Targeting Racist Sentiments," *The New York Times*, September 15, 2017. Retrieved from www.nytimes.com/2017/09/15/business/facebook-advertising-anti-semitism.html?rref=collection%2Fsectioncollection%2Fbusiness&action=click&contentCollection=business&region=rank&module=package&version=highlights&contentPlacement=2&pgtype=sectionfront.

Mai, Li-Wei and Hui Zhao, "The Characteristics of Supermarket Shoppers in Beijing," *International Journal of Retailing & Distribution* 32 no. 1 (2004): 56–62.

Malhotra, Naresh K., James Agarwal, and Mark Peterson, "Methodological Issues in Cross-Cultural Marketing Research: A State-of-the-Art Review," *International Marketing Review* 13 no. 5 (1996): 7–43.

Malone, Scott, "GE Uses Training to Appeal to Its Customers," *New York Times* (Online), November 26, 2007. Retrieved from www.nytimes.com/2007/11/26/business/worldbusiness/26iht-ge.1.8478485.html.

Martin, Susan F., "Heavy Traffics: International Migration in an Era of Globalization," *Brookings Review* Fall (2001): 41–44.

Matthes, J., M. Prieler, and K. Adam, "Gender-Role Portrayals in Television Advertising across the Globe," *Sex Roles* 75 no. 7 (2016): 314–327.

May, Meredith, "Microfinance's Next Frontier," *Stanford Social Innovation Review* 8 no. 4 (2010): 63–65.

Mehta, Rajiv, Pia Polsa, Jolanta Mazur, Fan Xiucheng, and Alan J. Dubinsky, "Strategic Alliances in International Distribution Channels," *Journal of Business Research* 59 (2006): 1094–1104.

Michaud, J., "Sweet Morsels: A History of the Chocolate-Chip Cookie," 2013. Retrieved from www.newyorker.com/culture/culture-desk/sweet-morsels-a-history-of-the-chocolate-chip-cookie.

Miller, John W., "China Complains to WTO about EU Tariffs; Petition against Antidumping Duties on Shoes Extends Fight against What Beijing Says Is Unfair Protectionism," *Wall Street Journal* (Online), February 5, 2010.

Milne, R., "Ikea Faces Cultural Challenge as Flat-Pack Empire Expands," *Financial Times*, November 28, 2013. Retrieved from https://www.ft.com/content/83389238-5819-11e3-82fc-00144feabdc0.

Miracle, Gordon E., Kyu Yeol Chang, and Charles R. Taylor, "Culture and Advertising Executions: A Comparison of Selected Characteristics of Korean and US Television Commercials," *International Marketing Review 9* no. 4 (1992): 5–18.

Miroff, N., "Mexico Gets a Taste for Eating Insects as Chefs Put Bugs Back on the Menu," *The Washington Post*, July 23, 2013. Retrieved from www.theguardian.com/world/2013/jul/23/mexico-insect-cuisine-sustainable-food.

Mitchell, R. and M. Oneal, "Managing by Values," *Business Week*, September 12, 1994.

Mittra, Debanjan and Peter N. Golder, "How Does Objective Quality Affect Perceived Quality?," *Marketing Science 25* no. 3 (2006): 230–247.

Moore, Marguerite, Karen McGowan Kennedy, and Ann Fairhurst, "Cross-Cultural Equivalence of Price Perceptions between U.S. and Polish Consumers," *International Journal of Retailing & Distribution Management 31* no. 4/5 (2003): 268–280.

Moreira, de L. Davyson, Sabrina Schaaf Teixeira, Maria Helena D. Monteiro, Ana Cecilia A. X. De-Oliveira, and Francisco J. R. Paumgartten, "Traditional Use and Safety of Herbal Medicines," *Revista Brasileira de Farmacognosia 24* no. 4 (2014): 248–257.

Morgan, M. J., "North Africa Leads Growth," *African Business* (London) no. 353 (May 2009): 54–55.

Morgan, Robert M. and Shelby D. Hunt, "The Commitment–Trust Theory of Relationship Marketing," *Journal of Marketing 58* no. 3 (1994): 20–38.

Morris, Stephen and Richard Partington, "Brexit: HSBC May Move 20% of Its London Banking Operations to Paris, Chief Executive Stuart Gulliver Says", *Independent* (Online), January 18, 2017. Retrieved from www.independent.co.uk/news/business/news/brexit-latest-news-hsbc-bank-move-20-per-cent-fifth-london-banking-operations-paris-chief-executive-a7532711.html.

Mortimer, Ruth, "Costa's £10m Tongue," *Marketing Week*, October 5, 2011. Retrieved from www.marketingweek.com/2011/10/05/costas-10m-tongue/.

Motavalli, Jim, "Transportation Inside the Think City Electric Car," *Forbes.com*, March 30, 2010.

Mullen, Michael R., "Diagnosing Measurement Equivalence in Cross-National Research," *Journal of International Business Studies 26* no. 3 (1995): 573–596.

Mullin, Rodney and Julian Cummins, *Sales Promotion: How to Create, Implement and Integrate Campaigns That Really Work* (4 ed.) (London: Kogan Page Publishers, 2008).

Murphy, James, "Giving Pizza Hut a Real Bit in Hong Kong," *Media*, January 13, 2006.

Murray, Janet Y., "Strategic Alliance-Based Global Sourcing Strategy for Competitive Advantage: A Conceptual Framework and Research Propositions," *Journal of International Marketing 9* no. 4 (2001): 30–59.

Nebenzahl, Israel D., Jaffe D. Eugene, and Shlomo L. Lampert, "Towards a Theory of Country Image Effect on Product Evaluation," *Management International Review 37* no. 1 (1997): 27–49.

Nelson, James, "What's Driving Globalisation?," *New Zealand Management*, June 23, 2006. Retrieved from http://findarticles.com/p/articles/mi_qn5305/is_20060623/ai_n24915192/.

Neuliep, J. W., *Intercultural Communication: A Contextual Approach* (Los Angeles, CA: SAGE, 2009).

Ngai, E. W. T. and Angappa Gunasekaran, "RFID Adoption: Issues and Challenges," *International Journal of Enterprise Information Systems 5* no. 1 (2009): 1–8.

Nidumolu, Ram, C. K. Prahalad, and M. R. Rangaswami, "Why Sustainability Is Now the Key Driver of Innovation," *Harvard Business Review* 87 no. 9 (2009): 56–64.

Njobeni, Siseko, "State Fury over Mittal's Latest Price Increase," *Business Day* (Johannesburg), October 4, 2006.

Nisbett, Richard E., *The Geography of Thought: How Asians and Westerners Think Differently . . . and Why* (New York: The Free Press, 2003).

Noah, Rick, "Home to 3 Million Turkish Immigrants, Germany Fears Rising Tensions," *The Washington Post*, July 18, 2016. Retrieved from www.washingtonpost.com/news/worldviews/wp/2016/07/18/home-to-3-million-turkish-immigrants-germany-fears-rising-tensions/?utm_term=.f6863c052d10.

Nobrega Ode, T., Andre Ricardo Marques, Ana Cleire Gomes de Aruajo, Margo Gomes de Oliveira Karnikowski, Janeth de Oliveira Silva Naves, and Lynn Dee Silver, "Retail Prices of Essential Drugs in Brazil: And International Comparison," *Revista Panamericana de Salud Pública/Pan American Journal of Public Health* 22 no. 2 (2007): 118–123.

Nolin, Robert, "Study Warns of Pollution from Ships," *Physorg.com* (Online), March 31, 2009. Retrieved from www.physorg.com/news157744326.html.

Noorbakhsh, Sarah, "Product Paradise in Tokyo's Consumer Hot Spot," *Japan Inc.*, October 3, 2008. Retrieved from www.japaninc.com/mgz_october_2008_sample-lab.

Notteboom, Theo and Jean-Paul Rodrigue, "The Future of Containerization: Perspectives from Maritime and Inland Freight Distribution," *GeoJournal* 74 no. 1 (2009): 7–22.

Oakley, David, "Gloom Hits Russia and Brazil," *Financial Times*, October 17, 2008.

O'Connell, Vanessa, "Diamond Industry Makeover Sends Fifth Avenue to Africa," *Wall Street Journal* (Eastern edition), October 26, 2009.

O'Grady, S. and H. W. Lane, "The Psychic Distance Paradox," *Journal of International Business Studies* 27 no. 2 (1996): 309–333.

Okazaki, Shintaro and Barbara Mueller, "Cross-Cultural Advertising Research: Where We Have Been and Where We Need to Go," *International Marketing Review* 24 no. 5 (2007): 499–515.

Okazaki, S., B. Mueller, and C. R. Taylor, "Global Consumer Culture Positioning: Testing Perceptions of Soft-Sell and Hard-Sell Advertising Appeals between U.S. and Japanese Consumers," *Journal of International Marketing* 18 no. 2 (2010): 20–34.

O'Neill, Brendan, "The Oreo Invades Britain," *Christian Science Monitor* (Boston), May 13, 2008.

O'Neill, Brendan, "Can the Lada Make a British Comeback?," *BBC News Magazine*, May 10, 2010. Retrieved from http://news.bbc.co.uk/2/hi/uk_news/magazine/8672464.stm.

Orlik, Tom, "Alibaba's Jewel Still Hidden," *Wall Street Journal* (Eastern edition), March 18, 2011.

Oviatt, B. M. and P. P. McDougall, "Toward a Theory of International New Ventures," *Journal of International Business Studies* 25 no. 1 (1994): 45–64.

Palmer, Brian, "Why do Foreigners Like Fanta So Much?," *The Slate Group, a Division of the Washington Post Company*, August 5, 2010. Retrieved from www.slate.com/id/2262956/.

Palumbo, Fred and Paul A. Herbig, "Trade Shows and Fairs: An Important Part of the International Marketing Mix," *Journal of Promotion Management* 8 no. 1 (2002): 93–108.

Parasuraman, A., V. Zeithaml, and L. Berry, "A Conceptual Model of Service Quality and Its Implications for Future Research," *Journal of Marketing 49* no. 4 (1985): 41–50.

Park, Daekeun and Changyong Rhee, "Measuring the Degree of Currency Misalignment Using Offshore Forward Exchange Rates: The Case of the Korean Financial Crisis," *Journal of Asset Management 2* no. 1 (2001): 84–96.

Parkhe, A., "Interfirm Diversity, Organizational Learning, and Longevity in Global Strategic Alliances," *Journal of International Business Studies 22* (1991): 579–601.

Patrick, Aaron O., "Unilever's Earnings Fall as Price Rises Hurt Sales," *Wall Street Journal* (Brussels), August 1, 2008.

Perkowski, Jack, "Protecting Intellectual Property Rights in China," April 18, 2012. Retrieved from www.forbes.com/sites/jackperkowski/2012/04/18/protecting-intellectual-property-rights-in-china/#39299f663458.

Pfanner, Eric, "Music Industry Counts the Cost of Piracy," *New York Times* (Online), January 22, 2010. Retrieved from www.nytimes.com/2010/01/22/business/global/22music.html.

Pham, Sherisse, "Samsung Is Making Huge Profits as Note 7 Crisis Fades," CNN Tech, January 24, 2017. Retrieved from http://money.cnn.com/2017/01/24/technology/samsung-earnings-note-7-profits/index.html.

Phatak, Arvind V. and Mohammed M. Habib, "The Dynamics of International Business Negotiations," *Business Horizons* (May–June 1996): 30–38.

Pignal, Stanley, "Carrefour Cuts 1,700 Jobs," *FT.com* (London), February 23, 2010.

Pilling, David, "China Has Every Right to Cheat, But Shouldn't," *Financial Times*, October 28, 2010.

Pitta, D. A., R. Guesalaga, and P. Marshall, "The Quest for the Fortune at the Bottom of the Pyramid: Potential and Challenges," *Journal of Consumer Marketing 25*, no. 7 (2008): 393–401.

Podoshen, Jeffrey S., Lu Li, and Junfeng Zhang, "Materialism and Conspicuous Consumption in China: A Cross-Cultural Examination," *International Journal of Consumer Studies 35* no. 1 (2011): 17–25.

Porter, M. E., "The Competitive Advantage of Nations," *Harvard Business Review* (March–April, 1990): 78. Retrieved from https://hbr.org/1990/03/the-competitive-advantage-of-nations.

Prahalad, C. K., *The Fortune at the Bottom-of-the-Pyramid: Eradicating Poverty through Profits* (Upper Saddle River, NJ: Pearson Education Inc., Wharton School Publishing, 2006).

Pralahad, C. K. and A. Hammond, "Serving the World's Poor, Profitably," *Harvard Business Review* (Sept. 2002): 4–11.

Prashantham, Shameen and Julian Birkinshaw, "Dancing with Gorillas: How Small Companies Can Partner Effectively with MNCs," *California Management Review 51* no. 1 (2008): 6–23.

Prasso, Sheridan, "Battle for the Face of China," *Fortune 152* no. 12 (2005): 156–178.

Prendergast, G., B. Ho, and I. Phau, "A Hong Kong View of Offensive Advertising," *Journal of Marketing Communications 8* no. 3 (2002): 165–177.

Prendergast, Gerard, Alex S. L. Tsang, and Chit Yu Lo, "Antecedents of the Intention to Seek Samples," *European Journal of Marketing 42* no. 11/12 (2008): 1162–1169.

Prestowitz, Clyde, "Why Isn't the iPhone Made in America?," *Foreign Policy*, March 8, 2011. Retrieved from http://prestowitz.foreignpolicy.com/posts/2011/03/08/why_isnt_the_iphone_made_in_america.

Qiblawi, Tamara, "Qatar Rift: Saudi, UAE, Bahrain, Egypt, Cut Diplomatic Ties," *CNN.com*, July 27, 2017. Retrieved from www.cnn.com/2017/06/05/middleeast/saudi-bahrain-egypt-uae-qatar-terror/index.html.

Queensland Government, "Calculating Your Stock Turnover," (n.d.). Retrieved from www.business.qld.gov.au/running-business/finances-cash-flow/stock-control/turnover.

Quelch, John A. and Katherine E. Jocz, "How to Market in a Downturn," *Harvard Business Review 87* no. 4 (2009). Retrieved from https://hbr.org/2009/04/how-to-market-in-a-downturn-2.

Quilter, James, "Kellogg's Gives Away Free Cereal in £3 Million Campaign," *Brand Republic*, April 1, 2009. Retrieved from www.brandrepublic.com/news/895368/Kelloggs-gives-away-free-cereal-3m-coupon-push/.

Rajagopal, "Brand Paradigm for the Bottom-of-the-Pyramid Markets," *Measuring Business Excellence 13* no. 4 (2009): 58–68.

Raji, Rafiq, "Doing Business: Can Nigeria Replicate the Singapore Model Like Mauritius Did?," *How We Made It in Africa*, May 12, 2017. Retrieved from www.howwemadeitinafrica.com/business-can-nigeria-replicate-singapore-model-like-mauritius/.

Ralston, David A., David H. Holt, Robert H. Terpstra, and Yu Kai-Cheng, "The Impact of National Culture and Economic Ideology on Managerial Work Values: A Study of the United States, Russia, Japan, and China," *Journal of International Business Studies 39* no. 1 (2008): 8–27.

Rathwell, Daniel, "The Qibla Cola Path of Least Resistance," October 8, 2004. Retrieved from www.thinking-east.net/indexa2ec.html?option=com_content&task=view&id=143.

Rawwas, Mohammed Y. A., K. N. Rajendran, and Gerhard A. Wuehrer, "The Influence of Worldmindedness and Nationalism on Consumer Evaluation of Domestic and Foreign Products," *International Marketing Review 13* no. 2 (1996): 20–38.

Reardon, J., C. Miller, B. Foubert, I. Vida, and L. Rybina, "Antismoking Messages for the International Teenage Segment: The Effectiveness of Message Valence and Intensity across Different Cultures," *Journal of International Marketing 14* no. 3 (2006): 115–138.

Reed, John, "Toyota Chief Vows 'Fresh Start' for Carmaker," *Financial Times*, March 24, 2010.

Reese, Andrew K., "Green Is Global: Is Your Supply Chain Ready?," *Supply & Demand Chain Executive*, June 9, 2011.

Reiss, Craig, "Why You Need to Know TED," *Entrepreneur* (Online), 2010. Retrieved from www.entrepreneur.com/article/217243.

Requejo, Hernandex William and John L. Graham, *Global Negotiation: The New Rules* (New York: Palgrave Macmillan, 2008).

Reynolds, N. L., A. C. Simintiras, and A. Diamantopoulos, "Theoretical Justification of Sampling Choices in International Marketing Research: Key Issues and Guidelines for Researchers," *Journal of International Business Studies 34* no. 1 (2003): 80–89.

Richardson, Craig, "China's New Landed Gentry: Foreigners," *Barron's*, October 27, 2008.

Riefler, Petra and Adamantious Diamantopoulos, "Consumer Animosity: A Literature Review and a Reconsideration of Its Measurement," *International Marketing Review 24* no. 1 (2007): 87–119.

Rigby, Chloe, "Working at M&S," *Internet Retailing*, November 8, 2016. Retrieved from http://global.marksandspencer.com/in/work-with-us/#.WVEOAZLyvIU.

Rilling, David, "TOTO Flushes Old Ways Down the Pan: Toilet Maker Sells to Remodellers and China's Super Rich," *Financial Times*, March 2, 2004.

Ritzer, G., *Essentials of Sociology* (London: SAGE, 2015).

Rocha, Roberto, "Tech Companies Use Fake Leaks to Create Buzz," *The Vancouver Sun* (Vancouver), September 1, 2006.

Rodionova, Z., "Half of All New Cars in Norway Are Now Electric or Hybrid," *Independent*, March 7, 2017. Retrieved from www.independent.co.uk/news/business/news/norway-half-new-cars-electric-hybrid-ofv-vehicle-registrations-a7615556.html.

Rogers, Charlotte, "What Is Programmatic? A Beginner's Guide," *Marketing Week*, March 27, 2017. Retrieved from www.marketingweek.com/2017/03/27/what-is-programmatic/.

Rogers, Dave, "Bed Store Signs a Nightmare for French Advocate," *The Ottawa Citizen* (Ontario), February 4, 2010.

Ronen, Simcha and Oded Shenkar, "Clustering Countries on Attitudinal Dimensions: A Review and Synthesis," *Academy of Management Review 10* no. 3 (1985): 435–454. Retrieved from www.grovewell.com/pub-GLOBE-intro.html.

Rosandic, Nina, "Dr. Martens Sets Sights on Fashion Positioning," *Marketing* (London), March 16, 2011.

Rostow, W. W., *The Stages of Economic Growth: A Non-Communist Manifesto* (Cambridge: Cambridge University Press, 1991).

Roth, Katharina P. and Adamantios Diamantopoulos, "Advancing the Country Image Construct," *Journal of Business Research 62* no. 7 (2009): 726–740.

Roy, Shubhajit and Yubaraj Ghimire, "SAARC Summit to Be Called Off as Dhaka, Kabul and Thimphu Too Slam Islamabad," *The Indian Express*, September 29, 2016. Retrieved from http://indianexpress.com/article/india/india-news-india/dhaka-kabul-thimphu-too-blame-islamabad-saarc-summit-to-be-called-off-3054953/.

Sanchanta, Mariko, "Tokyo's Luxury Market Matures," *Financial Times*, January 7, 2005.

Sanchez, Pablo, Joan Enric Ricart, and Miguel Angel Rodriguez, "Influential Factors in Becoming Socially Embedded in Low-Income Markets," *Greener Management International* no. *51* (2006): 19–38.

Schanen, N., "Demand for Exotic Kit Kats Is So High Nestle's Building a New Plant," July 25, 2017a. Retrieved from www.bloomberg.com/news/articles/2017-07-25/japans-exotic-kit-kats-entice-tourists-brand-new-nestle-plant.

Schanen, N., "Demand for Exotic Kit Kat Is So High Nestle Will Build a New Plant in Japan," July 26, 2017b. Retrieved from www.independent.co.uk/news/business/analysis-and-features/kit-kat-demand-exotic-flavours-nestle-new-plant-japan-wasabi-green-tea-sake-a7860641.html.

Schmidt, Joachim, "Mercedes-Benz: Sales and Marketing Strategy," *Daimler*, March 29, 2012. Retrieved from www.daimler.com/dokumente/investoren/kapitalmarkttage/daimler-ir-mercedesbenzcarsdivisiondayhungaryschmidt-20120329.pdf.

Schmutz, Armin, "Breakthrough in the World's Longest Tunnel," *Trains* (Milwaukee) *71* no. 3 (2011): 36–38.

Sexton, Timothy, "Weber's Law and Why Big Businesses Believe You Won't Notice a Price Increase Under 10%," *Associated Content* (n.d.) . Retrieved from https://www.slideshare.net/NakulPatel/webers-law-and-why-big-business-believes-you-wont-notice-a-price-increase-under-10-20029922

Shankarmahesh, Mahesh N., "Consumer Ethnocentrism: An Integrative Review of Its Antecedents and Consequences," *International Marketing Review 23* no. 2 (2006): 146–172.

Sharma, E. Kumar, "License to Download," *Business Today*, June 14, 2009.

Sharma, E. Kumar, "Microfinance Players Must Innovate, Recall Social Goals: The Sector's Rapid Growth Has Not Meant That the Financially Excluded Are Better Off," *Business Today* (New Delhi), August 8, 2010.

Shenkar, O., "Cultural Distance Revisited: Toward a More Rigorous Conceptualization and Measurement of Cultural Differences," *Journal of International Business Studies 43*, no. 1 (2012): 1–11.

Shi, Yi-Zheng, Ka-Man Cheung, and Gerard Prendergast, "Behavioral Response to Sales Promotion Tools: A Hong Kong Study," *International Journal of Advertising 24* no. 4 (2005): 467–486.

Shirouzu, Norihiko, "Toyota Tries to Shift Gears in China—Car Maker Sees Growth Slowing to 14%, Bets on Models with Smaller Engines," *Wall Street Journal*, November 27, 2009.

Sigal, Jane, "In Paris, Burgers Turn Chic," *New York Times* (Online), July 16, 2008.

Silayoi, Pinya and Mark Speece, "The Importance of Packaging Attributes: A Conjoint Analysis Approach," *European Journal of Marketing 41* no. 11/12 (2007): 1495–1517.

Sinha, Vivek, "Carrefour Plans to Open Stores in 7 Cities," *McClatchy–Tribune Business News* (Washington), December 11, 2009.

Smeltzer, Larry R. and Marianne M. Jennings, "Why an International Code of Business Ethics Would Be Good for Business," *Journal of Business Ethics 17* no. 1 (1998): 57–67.

Smith, Alex Duval, "How Africa's Party Animals Drank Themselves to Death," *Independent*, September 25, 2009.

Smith, Alison, "The Conundrum of Maintaining Image: Marketing Consolidating Brands," *Financial Times*, May 11, 1998.

Smith, Tony, "Sony Wins Nuplayer PSP Sales Ban," *The Register*, July 21, 2005. Retrieved from www.theregister.co.uk/2005/07/21/sony_vs_nuplayer/.

Songini, Marc L., "Quick Response," *ComputerWorld*, February 19, 2001. Retrieved from www.computerworld.com/article/2591779/vertical-it/quick-response.html.

Soni, Phalguni, "Why Is Foot Locker Eyeing Higher Growth in Europe?," *Market Realist*, June 21, 2016. Retrieved from http://marketrealist.com/2016/06/foot-locker-eyeing-higher-growth-europe/.

Sonne, Paul and Max Colchester, "France, the U.K. Take Aim at Digital Pirates: New Weapons Include Laws That Put Pressure on Internet-Service Providers to Assist in Crackdown on Illegal Downloads," *Wall Street Journal* (Eastern edition), April 15, 2010.

Sousa, C. M. and F. Bradley, "Cultural Distance and Psychic Distance: Two Peas in a Pod?," *Journal of International Marketing 14* no. 1 (2006): 49–70.

Spaulding, Mark, "Greenwashing: Seven Deadly Sins," *Converting 27* no. 6 (2009): 10.

Spears, N., X. Lin, and J. C. Mowen, "Time Orientation in the United States, China, and Mexico: Measurement and Insights for Promotional Strategy," *Journal of International Consumer Marketing 13* no. 1 (2000): 57–75.

Spencer, Jane, "China Shifts Pollution Fight; New Rules Target Export Industry with Stiff Penalties," *Wall Street Journal* (Eastern edition), November 1, 2007.

Spencer, Mimosa, "Carrefour, in Shift, to Exit Russia as It Reports 2.9% Drop in Sales," *Wall Street Journal* (Eastern edition), October 16, 2009.

Spencer, Richard, "China Bans Western Religious Music," *Telegraph*, September 30, 2008. Retrieved from www.telegraph.co.uk/news/worldnews/asia/china/3108810/China-bans-Western-religious-music.html.

Srinivasan, Raji, Gary L. Lilien, and Shrihari Sridhar, "Should Firms Spend More on Research and Development and Advertising during Recessions?," *Journal of Marketing 75* no. 3 (2011): 49–65.

Stanford, Duane, "Africa: Coke's Last Frontier," *Bloomberg Business Week*, October 28, 2010.

Stanley, Bruce, "Danger at Sea: Ships Draw Fire for Rising Role in Air Pollution; as Global Trade Grows, So Does the Spewing of Noxious Emissions," *Wall Street Journal* (Eastern edition), November 27, 2007.

Stanton, John L. and Kenneth C. Herbst, "Slotting Allowances: Short-Term Gains and Long-Term Negative Effects on Retailers and Consumers," *International Journal of Retail & Distribution Management 43* no. 3 (2006): 187–197.

Steenkamp, J.-B. E. M. and M. G. de Jong, "A Global Investigation into the Constellation of Consumer Attitudes toward Global and Local Products," *Journal of Marketing 74* no. 6 (2010): 18–40.

Steenkamp, Jan-Benedict E. M. and Frenkel Ter Hofstede, "International Market Segmentation: Issues and Perspectives," *International Journal of Research in Marketing 19* no. 3 (2002): 185–213.

Steinglass, Matt, "Vietnam Devaluation Fails to Stem Dong's Fall," *FT.com* (London), August 18, 2010a.

Steinglass, Matt, "Vietnam Motorbike Company in Trouble over Vespa Lookalike," *McClatchy–Tribune Business News* (Washington), September 27, 2010b.

Stelzer, I. M., "Euroland Moves from Tragedy to Farce," *Wall Street Journal* (Online), December 29, 2010.

Stern, Louis W., Adel I. El-Ansary, and Anne T. Coughlan, *Marketing Channels* (5 ed.) (Upper Saddle River, NJ: Prentice Hall, 1996).

Stock, James and Douglas Lambert, *Strategic Logistics Management* (Homewood, IL: Irwin, 2000).

Stokes, Bruce, "Hostile Neighbors: China vs. Japan," *Pew Research Center Global Attitudes and Trends*, September 13, 2016. Retrieved from www.pewglobal.org/2016/09/13/hostile-neighbors-china-vs-japan/.

Strachan, Honor, "Analysis: Why Did Gap's Banana Republic Fail in the UK?," *RetailWeek*, October 19, 2016. Retrieved from www.retail-week.com/sectors/fashion/analysis-why-did-banana-republic-fail-in-the-uk/7013094.article.

Stradley, Linda, "Vegemite," *What's Cooking America* (n.d.). Retrieved from http://whatscookingamerica.net/History/VegemiteHistory.htm.

Suder, G. S. (ed.), *Corporate Strategies under International Terrorism and Adversity* (Northampton, MA: Edward Elgar, 2006).

Survival, "Kalahari Bushmen Appeal to Dalai Lama," 2017. Retrieved from www.survivalinternational.org/news/11772.

Swibel, Matthew, "The 50 Top Microfinance Institutions," December 20, 2007. Retrieved from https://www.forbes.com/2007/12/20/microfinance-philanthropy-credit-biz-cz_ms_1220microfinance_table.html#18daf5dfb292

Swissinfo, "Languages," 2017. Retrieved from www.swissinfo.ch/eng/languages/29177618.

Tanaka, Norio, "Shoyu: The Flavor of Japan," *The Japan Foundation Newsletter 27* no. 2 (2000): 1–7.

Tapp, F., "Is La Tomatina a Waste of Food?," 2017. Retrieved from www.nationalgeographic.com/travel/destinations/europe/spain/la-tomatina-food-fight/.

Terada, Shinichi, "TOTO Ads Take Aim at America's Great Unwashed," *McClatchy–Tribune Business News* (Washington), November 15, 2007.

Thau, Barbara, "The Ugly (Retail) Truth: Which Stores Will Close or Survive?," *Forbes*, March 22, 2017. Retrieved from www.forbes.com/sites/barbarathau/2017/03/22/the-ugly-retail-truth-a-rundown-of-store-closings-and-survival-prospects/#6e969db75d02.

Thiessen, Tamara, "Shangri-La Works to Cross Cultures and Cuisines," *Hotel News Now*, June 24, 2010. Retrieved from www.hotelnewsnow.com/Articles/6853/Shangri-La-works-to-cross-cultures-and-cuisines.

Tinashe, Nyamunda, "Bond Notes, Wholesaler 'Tuckshops' and Zim's Irregular Economy," *The Herald*, September 20, 2017. Retrieved from www.herald.co.zw/bond-notes-wholesaler-tuckshops-and-zims-irregular-economy/.

Tiongson, J., "Mobile App Marketing Insights: How Consumers Really Find and Use Your Apps," 2015. Retrieved from www.thinkwithgoogle.com/consumer-insights/mobile-app-marketing-insights/.

Titus, Mark, "Farmers, Milk Processors Bicker over Price," *The Gleaner* (Jamaica, WI), August 10, 2010. Retrieved from www.jamaica-gleaner.com/gleaner/20100813/business/business4.html.

Trefas Team, "Diet Soda Slump to Lower Coca-Cola's Volumes: Still Beverages Could Offset Decline," *Forbes*, April 11, 2014. Retrieved from www.forbes.com/sites/greatspeculations/2014/04/11/diet-soda-slump-to-lower-coca-colas-volumes-still-beverages-could-offset-this-decline/#534778d5a0c3.

Trefas Team, "How Starbucks Plans to Grow Its International Operations," *Forbes*, January 18, 2016. Retrieved from www.forbes.com/sites/greatspeculations/2016/01/18/how-starbucks-plans-to-grow-its-international-operations/#551c5e7e1941.

Triandis, H. C., "Subjective Culture," *Online Readings in Psychology and Culture 2* no. 2 (2002): http://dx.doi.org/10.9707/2307-0919.1021.

Tung, R. L., "Managing in Asia: Cross-Cultural Dimensions," in *Managing across Cultures: Issues and Perspectives*, edited by P. Joyn and M. Warner, 233–245 (Albany, NY: International Thomson Business Press, 1996).

Ueltschy, Linda C., Michel Laroche, Axel Eggert, and Uta Bindl, "Service Quality and Satisfaction: An International Comparison of Professional Services Perceptions," *Journal of Services Marketing 21* no. 6 (2007): 410–423.

Underwood, Robert L., "The Communicative Power of Product Packaging: Creating Brand Identity via Lived and Mediated Experience," *Journal of Marketing Theory and Practice 11* no. 1 (2003): 62–76.

Usunier, J.-C. and J. A. Lee, *Marketing across Cultures* (5 ed.) (London: Pearson Education Limited, 2009).

Venkat, P. R., "Temasek Says It Will Pay Indonesia Fine," *Wall Street Journal Asia* (Hong Kong), January 19, 2011.

Ventola, C. L., "Direct-to-Consumer Pharmaceutical Advertising: Therapeutic or Toxic?," *Pharmacy and Therapeutics 36* no. 10 (2011): 669–684.

Versi, Anver, "How Do You Rebrand an Icon?," *African Business* (London) no. 346 (October 2008): 42–43.

Vijayraghavan, Kala and Chaitali Chakravarty, "Carrefour Sees Future in India, May Ink JV Soon," *McClatchy–Tribune Business News* (Washington), January 19, 2010.

Vrontis, Demetris, Alkis Thrassou, and Iasonas Lamprianou, "International Marketing Adaptation versus Standardisation of Multinational Companies," *International Marketing Review 26* no. 4/5 (2009): 477–500.

Wallin, Michelle and Matt Moffett, "Argentina Says It Is Devaluing Its Peso by 29%," *Wall Street Journal* (Eastern edition), January 7, 2002.

Walloga, April, "What People Eat for Breakfast Around the World," *Independent*, November 11, 2015. Retrieved from www.independent.co.uk/life-style/food-and-drink/features/what-people-eat-for-breakfast-around-the-world-a6730126.html.

Wang, G. and E. Y.-Y. Yeh, "Globalization and Hybridization in Cultural Products," *International Journal of Cultural Studies 8* no. 2 (2005): 175–193.

Ward, David, "Social Media Goes Global," *Direct Marketing News* (Online), October 3, 2008. Retrieved from www.dmnews.com/social-media-goes-global/article/118726/2/.

Warford, Luke, "Africa Is Moving toward a Massive and Important Free Trade Agreement," *The Washington Post*, July 14, 2016. Retrieved from www.washingtonpost.com/news/monkey-cage/wp/2016/07/14/the-7-things-you-need-to-know-about-africas-continental-free-trade-area/?utm_term=.ba1d55dbfc36.

Wassener, Betinna, "New Term for Emerging Economies Is Suggested," *The New York Times* (Online), November 15, 2010. Retrieved from www.nytimes.com/2010/11/16/business/global/16eagles.html.

Watkins, Kevin et al., "EFA Global Monitoring Report 2010: Reaching the Marginalized," *United Nations Educational, Scientific, and Cultural Organization*, Paris, 2010. Retrieved from http://unesdoc.unesco.org/images/0018/001866/186606E.pdf.

Watkins-Mathys, Lorraine, "Focus Group Interviewing in China: Language, Culture, and Sensemaking," *Journal of International Entrepreneurship 4* no. 4 (2006): 209–226.

Webber, Jude, "Argentina's Rivals Bite into Global Beef Export Market," *Financial Times*, October 6, 2010.

Weise, Elizabeth, "Maker of Artisanal Tofu Aims to Bring Sexy to Soybean Curd; Think of Another Funny, Creamy Foreign Food That's Now Popular—Yogurt," *USA Today* (McLean, VA), December 29, 2010.

Welsh, Diane H. B., Ilan Alon, and Cecilia M. Falbe, "An Examination of International Retail Franchising in Emerging Markets," *Journal of Small Business Management 44* no. 1 (2006): 130–149.

Wentz, Laurel and Rebecca A. Fannin, "Crest, Colgate Bare Teeth in Competition for China," *Advertising Age*, November 1996.

Wernerfelt, Birger, "A Resource-Based View of the Firm," *Strategic Management Journal* (September–October 1984): 171–180. Retrieved from http://onlinelibrary.wiley.com/doi/10.1002/smj.4250050207/abstract.

Wessel, David, "Did 'Great Recession' Live Up to the Name?," *Wall Street Journal* (Online), April 7, 2010.

Westjohn, S. A., N. Singh, and P. Magnusson, "Responsiveness to Global and Local Consumer Culture Positioning: A Personality and Collective Identity Perspective," *Journal of International Marketing 20* no. 1 (2012): 58–73.

Whalen, Jeanne and Andrew Osborn, "Corporate News: Glaxo at Loggerheads with Russia over HIV Drugs—Pharmaceutial Giant Rejects 15% Price Cut Sought by Government, Saying It Would Allow for Too Little Profit," *Wall Street Journal* (Eastern edition), June 12, 2009.

Wheeler, Carolynne, "Hummus Food Fight between Lebanon and Israel," *Telegraph*, October 11, 2008. Retrieved from www.telegraph.co.uk/news/worldnews/middleeast/3178040/Hummus-food-fight-between-Lebanon-and-Israel.html.

Whitney, Glenn, "A Year Later, Britain Reaps Dividends from Its Decision to Pull Out of the ERM," *Wall Street Journal* (Eastern edition), September 13, 1993.

Wilkinson, Melissa, "Marketing Plays Critical Role," *Charter* (Sydney) *81* no. 3 (2010): 24–27.

Wind, Y. and S. P. Douglas, "International Market Segmentation," *European Journal of Marketing, 6* no. 1 (1972): 17–25.

Winsted, K. F., "The Service Experience in Two Cultures: A Behavioral Perspective," *Journal of Retailing 73* no. 3 (1997): 337–360.

Winterman, Denise, "Tesco: How One Supermarket Came to Dominate," *BBC News Magazine*, September 9, 2013. Retrieved from www.bbc.co.uk/news/magazine-23988795.

Wise, Bambina, "South African Textiles Strike Ends, but Problems Remain," *WWD* (New York) *198* no. 73 (2009): 19.

Wongsamuth, Nanchanok, "TOTO Flush with Sales amid Industry Slump," *McClatchy–Tribune Business News* (Washington), October 21, 2009.

Wood, Van R., Dennis A. Pitta, and Frank J. Franzak, "Successful Marketing by Multinational Firms to the Bottom-of-the-Pyramid: Connecting Share of Heart, Global 'Umbrella Brands,' and Responsible Marketing," *Journal of Consumer Marketing 25* no. 7 (2008): 419–429.

Woodall, Pam, "Who's in the Driving Seat?," *The Economist 337* no. 7935 (1995): SS3–SS5.

Woodward, David, "The View from Here: Muhammad Yunus, Grameen Bank," *Director Magazine* (London) *62* no. 7 (2009): 12.

Yaprak, Attila, "Culture Study in International Marketing: A Critical Review and Suggestions for Future Research," *International Marketing Review 25* no. 2 (2008): 215–229.

Yeow, Jimmy, "Ganad Unipoles Alter Cambodia's Ad Scene," *Business Times* (Kuala Lumpur), June 19, 1996.

Zhang, Y. and B. D. Gelb, "Matching Advertising Appeals to Culture: The Influence of Products' Use Condition," *Journal of Advertising 25* (1996): 29–46.

Zikmund, William G. and Barry J. Babin, *Exploring Marketing Research* (10 ed.) (Eagan, MN: Southwestern/Cengage Publishing, 2010).

Zou, S. and S. T. Cavusgil, "The GMS: A Broad Conceptualization of Global Marketing Strategy and Its Effect on Firm Performance," *Journal of Marketing 66* no. 4 (2002): 40–56.

Zuckerman, Mortimer, "The Great Recession Continues," *Wall Street Journal* (Eastern edition), January 22, 2010.

GLOSSARY

absolute advantage theory: a theory that states that a country has the ability to produce a greater amount of a good or service using the same amount of resources used by another country

adaptation: changing a component of the marketing mix to better meet the needs of a local market

advertising management: the process of developing and overseeing a company's advertising program

aesthetics: concepts about what constitutes beauty

affective message strategies: advertising messages that invoke feelings or emotions and match those feelings with a product, service, or company

agent middlemen: marketing channel members that do not take title or ownership of the products that they market

analytics: statistical methods used to evaluate data

animosity: anger toward a country that is rooted in political, economic, or military conflict between countries

announcements: advertising presentations of facts without the use of people

arbitration: a formal conflict resolution process in which both parties agree to abide by the decision of a third-party arbitrator

association transfers: an advertising format in which a product is combined with another object, person, situation, or environment

back translation: a process in which a survey is translated from an original language into a targeted language and then back into the original language in order to check for accuracy and meaning

BATNA: best alternative to a negotiated agreement

bill of exchange: an agreement between parties in which one party, a drawer, directs a second party, the drawee, to issue a payment to another party, the payee

born-global firms: businesses that operate in two or more different countries from inception

bottom-of-the-pyramid: the approximately 4 billion people globally living on less than $2 per day

brand: a name, sign, symbol, or design, or some combination of these that identifies the products of a firm and distinguishes them from the competition

brand awareness: the strength of a brand's presence in the consumer's mind

brand equity: the unique outcomes a product enjoys due solely to its brand name

brand extension: a strategy utilized when a brand name is extended from one product to another

brand image: consumer perceptions of a brand

brand insistence: a condition where a customer will accept no substitutes for a specific brand

brand loyalty: a consumer's commitment to a product based on positive attitudes that leads to consistent purchase of the brand

brand parity: when brands within one product category are viewed as similar or undifferentiated

brand preference: a mental ranking in which the brand's attractiveness becomes foremost in the consumer's mind

brand valuation: the process of estimating the financial value of a brand

break-even analysis: a common method employed to discover the relationships between costs and price

capacity to consume: the power to use goods and services in the satisfaction of human wants

capital market: any location, online or physical, where businesses or individuals can raise funds

capitalist economic system: a marketplace in which transactions take place with limited government regulation or interference

civil law: a legal system in which law is based on written words or a legal code

clutter: the abundance of marketing messages that consumers routinely encounter

cobranding: placing two or more brand names on the same product

cognitive message strategies: advertising messages that present rational arguments or pieces of information to consumers

collusion: a pricing system in oligopolistic markets in which a set of major competitors sets prices at uniform levels, either overtly or covertly

command economy: an economy in which a central authority, normally the government, makes all key economic decisions

common law: a legal system where legal precedent and usage traditions are the basis of law

common market: a group of countries that have entered into an agreement to remove barriers to the movement of goods and services, to have a common tariff for non-members, and to allow the free movement of capital and labor within the market

communication: the process of sending, receiving, and interpreting information

communism: an extreme form of socialism where private ownership of property is outlawed

comparative advantage theory: a theory that states a country has an ability to produce a good or service at lower levels of opportunity cost than that in other countries

comparative advertising: product comparisons where two items are shown in use side by side

conative message strategies: advertising messages designed to lead directly to a consumer response, such as a store visit or purchase

conciliation: the various forms of mediation or conflict resolution that companies can pursue before beginning the more formal arbitration process

consumer culture: culture in which consumption and possessions are the primary source of meaning in life

consumer promotions: sales promotions directed at retail customers

contingency approach: marketers doing what is appropriate for individual markets, which typically leads to a combination of both standardized and adapted components

control: the process of comparing performance to standards, making corrections when needed, and rewarding success

core competence: the most proficiently performed internal activity that is central to the firm's strategy and competitiveness

cosmopolitanism: the view that a person is a member of a larger global community rather than merely maintaining an allegiance to a local culture and close-by circumstances

cost-based pricing: pricing based on a careful assessment of all costs associated with producing and selling an item

cost-plus pricing: setting a product's price based on fixed costs, variable costs, plus the desired profit margin for each item

countercultures: groups whose values set their members in opposition to the dominant culture

countertrade: when goods are traded or exchanged without the use of hard currency

country image: the attitudes and knowledge consumers have about a country

country-of-origin effect: the response a consumer has to a product due to the country that is the source, in the consumer's mind, for the product

cultural convergence: the increasing similarities between global consumers

cultural crossvergence: the emergence of a new, global value system as countries become more interconnected

cultural distance: the degree to which cultural values, norms, and beliefs in one country are different from those in another country

cultural divergence: persistence of specific values due to sociocultural influences

cultural electives: areas of behavior or customs that visitors may wish to, but are not required to, conform to or participate in

cultural exclusives: customs or behavior patterns reserved exclusively for the locals and from which the foreigner is barred

cultural imperatives: the customs and expectations that must be met and conformed to or avoided if international business relationships are to be successful

culture: the beliefs, customs, and attitudes of a distinct group of people

cultures of achievement: cultures in which egalitarianism, individualism, and orientation toward economic efficiency and productivity are important

cultures of honor: cultures which value religion, traditional gender roles, hierarchy, and strong authority

cultures of joy: individuals value well-being of individuals and society, and work is for achieving quality of life not to demonstrate economic productivity

currency: the form of money used by a specific country or region

customs union: a group of countries that have entered into an agreement to remove barriers to the movement of goods and services and to have a uniform tariff policy toward non-member countries

damage control: reacting to negative events caused by a company's mistake, consumer grievances, or unjustified or false claims made by the press or others seeking to injure a company

deceptive pricing: a pricing system in which the marketer promotes one price, yet charges more using hidden charges, add-ons, or higher prices for products with more than the minimum of features

demand: the amount of a good or service that consumers will buy at various price levels

differentiation: emphasis on a unique benefit or component of a product that separates that product from competitors

diffusion: the process by which an innovation slowly spreads through a culture or group

direct exporting: also called *export marketing,* a system in which the producer or supplier is responsible for marketing to foreign buyers

distinctive competence: a production activity a company performs at a level that is better than that of all competitive rivals

distribution intensity: the extent to which products are distributed throughout a country and the number of intermediaries that are utilized to carry the product

dual channel marketing: selling virtually the same goods or services to both consumers and businesses

dumping: the practice of selling goods below costs in another country in order to capture a market

economic system: the means by which countries allocate resources, goods, and services to citizens

economic union: a group of countries seeking to harmonize economic policies among members, and attempting to follow the same economic policy

economies of scale: the reduction in per unit costs as the total volume produced increases

economies of scope: efficiencies that emerge from producing a variety of similar products

emerging markets: economies in countries that have moved through the transformation from developing to developed

entertainment: when theatrical drama, musicals, shows, comedies, slapstick, humor, horror, or satire provide the primary advertising format

ethical absolutism: the philosophy that there are fundamental values that cross cultures, and companies must uphold them

ethical relativism: ethical values are relative to the norms of one's culture

ethnocentrism: the strongly held belief that one's culture is superior to that of others

event marketing: using marketing techniques to connect with buyers through specific live events including concerts, performances, or festivals to promote a product or brand

exchange rate: the rate at which one country's currency can be traded for another country's currency

exchange systems: the methods of facilitating payment for a product or service

exclusive distribution: an international marketing strategy that focuses on offering products at only one wholesaler or retailer in a particular market area

executional framework: the manner in which an advertising appeal and message strategy is delivered

experiments: research techniques that allow researchers to uncover cause-and-effect relationships by manipulating certain variables and controlling others

exporting: a mode of entry in which the product is shipped in one manner or another into a foreign market

express warranty: a document that spells out how a product promises to deliver its value and the remedies available when it does not

external validity: when cause-and-effect relationships are expected to be found in other situations or settings

family branding: a strategy wherein a number of products in a line or mix share the same brand name worldwide

flexible or floating exchange rate: the rate when the value of the currency is allowed to respond freely to market forces

focus groups: semi-structured or unstructured group discussions that generally take place in groups of eight to twelve individuals

forward rates: the exchange rates for the delivery of the currency at a specific time in the future

franchising: the contractual agreement to implement a business model

free trade: an economic situation in which goods travel across boundaries with little interference by individual governments

free trade area: a group of countries that have entered into an agreement to reduce tariffs, quotas, and other barriers to the movement of goods and services

free trade zones: specially designated areas within a country that have separate laws designed to encourage trade

future-oriented cultures: cultures in which planning for the future takes priority over enjoying the present or appreciating the past

futures contracts: contracts that allow the company to sell or buy a certain amount of a foreign currency at a set exchange rate on a specific date

global brand: identifies a company that uses the same brand name, image, and brand mark globally

Global consumer culture: globally recognized set of consumption behaviors, values, and brands associated with globalization and global culture

Global marketing strategy: a marketing strategy that encompasses several countries in the world and aims at coordinating a firm's marketing efforts in markets in these countries

globalization: the increased interconnectedness of consumers and businesses globally

globally integrated marketing communications program: a program that consists of a carefully designed combination of all communications with the company's internal and external publics

good: a physical product sold to and used by an individual, household, or business

gray market: the practice of distributing products through distribution channels that are not authorized by the marketer of the product

greenwashing: a practice in which a company exaggerates or even fabricates the degree of its sustainable or green activities

hard currency: currency that can be exchanged for other currencies worldwide

hedging: any financial process that lessens financial risk

high-context cultures: cultures that rely more on symbols and language with less explicit or spelled-out codes

High-cosmopolitanism: consumers view themselves as members of a larger global community rather than as merely maintaining an allegiance to a local culture and community

home country: the nation in which the business is located or the one that houses the company's main headquarters

horizontal channel conflict: conflict that occurs between members of a marketing channel at the same level

horizontal integration: a marketing strategy in which a company acquires or merges with another company

host country: the nation being targeted for expansion by a company

imagination: an advertising format that utilizes cartoon or other visual techniques to make unrealistic presentations of a make-believe world

importing: the transfer or shipping of goods into a country

indirect exporting: also called *export selling*, a system in which the manufacturer sells the product to intermediaries who then handle the foreign selling of the product

individual branding: a strategy in which distinct brand names are used for products

inflation: a situation in which the price of goods and services increases in a country or region

infrastructure: the organizational and physical structures present in a country, such as roads, technology, and information systems

intangible product benefits: the value drawn from the social, emotional, and non-physical aspects of consumption

integration: the process of using agreements between countries to lower limits on the movements of products, capital, or labor

intellectual property: creations of the mind or the intangible property that result from thought

intellectual property piracy: the unauthorized use or reproduction of intellectual property that has been legally protected

intensive distribution: an international marketing strategy in which a product is distributed through several wholesalers or retailers in a particular market

interest rates: the percentage rate charged or paid for the use of money

intermediaries: organizations that move products from producers to consumers and end users

internal validity: when accurate cause-and-effect relationships are identified in a research finding

international distribution: the process by which products and services flow between producers, intermediaries, and consumers, including the transfer of ownership

international finance: the study of currency exchange, investments, and how these processes influence business activities

international marketing: using the marketing mix to meet the needs and wants of consumers in foreign markets

international marketing channel: a marketing system that promotes the physical flow and ownership of products and services from producer to consumer, including producers, wholesalers, and retailers

international market segmentation: the process of identifying specific segments—whether they are country groups, other businesses, or individual consumer groups—of potential customers with homogeneous attributes across different countries, or within a single foreign market, that exhibit similar responses to a company's marketing mix

international retailing: the retail activities that occur across and inside national boundaries

international strategic planning: the plan for the overall direction of the firm

Internet interventions: identifying false statements about a company and then responding to the allegations in the same communication channel

joint venture: a legal partnership that involves an investment, a division of ownership, and the creation of a new legal entity, or when two companies combine to create a product

jurisdiction: the power to apply law

language: the system used to communicate between peoples, including verbal and nonverbal cues

legal systems: the methods for applying and implementing the laws of a country

lesson: a form of advertising presentation that applies facts and arguments to the audience

letter of credit: a document issued by a bank to signal the creditworthiness of a buyer to a seller

licensing: a contract that grants a company the legal right to use another company's brand, image, and other marketing components

litigation: a legal proceeding through a judicial system

logistics: the activities that manage the physical movement and storage of goods from the producer to the consumer

logistics: the management of the flow of products and services among marketing channel members

loss leader: pricing certain items at or below cost in order to build store traffic

low-context cultures: cultures that demonstrate high values toward and positive attitudes regarding words

market: people with wants and needs, money to spend, and the willingness to spend money on those wants and needs

market concentration: the strategy a company uses when it exports a small number of markets or just one key market and then slowly expands to export to new countries

market development: a strategy that focuses on increasing sales of existing products to new customers

market economy: an economy in which most economic decisions are made in the marketplace

market research: the systematic gathering, storing, and analyzing of marketplace information for use in managerial decision-making

market segment: a set of businesses or a group of individual consumers with distinct characteristics

market segmentation: a process that involves identifying specific groups based on their needs, attitudes, and interests; the grouping of consumers based on their needs, attitudes, and interests

market spreading: a marketing strategy of growing exports in many different markets simultaneously and rapidly expanding to new markets

marketing: discovering consumer needs and wants, creating the products that meet those needs, and then pricing, promoting, and delivering those products and services

marketing channel power: the ability of one channel member to control or influence the marketing decisions of another channel member

marketing mix: the major activities used to develop and sell goods and services, including products, prices, distribution systems, and promotional programs

markup pricing: a pricing method that simply adds a standard markup to the costs assigned to a product

material culture: physical elements of a culture such as clothing, food, houses, tools and machines, works of art, buildings

merchant middlemen: marketing channel members that take title and ownership of the products being marketed

message strategy: the primary tactic or approach used to deliver the key idea to be delivered in an advertisement

metrics: performance measures that serve as standards set during the planning process and that are used in the control process

mission statement: a document that delineates why an organization exists and guides the overall direction of the firm

mixed economy: an economic system in which part is guided by the marketplace and part is run by the government

monochronic-time orientation: cultural emphasis on schedules and punctuality

multinational corporations: organizations conducting business activities in at least one other country that differs from the home country in which the organization is headquartered

national competitive advantage: a circumstance in which a country has built a reputation with regard to an aspect of producing a product, such as technological superiority or lower labor costs

nationalism: the strong pride and devotion consumers have in their country or nation

needs: the necessities of life that all humans require for their survival and well-being

newly industrialized countries: nations that have experienced rapid economic expansion and industrialization that are neither less- nor most-developed countries

nonprobability sample: a sample in which the probability of an element of the population being included in a sample is unknown

offshoring: the movement of a business activity to another country

operational plans: plans that dictate the day-to-day entry-level activities that are crucial parts of successful international marketing programs

organizing: the process through which management designs the structure of the organization, assigns responsibilities, and ensures effective communication flows throughout the company

outsourcing: relinquishing organizational control of a business process and instead hiring a third party external to the company to operate the process

parallel translation: a process in which two translators are used for the back translation process with the results being discussed and one translation selected

past-oriented cultures: cultures in which people value tradition, history, and appreciate the past

pegged or fixed regime: the value of a currency when it is set to a predetermined band or par value

penetration pricing: setting the product's initial price as low as a company can afford, to discourage entry by competition

personal interviews: one-on-one discussions between a researcher and a respondent

pioneering advantage: the advantage that results from being the first mover in a market

planning: the process whereby managers develop goals, strategies, and activities that will best position the firm for success in the international marketplace

point-of-purchase materials: displays and materials that take a variety of forms, with the goal of encouraging the immediate sale of a product by the end user

political risk: the chance that political forces, such as government activities, will hamper and harm business activities within a country

political systems: the people with an organization, typically governments, who possess the power and how that power is structured

political union: the complete integration of political and economic policy by a group of countries

polychronic-time orientation: cultural emphasis on flexibility and performing multiple tasks at the same time

positioning: creating a perception in a consumer's mind regarding the nature of a company and its products relative to those of competitors

positioning maps: tools used to study a company and its competitors in terms of consumer attitudes or perceptions

positioning statement: a one- or two-sentence summary of the company's positioning strategy

predatory pricing: the direct attempt by a major competitor to drive other companies out of business by setting prices unrealistically low

present-oriented cultures: cultures which view time as a cyclical process in which the future cannot be controlled or predicted, and the past will repeat itself in the future

price: the amount a person, company, or government charges for a good or service

price elasticity of demand: a measure of the impact of price differences on demand and sales

price perceptual map: a map that depicts various companies or products along two dimensions, typically price and quality

primary data: data that are gathered by the researcher or research team for a specific project

probability sample: a sample in which each element in the population has a known, nonzero probability of being selected for a study

product: bundle of attributes, including tangible, intangible, and symbolic elements that provide value for exchange partners

product line: groups of similar products within a particular category

product line extension: a strategy that is utilized when new products are introduced that are in the related product category and that respond to specific opportunities in the marketplace

product mix: the total number of products that a firm carries

product position: what summarizes consumer opinions regarding the specific features of the product

product positioning: creating a perception in the consumer's mind regarding the nature of a company and its products relative to competitors

profit-based pricing: examining pricing from the perspective of what consumers are willing to pay rather than from the cost of the item

promotions mix: a company's combination of advertising, personal selling, sales promotion, and public relations efforts

protectionism: the desire to protect domestic businesses from the exports of foreign firms through governmental policy

psychic distance: the individual's subjective perception of the differences between the home country and the foreign country

public relations: the management of communication with all organizational stakeholders

qualitative research design: a research method that focuses on obtaining information without a reliance on numerical expression or measurement

quantitative research design: a research design that relies on numerical measurement and analysis

reliability: the internal consistency of a measure and its ability to be replicated over time

religiosity: the degree to which consumers within a country or region are religious

repositioning: the process of changing consumer perceptions of a brand relative to competitors on key attributes

sales promotions: marketing activities that are designed to stimulate consumer and marketing channel demand for a product or service

sampling: a process wherein only certain members of a set of consumers are used to represent the views of the larger population

scientific method: the use of observations, empirical evidence, and knowledge in order to make objective statements about certain phenomena

secondary data: data that have already been collected by an agency and are made available either free of charge or for a fee

selective distribution: an international marketing strategy of using only a limited number of channel intermediaries to sell products

self-reference criterion: when someone applies his or her own cultural values and background to the assessment of behaviors of others

service: an intangible product that generally centers on an act or performance that delivers value to individuals, households, and businesses

skimming: setting a product's initial price as high as the market will bear to allow the manufacturer or exporter to attain as much revenue as possible in a short period of time

socialism: an economic system in which the state owns at least some parts of industry

soft currency: currency that cannot be traded at major financial centers

sovereignty: governmental authority or control within its state

sovereignty debt ratings: a rating that represents the chance that a country will default on governmental debt

special effects: an advertising format used to deliver a wide variety of commercials by combining animation, cartoon, camera effects (camera motion), recording techniques, music, and other sounds

spin-off sales: sales that occur when individuals who buy a particular brand at work have positive experiences and, as a result, purchase the same brand for personal use

sponsorship: an agreement between a marketing organization and an individual, team, or a landmark

standardization: using the same marketing mix in all markets

STP approach: segmentation, targeting, and product positioning processes

strategic alliance: a formal agreement between companies to work together to achieve a common goal

strategic controls: performance measures that apply to the CEO and top-level management team that direct the portfolios of businesses or activities held by a single company or corporation

strategic planning: plans for the overall direction of the firm, the development of goals, and the allocation of resources in the pursuit of those goals, as prepared by top management

subcultures: groups whose values and related behaviors are distinct and set members off from the general or dominant culture

subjective culture: non-material elements of a culture such as ideas, values, beliefs

surveys: research instruments that can be administered to large numbers of consumers with relative ease

sustainability: meeting the needs of the current generation in a way that leaves future generations with the ability to also meet their needs

tactical planning: plans for specific activities and programs that support the overall direction set at the strategic level

tangible product benefits: the value drawn from the physical components of a product

target market: a specific, identifiable market segment that a company seeks to reach

target ROI pricing: a cost-based pricing technique that specifies a desired return on investment (ROI) for a particular product

terms of payment: the agreed-upon payment in return for the goods or services

test market: a type of experiment that is constructed within realistic marketplace conditions

theocratic law: a legal system based on religious writings

trade allowance: a price reduction or other consideration paid by a company to intermediaries as an incentive to purchase or promote a specific product

trade deficit: the balance of trade that occurs when a country imports more than it exports

trade promotions: sales promotions targeted at intermediaries, most notably wholesalers and retail outlets

trade surplus: the balance of trade that occurs when a country exports more than it imports

transition economies: rapidly developing economies that occur in what were formally communist countries with centrally planned economics

validity: the degree to which a concept is accurately measured by survey or research items

values: strongly held concepts that are pervasive within a culture

vertical channel conflict: conflict that occurs when there are disputes between channel members at different levels in the system

vertical integration: a marketing strategy in which one member of the market channel merges with or acquires another intermediary

vertical marketing system: a distribution arrangement in which the producer, wholesaler, and retailer perform marketing activities as a unified system

wants: the specific expression of needs through the desire for specific objects

wholly owned subsidiary: a company enters a country by establishing a 100% ownership stake in a business in that country

INDEX

Page numbers in italics indicate illustrations; page number in bold indicate tables; and page numbers in bold italic indicate maps.

quantity discounts, 372–373
quotas, 97

radio frequency identification development (RFID)
    technology, 476
railroad transportation, 473, **473–474**, 476
random sampling, 261–262
raw materials, 288
rebates, 542–543
regency theory, 500
referent power, 445
regiocentric companies, 10, 159
region-based organizations, 156–157, *157*
regional segmentation, 197, **197**, *198*
regulations, 223
reinforcement seekers, **548**
relationship-oriented cultures, 449, **449**
relationships, 448
reliability, 266–267
religion and religiosity, 58–59, 222–223, **223**
Renesas Electronics Corporation, 149
reports, 264–265
repositioning, 234, 299, 337
resident buyers, 465
retail price, 353
retailing, 478. *See also* international retailing
revaluation, 404
reverse-engineering, 318
reward power, 445
Ritzer, G., 40
Ronen, S., 197
Rostow modernization model, 114–115, **115**

safety needs, 12
sales promotions. *See* international sales promotions and
    public relations
sampling, 260–262, 543–544, **544**, 547
Samsung, 172–173
Schwartz, S., 47, **47–48**
scientific method, 265
seasonal discounts, 372
secondary data, 253–254, **253**
security, **48**
segmentation, 12, 182–183. *See also* international market
    segmentation
selective distribution, 428
self-actualization, 12
self-direction, **47**
self-reference criterion, 265
separate export departments, 462
service prices, 354
service quality, 330–331, **330**
service standardization, 325–326
services, 282, 292–295, **292–294**, 329–331, **329**, **330**
SERVQUAL method, 330, **330**
shadow pricing, 411
share of heart, 229–231
share of mind, 229–231
Shenkar, O., 197
shopping goods, 283
short-term orientation, **45**, **47**, 516, 521
simultaneous production and consumption, 329, **329**

situational analysis, 151
skimming, 365–366, *367*, 369, 465
sleeping patterns, 278–280
slice-of-life executions, 520
slotting fees and slotting allowances, 549–550
Slow Food movement, 51
smart phone apps, 532–533
snowball sampling, 262
social institutional demands for group welfare and
    survival, 47
social interactional requirements, 47
social media, 505, 537, 545, 557
socialism, 110, *110*, 111
socially desirable responses, 256–257
soft currencies, 391
sorting function, 442
South Asian Association for Regional Cooperation (SAARC),
    92, **93**
Southern African Customs Union (SACU), 94, **95**
Southern African Development Community, **95**
Southern Cone Common Market. *See* MERCOSUR (Mercado
    Común del Sur)
sovereignty, 223
sovereignty debt ratings, 407
soy sauce, 66–67, 76
space perceptions, 448
special drawing rights, 405
special effects, 523
specialty goods, 283–284
specialty stores, 480
spin-off sales, 194
sponsored consumers, 524
sponsorships, 555–556
spot rates, 393
Standard & Poor's, 407, **407–408**
standardization
    advertising and, 507–508
    international product marketing and, 323–326, **324–325**,
        331–332, 334–336, **334**, 339–340
    sales promotions and, 552–553
staple convenience goods, 282
statistical inference, 261–262
stereotypes, 527
stimulation, **47**
stock-outs, 470
stock turnover, 470–471, **471**
STP approach, 182–183, 216, 225. *See also* international
    market segmentation; international positioning; target
    marketing
strategic alliances, **127**, 130–131, 155–156
strategic business units, 147
strategic controls, 161, **162**
strategic corrections, 162–163
strategic planning, 145. *See also* international strategic
    planning
strong command economies, 111–112. *See also* communism
subcultures, 55–56
subjective culture, 42, **42**
subsidies, 98
success paradox, 513
supermarkets, 479
supply, 111